THE ROLE OF LAWYERS IN ACCESS TO JUSTICE

To a disturbing degree, we are at the mercy of our time and place. While law may provide relief for some of life's troubles, that requires access to justice. Accessibility is the focus of this volume, which expands analysis of access to justice beyond the US and the UK to Asia and other comparative jurisdictions. Chapters characterize access to justice dynamics in these jurisdictions by addressing how access is understood, how it is achieved or not achieved, and how the jurisdiction should improve. The book addresses some issues seldom addressed in analyses of western jurisdictions, such as paid mandatory legal services and mandatory public interest activities, and provides English translations of relevant regulations. The book expands our understanding of access to justice with a comparative perspective, one that allows readers to identify relationships between access and its constitutive environment.

HELENA WHALEN-BRIDGE is Associate Professor, National University of Singapore, Faculty of Law. Her publications include the co-authored *Litigants in Person: Principles and Practice in Civil and Family Matters in Singapore* (2021), and 'The Conceptualisation of Pro Bono in Singapore' (2014). Helena is an Expert with the UNODC's Education for Justice project and has been Faculty Advisor for the NUS Law Faculty's student Pro Bono Group since its inception in 2005.

The Role of Lawyers in Access to Justice

ASIAN AND COMPARATIVE PERSPECTIVES

Edited by

HELENA WHALEN-BRIDGE

National University of Singapore

CAMBRIDGE
UNIVERSITY PRESS

CAMBRIDGE
UNIVERSITY PRESS

Shaftesbury Road, Cambridge CB2 8EA, United Kingdom

One Liberty Plaza, 20th Floor, New York, NY 10006, USA

477 Williamstown Road, Port Melbourne, VIC 3207, Australia

314–321, 3rd Floor, Plot 3, Splendor Forum, Jasola District Centre, New Delhi – 110025, India

103 Penang Road, #05–06/07, Visioncrest Commercial, Singapore 238467

Cambridge University Press is part of Cambridge University Press & Assessment, a department of the University of Cambridge.

We share the University's mission to contribute to society through the pursuit of education, learning and research at the highest international levels of excellence.

www.cambridge.org
Information on this title: www.cambridge.org/9781009045476

DOI: 10.1017/9781009042253

First published 2022
First paperback edition 2024

A catalogue record for this publication is available from the British Library

ISBN 978-1-316-51745-1 Hardback
ISBN 978-1-009-04547-6 Paperback

This book is dedicated to Thomas and William, two fine, precious people.

Like love we seldom keep.

'Law Like Love', W. H. Auden

Contents

Figures

Tables

Appendices

Contributors

EDITOR

Helena Whalen-Bridge is Associate Professor of Law at the National University of Singapore. A recipient of multiple competitive research grants and the 2019 Teresa Godwin Phelps Award for Scholarship in Legal Communication, her research interests include legal ethics and access to justice, legal narrative, and legal education. Publications in the field of access to justice include *Litigants in Person: Principles and Practice in Civil and Family Matters in Singapore*, with Jaclyn Neo (SAL Academy Publishing, 2021), 'Automated Document Assembly: Access to Justice and Consumer Risk' (2020) *Singapore Academy of Law Journal*, and 'The Conceptualisation of Pro Bono in Singapore' (2014) *Asian Journal of Comparative Law*. Helena received the NUS Teaching Excellence Award and is a long-standing member of the Law Faculty's Teaching Excellence Committee. She is also an Expert with the UNODC's Education for Justice project. Helena is a founding member of the Law Society of Singapore's Project Law Help, which helps provide legal information and support to charities and social enterprises. She has been the Faculty Advisor for the Law Faculty's student Pro Bono Group since its inception in 2005.

CONTRIBUTORS

Ahmad Nizam Abbas was called to the Bar of Lincoln's Inn in the UK in July 1992 and was admitted as an Advocate and Solicitor of the Supreme Court of Singapore in January 1994. He has acted for clients from diverse countries in their family disputes involving cross-border disputes over the custody of children and matrimonial assets. He is the current Chairman of the Muslim Law Practice Committee of the Law Society and deals with Family Law and Probate work in both the Civil Law and Syariah Law systems. He was a member of the Law Society's team which participated in the Parliamentary Select Committee Hearing on the amendments to the Administration of Muslim Law Act back in 1997. In 2012, his paper on 'The Islamic Legal System in Singapore' was published in the *Pacific Rim Law & Policy Journal* of the University of Washington. Ahmad sits on the Panel of Advisors of the Youth Court and Vulnerable Adult Court of Singapore as well as on the Tribunal for the Maintenance of Parents.

Ahmad's passion for knowledge and teaching manifested in co-creating the first Islamic Family Law course at the Singapore University of Social Sciences. His zest for learning is also reflected in him undergoing the first Masters of Law programme at the Singapore Management University (SMU) in 2012, with a specialization in Islamic Finance. Ahmad has long been active in community and social work, with diverse organizations such as Central Singapore CDC, Feedback Unit, National Youth Council, Singapore International Foundation, and the Education Trust Fund (ETF). He received the PBM (Pingat Bakti Masyarakat – Public Service Medal) from the President during the 2007 Singapore National Day Awards.

Nick Cheesman is a senior fellow in the Department of Political and Social Change, Australian National University. A scholar of law and society, he does research at the nexus between law, politics, and state violence in mainland South East Asia, in particular Myanmar and Thailand. His 2015 book, *Opposing the Rule of Law: How Myanmar's Courts Make Law and Order* (Cambridge University Press), received the 2017 Distinguished Book Award of the Asian Law and Society Association.

Alice Esther Dawkins completed honours theses in Asian Studies and Law at the Australian National University. She did the research for this book while a research fellow at the Tharthi May Foundation in Yangon, Myanmar, where she was supported by a New Colombo Plan Scholarship. She is fluent in Mandarin and functional in Burmese and French.

Hualing Fu is Professor of Law and holder of the Warren Chan Professorship in Human Rights and Responsibilities, and Dean of the Faculty of Law, at the University of Hong Kong. Professor Fu is interested in the theoretical questions that explore authoritarian resilience and authoritarian fragility using China as a case study. A pivotal focus is the process through which regime type affects the particular institutional designs in a legal system, and how legal rules and institutions in turn discipline and regulate political power. His research in the past decades has explored political authoritarianism and its legal manifestation. The thread that ties his various projects together is the resilience of China's authoritarian political system and its impact on, and interaction with, legal institutions. His secondary research interest is the evolving constitutional relationship between Hong Kong and the rest of China.

Ching-Fang Hsu is a post-doctoral fellow at the Research Institute of Humanities and Social Sciences (RIHSS), Ministry of Technology, Taiwan. In 2020–1, she was also the holder of the Chiu Research Fellowship in Taiwan Studies at the Oregon State University. She received her PhD in political science from the University of Toronto, and an LLM from UC Berkeley. Her work focuses on the politics of legal professionals in varying power settings, with a regional interest in Asia. She publishes in both social sciences journals and law reviews, in both English and Chinese.

Arif A. Jamal is Associate Professor and Vice Dean of Graduate Studies at the Faculty of Law, National University of Singapore (NUS). He is also co-Editor-in-Chief of the *Asian Journal of Comparative Law*. Arif's research and teaching interests are in the fields of law and religion, Muslim legal traditions, comparative law, and legal and political theory. He is the author of *Islam, Law and the Modern State* and has published widely. Arif has held visiting appointments at law schools in the UK, Italy, Hong Kong, Israel, and the US, including with the Islamic Legal Studies Program at Harvard Law School.

JaeWon Kim is a professor of law at Sungkyunkwan University Law School, and he served his university as Vice President for Student Affairs. Professor Kim holds law degrees from both Korea and the US, and received a JSD degree from Cornell University, where he was a Clarke fellow. He was a visiting scholar at Harvard Law School. His teaching and research interests are law and society, legal ethics, disability law, and comparative law.

Helen Kruuse is an associate professor in the Faculty of Law, Rhodes University, South Africa, where she teaches jurisprudence, legal ethics, family law, and legal skills. She is an admitted attorney of the High Court of South Africa, and prior to lecturing, she worked in the legal services of the London Borough of Brent. She has also previously taught in the law faculties of the University of Cape Town and the University of the Western Cape. She is a review editor of the *South African Law Journal* and her research interests lie in law and social change.

Takgon Lee is an attorney who formerly worked at the Dongcheon Foundation. The Dongcheon Foundation is a public interest foundation offering pro bono and legal aid services for the socially disadvantaged and minorities, focusing on various areas including, but not limited to, refugees, migrants, gender, social enterprises, welfare, North Korean refugees, and the disabled. It supports, fosters, and connects non-profit organizations, activists, and pro bono lawyers, while engaging in research concerning public interest law, pro bono counselling, and legal and policy reforms. At the Dongcheon Foundation, Takgon focused on legal aid to, and policy reforms on, refugees, migrants, and pro bono coordination. Takgon received an MA from the Korea University College of Law in 2010 and his Juris Doctor from Korea University Law School in 2013. He was admitted into the Korea Bar Association in 2013, and to the California Bar in 2015. He currently works at the United Nations High Commissioner for Refugees as an associate legal officer.

Seh Lih Long is the co-founder of the Malaysian Centre for Constitutionalism and Human Rights, a human rights NGO based in Malaysia. Called to the Malaysian Bar in 2003, she worked with the Human Rights Commission of Malaysia (SUHAKAM), where she was the Head of the Law Reform and International Treaties Division. Internationally, she has worked with the United Nations as a human rights officer in Afghanistan, Timor Leste, and Somalia.

Setsuo Miyazawa is a legal sociologist who received an SJD from Hokkaido University and a PhD in sociology from Yale. He was a full-time faculty member at Hokkaido University, Kobe University, Waseda University, Omiya Law School, and Aoyama Gakuin University in Japan before reaching mandatory retirement in 2016. He also taught as a visiting professor at York University (Canada), the University of Washington, Harvard, UC Berkeley, UCLA, NYU, the University of Hawaii, the University of Pennsylvania, and Fordham. Since 2008, he has been teaching at UC Hastings College of the Law every autumn. He has been highly active in the promotion of judicial reform in Japan, where he was one of the most prominent proponents of the introduction of the American-style graduate professional law schools. He has also been active in the Law and Society Association (LSA) in the US, twice serving on its Board of Trustees. He co-founded the Collaborative Research Network 33 in East Asian Law and Society in the LSA in 2008 and the LSA awarded him the International Scholarship Prize in 2014 and the Stanton Wheeler Mentorship Award and the Legacy Award in 2021. He co-founded the Section on East Asian Law and Society in the Association of American Law Schools (AALS) in 2015 and the Asian Law and Society Association (ALSA) in 2016. He was the founding President of the ALSA in 2016 and 2017 and is currently the President of the Asian Criminological Society. He has a wide range of research interests, including police and criminal justice, legal education and the legal profession, and the judiciary and judicial politics. His first English book, *Policing in Japan* (SUNY Press, 1992), received the 1993 Distinguished Book Award of the Division of International Criminology of the American Society of Criminology.

Euis Nurlaelawati is a professor in Islamic (family) law at the faculty of Sharia and law, Sunan Kalijaga, State Islamic University (Universitas Islam Negeri/UIN), Yogjakarta. She teaches comparative family law in the Muslim world, contemporary Islamic family law, and judicial practices. Her publications include *Modernization, Tradition and Identity: The Kompilasi Hukum Islam and Legal Practices in Indonesian Religious Courts* (Amsterdam University Press, 2010); 'Muslim Women in Indonesian Religious Courts: Reform, Strategies, and Pronouncement of Divorce' (2013) 20:3 *Journal of Islamic Law and Society*; (with Arskal Salim) 'Female Judges at Indonesian Religious Courtrooms: Opportunities and Challenges to Gender Equality' in *Women Judges in the Muslim Countries: A Comparative Study of Discourse and Practice* (Brill, 2017); and 'Expansive Legal Interpretation: Muslim Judges' Approach to Polygamy in Indonesia' (2020) 18:2–3 *Hawwa Journal: Journal of Women in the Middle East and the Islamic World*.

Dr Michal Ofer-Tsfoni is a lecturer at the Law School of the Netanya Academic College in Israel. Her research focuses on both civil- commercial law and legal ethics. She is the head of the Center of Legal Clinics and Social Responsibility at the Netanya Academic College, and her initiatives have led to a significant increase in legal aid provided to the public through the clinics. She is a member of the David Weiner Center for legal ethics and professional responsibility.

Hiroshi Otsuka's area is socio-legal studies. Associate Professor Otsuka received his LLB and LLM from Kobe University. He has been a full-time faculty member at Nara Women's University (Faculty of Human Life and Environment). He teaches as an adjunct lecturer at Kindai University Law School and Ryukoku University. He has also taught at Doshisha Law School, Ritsumeikan University, and Kansai University of International Studies. His current research fields are social movements, public interest lawyering, and consumer law. The role of lawyers in consumer movements is his most important research theme.

Alpha Carole Pontanal is a lawyer from the Philippines with almost seven years' experience in non-profit programme management and human rights, as well as legal aid. She currently manages a project focusing on land rights issues concerning agrarian reform and indigenous peoples in the Philippines. Previously, Alpha worked in the Autonomous Region in Muslim Mindanao on human rights, peace processes, and transitional justice.

Nguyen Hung Quang is now acting as the Managing Partner of NH Quang & Associates law firm. He possesses deep experience in policy consultancy on institutional changes and public system reform, such as research on the Vietnamese court system, lawyers' roles, administrative procedure reform, and development projects. He conducts policy and law assessment and implementation, research framework development, Terms of Reference construction, and comment. Further, he has been involved in providing privatization consultancy, such as drafting and commenting on legislation regarding entrepreneurs, as well as acting as the facilitator between law-makers, implementation agencies, and beneficiaries. In addition, Quang is the respected author of numerous publications on Vietnam's legal environment, including 'Independence, Impartiality and Integrity of the Judiciary in Vietnam', with Professor Penelope (Pip) Nicholson, in *Asia-Pacific Judiciaries, Independence, Impartiality and Integrity* (H. P. Lee, Marilyn Pittard 2018); 'Between Authoritarian Governance and Urban Citizenship: Tree-felling Protests in Hanoi', with Professor John Gillespie in 2018; 'An Historical Overview of Land Law and Land Disputes in Vietnam', with Toan Le, in *Resolving Land Disputes in East Asia: Exploring the Limits of Law* (Hualing Fu and John Gillespie, 2014); and 'The Vietnamese Judiciary: The Politics of Appointment and Promotion', with Pip Nicholson in 2005.

George Baylon Radics received his PhD from the Department of Sociology at the National University of Singapore. He currently teaches law in society, selected topics in law and justice, social thought and social theory, and sociology of emotions. After receiving his PhD, Dr Radics studied law at the University of Washington, where he obtained his law degree with a concentration on Asian law. Dr Radics served as a research attorney at the Supreme Court of Guam for two years after graduating from law school. His articles have been published in a number of journals, including the *University of Pennsylvania Asian Law Review*, *Columbia Human Rights Law Review*, *Santa Clara Journal of International Law*, and the *Philippine Sociological Review*. Dr Radics has actively been engaged in research on the Philippines for the past 15 years.

Dr Kerstin Steiner is an associate professor at the Law School, La Trobe University. She is also a senior associate at the Centre for Indonesian Law, Islam and Society (CILIS) and Associate at the Asian Law Centre (ALC), both at the University of Melbourne. She specializes in South East Asian legal studies, and researches on the intersection of law, politics, economics, and society, especially with regard to Islam.

Dr Steiner has held numerous visiting positions, including the first (female) non-Muslim visiting scholar at the Department of Shariah and Law, Academy of Islamic Studies, University of Malaya in 2009 and 2014. She was also a visiting scholar at the Centre for Socio-legal Studies, Oxford University, in 2014. She has published widely on matters of Islam in South East Asia, including co-authoring two volumes with Tim Lindsey on Singapore, Malaysia, and Brunei in *Islam, Law and the State in Southeast Asia* (IB Tauris, 2012), as well as contributions on 'Comparative Law in Syariah Courts: A Case Study of Singapore, Malaysia and Brunei' in Mads Adenas and Duncan Fairgrieve, eds., *Comparative Law before the Courts* (Oxford University Press, 2015) and 'Islam, Law and Human Rights of Women in Malaysia' in Niamh Reilly, ed., *International Human Rights: Human Rights of Women* (Springer, 2019). She also has book chapters on 'The First Decade of Female Judges in the Malaysian Syariah Judiciary: Promises to Keep and Miles to Go' in Melissa Crouch, ed., *Women and the Judiciary in the Asia-Pacific* (Cambridge University Press, 2021) and 'The Challenges for Human Rights in Asia: Islam and the Patchwork System for Freedom of Religion in Malaysia' in Bernd Kannowski and Kerstin Steiner, eds., *Regional Human Rights: International and Regional Human Rights: Friends or Foe?* (Nomos Verlag, 2021).

Linda Yanti Sulistiawati is a senior research fellow at the Asia-Pacific Centre for Environmental Law (APCEL) and also an associate professor of law in Universitas Gadjah Mada. She is an internationally recognized scholar in Indonesian international environmental law and her research has established her as a leading expert who is frequently consulted by the Indonesian government and international organizations. Her research focuses on international environmental issues, such as climate change, REDD+, land issues, and customary (adat) issues. Linda was a member of the delegation leading Indonesia's negotiations of the Paris Agreement on Climate Change. From 2018 to 2021, Linda was a lead author of the Intergovernmental Panel on Climate Change's Sixth Assessment Report. Linda was a visiting fellow at APCEL from 5 August 2019 to 3 September 2019 under the APCEL Visiting Fellow Programme.

Sarasu Esther Thomas is a professor at the National Law School of India University. Her areas of interest include gender, human rights law, access to justice, and family law. She held the Ford Foundation Chair on Public Interest Law in addition to her research and teaching commitments. She currently heads the Centre for Women and the Law, and the Human Rights Lawyering Project at her University.

Yong-Ching Tsai is a research assistant at the Law Institute in Academia Sinica. She majored in law and accounting, and received her LLB and LLM from National Cheng Kung University. Before entering academia, she practised law in the greater Taipei area, handling civil and criminal litigation with a particular expertise in family law, contract disputes, real estate law, and tax law. Her research interests include legal anthropology, tax avoidance, international taxation, offshore banking units, comparative tax, tax policy, and tax justice. Yong-Ching conducts research on socio-legal studies, tax, and global finance, focusing on the technological infrastructures and legal techniques in regard to offshore financial services and cross-national economic governance.

Yunita is the country representative of Avocats Sans Frontières, an international NGO specializing in defending human rights and supporting justice. Previously, she was the head of the advocacy division of Lembaga Bantuan Hukum (LBH) Jakarta, one of the prominent legal aid organizations providing legal aid services in Jakarta, Indonesia. She has been providing legal aid services since 2010, and she has handled various cases using a structural legal aid approach, incorporating the education and empowerment of various communities in Indonesia. She is currently a lecturer at Parahyangan Catholic University.

Limor Zer-Gutman is a senior lecturer at the Law School of the College of Management Academic Studies (COMAS) in the city of Rishon LeZion in Israel. Dr Zer-Gutman received her PhD from Stanford Law School, her LLM from UCLA Law School, and her LLB from Tel Aviv University Law Faculty. Her research focuses on legal ethics and professional responsibility, the legal profession, the judiciary, and ethics education. She is the founder and the head of the David Weiner Center for legal ethics and professional responsibility. She served on two public committees that dealt with the legal profession in Israel. The first, in 2001, was the public committee for reviewing internships and certification exams. The second, in 2013, was the public committee for reviewing the Israel Bar Association. She wrote several bills for the Israel Bar Association, including advertising rules and various amendments to the Israeli Bar Act.

Foreword

Richard L. Abel

F. Scott Fitzgerald famously wrote: 'the very rich . . . are different from you and me'.[1] That may be a cliché; but it is uniquely true in law because of its adversarial nature. First class air travel is far more comfortable than the cattle cars to which most of us are relegated – but we all get to the same destination. Mega-mansions provide far more comforts and amenities than hovels, but the latter still offer some shelter. Concierge hospital care may be preferable to barefoot doctors, but some medical expertise is better than none. Private schools offer personal attention and college prep, but public schools also educate.

When those with the resources to hire lawyers confront those unable to afford lawyers, however, the result is not inferior justice but *injustice*. The US Supreme Court acknowledges this by proclaiming on its pediment 'Equal Justice for All' (although it routinely betrays that ideal). The Court sought to render justice more equal by declaring a constitutional right to counsel in criminal cases,[2] though it has declined to extend this to civil litigation. Yet there is ample evidence that having a lawyer makes a significant difference in outcome.[3]

Hence the vital need to explore the many ways to improve access to justice. US Supreme Court Justice Louis Brandeis praised the then 48 states as laboratories that could 'try novel social and economic experiments'.[4] But the literature on access to justice has, until recently, been focused on the global North. The editor of this essential book seeks to correct that bias by enlisting 24 eminently qualified scholars to describe such experiments in more than 16 jurisdictions. The fascinating and encouraging accounts will be invaluable to all those who retain the belief that law can and must produce justice.

[1] 'The Rich Boy', *Red Book* (1926) and in *All the Sad Young Men* (New York: Scribners, 1926).

[2] *Gideon* v. *Wainwright*, 372 U.S. 335 (1963); *Argersinger* v. *Hamlin*, 407 U.S. 25 (1972).

[3] Carroll Seron, Gregg Van Ryzin, and Martin Frankel, 'The Impact of Legal Counsel on Procedural Outcomes for Poor Tenants in New York City's House Court: Results of a Randomized Experiment', (2001) 35 *Law & Society Review* 419–34.

[4] *New State Ice Co.* v. *Liebermann*, 285 U.S. 262 (1932).

Acknowledgements

This volume was the work of many hands and would not exist without them.

First among them are of course the authors. Many of them travelled to Singapore for an initial conference in 2017, and they have revised and focused their work, producing chapters that contributed to the accomplishment of the volume's goal. I am primary among the readers who have learned from their work.

The research project and book were funded by a generous grant from the NUS Law Centre for Asian Legal Students (CALS), and CALS has supported the project enthusiastically throughout its duration. At the initial conference and afterwards, I was ably assisted by Margaret Peck Lin Ang, Elizabeth Chua, Suguna D/O Jeganathan, and Khairiyah Binte Abu. I received immensely helpful guidance and sustenance from CALS directors Andrew Harding, Dan Puchniak, and Jaclyn Neo.

I am grateful to Arif Jamal for helping to conceptualize the Syariah chapters and bring them to fruition, and I received helpful critique on different chapters from Sandra Booysen, Alvin Chen, Mike Dowdle, and Lim Tanguy.

Law students did the bulk of the essential tasks of formatting and cite checking, and I am grateful for their conscientious work and comradeship, from the original team of Jonathan Tan, Hairul Siddeeq, Jeremy Koo, and Megan Chua, to the final push team of Reesa Chua, Jared Yu Hern Sim, Russell Adam Rushi Whang, Stanley Wei Siang Woo, Zhang Yizhen, and Richmond Han Han Xiao, to the last man standing, Marc Tang.

Law librarians Carole Wee, Su-Lin Lee, and Bissy Ithack tirelessly procured books and materials, including ones that were difficult to find.

Lastly, I am the grateful recipient of observations regarding access to justice from lawyers, activists, and advocates, who opened my eyes to the many ways that justice and injustice function.

Helena Whalen-Bridge
June 2021

Abbreviations

AAI	*Asosiasi Advokat Indonesia* (Indonesian Advocates Association)
AALS	Association of American Law Schools
ABRI	*Angkatan Bersenjata Republik Indonesia* (Indonesian Army)
ACLS	Association of Criminal Lawyers of Singapore
ACLU	American Civil Liberties Union
AFTA	'Afta and Brothers' Law Firm
ALG	Alternative Law Groups (Philippines)
AMLA	Administration of Muslim Law Act (Singapore)
APIL	Advocates for Public Interest Law (South Korea)
APSI	Indonesian Association of Islamic Advocates
ASEAN	Association of South East Asian Nations
AWAM	All Women's Action Society
BAGUS	*Pusat Bantuan Guaman Shariah*
BAPPENAS	*Badan Pembangunan Nasional* (National Development Planning Agency, Indonesia)
BCLAS	Bar Council Legal Aid Scheme (Malaysia)
BHEUU	Prime Minister Department's Legal Affairs Division (Malaysia)
BKL	Bae, Kim, and Lee, LLC
BP4	*Badan Penasihatan Pembinaan dan Pelestarian Perkawinan* (Institution of Consultation, Development, and Resolution of Marriages)
BPHN	*Badan Pembinaan Hukum Nasional* (National Law Development Agency, Indonesia)
CCMA	Commission for Conciliation, Mediation and Arbitration (South Africa)
CDC	Community Development Council (Singapore)
CEDAW	Convention on the Elimination of All Forms of Discrimination against Women
CJC	Community Justice Centre (Singapore)
CLAS	Criminal Legal Aid Scheme (Singapore); Community Legal Aid Service (Philippines)

CLF	Christian Lawyers' Fellowship of Korea
CLS	Community Legal Services
CMC	Philippine National Police Command Memorandum Circular
COVID-19	Coronavirus disease 2019
CPC	Criminal Procedure Code (Malaysia/Vietnam)
CPD	Continuing Professional Development
CPRCG	Civil and Political Rights Campaign Group (Myanmar)
CRC	Convention on the Rights of the Child
Crores	ten million Indian rupees (10,000,000)
CSR	Corporate Social Responsibility
DLA	Developmental Legal Advocacy
DOJ	Provincial Department of Justice (Vietnam)
EU	European Union
FLAG	Free Legal Assistance Group (Philippines)
GDP	gross domestic product
GEC	General Electric Company
GO	governmental organization
IBA	Israel Bar Association
IBP	Integrated Bar of the Philippines
ICCPR	International Covenant on Civil and Political Rights
IDR	Indonesian rupiah
INR	Indian rupee
ISA	Internal Security Act 1960 (Malaysia)
ISL	New Israeli shekel
JCLU	Japan Civil Liberties Union
JFBA	Japan Federation of Bar Associations
JPY	Japanese yen
KAI	*Kongres Advokat Indonesia*
KBA	Korean Bar Association
KGS	Syariah Law Clinic
KLAC	Korea Legal Aid Corporation
KRW	Korean won
LAA	Legal Aid Act 1971 (Malaysia)
LAB	Legal Aid Bureau (Singapore)
LAC	Legal Aid Centre (Malaysia)
LAD	Legal Aid Department (Malaysia, *Jabatan Bantuan Guaman*)
LAF	Legal Aid Foundation (Taiwan)
LAR	Legal Aid Review (Singapore)
LASA	Legal Aid South Africa
LASCO	Legal Assistance Scheme for Capital Offences (Singapore)
LBH	*Lembaga Bantuan Hukum* (Legal Aid Institute, Indonesia)
LeIP	*Lembaga Kajian dan Advokasi Independensi Peradilan* (Indonesia)
LLA	Law on Legal Aid 2006 (Vietnam)

LPA	Legal Practice Act (South Africa); Legal Profession Act 1976 (Malaysia)
LPC	Legal Practice Council (South Africa)
LSO	Legal Service Officer
LSPBS	Law Society Pro Bono Services (Singapore)
LTRI	Legal Training and Research Institute (Japan)
MCCHR	Malaysian Centre for Constitutionalism and Human Rights
MCCY	Ministry of Culture, Community and Youth (Singapore)
MIG	Middle Income Group Schemes
MLAS	Mandatory Legal Aid Service (Philippines)
MLPC	Muslim Law Practice Committee (Singapore)
MOJ	Ministry of Justice (South Korea/Taiwan/Vietnam)
MUIS	*Majlis Ugama Islam Singapura* (Islamic Religious Council of Singapore)
MYR	Malaysian ringgit
NALSA	National Legal Services Authority (India)
NGO	non-governmental
NLAF	National Legal Aid Foundation (Malaysia)
NLD	National League for Democracy
NPO	non-profit organization
NUS	National University of Singapore
OECD	Organization for Economic Cooperation and Development
OFWs	Overseas Filipino Workers
PAO	Public Attorney's Office (Philippines)
PAP	People's Action Party (Singapore)
PCA	Prevention of Crime Act 1959 (Malaysia)
PDO	Public Defender's Office (Israel)
PEKKA	*Perempuan Kepala Keluarga*, or Female Heads of Households
PERADI	*Perhimpunan Advokat Indonesia*
PGSM	*Persatuan Peguam Syarie Malaysia* (Malaysian Syariah Lawyers Association)
PHP	Philippine peso
PIL	Public Interest Litigation
PJP	Primary Justice Project (Singapore)
PKPA	*Pendidikan Khusus Profesi Advokat* (Indonesia)
PO	Peoples' Organization
POTA	Prevention of Terrorism Act 2015 (Malaysia)
PPI	*Peguam Pembela Islam* (Lawyers in Defence of Islam)
PPMM	*Persatuan Peguam Muslim Malaysia* (Muslim Lawyers Association)
PSPD	People's Solidarity for Participatory Democracy
PWI	*Persatuan Wartawan Indonesia* (Indonesian Journalist Association)
RCA	Radio Corporation of America

RMB	Chinese renminbi
SAHRC	South African Human Rights Commission
SALAF	Structural Alternative Legal Assistance for Grassroots
SALRC	South African Law Reform Commission
SALSA	State Legal Services Authorities (India)
SCAP	Supreme Commander for the Allied Powers
SCLSC	Supreme Court Legal Services Committee (India)
SIS	Sisters in Islam
SLSA	State Legal Services Authority (India)
SOSMA	Security Offences (Special Measures) Act 2012 (Malaysia)
SSAR	Singapore Syariah Appeal Reports
SUHAKAM	Human Rights Commission of Malaysia
TLAF	Taipei branch of the Legal Aid Foundation
TWD	New Taiwan dollar
UK	United Kingdom
UN	United Nations
UNDP	United Nations Development Programme
UNICEF	United Nations Children's Fund
UPL	Unauthorized Practice of Law Rules
US	United States of America
US$	United States dollar
VND	Vietnamese dong
WAO	Women's Aid Organization
WWII	World War Two
YBGK	*Yayasan Bantuan Guaman Kebangsaan* (National Legal Aid Foundation)
YLBHI	*Yayasan Lembaga Bantuan Hukum Indonesia* (Indonesian Legal Aid Foundation)
ZAR	South African rand

1

Understanding and Comparing Access to Justice

Helena Whalen-Bridge

Abstract

Understanding access to justice in any jurisdiction requires identification of factors which create the dynamic in which access functions. Jurisdictions can have factors in common, but each jurisdiction has a dynamic of its own. Without an understanding of these factors and how they interact, proposed improvements in access may not accomplish much. Viewing access to justice in this way arguably allows for a clearer vision of positive change, because it acknowledges why particular changes may be difficult or unlikely. Establishing access to justice dynamics in sufficient complexity is also necessary for comparative understandings across jurisdictions, but comparative insight requires reference to an expanded set of jurisdictions, including Asia and beyond.

I. INTRODUCTION

We are to a disturbing degree at the mercy of our time and place. At the time of writing, a worldwide pandemic has served as a reminder of this. Resources such as money, education, and social capital can moderate some vagaries, but conditions such as political autocracy and instability, hatreds various and evergreen, and inequities of different sorts render us vulnerable.

Law may provide relief for some of life's troubles. In the resolution of legal disputes, law has the potential to provide justice,[1] if it is not derailed by corruption, undermined by systemic underfunding, or rendered inaccessible. People must have access to justice to get legal relief, but their access should be equal, 'so that the relative advantage or disadvantage of one citizen vis-à-vis another does not determine legal outcomes'.[2] Access to justice is therefore central to the rule of law.[3]

Accessibility is the focus of this volume. Simply stated, access to justice is the state's obligation to ensure that all members of a community can access law and dispute resolution equally and

[1] See Richard L. Abel, 'Epilogue: Just Law?' in Scott L. Cummings, *The Paradox of Professionalism: Lawyers and the Possibility of Justice* (Cambridge: Cambridge University Press, 2011) 296 [*Just Law?*] at 296, 309, and Marc Galanter, 'Why the "Haves" Come Out Ahead: Speculations on the Limits of Legal Change' (1974) 9:1 *Law & Society Review* 95.

[2] Tom Cornford, 'The Meaning of Access to Justice' in Ellie Palmer et al., *Access to Justice: Beyond the Policies and Politics of Austerity* (Oxford: Hart Publishing, 2016) 27 [*Meaning of Access*] at 29.

[3] See Yash Ghai and Jill Cottrell, 'The Rule of Law and Access to Justice' in Yash Ghai and Jill Cottrell, eds., *Marginalized Communities and Access to Justice* (Abingdon: Routledge, 2010) [*Marginalized Communities*] 1 at 3.

effectively.[4] But definitions of access to justice have varied over time.[5] Today access to justice emphasizes actual, effective access, and it can include legal advisors other than lawyers,[6] public legal education,[7] social services and political representation,[8] and informal legal resolution platforms,[9] all provided in a manner that respects human rights.[10] Critics of formal dispute resolution have pointed out that '[r]esolving justice problems lawfully does not always require lawyers' assistance',[11] and that alternatives to courts and lawyers are required.[12] However, Richard Abel has observed that while there have been historical examples of efforts to completely do away with legal rules and legal specialists, they re-emerge.[13] Civil or administrative matters may be amenable to different kinds of solutions, but disputes such as criminal matters normally end up in formal state-organized dispute systems such as courts.[14] In these forums, lawyers or suitably trained legal professionals[15] play a key role.[16] While it is possible in many countries to proceed without legal representation in venues that require legal and procedural knowledge, and unrepresented litigants are not uncommon, most unrepresented litigants encounter considerable difficulties.[17] Access to justice does encompass a wide variety of goals and strategies, but

[4] See European Union Agency for Fundamental Rights & Council of Europe, *Handbook on European Law Relating to Access to Justice* (Luxembourg: Publications Office of the European Union, 2016) at 16; and Daniel Bonilla Maldonado, 'The Right to Access to Justice: Its Conceptual Architecture' (2020) 27:1 *Indiana Journal of Global Legal Studies* 15 at 15.

[5] See Mauro Cappelletti and Bryant Garth, 'Access to Justice: The Newest Wave in the Worldwide Movement to Make Rights Effective' (1978) 27 *Buffalo Law Review* 181 [*The Newest Wave*] at 183–4.

[6] See Vivek Maru and Varun Gauri, eds., *Community Paralegals and the Pursuit of Justice* (Cambridge: Cambridge University Press, 2018).

[7] Christine Parker, *Just Lawyers: Regulation and Access to Justice* (Oxford: Oxford University Press, 1999) [*Just Lawyers*] at 30–1.

[8] Helen J. Ménard, *Accessing Justice through Mental Health Law Reform in the Pacific* (New York: Nova Science Publishers Inc., 2016) [*Mental Health Law Reform*] at 132.

[9] See Linn A. Hammergren, *Justice Reform and Development: Rethinking Donor Assistance to Developing and Transition Countries* (Abingdon: Routledge, 2015) [*Justice Reform*] at 129–30; and *Informal Justice Systems: Charting a Course for Human Rights-Based Engagement* (UNDP, 2012).

[10] See e.g. *Access to Justice for the Poor, Marginalised and Vulnerable People of Uganda* (Legal Aid Service Providers Network, 2015) at 18.

[11] Rebecca L. Sandefur, 'Access to What?' (2019) 148 *Dædalus* 49 at 51.

[12] In the US see Rebecca L. Sandefur, 'What We Know and Need to Know About the Legal Needs of the Public' (2016) 67 *South Carolina Law Review* 443 at 451; and Katherine S. Wallat, 'Reconceptualizing Access to Justice' (2019) 103 *Marquette Law Review* 581; but see Ugo Mattei, 'Access to Justice: A Renewed Global Issue?' (2007) 11:3 *Electronic Journal of Comparative Law* 1 [*Renewed Global Issue*] at 3 (the 'birth of the ADR industry . . . transformed *the issue of access to justice, by limiting as much as possible access to courts of law*' (emphasis in original)); and see *Justice Reform, supra* note 9, at 37 (those 'living in isolated, traditional communities typically have access to their own dispute system, albeit with its equally traditional biases') at 129–66.

[13] *Just Law?, supra* note 1, at 312–13.

[14] See *Justice Reform, supra* note 9, at 37; see generally, *Marginalized Communities, supra* note 3, at 6–7.

[15] This volume focuses on the lawyer's role in access to justice but is not meant to exclude other legally trained individuals who assist in court, as illustrated by the analysis of legal workers (and lay *litigants ad litem*) in the chapter on China. The chapter on Vietnam identifies the shift in defendant representation from civil servant to lawyer as an important development in effective representation.

[16] See e.g. *Meaning of Access, supra* note 2, at 28.

[17] See e.g. Liz Richardson, Genevieve Grant, and Janina Boughey, *The Impacts of Self-Represented Litigants on Civil and Administrative Justice: Environmental Scan of Research, Policy and Practice* (Sydney: Australasian Institute of Judicial Administration, 2018) 23–7; Bridgette Toy-Cronin, 'Keeping Up Appearances: Accessing New Zealand's Civil Courts as a Litigant in Person' (2015) (unpublished PhD dissertation, University of Otago, New Zealand); and Liz Trinder et al., *Litigants in Person in Private Family Law Cases* (UK: Ministry of Justice Analytical Series, 2014).

access to lawyers continues to be a 'central means to increase individuals' access to justice'.[18] This volume therefore focuses on the role of lawyers in making law and dispute resolution accessible, and, in this context, access to justice will refer to the ability of persons[19] to access fair, third-party dispute resolution processes, when they cannot afford a lawyer, or are vulnerable or marginalized from the law for other reasons.

II. EXPANDING ACCESS TO JUSTICE RESEARCH

Cappelletti and Garth famously described access to justice in three successive waves, a metaphor relevant at least in 'western-oriented countries':[20] legal aid for the poor; representation of group and collective interests rather than just individual rights; and a shift from access to lawyers to different mechanisms.[21] But the wave metaphor is not necessarily accurate in all western countries,[22] and in the comparative context it may send analysis in the wrong direction. When discussing comparative legal professions, Philip Lewis stated that discussion of '"waves" or "tendencies" is unsatisfactory', not just because comparative lawyers assume that similar kinds of changes fulfil similar needs, but because lawyers assume they have given 'a satisfactory account merely by showing the existence of apparently similar developments in different countries, whereas this only begins the inquiry into the circumstances underlying those similarities'.[23]

This volume starts from the position that understanding access to justice anywhere depends very much on the environment being studied.[24] In some ways, this approach is a continuation[25] of how Cappelletti, the quintessential comparative law scholar, initiated contemporary access to justice research in the 1970s,[26] when he 'launched a monumental comparative research project'

[18] Nourit Zimerman and Tom R. Tyler, 'Between Access to Counsel and Access to Justice: A Psychological Perspective' (2010) 37 *Fordham Urban Law Journal* 473 at 474; see also Tamara Goriely and Alan Paterson, 'Introduction: Resourcing Civil Justice' in Alan Paterson and Tamara Goriely, eds., *Resourcing Civil Justice* (Oxford: Oxford University Press, 1996) 1 at 1.

[19] The volume includes some discussion of collective actions: see Sarasu Thomas' chapter on India, Chapter 3. On representation of artificial persons such as corporations, associations, and governments, as opposed to natural persons, see Marc Galanter, 'More Lawyers than People: The Global Multiplication of Legal Professionals' in Scott L. Cummings, ed., *The Paradox of Professionalism: Lawyers and the Possibility of Justice* (Cambridge: Cambridge University Press, 2011) 68 at 80–2.

[20] *The Newest Wave, supra* note 5, at 196.

[21] *The Newest Wave, supra* note 5, at 197, 209, 222, and generally 196–289; there are different formulations, e.g. fives waves in Canada per Roderick Macdonald, 'Access to Justice in Canada Today: Scope, Scale and Ambitions' in Julia Bass, W. A. Bogart, and Frederick H. Zemans, eds., *Access to Justice for a New Century: The Way Forward* (Toronto: Law Society of Upper Canada, 2005) 19, 20–3.

[22] *Just Lawyers, supra* note 7, at 32; in South and South East Asia, see Ross Cranston, 'Access to Justice in South and South-East Asia' in Julio Faundez, ed., *Good Government and Law: Legal and Institutional Reform in Developing Countries* (London: Palgrave Macmillan, 1997) 233 [*Access to Justice in South and South-East Asia*] at 233–4.

[23] Philip S. C. Lewis, 'Comparison and Change in the Study of Legal Professions' in Richard L. Abel and Philip S. C. Lewis, eds., *Lawyers in Society: Comparative Theories* (Berkeley: University of California Press, 1989) 27 at 59, and see 47.

[24] See *Renewed Global Issue, supra* note 12, at 4 (comparative scholarship in access to justice is needed because 'access to justice is so intimately connected to the role of law in society . . .').

[25] See Andrew Harding, ed., *Access to Environmental Justice: A Comparative Study* (Leiden: Martinus Nijhoff Publishers, 2007) [*Environmental Justice*] at 5.

[26] The work originated from the comparative research project entitled 'Florence Access-to-Justice Project' and was published by Sijthoff (Leiden and Boston) and Giuffrè (Milan) under the general editorship of Cappelletti. The work

on access to justice.[27] After a hiatus,[28] access to justice research continued, although works in English focused primarily on western countries. In the UK, Lord Woolf's 1995 Interim[29] and Final Reports[30] on Access to Justice reviewed the civil justice system and made recommendations for reform.[31] In 1999, Christine Parker's *Just Lawyers: Regulation and Access to Justice*[32] provided an overview of lawyers and justice in primarily common law jurisdictions. Deborah Rhode revitalized access to justice scholarship in the US with her 2004 monograph *Access to Justice*[33] and articles such as the pointed 'Whatever Happened to Access to Justice?'[34] In 2005, Rhode followed this book with *Pro Bono in Principle and in Practice: Public Service and the Professions*;[35] one chapter included comparative jurisdictional analysis, with countries limited to the UK, Australia, and China.[36] Also in the US, Rebecca Sandefur has been a central figure in empirical access to justice research;[37] her 2009 edited book focused on the US, Canada, and the UK, with one chapter on Japan.[38] Robert Granfield and Lynn Mather's *Private Lawyers and the Public Interest: The Evolving Role of Pro Bono in the Legal Profession*,[39] similar to Rhode's work, focused on the US or provided a more conceptual overview.[40] *Access to Justice for*

includes the General Report introducing the project's four-volume series, *The Newest Wave*, *supra* note 5; Bryant G. Garth and Mauro Cappelletti, eds., *Vol. I, Access to Justice: A World Survey* (Milan: Giuffrè Editore/Alphen aan den Rijn, Sijthoff/Noordhoff, 1978); Mauro Cappelletti and John Weisner, eds., *Vol. II, Access to Justice: Studies of Promising Institutions* (Milan: Giuffrè Editore/Alphen aan den Rijn, Sijthoff/Noordhoff, 1978); Bryant G. Garth and Mauro Cappelletti, eds., *Vol. III, Access to Justice: Emerging Perspectives and Issues* (Milan: Giuffrè Editore/Alphen aan den Rijn, Sijthoff/Noordhoff, 1979); Klaus-Friedrich Koch, ed., *Vol. IV, Patterns in Conflict Management: Essays in the Ethnography of Law* (Milan: Giuffrè Editore/Alphen aan den Rijn, Sijthoff/Noordhoff, 1979); Klaus-Friedrich Koch, ed., *Access to Justice in an Anthropological Perspective* (Milan: Giuffrè, 2008).

27 *Renewed Global Issue*, *supra* note 12, at 1.

28 *Renewed Global Issue*, *supra* note 12, at 2.

29 Lord Woolf, 'Access to Justice – Interim Report' (*The National Archives*, 1995), online: webarchive.nationalarchives.gov.uk/20081106150907/www.dca.gov.uk//civil/interim/contents.htm.

30 Lord Woolf, 'Access to Justice – Final Report' (*The National Archives*, 1995), online: webarchive.nationalarchives.gov.uk/20060213223540/www.dca.gov.uk/civil/final/contents.htm.

31 Other jurisdictions also undertook comprehensive reviews; in Australia, see Access to Justice Advisory Committee, 'Access to Justice: An Action Plan' (Canberra, 1994).

32 *Just Lawyers*, *supra* note 7.

33 Deborah L. Rhode, *Access to Justice* (Oxford: Oxford University Press, 2004); and see Deborah L. Rhode, 'Colloquium: Deborah L. Rhode's Access to Justice' (2004) 73:3 *Fordham Law Review* 841; in addition to Rhode, see Earl Johnson Jr, 'Equal Access to Justice: Comparing Access to Justice in the United States and Other Industrial Democracies' (2000) 24 *Fordham International Law Journal* S83 (civil access to justice).

34 Deborah L. Rhode, 'Whatever Happened to Access to Justice?' (2009) 42 *Loyola of Los Angeles Law Review* 869; see also Deborah L. Rhode and Scott L. Cummings, 'Access to Justice: Looking Back, Thinking Ahead' (2017) 30 *Georgetown Journal of Legal Ethics* 485.

35 Deborah L. Rhode, *Pro Bono in Principle and in Practice: Public Service and the Professions* (Stanford: Stanford University Press, 2005) [*Pro Bono in Principle*].

36 *Pro Bono in Principle*, *supra* note 35, at 100–24.

37 See Rebecca L. Sandefur, 'Lawyers' Pro Bono Service and American-Style Civil Legal Assistance' (2007) 41:1 *Law & Society Review* 79 [*Civil Legal Assistance*]; Catherine R. Albiston and Rebecca L. Sandefur, 'Expanding the Empirical Study of Access to Justice' (2013) *Wisconsin Law Review* 101; and Scott L. Cummings and Rebecca L. Sandefur, 'Beyond the Numbers: What We Know – and Should Know – About American Pro Bono' (2013) 7 *Harvard Law and Policy Review* 83.

38 Rebecca L. Sandefur, ed., *Access to Justice* (Bingley: Emerald JAI, 2009).

39 Robert Granfield and Lynn Mather, eds., *Private Lawyers and the Public Interest: The Evolving Role of Pro Bono in the Legal Profession* (Oxford: Oxford University Press, 2009).

40 The work of Cummings and Rhode that highlights problems resulting from pro bono dominance also focuses on the US: see Scott L. Cummings, 'The Politics of Pro Bono' (2004) 52 *UCLA Law Review* 1 [*Politics of Pro Bono*] at 106–44; and Scott L. Cummings and Deborah L. Rhode, 'Managing Pro Bono: Doing Well by Doing Better' (2010) 78 *Fordham Law Review* 2357; *cf.* the more recent Scott L. Cummings, Fabio de Sa e Silva, and Louise G. Trubek, eds.,

Disadvantaged Communities, by Marjorie Mayo et al.,[41] provided a conceptual overview of access to justice and then focused on Law Centres in the UK after large cuts in legal aid expenditures. *Access to Justice: Beyond the Policies and Politics of Austerity*[42] also addressed access to justice in the UK, including one chapter on legal aid in the EU and one on access to justice in France, while *Access to Justice and Legal Aid: Comparative Perspectives on Unmet Legal Need* focused on Australia and Great Britain.[43]

There has been research on access to justice in countries outside western jurisdictions, although it is less well known and occasionally difficult to obtain. In terms of book treatments, an edited volume in 1985 by Harry Scoble and Laurie Wiseberg addressed South East Asia although the focus was human rights.[44] In 2002, Christina Jones-Pauly and Stefanie Elbern edited *Access to Justice: The Role of Court Administrators and Lay Adjudicators in the African and Islamic Contexts*,[45] and in 2009, Ayesha Kadwani Dias and Gita Honwana Welch published *Justice for the Poor: Perspectives on Accelerating Access*.[46] More recently, Yash Ghai and Jill Cottrell published *Marginalized Communities and Access to Justice*, which explores the rule of law via access to justice and focuses on the rights of communities or groups,[47] and Vinícius da Silva edited *Access to Justice in the Americas*.[48] A portion of this research focuses on access to justice regarding particular subject matter,[49] or has a constitutional or human rights,[50] international,[51] or gender

Global Pro Bono: Causes, Context, and Contestation (Cambridge: Cambridge University Press, 2022) [*Global Pro Bono*].

[41] Marjorie Mayo et al., *Access to Justice for Disadvantaged Communities* (Bristol: The Policy Press, 2014) [*Disadvantaged Communities*].

[42] Ellie Palmer et al., eds., *Access to Justice: Beyond the Policies and Politics of Austerity* (Oxford: Hart Publishing, 2016).

[43] Asher Flynn and Jacqueline Hodgson, eds., *Access to Justice and Legal Aid: Comparative Perspectives on Unmet Legal Need* (Oxford: Hart Publishing, 2017).

[44] Harry M. Scoble and Laurie S. Wiseberg, eds., *Access to Justice: Human Rights Struggles in South East Asia* (London: Zed Books, 1985).

[45] Christina Jones-Pauly and Stefanie Elbern, eds., *Access to Justice: The Role of Court Administrators and Lay Adjudicators in the African and Islamic Contexts* (The Hague: Kluwer Law International, 2002).

[46] Ayesha Kadwani Dias and Gita Honwana Welch, eds., *Justice for the Poor: Perspectives on Accelerating Access* (New Delhi. Oxford University Press, 2009).

[47] *Marginalized Communities*, *supra* note 3.

[48] Vinícius Alves Barreto da Silva, ed., *Access to Justice in the Americas* (Rio de Janeiro: Fórum Justiça, 2021) [*Access to Justice in the Americas*].

[49] Regarding access to mental health, see *Mental Health Law Reform*, *supra* note 8, at 132; regarding environmental justice, see Juan Miguel Picolotti and Kirstin L. Crane, 'Access to Justice Through the Central American Water Tribunal' in Carl Bruch et al., eds., *Public Participation in the Governance of International Freshwater Resources* (Tokyo: United Nations University Press, 2005) 460; *Environmental Justice*, *supra* note 25; and Engobo Emeseh, 'Environmental Victims, Access to Justice and the Sustainable Development Goals' in Chile Eboe-Osuji and Engobo Emeseh, eds., *Nigerian Yearbook of International Law 2017* (Cham: Springer, 2018) 291; regarding human rights in the Philippines, see Joselito S. Calivoso, Jr et al., *Access to Justice: Human Rights Abuses involving Corporations: Philippines* (Geneva: International Commission of Jurists, 2010); regarding microfinance in Peru, see Yasmine Olteanu, *Access to Justice in Microfinance: An Analytical Framework for Peru* (Cham: Palgrave Macmillan, 2018); and regarding Myanmar and democracy, see Helene M. Kyed and Aredth Maung Thawnghmung, *The Significance of Everyday Access to Justice in Myanmar's Transition to Democracy* (Singapore: ISEAS-Yusof Ishak Institute, 2019).

[50] See Kristina Bentley, 'Access to Justice: The Role of Legal Aid and Civil Society in Protecting the Poor' in Kristina Bentley, Laurie Nathan, and Richard Calland, eds., *Falls the Shadow: Between the Promise and the Reality of the South African Constitution* (Cape Town: University of Cape Town Press, 2013) 34; Chaloka Beyani, *Protection of the Right to Seek and Obtain Asylum under the African Human Rights System* (Leiden: M. Nijhoff, 2012); and Daniel Bonilla Maldonado, ed., *Constitutionalism of the Global South: The Activist Tribunals of India, South Africa, and Colombia* (Cambridge: Cambridge University Press, 2013).

[51] See Gaetano Pentassuglia, *Minority Groups and Judicial Discourse in International Law: A Comparative Perspective* (Leiden; Boston: Martinus Nijhoff Publishers, 2009).

focus.[52] Some work uses a development lens,[53] while other work takes place in the context of comparative legal systems.[54]

The volume seeks to expand this scholarship by providing different perspectives on access to justice, primarily via a strong focus on Asia. Many countries in Asia are economically or politically important,[55] and the region presents the kind of legal and social diversity which is well suited to a comparative project. Jurisdictions in Asia also offer important comparisons with western countries, challenging truisms regarding matters such as mandatory pro bono, and the role of legal aid and pro bono.

Most chapters examine access to justice within the context of the nation-state, one of the most common geographical structures of comparison.[56] Use of the nation-state is appropriate given the volume's focus on lawyers because, globalization notwithstanding, the regulation of lawyers is still handled primarily at the country (or in federations, the state) level. Methods of expanding access to justice 'are usually framed by local legal approaches'.[57]

Part I (Chapters 2 to 12) presents jurisdictions in Asia. Eleven chapters analyse a variety of legal traditions, political structures, and stages of socio-economic development: China, India, Indonesia, Japan, Malaysia, Myanmar, the Philippines, Singapore, South Korea, Taiwan, and Vietnam. Volume coverage is however not limited to nation-states, or to Asia, and the chapters in Part II provide comparative perspectives on particular aspects of access to justice. Michal Ofer-Tsfoni and Limor Zer-Gutman's chapter on Israel[58] addresses the challenges posed by a strong version of lawyer self-regulation. Helen Kruuse's chapter on South Africa presents an

[52] See Amanda Ellis, Claire Manuel, and Mark Blackden, eds., *Gender and Economic Growth in Uganda: Unleashing the Power of Women* (World Bank Publications, 2006); Amanda Ellis et al., eds., *Gender and Economic Growth in Kenya: Unleashing the Power of Women* (World Bank Publications, 2007); *Women's Access to Justice: Identifying the Obstacles & Need for Change: Thailand* (Geneva: International Commission of Jurists, 2012); *Women's Access to Justice in Kazakhstan: Identifying the Obstacles & Need for Change* (Geneva: International Commission of Jurists, 2013); Rachel Sieder and John-Andrew McNeish, eds., *Gender Justice and Legal Pluralities: Latin American and African Perspectives* (Abingdon: Routledge, 2013); Tim Luccaro and Erica Gaston, *Women's Access to Justice in Afghanistan: Individual Versus Community Barriers to Justice* (United States Institute of Peace, 2014); Sahar Maranlou, *Access to Justice in Iran: Women, Perceptions, and Reality* (New York: Cambridge University Press, 2015); Paul Bukuluki et al., 'Negotiating Restorative and Retributive Justice in Access to Justice for Survivors of Sexual and Gender Based Violence in Post-conflict Northern Uganda' in David Kaawa-Mafigiri and Eddy Joshua Walakiri, eds., *Child Abuse and Neglect in Uganda* (Cham: Springer, 2017) 201; and Rachel Sieder, ed., *Demanding Justice and Security: Indigenous Women and Legal Pluralities in Latin America* (New Brunswick: Rutgers University Press, 2017).

[53] See *Justice Reform, supra* note 9; Keith Crane et al., *Building a More Resilient Haitian State* (Rand Corporation, 2010); and *Access to Justice in South and South-East Asia, supra* note 22; and in the context of judicial reform, see e.g. Asia Pacific Judicial Reform Forum, *Searching for Success in Judicial Reform: Voices from the Asia Pacific Experience* (New Delhi: Oxford University Press, 2009).

[54] See Michèle Schmiegelow and Henrik Schmiegelow, eds., *Institutional Competition between Common Law and Civil Law: Theory and Policy* (Berlin: Springer, 2014) at 211–96.

[55] Prema-chandra Athukorala, 'Introduction and Overview' in Prema-chandra Athukorala, ed., *The Rise of Asia: Trade and Investment in Global Perspective* (Abingdon: Routledge, 2010) 1 at 1–2 (the twenty-first century 'has now come to be labeled the "Asian Century"'); and see Gao Zugui, 'The Effects of Asia's Overall Rise' (2014) 46 *China International Studies* 102 at 102–3, and Dale W. Jorgenson and Khuong M. Vu, 'The Rise of Developing Asia and the New Economic Order' (2011) *Journal of Policy Modeling* 698 at 699.

[56] Mark Van Hoecke, 'Methodology of Comparative Legal Research' (2015) *Law and Method* 1 [*Comparative Legal Research*] at 3.

[57] See *Access to Justice in the Americas*, supra note 48, at 8.

[58] Geographically, Israel is in the western tip of Asia, but it is understood primarily as part of the Middle East in socio-legal studies: see e.g. Richard L. Abel and Ole Hammerslev, eds., *Lawyers in 21st-Century Societies* (Oxford: Hart Publishing, 2020). This volume therefore includes Israel with other comparative perspective chapters as opposed to the jurisdiction-specific chapters of Asia.

environment of extreme economic inequality, a history of apartheid, and attempts at regulating mandatory pro bono; the latter enables comparisons with the mandatory schemes addressed in chapters on Japan and South Korea, and with US scholarship.[59]

Part II also includes four chapters on Syariah[60] law and courts. Syariah is a significant aspect of access to justice, particularly in South and South East Asia, where Syariah law and courts are primarily responsible for the personal law matters of marriage, divorce, maintenance, custody, and inheritance for Muslims.[61] Arif Jamal's chapter, 'Access to Justice and an Islamic Ethic of Justice', introduces the reader to the concept of access to justice in Syariah law. The Syariah chapters on Indonesia, Malaysia, and Singapore wrestle with how access to justice functions in their jurisdictions, and they provide an opportunity to compare access in different Syariah court systems. The Syariah chapters offer theoretical as well as practical interest. Some issues flow from a comparison of access to justice in different Syariah courts, such as whether non-Muslim lawyers should be allowed to practise in these courts,[62] and other issues are raised by comparing a nation-state structure to a religious structure, e.g. are there different conceptions of how to resolve disputes that impact the perceived necessity of lawyers?[63]

III. METHODOLOGY

Edited books that structure chapters via jurisdictional boundaries raise the question of how to engage in coherent comparison. The literature of comparative methodology is long and controversial,[64] and there is no agreement 'on the kind of methodology to be followed, nor even on the methodologies that could be followed'.[65] Maurice Adams, Jaakko Husa, and Marieke Oderkerk suggest that comparative law can be seen as a 'collection of methods that may be helpful in seeking answers to a variety of sorts of questions or problems about law', and that the method to use in any situation 'depends on the question one seeks to answer and the purpose one wants to achieve by doing a specific research project'.[66]

Access to justice can be understood as a right in itself or a means of accessing other rights,[67] and the volume focuses on the latter. This focus raised the following research questions for individual chapters: what needs to be known about the jurisdiction to grasp how access to justice is understood, how does access work or not work there, and based on this understanding how should the jurisdiction improve? With reference to Mark Van Hoecke's framework of compara-

59 See *Pro Bono in Principle*, *supra* note 35, at 37–45; Kendra Emi Nitta, 'An Ethical Evaluation of Mandatory Pro Bono' (1996) 29 *Loyola of Los Angeles Law Review* 909; and Rima Sirota, 'Making CLE Voluntary and Pro Bono Mandatory: A Law Faculty Test Case' (2017) 78 *Louisiana Law Review* 547 [*Making Pro Bono Mandatory*].

60 Per author preference, spellings of this word in the chapters include 'Shari'a', 'Sharia', 'Shariah', and 'Syariah'. In the Introduction and book headings, 'Syariah' is used as it is the usual transliteration in South East Asia.

61 See M. B. Hooker, *Islamic Law in South-East Asia* (Singapore: Oxford University Press, 1984); and Gregory C. Kozlowski, 'Islamic Law in Contemporary South Asia' (1997) 87:3–4 *The Muslim World* 221.

62 See Chapters 14, 15, and 16, and in Chapter 16, see Abbas' discussion of lawyer proficiency.

63 See Chapter 13.

64 See e.g. the research review by Maurice Adams, Jaakko Husa, and Marieke Oderkerk, 'Method and Methodology of Comparative Law: Introductory Remarks' in Maurice Adams, Jaakko Husa, and Marieke Oderkerk, eds., *Comparative Law Methodology* (Cheltenham: Edward Elgar, 2017) 1 [*Method and Methodology*].

65 *Comparative Legal Research*, *supra* note 56, at 1.

66 *Method and Methodology*, *supra* note 64, at 1.

67 *Disadvantaged Communities*, *supra* note 41, at 2.

tive law methodologies,[68] chapters in this volume use a combined functional and law-in-context approach. In terms of functionality,[69] all authors were asked to consider how their jurisdiction achieved or did not achieve access to justice. Chapters therefore prioritized how access to justice works in practice.[70] The contextualized aspect of this research prompted a number of chapters to include empirical research;[71] most chapters include existing quantitative data, and some chapters include qualitative data, pre-exising or produced for this volume.[72] Appendices include matters such as survey questions, as well as English translations of key legislative provisions related to access to justice, such as mandatory public interest regulations.[73]

The volume takes the view that access to justice can best be understood as a dynamic. Dynamics are produced by factors at work in particular jurisdictions, and while some factors are shared among certain jurisdictions, individual jurisdictions have a dynamic of their own.[74] Without an understanding of these factors and how they interact, proposed improvements in access may not accomplish much. Viewing access to justice in this way arguably allows for a clearer vision of positive change, because it acknowledges why and how certain change may be difficult or even unlikely.[75]

To respect the dynamics of individual jurisdictions as well as generate portraits that could offer some comparability,[76] authors were provided with categories of potentially relevant factors in their jurisdiction, including:

- Language: what words are used to discuss lawyers and access to justice, in English and in languages other than English? Why are the words used, and what connotations do they carry?
- Broader Currents: economy, history, legal system?
- Lawyers: conceptualization and types of lawyers, number of lawyers per capita, role of lawyers in society and law. Are lawyers required to contribute to access to justice, e.g. via legal services or monetary contributions, and what is the source of the requirement?
- Drivers: are there any legal guarantees of legal representation, e.g. right to counsel, right to legal aid? Are there key actors, such as non-governmental organizations ('NGOs'), or bar associations?
- Approach: what is the current approach to access to justice, and have there been major changes or shifts over time? What are the key institutions, who are the participants, and what are the sources of funding?
- Critique: what are the accomplishments and shortcomings, and how can shortcomings be improved?

68 *Comparative Legal Research*, *supra* note 56, at 9–11, 16–19, and see 20 (the common-core method is 'largely based on the functional method, to some extent combined with the law-in-context method').

69 *Comparative Legal Research*, *supra* note 56, at 9.

70 *Comparative Legal Research*, *supra* note 56, at 16.

71 *Comparative Legal Research*, *supra* note 56, at 17 ('[p]utting law in context aims at *understanding* the law, as a foreigner to that legal system and … *explaining* why the law is as it is. Inevitably, this implies empirical observation' (emphasis in original)).

72 See chapters on Japan (Chapter 5), Malaysia (Chapter 6), and Myanmar (Chapter 7).

73 See chapters on Japan (Chapter 5) and South Korea (Chapter 10).

74 In the context of legal rules, see the discussion of legal formants in Rodolfo Sacco, 'Legal Formants: A Dynamic Approach to Comparative Law (Installment I of II)' (1991) 39:1 *American Journal of Comparative Law* 1 at 21–34.

75 *Cf. Meaning of Access*, *supra* note 2, at 31–6.

76 *Method and Methodology*, *supra* note 64, at 3.

Authors were thus provided with an outline of potential factors, but they determined what aspects of access to justice were important. This approach led Ching-Fang Hsu and Yong-Ching Tsai's chapter on Taiwan to focus exclusively on the Legal Aid Foundation, and Sarasu Thomas' chapter on India to include the role played by alternative methods of dispute resolution such as *lok adalats*. In characterizing access to justice in their jurisdiction, chapters intend to go beyond country reports that answer the same series of questions.[77] Reports are extremely important sources of information and data, but the volume seeks to move further into the heart of access, by characterizing the relationship of lawyers and access to justice in that jurisdiction.

IV. POINTS OF COMPARISON

In addition to expanding our understanding of access to justice beyond the usual suspects, the volume suggests some potential relationships between the factors identified in the chapters. A few chapters, such as Hualing Fu's chapter on China and Hsu and Tsai's chapter on Taiwan, explicitly compare understandings of access to justice, legal aid, and pro bono to those of western democracies, and analyse how and why they are different. Alice Dawkins' and Nick Cheesman's Myanmar chapter characterizes lawyers as a 'legal occupation', not a legal profession, and the chapter acts as a point of comparison for any jurisdiction with a more developed legal profession. These non-western points of comparison, as well as inter-chapter comparisons, offer important diversity, because of a characteristic of comparison generally: the points chosen for comparison provide the structure of any resulting insight.[78] When read together the chapters raise an impressive array of comparative points, of which the main ones are highlighted here.

Language and Conception

One potential factor in the analysis of access to justice is language, and the interaction of English and other languages. English is not the dominant language in most of the jurisdictions covered in this volume, and because the language of the volume is English, authors were required to translate concepts and issues from other languages into English.[79] The volume though does not merely translate other languages into English, as differences between languages also contain the potential for conceptual insight.[80]

[77] See e.g. the International Legal Aid Group, online: www.internationallegalaidgroup.org/; *Thematic Study on Legal Aid* (ASEAN Intergovernmental Commission on Human Rights, 2019), online: https://aichr.org/wp-content/uploads/2019/09/AICHR-Thematic-Study-on-Legal-Aid-for-web.pdf; TrustLaw Index of Pro Bono 2020, 'Introduction', online: pbi.trust.org/introduction/?year=2020; and Presidents of Law Associations in Asia (POLA), online: www.polanet.org/main/main.php.

[78] See Esin Örücü, 'Developing Comparative Law', in Esin Örücü and David Nelken, eds., *Comparative Law: A Handbook* (Oxford: Hart, 2007) 43 at 62; regarding skills in comparative thinking, see Helena Whalen-Bridge, 'We Don't Need Another IRAC: Identifying Global Legal Skills' (2014) 10 *International Journal of Law in Context* 315 at 323–4.

[79] Managing different languages raised some citation issues. The volume's approach is to translate all article and book titles into English, but also provide some citation information in the original language to make chapters more accessible to readers fluent in that language. The authors' determinations are based on whether readers would need original language information to definitively locate a source.

[80] See e.g. Gerard-René de Groot, 'Legal Translation' in Jan M. Smits, ed., *Elgar Encyclopedia of Comparative Law*, 2nd edn (Cheltenham: Edward Elgar Publishing, 2012) 538.

Chapters discuss access to justice concepts and related usage in English and other languages in China, Indonesia, Japan, Malaysia, Myanmar, South Korea, Taiwan, Vietnam, and South Africa. This research constitutes initial steps toward the language of comparative access to justice. For example, many western countries define legal aid as government-funded legal services for deserving parties, while pro bono is understood as lawyer or law firm-funded legal services for deserving parties. Some chapters adopt this understanding, but not all the jurisdictions in the volume make this distinction; some use 'legal aid' as a catch-all phrase for any kind of legal assistance to low-income individuals. The latter usage could create confusion regarding contributions from different actors such as the government and lawyers, perhaps leading to less pro bono awareness among lawyers. This appears to be the case in Indonesia, where Yunita and Linda Yanti Sulistiawati note that there is widespread confusion among lawyers regarding the difference between legal aid and pro bono, and that lawyers do not agree that they have an obligation to serve low-income or vulnerable persons. This confusion continued after the passage of state-funded legal aid, when lawyers used legal aid funds to establish a 'pro bono' centre. In Malaysia, legal aid also applies to legal services from multiple sources, but Seh Lih Long observes a relatively clear understanding of lawyer obligations to provide access to justice and pro bono, even if it is not always carried out. One explanation for the difference is that Indonesia has multiple bar associations that compete for members and this leads to a lowering of standards generally, while Malaysia has one national bar association that has shown strong pro bono leadership.

Legal Aid and Pro Bono

Lord Denning observed in 1982 that the 'greatest revolution in the law' since World War II was 'the system of legal aid',[81] and governments now have a widely acknowledged obligation to provide some level of legal aid.[82] After recognizing the astronomical growth of legal aid in the US, Richard Abel suggested in 2009 that the 'most stunning contemporary development … is the concomitant rise of pro bono legal services',[83] i.e. law firm or lawyer-funded legal assistance. Today discussions of legal services and access to justice normally include both government-funded legal aid and pro bono.[84] What is the relationship between government-funded legal aid and pro bono? For example, does less legal aid generate more pro bono? There is some support for this equation, for example in the UK's historic development of expansive legal aid and a subsequent decline in voluntary associations providing free legal services.[85] The US suffered from cuts to legal aid that negatively impacted access to justice,[86] which in part gave rise to

[81] Lord Denning, *What Next in the Law* (London: Butterworths, 1982) at 81.

[82] See *Global Study on Legal Aid: Global Report* (United Nations Office of Drug and Crime, 2016) [*Global Report*] at 23.

[83] Richard L. Abel, 'State, Market, Philanthropy, and Self-Help as Legal Services Delivery Mechanisms' in Robert Granfield and Lynn Mather, eds., *Private Lawyers and the Public Interest: The Evolving Role of Pro Bono in the Legal Profession* (Oxford: Oxford University Press, 2009) 295 at 296.

[84] See *Global Pro Bono*, *supra* note 40.

[85] See Andrew Boon and Avis Whyte, '"Charity and Beating Begins at Home": The Aetiology of the New Culture of Pro Bono Publico' (1999) 2:2 *Legal Ethics* 169 at 175.

[86] See John Kilwein, 'The Decline of the Legal Services Corporation: "It's Ideological, Stupid!"' in Francis Regan et al., eds., *The Transformation of Legal Aid: Comparative and Historical Studies* (Oxford: Oxford University Press, 1999) 41 at 56–9.

expanded lawyer pro bono.[87] Examples from this volume include Singapore's historic refusal to implement broad-based criminal legal aid, which prompted the Law Society of Singapore's development of the Criminal Legal Aid Scheme in 1985.[88] George Radics and Alpha Pontanal also identified the supposed sufficiency of the government-funded Public Attorney's Office (PAO) in the Philippines as a barrier to pro bono legal practice.[89]

The relationship between government-funded and lawyer-funded legal services can also be more complex. In Hiroshi Otsuka and Setsuo Miyazawa's chapter on Japan, factors including the bar's desire to retain independence from the government, as well as limit the number of attorneys, have prompted the growth of extensive bar programmes of legal services and relatively large bar association fees. The largest bar associations in Japan have pursued not only voluntary pro bono, but also mandatory public interest activity requirements. In the editor's chapter on Singapore, after considerable success in increasing lawyer pro bono in the 2000s, the government reversed its historic position against criminal legal aid and greatly expanded funding for non-capital indigent defence.

Governments should bear the primary burden of legal services for low-income and vulnerable persons,[90] and Thomas notes that this is particularly true in countries with extreme levels of poverty, where a more profound lack of material resources greatly diminishes possibilities to participate in dispute resolution.[91] However, many countries have experienced legal aid cutbacks. Per Scott Cummings, the US demonstrates the 'promise and perils of the government-centered approach'.[92] The main lesson of legal services in the US is that 'a progressive law reform agenda that asserted the rights of the poor against government bureaucracies and private businesses was vulnerable to political backlash'[93] when the political winds changed. What might happen if government funding did bear the primary burden? Hsu and Tsai's chapter on Taiwan explores this question. They critique the literature on access to justice, which identifies the private practice lawyer, 'able and independent, volunteering outside the state' via pro bono. The literature of legal aid focuses on good governance, i.e. budgets, means and merits tests, the quality of representation, and other accountability issues. Hsu and Tsai argue that the Legal Aid Foundation in Taiwan restructures the access to justice debate by altering the relationship between the state, civil society, lawyers, and the legal profession. In part due to a budget within the Judicial Yuan which is relatively insulated from political shifts, this government-funded legal aid programme has become the major actor in access to justice, moving from individual client services to public advocacy and social justice, and exerting increasing control over individual lawyers in the process. However, having taken on more responsibilities to support access to justice, it has also encountered issues with accountability, as well as tensions with the state and the lawyers it employs.

87 See Richard Abel's brief discussion of the US, Australia, and civil-law countries in Richard L. Abel, 'The Paradoxes of Pro Bono' (2010) 78 *Fordham Law Review* 2443 at 2444; and in the US, see *Politics of Pro Bono, supra* note 40, at 23–4; for other factors in the US, see *Politics of Pro Bono, supra* note 40, at 6–41.

88 Chapter 9.

89 Chapter 8, Alpha Pontanal, Interview with Attorney Marlon Manuel, National Coordinator, Alternative Law Groups (March 2017, Manila, Philippines).

90 *Global Report, supra* note 82, at 2–3.

91 Chapter 3.

92 *Politics of Pro Bono, supra* note 40, at 20.

93 *Politics of Pro Bono, supra* note 40, at 21.

Pro Bono

Pro bono is commonly understood in North America as the provision of free legal services by a lawyer to benefit persons of limited means.[94] Radics and Pontanal briefly review the history of pro bono and observe that current conceptions of pro bono are relatively recent, emerging as a topic of study predominantly in the last few decades.[95] Pro bono has expanded in many western countries but expansion has not been uniform throughout the world, and pro bono only began to expand in the South East Asian region in the relatively recent past.[96]

The growth of pro bono is reflected in chapters on Malaysia, the Philippines, Singapore, and South Korea, but not all chapters identify pro bono as a major force. Hsu and Tsai's chapter on Taiwan identifies state-funded legal aid as the major player. Nor are all jurisdictions familiar with the phrase or the concept of pro bono. In Myanmar, where lawyers lack a unified and legal professional body or bar association, Dawkins and Cheesman note that terms like pro bono do not map neatly onto local usage.[97] In other jurisdictions, different ideas are central and must be reckoned with, e.g. public interest lawyering in South Korea[98] and Japan.[99] In Indonesia, Yunita and Sulistiawati observe that the concept of pro bono was historically understood to apply only to lawyers working in legal aid institutes and NGOs, not lawyers generally, and most lawyers and other legal actors engage in a highly commercialized practice. This practice environment is corroborated by Euis Nurlaelawati's chapter on Indonesian Syariah courts, which documents the pragmatic view that many lawyers take regarding legal practice, one that leads them to prioritize financial and professional interests above the law and sometimes client interests.

Pro bono and the contexts for it vary. Hsu and Tsai observe that '[s]tudies on pro bono lawyers, coming first from common law jurisdictions, naturally label lawyers as representatives of normative values, supported by a professional community with ample material means'.[100] But Thomas notes that in India, unlike the medical profession, lawyers as a whole do not earn large sums, and in fact the Bar Council has sought state support for lawyers in the form of pensions, health insurance, and stipends for young lawyers. In this jurisdiction, paying lawyers (relatively low amounts) to perform legal aid is the long-standing means of providing legal services to low-income and vulnerable persons.

Kerstin Steiner observes a different kind of issue in the Syariah courts of Malaysia, that of conflicting motivations in Syariah criminal cases. Criminal defence lawyers may well experience qualms about defending an accused criminal in other jurisdictions, but being a criminal defence lawyer in the Syariah context carries a moral stigma and creates a moral dilemma.

[94] Helena Whalen-Bridge, 'The Conceptualisation of Pro Bono in Singapore' (2014) 9:1 *Asian Journal of Comparative Law* 97 at 97.

[95] Chapter 8, citing Robert Granfield, 'The Meaning of Pro Bono: Institutional Variations in the Professional Obligations Among Lawyers' (2007) 41 *Law & Society Review* 113 at 113.

[96] See e.g. Daniel Lev, 'Lawyers' Causes in Indonesia and Malaysia' in Austin Sarat et al., eds., *Cause Lawyering: Political Commitments and Professional Responsibilities* (Oxford: Oxford University Press, 1998) 431, 432; and Stephen Ellmann, 'Cause Lawyering in the Third World' in Austin Sarat et al., eds., *Cause Lawyering: Political Commitments and Professional Responsibilities* (Oxford: Oxford University Press, 1998) 349, 350.

[97] Chapter 7.

[98] Chapter 10.

[99] Chapter 5.

[100] Chapter 11.

Lawyers may be criticized for 'defending wrongdoers against Islam' and being 'with the enemies of Islam against Islam'.[101]

If pro bono is understood as fulfilling a lawyer's professional obligation to justice, it has positive connotations, which is one of the reasons why lawyers and law firms want to be seen doing it. But in the Philippines, pro bono has different connotations. Here pro bono has been promoted by the state, and to the degree lawyers voluntarily participate in it, they may become associated with the state as an oppressive institution that has historically used law to oppress and avoid its own obligations.[102]

Mandatory Pro Bono

Some chapters explore schemes of mandatory requirements and whether they are feasible or desirable. In the US, where mandatory pro bono has been defined as requiring lawyers to provide legal services to low-income individuals without pay, it has been rejected by lawyers and bar associations for a number of reasons.[103] In this volume, chapters on the Philippines and Singapore document proposed schemes of mandatory pro bono that were defeated or not implemented. Kruuse describes how South Africa had bar-imposed mandatory requirements at one point, although they lacked a penalty for non-compliance, and she notes that pending legislation regarding mandatory community service allows for a wide variety of activities which cannot be characterized as pro bono. In Vietnam, Nguyen Hung Quang notes that lawyers are obligated by the Law on Lawyers to provide legal assistance. Some bar associations organize services at their offices or via tours to remote areas; however, lawyers are primarily requested to help disseminate legal information or settle protests. The Vietnam Bar Federation as well as local bars are responsible for guiding and monitoring these activities, and instruction from the Vietnam Bar Federation used to require eight hours of legal work per year or the monetary equivalent of 40 per cent of a basic monthly salary. However, in 2017 the Vietnam Bar Federation issued new instructions which reduced the number of required hours to four and removed the monetary contribution. The current sanction for non-compliance is merely that the lawyer will not be eligible for an award.

Two chapters in the volume, those on Japan and South Korea, explore functioning mandatory programmes that incorporate some legal services to low-income or vulnerable persons. Otsuka and Miyazawa note that in Japan, mandatory public interest activities were imposed by four major bar associations in urban areas in the 2000s: *Ichiben*, *Niben*, *Toben* (Tokyo region), and the *Kanagawa* Bar Association (Yokohama); in smaller bar associations, peer pressure appears sufficient to motivate members to do relevant work. Otsuka and Miyazawa examine the *Toben* rules in detail, and a recent revision of these rules indicates that the main purpose was not the provision of legal services to low-income persons but the need to staff all bar association activities.

In South Korea, Takgon Lee and JaeWon Kim point out that the Attorney-at-Law Act, not a bar association requirement, requires all Korean lawyers to perform a certain amount of public interest activities. The requirement arose out of a series of corruption scandals in which former

[101] Chapter 15.
[102] Chapter 8.
[103] See *Making Pro Bono Mandatory*, *supra* note 59, 574–8.

judges-turned-lawyers bribed large numbers of judges, prosecutors, and police officers. In response, the Ministry of Justice inter alia announced a plan to abolish the mandatory bar system, grant freedom to establish and join different bar associations, and transfer the Korean Bar Association's (KBA) authority to discipline its members to the government. The KBA then asserted that beyond being a professional organization, it existed to serve the public interest, and it petitioned for an amendment to the Attorney-at-Law Act that included mandatory public interest activities. The amendment was adopted but details of the requirement were delegated to the KBA, and under these guidelines working as a legal advisor as well as bar association matters qualify as mandatory activities. The requirement has been criticized because its broad scope is satisfied by many different activities and enforcement activity is lacking, but Lee and Kim argue that the requirement has encouraged law firm development of pro bono, with the annual requirement of 20 hours becoming the benchmark to exceed.

Abel has argued that the politics of legal aid were central to legal aid reforms.[104] In a similar fashion, chapters on Japan and South Korea suggest that there were strong reasons other than access to justice which motivated mandatory requirements. Fu also argues that China's system of mandatory paid legal aid, discussed further below, was imposed by the state on a potentially wealthy but politically weak profession, when lawyers' social status was relatively low.

The mandatory programmes analysed here also suggest that once an obligation becomes mandatory, there is pressure to create regulatory flexibility elsewhere, e.g. by expanding the list of activities that meet the requirement. Both the Japan and South Korea programmes have exemptions, and both programmes allow lawyers to make a monetary contribution in lieu of service. In practice, China's mandatory paid legal aid scheme allows law firms to designate a junior associate to handle cases on behalf of other lawyers in the firm.

As noted above, western countries have defined mandatory pro bono as free legal services that lawyers are obligated to provide to low-income individuals. It is of course not necessary to define mandatory pro bono this way, and if other aspects of compulsory lawyer contributions to access to justice are considered, there are more mandatory activities afoot than first appears. For example, Long points out that as part of the training qualifications for admittance as an advocate and solicitor to the High Court of Malaya, prospective lawyers have to participate in a compulsory 14-day internship with the Bar Council Legal Aid Scheme. Once they become qualified lawyers, they are required to make a yearly contribution to the Bar Council Legal Aid Scheme as part of the cost of renewing their practice certificate, a requirement for legal practice.

Mandatory, Paid Legal Service

There is relatively little discussion in the US and the UK of paid legal services which lawyers are required to perform for low-income or vulnerable individuals. Arguably this lack results from analysing access to justice via two accepted dichotomies: legal aid and pro bono on one hand, and voluntary and mandatory pro bono on the other. Compulsory legal services are understood to be unpaid pro bono only. There is a distinctively different possibility, that of requiring lawyers to provide legal services but paying them for it. Fu observes that when

[104] Richard L. Abel, 'Law without Politics: Legal Aid under Advanced Capitalism' (1985) 32 *UCLA Law Review* 474; *cf.* Francis Regan et al., 'Introduction' in Francis Regan et al., eds., *The Transformation of Legal Aid* (Oxford: Oxford University Press, 1999) 1 at 2.

lawyers were required to perform mandatory pro bono in China in 1996, they resisted. The state did not want to offend or alienate a potentially influential profession, and legal aid was a relatively low political priority. The law firm and bar association structures that enforce similar requirements in other countries were not in place; law firm structures were not strong, and bar associations were relatively weak because the authoritarian political system did not allow the creation of a bar independent of government control. Changes did ultimately support a paid mandatory requirement: legal aid was acknowledged to be a government responsibility, China developed the financial capacity to provide more legal aid funding, and a consensus grew that lawyers' work, like any work, should be adequately compensated. However, Fu argues that this approach has commercialized legal assistance in China and hollowed out public interest among lawyers in general, although some lawyers have developed a public interest spirit outside the official legal aid system. Fu's chapter raises the question of what kind of public spirit is sought in China.

Political Structure

Some chapters address the degree to which political structure and openness impacts access to justice. Quang recognizes the profound influence that democratic centralism has had on Vietnam, including the subordinate nature of the judiciary to the National Assembly, and the long-held understanding that lawyer activities and organizations are not independent of the government. A lack of lawyer independence historically diluted effective representation, for example by allowing state officials to represent criminal defendants, and it continues to hamper lawyer representation. Fu observes that China's authoritarian regime shapes access to justice in two ways. Legal professionals are more accountable to the state than to law, and courts are more receptive to political imperatives, giving priority to policy changes. Authoritarianism also ensures a weak legal system that lacks capacity and autonomy from the state, and this invites competition from other actors, leading to the resolution of many disputes without judicial involvement. Dawkins and Cheesman note that in Myanmar, the military dictatorship has stripped lawyers of professional characteristics to the extent that they are better characterized as an occupation, as opposed to a profession, although this has not prevented them from building identities and locating resources in more fragmented location- and politics-specific communities.

Structure and Strength of Lawyer Organizations

As described by Sandefur, there are two prominent accounts of lawyers' relationship to the market for their services, the classical theory and the market control theory.[105] Classically, professions are understood as largely self-regulating organizations, comprised of members that possess a strong professional identity which includes a duty of public service.[106] The market control theory regards professional behaviour as 'principally reflecting occupational self-interest'.[107] The market theory has been disputed,[108] but the thesis that a stronger bar association is

[105] *Civil Legal Assistance*, *supra* note 37, at 85–9.
[106] *Civil Legal Assistance*, *supra* note 37, at 85–6.
[107] *Civil Legal Assistance*, *supra* note 37, at 86; see *Just Law?*, *supra* note 1, at 297.
[108] See Scott L. Cummings, 'What Good are Lawyers?' in Scott L. Cummings, ed., *The Paradox of Professionalism: Lawyers and the Possibility of Justice* (New York: Cambridge University Press, 2011) 1 at 16–20.

more likely to pursue professional and financial interests over access to justice has some support in this volume. Ofer-Tsfoni and Zer-Gutman argue that while the State of Israel is the primary actor, the legal profession and the Israel Bar Association (IBA) are extraordinarily influential regarding whether access to justice is realized. The IBA has an expansive autonomy with little external oversight, and from this position of considerable strength it has worked against legal clinics in law school, blocked legal technology seeking to expand legal services, and only reluctantly participated in free legal assistance. Per Thomas, the strong bar in India is accompanied by low levels of pro bono, to the extent that data can be collected, and the legal profession has restricted the ability of law school clinics to assist low-income or vulnerable persons. Market control theory does not fully explain Japan though. Here the bar's historical insistence on a small number of attorneys restricted access to justice, but the imposition of mandatory public interest requirements by major bar associations expanded access to justice, although Otsuka and Miyazawa suggest that this was prompted by a variety of factors, including the need to retain independence from the authorities as well as service bar association activities.

Do relatively weaker bar associations translate into expanded access? In Myanmar, Dawkins and Cheesman establish that lawyers have had an impact on access to justice despite the lack of an organized bar association, and the bar in South Korea was in a severely compromised state when it proposed mandatory pro bono. In Singapore, the government and lawyer dynamic limits the power of lawyers, and pro bono has seen considerable growth; however, in many cases pro bono was initiated by lawyers, so Singapore cannot be explained in terms of a weak bar association being overcome by a more powerful government.

V. CONCLUSION

In the context of understanding legal aid, Abel has suggested that it is difficult but essential to maintain 'the inescapable tension between optimism and pessimism'.[109] Chapters in this volume have charted advances as well as obstacles to access to justice, but from the perspective of a non-expert user of law, the more important tension in access to justice is how to achieve fairness in the face of persistent inequality. By focusing on the factors that function in particular jurisdictions, this volume offers material to assist readers contemplating how to improve access. It also leaves the field with much research to be pursued. Despite the volume's 18 chapters, Part I does not include all jurisdictions in Asia, and Part II only includes a fraction of the jurisdictions which merit comparative attention. And beyond the volume's focus on formal dispute resolution lies the vitally important, larger area of informal dispute resolution, and how to resolve tensions between rights and resolution in that context, as well as between corrective and distributive justice,[110] across jurisdictions. True access to justice is an ideal, but there is much to do for those without it.

109 Richard L. Abel, 'The Paradoxes of Legal Aid' in Alan A. Paterson and Tamara Goriely, eds., *A Reader on Resourcing Civil Justice* (Oxford: Oxford University Press, 1996) 146 at 160.

110 See Marc Galanter, 'Access to Justice in a World of Expanding Social Capacity' (2010) 37 *Fordham Urban Law Journal* 115 at 128.

PART I

Access to Justice in Asia

2

Pro Bono, Legal Aid, and the Struggle for Justice in China

*Hualing Fu**

Abstract

This chapter examines the role of lawyers in providing legal services to indigent persons and facilitating access to justice in China. The chapter explores the degree to which access to justice in China is different from other countries, and addresses whether those differences are related to China's political and legal system or China's status as a middle-income country with a low level of GDP per capita. Under current Chinese law, the provision of legal services to the poor is both a government responsibility and a duty of practising lawyers. The principal argument of the chapter is that legal aid has reduced the scope of non-professional representation, and that increased legal aid funding has commercialized legal aid in China and hollowed out public interest among lawyers in general. However, as the legal profession grows, a public interest spirit has started to develop outside the official legal aid system, with some lawyers volunteering their services to assist those in legal need and promote public interest.

I. INTRODUCTION

China is a latecomer in developing its legal profession. Concepts like pro bono, legal aid, and access to justice were only introduced in China in the past 20 years.[1] In a mature legal system with an independent and effective judiciary at its core, access to justice tends to be court-centric, and pro bono services and legal aid, operating in the shadows of the legal system, are in general geared to providing effective access to courts. Is China's development following this trend? This chapter examines the role of lawyers in providing legal services to indigent persons and facilitating access to justice in China, exploring the degree to which access to justice in China is different from other countries, and addressing whether those differences are related to China's political/legal system and China's status as a middle-income country with a low level

* I am grateful to Tang Mei, Huang Yizhi, and Mike West for their comments on the earlier versions of this chapter. I would also like to thank Helena Whalen-Bridge for her meticulous editorship.

[1] Fu Hualing and Richard Cullen, 'The Development of Public Interest Litigation in China' in Po Jen Yap and Holning Lau, eds., *Public Interest Litigation in Asia* (London: Routledge, 2011) 14 [*Public Interest Litigation in Asia*] at 28; Benjamin L. Liebman, 'Legal Aid and Public Interest Law in China' (1994) 34 *Texas International Law Journal* 211 [*Legal Aid and Public Interest Law in China*] at 212; William P. Alford, 'Lawyers, Legal Aid, and Legitimacy in China' in William P. Alford, ed., *Raising the Bar: The Emerging Legal Profession in East Asia* (Cambridge, MA: Harvard University Press, 2007) 311 [*Legal Aid and Legitimacy*] at 311; Titi M. Liu, 'Transmission of Public Interest Law: A Chinese Case Study' (2008) 13 *UCLA Journal of International Law and Foreign Affairs* 263 [*Transmission of Public Interest Law*] at 275.

of GDP per capita. The chapter analyses the development of legal aid in China in general, with some specific examples of legal aid from the city of Chongqing, a province-ranking city under direct central control. Information regarding Chongqing, unless otherwise specified, was obtained through the author's interviews with lawyers from that city in 2017.

Under current Chinese law, the provision of legal services to the poor is both a government responsibility and a duty of practising lawyers. As interpreted and practised in China though, the government is duty-bound to provide legal aid funding, while lawyers must undertake a certain number of paid legal aid cases as a condition for renewing their annual practising certificates. The argument of this chapter regarding access to justice is twofold. First, the increase in legal aid has reduced the scope of non-professional representation in Chinese courts and thus the level of social participation in the legal system, but it has also reduced the involvement of police in individual disputes and social conflict, thus symbolizing a baton-to-gavel transition in dispute resolution. Second, increased legal aid funding has commercialized legal aid in China and hollowed out public interest among lawyers in general, but as the legal profession grows, a public interest spirit has started to develop outside the official legal aid system, with some lawyers volunteering their services to assist those in legal need and promote public interest. However, public interest lawyering continues to face unique political challenges under China's authoritarian political system.

II. ACCESS TO JUSTICE TERMINOLOGY IN CHINA

Although the English phrase access to justice is frequently referred to in the literature in China, the term does not have a concise Chinese translation. The translation, getting close to justice, is awkward. Users of the English term are aware of the lack of equivalence in Chinese, and when the term access to justice is used, both the English term and its Chinese translation are displayed. Instead of access to justice, the term legal aid (*falu yuanzhu* or 法律援助), which refers to the system of government-organized and government-funded legal assistance to poor persons, is the official term used to describe the legal process of facilitating access to justice. More recently, the idea of providing justice to all, as exhorted by President Xi through legal aid to the poor and those in need, is strongly promoted by the government as a core component of socialist law and has gained popularity among the general public.

On the other hand, pro bono, defined as free legal services provided by lawyers for the poor and those in need, is not well known as an English phrase or as a general concept. China does not have an institutionalized pro bono practice. When used in China, the concept of pro bono is intertwined with the official legal aid system and is often regarded as an integral part of that system. Indeed, there is no equivalent Chinese phrase for pro bono as such.

In this chapter, the phrase legal aid will be used in the sense most often used in China: the government organized and funded process of facilitating access to justice for poor persons. In contrast, pro bono will refer to the idea that lawyers not funded by the government should provide free legal services to poor people.

III. LEGALITY IN AUTHORITARIAN STATES

China is an authoritarian state where the Chinese Communist Party ('Party') monopolizes all political power. The 1982 Chinese Constitution ('Constitution')[2] entrenched the

[2] *Constitution of the People's Republic of China*, 1982 (as amended 11 March 2018).

Party's leadership role in China, which renders any challenge to its monopoly over political power unconstitutional and illegal. Article 1 of the Constitution openly asserts that China is 'a socialist state under the people's democratic dictatorship'. China's authoritarian state limits the autonomy of law, the independence of legal institutions, and the professionalism of legal actors.

Although politically authoritarian at the core, the Party has proven adaptable in reforming its political and legal institutions to meet external and internal challenges. Like many other authoritarian states,[3] the Chinese Party-state has embraced and promoted the concept of a socialist rule of law, and has undertaken to respect human rights. The Party-state has reiterated its commitment to strengthen legal institutions around the margins and to rely on legal rules and institutions in dispute resolution. Significantly, Article 5 of the Constitution provides for the principles of the rule of law, equality before the law, and supremacy of Constitution and laws. Article 24 further states that 'the state respects and protects human rights'. Beneath the periodical political repression that often sweeps through China's legal landscape, China's emerging legal system has been struggling for institutionalization.[4] Legal reforms aimed at enhancing judicial autonomy and power have even continued since 2015, during one of the worst crackdowns on human rights lawyers and civil society in recent history.[5]

Since the decisive shift in the late 1970s from revolution to modernization, legal rules and legal institutions have been playing a more meaningful role in social and economic governance.[6] In relative terms, there has been a gradual process of juridification in areas beyond the political core, whereby ordinary disputes are increasingly resolved through legal institutions including the courts, and facilitated by lawyers in accordance with legal rules. While political control over the legal process continues to take place and is even tightening in some spaces, legal rules are important and consequential in a vast majority of areas constituting the ordinary range of justice. Within this institutional design, China follows a global trend and faces the common challenges of capacity building in the courts and improving access to justice.

China's type of authoritarian regime shapes access to justice in two different ways. First, it directly affects the operation of legal institutions. Under China's authoritarian system, legal professionals are more politically accountable to the Party-state than they are legally accountable to the law. Courts are also more receptive and responsive to political imperatives, giving priority to government policy changes. Depending on the prevailing political economy, for example, courts handling labour disputes can be friendly to labour, indifferent to labour, or hostile to labour,[7] and

[3] Tom Ginsburg and Tamir Moustafa, eds., *Rule by Law: The Politics of Courts in Authoritarian Regimes* (Cambridge: Cambridge University Press, 2008) at 4–10; Mark Tushnet, 'Authoritarian Constitutionalism' (2015) 100 *Cornell Law Review* 391 at 423.

[4] Fu Hualing, 'Challenging Authoritarianism through Law: Potentials and Limit' (2011) 6 *National Taiwan University Law Review* 339 at 342.

[5] Fu Hualing, 'The July 9th (709) Crackdown on Human Rights Lawyers: Legal Advocacy in an Authoritarian State' (2018) 112 *Journal of Contemporary China* 554 [*July 9th Crackdown*] at 566.

[6] Randall Peerenboom, *China's Long March Toward Rule of Law* (Cambridge: Cambridge University Press, 2002) [*March Toward Rule of Law*] at 55; Albert Chen, *An Introduction to the Legal System of the People's Republic of China*, 4th edn (Hong Kong: LexisNexis, 2011) [*PRC Legal System*] at 41–5.

[7] For examples of the situational application of law on labour cases, see Yang Su and Xin He, 'Street as Courtroom: State Accommodation of Labour Protest in South China' (2010) 44 *Law & Society Review* 157; and Aaron Halegua, 'Getting Paid: Processing the Labor Disputes of China's Migrant Workers' (2008) 26 *Berkeley Journal of International Law* 254 [*Getting Paid*]. For a careful study of the political use of labour law, see Mary E. Gallagher, *Authoritarian Legality in China: Law, Workers, and the State* (Cambridge: Cambridge University Press, 2017) [*Authoritarian Legality in China*] at 213.

judges can be accordingly lenient or harsh in sentencing in relative terms.[8] The political identity of legal actors is in general stronger than their professional identity.

Second, authoritarianism ensures a weak legal system that lacks capacity and autonomy. A weak legal system allows the diversion of disputes away from courts and invites competition for jurisdiction from other political and administrative entities. Because of this diversion and competition, a significant proportion of disputes are settled without judicial involvement and resolved or otherwise managed through informal justice spaces such as mediation.[9] Moreover, the police are empowered to intervene in disputes and conflict at an early stage through multiple means, including force. The political imperative to pre-empt disputes allows a high degree of informality and political control in dispute resolution.[10]

A country's economic environment significantly impacts on the implementation of its rule of law.[11] Justice is economically costly as well as politically risky. China has become well known for its economic growth over the past 40 years, having achieved a status of being the second largest economy in terms of total GDP within a relatively short time span. The irony is that while China's economic resources allow it to invest more in legal institutions and expand legal aid spending, its 2016 GDP per capita was slightly over US$8,000, a figure far below the average level of an advanced economy,[12] even though that constitutes a significant increase since the beginning of economic reform. The availability of increased legal aid funding has proved essential to incentivizing lawyers, and it has allowed the government to openly state that legal aid is a public good to be paid for by the state. Ultimately however, financial capacity is limited when faced with the scale of the demand for justice from the society. Indeed, the legal aid services available in different Chinese provinces and cities largely depend on the amount of legal aid funding from the respective local governments. Wealthy areas by and large do better in providing legal aid, soliciting support from the wider society to those in need, and compensating lawyers who provide legal aid services.[13]

IV. FROM LEGAL PLURALISM TO ACCESS TO THE COURTS

Currently, China has a pluralist legal services structure. There is first and foremost a distinction in the delivery of legal services between rural and urban areas. China operates a dual

[8] Susan Trevaskes, *Policing Serious Crime in China: From Strike Hard to Kill Fewer* (Abingdon: Routledge, 2010) at 170–1.

[9] Fu Hualing, 'Mediation and the Rule of Law: The Chinese Landscape' in Joachim Zekoll, Moritz Balz, and Iwo Amelung, eds., *Formalization and Flexibilisation in Dispute Resolution* (Leiden: Brill–Nijhoff, 2015) 108 at 114.

[10] Ibid.; Fu Hualing and Michael Palmer, 'Mediation in Contemporary China: Continuity and Change' in Fu Hualing and Michael Palmer, eds., *Mediation in Contemporary China: Continuity and Change* (London: Wildy, Simmonds & Hill Publishing, 2017) 1 at 7–9; Cynthia Estlund and Aaron Halegua, 'What is Socialist about Labour Law in China?' in Fu Hualing et al., eds., *Socialist Law in Socialist East Asia* (Cambridge: Cambridge University Press, 2018) 257 at 272–3; and Zhou Kai and Yan Xiao Jun, 'The Quest for Stability: Policing Popular Protest in the People's Republic of China' (2014) 61 *Problems of Post-Communism* 3 at 6–7. For a general comparative study, see Richard L. Abel, *The Politics of Informal Justice: Vol. II, Comparative Studies* (New York: Academic Press, 1982).

[11] Randall Peerenboom, 'Law and Development in Middle-Income Countries' in Randall Peerenboom and Tom Ginsburg, eds., *Law and Development of Middle-Income Countries: Avoiding the Middle-Income Trap* (Cambridge: Cambridge University Press, 2014) 1 at 7.

[12] *GDP per capita (current US$) – China* (The World Bank), online: https://data.worldbank.org/indicator/NY.GDP.PCAP.CD?contextual=max&end=2016&locations=CN&start=1960.

[13] China, Department of Legal Aid Work, Ministry of Justice, 健全法律援助制度调研报告汇 (Collection of Research Reports for Legal Aid System Improvement) (Beijing: Beijing University Press, 2014) [*Legal Aid Improvement Reports*] at 372–5 (Zhengzhou), 398–402 (Guangzhou), and 430–2 (Yinchuan).

legal profession, with lawyers serving cities, and another less standardized class of legal workers (法律工作者) who provide more limited services in rural areas. In rural areas, access to lawyers has remained limited. In response to unmet legal need in rural communities, the government created the quasi-legal profession of legal workers. Unlike their professional peers, the minimum educational requirement for legal workers is a sub-university qualification, and they are qualified through provincially based examinations as opposed to national examinations. Legal workers are barred from practising criminal law, and their practices are limited to rural counties where they are registered. Totalling around 120,000,[14] legal workers principally serve the legal needs of farmers. Concentrated in county seats, legal workers compete directly with lawyers at the county and sub-county levels. While lawyers have tried to eliminate or otherwise restrict the practice of their less qualified peers, the latter have proven resilient. The existence of legal workers has always been a contentious issue and their partial practice is a compromise between the legal profession that demands abolition and the government that wants to preserve the dual system to meet legal needs in vast rural areas. The wider political and legal circumstances are hostile to their continuation,[15] but given the scarcity or absence of qualified lawyers in rural areas, legal workers are likely to survive in the foreseeable future.

The Lawyers Law governs the regular legal profession.[16] Prior to the enactment of this law, lawyers were defined as state legal workers, who were part of the state legal establishment and directly accountable to the government.[17] In the initial stage of China's market economic reforms in the early 1990s, the rule of law and an independent legal profession were regarded as indispensable pillars to support the growing edifice of market transactions. Under the able leadership of Xiao Yang, the Ministry of Justice privatized an essential public service against strong political opposition. A landmark piece of legislation, the Lawyers Law was enacted in 1996 to delink the legal profession from the government in order to facilitate an emerging socialist market economy.

Since 1996, lawyers have also become a socialized profession, and they are, in the legal aid colloquialism, often referred to as social lawyers. This phrase refers to private lawyers who take legal aid cases paid for by the government, as distinguished from salaried legal aid lawyers, government employees who provide legal aid services. There are currently nearly 330,000 lawyers in China,[18] and as of 2012, about 1 per cent were salaried legal aid lawyers,[19] mostly practising law

[14] 司法部关于组织全国基层法律服务工作者执业资格考试和考核工作的通知 (Notice by the Ministry of Justice on the Organization of National Practising Qualification Examination and Assessment of Legal Workers) (issued 7 June 2000).

[15] William P. Alford, '"Second Lawyers", First Principles: Lawyers, Rice-roots Legal Workers, and the Battle over Legal Professionalism in China' in William P. Alford, Kenneth Winston, and William C. Kirby, eds., *Prospects for Professionalism in China: Essays on Civic Vocations* (London: Routledge, 2013) 51 at 52; Fu Hualing, 'Away from Grass-roots? The Irony of the Chinese Rural Legal Service' (2015) 60 *Diogene* 116 at 126.

[16] 律师法 (Lawyers Law), China 2007, c 76 (with effect from 28 October 2007), online: www.gov.cn/flfg/2007-10/28/content_788495.htm.

[17] *PRC Legal System*, *supra* note 6, at 220.

[18] 司法部首次举行新闻发布会 关注律师执业权利保障 (The Ministry of Justice Holding its First Press Conference, Responding to the Questions Relating to the Protection of Lawyers' Rights and Lawyers' Classification by Expertise), *CCTV* (26 April 2017), online: news.cctv.com/2017/04/26/ARTI6mlNRg3akY534QjW0884170426.shtml.

[19] The 1 per cent estimation is based on provincial statistics gathered in *Legal Aid Improvement Reports*, *supra* note 13, at 6, 13, 19, 31, 39, 51, 60, 71, 85, 96, 107, 115, 125, 136, 147, 156, 166, 176, 192, 204, 220, 232, 245, 257, 272, 280, 285, 289, 300, 310, 329, 340, 359, 368, 373, 390, 405, 413, 421, and 425; China, State Council Information Office,《中国的司法改革》白皮书 (White Paper: Judicial Reform in China) (9 October 2012), online: www.scio.gov.cn/zfbps/ndhf/2012/Document/1226620/1226620_5.htm [*White Paper: Judicial Reform*].

in big cities. Nearly 94 per cent of lawyers were social lawyers, and the other 6 per cent were government lawyers, corporate in-house counsel, legal aid lawyers, and military lawyers.[20]

The number of lawyers had hovered around 100,000 before the late 2000s. A relaxation of the pass rate for the Bar exam in China, which rose about 20 per cent (of approximately 300,000 candidates per year) for four consecutive years between 2007 and 2010,[21] pushed the number of lawyers to nearly 200,000.[22] For decades, the Chinese legal system operated with more judges than lawyers, but with the recent increase, the number of lawyers has finally surpassed that of judges.

With recent social and economic developments, the Chinese legal profession has made progress in its degree of professionalism and the level of institutionalization. As the number of lawyers has steadily increased, their quality, as defined by level of education, has also improved. There is now a rigorous national judicial examination for judges, prosecutors, and lawyers, and the eligibility requirement to take the examination has changed in turn from a sub-degree, to a general university degree,[23] to the current requirement of a full law degree.

In addition, there is a division between lawyers and notary publics. The latter form a government department that offers document verification and certification services, work that would be done by lawyers in common law jurisdictions. The government has made these important services available to poor persons via legal aid. Attempts in the early 2000s to socialize notary publics failed and there has been no further discussion to delink them from the government. Notary publics remain part of a state-controlled public service organization whose services are compulsory in certain transactions, such as real estate transfers. The notary public business in cities is well known for its huge profitability, and the fees it generates are commonly shared between the state, the Department of Notary Publics, and individual notary publics.

Finally, there is a division in civil cases between trained legal personnel and non-lawyer citizen representatives (公民代理 or *litigants ad litem*). With the approval of the court, citizens had been allowed to act as legal representatives in administrative, civil, and criminal litigation. Chinese law has historically been liberal in legal representation; in addition to lawyers and legal workers, family members and relatives, individuals recommended by the residential community and workplaces, or perhaps most importantly any citizen could be a legal representative in civil litigation.[24] This layperson backstop compensated for the shortage of lawyers and at the same time reduced the dependence on professionals, making their shortage less of a concern for ordinary people. This approach to representation, while allowing legal assistance from untrained persons, was justified because of the shortage of lawyers. The approach was deemed feasible because of the central judicial role in fact-finding as well as previously limited concerns with procedures and evidential niceties. It was also politically correct because it enabled citizens' public participation in the judicial process. Since the early 1990s, another effect of this open door policy was that it created tremendous opportunities at law school legal clinics and public interest-oriented non-governmental organizations ('NGOs') to provide free legal aid services to vulnerable groups in society. Foreign

[20] *Legal Aid Improvement Reports*, *supra* note 13, at 11, 16, 26, 37, 46, 57, 68, 82, 92, 122, 133, 145, 152, 162, 186, 202, 215, 227, 242, 254, 264, 306, 322, 336, 366, 386, 399, 411, and 418; *White Paper: Judicial Reform*, *supra* note 19.

[21] Rachel E. Stern, 'Political Reliability and the Chinese Bar Exam' (2016) 43 *Journal of Law and Society* 506 at 512.

[22] *White Paper: Judicial Reform*, *supra* note 19.

[23] *PRC Legal System*, *supra* note 6, at 223–4.

[24] Zhao Junsheng, Li Jijun, and Song Jiangtao, 浅谈新民事诉讼法实施后公民代理的规范 (The Regulation of Citizen Representation after the Implementation of New Civil Procedures), *Zhengzhou Intermediate People's Court* (8 June 2015), online: zzfy.hncourt.gov.cn/public/detail.php?id=22393.

donors such as the Ford Foundation and the American Bar Association played a crucial role in supporting, facilitating, and shaping the growth of legal clinics and advocacy NGOs in China.[25]

This approach to representation changed when civil procedure was reformed in 2013.[26] At present, although family members and direct relatives can still serve as litigation representatives, open-ended citizen representation has been placed under stricter control. Under the new rules, citizen representation is not allowed until the workplace or the residential committee of a party to a litigation so recommends. It appears that citizen representation among family members has continued in practice, but representation provided by NGOs, activist citizens, and law school clinics has diminished significantly, if not vanished completely.

V. THE GENERAL PROFILE OF LEGAL AID IN CHINA

Legal aid in China was formally created in 1996, immediately after the enactment of the Lawyers Law.[27] Legal aid was not available before 1996 except in a limited number of criminal cases, such as those involving juvenile offenders where assistance from lawyers was mandatory. The governing law is the Legal Aid Regulations which were enacted by the State Council in 2003.[28] Each province has also enacted its own rules to implement the national regulations.

The government has been the principal source of legal aid funding and the key driver for its development. The total legal aid funding in China in 2013, for example, was over RMB1.6 billion (US$225.9 million),[29] of which nearly 99 per cent was sourced from government budgets, in particular local county and district governments, which have contributed the lion's share of over RMB1 billion (US$141.2 million).[30] Legal aid is mostly a local government responsibility. At slightly over RMB1 (US$0.14) per person, the legal aid spending per capita in China is tiny, but its mere existence represents a significant change in the Chinese legal system.[31] Before and during the early stages of China's social and economic development, dispute resolution relied heavily on community-based mediation, in which justice was administered with minimal contribution from lawyers or even judges. China's closely knit, communitarian society was perceived to have the capacity to resolve its own disputes without resorting to external

[25] Fu Hualing and Richard Cullen, 'Climbing the Weiquan Ladder: A Radicalizing Process for Rights-Protection Lawyers' (2011) 205 *The China Quarterly* 40 at 55; *Legal Aid and Public Interest Law in China*, *supra* note 1, at 268; *Transmission of Public Interest Law*, *supra* note 1, at 282.

[26] *The Civil Procedure Law of the People's Republic of China* (adopted on 31 August 2012, with effect from 1 January 2013).

[27] *Legal Aid and Public Interest Law in China*, *supra* note 1, at 220; *Legal Aid and Legitimacy*, *supra* note 1, at 311; Gong Xiaobing, 'Decision-making and Reflections on the Establishment of China's Legal Aid System' in Zhang Geng and Gong Xiaobing, eds., 中国法律援助制度诞生的前前后后 (The Creation of the Chinese Legal Aid System) (Beijing: China Fangzheng Press, 1998) 3 at 21.

[28] 法律援助条例 (*Legal Aid Regulations*), China 2003 (with effect from 1 September 2003), online: www.law-lib.com/law/law_view.asp?id=78770 [*Legal Aid Regulations*].

[29] XE Currency Converter, online: www.xe.com/currencytables/?from=CNY&date=2018-07-26. Unless another reference was cited, US$ denominations in the chapter were derived from www.xe.com at the time of publication; they are intended for general reference and may have been rounded up or down for ease of reference.

[30] See *Legal Aid Improvement Reports*, *supra* note 13, at 5, 12, 17, 28, and 38. See also China, Legal Aid Centre, Ministry of Justice, 中国法律援助年鉴 2013 (Yearbook of Legal Aid in China: 2013) (Beijing: China Democracy and Legal System Publishing House, 2014) [*2013 Legal Aid Yearbook*] at 204.

[31] Fu Hualing, 'Access to Justice and Constitutionalism in China' in Stephanie Balme and Michael W. Dowdle, eds., *Building Constitutionalism in China* (New York: Palgrave Macmillan, 2009) 163 [*Access to Justice and Constitutionalism*] at 168–70.

assistance.[32] Legal aid and access to courts became relevant and gained importance as the capacity of traditional communities in dispute resolution diminished,[33] and the evolution of social and economic disputes gradually demanded more formal legal intervention.[34]

The central government initiated the delivery of legal aid through the creation of Legal Aid Centres ('LAC'), which function at four levels. The national level coordinates legal assistance across the country, while LACs in provinces and autonomous regions supervise the actual legal aid work in their jurisdictions. LACs in cities and counties are also responsible for providing legal aid. LACs are staffed by salaried lawyers paid by the government, who provide full-time legal aid services within jurisdictional limits. The institutionalization of LACs created a stable team of professional lawyers in each jurisdiction, able to exercise hands-on quality control in the delivery of legal aid services.

A significant proportion of legal aid funding is used to pay for government-run LACs, mostly to cover the costs of the salaried legal aid lawyers. In 2014, there were 14,548 legal aid personnel, including lawyers, working in LACs, with most of them (11,755) working for county or district level LACs.[35] Chongqing's funding and performance were better than the national average. The total legal aid funding in the city in 2016 was close to RMB80 million (US$11.3 million), including RMB36 million (US$5.1 million) as legal aid fees for lawyers, RMB20 million (US$2.8 million) to pay for the salary of 110 legal aid lawyers, and RMB18 million (US$2.5 million) to cover LAC administrative costs.[36] In addition to salaried legal aid lawyers, the government relies extensively on providers in private practice, both social lawyers and legal workers, to deliver legal aid services.

In total, over 1.24 million legal aid cases including mediation were approved in 2014; there were over 997,000 civil cases, 240,000 criminal cases, and over 5,800 administrative law cases.[37] The three categories of legal aid providers – salaried lawyers, social lawyers, and legal workers – each handle approximately one third of the national legal aid caseload. The percentage of cases handled by legal workers has been fairly stable and ranges from around 36 to 38% of the total number of legal aid cases. Cases handled by social lawyers have been on the increase, reaching 38% in 2013, partially due to an overall increase in legal aid funding. In contrast, the volume of cases handled by salaried lawyers has been declining, from over 29% in 2009 to about 20% in 2013. There are significant regional variations in these percentages, with legal workers handling half of the legal aid cases in the western provinces with larger rural populations.[38] Legal aid services offered by other social groups, including NGOs or university-based legal aid centres, can

[32] Victor Li, *Law Without Lawyers: A Comparative View of Law in the United States and China* (Boulder: Westview Press, 1978) at 59; Stanley B. Lubman, *Bird in a Cage: Legal Reform in China After Mao* (Stanford: Stanford University Press, 2000) at 218–19.

[33] *Access to Justice and Constitutionalism*, *supra* note 31, at 172; Fu Hualing, 'Understanding People's Mediation in Post Mao China' (1992) 6:2 *Journal of Chinese Law* 211 at 216–18.

[34] Donald Clarke, Peter Murrell, and Susan Whiting, 'The Role of Law in China's Economic Development' in Loren Brandt and Thomas G. Rawski, eds., *China's Great Economic Transformation* (Cambridge: Cambridge University Press, 2008) 375 at 405.

[35] China, Legal Aid Centre, Ministry of Justice, 中国法律援助年鉴：2014 (Yearbook of Legal Aid in China: 2014), (Beijing: China Democracy and Legal System Publishing House, 2015) [*2014 Legal Aid Yearbook*] at 206.

[36] Communications with legal aid lawyers from Chongqing (December 2018).

[37] *2014 Legal Aid Yearbook*, *supra* note 35, at 208.

[38] Huang Dongdong, 法律援助案件质量: 问题、制约及其应对——以 C 市的调研为基础 (Quality of Legal Aid Cases: Problem, Regulations, and Reaction – A Search Focused on C City) (2015) 4 *Research on Law and Commerce* 54 at 59.

have a considerable social impact but are negligible in number, with the exception of those in Beijing.[39]

The scope of civil cases that are eligible for legal aid is limited. Under the Legal Aid Regulations, legal aid is available only for a listed category of cases relating to state compensation, social insurance payment, support for family members, relief payment, labour remuneration, or traffic accidents, medical malpractice, or industrial injuries.[40] The types of legal aid recipients, as categorized by the official statistics, are also telling. In 2014, over 1.38 million recipients were recorded. They included approximately 476,000 migrant workers, 471,000 farmers, 351,000 females, 65,000 persons with disabilities, 154,000 juveniles, and 112,000 senior citizens.[41] The classification reflects how the Party prioritizes legal aid services, many of which are directed to migrant labourers whose grievances have attracted significant political attention.

Legal aid in China is a rare public good that is in short supply, even with a restricted application, and the government exercises further control over the legal aid threshold by means and merits tests. The means test is straightforward. It is standard practice for LACs to use the poverty line in China, i.e. those who receive a welfare payment calculated for the poorest persons (*dibao* or 低保), as a cut-off line. While the *dibao* varies from one jurisdiction to another, it is generally so low[42] that it limits legal aid to extremely poor persons. There is also a merits test, which the government uses to screen out contentious cases and which ensures a virtual certainty of winning. While there has been criticism that the merits test lacks consistency, its enforcement is rigorous enough that the majority of legal aid cases win. The courts found against legal aid recipients in only 5 per cent of legal aid cases in 2011 and 2012.[43]

As the Chinese economy improved and more people were lifted out of poverty, a diminishing number of people became eligible for legal aid. In response, nearly every province has raised the threshold to reflect China's changing economic reality and to increase access to justice. In Chongqing, the poverty line was drawn in 2016 at RMB460 (US$64.95) per month for urban residents and RMB300 (US$42.36) per month for rural residents, but the legal aid cut-off line is twice the poverty line.[44] There are close to 1 million residents of Chongqing who live under the poverty line, but between 2 and 3 million residents are eligible for legal aid, about 10 per cent of the population in the city.[45]

A significant characteristic of access to justice in China is that the government no longer regards legal aid merely as a tool to meet the legal needs of the poorest of the population. It uses

[39] The Beijing government has been providing funding to a few NGOs to provide legal aid services, including the well-known Zhicheng Legal Aid and Research Centre for Migrant Workers and the Yilian Labour Law Legal Aid and Research Centre. See *Legal Aid Improvement Reports*, *supra* note 13, at 6–8.

[40] *Legal Aid Regulations*, *supra* note 28, s 10.

[41] 2013 *Legal Aid Yearbook*, *supra* note 30, at 208–9.

[42] In Chongqing, for example, the poverty line was drawn in 2016 at RMB460 per month (US$64.96) for urban residents and RMB300 (US$42.36) per month for rural residents; see 重庆市提高城乡低保标准 (Chongqing Raises Urban and Rural Poverty Line Standards), *Chongqing Daily* (19 September 2016), online: www.gov.cn/xinwen/2016-09/19/content_5109332.htm.

[43] In 2012, legal aid lawyers won in 58.4% of the cases and lost in 4.9% of the cases; 30.3% of the cases were mediated and 5.8% of the cases were withdrawn. See *Legal Aid Improvement Reports*, *supra* note 13, at 152.

[44] 重庆市法律援助条例 (Regulation of Chongqing Municipality on Legal Aid), China 2004 (as amended 26 March 2014), s 17.

[45] 新修订的《重庆市法律援助条例》5 月1 日起施行 (The Newly Amended 'Regulation of Chongqing Municipality on Legal Aid' Came into Force on 1 May), *China National Radio* (29 April 2014), online: news.cnr.cn/native/city/201404/t20140429_515399506.shtml.

legal aid as a policy tool for legal intervention in matters of high-profile social concern. The plight of Chinese workers migrating to the cities for work has in particular attracted wide political attention,[46] and as a result legal aid is now extended to legal disputes between these migrant workers and their employers, without having to satisfy a means test. Facing collective disputes such as those involving labour and the environment, the authoritarian government is sending legal aid lawyers, instead of police as it used to do, to manage delicate and potentially explosive issues.[47] Other cases that are regarded as sensitive or significant, such as those involving the spouses of soldiers, Good Samaritans in legal need, victims of domestic violence, or collective disputes involving low-income groups particularly in the areas of consumer rights and environmental pollution, have also been brought into the fold of legal aid cases.[48]

Because of its politicization, China's legal aid caseload shows some features that may be uniquely Chinese. Civil legal aid funding elsewhere may be spent mostly on family law matters, including divorce or custody of children.[49] For clear policy reasons, a wide range of labour law issues relating to migrant workers have now become the largest type of case to receive legal aid funding. Ordinarily, a legal aid case must pass a means test to qualify, but the means test is waived for migrant workers for claims based on labour law rights. Migrant workers were brought within legal aid coverage without a means test in part because of the prevalence of violation of their rights and in part because migrants had acted collectively, extra-legally, and occasionally violently in their advocacy.[50] In China, law in general and legal aid in particular are used to disaggregate collective conflict among migrants to bring them from the streets back into the courts.[51]

Legal aid priority is also given to criminal cases. There is a general legal right to counsel for all criminal suspects after the first interrogation by the police,[52] and legal aid is available for all indigent suspects if they wish to have a lawyer.[53] The circumstances in which access to a lawyer is mandatory for suspects and defendants under the Criminal Procedural Law[54] have been widening. They now include death penalty cases, juvenile offenders, and offenders who are senior or with certain disabilities. In detaining criminal suspects, police generally advise the detainees of their right to be represented by a lawyer. As a pilot project, the government has set

46 *Authoritarian Legality in China*, *supra* note 7, at 2; *Getting Paid*, *supra* note 7, at 256.

47 *Access to Justice and Constitutionalism*, *supra* note 31, at 170.

48 China, The General Office of the Central Committee of the CPC and the General Office of the State Council, 关于完善法律援助制度的意见 (Opinions on Perfecting the Legal Aid System) (29 June 2015), online: www.gov.cn/gongbao/content/2015/content_2897153.htm; China, Ministry of Justice, 军人军属法律援助工作实施办法 (Measures for the Implementation of the Work of Legal Aid for Servicemen and Their Family Members) (29 September 2016), online: www.gov.cn/gongbao/content/2017/content_5197025.htm; *Legal Aid Regulations*, *supra* note 28, s 10.

49 Richard L. Abel, 'Law without Politics: Legal Aid under Advanced Capitalism' (1985) 32 *UCLA Law Review* 474 [*Law without Politics*] at 608.

50 *Getting Paid*, *supra* note 7, at 281, 283–6.

51 Yang Su and He Xin, 'Street as Courtroom: State Accommodation of Labor Protest in South China' (2010) 44 *Law & Society Review* 157 at 164.

52 中华人民共和国刑事诉讼 (Criminal Procedure Law of the People's Republic of China), 1979 (as amended 14 March 2012) [*Criminal Procedure Law*], s 33. Under s 37, access to lawyers can be restricted in cases concerning national security, terrorism, and major corruption.

53 *Legal Aid Regulations*, *supra* note 28, s 13.

54 *Criminal Procedure Law*, *supra* note 52, ss 34, 267. Under s 267, for a juvenile criminal suspect or defendant who has not retained a defender, a people's court, a people's procuratorate, or a public security authority shall serve a notice on a legal aid agency requiring assignment of a lawyer to defend him or her.

up legal aid offices in detention centres and courts in which duty lawyers, private lawyers paid for by the legal aid fund, provide legal advice or defence when needed.

At a policy level, criminal justice reform and better access to lawyers for suspects in custody has been a major focus since the 1990s. The lack of access to effective legal advice has been a perennially sensitive international concern, with China receiving consistent criticism for lack of criminal representation.[55] Because the right to defence in criminal cases is widely regarded as a core human right, the central government is strongly incentivized to improve access to lawyers in criminal cases as soon as the police finish their first round of interrogation. In another pilot project in eight provinces, the Ministry of Justice and the Supreme People's Court have provided comprehensive legal aid coverage for all criminal cases at trial, appeal, and for post-conviction reviews, where the defendant has no legal representative. The court is invested with the duty to inform a competent legal aid centre of a defendant's need for legal aid, and where a failure to notify this leads to the deprivation of the defendant's right to a lawyer, the appellant court 'shall' automatically quash the conviction and remand the case for a retrial.[56] China has sufficient lawyers to handle the current legal aid caseload, but whether the local legal aid budget is adequate remains uncertain.

Overall legal aid capacity is limited in any given jurisdiction, and choices among priorities are made. It is more likely than not that criminal cases are given priority in funding allocation. Criminal cases generally account for fewer than 10 per cent of the total cases that courts adjudicate each year, but more than 20 per cent of total legal aid funding. In places where duty lawyer schemes in detention centres have been implemented, a much larger percentage of the legal aid budget, as limited as it is, has to be diverted to subsidize lawyers for advising suspects during their lengthy pre-trial detention.[57]

Other unique features of access to justice in China include the cooperation and coordination in case-handling between legal aid centres and government-controlled women's confederations, associations for disabled persons, and trade unions. Those groups are often the first port of call for their respective constituents when disputes arise, and they can effectively channel those disputes to legal aid services.[58] Another feature of legal aid is the extensive use of legal advice from lawyers via government run telephone hotlines. Each year, the National Legal Aid Centre reports over a million instances of the provision of such legal advice. There were over 6 million cases of legal advice given via hotline each year in 2013 and in 2014.[59] The 12348 hotline is now well established and has become an important starting point for people with legal needs. Settlement through mediation by legal aid lawyers is another feature of legal aid in China. Lawyers are generally encouraged to settle cases through mediation, although the rate of

[55] Zuo Weimin and Ma Jinghua, 'The Role of Criminal Defence Lawyers in China: An Empirical Study of D County, S Province' in Mike McConville and Eva Pils, eds., *Comparative Perspectives on Criminal Justice in China* (Cheltenham: Edward Elgar, 2013) 234 at 234; for a broad review of the issues, see Sida Liu and Terence G. Halliday, *Criminal Defense in China: The Politics of Lawyers at Work* (Cambridge: Cambridge University Press, 2017) [*Criminal Defense in China*].

[56] The Ministry of Justice and the Supreme People's Court, 最高法司法部联合出台办法 开展刑事案件律师辩护全覆盖试点 (The Ministry of Justice and the Supreme People's Court Jointly Issuing Measures to Offer Blanket Coverage of Legal Aid by Lawyers for Criminal Cases), *Xin Hua* (12 October 2017), online: news.xinhuanet.com/politics/2017-10/12/c_129719121.htm.

[57] Proceedings from the 'Conference on Human Rights Protection Mechanism for Criminal Detainees' (Conference delivered in Wuhan, China, 14–15 September 2013) (copy on file with author).

[58] *Access to Justice and Constitutionalism*, *supra* note 31, at 173.

[59] 2013 *Legal Aid Yearbook*, *supra* note 30, at 206.

mediation varies significantly in any given period of time, depending on whether judicial policies are pro-mediation or anti-mediation. In both 2011 and 2012, for example, the mediation rate for applicable cases was approximately 30 per cent.[60]

VI. LAWYERS AND MANDATORY LEGAL SERVICES

Chinese lawyers have a mandatory statutory duty to provide legal aid services, which means that they are required to take a certain number of legal aid cases each year as determined by the jurisdiction, and for which they will be paid. According to Article 42 of the Lawyers Law,[61] lawyers should provide legal services according to state regulations and should do so diligently and dutifully. A 2007 amendment of that Article expanded the duty to law firms.[62] The Legal Aid Regulations also reiterate the duty for mandatory legal aid services on the part of lawyers.[63]

While the particular requirements of the obligation have varied historically, and currently differ from one jurisdiction to another, the requirement is normally within the range of one to three legal aid cases per lawyer per year. Failure to provide the mandatory legal aid services may lead to disciplinary sanctions. Indeed, all lawyers are required to have their practising certificates renewed by their respective provincial government each year, and completion of legal aid cases is one of the conditions for licence renewal. Government regulators often state expressly on their official websites that lawyers may be subjected to a wide range of disciplinary actions, including disbarment, for failing to provide this mandatory legal aid service. In practice, however, lawyers and their law firms are always able to meet the mandatory legal aid requirement. Law firms may organize legal aid duties by designating one junior associate to handle multiple legal aid cases on behalf of the lawyers in the firm, or lawyers may help each other out by registering a legal aid case under the name of a lawyer who falls short of the mandatory requirement. As long as the total number of legal aid cases is higher than the number of lawyers in a jurisdiction, it is assumed that lawyers are doing their duty and the legal aid performance of individual lawyers is not questioned.[64]

There is little articulation or conceptualization of the basis of the legal duty to provide mandatory legal aid services. Is it the socialist ambition to create an egalitarian and equal society through legal intervention, a moral responsibility of lawyers due to their status and privilege, or simply an authoritarian tradition that allows the government to impose whatever duties on lawyers it sees fit?

A typical argument put forth to justify pro bono in liberal democracies, compulsory or not, is an appeal to the sense of professionalism of lawyers,[65] as defined by the particular institutional settings in which lawyers work.[66] This argument asserts that lawyering is a noble profession that

60 China, Legal Aid Centre, Ministry of Justice, 中国法律援助年鉴：2011 (Yearbook of Legal Aid in China: 2011), (Beijing: China Democracy and Legal System Publishing House, 2012) at 232; China, Legal Aid Centre, Ministry of Justice, 中国法律援助年鉴：2012 (Yearbook of Legal Aid in China: 2012), (Beijing: China Democracy and Legal System Publishing House, 2013) at 215.

61 中华人民共和国律师法 (Lawyers Law of the People's Republic of China), 1996 (as amended 29 December 2001), s 42.

62 Ibid.

63 *Legal Aid Regulations*, *supra* note 28, s 6.

64 Interviews with two Chinese lawyers (2017, Chongqing, China).

65 Deborah L. Rhode, *Access to Justice* (New York: Oxford University Press, 2004) at 77–8.

66 Robert Granfield, 'The Meaning of Pro Bono: Institutional Variations in Professional Obligations among Lawyers' (2007) 41 *Law & Society Review* 113 [*The Meaning of Pro Bono*] at 114–15.

facilitates the supply of justice, and that if the poor cannot afford it, lawyers should provide it for free. There is indeed a moral and professional duty on lawyers to do so, because lawyers have a monopoly over the supply of legal services. Since only qualified lawyers can satisfy legal demand, lawyers have a duty to satisfy unmet legal needs though pro bono services. The monopolistic nature of legal services and the related privileges that lawyers enjoy underlie this pro bono duty. Related to this main argument, there are more pragmatic arguments for lawyers to participate in pro bono, such as gaining practical experience, developing potential clients, and improving the public image of the legal profession by serving the poor.[67]

The conceptualization of pro bono in western democracies is less relevant to understanding access to justice, and in particular mandatory legal services, in China. As new concepts, legal aid, access to justice, and pro bono became relevant in China only after it decided to embark on market reforms, including delinking of the legal profession from the state. The prevailing view was that a market economy required an independent legal system to facilitate economic transactions,[68] and it was at this historical juncture that mandatory legal service provision duties were imposed on lawyers, who otherwise had no indigenous pro bono tradition.

When mandatory legal services were imposed on Chinese lawyers in 1996, lawyers' social status was relatively low. Lawyers also faced fierce competition from legal workers and citizen representation in a limited legal market. Lawyers were a newly socialized profession, recently delinked from a powerful government, and yet to establish wealth, reputation, or status. Although lawyering might be a profession with potential to prosper in the future, it was hardly a privileged one in the American sense that called for a corresponding responsibility.

A more viable explanation for the growth of mandatory legal services in China is that it provided lawyers with better economic prospects. At the beginning of market reforms, lawyers were largely content with the socialization of their profession and the corresponding improvement in financial prospects. It was taken for granted by all stakeholders in the larger legal community that once freed from government control, lawyers would be financially independent, and certainly better off than judges, prosecutors, and legal advisors in government positions. Mandatory legal services were most likely imposed not because of lawyers' prestige in a political or social sense, but rather their potential financial profitability. Mandatory legal services imposed an additional tax on a potentially wealthy but politically weak profession. Historically, judges and prosecutors have treated lawyers poorly, in part because of a common perception that the lawyers could make a lot of money by doing very little in a case.[69]

The requirement to provide mandatory legal services, however, was not well enforced. Without the government reimbursing at least the cost of transportation for rendering legal services, lawyers simply refused to assist, and there was little the government could do. Several factors may be relevant in explaining this lack of enforcement. Legal aid for the poor was a relatively low political priority, not something that merited resort to compulsion. Also, demand for lawyers in 1996, when the obligation was introduced by the Lawyers Law, remained limited. At the beginning of lawyers' socialization, use of professional legal representation by parties was low in both civil and criminal cases, and in the vast majority of the cases the parties did not have

[67] Ibid.

[68] Albert Chen, 'Rational Law, Economic Development and the Case of China' (1999) 8 *Social and Legal Studies* 97 at 111.

[69] Fu Hualing, 'When Lawyers are Prosecuted ... The Struggle of a Profession in Transition' (2007) 2 *Journal of Comparative Law* 95 at 112; *Criminal Defense in China*, *supra* note 55, at 136–7.

any professional legal representation. China's proactive, inquisitorial judges needed little assistance from lawyers in their fact-finding and legal analysis, effectively rendering the lawyers' role marginal.

Another reason for non-enforcement of mandatory duties was the state of law firm structures and bar associations. The experience of mature legal systems suggests that compliance with a pro bono requirement requires support and oversight from law firms and bar associations. In the American experience, voluntary pro bono works when the law firms employing lawyers, especially larger firms, encourage or insist on this requirement. Pro bono tends to be most sustainable when it is embedded within its institutional settings, for example when law firms count pro bono work toward billable hours. Mandatory pro bono, where it exists, works because of the existence of a well-organized and resourceful bar, which can coordinate, monitor, and enforce compulsory pro bono. Compulsory pro bono would not exist without a well-organized bar or other organization with resources to organize and power to discipline.[70]

These enforcement mechanisms from law firms and bar associations are not available in China. Before the enactment of the 1996 Lawyers Law, Chinese lawyers were state legal workers, and law firms were state owned or attached to government departments and other public entities such as universities. Law firms were small in size, and lawyers' associations were largely irrelevant in the regulation of the legal profession, itself a marginal institution.[71]

While the Lawyers Law has freed lawyers and law firms from direct government control, the road to building genuine partnerships within law firms has been a tortuous one. It is well documented that Chinese law firms, until recently, were composed of individual partners and associates, who worked largely in isolation as solo practitioners. The influence of a firm on its lawyers is limited, and firms lack the effective tools to motivate lawyers to join public interest work that international firms typically have.[72]

Similarly, lawyers' associations in China do not have organizing abilities or disciplinary powers over law firms or lawyers. The authoritarian political system does not permit the creation of a free and powerful bar to represent lawyers independent of government control. Economic imperatives may require the state to create a free legal profession to serve the market economy, but the political concerns of an authoritarian state do not allow for the creation of an autonomous and vibrant civil society association.[73] Thus, the creation of a socialized legal profession did not witness the parallel institution of a powerful representative body. The bar is intentionally weak for political reasons, and is therefore not well placed to serve, monitor, or discipline its members. A weak bar association has neither the will nor the capacity to enforce mandatory legal aid. While the government may intervene in matters that it perceives to be significant, such as political challenges raised by human rights lawyers, it typically leaves lawyers alone in relation to minor matters such as legal aid or pro bono. Indeed, whenever the lawyers' association or government regulators did discipline lawyers, they took this action primarily on political grounds

[70] Rebecca L. Sandefur, 'Lawyers' Pro Bono Service and American-Style Civil Legal Assistance' (2007) 41 *Law & Society Review* 79 at 91–2; *The Meaning of Pro Bono, supra* note 66, at 138.

[71] *PRC Legal System, supra* note 6, at 226; *March Toward Rule of Law, supra* note 6, at 348–9.

[72] Ethan Michelson, 'The Practice of Law as an Obstacle to Justice: Chinese Lawyers at Work' (2006) 40 *Law & Society Review* 1 at 10; for official criticisms of the lack of supervision and monitoring, see Meng Jianzhu, 律师事务所要加强日常监管不能养痈遗患 (Law Firms Must Solidify Routine Supervision and Not Leave Wrongdoers Unchecked), *The Procuratorate Daily* (16 September 2015), online: www.chinanews.com/gn/2015/09-16/7526556.shtml.

[73] Anthony J. Spires, 'Contingent Symbiosis and Civil Society in an Authoritarian State: Understanding the Survival of China's Grassroots NGOs' (2011) 117 *American Journal of Sociology* 1 at 8.

and for the purpose of exerting political control, i.e. 'to safeguard the Communist Party's rule by keeping lawyers in bounds'.[74]

The position of bar associations may change. As the profession has developed, lawyers have amassed wealth and gained a certain political clout and social status, which could be used to advance the professional interest of the legal profession.[75] For example, lawyers have lobbied the government to limit competition from others in the legal services market, with varying degrees of success. They had some success pushing legal workers out of cities and back to their rural counties. They were also successful in prohibiting barefoot lawyers, law students, and other activist citizens from representing civil cases in court. In relation to the mandatory legal service provision duty, they succeeded in persuading the government to expand legal aid spending and to offer better compensation for their legal aid services.

Indeed, the increase in legal aid funding in general, and funding to subsidize legal aid cases by social lawyers who take legal cases for a fee, reflects the increased power of lawyers. The total legal aid budget in 2003, for example, was RMB155 million (US$21.9 million), the vast proportion of which was earmarked for salaried lawyers and their operating costs. A mere 17 per cent was spent on legal aid cases by social lawyers in that year, with a national average of slightly over RMB400 (US$56.48) per case, which reflected an increase of RMB100 (US$14.12) from its 2002 level. By 2014, China's legal aid spending rose to over RMB1.7 billion (US$240.1 million).[76]

While the national average case subsidy remains low, the situation has started to change in wealthy cities, where increased spending has made legal aid cases an attractive source of income for young lawyers struggling to find work. With increased spending on case subsidies, there is a distinct change in lawyers' attitude toward legal aid: the mandatory legal aid quota imposed on lawyers, which was regarded as a burden to be avoided if possible, is becoming a source of income to be fought for. The case fee has been increasing steadily in Chongqing and elsewhere in China.[77] In 2013, the legal aid fee per civil case in Chongqing was approximately RMB800 (US$112.97), increasing to RMB1,800 (US$254.17) in 2017.[78]

Legal aid cases have become attractive not only because the pay has increased, but also because they are a stable source of income. The way the legal aid fee is calculated and offered is modelled on market fee arrangements. For civil cases, the government offers a lump sum to the social lawyers selected for cases. For criminal cases, the fee is calculated in phases, with lawyers paid different amounts for their participation in different stages of the criminal process.[79] While it is difficult to estimate the gap between legal aid fees and market prices for a comparable case, an educated guess is that the legal aid fee is a third to a half of the market fee that a lawyer would charge in Chongqing for a simple civil case.

Why have legal aid fees been increased and how are they justified? Moreover, how does the government justify the practice of paying lawyers to fulfil their duty to assist the poor? First, as the 2003 Legal Aid Regulations[80] clearly state, legal aid is a government responsibility, and

74 Judith A. McMorrow, Sida Liu, and Benjamin Van Rooij, 'Lawyer Discipline in an Authoritarian Regime: Empirical Insights from Zhejiang Province, China' (2017) 30 *Georgetown Journal of Legal Ethics* 267 at 267.

75 *Criminal Defense in China*, *supra* note 55, at 150.

76 Jiang Jianfeng and Guo Jie, 2003 年全国法律援助统计分析 (Statistical Analysis of National Legal Aid Work: 2003) (2004) 3 *Justice of China* 79; 2014 *Legal Aid Yearbook*, *supra* note 35, at 209.

77 *Legal Aid Improvement Reports*, *supra* note 13, at 230.

78 Communications with legal lawyers in Chongqing (December 2018).

79 For detailed description of the pay-scale for legal aid cases in different provinces, see *Legal Aid Improvement Reports*, *supra* note 13, at 402 (Guangzhou).

80 *Legal Aid Regulations*, *supra* note 28.

governments at the county level and above are required to take active measures to promote legal aid work and provide financial support for legal aid within their respective jurisdictions.[81] Local legislation on legal aid confirms the statutory duty of the local government to provide adequate financing to satisfy local legal needs. Legal aid is now a regular budgetary item in government budgets and revenue for legal aid is relatively stable. There is a genuine commitment from both the central and local governments to expand legal aid funding to improve access to justice. Significant policy leadership is also provided by the Party, and the Party has repeatedly undertaken different kinds of legal reforms. Starting in 2014, the Party adopted a number of policy responses emphasizing the significance of legal aid, and together with the expansion of legal aid, these measures indicate a strong political desire to replace the police and other coercive apparatuses of the state with legal procedures as the predominant method for dispute resolution.[82] For example, in 2015, the Party's General Office and that of the State Council, two key policy-making bodies in China's political structure, jointly issued a document entitled 'Opinions on Improving the Legal Aid System'. The Opinions demanded that concrete measures be taken to channel disputes and conflicts into the legal process via the expansion of legal aid for disputes involving labour, family, food and medicine, education, and medical care. The Opinions also required the creation of a duty lawyer scheme in courts and detention centres. For those who promote legal aid in China, the Party has offered a target list of commitments.[83] Beyond the broader rule of law promotion, the Party is also increasing public spending on public services to improve the livelihood of the poor, specifically referencing the constitutional right of equality for all.[84] Legal aid is regarded as part of the wider provision of public services in state planning. The 13th Five Year Plan, in particular, refers to the improvement of public legal services through improving legal aid.[85]

Second, China has developed the financial capacity to provide more legal aid funding. China's GDP per capita has increased steadily over the past four decades, particularly in the wealthy provinces and cities in the past 15 years. This enhanced financial capacity, coupled with a political commitment to legal aid spending, means a larger and more stable budget for legal aid in general and increased subsidies for lawyers handling individual cases throughout the country.[86]

Third, there seems to be a consensus that lawyers' work, like any work, should be adequately compensated. While legal aid is both a government responsibility and a duty of lawyers, Chinese discourse has decisively shifted from lawyers' duty to government responsibility. The argument that lawyers are a special profession that provides a crucial public service remains relevant, and the notion that serving the people defines socialist lawyers has not entirely evaporated, but lawyers' voluntary and free contributions no longer dominate public discourse or government decision-making. The government has the money and lawyers have the expertise. The only

[81] *Legal Aid Regulations*, *supra* note 28, s 3.

[82] *Access to Justice and Constitutionalism*, *supra* note 31, at 170.

[83] China, Ministry of Justice and Ministry of Finance, 关于完善法律援助制度的意见 (Opinions on the Provision of Legal Aid by Lawyers) (29 June 2015), online: www.chinalawedu.com/falvfagui/21752/wa1507079100.shtml.

[84] 司法部就《关于完善法律援助制度的意见》答记者问 (The Press Conference of the Ministry of Justice on the Opinions on Improving the Legal Aid System), *Xin Hua* (30 June 2015), online: news.xinhuanet.com/politics/2015-06/30/c_127966971.htm.

[85] China, *The 13th Five-Year Plan for Economic and Social Development of the People's Republic of China* (17 March 2016), at chapter 75, section 4.

[86] *Legal Aid Improvement Reports*, *supra* note 13, at 166 (Hubei).

remaining challenges are for lawyers to bargain for higher fees from the legal aid authority, and for the national legal aid authority and local governments to bargain about the balance of funding. Adequate compensation for legal aid is mostly taken for granted due to a combination of reasons, including acknowledged increases in inflation and related cost of living allowances, and recognition that lawyers need time to prepare a case. The clear intention of the Party is to increase spending on quality legal services from lawyers to cover a wide range of social issues.[87]

Expanded legal aid funding and the corresponding increase in legal aid fees per case, however, have arguably led to the commercialization of legal services for the poor. While commercialization may have motivated some lawyers to contribute to legal aid, it creates its own difficulty. Before the increase in legal aid funding, the difficulty was one of motivation, in other words how to incentivize lawyers to provide services largely for free. For the reasons stated above, neither the socialist ideology of serving the people nor a professional commitment based on a newly found lawyer identity were strong enough to nurture a pro bono culture. Lawyers who participated in legal aid work bargained for higher pay, and with the availability of more resources, the government met market demand. With steady increases in funding and acceptance of legal aid as a government responsibility, it became possible and necessary to offer enhanced financial compensation for lawyers for legal services to the poor. Indeed, a new difficulty has emerged with the increase of the legal aid budget, namely how to distribute legal aid funding among lawyers demanding legal aid cases in an equitable and efficient manner.

The availability of legal aid funding has solved, in part at least, the incentive difficulty. With more lawyers providing legal aid services, the main difficulty becomes one of monitoring. The dominant discussion in policy and academic circles now is how to increase the legal aid budget and how to put the increased legal aid funding to better use, including how to monitor lawyers effectively to ensure compliance and to maintain quality control. The clear agenda is for the government to purchase legal services from the private sector and put them into effective use in solving disputes and improving governance. However, for junior lawyers and small law firms, the increased budget means little more than a steady source of income. Regardless of how the quality issue will be resolved, the embryonic spirit of pro bono has diminished in the official system. By commercializing pro bono, the state has ended it.

VII. LEGAL AID AS A SITE OF CONTENTION

Legal aid serves a political function. It is political in the classic Abelian sense[88] in that legal aid reproduces labour relations, disciplines capital and bureaucrats, and mitigates social and economic repression of the poor. Structurally, legal aid legitimizes the underlying political system and maintains the status quo. The endowment of rights on individual legal subjects is fundamental to the operation of China's emerging market economy, yet at the same time the law and the legal rights it endows atomize society and individualize disputes. The enshrinement of rights in law, under contract and through the legal process, creates an impression of neutrality and a sense of justice, which in turn render the legal regime legitimate in the eyes of its users, even though the legal system operates in a passive, reactive fashion, with courts responding to particular allegations of infringements and demands for remedies. Private rights rely on private

[87] *Legal Aid Regulations*, *supra* note 28, s 3.
[88] *Law without Politics*, *supra* note 49, at 586.

dispute resolution, and litigants are presumed to have the capacity to enforce their individual rights. Access to justice in this context is narrowly construed and indeed dependent on the willingness and ability of parties to take legal action.[89] Legal aid, while empowering those who are weak and cannot initiate a legal action,[90] can hollow out the political substance of social conflict and reduce collective conflict to matters of mere legal technicality. Through the legal process, collective or class conflict is turned into isolated legal disputes between individuals. While legal aid reduces real harm, as Abel acknowledges,[91] it also serves an anti-solidarity function that prevents the poor and the vulnerable from organizing themselves and projecting a collective voice.

Although the state commercializes legal aid and uses it to depoliticize conflict, progressive forces can potentially use similar legal tools to recreate a collective identity, class awareness, and a sense of shared community. Rights-based NGOs and university-based legal clinics can recruit lawyers and organize their own pro bono work independent of the official legal aid system. Coordinated and supported by overseas and domestic NGOs of various kinds, lawyers have offered a variety of legal intervention on a wide range of legal issues touching on gender equality, disability rights, environmental protection, labour rights, and criminal defence in general. The NGO-facilitated pro bono cases may be small in number, but they are significant in the social impact they create.[92]

While NGO-coordinated pro bono cases share some common characteristics with government-run legal aid services, there is a significant divergence in both the case selection process and its objectives. Legal aid aims to serve individual legal needs of the poor, and lawyers generally accept cases according to a means and merits test without considering the political implication or social impact of the case. The clear objective is to offer immediate remedies for the particular legal predicament that a client faces. Public interest lawyers on the other hand strategically choose cases for the purpose of generating a larger social impact, either to raise awareness among the general public, to highlight some systematic abuses, or to lobby for certain legal or policy changes.[93] The immediate grievance of a particular individual is of less concern than the larger public interest behind it. These kinds of lawyers are concerned with structural issues and aim to obtain transformative remedies. The particular case is used as an entry point into the legal system, and pro bono here serves a larger political agenda for social transformation.

The provision of legal services for the majority of poor persons is better left to the extensive official legal aid programmes that the government runs or sponsors. NGOs and public interest groups can better serve their objectives by moving beyond individual grievances and concentrating their limited resources on structural issues with larger social and legal impact. Some NGOs and law-school-based clinics have a long-standing strategy of shifting from providing legal aid for individual cases to proactively selecting cases for legal or policy changes. If the political

89 Fu Hualing, 'Bringing Politics Back: Access to Justice and Labour Disputes' in Flora Sapio et al., eds., *Justice: The China Experience* (Cambridge: Cambridge University Press, 2017) 356 at 357.

90 *Access to Justice and Constitutionalism*, *supra* note 31, at 168.

91 *Law without Politics*, *supra* note 49, at 554.

92 *Public Interest Litigation in Asia*, *supra* note 1, at 20; *Legal Aid and Public Interest Law in China*, *supra* note 1, at 248–50; *Transmission of Public Interest Law*, *supra* note 1, at 279.

93 *Public Interest Litigation in Asia*, *supra* note 1, at 24; Wang Zhenyu and Chen Shengqiang, 'Public Interest Litigation and Social Media – Commenting on the Case of Cui Yingjie Murdering an Urban Management Officer' in Yan Xiang, ed., 公益诉讼的理念与实践 (Public Interest: Philosophy Through Litigation) (Wuhan: Wuhan University Press, 2010) 81 at 95.

agenda of legal aid is to individualize conflict and maintain the status quo, public interest law promotes a collective identity, aggravates isolated grievances and disputes, and seeks social changes through law. However, it is this organization and collective action, with the political objective of social transformation, that invites suspicion and hostility from the government. For China's authoritarian system, legal advocacy of the public interest independent of the Party-state poses a potential risk to social and political stability. It challenges the Party's governance and legitimacy, and it must be restricted and suppressed because of its potential to nurture independent social forces.[94]

The rise and fall of Wuhan University Law School's Centre for the Protection of Rights of Disadvantaged Citizens ('Centre') is illustrative of this dynamic process. The Centre was created in 1992 with the support of the Ford Foundation. It was modelled on American public interest law firms, and it was the first legal aid centre that was created by a law school in China.[95] Like other clinical programmes that became popular in subsequent years, law students in Wuhan University provided free legal advice under faculty supervision and assisted in case preparation for those requesting their services. There was an open door policy and clients were invited to walk in for legal assistance. As the Centre developed, its management started to reconsider the direction of the Centre's development. As a result of that reflection, the Centre shifted its priority from providing legal aid for vulnerable groups to promoting policy challenges through impact litigation. As it turned out, the Centre was successful in instituting a number of high-profile judicial review cases challenging a variety of practices, including the police power to randomly check ID cards, age discrimination in civil service recruitment, and governmental refusal to publicize information in response to open government information applications.[96] The Centre's success soon attracted wide public attention and hostility from a range of authorities, including the security forces. When the government launched a new round of crackdowns on civil society and public interest activism in 2014, the Centre had to abandon its public interest law practice. Its director was forced to resign, and the Centre was coerced into having its name changed to a Legal Aid Centre to symbolize a retreat from impact litigation for social change to legal aid to assist the poor. A similar shift from providing legal aid services to creating legal impact through public interest law has also taken place in other university-based legal aid centres or legal aid NGOs.[97]

Public interest litigation, initiated by civil society actors including lawyers, can become politically sensitive, inviting pushbacks and even repression, as human rights lawyers have experienced since 2015.[98] The political risk marks a fundamental difference in legal aid and access to justice between democracies and authoritarian states. However, grassroots public

[94] *July 9th Crackdown*, *supra* note 5, at 567; Eva Pils, *China's Human Rights Lawyers: Advocacy and Resistance* (Abingdon: Routledge, 2014) at 274.

[95] *Public Interest Litigation in Asia*, *supra* note 1, at 14; *Legal Aid and Public Interest Law in China*, *supra* note 1, at 233.

[96] Details of the cases are provided in Shen Xiaoping, 'Public Interest Litigation and the Making of Government under Sunshine' in Yan Xiang, ed., 公益诉讼的理念与实践 (Public Interest: Philosophy Through Litigation) (Wuhan: Wuhan University Press, 2010) 3 at 7; Shen Xiaoping and Xiong Yongxian, 'Police ID Check Challenged by Public Interest Litigation' in Yan Xiang, ed., 公益诉讼的理念与实践 (Public Interest: Philosophy Through Litigation) (Wuhan: Wuhan University Press, 2010) 35 at 35; Chen Shengqiang and Liu Jiahai, 'Do Eligibility Requirements for Civil Service Exams Constitute Discrimination?' in Yan Xiang, ed., 公益诉讼的理念与实践 (Public Interest: Philosophy Through Litigation) (Wuhan: Wuhan University Press, 2010) 64 at 66.

[97] Interviews with five current and former lawyers from legal aid centres in Wuhan and Beijing (2016 and 2017, Wuhan and Beijing, China).

[98] *July 9th Crackdown*, *supra* note 5, at 560.

interest promotion in China has proven resilient. While the ongoing crackdown has had a chilling impact on public interest law, it has not put all NGO-facilitated social-legal activism on hold. NGOs in different parts of China have continued to organize lawyers to participate in pro bono work in relation to the promotion of rights equality. The narrowing of space for civil society activism in general is making public interest litigation much harder, but it has not prevented lawyers from offering pro bono legal aid services in cases relating to domestic violence, and gender and sexual orientation-based discrimination.[99]

VIII. CONCLUSION

Before the 1996 landmark legal changes, lawyers were part of the state, hired by and accountable to the state. There was no pro bono tradition or public interest spirit in what was a government-controlled legal profession. The 1996 reforms delinked the profession from the government, and at the same time China's authoritarian government imposed a duty of mandatory legal aid on lawyers. However, the government did not secure lawyers' compliance. The mandatory legal aid duty was imposed at a moment when the legal profession had just been freed from direct government control, and after the practice of law became a socialized profession, the government had little leverage over lawyers to enforce its mandatory rule.

To manage China's post-revolutionary transition, lawyers became indispensable in channelling rising social conflict into legal institutions for effective resolution. Unmet legal demands attracted official attention because of their potential to trigger social and political instability. Lawyers gained wealth and status after socialization, and to motivate lawyers to work for poor or vulnerable persons, the government first created a legal aid system and then increased legal aid spending following demands from lawyers. With both carrots and sticks in hand, the government proved successful in bringing lawyers back to meet the legal needs of the poor and other vulnerable groups. However, although the commercialization of legal aid may have motivated lawyers to provide legal aid for the poor, it also diminished and for many lawyers perhaps even killed an embryonic pro bono spirit.

A pro bono, or perhaps more accurately in China, a public interest spirit, managed to survive in the legal profession, outside the official legal aid system. As the legal profession in China developed and matured, lawyers started to volunteer their services to promote public interest law, with the coordination of public interest NGOs. Gradually, a pro bono or public interest ethos started to take root and grow. Lawyers, of their own volition and with some support from the international community, are advocating for equality rights in the court of law as well as in the broader court of public opinion. The main challenge to this ethos lies in China's authoritarian political system, which has definitively acted to prohibit activity perceived to conflict with sensitive areas, and it is this tension which will test access to justice in the coming years.

[99] Fu Hualing, 'What Future is there for Human Rights Lawyering in China?' (2017) 2 *Made in China: A Quarterly on Chinese Labour, Civil Society, and Rights* 11 at 15; *July 9th Crackdown*, *supra* note 5, at 561.

3

Access to Justice in India: Managing Multiple Mechanisms in a Restrictive Practice Environment

*Sarasu Esther Thomas**

Abstract

India currently has the largest number of poor persons in the world, as well as the largest illiterate population, which creates tremendous challenges for access to justice. While free legal aid is a fundamental right for indigent litigants in India, accomplishing this standard remains elusive, and the system struggles with poor-quality state-empanelled lawyers and other challenges. There is also considerable emphasis on dispute settlement through alternative means such as lok adalats, *where there is no legal aid. Although the bar calls itself a noble profession, giving back to society is not something the legal profession feels duty bound to do, and pro bono or low bono lawyers remain few and intermittent. Legal aid clinics in law schools could play a key role in this environment, but they are fettered by stringent practice rules which prevent teachers or students from assisting and representing clients. Access to justice could be enhanced if the quality of state-empanelled lawyers is improved, the appropriateness of* lok adalats *is considered in a more nuanced manner, and barriers to law school clinics are removed.*

I. INTRODUCTION

India has the largest number of poor people in the world, and in fact one in three poor persons live in India.[1] In addition to providing basic necessities to this large and vulnerable population, access to justice for the poor is a very real concern for the state. The fact that India also has the largest illiterate population in the world[2] means that legal literacy is low and vulnerable populations are unaware of what their rights are. Access to justice therefore involves not just the provision of necessary legal services free of cost, but also popularizing them and making sure that the pathways to access such services are smooth.

* The author would like to thank the following persons for their assistance in finding materials for the chapter: Mr Wilfred Thomas, Ms Shriyanka Dash, Mr Arjun Varma, Ms Jasoon Chelat, and Ms Priti.

[1] *Poverty and Shared Prosperity 2016: Taking on Equality* (World Bank Group, 2016) at 40, online: https://openknowledge.worldbank.org/bitstream/handle/10986/25078/9781464809583.pdf.

[2] 'India Tops in Adult Illiteracy: UN Report', *The Hindu* (13 May 2016), online: www.thehindu.com/features/education/issues/india-tops-in-adult-illiteracy-un-report/article5629981.ece.

This chapter looks at access to justice for marginalized groups, examines the need to provide adequate legal representation in an adversarial system, and considers the challenges faced by the mechanisms currently in place. While mechanisms to support access to justice, such as government-funded legal aid, were introduced to dilute the rigour of the adversarial system inherited from the British, a lack of access has persisted even after 65 years of independence. Barriers to access to justice are unlikely to go away soon, and it is therefore essential to ensure that vulnerable parties are protected.

In India, case dockets for judges in the lower judiciary are high and result in unjustifiable delays, imposing monetary and non-monetary costs for litigants who can ill afford them. Pro bono services, understood as legal services underwritten by lawyers to poor or vulnerable persons, are not common in India. The question is therefore not whether legal aid or pro bono services are needed, or even whether the state or lawyers should shoulder the burden, but how to implement current legal guarantees. Increased access to justice may be obtained through a combination of approaches: upgrading existing mechanisms, bringing about volunteerism in the legal community, and creating a greater participatory role for legal educational institutions.

II. EARLY DEVELOPMENTS

The early history of access to justice in India is primarily the history of the legal aid movement. There have been initiatives starting from 1945, like the Bombay Legal Aid Society. These early lawyers received some funds from the municipal government,[3] and the Civil Procedure Code 1908 provided for suits and appeals for indigent persons and exempted them from paying a court fee.[4] State governments did see the need to liberalize the availability of legal aid in criminal proceedings, but they were reluctant to take measures due to financial constraints.[5] A Committee appointed by the government of Bombay under the chairmanship of Justice Bhagwati in 1949 proposed legal aid grants to support legal representation and provided detailed suggestions. The Committee asserted that the government had responsibility for legal aid, which must be made available in order to uphold the equality guarantee, a position also held by the Trevor Harries Committee in Calcutta.[6]

The Law Commission of India examined suggestions for replacing the adversarial system with an indigenous system of judicial administration to suit the socio-economic conditions of India, especially in providing for the poor who would not be able to afford the costs of representation in court.[7] However, the Law Commission pointed out that the system, which was British in origin, was now firmly rooted in India, and stated that reverting to ancient practices would be unsuitable to modern times.[8] The adversarial system, with parties represented by lawyers, was thus retained.

A. *The Constitution and Legal Aid in India*

The history of state-sponsored legal aid in India arguably begins with independence. While initiatives did exist before this, after independence they were identified as having a constitutional

[3] Laxmi Mall Singhvi, *Evolution of Indian Judiciary* (New Delhi: Ocean Books, 2008) at 125.

[4] *Code of Civil Procedure*, India 1908, as amended 20 March 2018 [*Civil Procedure Code*], Orders 33 and 44.

[5] Law Commission of India, *Reform of Judicial Administration*, 14th report (India: 1958) [*Reform of Judicial Administration*] at 587–9, online: https://lawcommissionofindia.nic.in/1-50/Report14Vol1.pdf.

[6] *Reform of Judicial Administration*, *supra* note 5, at 588.

[7] *Reform of Judicial Administration*, *supra* note 5, at 24.

[8] Ibid.

goal and were legislated in a fair amount of detail.[9] Having inherited an adversarial judicial system as a colonial legacy from the British, it was clear that the system could not work without adequate representation.

Rights in the Constitution of India may be divided into three categories:

1. Fundamental Rights – enumerated in Part III of the Constitution, a violation of these rights, such as the right to equality, the right to life, etc.,[10] can be challenged directly in the High Court or the Supreme Court of India.[11]
2. Directive Principles of State Policy – these protections are not considered justiciable, but are broad guidelines to be followed by the state, for example environment protection and a better standard of living.[12]
3. Other Constitutional Rights – found in other parts of the Constitution, such as the right to vote, right to hold property, etc., these rights are justiciable by additional means other than a direct challenge in the High Court or the Supreme Court of India.[13]

It was a long journey from the recognition that free legal aid was necessary, to implementing free legal aid as a legal right, and then to a constitutional right. Several Committee Reports[14] and the Law Commission of India[15] had recognized the need for legal aid to be a fundamental right, which would render it justiciable with the state bound in law to provide for it. However, the Constitution of India listed free legal aid as a Directive Principle of State Policy through a Constitutional Amendment in 1976, which stated that '[t]he State shall secure that the operation of the legal system promotes justice, on a basis of equal opportunity, and shall, in particular, provide free legal aid, by suitable legislation or schemes or in any other way, to ensure that opportunities for securing justice are not denied to any citizen by reason of economic or other disabilities'.[16]

While Directive Principles of State Policy are generally considered non-justiciable, some of them have been elevated to the status of fundamental rights though a series of judicial decisions from the Supreme Court and the High Courts of different states. The right to free legal aid developed in this way. In 1978, in the Supreme Court of India, in the case of *M. H. Hoskot* v. *State of Maharashtra*,[17] Justice Krishna Iyer pointed out that free legal aid was the state's duty and not charity. In *Hussainara Khatoon* v. *State of Bihar*,[18] the Supreme Court of India passed a landmark judgment regarding free legal aid. The case involved a number of undertrials, procedures in which men, women, and children accused of crimes were awaiting the trial process to be completed. For the duration of this period, if defendants were unable to get bail,

9 For positions prior to Independence, see generally S. Muralidhar, *Law, Poverty and Legal Aid: Access to Criminal Justice* (New Delhi: LexisNexis Butterworths, 2004) [*Law, Poverty and Legal Aid*]; *Reform of Judicial Administration*, *supra* note 5.

10 *Constitution of India*, India 1950, as amended 21 January 2020 [*Constitution* 1950], Part III.

11 *Constitution* 1950, *supra* note 10, Article 226.

12 *Constitution* 1950, *supra* note 10, Part IV.

13 *The Representation of the People Act*, India 1951, as amended 20 September 2013, s 62; *Constitution* 1950, *supra* note 10, Article 326.

14 For the findings of the Committee on Legal Aid and Legal Service in the State of Bombay, see generally Sarah Leah Whitson, '"Neither Fish, Nor Flesh, Nor Good Red Herring". *Lok Adalats*: An Experiment in Informal Dispute Resolution in India' (1992) 15 *Hastings International and Comparative Law Review* 391 at 393.

15 *Reform of Judicial Administration*, *supra* note 5, at 599.

16 *Constitution* 1950, *supra* note 10, Article 39A.

17 [1978] AIR 1548 (SC).

18 [1979] AIR 1369 (SC).

they stayed in prison. Many times lengthy incarceration occurred because defendants did not have or could not afford legal representation. Some undertrials were charged with minor offences, and many persons had spent between three to ten years waiting for their cases to come up for trial. The Supreme Court ordered their release, and it established the right of a prisoner to free legal aid. The Court stated that the state could not be permitted to deny the constitutional right to a speedy trial to a prisoner on the grounds of inadequate financial resources to improve administrative and judicial mechanisms and provide a speedy trial.[19] The Supreme Court stated categorically that unless there is free legal aid provided to an accused at the cost of the state, the trial would be vitiated. The only exception would be if the accused had refused free legal aid.[20]

In addition to its basis in the Constitution, the right to free legal aid was given effect through statutes, such as the Code of Criminal Procedure 1973 and the Code of Civil Procedure 1908. Section 304 of the Criminal Procedure Code, 1973 provides for a court-assigned pleader for defence in a court of sessions if the accused does not have sufficient means to hire a lawyer to represent her.[21] The Civil Procedure Code, in Order 33, provides such an assignment if there is a suit or defence of a suit by an indigent person.[22]

The right to legal aid was thus established. A paradigm shift began with operationalization of the right to be represented, which came through the Legal Services Authorities Act 1987, under which legal aid lawyers would be reasonably remunerated for their services.[23] Lawyer provision of free legal services was seen as desirable, but it was and still is considered the personal choice of the lawyer. There are more than 2 million lawyers in India[24] who could potentially assist poor and vulnerable individuals, but the Advocates Act 1961 nowhere requires lawyers to render free legal services. Pro bono services, understood to be lawyers providing and underwriting the cost of free legal services to poor or vulnerable persons, are not common in India, and legal representation for those who otherwise cannot afford it is uniformly referred to as legal aid. Even more unusual in view of current approaches to access to justice in other jurisdictions, the profession itself has not considered asking lawyers to perform free services. The state therefore had to develop mechanisms for providing legal aid. The bulk of legal services to indigent and vulnerable persons in India is state-sponsored, although there are some private actors who provide legal services pro bono. These include individual lawyers and lawyers working through non-governmental organizations.

III. MECHANISMS PROVIDING LEGAL ASSISTANCE TO POOR OR PROTECTED PERSONS

The mechanisms through which lawyers provide access to justice in India include:

- Legal aid and state-empanelled lawyers
- Private pro bono lawyers

[19] *Hussainara Khatoon* v. *State of Bihar* [1979] AIR 1369 (SC) at [10].

[20] *State of Maharashtra* v. *Manubhai Pragaji Vashi* [1996] AIR 1 (SC) at [16].

[21] *The Code of Criminal Procedure*, India 1973, as amended 21 April 2018, s 304, online: legislative.gov.in/sites/default/files/A1974–02.pdf.

[22] *Civil Procedure Code*, *supra* note 4, Order 33.

[23] *The Legal Services Authorities Act*, India 1987, as amended 29 October 1994, online: https://nalsa.gov.in/acts-rules/the-legal-services-authorities-act-1987 [*LSA Act*].

[24] Based on 2016 statistics, a big jump from 1.3 million in 2011. Statistics received from the Bar Council on a Right to Information petition filed by Advocate Kush Kalra for Legally India: see Kian Ganz, 'RTI Reveals: 1.3m Advocates; 1 in 300 Delhi-ites a Lawyer; Maharashtra Lawyers "Richest"; Jharkand, Assam, J&K fastest', *legallyindia* (18 February 2013), online: www.legallyindia.com/the-bench-and-the-bar/rti-reveals-number-of-lawyers-india-20130218-3448.

- Non-governmental organizations
- Public interest litigants
- Legal aid clinics in law schools

A. *Legal Aid and State-Empanelled Lawyers*

The Legal Services Authorities Act 1987 set up the Legal Services Authorities, and it is the primary legislation regarding legal aid in India. In its Vision Statement, the National Legal Services Authority states that its purpose is '[t]o promote an inclusive legal system in order to ensure fair and meaningful justice to the marginalized and disadvantaged sector'.[25]

The Authority seeks to carry out this purpose in two ways:

1. Empowering marginalized and excluded groups by providing legal representation among other services; and
2. Strengthening Alternative Dispute Resolution mechanisms to provide for speedy dispute settlement, including through *lok adalats*.[26]

The Legal Services Authorities Act 1987 also set up a National Legal Services Authority ('NALSA') at the central level. NALSA is the apex body developing policies on legal aid and channelling the funds allotted to different states for the primary purpose of delivering legal aid. Operations were distributed by setting up State Legal Services Authorities ('SALSA') at the states level, followed by District level and *taluk*[27] level authorities at the grassroots level. As a quasi-federal system, individual states have their own rules and authorities to ensure delivery of legal services. At all levels, there are two main aims: to provide litigation-oriented legal services for vulnerable groups, and to organize *lok adalats*,[28] literally people's courts, an alternative dispute resolution mechanism for speedy settlement of certain kinds of disputes.

Under the Legal Services Authorities Act, advocates are empanelled with NALSA or the SALSA in their state, and then they request to be a part of the scheme. When a poor or vulnerable litigant approaches the Authority, she is assigned one of the empanelled advocates. Finances are largely taken care of by grants from the central government. After independence but prior to the Act, the central government believed that legal aid was the responsibility of states within the federal structure, but states were reluctant to make financial provisions in view of their limited budgets, and some made only token provisions of INR1,000 (US$13.12)[29] to INR2,000 (US$26.24).[30] Today we see clear budgeted amounts for legal services, which are used to pay lawyers who provide services to litigants,[31] a change in government policy which came about mainly because of the judicial holdings noted earlier. Legal aid includes not just representation by an advocate in legal proceedings, but also payment of court fees, process fees,

25 National Legal Services Authority, 'Vision Statement', online: nalsa.gov.in/content/vision-statement.

26 Ibid.

27 A *taluk*, also referred to as a *mandal*, *taluka*, or *tehsil* in some districts, is an administrative unit consisting of a group of villages or a small town or village. A District consists of several *taluks*.

28 *Lok adalats* are an alternative dispute mechanism process. Judges or retired judges, lawyers, teachers, and social workers come together with disputants to settle the matter outside court amicably.

29 XE Currency Converter: www.xe.com/currencyconverter/convert/?Amount=1000&From=INR&To=USD. All subsequent references to US$ denominations in the chapter were derived from www.xe.com at the time of publication, and may have been rounded up or down for ease of reference.

30 *Reform of Judicial Administration*, *supra* note 5, at 589.

31 See Table 3.1, Appendix, p. 55.

and other charges payable or incurred in connection with legal proceedings, obtaining documents and certified copies, preparation of appeal, printing documents, etc.[32]

While it is generally understood that legal aid is for poor clients, persons entitled to free legal services can be broadly divided into two categories, by income level and criteria of vulnerability. Based on income level, any person who has an annual income of not more than the amount fixed by each state in India is entitled to free legal services; these figures range from INR9,000 (US$122.31) to INR3,00,000 (US$4,077).[33] Based on criteria of vulnerability, eligible persons include women and children, members of marginalized groups such as Scheduled Castes and Scheduled Tribes, industrial workmen, victims of mass disasters, persons with disabilities, and persons in custody.[34] In India, the caste system is still extant, even though the Constitution prohibits untouchability.[35] Penal laws punish derogatory and harmful behaviour by upper caste individuals to those they consider 'lower caste'.[36] Scheduled Castes, as they are known, are protected by affirmative action provisions in the Constitution of India.[37] Since they are especially vulnerable to violence and discrimination by upper castes, these individuals are protected by laws punishing such violence, and legal aid is made available to them to supplement this protection.

Every person who is qualified, under either income or vulnerability criteria, will receive legal aid on application, provided that they meet the merits test of having a 'prima facie' case.[38] However, despite this legal aid coverage, many persons within this group still end up paying for their own legal representation from private counsel, either because they lack awareness or access to legal aid, or because they feel private counsel will do a better job. Also, many who are not actually in a position to afford legal counsel are not covered by this scheme because they are not considered poor enough.

Lawyers empanelled with the legal aid authorities should be the backbone of the legal aid system, as they are paid by the state to provide legal services to those who qualify. However, two major criticisms have been levelled against this system in India. It is generally felt that first, the quality of services empanelled lawyers render is poor, and second, that the Legal Services Authorities spend more time and resources on settling disputes through *lok adalats* than providing legal aid for the poor.

1. *Lok Adalats* and Access to Justice

Despite studies going back 25 years on the ineffectiveness of *lok adalats*, these tribunals continue to be promoted by the NALSA and SALSAs.[39] *Lok adalats* or 'People's Courts' were an attempt to indigenize legal proceedings by providing quick and informal resolution of disputes outside court proceedings primarily through conciliation and mediation.[40]

Lok adalats may be organized from time to time on a need or convenience basis, while the Permanent *Lok Adalat* is a permanent three-member body set up to provide compulsory pre-litigative conciliation and settlement of cases regarding public utility services such as electricity

[32] National Legal Services Authority, 'Services Provided', online: nalsa.gov.in/node/13#history [*NLSA Services Provided*].

[33] *LSA Act*, *supra* note 23, s 12; see also National Legal Services Authority, 'Eligibility', online: https://nalsa.gov.in/services/legal-aid/eligibility.

[34] *LSA Act*, *supra* note 23, s 12. See also *NLSA Services Provided*, *supra* note 32.

[35] *Constitution* 1950, *supra* note 10, Article 17.

[36] *Scheduled Castes and Scheduled Tribes (Prevention of Atrocities) Act*, India 1989, as amended 17 August 2018, s 3.

[37] *Constitution* 1950, *supra* note 10, Articles 15 and 16.

[38] *LSA Act*, *supra* note 23, s 13.

[39] See National Legal Services Authority, 'Lok Adalat', online: https://nalsa.gov.in/lok-adalat.

[40] Ibid.

and water. *Lok adalats* are empowered to make a binding decision if there is a failure of amicable settlement.[41] The disposal of cases from April 2018 to March 2019 across 239 Permanent *Lok Adalats* was 102,625, with a total settlement amount of INR3,870,578,815 (US$50.79 million) achieved through 26,615 sittings during that time.[42]

Lok adalats account for a large number of claim settlements, but there are criticisms that it is unclear what is actually happening to litigants who vanish behind this mass approach to settlement of cases.[43] In some matters, cases had already been settled before they were brought before the *lok adalat*, but the cases were included in statistics to shore up numbers.[44] There have also been critiques of the manner in which the tribunal was conducted. Usually judges or retired judges hear the matters, and they are not fettered by court regulations. Sometimes litigants have had outcomes thrust on them, normally without the benefit of legal representation through legal aid.

2. Quality of Legal Aid

As it is currently implemented, legal aid has also been criticized. One problem is that poor litigants entitled to legal aid still end up bearing some costs. For example, certified copies of orders or judgments are made available to the litigant free of cost, but the litigant must pay for copies of books or articles necessary for the preparation of the case, as well as unlisted expenses. Incidental costs, such as transport to the place where the court is located and the litigant's loss of earnings, though important for a poor litigant, are also not counted as covered costs.

Studies have shown that the quantum of legal aid is very little in practical terms,[45] particularly if there are unanticipated extralegal fees.[46] The inadequacy of funding is compounded by the long pendency of proceedings and the heavily burdened lower judiciary, who carry a heavy caseload and work in conditions of poor staffing and infrastructure.[47]

Budgetary allocations for legal aid must increase, but they must also be utilized to their full potential, which is not currently being done.[48] At the time of writing, at least 10 per cent of the funding allocated for legal aid remains unspent.[49] Considering the large numbers of poor litigants and accused persons, the existence of unspent portions of the allocation is not because there are no takers for these schemes, but rather because knowledge of them has not penetrated sufficiently, and the quality of representation is doubted by potential applicants. These problems can be combatted by increasing awareness of legal aid and improving the quality of legal services. While *lok adalats* may be a good alternative dispute resolution mechanism, their

[41] *LSA Act*, *supra* note 23, s 22C(5).

[42] National Legal Services Authority, 'Permanent Lok Adalat', online: https://nalsa.gov.in/statistics/permanent-lok-adalat-april-2018-to-march-2019.

[43] See generally *Law, Poverty and Legal Aid*, *supra* note 9, at 122.

[44] See generally *Law, Poverty and Legal Aid*, *supra* note 9, at 122, n 97, citing Sujan Singh, *Legal Aid: Human Right to Equality* (New Delhi: Deep & Deep Publications, 1997); N. R. Madhava Menon, 'Legal Services Act and Justice to the Poor' (1987) 14:3 *Indian Bar Review* 99; Rajeev Dhavan, 'The Unbearable Lightness of India's Legal Aid Programme' in Sara Hossain, Shahdeen Malik, and Busra Musa, eds., *Public Interest Litigation in South Asia: Rights in Search of Remedies* (Dhaka: The University Press, 1997).

[45] Jayanth K. Krishnan et al., 'Grappling at the Grassroots: Access to Justice in India's Lower Tier' (2014) 27 *Harvard Human Rights Journal* 151 [*Grappling at the Grassroots*] at 168.

[46] *Grappling at the Grassroots*, *supra* note 45, at 171.

[47] *Grappling at the Grassroots*, *supra* note 45, at 165.

[48] See Table 3.1, Appendix.

[49] Ibid.

availability must not detract from the stated goals of legal aid, and cases should not be pushed from the courts to *lok adalats* without providing the parties with free legal aid.

B. Law Firm and Lawyer Pro Bono

To what extent should lawyers be required to play a part in indigent legal services? The Law Commission of India in its early days recognized the moral and social obligations of lawyers but did not feel that they should be legally compelled, because of the view that unwilling, forced services would not be satisfactorily performed.[50] The Law Commission also said that 'lawyers in India would not be worthy of the great traditions of the profession if they failed to render this social service which can be so usefully and appropriately rendered by them'.[51] The Bhagwati Committee felt that a maximum of six free cases every year should be done by every lawyer.[52] More recently, on 20 April 2017, the Union Law Minister Ravi Shankar Prasad said that credible pro bono legal services rendered by a lawyer would be considered while assessing a person for elevation to the bench. He also stated that services of retired judicial officers would be utilized to provide free legal aid to poor litigants through digital platforms.[53] However, these suggestions have not come to fruition.

Part of the difficulty regarding pro bono in India is that, unlike practitioners of medicine, it cannot be said that lawyers as a whole are wealthy and earn large sums. In fact, in 2017 the Bar Council sought state support for lawyers in terms of pensions, health insurance, and stipends to young lawyers.[54] The concept of 'giving back' to the community via pro bono services has no meaning for many members of the profession, who are struggling to make ends meet.

There are no reliable statistics on lawyer pro bono, and a field study on pro bono in India would face considerable challenges. In a study carried out by the Human Rights Lawyering Project, National Law School of India University,[55] the researcher observed that in his research he:[56]

> anticipated that a mixed-methods approach, involving semi-structured/informal interviews and direct observation combined with open-ended questionnaire based surveys will generate relevant local data. However, none of the law firms responded officially. Very few senior partners and associates responded in their personal capacities, and strictly 'off-the-record'.

This low response rate occurred because, while very few lawyers actually do pro bono work, they are not comfortable admitting that openly. It also appears that many lawyers and firms who have

[50] *Reform of Judicial Administration*, *supra* note 5, at 594–6.

[51] *Reform of Judicial Administration*, *supra* note 5, at 594–7.

[52] *Reform of Judicial Administration*, *supra* note 5, at 595–6.

[53] Prabhati Nayak Mishra, 'Free Legal Services By Lawyer Will Be Considered for Elevation to Bench: Law Minister', *LiveLaw.in* (20 April 2017), online: www.livelaw.in/free-legal-services-lawyer-will-considered-elevation-bench-law-minister/.

[54] Bar Council of India, *Press Release* (India: 2017), online: www.barcouncilofindia.org/wp-content/uploads/2017/04/Press-Realese.pdf [*Bar Council Press Release*].

[55] Suman Saha, *Pro Bono Lawyering in India* (India: National Law School of India University, 2017) [*Pro Bono Lawyering*] at viii.

[56] *Pro Bono Lawyering*, *supra* note 55, at 118.

provided legal services for free or a reduced fee[57] do so for clients with whom they have some kind of personal relationship.[58]

Barriers to pro bono include the fact that only an 'advocate' can represent clients in court, and 'advocate' has been narrowly defined as an advocate entered in any roll under the provisions of the Advocates Act 1961.[59] As discussed further in Section III(E), this definition has been interpreted in a restricted fashion that essentially confines practice to individuals working in law firms. This approach limits the individuals who could provide pro bono legal services, because it leaves out qualified lawyers in full-time employment, for example someone working in the legal department of a company or the government, as well as those in teaching positions. Current amendments proposed by the Law Commission suggest that, going ahead, a law firm may be formed and registered under the Limited Liability Partnership Act 2008, or as a private or public limited company incorporated under the Companies Act 2013.[60] The Law Commission has also recommended that Limited Liability Partnerships be registered and regulated within the territorial jurisdiction of the state Bar Councils.[61] The Law Commission felt that there was a need to change the definition of a lawyer in legal provisions to reflect changes in the practice structures in which lawyers work. In its proposal, the rolls of advocates would include rolls of lawyers in law firms, partnerships and so on.[62] If accepted, the Law Commission's recommendations would also recognize law firms larger than the current limit of 20 lawyers under the Limited Liability Partnership Act 2008.

It is possible that very large firms in India would not be averse to having dedicated pro bono staff. This belief however does not appear accurate across the board, as Indian law firms that do very well commercially usually do not have dedicated pro bono staff or do any pro bono work.[63] The effect of allowing large law firms in India to represent clients in court is therefore questionable. The viability of this approach is also under question, as the Bar Council has opposed the Law Commission's recommendations in toto in an extremely emotional response.[64] Despite the Bar's opposition, the entry of foreign law firms and their impact on pro bono practice has also been speculated about, with some writers claiming that pro bono legal work would be enhanced, as major international law firms spend resources in terms of staff time promoting pro bono work,[65] which could help to create a substantive culture of pro bono legal services.

Complementing the limited pro bono work done by individual lawyers is the system of *amici curiae*. According to the Supreme Court Rules 2013, the Registrar may require the Supreme Court Legal Services Committee to appoint an *amicus curiae* in petitions or appeals received

57 *Pro Bono Lawyering, supra* note 55, at 122, citing Thomas H. Morsch, 'Discovering Transactional Pro Bono' (2003) 72 *UMKC Law Review* 423.

58 *Pro Bono Lawyering, supra* note 55, at 122.

59 *The Advocates Act*, India 1961, as amended 31 October 2019 [*Advocates Act*], s 2(1)(a).

60 Law Commission of India, *The Advocates Act, 1961 (Regulation of Legal Profession)*, 266th Report (India: March 2017) [*Report on Advocates Act*] at 94, online: https://lawcommissionofindia.nic.in/reports/Report266.pdf.

61 *Report on Advocates Act, supra* note 60, at 68.

62 *Report on Advocates Act, supra* note 60, at 68 and 89.

63 Chockalingam Raj Kumar, 'Globalization of the Indian Legal Profession', *The Sentinel*, online: crajkumar.net/LatestNews/TheSentinel.pdf [*Indian Legal Profession*].

64 The Bar Council's demand that the government throw the recommendations and bill of law Commission in the dustbin: see *Bar Council Press Release, supra* note 54.

65 *Indian Legal Profession, supra* note 63.

from jail, or a matter filed by a party-in-person, or where a respondent is not represented.[66] The fee paid to an *amicus curiae*,[67] which is funded by the courts,[68] would be on par with the fee payable under services provided by the Supreme Court Legal Services Committee.[69]

Historically, High Courts and Supreme Courts have been appointing *amici curiae* in individual cases, where the *amicus* did the case without remuneration.[70] However, now there is a system for paying *amici curiae*. The fees payable to them vary widely, with Supreme Court *amici curiae* getting up to INR16,000 (US$209.94) according to the Rules, but some High Court *amici* getting only around INR500 (US$6.56) with INR100 (US$1.31) for each additional day.[71] However, courts have discretion to fix a higher fee, keeping in mind the standing at the Bar of the *amicus curiae* and the experience she has,[72] or according to the rates applicable to that state for legal aid work.[73] There are also lawyers who submit *amicus* briefs voluntarily in a case, especially in one involving the public interest.

Anecdotal evidence seems to indicate that the *amicus curiae* mechanism can be better tapped to incorporate unpaid lawyer pro bono work if a system can be better organized to connect poor clients with lawyers.

C. *Non-Governmental Organizations*

Non-governmental organizations ('NGOs') play an important role in access to justice in India. NGOs may have a consultant lawyer, who can deal with legal issues as well as provide non-legal services. Some NGOs may address legal issues via paralegals.[74] Some NGOs focus on the delivery of legal services, while some serve as a conduit or referral mechanism. Some NGO lawyers identify themselves as human rights lawyers or cause lawyers, and work to bring about systemic change together with representing individual clients.[75]

A recent study by the Alternative Law Forum interviewed 50 lawyers who saw themselves as human rights lawyers.[76] Motivations of lawyers included critical events in the collective life of the people, such as the 1975–7 Emergency and the 1984 Bhopal Gas Tragedy.[77] When lawyers

66 *Supreme Court Rules*, India 2013, as amended 17 September 2019 [*Supreme Court Rules*], Order IV, Rule 1(c).

67 *Supreme Court Rules*, *supra* note 66, Second Schedule Part I Item 11.

68 Ibid.

69 INR6,000 (US$78.72) up to admission stage and INR10,000 (US$131.20) on final disposal stage or hearing on regular side after admission, or as directed by the Court. See *Supreme Court Rules*, *supra* note 66, Second Schedule Part I Item 11.

70 See *Law, Poverty and Legal Aid*, *supra* note 9, at 132–4.

71 *The High Court of Karnataka Rules*, India 1959 [*Karnataka High Court Rules*], Chapter V, Rule 2A(v) at 19, online: www.karnatakajudiciary.kar.nic.in/hcklibrary/PDF/hckrules.pdf.

72 *Karnataka High Court Rules*, *supra* note 71, Rule 2A(v).

73 Amendment to Chapter 4-E of *The Legal Aid to the Indigent Persons (Punjab Haryana & Chandigarh Administration) Rules*, India 1981, with effect from 31 October 2007, online: highcourtchd.gov.in/sub_pages/left_menu/Rules_orders/high_court_rules/Vol-V-PDF/New%20Amendments%20vol.V.pdf.

74 Centre for Advocacy and Research, 'Ensuring an Enabling Ecosystem Through Legal Protection and Reduction of Violence', online: cfar.org.in/social-inclusion-button-5/.

75 For example, Human Rights Law Network, 'Human Rights Law Network', online: www.hrln.org/hrln/karnataka.html; Lawyers Collective, 'Lawyers Collective', online: www.lawyerscollective.org/; Majlis Legal Center, 'Majlis', online: www.majlislaw.com/; Alternative Law Forum, 'Alternative Law Forum', online: altlawforum.org/; Centre for Social Justice, 'Centre for Social Justice', online: www.centreforsocialjustice.net/.

76 Arvind Narrain and Saumya Uma, *Breathing Life into the Constitution: Human Rights Lawyering in India* (Bengaluru: Alternative Law Forum, 2017) [*Breathing Life*] at 197.

77 *Breathing Life*, *supra* note 76, at 16–21.

are involved in people's movements, it often motivates them to provide legal services for issues arising out of the movement. One example is the number of women lawyers who have taken up women's issues.[78] Many of these cases have been brought in the form of public interest litigation, a procedural tool often used to take up matters involving substantial public interest in the Supreme Court of India or the High Courts of states. Besides public interest litigation, a significant number of test cases have been brought in lower courts as well.[79] The women lawyers who take up such cases may have been brought up in traditional patriarchal homes, but they have become advocates for women's issues through personal experiences and being exposed to political movements.[80]

While filing public interest litigation is often newsworthy and considered to be what human rights lawyers do, lawyers working for NGOs also work in different ways, engaging in pro bono, low bono, or charging a full fee to protect the rights of poor and marginalized individuals. A new phenomenon among NGOs is that of online portals. iProbono is an online portal which seeks to match NGO clients with lawyers, who provide credible legal help which would otherwise be unaffordable.[81] Profiles of the legal professional and the NGO client are created, and there will be a matching of needs. Once the lawyer finds an interesting project, they can 'connect' to that project and then the project can be allocated to the lawyer to work on.[82] This portal provides lawyers who want to give back to society an avenue to do so. While the organization has listed some case studies showing successes in connecting firms and NGOs, there is no study to show how effective the portal has been, and it has not been able to offer pro bono service to individual clients, only to NGO clients.

Other portals are now being offered by other organizations which offer pro bono schemes.[83] Cyber platforms such as Lex Mundi Pro Bono Foundation provide services similar to those of iProbono, linking law firms with social projects.[84] Ashoka Foundation began 'Law for All' to ensure that its Fellows, who are social entrepreneurs, had access to legal support in different forms.[85] The Society of Women Lawyers set up a pro bono committee to link women-centric projects with lawyers and law firms in India and globally.[86] However, much of the pro bono service provided by portals comprises transactional legal advice, which, while important, does not meet the needs of individual poor or vulnerable litigants.[87]

78 The contributions of Indira Jaising through the Lawyers Collective and Flavia Agnes through Majlis are to be especially noted. For details, see Sarasu Esther Thomas, 'The Personal is Political: A Struggle for Equality in the Private Realm of Family Law' in Payal Kumar, ed., *Unveiling Women's Leadership: Identity and Meaning of Leadership in India* (London: Palgrave Macmillan, 2015) [*Personal is Political*] at 181.

79 *Personal is Political, supra* note 78, at 184–7.

80 Ibid.

81 'Young Lawyers Help NGOs Access Free Specialized Legal Help Through Online Portal', *iProbono* (December 2012), online: www.news18.com/videos/india/i-probono-ip-526045.html.

82 iProbono, 'Frequently Asked Questions', online: www.i-probono.com/faq.

83 Lubna Kably, 'Legal Fees are on the House', *The Times of India* (24 July 2013), online: timesofindia.indiatimes.com/business/india-business/Legal-fees-are-on-the-house/articleshow/21293375.cms.

84 Ibid.

85 Ibid.

86 Ibid.

87 Arpita Gupta, 'Pro Bono and Corporate Legal Sector in India' in David B. Wilkins, Vikramaditya S. Khanna, and David M. Trubek, eds., *The Indian Legal Profession in the Age of Globalization: The Rise of the Corporate Legal Sector and its Impact on Lawyers and Society* (Cambridge: Cambridge University Press, 2017), online: https://ssrn.com/abstract=2344257.

The multiplicity of roles played by NGOs is to be lauded. But in terms of legal services for indigent and vulnerable persons, NGOs can only perform the supporting role of complementing the work being done by the state. They do not have the reach or resources to dispense legal aid to every eligible person. This responsibility must be squarely on the state, and it should not be abdicated and left to other entities.

D. *Public Interest Litigants*

Public interest litigation ('PIL') is often used in India to access justice in cases where there has been a rights violation. The mechanism works via a direct approach to the Supreme Court of India or the High Courts of states. PIL in India is unusual because of the dilution of the requirement of *locus standi* to submit a motion to the Supreme Court or High Courts, the reduction of procedural requirements, and sometimes a shift from an adversarial proceeding to an inquisitorial one, where the Court may call for information and sometimes also follow up on a case. The Supreme Court can be petitioned, or 'moved',[88] when there is a violation of fundamental rights,[89] and the High Courts can be moved for violation of all rights, both constitutional and other rights.[90]

Individuals directly impacted by rights violations may be poor or otherwise marginalized and find it difficult to access courts. In view of the difficulties that claimants face, third-party representations have been allowed through a diluting of the *locus standi* requirement in relevant cases. As Bhagwati J stated, access should not be denied to large masses of people who, due to lack of awareness, assertiveness, and resources, are unable to access justice.[91]

Legal remedies for the poor and underprivileged have historically been one of the major gains of PIL, and guarantees of economic opportunities and making sure that the poor were protected have been established in many PIL decisions.[92] For example, the right to livelihood of pavement and slum dwellers and the prevention of their eviction without alternatives for shelter were upheld as part of their right to live in *Olga Tellis* v. *Bombay Municipal Corporation*.[93] The right of children to be free from hazardous labour was also established through a PIL.[94] The right to free and compulsory primary education was first recognized as a fundamental right through PIL,[95] before finally being established as a fundamental right through constitutional amendment[96] and other legal means.[97]

The sheer numbers of PIL cases have complicated any empirical assessment of their effectiveness,[98] because there is no clear, comprehensive record of PIL cases.[99] Currently there is even some debate regarding whether PIL actually serves the poor. Some feel that since the middle classes have better access to courts and resources, and they are aware and alert to middle-class

[88] *Constitution 1950*, *supra* note 10, Article 32.
[89] *Constitution 1950*, *supra* note 10, Part III.
[90] *Constitution 1950*, *supra* note 10, Article 226.
[91] *Bandhua Mukti Morcha* v. *Union of India* [1984] AIR 802 (SC) at [15].
[92] Sarbani Sen, 'Public Interest Litigation in India: Implications for Law and Development' (2012) 47 *Policies and Practices* 4 at 10.
[93] [1985] SCC (3) 545.
[94] *People's Union for Democratic Rights* v. *Union of India* [1982] *AIR* 1473.
[95] *Mohini Jain* v. *State of Karnataka* [1992] AIR 1858; *Unni Krishnan JP* v. *State of Andhra Pradesh* [1993] 1 SCC 645.
[96] *Constitution 1950*, *supra* note 10, Article 21A.
[97] *Right to Education Act*, India 2009, as amended 10 January 2019.
[98] *Public Interest Litigation in India: Overreaching or Underachieving?* (The World Bank, Development Research Group, 2009) by Varun Gauri [*Overreaching or Underachieving*] at 14.
[99] *Overreaching or Underachieving*, *supra* note 98, at 11.

concerns, they are in a better position to use PIL in a way that benefits them; the poor will not be able to utilize it in the same manner.[100] Some studies have shown that claims on behalf of the poor have been less successful in recent years, but the reasons for this are unclear.[101] Human rights movements and other social movements have relied heavily on the Supreme Court for remedies through PIL,[102] but more recent court activism has largely been in favour of the state's development agenda and the urban middle class, and not in favour of the poor rural farmers and workers.[103] There is also substantive ad hocism,[104] and increasingly, economic, social, and cultural rights protection is not happening,[105] of particular concern in this era of globalization, privatization, and liberalization. Dr Upendra Baxi referred to this shift in PIL as the structural adjustment of judicial activism.[106] There are also views that India's rights revolution has failed.[107]

Additionally, the focus of PIL has largely been on procedural justice. Even in *Olga Tellis*, reviewed above, the court did not rule that slum dwellers had rights to adequate housing, but that eviction without notice and due process violated fundamental rights.[108] In *Narmada Bachao Andolan* v. *Union of India*,[109] the court approved the world's largest court-sanctioned eviction even though there was sufficient evidence to show that it would violate legal standards.[110]

The Supreme Court has promoted social rights, but it has no direct constitutional responsibility for such rights, that function being vested in the legislature and executive.[111] In his 2017 book, Anuj Bhuwania pointed out that 'the Indian Supreme Court has repeatedly upheld a whole alphabet soup of repressive statutes which violate basic civil and political rights. For a populist judiciary, a counter-democratic role comes much more naturally than its classic democratic function of reinforcing representation.'[112]

PIL has been a mechanism for access to justice, but stronger safeguards for legal aid must come from rights-giving legislation, to promote access to all levels of the judiciary.

E. Legal Aid Clinics in Law Schools

Legal aid clinics have since the 1970s been seen in India as one way that legal services can reach the poor. Law school clinics involve teachers, students, and lawyers working together. Clinics in

100 *Overreaching or Underachieving*, *supra* note 98, at 8.
101 *Overreaching or Underachieving*, *supra* note 98, at 16.
102 Balakrishnan Rajagopal, 'Judicial Governance and the Ideology of Human Rights: Reflections from a Social Movement Perspective' in C. Raj Kumar and K. Chockalingam, eds., *Human Rights, Justice and Constitutional Empowerment*, 2nd edn (New Delhi: Oxford University Press, 2010) [*Judicial Governance*] at 200.
103 *Judicial Governance*, *supra* note 102, at 202.
104 *Judicial Governance*, *supra* note 102, at 205.
105 Ibid.
106 Upendra Baxi, 'The Structural Adjustment of Judicial Activism' in Jagga Kapur, ed., *Supreme Court on Public Interest Litigation: Cases and Materials* (New Delhi: LIPS Publications, 2002) at A-145-B.
107 See generally Charles R. Epp, *The Rights Revolution: Lawyers, Activists and Supreme Courts in Comparative Perspective* (Chicago: University of Chicago Press, 1998).
108 *Olga Tellis* v. *Bombay Municipal Corporation* [1986] AIR 180.
109 [2000] 10 SCC 664.
110 *Judicial Governance*, *supra* note 102, at 208.
111 Arun Thiruvengadam, 'The Global Dialogue Among Courts: Social Rights Jurisprudence of the Supreme Court of India from a Comparative Perspective' in C. Raj Kumar and K. Chockalingam, eds., *Human Rights, Justice and Constitutional Empowerment*, 2nd edn (New Delhi: Oxford University Press, 2010) at 264, 284–6.
112 Anuj Bhuwania, *Courting the People: Public Interest Litigation in Post-Emergency India* (Cambridge: Cambridge University Press, 2017) at 142.

India generally use a paralegal strategy, in which the clinic investigates problems and attempts to resolve them, and resorts to a legal remedy where required, either by referring the client to the state legal aid authority or to a lawyer attached to the clinic.

The history of this model of clinical legal education includes early recommendations regarding practical courses and vocational training by bodies like the Law Commission (1958) and the Bombay Legal Education Society (1949).[113] However, the goal of these recommendations was to expose students to practical dimensions, not to contribute to assisting clients in any way. In any case, students were prohibited from representing clients because professional regulation practice prohibited that. This approach to legal clinics continued until the 2000s. In 2002, the Law Commission suggested making clinical legal education mandatory,[114] and the second University Grants Commission Report of 2001, prepared by a curriculum development committee asked to upgrade the undergraduate law course, suggested this as well.[115] Some law colleges/universities did implement this suggestion, introducing what they called clinics. While exposing students to some practical elements, the clinics did not involve client representation in courts. Most clinics are not mandatory.

Today, many national law schools as well as private law schools have legal aid societies or clinics. They deal with practical situations and advise clients, often referring them to lawyers.[116] The goal of these societies or clinics is not so much practical training, but rather to encourage students to give back to society and educate people about their legal rights. Some clinics focus exclusively on particular groups, such as undertrials in prison.[117] They also help organize community participatory meetings, and link clients with the state Legal Services Authority to enable them to get free legal aid.[118]

The biggest reason why law clinics do not deliver a fuller range of services to poor clients is the ban on full-time teachers practising in courts. Two court decisions have dealt with different aspects of this issue, including (1) the position of full-time law teachers, and (2) the position of non-law professionals who are also qualified in law.

In *Anees Ahmed* v. *University of Delhi*,[119] the court held that a full-time teacher could not practise law in the courts. In a second case, *Dr Haniraj L. Chulani* v. *Bar Council of Maharashtra & Goa*,[120] a medical doctor who was also a qualified advocate sought the right

[113] Archana K., 'Practicability of Clinical Legal Education in India – An Overview' (2013) 4:26 *Journal of Education and Practice* 157 at 158.

[114] Law Commission of India, *The Legal Education and Professional Training and Proposals for Amendments to the Advocates Act 1961 and the University Grants Commission Act 1956*, 184th Report (India: 2002) [*Proposals for Amendments*] at 95.

[115] University Grants Commission, *Curriculum Development Committee Law Report* (2001) at 9, online: www.ugc.ac.in/oldpdf/modelcurriculum/law.pdf.

[116] Bhargavi Raman, *Law Clinics and Clinical Legal Education in Human Rights* (India: National Law School of India University, 2017) at 13.

[117] The Shadhinota Project of the National University of Juridical Sciences in Kolkata is an example of a paralegal programme which put inmates of prisons in touch with legal aid lawyers for effective legal aid. This was initiated by one of the members of the faculty and run with student assistance. See West Bengal National University of Juridical Sciences Legal Aid Society, 'Legal Aid Society Convenor's Report' at 6, online: www.nujs.edu/downloads/legal-aid-activities-for-2010-11-conveners-report.pdf.

[118] See generally Sital Kalantry, Elizabeth Brundige, and Priya S. Gupta, *Promoting Clinical Legal Education in India: A Case Study of the Citizen Participation Clinic* (Cornell University Law School and Jindal Global Law School, 2012), online: https://scholarship.law.cornell.edu/cgi/viewcontent.cgi?article=2538&context=facpub.

[119] [2002] AIR 440 (Delhi).

[120] [1996] AIR 1708 (SC).

to practise law. In rejecting the request, the court stated that every advocate must be devoted full time to the legal profession.[121]

Today, the Bar Council and the Law Commission require law schools to provide practical training;[122] however, the prohibition on teachers representing cases in court leads to a situation where teachers are unable to run clinics effectively. A blanket ban on teachers prevents interested teachers who are willing to give time from participating effectively in access to justice for poor persons. Of course, students are also barred, even with a lawyer assisting them.

There are other limitations on the abilities of clinics to contribute to access to justice, related to their location within the university environment. In many law faculties, clinical courses usually have a limited enrolment due to heavy supervisory responsibilities, but in India they are viewed as a regular course with an equal workload, and so teachers are reluctant to offer them. Additionally, most universities are situated beyond the city limits, making it difficult for poor clients to reach them. Their location makes them fairly invisible to the public. Also, resources in terms of funding for such courses are not widely available. In terms of pedagogy, the manner of evaluating student performance on such courses must be properly determined. Also, class size needs to be restricted; some clinics have a regular class size of up to 60 students, which makes them difficult to manage.

Formal clinical legal education is widely considered necessary for education, but it is largely missing in law schools in India, and existing directives regarding practice restrictions make it near to impossible.

IV. LOW BONO LAWYERING

The term 'low bono', understood as legal services priced below market rates and based on the client's ability to pay, is not in use in India, but it is an apt term for two kinds of legal representation. First, there is a category of cases in which lawyers provide paid assistance to low- and middle-income groups but subsidize the costs of legal representation to some degree. It is well known that although some lawyers do not do pro bono work, they may subsidize the client's case, either by using a differential fee system or waiving some of the costs.

A low bono system is also evident in an official legal aid mechanism, the Middle Income Group Schemes ('MIG Schemes'), which offer government-subsidized services to middle-class litigants. MIG Schemes for non-legal matters have been in effect for a while, but in February 2017, the Supreme Court introduced a variation of these schemes, intended to be self-funding, which provides low bono legal services to citizens who are not poor but earn no more than INR60,000 (US$787.29) per month.[123] This is a fairly high amount, for example about what an assistant professor in a university would earn. This Scheme is definitely not aimed at the poor.

The Scheme works through a registered Society which is a separate legal entity,[124] with the Chief Justice of India as Patron in Chief.[125] While services are not cheap, they are still

[121] *Dr Haniraj L. Chulani* v. *Bar Council of Maharashtra & Goa*, MANU/SC/1120/1996 at 14.

[122] *Proposals for Amendments*, *supra* note 114, at para. 12.23.

[123] India, Ministry of Law and Justice Press Information Bureau, *Now it is Easier to File Petition for the Poor* (India: 2017), online: pib.nic.in/newsite/PrintRelease.aspx?relid=158509.

[124] The Supreme Court Middle Income Group Legal Aid Society, established under *Societies Registration Act*, India 1860, as amended on 25 March 2019, s 2.

[125] Details can be accessed at Supreme Court of India, 'Middle Income Group Scheme', online: https://main.sci.gov.in/legal-aid.

reasonably priced. The setting up of the Society provides persons who can afford to pay access to empanelled lawyers, who then assist for a reduced fee. The scheme does support access to justice for these clients, but this state of affairs can be criticized as providing subsidized, better-paid lawyers for the middle class, and poor quality, low-paid lawyers for poor litigants under legal aid.

V. CONCLUSION

Early in its history as an independent nation, India considered but rejected the exclusive use of a more traditional approach to access to justice, because the adversarial system had already been established under colonial rule. That approach requires significant amounts of legal aid, and India today can be seen to be struggling to balance multiple mechanisms to allow access to justice, including the primary mechanism of legal aid and others such as public interest litigation. Remnants of traditional approaches to justice do actively influence access to justice, such as the categories of persons eligible for legal aid and the extensive use of *lok adalats*. The multiple mechanisms in place are not necessarily in conflict, but inadequate coordination, such as a lack of legal aid in *lok adalats*, can interfere with access. While *lok adalats* play an important role and may reduce the burden of cases on the court, they may not always be the best solution for litigants.

The poverty levels in India mean that the state's role in guaranteeing the fundamental right to legal aid, the main mechanism in accessing justice for poor and vunerable persons, cannot be overemphasized. The current lack of adequate legal aid indicates that this access is underfunded and tenuous.[126] This lack of access in India is compounded by factors such as illiteracy, caste divides, and sex discrimination.[127] Legal aid lawyers have often had poor legal education to begin with, and the focus must shift to improving the quality of legal aid and representation. Investing in training programmes or continuing legal education programmes for legal aid lawyers would not only equip them to provide better-quality assistance to poor clients, but also allow them to perform better in private practice.

There is immense potential value in private pro bono lawyering, but as yet it is not a significant factor. Bar organizations have a role to play here. The functions of state Bar Councils include making legal aid available according to the Advocates Act 1961.[128] Bar Councils are empowered to create funds to give legal aid or advice.[129] The Bar Council of India also has a similar function, to 'organise legal aid to the poor',[130] and to create funds for this purpose,[131] as well as legal aid committees.[132] It is high time that, as the representative bodies for lawyers, the Bar Councils and Bar Associations play their intended role in access to justice. At the very least, they should remove the practice barriers that stand in the way of allowing others to provide access to justice, and ensure that law clinics are protected from prohibitions which ban teachers from practising in these cases. Clinics have the potential to be an effective mechanism

[126] *Grappling at the Grassroots*, *supra* note 45, at 165.
[127] *Grappling at the Grassroots*, *supra* note 45, at 172.
[128] *Advocates Act*, *supra* note 59, s 6(1)(eee).
[129] *Advocates Act*, *supra* note 59, s 6(2)(b).
[130] *Advocates Act*, *supra* note 59, s 7(1)(ib).
[131] *Advocates Act*, *supra* note 59, s 7(2)(b).
[132] *Advocates Act*, *supra* note 59, s 9A.

supporting access to justice in India, but that will not happen until more reasonable practice restrictions are in place. Encouraging volunteerism by exposing law students to clinics, publicizing volunteer work, and having eminent members of the Bar endorse it by setting an example, are all ideas worthy of exploration.

The current movement to allow large firms and even foreign firms into the practice picture may not necessarily benefit poor and vulnerable persons who need access to legal services. These moves could further marginalize poor or vulnerable clients by bringing about a corporatization of the legal profession, and they do not address pro bono for the majority of practitioners in India, who still largely practise in individual or small settings. Creating systemic changes in local and foreign law firms must not be done without sufficient study of the impact on access to justice. A final point arising from the historically closed Indian legal profession is that although the profession has effectively protected itself from perceived competition by restricting the practice of law to licensed advocates, the pressure from globalization and the move to open up the market indicates that, try as it might, the Bar is not immune to change. It should concern itself with the justice delivery process before others make changes for it.

APPENDIX 3.1 BUDGET AND EXPENDITURE OF THE NATIONAL LEGAL SERVICES AUTHORITY

TABLE 3.1. *Budget and expenditure of the National Legal Services Authority, 2015–2016*[133]

Budget 2015–16		
Budget estimates of NALSA	Rs.145 Crores	US$20,522,551
Grant received from Ministry of Law and Justice	Rs.67.97 Crores	US$9,621,497
Grant released to SLSA/SCLSC etc.	Rs.60.30 Crores	US$8,535,537
Other expenses	Rs 35.72 Lakhs	US$50,564
Total expenses	Rs.60.66 Crores	US$8,584,500

TABLE 3.2. *Budget and expenditure of the National Legal Services Authority, 2016–2017*[134]

Budget 2016–17		
Budget estimates of NALSA	Rs.142 Crores	US$19,252,275
Grant received from Ministry of Law and Justice	Rs.63.67 Crores	US$8,632,340
Grant released to SLSA/SCLSC etc.	Rs.110.09 Crores	US$14,913,734
Other expenses	Rs.2.92 Crores	US$395,892
Total expenses	Rs.113.01 Crores	US$15,401,059

[133] India, National Legal Services Authority, *Accounts, Audit Report & Annual Report 2015–16*, at 4, online: https://nalsa.gov.in/grants-and-accounts/accounts-audit-report-annual-report-2015-16.

[134] India, National Legal Services Authority, *Annual Accounts 2016–17*, at 4, online: https://nalsa.gov.in/grants-and-accounts/annual-accounts-2016-17-english.

4

Access to Justice in Indonesia: Searching for Meaning

Yunita with Linda Yanti Sulistiawati*

Abstract

Advocates in Indonesia do not generally provide free legal assistance to poor persons. Advocates largely believe that these matters should be handled by non-governmental organizations, and it is these organizations that have been the drivers of legal services to the poor, not lawyers. Indonesia also faces some confusion between 'legal aid' and 'free legal assistance', as both terms can be translated as 'bantuan hukum', *and the historical conflation of these two terms has not supported identification of a lawyers' responsibility in access to justice. Historically the state did not have an obligation to provide legal services to poor persons, although this changed in 2011 with the Law on Legal Aid, which created a state obligation to provide legal aid. This law is a major step forward, but there are indications that state-paid legal aid services from the 'legal aid organizations' recognized under the law will now take centre stage, and that pro bono will not develop. Access to justice in Indonesia therefore continues to search for meaning: literally in the sense that neither legal aid nor pro bono are clearly understood, figuratively, as there is no vision of how to proceed, and practically, as many barriers impede current programmes.*

I. INTRODUCTION

A broad view of access to justice examines formal as well as informal justice mechanisms to improve the equality of justice in daily life.[1] Access to justice, for all members of society, has three components:[2]

1. Normative protections, e.g. the existence of a remedy, through laws and law reform, legal and regulatory frameworks, and customary norms;
2. Institutions and mechanisms, both formal and informal, which create the capacity to provide an effective remedy; and
3. Legal empowerment, or the capacity to seek a legal remedy.

* The author wishes to thank LBH Jakarta, especially Yanti, the librarian.

[1] Access to Justice Task Force, *A Strategic Framework for Access to Justice in the Federal Justice System* (Sydney: Attorney General's Department, 2009) at 4.

[2] Ramaswamy Sudarshan, 'Rule of Law and Access to Justice: Perspectives from UNDP Experience' (Paper presented to the European Commission Expert Seminar on Rule of Law and the Administration of Justice as part of Good Governance, Brussels, 3–4 July 2003) at 2.

These three components are linked to one another, and they are all necessary for access to justice, but Indonesia faces many obstacles in fulfilling these components. In March 2020, the number of Indonesian persons living in poverty was 26.42 million.[3] Out of a total population of 270.20 million people in September 2020,[4] there were around 35,504 lawyers registered with one of the bar associations, PERADI, in 2019,[5] and 524 accredited legal aid organizations in 2019–21.[6] According to this data, if free legal assistance for the poor is conducted only by legal aid organizations, then one organization must serve 50,419 people. The need for legal assistance for the poor, referred to as 'legal aid' (*bantuan hukum*) in Indonesia,[7] can also be seen in the number of cases received by one of the legal aid institutes in Jakarta, named *Lembaga Bantuan Hukum* ('LBH') *Jakarta* (together, 'LBH Jakarta').[8] In 2019, LBH Jakarta alone accepted 1,496 cases serving 60,793 justice-seekers.[9] In the years 2015–19 LBH Jakarta accepted 6,634 cases.[10]

In this environment of great need, the state and lawyers have either been absent or not had an effective impact on access to justice. Advocates[11] in Indonesia do not generally provide pro bono, understood as a lawyer's or law firm's provision of free legal assistance to poor persons. Pro bono is an obligation for every advocate in Indonesia,[12] and there is even a sanction for those who violate the requirement,[13] but the law is not enforced. Advocates largely believe that these matters should be handled by legal aid institutes such as LBH under *Yayasan Lembaga Bantuan Hukum Indonesia* ('YLBHI'),[14] and these organizations are the drivers of legal services to the poor, not individual lawyers.

[3] Badan Pusat Statistik, *Presentase Penduduk Miskin Maret 2020 Naik Menjadi* 9.78% (Percentage of Poor Population in March 2020 Increases to 9.78%) (15 July 2020), online: www.bps.go.id/pressrelease/2020/07/15/1744/persentase-penduduk-miskin-maret-2020-naik-menjadi-9-78-persen.html.

[4] Badan Pusat Statistik, Hasil Sensus Penduduk 2020 (Population Census Result 2020) (21 January 2021), online: www.bps.go.id/pressrelease/2021/01/21/1854/hasil-sensus-penduduk-2020.html.

[5] Moch. Dani Pratama Huzaini, Terbitkan Buku Daftar Anggota Tahun 2019, Sebanyak 35,504 Advokat Terdaftar di Peradi (Publishing the Member List Book for 2019, A total of 35,504 advocates registered in PERADI), *Hukumonline* (6 July 2020), online: www.hukumonline.com/berita/baca/lt5f02c9e79a120/terbitkan-buku-daftar-anggota-tahun-2019–sebanyak-35504-advokat-terdaftar-di-peradi/.

[6] *Badan Pembinaan Hukum Nasional*, Perluas Jangkauan, BPHN loloskan 524 Organisasi Bantuan Hukum (Expanding its Reach, National Legal Development Agency has passed 524 legal aid organizations) (4 January 2019), online: https://lsc.bphn.go.id/news/?nid=887.

[7] Under the current *Undang-Undang Tentang Bantuan Hukum* (Law on Legal Aid 2011), Indonesia Law No. 16/2011 [*Law on Legal Aid 2011*], s 1, legal aid (*bantuan hukum*) is defined as legal services given by a legal aid provider to a legal aid beneficiary free of charge, and legal aid providers are limited to legal aid organizations giving legal aid.

[8] *Lembaga Bantuan Hukum Jakarta* is a legal aid organization providing legal aid since its establishment in 1970, currently functioning within the *Yayasan Lembaga Bantuan Hukum Indonesia* (YLBHI)/Indonesian Legal Aid Foundation: see the *Lembaga Bantuan Hukum Jakarta* website, online: https://bantuanhukum.or.id/tentang-kami/.

[9] Lembaga Bantuan Hukum Jakarta, Reformasi Dikorupsi Demokrasi Direpresi: Catatan Akhir Tahun Refleksi Hukum dan HAM Indonesia 2019 (Reform is Corrupted, Democracy is Repressed: Annual Report of Reflection of Legal and Human Rights in Indonesia 2019) (Lembaga Bantuan Hukum Jakarta, 2019) at 20, online: www.bantuanhukum.or.id/wp-content/uploads/2019/12/Catahu-2019-reformasi-dikorupsi.pdf.

[10] Ibid.

[11] Per the *Law of Advocates*, Indonesia Law No. 18/2003 [*Law of Advocates*], s 1(1), an advocate is a person who is in the profession of giving legal service, both in and out of the court, and who has fulfilled the requirements under the *Law of Advocates*. In Indonesia and in this chapter, the terms 'advocate', 'lawyer', and 'attorney' are used interchangeably.

[12] *Law of Advocates, supra* note 11, s 22; *Government Regulation*, Indonesia, No. 83/2008 [*Government Regulation* 83], s 2; PERADI Instruction No. 1/2010, s 2.

[13] *Government Regulation* 83, *supra* note 12, s 14.

[14] Agus Raharjo et al., Akses Keadilan Bagi Rakyat Miskin (Dilema Dalam Pemberian Bantuan Hukum Oleh Advokat) (Access to Justice for the Poor (Dilemma in Providing Free Legal Representation by Advocate)) (2015) 27:3 *Jurnal Mimbar Hukum* at 1, online: https://jurnal.ugm.ac.id/jmh/article/view/15881.

The chapter also addresses the fundamental challenge posed by the confusion between 'legal aid' and 'free legal assistance' by lawyers, as both of the terms can be translated as '*bantuan hukum*'. The historical conflation of these two terms has left no room for identification of a lawyer's responsibility in access to justice. Historically the state has not had an obligation to provide legal services to poor persons, but a major development occurred in 2011, when the Law on Legal Aid (*Undang-undang tentang Bantuan Hukum*)[15] created a state obligation to provide legal aid. The law also defined and institutionalized legal aid and provided a standardized delivery mechanism. The Law on Legal Aid 2011 is a major step forward, but there are indications that paid legal aid services will now take centre stage and pro bono will not develop. Also, the law still does not answer the problem of access to justice for the poor, because access is a complicated issue involving Indonesian politics, culture, the organization of bar associations, and even the economy.[16] Access to justice in Indonesia therefore continues to search for meaning, literally in the sense that neither legal aid nor pro bono are clearly understood, figuratively as there is no vision of how to proceed, and practically, as many barriers impede current programmes.

II. THE CONTEXT FOR ACCESS TO JUSTICE IN INDONESIA

A. *Normative Protections*

1. Legal Guarantees and National Policy Guidance

Access to justice serves as an essential component in providing the rule of law[17] and the protection of the fundamental human rights guaranteed by the Indonesian Constitution.[18] It has two basic aims in any legal system, ensuring that all people have access to the legal system, and delivering justice to all. Indonesia acknowledges the significance of access to justice, in part because it serves as one of the key strategies to eliminate poverty.[19] Indonesian citizens also have the right to obtain legal assistance from a lawyer. As stated in Article 37 of Law No. 4 of 2004 regarding judicial power, 'every person involved in a case has the right to the assistance of a lawyer'.[20] The right to legal assistance must be implemented without regard to the background of the individual, such as religion, heritage, race, ethnicity, political beliefs, socio-economic stratum, skin colour, and gender.[21]

[15] *Law on Legal Aid 2011*, *supra* note 7, ss 6 and 7.

[16] Adnan Buyung Nasution, 'Legal Aid and Access to Justice in Indonesia' (Paper delivered at the First International Colloquium on Legal Aid and Legal Service, United Kingdom, London, 25–28 October 1976).

[17] *Indonesian Constitution 1945* (as amended by the Fourth amendment, 11 August 2002) [*Indonesian Constitution 1945*], Article 1.

[18] *Indonesian Constitution 1945*, *supra* note 17, Article 28.

[19] *Making the Law Work for Everyone* (UNDP Commission on Legal Empowerment of the Poor, 2008) at 48–9, online: www.un.org/ruleoflaw/files/Making_the_Law_Work_for_Everyone.pdf; *Kementerian Perencanaan Pembangunan Nasional, Strategi Nasional Akses Pada Keadilan 2016–2019* (National Strategy of Access to Justice) (UNDP Indonesia, 10 May 2016) [*National Strategy of Access to Justice*] at ii, online: www.id.undp.org/content/dam/indonesia/2016/press-doc/buku%20SNAK%20rev(2)%20-4-5-16.pdf.

[20] *Law of Judicial Power*, Indonesia Law No. 4/2004, s 37.

[21] The principle of equality before the law as mentioned in the *Indonesian Constitution 1945*, *supra* note 17, Article 28D; *International Covenant on Civil and Political Rights* (ratified by Indonesia 2006), Articles 16 and 26; *Law of Human Rights*, Indonesia Law No. 39/1999, ss 17, 18, 19, and 34.

2. Legal Pluralism

Indonesian law itself poses some challenges for access to justice. Indonesia's rich cultural history had led to incorporation of a variety of legal traditions, including the national legal system, the Islamic legal system, and the Adat legal system.[22] As the Islamic and Adat legal systems are subordinate to national laws, national laws almost always dominate in dispute settlement. The hierarchy of laws hinders flexibility in reaching a fair result,[23] and as a result, vulnerable or minority groups are disadvantaged, for example in the case of land or *ulayat* rights of Adat communities.[24]

B. *Resources to Accommodate Access to Justice*

A fundamental requirement of access to justice is the existence of proper resources, including judges and venues for dispute resolution. Indonesia faces a large imbalance in the ratio of judges to population, as well as inadequate venues for the amount of legal issues. These challenges impact all litigants, but particularly poor and vulnerable individuals.

1. Imbalance of Population and Judges

Indonesia struggles to provide an adequate number of judges for its large population. Based on an earlier total population of 237,641,326, there are only 7,000 judges.[25] These numbers depict a heavy imbalance, with only one judge for every 34,000 persons. The Supreme Court's spokesperson, Y. M. Suhadi, asserts that Indonesia needs an additional 4,000 judges to accommodate the people, and that a total of 11,000 judges would be ideal.[26] However, achieving this number has proven difficult. Since 2015, several courts have experienced a 'judge crisis', in which courts faced an immense decrease in the number of judges available.[27] There are several examples of insufficient numbers of judges in District Courts around Indonesia. For example, in Manggarai District of Eastern Nusa Tenggara, Flores, there are only four judges, and with one judge acting as interim head of the District Court Office, in practice there are only three judges, comprising only one bench; none of them can take even a sick day due to the caseload and lack of human

[22] Sulistyowati Iranto, 'Menuju Pembangunan Hukum Pro-Keadilan Rakyat dan Perempuan' (Towards the Legal Development of Pro-Justice for People and Women) (Paper delivered at the PGA Parliamentary Seminar on Promoting Gender Justice and the Rule of Law through National Mechanisms, 2011) at 6, online: www.pgaction.org/pdf/Menuju-Pembangunan-Hukum-Pro-Keadilan-Rakyat-Perempuan.pdf.

[23] Franz von Benda-Beckmann, 'Legal Pluralism and Social Justice in Economic and Political Development' (2009) 32:1 *IDS Bulletin* 46.

[24] See e.g. *Basic Agrarian Law*, Indonesia Law No. 5/1960, s 3, which states that 'the implementation of *ulayat* rights and other similar rights of *adat*-law communities – as long as such communities in reality still exist – must be such that it is consistent with the national interest and the State's interest and shall not contradict the laws and regulations of higher levels'.

[25] Ihsanuddin, CNN Indonesia, Mahkamah Agung: Indonesia Kekurangan 4.000 Hakim (Supreme Court: Indonesia Lack of 4,000 Judges), *CNN Indonesia* (19 July 2018), online: www.cnnindonesia.com/nasional/20180719065206-12-315260/mahkamah-agung-indonesia-kekurangan-4000-hakim.

[26] Ihsanuddin, Ketua MA: Indonesia Kekurangan Hakim (Chief Justice of Supreme Court: Indonesia Lacks Judges), *KOMPAS Jakarta* (27 February 2019), online: https://nasional.kompas.com/read/2019/02/27/14423441/ketua-ma-indonesia-kekurangan-hakim.

[27] Marwan, S.Ag. M.Ad (Ketua Pengadilan Agama Pasarwajo), *Fenomena Kekurangan Hakim dan Status Hakim Tunggal* (The Phenomena of Lack of Judges and Single Judge Status), Supreme Court of the Republic of Indonesia (21 February 2019), online: https://badilag.mahkamahagung.go.id/artikel/publikasi/artikel/fenomena-kekurangan-hakim-dan-status-hakim-tunggal-oleh-marwan-s-ag-m-ag-21-2.

resources.[28] Many districts in Indonesia experience similar situations. The District Court of Melongaune, in the Talau Islands Regency in North Sulawesi, is newly established, but it faces similar issues. It has only one panel of judges, consisting of a total of three judges.[29] These judges were also advised not to fall sick, nor take leave because it could hamper trials and delay proceedings. Yet another example is the Surabaya District Court. Although Surabaya possesses a total of 30 judges, the case burden is heavy.[30] The number of civil and criminal cases in the Surabaya District Court reaches 6,000–7,000, or 233 cases per judge. The extent of the judge crisis reduces the productivity of courts and their ability to deliver justice.

2. Inadequate Court Venues

Indonesia also lacks an appropriate number of venues to be an effective and efficient platform to solve legal conflicts. There is a total of 886 courts in Indonesia, which includes the District Court, Religious Court, Military Court, and Administrative Court,[31] and this number is not enough to handle the caseload. In 2019, in the Supreme Court alone, the caseload totalled 20,021 cases, an increase of 12.91 per cent compared to the previous year,[32] and all of these 20,000-odd cases had already gone on appeal twice before reaching the Supreme Court.

In addition to the lack of sufficient venues, the courts are not sufficiently well resourced to resolve all the disputes within their jurisdiction, in terms of judicial training or investigation.[33] A few specialized courts exist, covering areas such as banking, agriculture, tax, or fisheries. There are three key aspects of specialized courts in Indonesia: the subject matter or distinct jurisdiction of the court, the judicial selection process consisting of expert judges, and an investigation procedure differing from the general courts. These specialized courts are designed to be more efficient,[34] and their tailored organization also eases the judicial burden in handling cases. Having expert judges also helps provide credible judgments on disputed matters. However, while having more specialized courts is ideal, the capacity to establish them is debatable. Also, the specialized courts focus on matters that require investigation and careful analysis, and not all cases from the general courts require the same investigation.

[28] Linda Yanti Sulistiawati et al., *Identification and Mapping of Adat Land Conflicts in Manggarai, Eastern Nusa Tenggara, Indonesia* (Research Report CaRED UGM, 2017–19).

[29] Robert Tamaroba, Pengadilan Negeri Melonguane Talaud Kekurangan Tenaga Hakim (Melonguane Talaud District Court lacks Judges), *Radio Republik Indonesia* (2018).

[30] Samsul Arifin, PN Surabaya Kekurangan Hakim untuk Tangani Ribuan Perkara Seusai Tiga Ketua Sidang Dipindah Tugaskan (Surabaya District Court Lacks Judges to Handle Thousands of Cases After Three Chiefs of Trials were Transferred), *Tribun Jatim* (28 July 2018), online: https://jatim.tribunnews.com/2018/07/28/pn-surabaya-kekurangan-hakim-untuk-tangani-ribuan-perkara-seusai-tiga-ketua-sidang-dipindah-tugaskan; Zaenal Effendi, Duh, PN Surabaya Kekurangan Hakim (Duh, Surabaya District Court Lacks Judges), *Detik News* (31 July 2018), online: https://news.detik.com/berita-jawa-timur/d-4142146/duh-pn-surabaya-kekurangan-hakim.

[31] Chief Justice of Supreme Court Decision No. 200/KMA/SK/X/2018 Regarding Class, Type and Legal Area of Courts of First Instance and High Courts in Four Judicial Environments, ss 3–6.

[32] Supreme Court of the Republic of Indonesia, Sepanjang MA RI Berdiri, Tahun 2019 Adalah Rekor Terbaik Pencapaian Penyelesaian Perkara (As Long as Supreme Court was Established, 2019 is the Best Achievement Record for Case Settlement) (27 December 2019), online: www.mahkamahagung.go.id/id/berita/3943/sepanjang-ma-ri-berdiri-tahun-2019-adalah-rekor-terbaik-pencapaian-penyelesaian-perkara.

[33] Lembaga Kajian dan Advokasi Independesi Peradilan (Indonesian Judicial Reform Forum), Capaian, Tantangan, dan Rekomendasi Pembaruan Peradilan (Achievement, Challenge, and Recommendation for Judicial Reform) (2018), online: https://leip.or.id/wp-content/uploads/2018/01/Capaian-Tantangan-dan-Rekomendasi-IJRF-2018.pdf.

[34] Ibid.

3. Legal Services Generally

A. LEGAL EDUCATION. The standard of legal education in Indonesia lacks the ability to shape future lawyers in a manner that maximizes their potential.[35] The pathway to become a lawyer begins with a four-year law degree, followed by a two-year internship at a law firm, and it ends with taking the bar exam.[36] The four-year law degree is a key step in the transition from student to lawyer. However, the quality of legal education in Indonesia has many flaws.[37] While a broad spectrum of subjects is taught, teaching relies heavily on memorizing and describing legal subject matter, rather than critical analysis and application. It is beyond dispute that application of the law is not necessarily clear and requires critical analysis and creative thinking. However, the lack of a carefully designed teaching mechanism to stimulate critical and creative thinking hinders students from fully mastering the law and its application for Indonesia. While some universities are improving their law faculties, many others fail to keep up and provide an acceptable standard of education. Admittedly, students can gain a lot of skills during their two-year internship, however legal education is not pulling its weight to produce top lawyers for Indonesia.

B. AVAILABILITY OF LAWYERS. As noted above, all Indonesian citizens have the right to obtain legal assistance from a lawyer.[38] Yet despite the existence of this right, the citizens' access to the current population of lawyers is not maximally achieved due to their geographic distribution.[39] Law firms and courts are typically found in the larger or main cities within a region, and most lawyers seek work from these law firms. It is very rare to find law firms in the suburbs or villages. This means that those seeking lawyers for representation must go to inner cities.

However, even big cities present issues in accessing lawyers. The lack of representation from lawyers is particularly evident in criminal cases. *Lembaga Kajian dan Advokasi Independensi Peradilan* ('LeIP') conducted a study in 2010 which depicted the difficulty in accessing a lawyer in Jakarta.[40] In a survey of 100 respondents, 95 of the respondents admitted that during the police investigation phase, they were not accompanied by lawyers. Although five others were accompanied during that phase, the number decreased again in the court proceedings stage. Legal representation in criminal proceedings, where the sanction is five to fifteen years of imprisonment, is crucial, but the majority of respondents did not have it.

III. LAWYERS AND ACCESS TO JUSTICE

After students of law or an equivalent major[41] graduate, they must participate in several weeks of special education for lawyers (*pendidikan khusus profesi advokat*) ('PKPA'), conducted by an

[35] Agus Raharjo and Sunarnyo, Penilaian Profesionalisme Advokat Dalam Penegakan Hukum Melalui Pengukuran Indikator Kinerja Etisnya (Assessment of Advocate Professionalism in Law Enforcement through the Measurement of its Ethical Performance) (2014) 21:2 *Jurnal Media Hukum* 182 [*Assessment of Advocate Professionalism*] at 187–8, online: https://journal.umy.ac.id/index.php/jmh/article/view/1186.

[36] *Law of Advocates, supra* note 11, s 3(1).

[37] H. Juwana, Reformasi Pendidikan Hukum di Indonesia (Legal Education Reform in Indonesia) (2014) 35:1 *Jurnal Hukum dan Pembangunan* at 6–8, online: jhp.ui.ac.id/index.php/home/article/view/1458.

[38] *Law on Judicial Power*, Indonesia Law No. 4/2004, s 37.

[39] Micah B. Rankin, 'Access to Justice and the Institutional Limit of Independent Courts' (2012) 30:1 *Windsor Yearbook of Access to Justice* 101 at 101–38.

[40] *National Strategy of Access to Justice, supra* note 19, at 39.

[41] Graduates from Syaria Faculties and Military Law, and Police graduates, can also participate. See the explanation of Article 2(1) in *Law of Advocates, supra* note 11.

organization that coordinates with the bar and charges fees of approximately IDR5,000,000 (US$355.47)[42] to IDR6,000,000 (US$426.56).[43] This is a prerequisite for taking the examination conducted by the bar, which cost IDR2,000,000 (US$142.17) in 2020.[44] After applicants have completed an internship for two continuous years, they can then be sworn in as an advocate at the court.[45] Every advocate must register themselves with a bar association in order to practise at the court, and as of October 2019 they were charged a fee of around IDR4,000,000 (US$284.29), which is paid to the bar.[46] After that, advocates only pay the administration fee for the bar card extension, which in 2018 cost IDR400,000 (US$28.45)[47] to IDR750,000 (US$53.35).[48] Bar associations have considerable potential to expand access to justice, but in Indonesia they not have fulfilled this role, a matter addressed below in Section III(B).

As the actors who provide legal services, advocates are main players in schemes of free legal assistance. Lawyers in Indonesia participate in two main institutions, *Lembaga Bantuan Hukum* ('LBH') and legal aid, and to a very limited extent, pro bono, or legal services provided for free by law firms to poor and vulnerable persons.

A. *The Concept and History of Legal Aid*

Since independence in 1945, legal aid has moved from being a non-state, poorly organized charitable act, to a state responsibility, although significant budget and quality issues remain. An important aspect of access to justice in Indonesia is that the concept of free legal assistance is strongly intertwined with the legal aid movement, which has arguably confused and delayed the development of a separate professional obligation.

In the years 1945–70, many advocates devoted themselves to government service, because they had been involved in the struggle for independence. However, the legal profession declined from 1959 to 1965, because of the influence of the executive branch on the courts. Court verdicts were discussed with the prosecutor, and therefore people preferred to ask for help from the prosecutor rather than the advocate.[49] In 1970, the bar association PERADIN, which had been

[42] XE Currency Converter, online: www.xe.com/currencyconverter/convert/?Amount=10&From=IDR&To=USD. Unless another reference was cited, US$ denominations in the chapter were derived from www.xe.com at the time of publication; they are intended for general reference and may have been rounded up or down for ease of reference.

[43] PERADI, Tempat dan Waktu Penyelenggaraan PKPA Seluruh Indonesia (Place and Time of PKPA throughout Indonesia) (25 January 2019), online: www.peradi.or.id/index.php/profil/detail/10.

[44] PERADI, Pengumuman Pelaksanaan Ujian Profesi Advokat Tahun 2020 (Announcement of Bar Exam Year 2020) (3 December 2019), online: www.peradi.or.id/index.php/berita/detail/pengumuman-ujian-profesi-advokat-upa-tahun-2020.

[45] *Law of Advocates, supra* note 11, s 3.

[46] PERADI, Pengumuman Persyaratan Pengangkatan dan Pengambilan Sumpah Atau Janji Advokat di Wilayah Pengadilan Tinggi di Seluruh Indonesia Tahun 2019 (Announcement of Requirement for Appointment to Advocates Sworn in All High Courts in Indonesia Year 2019) (21 October 2019), online: www.peradi.or.id/index.php/berita/detail/pengumuman-persyaratan-pengangkatan-dan-pengambilan-sumpah-atau-janji-advokat-di-wilayah-pengadilan-tinggi-di-seluruh-indonesia-tahun-2019-update-21-oktober-2019.

[47] PERADI RBA, Circular Letter of National Leadership Council of PERADI No. 30/SE-DPN PERADI/IV/2018 regarding extension of advocate identification card, s 5, online: www.peradi.co/media/file/pengumuman/surat-edaran-peradi-perpanjangan-ktpa.pdf.

[48] PERADI, Pengumuman Data Ulang Advokat Perhimpunan Advokat Indonesia Tahun 2018 (Announcement of advocate re-registration of Indonesian Advocate Association Year 2018) (2 April 2018), online: www.peradi.or.id/index.php/berita/detail/pengumuman-data-ulang-advokat-perhimpunan-advokat-indonesia-tahun-2018.

[49] Frans Hendra Winarta, *Hak Konstitusional Fakir Miskin Untuk Memperoleh Bantuan Hukum Dalam Rangka Pembangunan Hukum Nasional* (The Constitutional Right of the Poor to Get Free Legal Representation in the Context of National Legal Development) (Indonesia: Padjadjaran University, 2007) at 38.

established in 1964, launched a pilot project relating to legal assistance in Jakarta called *Lembaga Bantuan Hukum* ('LBH') (Legal Aid Institute, now LBH Jakarta or YLBHI). LBH was an independent organization with its own charter and management.[50] The initiative was supported by the governor of DKI Jakarta, Ali Sadikin, who was also one of the founders of LBH. He understood the importance of legal aid to access to justice, and the Jakarta government provided non-binding funding and facilities to LBH.[51] Relations were not smooth however, and even though the DKI government was LBH's main funder, LBH sued Ali Sadikin approximately 200 times. Yet, when there was an initiative to disband LBH, he rejected the idea, because as governor he wanted a degree of control over organizations like LBH.[52]

Other legal aid organizations were established, such as *Persatuan Wartawan Indonesia* ('PWI') (Indonesian Journalist Association), which provided legal aid to journalists. In the 1970s, the bar association PERADIN Jakarta established a legal aid post (*pos bantuan hukum*, or *posbakum*). The *posbakum* cooperated with all district courts in Jakarta, and the court provided one special room at every court for *posbakum*. This approach, which focused on litigation representation for poor persons, became the model for the legal aid organizations later developed by other institutions. However, these *posbakum* were not well managed, faced problems with case management and finances, and did not have much of an impact.[53]

In the years 1974–6, LBH expanded its methods of representation, from only litigation to litigation as well as non-litigation matters. Lawyers, particularly within LBH, also began to recognize barriers to access to justice, including a lack of resources and a lack of legal awareness. Other parties were needed to contribute to legal aid.[54] In 1976–9, awareness grew of the importance of non-legal issues to the legal aid movement, such as the economy, politics, and psychology.

Beginning in 1979, LBH undertook a fundamental shift, from traditional legal aid to structural legal aid. Introduced by Prof. Paul Moedikdo, structural legal aid is legal aid that creates legal awareness within the community, so community members can identify and defend their rights, and ultimately change the social structure that oppresses them.[55] Progress had been made using the traditional approach to legal aid, but by the end of the 1970s there was discomfort with the inability of traditional legal aid to solve poverty issues in Indonesia. Structural legal aid relied on the concept of structural poverty, which is defined as poverty caused by an unequal social structure that unfairly limits access to resources and technology, thereby violating basic human rights.[56] The theory of structural poverty asserts that law is not neutral, because it is a product of imbalanced social processes in society.[57] Because the social system is more protective of those

[50] Ibid.

[51] Ramadhan KH, *Bang Ali: Demi Jakarta (1966–1977): Memoar* (Brother Ali: For Jakarta (1966–1977)) (Jakarta: Pustaka Sinar Harapan, 1995) at 39.

[52] Ibid.

[53] Ibid.

[54] Todung Mulya Lubis, *Bantuan Hukum dan Kemiskinan Struktural* (Legal Aid and Structural Poverty) (Jakarta: Lembaga Penelitian, Pendidikan dan Penerangan Ekonomi dan Sosial, 1986) at 70.

[55] Gatot and Virza Roy Hizzal, eds., Dimas Prasidi and Febi Yonesta, tr., *Bantuan Hukum: Akses Masyarakat Marjinal Terhadap Keadilan* (Legal Aid: Access to Justice for the Poor) (Jakarta: Lembaga Bantuan Hukum Jakarta, 2007) [*Access to Justice for the Poor*] at 14–16.

[56] *Access to Justice for the Poor*, *supra* note 55, at 27–8.

[57] *Access to Justice for the Poor*, *supra* note 55, at 27.

with greater resources, the rights of the poor cannot be defended in an individualistic, legal-normative way.[58]

To be effective, structural legal aid was required to articulate all systemic problems, which in Indonesia included an authoritarian regime, one that was not restricted by other actors such as political parties, the legislature, or the media. When Soeharto was in power, LBH used the immunity of advocates to articulate LBH's views regarding democracy, justice, and rule of law at the court. The goal in these cases was not to win, since all cases defended by LBH against the government were bound to lose, but to use legal aid to critique the authoritarian government and its ideology.[59]

Structural legal aid was criticized, especially by Ali Moertopo, ex-Information Minister and a military general loyal to Soeharto, as changing LBH from a legal movement to a political movement, and thereby ignoring the lawyer's role. In response, Mulyana stated that although LBH prioritized structural cases and became more political, it did not ignore legal issues.[60] Adnan Buyung Nasution also stated that as a civil society organization, LBH could not be separated from political matters, and it should not restrict itself to traditional legal service at the court, but also empower society to defend their rights, especially when they were violated by oppressive parties.

At the same time that it was changing the entire approach to legal aid, LBH was also changing itself. It adopted a regeneration system that imposed maximum time limits for LBH positions. If a person wanted to become a public interest lawyer with LBH, they had first to attend and pass a training period called *Karya Latihan Bantuan Hukum* ('*Kalabahu*'). *Kalabahu* was an annual training session that provided participants with perspective, knowledge, and skills. If participants passed this stage, they would enter the next stage where they served as assistants of legal aid/volunteers for about one year.[61] During this phase, participants helped a public interest lawyer but earned no salary at all, although they could receive small amounts of money to cover transportation and meal costs. After completing this phase, participants could apply to become a public interest lawyer, but only for a maximum of eight years. In those eight years, the public interest lawyer could progress through three roles: junior lawyer, middle lawyer, and senior lawyer. Only if there was exceptional organizational need, e.g. no available younger generation members, or being chosen to serve as LBH Director, would a participant be allowed to serve a longer term. If these exceptions did not occur, the participant would have to leave the organization. The goals of the regeneration system were to sustain LBH as a healthy organization, ensure that participants did not prioritize retention of their position over organizational goals, and actively develop and reformulate LBH ideas. After their departure from LBH, public interest lawyers were free to move to other civic organizations, further enriching and strengthening civil society and contributing to democracy and the rule of law.[62]

[58] Irawan Saptono, 'Kisah Panjang Gerakan Bantuan Hukum' (The Long Story of the Legal Aid Movement), in Irawan Saptono and Tedjabayu, eds., *Verboden Voor Honden en Indlanders dan Lahirlah LBH: Catatan 40 Tahun Pasang Surut Keadilan* (Jakarta: Yayasan Lembaga Bantuan Hukum Indonesia, 2012) [*The Long Story*] at 49.

[59] *The Long Story*, *supra* note 58, at 34–5.

[60] *The Long Story*, *supra* note 58, at 59.

[61] Lembaga Bantuan Hukum Jakarta, Pengumuman Hasil Rekrutmen Asisten Pengabdi Bantuan Hukum 2020–2021 (Announcement of Recruitment Result of Legal Aid Assistants 2020–2021) (15 December 2020), online: https://bantuanhukum.or.id/pengumuman-hasil-rekrutmen-asisten-pengabdi-bantuan-hukum-lbh-jakarta-2020-2021/.

[62] Mas Achmad Santosa, 'Menakar Relevansi Bantuan Hukum Struktural dan Tantangan ke Depan' (Measuring the Relevance of Structural Legal Aid and Future Challenge) in Irawan Saptono and Tedjabayu, eds., *Verboden Voor*

LBH has become an organization independent from the government, donors giving financial support, the bar association, and even political parties.[63] The role of LBH is currently understood as:[64]

(1) providing legal representation of individual indigent clients through public interest litigation;
(2) strengthening marginalized communities through legal awareness programmes;
(3) being at the forefront of critiquing ideology, state administration, state practice, and law enforcement;
(4) becoming the 'host' of critical people and communities; and
(5) pushing policy and legislative reform.

By demanding reformation through the disclosure of human rights violations, LBH and its related organizations played a significant role in helping to end the Soeharto era.[65] But despite the significant accomplishments of LBH, it must be noted that during this period, traditional legal aid services remained relatively weak, primarily because of a lack of resources. The state was not responsible for providing legal aid, and if it did, assistance was limited.

In addition to Indonesia's failure to implement widespread free legal representation, the internal regulations of state ministries demonstrated that the definition and purpose of legal aid was not understood. According to the *Badan Pembangunan Nasional* (National Development Planning Agency) ('BAPPENAS'), 44 ministries or state bodies used the term 'legal aid', but most did not provide legal aid to the poor,[66] and instead provided legal assistance to their own internal personnel who faced legal issues. This use of funds, intended for the poor but diverted to government employees, violated the written law,[67] which includes prohibitions on giving parties legal aid where there are special funds dedicated to government officials, such as government employees and *Angkatan Bersenjata Republik Indonesia* (Indonesian Army) ('ABRI').[68] This activity is also a systematic and institutionalized deviation from the state budget. The deviation occurred in part because of the lack of a monitoring mechanism for the legal aid budget. There were some positive achievements during this time, such as the Supreme Court's programme of legal aid for the poor.[69] However, there was an urgent need to enforce compliance with the concept of legal aid and ensure that its budget was only used for the poor.[70] The combined impact of very limited implementation of free legal assistance, practices counter to the goals of legal aid, as when some legal aid organizations asked the client for a fee, and the use of legal aid funds as a way to get inappropriate public support, led to demands to establish a legal aid law,[71] which produced the Law on Legal Aid 2011.[72]

Honden En Inlanders dan Lahirlah LBH (Menteng, Jakarta Pusat: Yayasan Lembaga Bantuan Hukum Indonesia, 2012) at 326.

63 Lembaga Bantuan Hukum Jakarta, *Bantuan Hukum: Akses Masyarakat Marjinal Terhadap Keadilan* (Legal Aid: Access to Justice for Marginalized People) (Lembaga Bantuan Hukum Jakarta, 2007) [*Legal Aid: Access to Justice for Marginalized People*] at 7–18.

64 Ibid.

65 *Legal Aid: Access to Justice for Marginalized People*, *supra* note 63, at 32–4.

66 *Legal Aid: Access to Justice for Marginalized People*, *supra* note 63, at 21.

67 *Law on Legal Aid* 2011, *supra* note 7, s 1(2) stating that legal aid is only for the poor.

68 Supreme Court Circular Letter No. 10 of 2010 relating to legal aid guidance.

69 *Access to Justice for the Poor*, *supra* note 55, at 21.

70 Ibid.

71 *Assessment of Advocate Professionalism*, *supra* note 35, at 432.

72 *Law on Legal Aid* 2011, *supra* note 7.

The distinguishing characteristic of the current phase of legal aid can be understood as the state's assumption of responsibility for providing legal aid. Law No. 16 of 2011 defines and regulates legal aid, and even identifies the state budget as part of the state's obligation to guarantee that legal aid is recognized and legally protected. State responsibility for legal aid requires the state to allocate the state budget to fund legal aid activities, which can be obtained from: (1) the central government budget; (2) state grants; (3) local government budgets; and (4) other non-binding financial sources.[73] Funds are distributed through a reimbursement system,[74] and they must be reported.[75]

The legal aid law identifies three main actors: (1) the executor, i.e. the Ministry of Law and Human Rights through the *Badan Pembinaan Hukum Nasional* (National Law Development Agency) ('BPHN'); (2) the legal aid provider, comprising accredited legal aid organizations,[76] which in addition to advocates, provides opportunities for involvement by lecturers, students, and paralegals;[77] and (3) the legal aid beneficiary, the economically poor individuals who receive legal aid services.[78] The Law on Legal Aid does not expressly refer to pro bono, but the structure of the law can be seen as implicitly distinguishing legal aid, which is a state responsibility, from pro bono, which is part of an advocate's professional responsibility.

Even though legal aid focuses on litigation, the law regulates two types of legal services, litigation and non-litigation,[79] and it covers criminal, civil, and administrative cases.[80] Legal aid is provided via the following procedures. First, the legal aid beneficiary must file a petition to a legal aid organization, which at a minimum must: (1) identify the applicant; and (2) provide a short explanation about the case. The petition must also include at least two documents: (1) a 'poverty proof' letter or certificate from an authority, stating that such person is economically poor;[81] and (2) documents related to the case.[82] After the petition is submitted, the legal aid organization must examine the documents, for no more than one working day. After all documents have been reviewed, the legal aid organization must inform the applicant of the result in writing within three working days. If the legal aid organization accepts the case, they must provide legal aid using a power of attorney.[83] Legal aid must be provided until the case reaches its final verdict, unless the legal aid beneficiary revokes the power of attorney before that.[84]

The first actions taken to implement the Law on Legal Aid were the verifications of legal aid organizations, in which the Ministry of Law and Human Rights provided opportunities to all legal aid organizations to register themselves.[85] The verification process resulted in the

[73] *Law on Legal Aid 2011, supra* note 7, s 16.

[74] *Badan Pembinaan Hukum Nasional,* Implementasi Undang-Undang Nomor 16 Tahun 2011 Tentang Bantuan Hukum (The Implementation of Law No. 16 of 2011 Relating to Legal Aid) (Kementerian Hukum dan HAM, 2014) [*The Implementation of Law No. 16 of 2011*] at 8.

[75] *The Implementation of Law No. 16 of 2011, supra* note 74, at 12.

[76] *Law on Legal Aid 2011, supra* note 7, s 1(3).

[77] *Law on Legal Aid 2011, supra* note 7, s 9.

[78] *Law on Legal Aid 2011, supra* note 7, s 1(2).

[79] *Law on Legal Aid 2011, supra* note 7, s 4(2).

[80] Ibid.

[81] *Law on Legal Aid 2011, supra* note 7, s 14.

[82] Ibid.

[83] *Law on Legal Aid 2011, supra* note 7, s 15.

[84] *Law on Legal Aid 2011, supra* note 7, s 12.

[85] *The Implementation of Law No. 16 of 2011, supra* note 74, at 23.

registration of 310 legal aid organizations from 2013 to 2015, 405 organizations from 2016 to 2018, and 524 organizations from 2019 to 2021.[86]

The verification process is conducted every three years, and it has produced a growing number of legal aid organizations in Indonesia. In this three-year cycle, the National Law Development Agency reverifies every single legal aid organization, based on their absorption of the budget.[87] The National Law Development Agency has reported that the budget absorption in 2016 was 96 per cent of the total budget of IDR44,983,620,000 (US$3,199,714.23), with 38,543 legal aid beneficiaries.[88] However, a problem occurred in 2017, when the state budget for legal aid was incorrectly reduced.[89] This occurred because of an error in the planning process when the government used the 2014 budget report and wrongly stated that only 46 per cent of the total budget was absorbed.[90] These decreases in the state budget hampered programme effectiveness and led the state to seek support from local governments, via contributions and enacting local regulation relating to legal aid, e.g. adding new activities covered by legal aid law.[91]

With the passage of the Law on Legal Aid, there is now a legal basis to require the state to provide legal aid, which is a major accomplishment. However, the current legal aid system has been subject to significant criticism. First, evaluation of legal aid is tied to budget absorption, not the benefit to the people. The performance of legal aid organizations is therefore measured based on the quantity of cases they have handled, resulting in larger budget absorption rates, but that does not guarantee the quality of service. Budget absorption is one aspect of performance, but it cannot be used as the sole indicator of legal aid organization performance.

Second, some legal aid organizations have faced problems getting reimbursement for the legal aid expenses they incurred, because of administrative issues.[92] Lastly, there is the problem of service quality. According to monitoring carried out in 2016, the National Law Development Agency received several complaints relating to service quality, such as: (1) several legal aid organizations asking for a fee from the beneficiary; (2) some legal aid providers being silent in court and demonstrating substandard legal representation; (3) some legal aid providers failing to provide continuous representation, appearing for the first trial and the verdict only; and (4) some

[86] *Badan Pembinaan Hukum Nasional*, BPHN Jamin Objektivitas Proses Verifikasi dan Akreditasi OBH Periode 2022–2024 (BPHN Guarantees the Objectivity of the Verification and Accreditation of Legal Aid Organizations for the Period 2022–2024) (17 February 2021), online: https://bphn.go.id/pubs/news/read/2021021801075675/bphn-jamin-objektivitas-proses-verifikasi-dan-akreditasi-obh-periode-2022-2024.

[87] *The Implementation of Law No. 16 of 2011, supra* note 74, at 8.

[88] There were 9,906 reimbursed cases, consisting of 73% criminal cases, 27% civil cases, and 0% administration cases. In litigation cases, 41% of criminal cases were drug-related, and 87% of civil cases were domestic cases. Of the 2,172 non-litigation cases, 40% were legal education, or street law activities: see *Badan Pembinaan Hukum Nasional*, by Audy Murfi MZ, *Kebijakan Program Bantuan Hukum* 2017 (2017 Legal Aid Programme Policy) (Bogor: Kementerian Hukum dan HAM, 2017) [2017 *Legal Aid Programme Policy*].

[89] The legal aid budget in 2016 was IDR44.9 billion (US$3.3 million), yet in 2017 the budget was cut to IDR18 billion (US$1.27 million): see Meski Serapannya Tinggi Anggaran Bantuan Hukum Turun Drastis (Despite High Absorption, Legal Aid Budget Drastically Reduced), *Hukumonline* (12 December 2016), online: www.hukumonline.com/berita/baca/lt584e5aa031816/meski-serapannya-tinggi–anggaran-bantuan-hukum-turun-drastis.

[90] 2017 *Legal Aid Programme Policy, supra* note 88.

[91] Maulana Rahmat, Perluasan Pemberian Bantuan Hukum Melalui Peraturan Daerah (The Expansion of Legal Aid Through Legal Regulation) *Info Publik Solok* (29 July 2020), online: https://infopublik.solokkota.go.id/perluasan-pemberian-bantuan-hukum-melalui-peraturan-daerah/.

[92] Muhamad Kodim, *ed., Perluasan Akses Keadilan Melalui Optimalisasi Layanan Bantuan Hukum yang Berkualitas* (Expanding Access to Justice Through Optimizing Good Quality Legal Aid Service) (Yayasan Lembaga Bantuan Hukum Indonesia, 2019), online: http://mappifhui.org/wp-content/uploads/2020/03/Perluasan-Akses-Keadilan-Melalui-Optimalisasi-Layanan-Bantuan-Hukum-yang-Berkualitas.pdf.

legal aid organizations refusing to file an appeal to the court, even though the legal aid beneficiary asked them to do so.[93] Poor quality legal aid services could occur because individual providers lack competence, or because they lack integrity, such as when a non-committed lawyer agrees to take a legal aid case, not to represent poor people but to get legal aid funds for their own financial benefit.

Legal aid beneficiaries can make a complaint to the Ministry of Law and Human Rights through the National Law Development Agency,[94] but in practice this monitoring is weak. The National Law Development Agency is developing online monitoring tools to measure legal aid organization performance. There was a proposal to interview legal aid beneficiaries and then upload this information. However, large amounts of human resources are needed to monitor all legal aid beneficiaries, so in addition to interviews, there must be an open complaint mechanism, with an effective investigation procedure to determine whether any violations of legal aid standards or rules have occurred, and the ability to impose sanctions on the organization. This proposal, although nearing completion, was interrupted by the COVID-19 pandemic at the time of writing.

When the state-funded legal aid mechanism adopted by Indonesia is compared to the work of LBH, it is clear that legal aid is not suited to structural legal aid for a number of reasons. First, the goal of structural legal aid is legal reform, while the legal aid law only supports traditional legal aid using individual representation. Legal aid beneficiaries are limited to economically poor persons and do not include vulnerable persons. Legal aid is also managed by government institutions, not an independent body, so it is vulnerable to influence from political interests. Even with these drawbacks, the dual institutions of LBH and legal aid arguably hold at least the potential to address the different kinds of legal issues raised by access to justice.

B. Pro Bono Legal Services

In Indonesia, the provision of free legal assistance for the poor is a professional responsibility of the advocate as a member of an honourable profession (*officium nobile*).[95] This responsibility must be distinguished from the legal aid provided as part of state responsibility, because advocates should be seen as independent from state organs.[96]

A number of factors in Indonesia have created conditions that are not conducive to the fulfilment of pro bono obligations. The long absence of a state responsibility to provide legal aid has meant that access to justice was in fact obtained only by a few people. Neoliberalism has impacted the structure of society, and social relationships are now guided by the principle of profit–loss transactions in a market economy system.[97] These principles have in legal circles produced legal commercialization, especially in the judicial system and the legal profession. In the judicial system, commercialization can be seen in the recognition of the 'judicial mafia' that

[93] 2017 *Legal Aid Programme Policy*, *supra* note 88.

[94] *Law on Legal Aid 2011*, *supra* note 7, s 12.

[95] *Komite Kerja Advokat Indonesia* (Work Committee of Indonesian Advocates); *Advocate Ethic Code*, Jakarta (23 May 2002), Article 3.

[96] Constitutional Court Verdict No. 014/PUU-IV/2006 (2006).

[97] B. Herry Priyono, Neoliberalisme dan Sifat Elusif Kebebasan (Neoliberalism and the Elusive Nature of Freedom) (*Pidato Kebudayaan Kesenian Jakarta* (Jakarta Art Culture Speech) delivered at the Taman Ismail Marzuki, Jakarta, 2006).

sells the result in cases, prompting many advocates to follow suit, e.g. by agreeing to change facts and bribery, which greatly disfigures the profession.[98] In addition, the commercialization of the legal profession can be seen in competition among advocates to generate profit. As a commercialized profession, advocates choose the cases that generate the most benefit for themselves, especially a big financial benefit. Cases involving the poor never become a priority, and the community of the poor face major difficulties finding a lawyer.[99]

1. Lack of Bar Associations and Organizational Conflict

In Indonesia, there was a long period when advocates were not well organized. The absence of a central bar association meant that there was no organization to guarantee ethical and high-quality advocates, or create awareness of pro bono obligations. Before the Law of Advocates in 2003,[100] no law addressed bar associations; the bar associations that did exist had different rules and membership was voluntary. Supervision of ethical responsibilities depended on the particular bar itself. After the enactment of the Law of Advocates in 2003, the eight existing bar organizations merged to form one bar association, *Perhimpunan Advokat Indonesia* ('PERADI'). More recently, PERADI was divided into several organizations which now retain common rules, although ethical regulation varies. Even today, no bar association asserts a pro bono obligation for advocates. Law No. 16 of 2003 establishes the obligation of advocates to give pro bono, but while PERADI Regulation No. 1 of 2010 recommends that advocates carry out 50 hours of pro bono per year,[101] the recommendation is not implemented.

Bar associations in Indonesia do not monitor advocate quality or implement pro bono obligations, perhaps because they are fighting to maintain their individual existence, by competing with each other to attract more members and increase their power. Article 32, point 4 of Law No. 18 of 2003 stated the obligation to establish the first bar associations, establishing a deadline of two years after the law was enacted. This law became the basis for the establishment of PERADI on 21 December 2004, which, as noted above, was formed from eight bar associations. These eight established organizations still exist, but the authority to formulate ethical rules, and verify, monitor, and dismiss advocates, resides with PERADI.

In 2008, PERADI separated into two bar associations which exist today, PERADI and *Kongres Advokat Indonesia* ('KAI'), both of which once claimed to be the sole legitimate bar association. On 24 June 2010, both organizations agreed to recognize PERADI as the sole bar association.[102] This agreement became the basis of Supreme Court Decree No. 089/KMA/VI/2010,[103] but the decree was subjected to a lawsuit in 2015, and the Constitutional Court ordered the High Court to

98 See Simon Butt and Tim Lindsey, 'Judicial Mafia: The Courts and State Illegality in Indonesia' in Edward Aspinall and Gerry van Klinken, eds., *The State and Illegality in Indonesia* (Leiden: KITLV Press, 2011) at 189–213.

99 Asfinawati, Bantuan Hukum Cuma-Cuma Versus Komersialisasi (Free Legal Representation versus Commercialism) (Prologue), in *Legal Aid: Access to Justice for Marginalized People*, *supra* note 63, at 10.

100 *Law of Advocates*, *supra* note 11.

101 *PERADI Regulation*, Indonesia Law No. 1/2010, Article 48, online: https://pbhperadi.files.wordpress.com/2010/10/peraturan-peradi-no-1-tahun-2010.pdf.

102 Constitutional Court Verdict No. 112/PUU-XII/2014 [2014]; modified by Constitutional Court Verdict No. 36/PUU-XIII/2015 [2015].

103 Arry Anggaha and Suryanta Bakti Susila, KAI dan PERADI Akhiri Konflik (KAI and PERADI End Conflict), *Viva News* (24 June 2010), online: http://nasional.news.viva.co.id/news/read/159961-kai-dan-peradi-akhiri-konflik; Menkumham: PERADI Wadah Tunggal Adalah Kesepakatan Sementara (Ministry of Law and Human Rights: PERADI Single Bar is Temporary Agreement), *Hukumonline* (24 September 2010), online: www.hukumonline.com/berita/baca/lt4c9c8878b512e/menkumham-peradi-wadah-tunggal-advokat-adalah-kesepakatan-sementara; Konflik Advokat Bikin

recognize and inaugurate advocates from both PERADI and KAI. The conflict did not stop there. On 26–28 March 2015, there was turmoil during the election of PERADI's chairman,[104] which led to the separation of PERADI into three organizations: PERADI led by Fauzi Yusuf Hasibuan, PERADI led by Juniver Girsang, and PERADI led by Luhut M. P. Pangaribuan. Each one claimed to be the lawful chairman of PERADI. Responding to this conflict, the Supreme Court ordered the High Court to recognize every qualified advocate from any bar association.[105] At the time of writing, this decree is the basis upon which a member of PERADI from any group, KAI, and the other previous eight bar associations can submit themselves to become an advocate.

2. Bar Associations and Bar Exam Oversight

The Advocates Act, Law No. 18 of 2003, Article 6, states that a lawyer candidate must pass a bar exam set by a Law Association.[106] The most popular Law Association is *Perhimpunan Advokat Indonesia* ('PERADI'), which hosts two examinations a year. However, candidates can also opt to take the bar exams hosted by *Kongres Advokat Indonesia* ('KAI') or *Asosiasi Advokat Indonesia* ('AAI'). Two issues regarding the quality of advocates are raised by these three hosts for bar examinations, the standard for passing, and the impact of having multiple hosts.

While there may be advantages in having different bar associations host the bar examination, problems are posed regarding the standard of the tests given out.[107] Also, the test for bar examinations is not standardized, which enables people who may not yet be ready or competent to become advocates.[108] In fact, individual bar exams do not impose much of a barrier. PERADI has a pass rate of 89%,[109] suggesting that it does not act as much of a filter, but merely an additional stage along the candidate's pathway. Of the 5,887 candidates who sat the 2018 second round PERADI bar exam, 5,238 passed with a grade of 70% or above.[110] The number of advocates escalates without strict examination of an advocate's quality.

An even more serious problem is an applicant's ability to take the bar exam hosted by another association upon failure to pass a previous exam. For example, if a candidate fails in the bar examination hosted by PERADI, the candidate has the option to take the examination of a different standard with either KAI or AAI, where they may easily pass. This situation is highly problematic. The bar exam is too easy to pass, and thus anyone can become an advocate. Bar passage does not therefore guarantee the competency of advocates. Bar passage does not even guarantee basic subject matter knowledge, which means that lawyers may fail to guide and represent citizens competently.

bingung Hakim di Daerah (Conflict of Advocates Confuses Judges in the Regions), *Hukumonline* (12 October 2010), online: www.hukumonline.com/berita/baca/lt4cb3fd590a635/konflik-advokat-bikin-bingung-hakim-di-daerah.

104 Munas PERADI 2015 Diwarnai Insiden Kericuhan (National Forum of PERADI 2015 Chaos), *Hukumonline* (26 March 2015), online: www.hukumonline.com/berita/baca/lt5513f46013f30/munas-peradi-2015-diwarnai-insiden-kericuhan.

105 Supreme Court Decree No. 73/KMA/HK.01/IX/2015.

106 *Law of Advocates*, *supra* note 11, s 16.

107 Hanya PERADI Yang Berhak Adakan Ujian Advokat (Only PERADI has the Right to Hold Bar Exam), *PERADI* (5 September 2018), online: www.peradi.or.id/index.php/berita/detail/siaran-pers-hanya-peradi-yang-berhak-adakan-ujian-advokat.

108 Aida Mardatillah, Beragam Pandangan Tolak Peradi Sebagai Wadah Tunggal (Various Views Reject PERADI as Single Bar), *Hukumonline* (15 October 2018), online: www.hukumonline.com/berita/baca/lt5bc4932056bbd/beragam-pandangan-tolak-peradi-sebagai-wadah-tunggal.

109 Daftar Kelulusan UPA Peradi 2018 Gelombang II, 45 Persen Didominasi DKI (List of Graduates of PERADI Bar Exam 2018 Batch II, 45 per cent is Dominated by DKI), *PERADI* (9 February 2019), online: www.peradi.or.id/index.php/berita/detail/daftar-kelulusan-upa-peradi-2018-gelombang-ii-45-persen-didominasi-dki.

110 Ibid.

3. Bar Associations and Pro Bono Activity

The long absence of bar associations from effective participation in access to justice has generated an environment in which there is no nurturing and monitoring of pro bono. There is no data regarding advocates who do pro bono. Most law firms in Indonesia do not document and register their pro bono activities, if they do them at all. Only one law firm in Indonesia was included in the 2016 Thomson Reuters Foundation's pro bono index, an index produced by the Thomson Reuters Foundation to map the global scale and trends of the pro bono legal sector, an example which illustrates the low amount of pro bono practice conducted by law firms in Indonesia.[111] There is no systematic approach that provides advocates with an awareness and understanding of the role the advocate plays in access to justice and pro bono, in the early stage of legal education or any later stages of professional training. If the advocate provides any pro bono in this environment, they do so as an individual choice based on their own morality.

In fact, there is widespread confusion among lawyers about the difference between pro bono and legal aid.[112] Misconceptions were illustrated when some law firms, or free legal assistance divisions/pro bono centres within bar associations, registered themselves as a legal aid organization with rights to receive funds from the state budget – reportedly as a fulfilment of their pro bono responsibility. The misunderstanding worsens access to justice, because it is a departure from the concept of legal services provided for free by law firms to the idea that services are offered solely because the state budget provides funds. The state budget is not enough to cover the need for free legal assistance to the poor, and pro bono is needed to cover the legal need that cannot be covered by the state budget, especially for middle–low income persons who are not considered poor under the regulations but are still unable to pay for a lawyer.

In the void created by the absence of the state and bar associations, there appear to be two ways that pro bono occurs in Indonesia, when it is performed. Organization-driven initiatives arise from an order from the law firm to all of its lawyers to do pro bono. This method is usually employed by regional or international law firms that have a branch or a cooperation with a local law firm in Indonesia. This approach raises the question of whether the local firm would engage in pro bono activities if they did not have any connection to the regional/international firm. The other approach involves individually driven initiatives, which arise from the moral obligations of particular lawyers. One pro bono initiative, SOCOLAS, was formed by a group of corporate lawyers. If the lawyer is working at a law firm, and pro bono is not supported by the firm, the initiative will be stopped.

The more prevalent trend among bar associations, after the enactment of the Law on Legal Aid, is to use the state legal aid budget to fund a limited free legal assistance centre at the bar association, e.g. as part of a bar association's incorrectly named 'pro bono award'.[113] These activities do increase the provision of legal assistance, which is free for the recipients, but the

[111] Thomson Reuters Foundation, *Index of Pro Bono 2016, Asia Pacific*, online: pbi.trust.org/data/?year=2016; Kartini Laras Makmur, Hanya Satu Law Firm Indonesia Masuk Pro Bono Index 2016 (Only One Law Firm in Indonesia Gets Into Pro Bono Index 2016), *Hukumonline* (1 August 2016), online: www.hukumonline.com/berita/baca/lt579f1b27e6ce4/hanya-satu-law-firm-indonesia-masuk-pro-bono-index-2016.

[112] Discussion at the Clearing House Pro Bono Initiative, 5th Asia Pro Bono Exchange, organized by PILnet, Bali, Indonesia, 30 August 2016 (unpublished).

[113] See e.g. Ini Dia Pemenang Pro Bono Awards 2016, *Hukumonline* (27 February 2016), online: www.hukumonline.com/berita/baca/lt56d12931df31f/ini-dia-pemenang-pro-bono-awards-2016.

model is actually closer to a legal aid organization model, and it is completely at odds with a pro bono ethic in which the legal service providers bear the costs. However, since 2018, *Hukumonline* has conducted a similar award called 'Hukum Online Award Pro Bono Champion', one that only applies to commercial law firms that offer pro bono, not legal aid.[114]

IV. CONCLUSION

Access to justice in Indonesia is still in the process of searching for meaning. It is in an early stage, as illustrated by the fact that there is still confusion on basic definitions, such as the difference between legal aid and pro bono. Of all the methods of free legal assistance, legal aid has been the most significant, but although the right to legal aid has been acknowledged since before independence, the concept of legal aid as a state responsibility is a new idea in Indonesia. The long absence of both the state and bar associations in effectively supporting access to justice, together with the commercialization of both the judicial system and the legal profession, has led to justice for the poor being ignored. There are also misconceptions about legal aid, illustrated by various internal regulations of state bodies providing legal aid for their internal members only, not for the poor. The 2011 Law on Legal Aid has the potential to address some of these problems, but other matters are required for better access to justice for the poor, including expansion of legal aid coverage, extending local governments' responsibility through local regulation, correction of budget problems, and improvement of poor quality legal aid services.

While state responsibility for legal aid has at least been established, pro bono as the professional responsibility of lawyers is still far away. The law obliges advocates to do pro bono, but there is no supporting structure in place and very little implementation. The historical absence of the state and bar associations from access to justice has in large part brought about this condition, and the prolonged internal conflict between bar associations has worsened it. Pro bono culture does not exist, and the provision of free legal services from advocates depends solely on individual morality. Confusion between legal aid and pro bono among lawyers, and a lack of awareness of pro bono, has also contributed to the current form of professional obligations, in part because the primary role that legal aid organizations played in giving free legal assistance for almost half of century resulted in the merging of the concept of free legal assistance with legal aid organizations.

Looking forward, several matters stand out. Legal practice does need to generate fees, but that does not require the current commercialization and self-serving nature of the legal profession. The regeneration approach taken by LBH demonstrates that a healthy approach to the provision of legal services and legal practice can be undertaken, even in an extremely challenging environment. The main vehicles for lawyers and access to justice, LBH and legal aid, are not well suited to do each other's work, but together they have the potential to address many of the legal problems faced by poor and vulnerable persons in Indonesia.

[114] Normand Edwin Elnizar, Ini Dia Para Juara Hukum Online Award Pro Bono Champion 2019 (This is the Champion of Hukum Online Award Pro Bono Champion 2019), *Hukumonline* (11 December 2019), online: www.hukumonline.com/berita/baca/lt5df103d90cb83/ini-dia-para-juara-hukumonline-award-pro-bono-champions-2019/.

5

Access to Justice and Lawyer Independence in Japan

Hiroshi Otsuka and Setsuo Miyazawa

Abstract

Historically Japanese attorneys were understood to function outside the government, and compared to judges and prosecutors they occupied a lower position but one with the potential to be more independent. The government control exerted prior to and during WWII had a long-lasting impact on Japanese attorneys, motivating the bar to retain its independence despite high costs over many years. The prioritization of independence is particularly evident in the somewhat unusual adoption of mandatory 'public interest' activities by the larger bar associations in Tokyo and other major cities. The chapter examines the process of making and revising mandatory rules, and argues that the divergence of views regarding what constitutes 'public interest activities' suggests that mandatory rules serve multiple purposes, not necessarily related to access to justice. The chapter also suggests a four-part typology to examine the different public interest activities which attorneys in Japan carry out: (1) professional work, paid and unpaid, undertaken for those unable to afford it; (2) criminal and civil legal aid paid for with public funds; (3) activities for bar associations; and (4) other activities recognized by bar associations as public interest activities even though they do not utilize legal skills.

I. INTRODUCTION

Generally defined, pro bono usually means professional work undertaken without payment for those unable to afford it, and while 'public interest activities' include these services, it is much broader. To analyse the role of lawyers in Japan in access to justice, this chapter explores public interest activities, the English translation of the Japanese phrase *koeki katsudo*, as this is the phrase used by Japanese bar associations and attorneys. As we discuss them, public interest activities by Japanese attorneys can include (1) professional work, paid and unpaid, undertaken for those unable to afford it, including cause lawyering; (2) criminal and civil legal aid works paid for with public funds; (3) activities for bar association committees or as bar association officers; and (4) other forms of activities recognized by bar associations as public interest activities, even though they do not use professional skills for any specific beneficiaries. Given its dominance in Japan, this broad concept of public interest activities should be the focus for a comparative analysis of the role of lawyers in access to justice.

Bar associations play a central role in how lawyers support access to justice in Japan, and they are organized in the following fashion. Japan is divided into 50 district court jurisdictions. Each jurisdiction has a local bar association. The exception is the jurisdiction of the Tokyo District Court, which has three bar associations due to pre-war conflicts among practising attorneys (*bengoshi*) in this region. These bar associations are the Tokyo Bar Association (*Toben*), the Daiichi Tokyo Bar Association (*Ichiben*), and the Daini Tokyo Bar Association (*Niben*).[1] Every practising attorney is required to register with the local bar association in the jurisdiction where he/she wants to maintain an office, as well as with the national association called the Japan Federation of Bar Associations ('JFBA').

Currently at least six of the largest bar associations in Japan have rules requiring attorneys to do mandatory public interest activities, a feature which distinguishes Japan from many other jurisdictions. They are the *Toben* (7,737 members as of March 2016), the *Ichiben* (4,786 members), the *Niben* (5,042 members), the Osaka Bar Association (4,333 members), the Aichi Prefectural Bar Association (jurisdiction of the Nagoya District Court; 1,857 members), and the Kanagawa Prefectural Bar Association (jurisdiction of the Yokohama District Court; 1,535 members).[2] We explored this aspect of access to justice in Japan via surveys and interviews. We collected information from the JFBA and mailed a questionnaire survey to all 52 bar associations, to which 46 responded.[3] We also conducted interviews of relevant officers of the three bar associations in Tokyo and the Kanagawa Prefectural Bar Association,[4] and a survey via questionnaire with members of JFBA's Law School Centre.[5] Consent was provided for all survey respondents and interviews, and approval was provided by the Secretary General of JFBA.

This chapter analyses the survey and interview data, as well as the background and content of these rules, and discusses the implications of the mandatory rules for a comparative analysis of public interest lawyering. The chapter argues that historically Japanese attorneys were understood to function outside the government, and compared to judges and prosecutors they occupied a lower position but one with the potential to be more independent. The defeat of Japan in World War II provided attorneys with an opportunity to equalize their status. The government control exerted prior to and during WWII also had a long-lasting impact on Japanese attorneys, motivating the bar to retain its independence despite high costs over many years. The prioritization of independence is particularly evident in the somewhat unusual adoption of mandatory public interest activities by the larger bar associations in Tokyo and other major cities. To explore these points, the chapter first provides a historical background of the commitment to public interest activities in Section II, and then provides a typology of individual and organized forms of public interest activities in Section III. Mandatory public interest requirements are analysed in Section IV.

[1] *Daiichi* and *Daini* can be respectively translated as 'First' and 'Second', but those bar associations avoid using such translations in order to avoid a misleading impression of superiority and inferiority.

[2] *Kanagawa Bar Association*, online: www.kanaben.or.jp/profile/gaiyou/history/member/index.html.

[3] In this questionnaire, we simply asked bar associations if they had mandatory rules, and if so to provide them. The research team for this work included Hiroyuki Kabashima, a member of the *Toben* and a former Vice Secretary General of the JFBA.

[4] We conducted four sets of interviews with officers of each of the following bar associations: (1) Tokyo Bar Association, 2 July 2017, Bar Association Building, Tokyo; (2) Daini Tokyo Bar Association, 3 January 2017, Bar Association Building, Tokyo; (3) Daiichi Tokyo Bar Association, 3 February 2017, Bar Association Building, Tokyo; (4) Kanagawa Bar Association, 3 August 2017, Kanagawa Bar Association Building, Yokohama.

[5] Surveys were conducted in Tokyo in February 2017; see Appendix 5.3 for a translation of the survey questions.

II. HISTORICAL BACKGROUND OF THE COMMITMENT TO PUBLIC INTEREST ACTIVITIES

Japanese practising attorneys have been proud of their commitment to public interest activities. The history of public interest activities can be traced to the Meiji era, when many members of the Freedom and Popular Rights Movement (*Jiyu Minken Undo*) in the 1870s to the 1890s were lawyers.[6] While there were attorneys who worked for big businesses and wealthy landlords, the attorneys who represented workers, tenant farmers, and criminal defendants against businesses, landlords, and the government had a stronger influence in forming the predominant self-concept of attorneys as 'lawyers outside the government' (*zaiya hoso*) as opposed to 'lawyers inside the government' (*zaicho hoso*), namely judges and prosecutors.

Before World War II, the self-concept of lawyers as outside the government, or anti-establishment lawyers, was also reflected in their professional status vis-à-vis judges and prosecutors. When precursors of practising attorneys called *daigennin* (meaning a person who speaks on behalf of another) were first introduced in 1872 along with those of judges and prosecutors, the government did not set any professional qualifications for them. Their professional status was clearly lower than that of judges and prosecutors. It improved slightly when the first Practising Attorney Act was enacted in 1893 and the term *bengoshi* (meaning a person who defends by speaking) replaced the term *daigennin* as their title.[7] A qualifying examination was introduced for attorneys. However, the examination was still separate from the qualifying examination for judges and prosecutors. Furthermore, while apprenticeship training was provided to those who passed the qualifying examination for judges and prosecutors, there was no such training for practising attorneys. Attorneys were also subordinate to the state; for example, in the matter of professional discipline, bar associations could not discipline their members, and disciplinary actions against attorneys were initiated by prosecutors and the Justice Minister-supervised bar associations.[8]

The second Practising Attorney Act was enacted in 1933.[9] It finally combined the attorney-qualifying examination with that of judges and prosecutors, and apprenticeship training was introduced. Yet, the apprenticeship training was still separate from that of judges and prosecutors and considered inferior. Overall, these institutional developments contributed to the creation and continuation of attorneys' self-concept as lawyers outside the government. They also produced a strong movement among attorneys to seek equalization of their professional status with that of judges and prosecutors and to ensure their independence from the state.

[6] On the history of practising attorneys in Japan, see Takaaki Hattori, 'The Legal Profession in Japan: Its Historical Development and Present State' in Arthur Taylor von Mehren, ed., *Law in Japan: The Legal Order in a Changing Society* (Cambridge, MA: Harvard University Press, 1963) 111 at 117–19, 126–9, 136–8; Setsuo Miyazawa and Hiroshi Otsuka, 'Legal Education and the Reproduction of the Elite in Japan' in Yves Dezalay and Bryant G. Garth, eds., *Global Prescriptions: The Production, Exportation, and Importation of a New Legal Orthodoxy* (Ann Arbor: University of Michigan Press, 2002) 162 [*Reproduction of the Elite in Japan*] at 170; Malcolm M. Feeley and Setsuo Miyazawa, 'The State, Civil Society, and the Legal Complex in Modern Japan: Continuity and Change' in Terence C. Halliday, Lucien Karpik, and Malcolm M. Feeley, eds., *Fighting for Political Freedom: Comparative Studies of the Legal Complex and Political Liberalism* (Oxford: Hart Publishing, 2007) 151 [*Legal Complex in Modern Japan*]; Malcolm M. Feeley and Setsuo Miyazawa, 'Legal Culture and the State in Modern Japan' in Robert W. Gordon and Morton J. Horwitz, eds., *Law, Society, and History: Themes of the Legal Sociology and Legal History of Lawrence M. Friedman* (Cambridge: Cambridge University Press, 2011) 169; Darryl E. Flaherty, *Public Law, Private Practice: Politics, Profit, and the Legal Profession in Nineteenth-Century Japan* (Cambridge, MA: Harvard University Asia Center, 2013).

[7] *Practising Attorney Act*, Japan 1893, Act No. 7, [*Practising Attorney Act* 1893], Article 1.

[8] *Practising Attorney Act* 1893, *supra* note 7, Articles 23, 30, 31.

[9] *Practising Attorney Act*, Japan 1993, Act No. 53.

The 1945 defeat of Japan in World War II provided attorneys with an opportunity to realize these goals. The current Practising Attorney Act of 1949[10] was introduced as a member bill by members of the *Diet* (parliament) who were practising attorneys.[11] The Justice Ministry opposed it, but the Supreme Commander for the Allied Powers ('SCAP') supported it and the bill was passed. Article 1(1) of the Act clearly reflects a self-concept of an attorney and proudly proclaims that the mission of an attorney is to protect 'fundamental human rights and [achieve] social justice'.[12] This provision provided the legal basis for development of public interest activities of attorneys after the war.

Attorneys also succeeded in elevating their professional status. In addition to the unification of the qualifying examination introduced by the Practising Attorney Act of 1933, the apprenticeship training was unified in 1947 by the Legal Training and Research Institute ('LTRI'), which is operated by the Supreme Court.[13] Attorneys also obtained independence from the state. The power to bring disciplinary actions against attorneys was transferred from prosecutors to local bar associations and the JFBA. Attorneys' desire for independence was so strong that their employment by profit-making organizations was clearly discouraged and their employment by governments was flatly prohibited.[14]

III. INDIVIDUAL AND ORGANIZED FORMS OF PUBLIC INTEREST ACTIVITIES AND THEIR MUTUAL RELATIONSHIPS

This chapter uses the concept of public interest activities to explore the role of attorneys in access to justice in Japan. The chapter suggests the following typology of public interest activities: (1) professional work, paid and unpaid, undertaken for those unable to afford it, including cause lawyering; (2) criminal and civil legal aid works paid for by public funds; (3) activities in bar association committees or as bar association officers; and (4) other forms of activities recognized by bar associations as public interest activities, even though they do not include the use of professional skills for specific beneficiaries. Type (1) and type (2) are best understood as activities undertaken for individual clients, which directly provide legal skills to specific clients for no or a reduced cost, while most type (3) and type (4) activities are undertaken for organizations and do not directly provide legal skills to specific clients. Yet, in Japan, individual and organized forms of public interest activities are often intertwined, and an appreciation of this point may be helpful to understand the contents of the rules on mandatory public interest activities discussed later in the chapter.

A. *Cause Lawyering as an Individual Form of Public Interest Activity and Relevant Organizational Settings*

Does the category of cause lawyering assist in understanding the role of attorneys in access to justice in Japan? Austin Sarat and Stuart Scheingold suggested that a cause lawyer 'shares and aims to share with her client responsibility for the ends she is promoting in her representation'.[15]

[10] *Attorney Act*, Japan 1949, Act No. 205 (as amended on 29 May 2020) [*Attorney Act 1949*].
[11] See *Reproduction of the Elite in Japan*, *supra* note 6, at 167.
[12] *Attorney Act 1949*, *supra* note 10, Article 1(1).
[13] *Court Act*, Japan 1947, Act No. 59 (as amended in March 2017), Article 66(1).
[14] *Attorney Act 1949*, *supra* note 10, Article 30.
[15] Austin Sarat and Stuart Scheingold, 'Cause Lawyering and the Reproduction of Professional Authority: An Introduction' in Austin Sarat and Stuart Scheingold, eds., *Cause Lawyering: Political Commitments and Professional Responsibilities* (Oxford: Oxford University Press, 1998) 3 at 3.

In other words, cause lawyers provide their legal skills because they share a certain cause or causes with their clients. The concept of cause lawyering was formally introduced into Japan when Miyazawa invited Scheingold to Kobe University in February to March 1995. Scheingold gave talks at the JFBA, the Osaka Bar Association, and Kobe, Kyoto, and Doshisha Universities, and Miyazawa and Otsuka translated his talk 'Something to Believe In: Profiles in Cause Lawyering' in a Japanese law journal, *Hanrei Jiho*, in December 1995.[16]

Although cause lawyering was not introduced as a concept in Japan until 1995, Japanese attorneys have participated in activities that could be called cause lawyering from the very beginning of their history. As noted above, attorneys participated in the Freedom and Popular Rights Movement in the Meiji era (1868–1912). They not only engaged in legislative activities, but also defended fellow members of the movement who were persecuted by criminal charges, often risking their own persecution. In the Taisho era (1912–26), 30,000 workers in Kobe engaged in a strike in 1921, considered to be the largest labour dispute before World War II. Those workers were brutally suppressed by the police and the army. A group of lawyers gathered there to investigate the incident and defend prosecuted workers. This event gave birth to an organization called the Japan Lawyers Association for Freedom (*Jiyu Hosodan*), which is still quite active, with more than 2,000 members and a tie to the United States organization the National Lawyers Guild.[17]

After the war, probably the best-known examples of cause lawyering were activities to help victims of environmental pollution. Such cases included not only the so-called Four Large Pollution Cases (*Yondai Kogai Sosho*)[18] filed in the 1960s, but also many other environmental cases which followed them.[19] A number of lawyers donated their skill and time without compensation from clients in those cases, and some even moved to the areas where their clients lived. They participated in those cases not only because they wanted to help their clients, but also because they wanted to change governmental policies on the environment. Similar forms of cause lawyering can be seen in a wide range of cases, including drug poisoning cases (*yakugai sosho*),[20] cases on religious freedom,[21] and death-row inmates who wanted to overturn their false conviction (*enzai jiken*).[22]

How prevalent is cause lawyering among Japanese attorneys, and what are the major causes of this activity? Miyazawa tried to answer those questions in research carried out in 1994 and 1995.[23]

16 Stuart A. Scheingold, アメリカにおける公益的弁護士活動—コーズローヤリングのプロフィール (Something to Believe In: Profiles in Cause Lawyering) (Japan: Hanrei Jiho, 1995) at 9–17.

17 自由法曹団とは (Japan Lawyers Association for Freedom), *JLAF*, online: www.jlaf.jp/; *Legal Complex in Modern Japan, supra* note 6, at 166.

18 Mercury poisoning in Kumamoto and Niigata, cadmium poisoning in Toyama, and air pollution in Yokkaichi. See e.g. Frank K. Upham, *Law and Social Change in Postwar Japan* (Cambridge, MA: Harvard University Press, 1987), Chapter 2.

19 See e.g. Robert L. Kidder and Setsuo Miyazawa, 'Long Term Strategies in Japanese Environmental Litigation' (1993) 18:4 *Law & Social Inquiry* 605 at 605–27.

20 See e.g. Eric A. Feldman, *The Ritual of Rights in Japan: Law, Society, and Health Policy* (Cambridge: Cambridge University Press, 2000), Chapter 6.

21 See e.g. David M. O'Brien and Yasuo Okoshi, *To Dream of Dreams: Religious Freedom and Constitutional Politics in Postwar Japan* (Honolulu: University of Hawai'i Press, 1996), Chapter 3.

22 See e.g. Kazuko Ito, 'Wrongful Convictions and Recent Criminal Justice Reform in Japan' (2012) 80 *University of Cincinnati Law Review* 1245 [*Wrongful Convictions*] at 1253–6.

23 Setsuo Miyazawa, 'Lawyering for the Underrepresented in the Context of Legal, Social, and National Institutions: The Case of Japan' in Louise G. Trubek and Jeremy Cooper, eds., *Educating for Justice Around the World: Legal Education, Legal Practice and the Community* (Aldershot: Ashgate, 1999) 19 [*Lawyering for the Underrepresented*] at 27–38.

He chose the Osaka, Kobe (now Hyogo Prefectural), and Shiga Bar Associations as representatives of large, medium, and small bar associations in the Kansai region of Japan, and sent a questionnaire to a random sample of 410 attorneys in Osaka and all the members in Kobe and Shiga, for a total of 774 attorneys. There were responses from 329 attorneys, a response rate of 42.5 per cent. The questionnaire defined cause lawyering as:[24]

> activities of the attorney (*bengoshi*) to take charge of litigation, participate in a movement, or otherwise make use of the knowledge, ability, or qualification as a lawyer (*horitsuka*), not simply for the immediate purpose of the protection or realization of rights or interests of the client or party, but rather out of one's own sympathy or support of the social cause, namely some value, ideal, principle, or purpose which the given litigation or movement is deemed to realize.

In the survey, 159 out of 329 responding attorneys, or 48.3%, indicated that they were engaging in cause lawyering. Among these 159 attorneys, the proportion of their time spent on cause lawyering varied from less than 5% (18.3%) to more than 35% (15.7%), with 5–10% as the most frequent response (23.5%). When they were asked about the proportion of income earned through cause lawyering, the most frequent response was zero (45.3%); only 8.7% of the respondents answered that more than 10% of their income was earned through cause lawyering. One attorney told Miyazawa that when one of the four Large Pollution Cases was settled, a part of the damages paid to the plaintiffs was used as belated fees to their attorneys. Such cases were rare, however, and cause lawyering in Kansai was generally provided free of charge.

In February and March 1995, Miyazawa interviewed 15 lawyers who indicated that they spent more than 30 per cent of their time on cause lawyering. On the basis of these interviews, Miyazawa found that cause lawyering in Japan is not simply undertaken by individual attorneys, but it can also take place in the context of committees and other projects organized by the JFBA or regional[25] or local bar associations. Bar association activities can help cause lawyers via networking and policy-oriented activities. Nevertheless, cause lawyer achievements can be viewed as conceptually distinct from bar association activities, since participation in bar association activities is normally understood as a matter of general duty for bar members, while individual activities require a stronger commitment to particular causes.

Among the bar association activities that these lawyers participated in, the most frequently mentioned areas were human rights protection committees and related activities, criminal defence and other criminal justice issues, and children's rights and juvenile law. Environmental protection, consumer issues, and training of lawyers were also mentioned.[26] For activities outside bar associations, the most frequently mentioned areas were environmental cases and issues, criminal defence and criminal justice issues, labour issues, and children's rights, juvenile law, and school rules. The above subject-matter areas suggest that these lawyers worked mostly on liberal or leftist causes. It is clear from these interviews that lawyers pursued their chosen causes both inside and outside bar associations, and that they pursued more than one cause.

[24] *Lawyering for the Underrepresented*, *supra* note 23, at 27.

[25] Japan is divided into eight jurisdictions of high courts. Local bar associations in each high court jurisdiction form a regional federation; see *Japan Federation of Bar Association*, online: www.nichibenren.or.jp/jfba_info/bar_association.

[26] The Human Rights Protection Committee is listed at the top of the list of the standing committees on the JFBA website. Most of the other areas are also listed as a standing or a special committee: see Japan Federation of Bar Associations, 'Committees' online: www.nichibenren.or.jp/en/about/us/committee.html. Local bar associations also have similar committees, though the number varies depending on the size of the association.

One aspect of cause lawyering that is different in Japan is that there is no equivalent to the non-profit and legal services organizations ('NPO')[27] apparent in other jurisdictions such as the United States. An example of a US NPO is the American Civil Liberties Union ('ACLU'),[28] which proclaims that they are 'the nation's largest public interest law firm . . . [which appears] before the United States Supreme Court more than any other organization except the US Department of Justice. About 100 ACLU staff attorneys collaborate with about 2,000 volunteer attorneys in handling close to 2,000 cases annually.'[29] Japan has the Japan Civil Liberties Union ('JCLU'),[30] which was actually established by one of the founders of the ACLU, Roger Baldwin, when he was invited to Japan by General Douglas MacArthur, the Supreme Commander of the Allied Powers. However, while the ACLU engages in advocacy of clients on specific cases with its staff and cooperating lawyers, the JCLU has no staff attorneys, and it engages only in policy advocacy.

B. *Criminal Legal Aid and Duty Attorneys*

Criminal legal aid in Japan is called *kokusen bengonin*, or court-appointed attorney. This kind of legal representation is based on Article 37 of the Constitution, which provides that '[a]t all times the accused shall have the assistance of competent counsel who shall, if the accused is unable to secure the same by his own efforts, be assigned to his use by the State'.[31] The word for 'the accused' in the Japanese version of the Constitution is *hikokunin*, meaning 'the defendant'. Historically, the Japanese government did not provide free defence counsel until after indictment. The system of court-appointed defence was administered by the court and a counsel was appointed after indictment from the list of attorneys signed up for the system in each jurisdiction. However, in the Japanese criminal justice system, the investigation stage is crucial. This is the stage when the police and the prosecutor try to obtain a confession from the suspect.[32] After arrest, the suspect may be detained in a police station for 48 hours, which can be expanded for another 24 hours by the prosecutor. The prosecutor may at that point ask the judge to detain the suspect for ten days, and then to extend it for another ten days. Though detention facilities are maintained by the Justice Ministry for suspects who are detained by a judicial authorization, the practice is that most of them are still detained in a police station. Thus, the arrested suspect may be detained for a total of 23 days, for each count. If the police or the prosecutor add more counts in proper intervals, the entire detention period can be multiplied. The suspect may of course employ a defence counsel, but that counsel could not be present during interrogations; counsel can only meet the client briefly and give advice. This system of criminal investigation has been criticized as hostage-taking justice and a hotbed for false convictions.[33]

27 On public service practice settings, public interest work types, and public interest issue areas in the US, see e.g. Office of Public Interest Advising, 'What Is Public Interest Law?', *Harvard Law School*, online: https://hls.harvard.edu/dept/opia/what-is-public-interest-law/

28 'Private Public Interest and Plaintiffs' Firm Guide', *Bernard Koteen Office of Public Interest Advising at Harvard Law School (OPIA) and Center for Public Interest Law at Columbia Law School (CPIL)* at 3, online: https://hls.harvard.edu/dept/opia/private-public-interest-law-and-plaintiffs-firm-guide/.

29 American Civil Liberties Union, 'ACLU History', online: www.aclu.org/about/aclu-history.

30 Japan Civil Liberties Union, 'About JCLU', online: jclu.org/english/.

31 *Constitution of Japan*, 1947, Article 37, online: japan.kantei.go.jp/constitution_and_government/frame_01.html.

32 On the relevant legal provisions, see e.g. Setsuo Miyazawa, *Policing in Japan: A Study on Making Crime* (Albany: State University of New York Press, 1992) at 11–25; David T. Johnson, *The Japanese Way of Justice: Prosecuting Crime in Japan* (New York: Oxford University Press, 2002) at 33–47.

33 See *Wrongful Convictions*, *supra* note 22, at 1249–50.

Attorneys had proposed on different occasions that the government provide state-appointed counsel for suspects, but the government did not accept their proposal. In order to ameliorate the situation by themselves, local bar associations introduced the duty attorney (*toban bengoshi*) system in 1992. This system was inspired by the British duty solicitor scheme. When an arrested or detained suspect wanted a meeting with an attorney, the local bar association would send an attorney from the list of attorneys signed up for the given day. The meeting was free, and the local bar association would cover travel expenses and pay the attorney a small fee.

While running this duty attorney system, the JFBA continued to demand that the government extend the state-appointed attorney system to the investigation stage. In 1999, when the government established the Justice System Reform Council (*Shiho Seido Kaikaku Shingikai*) with a broad mandate to draw up a comprehensive set of proposals to improve the justice system,[34] the JFBA managed to persuade the Justice System Reform Council to include a proposal to extend the provision of free defence counsel to the investigation stage. In its final opinion, the Council proposed that:[35]

- A public defence system for suspects should be introduced, and a continuous defence structure covering both the suspect stage and the defendant stage should be established;
- The organization that manages the public defence system should be fair and independent, and public money should be introduced for operation of the system through a proper mechanism;
- While it is appropriate that technically the courts appoint and remove the defence counsel as in the case of the current court-appointed defence counsel system for the defendant, the public defence system should be responsible for other aspects of services; and
- The public defence system should take responsibility for the administration of the system vis-à-vis the people, and should establish a system that can offer thorough defence activity nationwide.

Based on this recommendation, the government introduced the court-appointed attorney system for suspects in 2006.[36] Initially an attorney was provided to suspects for whom detention was authorized by the judge for a crime punishable by death, indefinite imprisonment, or imprisonment for the minimum term of one year or longer, but it was expanded to include crimes punishable by imprisonment of the maximum term of three years or longer.[37]

Based on the Justice System Reform Council's second recommendation, a new organization called the Japan Legal Support Centre ('JLSC') was established in 2006.[38] Partly inspired by public defender offices in the US, JLSC is a public corporation totally funded by the Japanese government under the jurisdiction of the Justice Ministry. Unlike public defender offices in the US, JLSC administers both criminal and civil legal aid; it also disseminates legal information, and provides support to crime victims (see Tables 5.1–5.3 on pp. 81–4). JLSC has a regional office

34 On the background to this Council, its recommendations, and impacts of its recommendations, see Setsuo Miyazawa, 'Successes, Failures, and Remaining Issues of the Justice System Reform in Japan: An Introduction to the Symposium Issue' (2013) 36:2 *Hastings International and Comparative Law Review* 313, sources cited in this article, and other articles in the same issue.

35 'Recommendations of the Justice System Reform Council – For a Justice System to Support Japan in the 21st Century', *The Justice System Reform Council* (12 June 2001), online: japan.kantei.go.jp/policy/sihou/singikai/990612_e.html [*Recommendations*].

36 *Code of Criminal Procedure*, Japan 1948, Act No. 131 (as amended in 2011), Article 37-2.

37 Ibid.

38 Japan Legal Support Centre, 'Home', online: www.houterasu.or.jp/en/index.html.

TABLE 5.1. *Services and support provided by Japan Legal Support Centre*[39]

Support/Services	2010	2011	2012	2013	2014	2015	2016	2017	2018
1. Information services									
Inquiries at Houterasu Support Dial by telephone[40]	350,654	321,781	308,825	298,889	307,756	295,600	322,595	305,130	322,150
Inquiries at Houterasu Support Dial by email	19,470	17,553	18,934	14,599	22,982	22,920	27,004	34,214	40,559
Inquiries at local offices	234,149	198,963	210,432	209,093	198,692	202,987	204,837	196,135	206,269
2. Civil legal aid									
Number of contracted attorneys	15,037	16,570	17,863	19,159	20,176	21,033	21,885	22,346	23,371
Number of contracted judicial scriveners[41]	5,617	6,065	6,355	6,714	6,897	7,128	7,193	7,294	7,440
Cases supported by Legal Consultation Aid[42]	256,719	280,389	271,554	273,594	282,369	286,602	298,220	302,410	314,614
Cases supported by Representation Aid[43]	110,217	103,751	105,019	104,489	103,214	107,358	108,583	114,770	115,830
Cases supported by Documentation Aid[44]	7,366	6,164	5,441	4,620	3,982	3,993	3,877	4,278	3,522
3. Services relating to court-appointed defence counsel									
Number of contracted attorneys for court-appointed defence counsel	19,566	21,259	22,550	24,055	25,218	26,370	27,667	28,585	29,297
Cases with court-appointed defence counsel appointed for suspects	70,917	73,209	73,664	72,118	70,939	70,393	66,579	63,839	78,780

(*continued*)

[39] Table 5.1 is based on the brochure 'Japan Legal Support Centre' as of 2019: see Japan Legal Support Centre, 'Publications', online: www.houterasu.or.jp/en/about_jlsc/publications.html.

[40] Houterasu Support Dial is operated by the JLSC. It provides free information on relevant laws and the justice system in response to questions and makes referrals to an appropriate authority or organization.

[41] Unlike practising attorneys (*bengoshi*) who are generally licensed to represent clients in litigation, judicial scriveners (*shiho shoshi*) are generally licensed only to prepare legal documents; however, judicial scriveners may also represent clients in civil litigation worth less than JPY1,400,000 (US$12,987.88) if they are specially certified by the Minister of Justice: see *Judicial Scriveners Act*, Japan 1950, Act No. 197 (as amended in 2011), Article 3.

[42] Each user of Legal Consultation Aid is allowed up to three legal consultations at no charge on a single matter. The consultation is available either at the JLSC's local offices or the offices of attorneys or judicial scriveners under contract with the JLSC.

[43] The JLSC will make a payment of fees for an attorney's services as Representation Aid if legal representation at trial, mediation, or arbitration is needed.

[44] Documentation Aid means judicial scrivener's services for the preparation of legal documentation to be submitted to the court for self-representation.

TABLE 5.1. (*cont.*)

Support/Services	2010	2011	2012	2013	2014	2015	2016	2017	2018
Cases with court-appointed defence counsel appointed for defendants	69,634	67,374	63,695	60,269	59,816	59,504	56,388	53,655	53,862
Number of contracted attorneys for court-appointed attendants for juveniles	6,564	7,701	8,703	9,637	12,512	13,409	14,272	14,867	15,177
Cases with court-appointed attendant appointed for juveniles	423	469	419	445	2,955	3,698	3,427	3,417	3,489
4. Services concerning JLSC staff attorneys									
Number of staff attorneys	217	220	233	246	252	250	232	215	198
Number of local law offices	29	31	32	33	34	35	35	35	35
5. Crime victims support									
Inquiries through crime victim support number at Houterasu Support Dial	10,482	9,780	11,048	11,321	13,137	13,056	12,014	13,461	15,145
Inquiries at local offices	14,089	13,096	15,582	14,081	12,695	13,380	13,825	12,717	14,035
Reference to attorneys with expertise in crime victims support	929	877	1,013	1,330	1,491	1,603	1,677	1,705	1,795
6. Other legal aid cases entrusted to the JFBA (without civil legal aid or court-appointed defence)	17,587	19,826	23,160	25,313	24,096	22,316	22,444	22,206	15,158

in the jurisdiction of each district court, with additional local offices in areas which have very limited access to legal services.

JLSC has approximately 210 staff attorneys, but their number is too small to handle all the legal aid cases, and most cases are handled by private attorneys who contract with JLSC. The JFBA has been supporting JLSC's operations.[45]

In spite of the extension of the system of court-appointed attorneys to cover criminal suspects, there are still suspects who are not covered by the system, and the JFBA continues to maintain the duty attorney system as well as the Criminal Suspects Defence Legal Aid System, which is self-funded by the JFBA.[46] As of 2014, 47% of attorneys signed up for the duty attorney (16,590

[45] 弁護士白書 2015 年版 (White Paper on Attorneys 2015), *Japan Federation of Bar Associations* at 90–1, online: www.nichibenren.or.jp/en/about/whitepaper/whitepaper2015.html [*White Paper on Attorneys 2015*].

[46] *White Paper on Attorneys 2015*, *supra* note 45, at 36–9. See also, 弁護士制度の改善 (Improvement of Attorney System), *Japan Federation of Bar Associations*, online: www.nichibenren.or.jp/activity/improvement.html.

TABLE 5.2. *Japan Legal Support Centre funding*[47]

Item	2010	2011	2012	2013	2014	2015	2016	2017	2018
Income									
Government subsidies	15,542	16,554	16,147	12,836	15,507	15,206	15,117	15,396	15,391
Business income (e.g. repayments of civil legal aid by recipients)	11,141	11,394	10,853	10,663	10,737	10,958	11,469	11,859	12,206
Grant income	149	84	65	79	68	69	69	46	45
Income from Entrusted Business[48]	16,451	17,150	17,465	17,446	18,079	17,230	17,411	17,014	17,950
Other business income	541	1,342	3,789	5,676	532	1,064	1,119	1,495	1,667
Total	43,824	46,525	48,319	46,701	44,923	44,526	45,185	45,811	47,260
Expenses									
Business expenses (e.g. civil legal aid)	19,085	17,987	17,914	17,666	17,815	18,337	–	–	–
Expenses concerning Entrusted Business relating to court-appointed defence counsel	14,786	15,323	15,405	15,200	16,066	15,458	–	–	–
Expenses concerning Entrusted Business (aid services entrusted by the JFBA and others)	1,665	1,827	2,060	2,246	2,012	1,772	–	–	–
Other expenses such as personnel costs (excluding those of Entrusted Business)	7,120	7,729	7,397	8,083	8,046	7,911	–	–	–
Total	42,656	42,866	42,776	43,195	43,939	43,477	43,733	44,382	45,642

attorneys) and 48% of the requests for a duty attorney (21,554 cases) were undertaken. Also, as of 2014, almost 68% of attorneys contracted with the JLSC for the court-appointed attorney system (24,055 attorneys).[49]

Among the attorneys who sign up for the duty attorney system or contract with the JLSC for the system of court-appointed attorneys, it is difficult to know the proportion who perform criminal defence as a cause lawyer. It is clear, however, that the systems of duty attorney and

[47] Table 5.2 is based on 2019 figures: see Japan Legal Support Centre, 'Publications', online: www.houterasu.or.jp/en/about_jlsc/publications.html. Figures represent millions of Yen and have been rounded off.

[48] The JLSC provides services for two organizations (JFBA and the Assistance Fund for Remaining Japanese Orphans in China) that fully fund the services. Entrusted Business includes services for suspects in custody, juveniles transferred to the family court, victims of crime, refugees, mentally challenged people, foreigners, or elderly persons.

[49] *White Paper on Attorneys 2015*, *supra* note 45, at 91, 264.

TABLE 5.3. *Changes in government funding for Japan Legal Support Centre court-appointed defence counsel*[50]

	2012	2013	2014	2015	2016	2017	2018	2019
Government subsidies	16,402	12,836	15,507	15,206	15,117	15,396	15,391	15,508
Funding for entrusted business relating to court-appointed defence counsel	15,445	15,686	16,429	16,110	16,067	15,478	16,851	16,613
Total	31,847	28,522	31,936	31,316	31,184	30,874	32,242	32,121
Growth against previous year (%)	1.60	−10.44	11.97	−1.94	−0.42	−0.99	4.43	−0.38

court-appointed attorney provide financial support, at least to a limited extent, to cause lawyers as well as other attorneys.

C. *Civil Legal Aid*

Unlike criminal legal aid, there is no constitutional provision which clearly requires the state to provide civil legal aid. Article 32 of the Constitution provides that 'No person shall be denied the right of access to the courts',[51] but this Article has not been understood to require the state to provide civil legal aid. On the other hand, Article 33(2) of the Practising Attorney Act of 1949 provides that the by-laws of a local bar association should include provisions on the legal support to be provided to indigent persons.[52] This provision clearly indicates that practising attorneys have civil legal aid as part of their mission, as provided in Article 1 of the same Act: 'An attorney is entrusted with the mission of protecting fundamental human rights and achieving social justice.'[53] Following this obligation, practising attorneys donated funds to establish the Japan Legal Aid Association in 1952.[54] Because it was funded by contributions, however, the civil legal aid provided was very limited. It covered attorney fees and litigation filing fees, but aid was considered to be available only to people in the bottom fifth income level,[55] and it was limited to cases where the recipient was not deemed totally lacking a chance of winning. Furthermore, the aid was not really free, because the recipient was required to repay the aid after the conclusion of the case. In fact, the largest income source of the Japan Legal Aid Association was repayments from recipients,[56] and the system was essentially an interest-free loan. The government started to

[50] Table 5.3 is based on the brochure 'Japan Legal Support Centre' as of 2019: see Japan Legal Support Centre, 'Publications', online: www.houterasu.or.jp/en/about_jlsc/publications.html. Figures represent millions of Yen. The decrease in the government funding for 2013 is due to inclusion of the funding rolled over from the government funding of previous years, which was added up in the income for 2013.

[51] *The Constitution of Japan*, 1946, Article 32.

[52] *Attorney Act 1949*, *supra* note 10, Article 33(2)(ix), which provides that '[t]he following matters shall be stipulated in the articles of association of a bar: Rules pertaining to legal support to be provided to indigent persons'.

[53] *Attorney Act 1949*, *supra* note 10, Article 1(1).

[54] On the history of the civil legal aid system in Japan and the reform movement up to the late 1990s, see *Lawyering for the Underrepresented*, *supra* note 23, at 38–46; Gotaro Ichiki and Tetsuo Ohishi, 'Current Issues for Legal Aid in Japan – Reform Perspective' in Louise G. Trubek and Jeremy Cooper, eds., *Educating for Justice Around the World: Legal Education, Legal Practice and the Community* (Aldershot: Ashgate, 1999) 51 at 52–3.

[55] See *Lawyering for the Underrepresented*, *supra* note 23, at 40.

[56] See *Lawyering for the Underrepresented*, *supra* note 23, at 39.

provide funding in 1952, but it was very limited and could not be used to cover the costs of personnel and facilities.

The creation of the Justice System Reform Council in 1999 provided an opportunity for JFBA and the Japan Legal Aid Association to demand that the civil legal aid system be strengthened. However, the recommendation by the Justice System Reform Council in 2001 was lukewarm on this issue. It simply stated that '[t]he civil legal aid system should be further reinforced after comprehensive, systematic studies are made on the scope of cases and persons to be covered, what burdens should be borne by users, how the system should be managed, etc.'.[57] The ultimate result was the transfer of civil legal aid to JLSC in 2006. This restructuring greatly increased funding for civil legal aid as operational costs such as personnel and facilities are now completely supported by the state budget. However, the fundamental character of the civil legal aid as an interest-free loan has not changed.

Again, it is difficult to know the proportion of lawyers who provide civil legal aid services as a form of cause lawyering compared to other motivations. However, cause lawyers can use the civil legal aid system in cases where they do not want to donate their time completely free of charge.

D. JFBA's Efforts to Address Geographical Inequalities in Public Access to Legal Services and Financial Burdens on Individual Members

Criminal and civil legal aid are systems to alleviate economic inequalities in public access to legal services, but Japan also has a serious problem regarding geographical inequalities. In 2016, there was one attorney per 3,373 people in Japan,[58] but their geographical distribution was highly skewed. While Tokyo had one attorney per 769 residents, Akita Prefecture had one attorney per 13,113 residents. This skewed distribution was much worse in earlier periods when Japan had an even smaller number of attorneys.

The JFBA tried to ameliorate this problem through its own efforts. Japan's 50 district court jurisdictions comprise approximately 200 court branches, and about one third of those branch court jurisdictions had one or no attorney, referred to as 'zero–one areas'. The JFBA tried to eliminate zero–one areas by encouraging attorneys to open offices in those areas with JFBA funding. JFBA provided the funding through a programme called the Himawari Fund Law Offices in 2000.[59] *Himawari* means sunflower, which is the official symbol of Japanese attorneys and is reflected in their lapel badge. JFBA funded the programme by allocating a part of member dues to provide loans to cover opening and administrative costs for law firms. Law offices which received this financial assistance are called Himawari Fund Law Offices. Nearly 120 such offices were opened in the 15 years after the progamme started in 2000, and approximately half of them have become regular offices without further financial assistance. The zero–one areas had virtually disappeared by 2015.[60] The JFBA continues to address the issue, and is now trying to

[57] *Recommendations*, *supra* note 35, at Chapter 2, Part 1, 7(2).

[58] 弁護士白書2016年版 (White Paper on Attorneys 2016), *Japan Federation of Bar Associations* at 40, online: www.nichibenren.or.jp/en/about/whitepaper/whitepaper_2016.html.

[59] Kenji Utsunomiya, 'Comment on the 10th Anniversary of Himawari Law Offices', *Japan Federation of Bar Associations* (11 June 2010), online: www.nichibenren.or.jp/en/document/statements/20100611.html.

[60] *White Paper on Attorneys 2015*, *supra* note 45, at 216.

encourage attorneys to open offices in other areas where, for instance, there is one attorney for more than 30,000 residents.[61]

The Himawari Fund raises an important question regarding attorneys and access to justice in Japan, that of the financial burden on individual attorneys. Except for criminal and civil legal aid, which is supported by the government budget, activities of the JFBA and local bar associations are self-funded, and a variety of dues and fees are used to support the many activities of the JFBA[62] and bar associations. The bar associations incur these costs to maintain their independence from the government. For example, at the *Toben*, the largest bar association in Tokyo with approximately 8,600 members, a member with more than four years' experience in 2016 was required to pay a total of JPY34,800 (US$322.90)[63] as combined monthly dues for the *Toben* and the JFBA.[64] In addition, *Toben* members are required to pay temporary dues to cover the cost of maintaining the *Bengoshi Kaikan* (Bar Association Building), the building in central Tokyo which houses the headquarters of the JFBA and the three bar associations of Tokyo,[65] at the rate of JPY4,000 (US$37.12) to JPY10,000 (US$92.80) per month. The yearly total is JPY400,000 (US$3,711.53) to JPY1,300,000 (US$12,062.46), depending on the year of registration. On top of this payment, in cases referred to attorneys by various programmes operated by the *Toben*, attorneys are required to donate a certain percentage of their fees to the *Toben*.

As a point of comparison, the State Bar of California, the mandatory bar association for lawyers in the State of California with approximately 190,000 active members, charges its members annual dues of approximately US$430.[66] The annual dues in California are one month's dues in Tokyo. The financial burden is even higher in the smallest bar associations with 100 or fewer members, where fees can be twice as much as those at the *Toben*.

One way to reduce the financial burden would be to increase the number of attorneys and bar members, but this is not the position taken by the JFBA. Its position is the opposite. When the bar examination, which is administered by the Justice Ministry, passed 2,102 people, or 25.1 per cent, in 2012, the JFBA President issued a statement that the increase in the number of new attorneys was outpacing the increase in demands for legal services, so that the number of passers should be reduced to 1,500.[67] The JFBA President issued similar statements every year until 2016, when the government formally announced the policy to produce 'at least 1,500 new legal professionals (*hoso*)'[68] per year in 2016. The bar exam in 2016 actually passed 1,583 people, or 22.9 per cent, and

[61] *White Paper on Attorneys 2015*, *supra* note 45, at 189.

[62] On the JFBA's finances, see Japan Federation of Bar Associations, 'What is the JFBA?', online: www.nichibenren.or.jp/en/about/us/profile.html.

[63] XE Currency Converter, online: www.xe.com/currencyconverter/convert/?Amount=34%2C800&From=JPY&To=USD. Unless another reference was cited, US$ denominations in the chapter were derived from www.xe.com at the time of publication; they are intended for general reference and may have been rounded up or down for ease of reference.

[64] 2016（平成28）年度 東京弁護士会会費のご案内 (Membership dues), *Tokyo Bar Association*, online: www.toben.or.jp/news/file/pdf/LIBRA201604_kaihi.pdf.

[65] Japan Federation of Bar Associations, 'Access to Bar Associations Building', online: www.nichibenren.or.jp/en/about/us/access.html.

[66] Lyle Moran, 'California Legislature Approves Bill Hiking State Bar Fees by 27 Percent', *Above the Law* (19 September 2019), online: https://abovethelaw.com/2019/09/california-legislature-approves-bill-hiking-state-bar-fees-by-27-percent/.

[67] Kenji Yamagishi, 平成24年司法試験最終合格発表に関する会長談話 (The Presidential Statement on the 2012 Bar Examination Result), *Japan Federation of Bar Associations* (11 September 2012), online: www.nichibenren.or.jp/activity/document/statement/year/2012/120911.html.

[68] *Hoso* means judges, prosecutors, and practising attorneys. Those who want to become one of them must take the bar examination administered by the Justice Ministry. Most of those who pass the bar examination become practising attorneys.

the JFBA President responded by issuing a statement which welcomed this result and demanded further reductions to 1,500.[69] This position reflects the prevailing opposition among bar members to an increase in the number of attorneys. In fact, some small bar associations demand more radical reductions. Therefore, as long as the JFBA and local bar associations maintain their efforts to self-finance their activities to ameliorate economic and geographical inequalities in public access to legal services, the financial burden on individual members is unlikely to shrink. Ultimately it will also limit the ability of attorneys to support access to justice.

IV. MANDATORY RULES ON PUBLIC INTEREST ACTIVITIES

The *Toben* introduced its first set of Rules on Public Interest Activities and Other Matters (*Koeki Katsudo To*) ('Rules') in 1998.[70] At this stage, the Rules merely encouraged its members to take state-appointed criminal defence cases and civil legal aid cases and participate in committee activities. However, the number of members who signed up for court-appointed criminal defence cases and civil legal aid cases did not increase as much as expected, while association affairs (*kaimu*) were also handled by a limited range of members who took increasingly heavier burdens. The *Toben* examined various ways to alleviate this situation. It finally introduced the new Rules in December 2003 ('new Rules') and implemented them in April 2004.[71]

In addition to the practical needs of bar associations, the recommendations by the Justice System Reform Council were also a factor which contributed to the introduction of the new Rules. The Justice System Reform Council recommendations in 2001 included the following demands for practising attorneys:[72]

- Lawyers should carry out their social responsibility by faithfully pursuing their duties and rendering services to fulfil the public's rights and benefits (for the public interest), as well as by making continuous efforts to improve their professional activities while retaining professional ethics that are suitable for their missions;
- Performing activities for the public interest should be deemed to be one of the lawyers' duties, with the details of such activities being clearly defined. Lawyers should secure the transparency of such details and demonstrate their accountability to the public.

These demands were not objectionable to the JFBA because it was already engaging in various forms of public interest activities as described above. When first introduced, the Rules merely reconfirmed what bar associations had already been doing. The rules on mandatory public interest activities were therefore partly a response of bar associations to the Justice System Reform Council, to reconfirm their commitment to public interest activities, but they were implemented primarily for the more immediate and practical requirements of the bar.

[69] Kazuhiro Nakamoto, 平成28年司法試験最終合格発表に関する会長談話 (The Presidential Statement on the 2016 Bar Examination Result), *Japan Federation of Bar Associations* (6 September 2016), online: www.nichibenren.or.jp/activity/document/statement/year/2016/160906.html.

[70] 公益活動等に関する会規 (Rules on Public Interest Activities and Other Matters), Tokyo Bar Association, 1998.

[71] 公益活動等に関する会規 (Rules on Public Interest Activities and Other Matters), Tokyo Bar Association, 2003 [*2003 Rules on Public Interest Activities*], Article 2; see also *Libra*, vol. 4:5 (Toben 2004) [*Libra* 2004] at 2.

[72] *Recommendations*, *supra* note 35, at Chapter 3, Part 3, 1.

This chapter explores the mandatory public interest activities requirement by focusing on the rules of one of the Tokyo bar associations, *Toben*, the largest bar association in Japan. When they were first introduced in 2003, the main points of the new Rules were as follows:[73]

1. Members have a duty to participate in one of the following activities:
   (1) Committee activity (at least four meetings a year in a committee)
   (2) Legal advising activity (at least once a year)
   (3) Court-appointed defence activity in a criminal or juvenile case (at least once a year)
   (4) Duty attorney activity in a criminal or juvenile case (at least once a year)
   (5) Civil legal aid activity (at least once a year).
2. The duty may be exempted for the following reasons:
   (1) 70 years or older
   (2) Illness, childbirth, study abroad, assignment to foreign countries, and other reasons deemed to justify exemption for a certain period.
3. The following members are considered to have fulfilled the duty:
   (1) President, Vice President, Auditor, member of the Permanent Committee (*jogiin*), and attorney employed to handle association affairs (*shokutaku*) of the *Toben*
   (2) President, Vice President, Board Member, Auditor, member of the House of Delegates (*daigiin*), Secretary General, and Vice Secretary General of the JFBA
   (3) Chairperson of the Board, Vice Chairperson of the Board, Board Member, and Auditor of the Kanto Federation of Bar Associations (*Kanbenren*)
   (4) Faculty and other members assigned to the Legal Training and Research Institute (*Shiho Kenshujo*)
   (5) Full-time faculty members of a law school
   (6) Those who contributed JPY50,000 (US$463.94) as a substitute.
4. The following measures may be taken by the President against a member who failed to perform the duty:
   (1) Advice for improvement
   (2) Posting the name of the member who refused to follow the advice in the bar association building after giving them an opportunity to explain.

Members could also file a petition for exemption giving a specific reason.

The required activities included both bar committee activities and activities in which attorneys provided legal assistance to clients. The contribution of JPY50,000 (US$463.94) a year was understood not as a penalty for the failure of performance, but as an alternative contribution to support *Toben*'s public interest activities. *Toben* officials explained that the amount was set at JPY50,000 (US$463.94) based on two factors: the amount charged by the Daini Tokyo Bar Association (*Niben*), which could reach as much as JPY120,000 (US$1,113.46) a year, and the average amount of the fee paid in civil legal aid cases, which was JPY80,000 (US$742.31).[74] As a point of comparison, the JPY50,000 (US$463.94) payment in lieu of service was approximately JPY10,000 (US$92.80) more than the amount a Japanese attorney might pay in monthly dues.

[73] 2003 *Rules on Public Interest Activities*, *supra* note 71, Articles 2, 3.

[74] *Libra* 2004, *supra* note 71, at 5. *Niben*'s maximum amount has been reduced to the same level as that of the *Toben* as we will explain later.

A significant change to the rules was made in 2006 ('2006 Rules').[75] First, the 2006 Rules were renamed as the Rules on Association Affairs and Other Matters (*Kaimu To*). Bar officials explained that the reason for the new name was that the term public interest activities (*koeki katsudo*) was misleading, because of different understandings in the bar association compared to the general public.[76] Second, bar committee activities became more broadly defined, activities in connection with outside organizations assigned by committees were added, and activities in ADR programmes operated or assigned by the *Toben* were included. Additionally, the list of positions which justify exemption was extended considerably, and new additions have been added since then.[77] The age for exemption was also brought down to 65.

Although the prior version of the rules recognized bar duties as satisfying the requirement, the 2006 Rules indicate that the main purpose of the rules was not the provision of legal services to indigent people, but the staffing of bar association activities. Interviews with bar officers suggested that changes were prompted by an increasing number of younger members, which made it easier to find members to take court-appointed defence work or civil legal aid cases.[78]

In 2015, 879 members, slightly more than 10% of the members, were exempted from the duty by contributing JPY50,000 (US$463.94). The total amount of contributions was JPY43,950,000 (US$407,803.89), which was about 2.5% of *Toben*'s income in 2016.

The mandatory rules of other bar associations are still called the Rules on Public Interest Activities. The Daiichi Tokyo Bar Association (*Ichiben*) introduced its rules in 2007.[79] The amount of the contribution in lieu of the duty was exactly the same, JPY50,000 (US$463.94). The Daini Tokyo Bar Association (*Niben*) introduced its rules in 2003.[80] It now requires its members to spend more than ten hours in specified activities, and it determines the amount of the contribution in terms of the missed hours, at the rate of JPY5,000 (US$46.39) per hour.[81] The Kanagawa Bar Association introduced its rules in 2007.[82] It has an elaborate point system which requires members to earn 12 points a year and requires them to contribute JPY10,000 (US$92.80) for each missed point.[83]

We were puzzled to see some well-paid positions included in the activities qualifying as required public interest activities. One example is law school faculty member. Our interviewees told us unanimously that the category of law school faculty member was included because bar associations should contribute to the development of new law schools, recently introduced at that time as part of the comprehensive justice reform.[84]

[75] 会務活動等に関する会規 (*The Rules on Association Affairs and Other Matters*), Tokyo Bar Association (as amended in 2006) [*2006 Rules on Association Affairs*]; see Appendix 5.1 for an English translation of the 2016 version of the 2006 rules.

[76] *Libra*, vol. 6:9 (Toben 2006) [*Libra 2006*] at 24.

[77] *2006 Rules on Association Affairs*, *supra* note 75, Article 3.

[78] Interviews with Tokyo Bar Association officials (2 July 2017, Bar Association Building, Tokyo).

[79] 公益活動に関する会規 (*The Rules on Public Interest Activities*), Daiichi Tokyo Bar Association, 2007; see Appendix 5.2 for an English translation of the 2015 version of these rules.

[80] 会員の公益活動等に関する会規 (*The Rule on Public Interest Activities*), Daini Tokyo Bar Association, 2003.

[81] 会員の公益活動等に関する会規 (*The Rule on Public Interest Activities*), Daini Tokyo Bar Association (as amended in 2015), Article 6; the maximum amount is no longer JPY120,000 (US$1,113.25), but only JPY50,000 (US$463.94).

[82] 会員の公益活動及び委員会活動等に関する会規 (*The Rules on Public Interest Activities and Association Affairs*), Kanagawa Bar Association, 2007.

[83] 公益活動・委員会活動等分担金に関する規則 (*The Rules on the Contributions to Public Interest Activities, Committee Activities, and Related Matters*), Daini Tokyo Bar Association, 2008, Article 2.

[84] Interviews with Tokyo Bar Association officials (2 July 2017, Bar Association Building, Tokyo); Interviews with Daini Tokyo Bar Association officials (3 January 2017, Bar Association Building, Tokyo); Interviews with Daiichi Tokyo Bar Association officials (3 February 2017, Bar Association Building, Tokyo); Interviews with Kanagawa Bar Association

An interesting question is why smaller bar associations in Japan do not have similar rules. Our interviewees were unanimous in saying that peer pressure in smaller bar associations is so strong that they do not need formal rules to require their members to take court-appointed work and civil legal aid cases or participate in bar association committees. Many interviewees told us that members of such bar associations know that those systems and committees would not work unless every member performs their obligations.[85]

A. *How Do Mandatory Public Interest Rules Work in Practice?*

Is it easy or difficult for bar association members to satisfy these requirements? To delve further into how the mandatory public interest rules work in practice, in 2016 we conducted a preliminary survey via questionnaire with members of JFBA's Law School Centre.[86] Six *Toben* members, two *Ichiben* members, four *Niben* members, and two members of the Osaka Bar Association responded. Eleven respondents answered that it was easy, one answered that it was rather easy, one answered that it was difficult to judge the difficulty, and one answered that he was exempted because he worked as his bar association's full-time staff member.

We also asked respondents whether they satisfied the requirement by doing (a) work directly for members of the general public, such as court-appointed defence work and civil legal aid, or (b) work in committees and other public activities. Excluding the exempted individual, there was a preference for not working directly with clients; seven participants answered (b), two answered 'somewhat (b)', and three answered both (a) and (b). Only one answered 'somewhat (a)'.

Our next question was whether the requirement was effective in facilitating public interest activities and bar association activities. Seven answered yes, four answered rather yes, two answered 'difficult to tell', and one did not provide an answer.

We then inquired about compensation, and asked respondents whether they wanted to ask their association to recognize the activities they do for no or small compensation, even where such activities were not listed in the relevant rules. Our respondents were split on this question. Four answered positively or rather positively, four said it was 'difficult to tell', five answered negatively or rather negatively, and one respondent did not answer. Their ambivalence is interesting, because the association officers we interviewed told us that they rarely receive such requests. One hypothesis may be that attorneys hesitate to ask for inclusion of their individual causes by the bar association, because in many cases their causes are deeply felt, a matter independent from any authorities including bar associations.

One question raised by the survey results is whether the required public interest activities of court-appointed defence, civil legal aid cases, and bar association activities hinder cause lawyering or other forms of activities which would directly benefit individual clients. Some of our

officials (3 August 2017, Kanagawa Bar Association Building, Yokohama). Japan used to have only undergraduate law faculties which were not considered professional schools, and the bar examination used to require no formal legal education from its takers. Post-graduate professional law schools were introduced in 2004 and the bar examination now requires in principle a JD degree. On the introduction and the current crisis of the Japanese law school system, see Daniel H. Foote, 'The Trials and Tribulations of Japan's Legal Education Reforms' (2013) 36:2 *Hastings International and Comparative Law Review* 369.

85 Interviews with Tokyo Bar Association officials (2 July 2017, Bar Association Building, Tokyo); Interviews with Daini Tokyo Bar Association officials (3 January 2017, Bar Association Building, Tokyo); Interviews with Daiichi Tokyo Bar Association officials (3 February 2017, Bar Association Building, Tokyo); Interviews with Kanagawa Bar Association officials (3 August 2017, Kanagawa Bar Association Building, Yokohama).

86 For a translated version of the survey, see Appendix 5.3.

interviewees told us that the lawyers engaging in these activities are also likely to participate in bar association activities, so the requirement would not hinder their representation of individuals in need. The interaction between a mandatory requirement and non-qualifying activities in support of access to justice remains a question for future, systematic empirical investigation.

The survey results also raise a conceptual issue regarding how mandatory public interest activities should be defined, and the normative question of whether mandatory activities should include bar committee activities. It is easier to characterize bar committee activities as public interest activities if the activities facilitate the provision of legal services for indigent people or social causes, but is it appropriate to include bar committee work that promotes the bar association as a trade association, or include positions which carry large amounts of prestige? As noted in the discussion of cause lawyering above, individual forms of public interest lawyering can be supported and facilitated by bar association committees and bar association officials. Some findings from Otsuka's participant observation of the consumer movement in Japan, mainly organized by cause lawyers in Osaka and Nara, Japan, may be relevant.[87] In many cases, attorneys had chances to meet each other in committee activities, and networks formed through committees also exposed young attorneys to various types of cause lawyering. More senior attorneys could also recruit new cause lawyers through the networks. We can say here that committee activities promoted cause lawyering, at least indirectly, so mandatory rules may play a role in cultivating public interest lawyering to some extent. However, if all bar committees and officials do not have this impact, how does their characterization as public interest activities effect access to justice?

B. *The Influence of Mandatory Rules and the Definition of Public Interest*

What is the ultimate effect of the mandatory public interest requirement? The recommendations of the Justice System Reform Council (2001) stated that bar associations should clarify the contents of public interest activities and make it mandatory.[88] In response to this recommendation, and for their own reasons, mandatory rules were established at the larger bar associations. But there is ambiguity and tension regarding these public interest activities, because Japanese lawyers do not share a specific understanding of what is meant by public interest activities.

In our interviews at *Ichiben*, some lawyers asserted that lawyer activities that result in monetary rewards should not be recognized as public interest activities.[89] The opposing view is indicated in the rules themselves. For example, *Toben* changed the title of the mandatory rules from 'The Rules on Public Interest Activities and Other Matters' to 'The Rules on Association Affairs and Other Matters'. A different view again is expressed by other lawyers that the general definition of public interest activities is broader than that of the mandatory rules. However, even with the broadening of the rules, some *Toben* lawyers complain that the mandatory rules exclude their public interest activities.[90] The renaming of the rules may also suggest that some *Toben* lawyers see a contradiction in the current definition of public interest. On the one hand, the rules include teaching in a law school, which is accompanied by relatively high rewards, while on the other hand, public interest litigation, for example for victims of public nuisance and consumers, is excluded from the mandatory rules.

87 Hiroshi Otsuka, コーズ・ローヤリングにおける弁護士-依頼者関係の実態と弁護士倫理 (Ethical Problems of Lawyer–Client Relationships in Cause Lawyering) (2009) 70 *The Sociology of Law* 129 at 129–43.

88 *Recommendations, supra* note 35, at Chapter 3, Part 3, 1.

89 Interviews with Daiichi Tokyo Bar Association officials (3 February 2017, Bar Association Building, Tokyo).

90 Interviews with Tokyo Bar Association officials (2 July 2017, Bar Association Building, Tokyo); and see *Libra 2006*, *supra* note 76, at 24.

At all the bar associations where we did interviews, public interest activities in the mandatory rules mainly meant activities which the bar associations undertook with local and national governments or law schools and so on. They included such activities as those of law school professors who are paid a relatively high salary, and it may seem inappropriate to call them public interest activities. On the other hand, activities for public interest litigation such as public nuisance cases, consumer cases, or phytotoxicity cases are excluded from public interest activities in the mandatory rules, even if the purpose of those activities is to improve the public interest, because those cases may eventually bring a large amount of money to the attorneys who undertake them.

Classification of public interest activities in mandatory rules seems to cause contradictions, although it does appear difficult to set specific criteria to distinguish public interest activities from others. Even the categories of cause lawyering and pro bono cannot express all aspects of public interest activities. Why would it be difficult to define public interest activities in Japan? While lawyers may conceive of service without charge as the core of the work attorneys should do in the public interest, in Japan there is also a long history of cause lawyering. These two different streams of public interest activities have coexisted but their differences have only surfaced in the need to define mandatory public interest activities. We could say that the establishment of mandatory rules was the opportunity to reveal the tension between the two approaches.

Do mandatory rules promote public interest activities? Mandatory rules may bring about public interest activities, but it is difficult to find evidence of the influence of the rules on public interest activities. If public interest is defined broadly, we can expect that a mandatory requirement will have only an indirect effect on the public interest activities.

V. CONCLUSION

Attorneys have a long history of supporting access to justice in Japan. Raising the status of their profession and maintaining independence from the government has prompted a considerable amount of the activities organized by bar associations over the years, and the need to staff these activities has been the primary reason for mandatory public interest requirements. The scope of these bar-funded and attorney-funded activities, particularly when compared to other jurisdictions, is impressive. However, the question for Japan is whether access to justice can be improved if this degree of independence is maintained. The bar's insistence on low numbers of attorneys per capita suggests that, in the long run, complete independence will not allow Japan to reach optimal levels of access to justice.

APPENDIX 5.1 THE RULE ON ASSOCIATION AFFAIRS AND OTHER MATTERS (TOKYO BAR ASSOCIATION, 2016)

(Purpose)

Article 1

The purpose of the rule is to provide the duties to participate in one of the following activities ('association affairs and other matters' among public interest activities provided in Article 26-2 of the Tokyo Bar Association Constitution) to continue public interest activities as a social responsibility for the Tokyo Bar Association.

(Obligation to participate in association affairs)

Article 2

1. Each year a lawyer member shall participate in any activities listed in the following items (hereinafter referred to as 'association affairs and other matters').
   (1) Activities as a member of committees of the Japan Federation of Bar Associations (JFBA), the Kanto Federation of Bar Associations, and the three bar associations in Tokyo.
   (2) Activities as a member of committees outside the bar by the request of any committee of Tokyo Bar Association.
   (3) Legal counselling, document preparation, and to undertake cases of legal counselling at Centres of Tokyo Bar Association and other counselling institutions.
   (4) Arbitration and mediation in the Dispute Resolution Centre of Tokyo Bar Association and other ADR.
   (5) Activities for Criminal legal aid.
   (6) Activities as a duty attorney.
   (7) Activities for crime victims.
   (8) Activities for civil legal aid.
2. With regard to the activities of item 1 of the preceding paragraph, by participating in meeting of the same committee at least four times in a year, a lawyer member is deemed to participate in the committees.
3. The activities conducted by a lawyer member in response to a request from a committee of Tokyo Bar Association are included in association affairs by admission of the president.
4. A lawyer member engaging in an activity prescribed by association rules shall be deemed to have participated in association affairs.
5. A lawyer member, who offers to the association not to participate in association affairs in writing with some reasons, is deemed to participate in association affairs by payment of a contribution fee of JPY50,000 (US$463.94) for association affairs a year.
6. When a newly registered lawyer participates as a trainee in a committee of the association, he or she shall be deemed to participate in the activities of item 1 of paragraph 1.

(Exemption of association affairs and other matters)

Article 3

1. A lawyer member who is over 65 years does not have an obligation to participate in association affairs.
2. The president may exempt a lawyer member from the obligation to participate in association affairs, when he or she falls under any of the following items.
   (1) Those who are unable or have extreme difficulty participating in association affairs for reasons such as sickness, nursing care and other similar reasons.
   (2) Those who are unable or have extreme difficulty participating in association affairs because they do not live in Japan due to study abroad, work in other countries, or for other reasons.

(3) Those who are allowed reduction or exemption of membership fees under the provisions of Article 27 of the Constitution of Tokyo Bar Association.
(4) Members of the Diet, members of a prefectural or city assembly, prefectural governors and mayors.
(5) Civil servants.
(6) Those who gave birth during the fiscal year or the previous fiscal year.
(7) Any person who raises a child who is under 6 years old.
(8) Others who have reasonable grounds.

3. A lawyer member who joined Tokyo Bar Association in the middle of the fiscal year shall be exempted from the participation obligation of association affairs in that year.

(Guidance and recommendation for the participation obligation)

Article 4

The president may give guidance and recommendation to lawyer members to fulfil their participation obligation through investigating the status of association affairs.

(Obligation of consideration)

Article 5

1. A lawyer member shall encourage and cooperate with other lawyer members to participate in activities on association affairs.
2. The president may instruct a lawyer member who does not fulfil the obligation of the preceding paragraph to do his or her duty.

(Publication)

Article 6

1. The president can announce the name, his or her registration number, and office address of a lawyer member who does not or is not deemed to participate in association affairs despite guidance or recommendation from the president based on article 4.
2. The president can announce the name of a lawyer member or a legal professional corporation who does not make improvements despite guidance or recommendation from the president based on article 5.
3. The president can notify in a document to a lawyer member or a legal professional corporation the fact that he or she is a target of announcement, before making an announcement based on the preceding two paragraphs.
4. The president shall give an opportunity for defence to a lawyer member before making an announcement based on paragraph 1 or 2.
5. The president shall notify in a document to a lawyer member or a legal professional corporation, when making an announcement based on paragraph 1 or 2 after giving an opportunity for defence.
6. An announcement based on paragraph 1 or 2 shall not be made unless 15 days pass from the date on which a lawyer member or a legal professional corporation receives the notification in a document.

(Appeal)

Article 7

1. A lawyer member can make an appeal to the association in a document within 14 days from the date of receiving the notification based on paragraph 5 of the preceding article.
2. When the association accepts an appeal based on the preceding paragraph, the association shall make a decision whether to approve the appeal or not, after the decision of the Appeal Examination Board.
3. The procedures of the Appeal Examination Board shall be subject to the Appeal Examination Board Rules.
4. When an appeal based on paragraph 1 has been made, the president shall not make an announcement on paragraphs 1 and 2 of the preceding article until the decision of the Appeal Examination Board.

(Special Committee for Association Affairs)

Article 8

1. In order to implement this rule, the Special Committee for Association Affairs shall be established based on article 57 of the Constitution of the association.
2. Matters concerning the Special Committee for Association Affairs shall be prescribed by the Regulations.

(Fiscal year calculation)

Article 9

A fiscal year in this rule is from 1 April of each year to 31 March of the following year.

APPENDIX 5.2 THE RULES ON PUBLIC INTEREST ACTIVITIES, EXCERPTS (DAINI TOKYO BAR ASSOCIATION, 2015)

(Purpose)

Article 1

Matters relating to obligations of lawyer members, legal professional corporations, registered foreign lawyer members, registered foreign lawyer corporation members, to do public interest activities and others, shall be provided by this rule.

(Public interest activities)

Article 2

Public interest activities and others are listed in the following items.

1. Legal services to citizens
   (1) Activities for Criminal Legal Aid.
   (2) Activities as a Duty Attorney.

(3) Activities for Civil Legal Aid.
(4) Legal Consultation prescribed in the regulation of the association.

2. Association affairs and others
   (1) Activities as an officer of the Japan Federation of Bar Associations (JFBA), the Kanto Federation of Bar Associations, and the Daini Tokyo Bar Association.
   (2) Activities as a member of committees of the Japan Federation of Bar Associations (JFBA), the Kanto Federation of Bar Associations, and the Daini Tokyo Bar Association.
   (3) Arbitration and mediation in ADR which is operated by the association.

(Practice of public interest activities)

Article 3

A lawyer member shall accept at least one of the activities which are listed in item 1 of the preceding article.

...

(Contribution fee)

Article 6

Instead of participating in public interest activities or association affairs, a lawyer member can pay a contribution fee of JPY5,000 for an hour to make up for the obligation, if he or she participates in such activities less than 10 hours a year.

APPENDIX 5.3 QUESTIONNAIRE: 'MANDATORY RULES ON PUBLIC INTEREST ACTIVITIES'

The bar association to which you belong: __________
Your graduating class from The Legal Training and Research Institute of Japan: ___
Type of your office (please circle the number of the applicable item)

① General law office
② Himawari Fund Law Office
③ Company Legal Department
④ Japan Legal Support Centre
⑤ Other (Please fill in): __________

Size of your office (please fill in the number of lawyers): ___

Question 1: Does the bar association to which you belong have rules or regulations called 'Mandatory Rules on Public Interest Activities', or 'Mandatory Rules on Association Affairs', etc.? Please circle the number of the corresponding item.

① There are rules or regulations imposing some obligations, which stipulate 'contribution fee' if one can't fulfil the obligations.
   → Go to question 2.
② There are rules or regulations imposing some obligations, which do not stipulate 'contribution fee' if one can't fulfil the obligations.
   → Go to question 3.

③ There are rules or regulations stipulating the obligation to make efforts, but it is not obligatory to require certain activities.
→ Go to question 3.
④ There are rules or regulations that provide a 'daily allowance' to members whose burden of public interest activities or association affairs is seriously heavy.
→ Go to question 4.
⑤ There are no applicable rules or regulations.
⑥ I do not know whether there are applicable rules or regulations.

Question 2: Is it easy or difficult to fulfil the required obligation? Please circle the number of the item. → Next please answer question 2-1.

① easy
② somewhat easy
③ neither easy nor difficult
④ somewhat difficult
⑤ difficult

Question 2-1: By which activities do you meet the criteria?

(A) Activities to offer directly to citizens such as Court Appointed Defence Counsel or Civil Legal Aid.
(B) Bar Association Affairs.

Please circle the number of the item.

① A
② somewhat A
③ either
④ somewhat B
⑤ B

Question 3: Do you think such rules or regulations have any effect to encourage 'public interest activities' or 'association affairs'?
Please circle the number of the item that applies.

① effective
② somewhat effective
③ neither effective nor ineffective
④ somewhat ineffective
⑤ ineffective

Question 4: Do you think that such a system has some effect to encourage 'public interest activities' or 'association affairs'? Please circle the number of the item.

① effective
② somewhat effective
③ neither effective nor ineffective
④ somewhat ineffective
⑤ ineffective

6

Improving Access to Justice in Malaysia: Introspection, Purpose, and Dynamism

*Seh Lih Long**

Abstract

Malaysian lawyers have a number of formal structures in which to meet their access to justice obligations, including the government-funded National Legal Aid Foundation and the lawyer-funded Bar Council's semi-mandatory pro bono scheme. These systems, together with the constitutional guarantee of the right to legal counsel, establish the foundation for access to justice in Malaysia. This chapter critiques current pro bono practices in support of access to justice and presents the first survey of Malaysian lawyers on pro bono lawyering. While acknowledging the lack of publicly available information and empirical data, the chapter argues that access to justice is hampered by budgetary constraints and piecemeal reforms in civil legal aid, the limited extent of access to justice for women and foreigners, and a politically visible but relatively unimpressive pro bono culture amongst lawyers overall. There is a critical need to challenge the primacy of current thinking and discourse, regarding participation from the government, the Bar, and leadership, at every level. For a start, the chapter recommends a baseline study on criminal legal aid, an open and transparent reform of civil legal aid, and approaches to strengthen pro bono culture amongst lawyers.

I. INTRODUCTION

A. *Overview*

From an economic standpoint, Malaysia's status as an upper middle-income nation[1] with a GDP of MYR1,106.1 billion (US$267.56 billion)[2] has much to celebrate,[3] but the well-being of a nation also concerns sustainable development, with equal access to justice as one of its targets. As a

* The author is grateful to Chan Jin Ai, Priscilla Chin, and Sarah-Ann Yong, who took time out of their busy schedules to provide invaluable and important contributions to this research.

1 'Data – Malaysia', *The World Bank* (2020), online: data.worldbank.org/country/malaysia.

2 XE Currency Converter, online: www.xe.com/currencyconverter/convert/?Amount=10&From=MYR&To=USD. Unless another reference was cited, US$ denominations in the chapter were derived from www.xe.com at the time of publication; they are intended for general reference, and may have been rounded up or down for ease of reference.

3 Malaysia, Prime Minister's Department: Economic Planning Unit, *The Malaysian Economy in Figures 2016* (2016).

member of the United Nations, Malaysia has committed to the 2030 Agenda for Sustainable Development, and Goal 16 recognizes access to justice for all as part of improving the lives of citizens. Malaysia has the fundamentals for this in place: the Federal Constitution recognizes the right to legal counsel, and the combined efforts of the government, the judiciary, and the Malaysian Bar have to a certain extent delivered equal access to justice. Malaysia's challenge is therefore how to improve access to justice. When analysing these challenges, it is difficult to achieve an evidence-based understanding of the impact of available legal aid and pro bono mechanisms beyond basic figures or information. The chapter therefore provides an overview of the current state of access to legal assistance available to indigent persons, the information and knowledge needed, and the responsibility gap of lawyers in ensuring access to justice. Additionally, the chapter highlights priority areas and innovative approaches in other jurisdictions which could inspire new initiatives. It is hoped that this research will be the first step toward comprehensive reforms to ensure that all who live in Malaysia enjoy equal access to justice.

B. *Empirical Methodology*

To generate additional data for this research, the Malaysian Centre for Constitutionalism and Human Rights ('MCCHR') carried out an online survey on pro bono for members of the Malaysian Bar between March and October 2017. The survey was distributed through social media, emails, and in-person encouragement. MCCHR also requested chairpersons of all state Bars via email to distribute and encourage their members to participate in the survey. The survey was divided into four parts: general demographic, participation in pro bono work, views on pro bono, and the future of pro bono in Malaysia; survey questions can be found in the Appendix, with the parts of the survey indicated by dotted lines.

The survey was supplemented by interviews with lawyers. MCCHR contacted approximately 50 lawyers with whom the MCCHR was familiar, ensuring that male and female lawyers and lawyers of varying seniority were interviewed. However, only 22 lawyers agreed to be interviewed, 10 female and 12 male lawyers, and within this group there were 8 young lawyers,[4] 7 mid-level lawyers,[5] and 7 senior lawyers.[6]

Given the limited number of survey respondents and interviews, the results may not be representative of Malaysian lawyers. The survey collected 202 responses, representing 1 per cent of the Malaysian Bar, and the demographics do not correspond with the wider profession. Nevertheless, the survey and interviews still provide a glimpse of the pro bono culture within the Bar, and a basis for further research.

II. THE LANGUAGE OF ACCESS TO JUSTICE IN MALAYSIA

A. *Access to Justice*

Access to justice as investigated in this chapter refers to the more narrow meaning of access to legal services and formal remedies. This description appears consistent with how Malaysian courts have interpreted it, and how lawyers understand the concept of access to justice.

[4] Less than seven years in practice.
[5] Defined as between 7 and 15 years in practice.
[6] More than 15 years in practice.

The courts have held that access to justice is a human right,[7] one that includes, inter alia, the right to a fair and expeditious trial,[8] the right to be heard by an impartial tribunal,[9] the right to have a fair and just decision,[10] the right of the economically weaker class to realize their fundamental rights by using the courts,[11] legal representation for individuals who have been arrested, detained, charged, or prosecuted,[12] and justice for victims of deaths in police custody.[13] When asked how they understand access to justice, all the lawyers interviewed raised the concept of fairness.[14] To them, access means having the relevant capabilities, including the financial means, to underwrite the costs of pursuing justice. It is also observed that in public discourse, the provision of legal services to indigent persons is almost always linked to access to justice.[15] The Bar's National Legal Aid Committee states that its objective is to ensure 'access to justice is available fairly and impartially to everyone'.[16] Similarly, the Legal Aid Department sees its role as providing access to justice through the legal process.[17]

B. *Pro Bono is Synonymous with Legal Aid*

Although no formal study has been conducted, a rudimentary perusal of websites, media articles, and speeches suggests that the judiciary, government authorities, and lawyers are familiar with the terms 'pro bono' and 'legal aid', although the meanings of these phrases differ from other jurisdictions. Whilst scholarly literature frequently defines legal aid as government-funded legal services to indigent persons and pro bono as the provision of lawyer-funded legal services by private lawyers, in Malaysia the terms 'pro bono' and 'legal aid' are used interchangeably. The previous Chief Justice of Malaysia defined pro bono in a speech as 'a mechanism intended to help the poor or public to have a better access to the judicial process'.[18] Government-funded

[7] *Tengku Aziz Ku Jusoh* v. *Public Prosecutor* [2017] 1 LNS 170 [*Tengku Aziz* v. *PP*] and *PP* v. *Gan Boon Aun* [2017] 4 CLJ 41 [*PP* v. *Gan Boon Aun*].

[8] *Tengku Aziz* v. *PP*, *supra* note 7.

[9] *PP* v. *Gan Boon Aun*, *supra* note 7.

[10] *Racha Urud* v. *Ravenscourt Sdn Bhd* [2014] 4 CLJ 393.

[11] *Malik Brothers* v. *Narendra Dadhich* AIR 1999 SC 3211, cited in *Hotel Sentral (JB) Sdn Bhd* v. *Pengarah Tanah Dan Galian Negeri Johor* [2016] 1 LNS 1671.

[12] Lim Chee Wee, 'Welcome Address' (Speech delivered by the President of the Malaysian Bar at the International Malaysia Law Conference, Kuala Lumpur, Malaysia, 26 September 2012).

[13] Kuthubul Zaman, 'Fundamental Right of Access to Justice', *Free Malaysia Today* (24 March 2017), online: www.freemalaysiatoday.com/category/opinion/2017/03/24/fundamental-right-of-access-to-justice/ [*Right of Access to Justice*].

[14] Interviews with Lawyers (12 July 2017 – 26 October 2017, Kuala Lumpur, Malaysia) [*Interviews with Lawyers*].

[15] Veerasamy Anbalagan, 'Government Legal Aid Scheme Allows Lawyers to Hone Their Skills', *Free Malaysia Today* (22 September 2016), online: www.freemalaysiatoday.com/category/nation/2016/09/22/govt-legal-aid-scheme-allows-lawyers-to-hone-their-skills/ [*Hone Their Skills*]; see also *Right of Access to Justice*, *supra* note 13; Malaysia, Bar Council Malaysia, 'Information Sheet: Malaysia' (Tokyo: 3rd Conference on Access to Justice and the Role of Bar Associations and Law Societies in Asia, 2011) [*Information Sheet: Malaysia*]; and Steven Thiruneelakandan, 'Closing Keynote' (Speech delivered by the President of the Malaysian Bar at the London Annual Bar and Young Bar Conference, 15 October 2016).

[16] *Annual Report 2016/17* (The Malaysian Bar, 71st AGM of the Bar, 18 March 2017) [*Annual Report 2016/17*] at 263.

[17] Datuk Haini binti Hassan, Ketua Pengarah Jabatan Bantuan Guaman, 'Perutusan Tahun Baru 2016' (Speech delivered by the Director of the Legal Aid Department at the Legal Aid Department New Year's Message 2016, Kuala Lumpur, 29 December 2015).

[18] Tun Arifin Zakaria, 'Fostering an Efficient and Competent Legal Profession to Support the Court Development of Pro Bono Civil and Criminal Programs: Malaysian Perspective' (Speech delivered by the Chief Justice of Malaysia at the Singapore Conference of Chief Justices of Asia and the Pacific 2013, 27–30 October 2013) [*Competent Legal Profession*].

legal service providers such as the Legal Aid Department and the National Legal Aid Foundation ('NLAF') often refer to their services as pro bono services.[19] Conversely, the name of the Bar Council's programme that provides legal assistance to the poor contains the word 'legal aid'; it is named the Bar Council's *Legal Aid* Scheme and *Legal Aid* Clinics (emphasis supplied). In the survey, when lawyers were asked what best describes pro bono, a large proportion of lawyers associated pro bono with 'Bar Council Legal Aid' and the 'NLAF'.

For the minority of lawyers who differentiated 'pro bono' and 'legal aid', the distinction was not the source of funding but the use of a means test. To them, legal aid uses a means test to determine eligibility, while in pro bono, the question of whether a client can afford to pay for legal services was not an important factor, and some lawyers would take up a pro bono case because it had a public interest element.[20] There is broad consensus that a pro bono lawyer is one who takes up cases voluntarily, either without legal fees or for low fees below the usual rate.[21]

In light of the blurred distinction between the terms 'pro bono' and 'legal aid', this chapter will use the terms as they are used in Malaysia. However, where possible, the nature of the legal service as a government-funded or lawyer-funded service will be identified.

III. CONSTITUTIONAL AND LEGAL GUARANTEES

A. *The Malaysian Legal System*

The Malaysian legal system is based on the English legal system of parliamentary democracy and constitutional monarchy. The *Yang di-Pertuan Agong* (King) is the ceremonial Head of the Federation who is elected by the Conference of Rulers for a term of five years. The doctrine of separation of powers is preserved in the Federal Constitution, which defines the executive, legislature, and judiciary. In terms of lawyers, the Malaysian Bar comprises 19,305 legal practitioners in Malaysia,[22] which is approximately 59.1 lawyers per 100,000 people.[23] The legal profession in Malaysia is a fused one in which a legal practitioner is both barrister and solicitor.

The Executive segment of the government is headed by the Prime Minister[24] and legislative authority is vested in Parliament, which consists of the *Dewan Negara* (Senate) and *Dewan Rakyat* (House of Representatives). The judicial powers of the Federation are vested in the Federal Court, Court of Appeal, and two High Courts of coordinate jurisdiction (the High Court in Malaya and the High Court in Sabah and Sarawak).[25]

[19] 'Pro Bono Legal Aid Benefits 140,000 – Nancy', *Borneo Times Online* (19 January 2014), online: www.theborneopost.com/2014/01/19/pro-bono-legal-aid-benefits-140000-nancy/.

[20] Interview with 22L (21 July 2017, Kuala Lumpur); Interview with 12J (12 July 2017, Kuala Lumpur) [*Interview with 12J*]; Interview with 12M (12 July 2017, Kuala Lumpur) [*Interview with 12M*]; Interview with 473WB (11 August 2017, Kuala Lumpur) [*Interview with 473WB*]; Interview with 682TR (23 August 2017, Kuala Lumpur) [*Interview with 682TR*]; and Interview with 832W (24 July 2017, Kuala Lumpur).

[21] *Interviews with Lawyers, supra* note 14.

[22] 'Bar Council General Statistics', *Bar Council Malaysia* (31 January 2019), online: www.malaysianbar.org.my/article/about-us/malaysian-bar-and-bar-council/about-us/figures/general-statistics [*General Statistics*].

[23] Ibid. This figure is based on the number of lawyers as at 31 January 2019 (19,305), and the population of Malaysia in the first quarter of 2019 of 32.66 million, Department of Statistics Malaysia, *Selected Demographic Indicators Malaysia*, 2019, Official Portal (15 August 2019), online: www.dosm.gov.my/v1/index.php?r=column/cthemeByCat&cat=397&bul_id=bFhLclp4ZnpSMHRIa21haFNLR2JqZz09&menu_id=LopheU43NWJwRWVSZklWdzQ4TlhUUT09.

[24] *Federal Constitution*, Malaysia 1957 (as amended 1 November 2010) [*Federal Constitution Malaysia*], Article 43.

[25] *Federal Constitution Malaysia, supra* note 24, Article 121.

B. *Right to Legal Counsel in Criminal Cases*

Article 5(3) and (4) of the Federal Constitution[26] and Section 28A of the Criminal Procedure Code ('CPC')[27] guarantee the right to legal counsel, as long as it would not impede police investigations,[28] and it should be given with 'all convenient speed'.[29] The right can be suspended if the Deputy Superintendent of Police[30] reasonably believes that consulting a legal practitioner is likely to result in: the avoidance of apprehension of an accomplice; the concealment, fabrication, or destruction of evidence or intimidation of a witness; or, if having regard to the safety of another person, questioning or recording should not be delayed due to the urgency of the situation.[31] Section 28A of the CPC was seen as a major shift in a lawyer's role in the criminal justice system, as it compelled the police to allow an arrested person to communicate with and consult a legal practitioner of his or her choice, prior to questioning or recording of the statement. However, a number of security and anti-terrorism laws now contain provisions limiting access to legal counsel, e.g. the Prevention of Terrorism Act 2015 ('POTA'),[32] the Prevention of Crime Act 1959 ('PCA'),[33] and the Security Offences (Special Measures) Act 2012 ('SOSMA').[34]

C. *Right to Legal Representation in Civil Cases*

The right to legal representation in civil cases is not expressly guaranteed in the Federal Constitution or any written law. It was read into the constitutional right to equality before the law[35] and the principle of procedural fairness.[36]

D. *Right to Legal Aid*

There is no explicit right to legal aid in Malaysia. The Legal Aid Act 1971[37] provides civil and criminal legal aid in matters prescribed in the Second, Third, and Fourth Schedules, and Section 10(2A) of the 1971 Act gives the Minister wide powers to authorize criminal legal aid if it is in the interest of justice to do so, whether or not included in the Second Schedule. Section 10(3) of the Legal Aid Act 1971 gives any person the right to apply in writing for legal aid for his or her defence within 14 days after committal under the CPC, or charge or conviction by any court, while Section 13(1) provides for legal aid in civil matters. Additionally, Rule 32 of the Rules of the Court of Appeal 1994 allow any 'poor person' to apply to the court for leave to proceed in any

26 *Federal Constitution Malaysia*, *supra* note 24.

27 *Criminal Procedure Code*, Malaysia 1935, Act 593 (as amended 1 November 2012) [*Criminal Procedure Code*].

28 *Ooi Ah Phua* v. *Officer-in-Charge Criminal Investigation, Kedah/Perlis* [1975] 2 MLJ 198.

29 *Public Prosecutor* v. *Mah Chuen Lim* [1975] 1 MLJ 95.

30 *Criminal Procedure Code*, *supra* note 27, s 28A(9).

31 *Criminal Procedure Code*, *supra* note 27, s 28A(8).

32 *Prevention of Terrorism Act 2015*, Malaysia 2015, Act 769 (as amended 4 June 2015), s 10(6), online: www.federalgazette.agc.gov.my/outputaktap/aktaBI_20150604_Act769%28BI%29.pdf.

33 *Prevention of Crime Act 1959*, Malaysia 1959, Act 297 (as amended 1 January 2018), s 9(5), online: www.agc.gov.my/agcportal/uploads/files/Publications/LOM/EN/002%20-%20Act%20297%20(11_3_2018).pdf.

34 *Security Offences (Special Measures) Act 2012*, Malaysia 2012, Act 747 (as amended 1 August 2015), s 5(2), online: www.agc.gov.my/agcportal/uploads/files/Publications/LOM/EN/Act%20747%20-TPPUU).pdf.

35 *Doresamy* v. *Public Services Commission* [1971] 2 MLJ 127.

36 *Federal Hotel Sdn Bhd* v. *National Union of Hotel, Bar and Restaurant Workers* [1983] 1 MLJ 175 and *Marathaei d/o Sangalullai (suing on behalf of the estate of Thangayah Aupulley)* v. *Syarikat JG Containers (M) Sdn Bhd* [2003] 2 MLJ 337.

37 *Legal Aid Act 1971*, Malaysia 1971, Act 26 (as amended 1 November 2013) [*Legal Aid Act 1971*].

appeal as a pauper and the court will then appoint a solicitor to represent the pauper,[38] who is not required to pay court fees or security for costs.[39]

IV. THE ACCESS TO JUSTICE LANDSCAPE

The extent of a person's access to legal services and formal remedies in Malaysia is very much shaped by three main stakeholders, the judiciary, the government, and the Malaysian Bar. These three entities appear to take extra care to ensure that the services they provide do not overlap.

A. *Government-Funded Initiatives*

1. Court-Assigned Counsel Scheme and Other Programmes

The judiciary spearheaded one of Malaysia's earliest efforts to increase access to justice, the Court-assigned Counsel scheme, which was established by the British before World War II.[40] Under the purview of the Chief Registrar of Malaysia, a counsel is assigned to unrepresented accused persons facing the death penalty. Counsels receive fees paid by the court based on the practice direction of the Chief Justice of Malaysia.[41]

In addition to the above judicial schemes, given the vast rural geography of East Malaysia, since March 2007 the Mobile Court has visited rural villages in Sabah and Sarawak in customized buses twice a month, where it spends typically eight to nine hours in a village.[42] The Mobile Court usually comprises Sessions Court judges, magistrates, and government departments such as the National Registration Department, the hospital, and the Information Department. The Mobile Court holds inquiries on pending applications for endorsement of late registration of birth certificates. Civil and criminal disputes are rare, and according to the former Chief Judge of Sabah and Sarawak Tan Sri Richard Malanjum, the Mobile Court serves districts which do not have a courthouse and where court cases are unusual.[43]

Whilst the Court-assigned Counsel scheme and the Mobile Court continue to operate, it appears that efforts by the judiciary in the past decade have primarily focused on reducing the backlog of cases. Pre-2010, it could take 10 to 15 years to dispose of a case,[44] but since 2010, the courts have engaged in extensive reform, including for example increasing the number of judges, establishing specialized courts[45] and a case management system,[46] introducing mediation as an alternative dispute resolution mechanism,[47] and stipulating strict timelines for *habeas*

[38] *Rules of the Court of Appeal 1994*, Malaysia 1994, P.U.(A) 524/1994 (as amended 1 August 1994) [*Court of Appeal Rules*], r 32.

[39] *Court of Appeal Rules*, *supra* note 38, r 33.

[40] *Information Sheet: Malaysia*, *supra* note 15.

[41] Federal Court of Malaysia, *Chief Justice Practice Direction 5/2013* (Putrajaya, June 2013), online: library.kehakiman.gov.my/digital/Arahan%20Amalan%20Dan%20Nota%20Amalan/Arahan%20Amalan%20Bil%205%20Tahun%202013.pdf.

[42] Zainun Ali, ed., *The Malaysian Judiciary: Yearbook 2014* (The Malaysian Judiciary, 2014) at 43, 52, and 77.

[43] Avila Geraldine, 'New Fleet of Mobile Courtrooms Delivers Justice for Rural Sabahans', *The New Straits Times* (5 January 2017).

[44] *Competent Legal Profession*, *supra* note 18.

[45] Federal Court of Malaysia, *Chief Justice Practice Direction 3/2012* (Putrajaya, 27 August 2012), online: www.praktis.com.my/practical-tools/practice-directions/chief-justice-s-practice-directions-notes/chief-justice-of-malaysia-practice-direction-no-1.

[46] Kwan Will Sen, 'Key Points from Practice Direction 1 of 2020 (Malaysian Civil Court Practice)' (31 January 2020), online: www.linkedin.com/pulse/key-points-from-practice-direction-1-2020-malaysian-civil-will-sen.

[47] Federal Court of Malaysia, *Chief Justice Practice Direction 4/2016* (Putrajaya, 30 June 2016), online: library.kehakiman.gov.my/digital/Arahan%20Amalan%20Dan%20Nota%20Amalan/Practice%20Direction%20No.%204%20of%202016.pdf.

corpus applications.[48] The judiciary has also begun diligently tracking and publishing, on a monthly basis, its rate of disposal of cases.[49]

2. Legal Aid Department

The government's efforts in legal aid can be divided into two stages. The first stage was a foundational development in the early years after independence, in which the Legal Aid Bureau, the predecessor to the Legal Aid Department, was established to provide legal advice and assistance to the lower income group.[50] The scope of legal services currently provided by the Legal Aid Department includes inter alia:[51]

- Criminal proceedings, limited to pleading guilty and making a plea of mitigation; offences under the Child Protection Act 1991; and minor offences;
- Civil proceedings, e.g. maintenance; divorce and custody; probate and letters of administration; rent and security of tenure of *padi* cultivators; moneylenders; and consumer claims;
- Syariah proceedings, e.g. for betrothal (damages); maintenance; custody; divorce; gifts *inter vivos* (*hibah*); and wills; and
- Legal advice, for all legal matters.

The registration fee for any legal aid service is MYR10[52] (US$2.41). The eligibility criteria, contributions, and registration fees were amended on 1 December 2017 (see Table 6.1 opposite).[53]

In 2016, the Legal Aid Department provided the following number of legal services (see Table 6.2 opposite).[54]

It is observed that the Legal Aid Department operates on parameters set some 40 years ago, except for piecemeal revisions such as the introduction of mediation in 2003,[55] the introduction of legal companion services for victims of child sexual offences,[56] and the revised means test. Unsurprisingly, some lawyers opined that the scope of the Legal Aid Department's civil legal aid should be reviewed and expanded to include matters of current importance, inter alia, employment, debt collection matters, child rights issues, and domestic violence.[57]

[48] Federal Court of Malaysia, *Chief Justice Practice Direction 1/2010* (Putrajaya, 23 June 2010), online: library.kehakiman.gov.my/digital/Arahan%20Amalan%20KHN/2010/Arahan_Amalan_KHN_Bil_1_2010.pdf.

[49] Pejabat Ketua Pendaftar Mahkamah Persekutuan Malaysia (Office of the Registrar of the Federal Court Malaysia), *Statistik* (Statistics) (Putrajaya, 2020), online: www.kehakiman.gov.my/ms/statistik.

[50] The Legal Aid Bureau was not established by the *Legal Aid Act 1971, supra* note 37. The Bureau was established in 1970 by the Government of Malaysia, and then in 1971 the *Legal Aid Act 1971* was passed, to support the functions and mandate of the Bureau: see Malaysia, JBG Legal Aid Department, *Historical Background*, online: www.jbg.gov.my/index.php/en/info-jbg/history, and see *Thematic Study on Legal Aid* (ASEAN Intergovernmental Commission on Human Rights, July 2019) [*Thematic Study*] at 82, online: aichr.org/wp-content/uploads/2019/09/AICHR-Thematic-Study-on-Legal-Aid-for-web.pdf.

[51] *Legal Aid Act 1971, supra* note 37, Second, Third, and Fourth Schedules.

[52] Malaysia, JBG Legal Aid Department, *What are the Privileges of an Aided Person?*, online: www.jbg.gov.my/index.php/en/faq/general#6-what-are-the-privileges-of-an-aided-person.

[53] *Legal Aid (Fees and Contributions) Regulations 2017*, Malaysia (30 November 2017), online: www.jbg.gov.my/images/doc/Akta/Peraturan-Peraturan%20Bantuan%20Guaman%20(Fi%20dan%20Sumbangan)%202017.pdf.

[54] Malaysia, Legal Affairs Department, Prime Minister's Department, *Annual Report 2016*, online: www.bheuu.gov.my/pdf/Penerbitan/Laporan%20Tahunan%20BHEUU%202016.pdf.

[55] *Legal Aid (Amendment) Act 1995*, Malaysia, Act A911 (17 February 1995); *Legal Aid (Amendment) Act 2003*, Malaysia, Act A1188 (15 July 2003).

[56] *Legal Aid (Amendment) Act 2017*, Malaysia, Act A1548 (17 October 2017) [*Legal Aid (Amendment) Act 2017*].

[57] Interview with Ravi Nekoo, former Chairperson, National Legal Aid Committee, Malaysian Bar (21 September 2017, Kuala Lumpur) [*Interview with Nekoo*]; *Interview with 12J, supra* note 20; *Interview with 473WB, supra* note 20.

TABLE 6.1. *Legal aid fees and contributions*

Financial resources (per annum) (MYR)	Contributions under Section 16(2) (MYR)	Contributions under Section 16A(2) (MYR)	Contributions under Section 29H(3) (Legal Companion Services) (MYR)
0–30,000 (US$7,017)	–	–	–
30,001–35,000 (US$7,018–8,186)	500–2,000 (US$117–468)	500–2,000 (US$117–468)	500–2,000 (US$117–468)
35,001–40,000 (US$8,187–9,356)	2,001–3,000 (US$469–701)	2,001–3,000 (US$469–701)	2,001–3,000 (US$469–701)
40,001–50,000 (US$9,357–11,696)	3,001 – 5,000 (US$702–1,170)	3,001–5,000 (US$702–1,170)	3,001–5,000 (US$702–1,170)
50,001 and above (US$11,697)	N/A	5,001–50,000 (US$1,170–11,696)	5,001–50,000 (US$1,170–11,696)

TABLE 6.2. *Legal services provided by the Legal Aid Department (2016)*

2016	Civil	Criminal	Syariah	**Total**
Legal advice provided	16,698	3,220	42,318	62,236 clients
New cases registered	3,753	1,928	13,333	19,014 cases

Additionally, the budget that the Legal Aid Department receives from the government is relatively small. By way of comparison, the legal aid expenditure is about 0.14 per cent of the budget allocated for education expenditure (approximately MYR16.8 billion (US$4.056 billion)), and slightly less than the budget earmarked for Islamic religious (*tahfiz*) education (MYR30 million (US$7.02 million)).[58] There is also a valid concern that the economic downturn could reduce allocations to government-funded legal services, further weakening the civil legal aid system.[59] The budget allocation to the Legal Aid Department in 2017 was MYR23 million (US$5.55 million), a reduction of 14 per cent compared to 2016 when it received approximately MYR27.4 million (US$6.62 million).[60]

3. National Legal Aid Foundation

The second phase of legal aid development in Malaysia was prompted by a deficit of services within criminal legal aid, which at that time did not extend to trials and was limited to guilty pleas. In 2010, the Malaysian Bar observed that 80 per cent of accused persons in criminal cases were not represented, resulting in many accused persons pleading guilty and being sentenced to stiffer punishments as there was no lawyer to mitigate on their behalf.[61] This was brought to the

[58] YAB Dato' Sri Mohd Najib Tun Haji Abdul Razak, 'Ensuring Unity and Economic Growth, Inclusive Prudent Spending, Wellbeing of the Rakyat' (Speech delivered by the Prime Minister and Minister of Finance at the 2017 Budget Speech, 21 October 2016), online: www.bnm.gov.my/documents/20124/761691/Budget_Speech_2017.pdf/a34756a5-aa98-0dd7-3aea-29a9ce897f0b?t=1580452296331.

[59] Ida Lim, 'Legal Aid Shrinking Due to Delayed Payments, Malaysian Bar Report Says', *The Malay Mail Online* (18 March 2017), online: www.malaymail.com/news/malaysia/2017/03/18/legal-aid-shrinking-due-to-delayed-payments-malaysian-bar-report-says/1337793 [*Legal Aid Shrinking*].

[60] Ibid.

[61] Interview with YA Tuan George Varughese, Former President of the Malaysian Bar 2017–19 (11 October 2017, Kuala Lumpur) [*Interview with Varughese*].

attention of the Prime Minister by the Malaysian Bar, which led to the establishment of the NLAF on 25 January 2011.[62]

NLAF is an exemplary case of government–bar partnership. While funding comes from the government, the Bar was involved in the formative stages of NLAF,[63] the President of the Bar sits on the Board of Directors of NLAF, NLAF shares its offices with the Bar's Legal Aid Centres ('LAC'), and training for NLAF lawyers is provided by the Bar. NLAF started with a MYR5 million budget (US$1.2 million);[64] in 2012 it received an allocation of MYR10 million (US$2.46 million), and in 2013 a further MYR20 million (US$4.8 million).[65] According to YA Tuan George Varughese,[66] 2018–19 President of the Malaysian Bar, no further funds were provided thereafter as the allocated funds have been sufficient to administer NLAF.[67] YA Varughese elaborated that the MYR20 million (US$4.8 million) was the government's way of showing support for NLAF; it was not in accordance with a specific budget and the utilization of the funds was not linked to a defined period.[68]

NLAF provides legal aid only in criminal matters, including Syariah criminal matters, but only to Malaysian citizens, with the exception of non-Malaysian children accused of offences.[69] Death penalty cases are not covered as these are already provided for by the judiciary's Court-assigned Counsel scheme.[70]

In order to qualify for legal assistance under NLAF, a person's income must not exceed MYR36,000 (US$8,692) per annum. No fee will be charged for a person whose income is less than MYR25,000 (US$6,036) per annum, but those whose annual income is between MYR25,000 (US$6,036) and MYR36,000 (US$8,692) will be charged rates determined by NLAF's Board of Directors.[71]

Payment to NLAF volunteer lawyers varies according to the work, and ranges from MYR30 (US$7.24) for a remand hearing to MYR1,200 (US$289) for an appeal to the Court of Appeal.[72] In 2016, NLAF provided legal assistance to 181,993 clients,[73] a decrease from 231,655 clients in 2015.

Lawyers intending to volunteer for NLAF are required to undergo training and assessment. If a candidate is successful, he or she is certified as a NLAF lawyer. In 2015, NLAF established an audit team consisting of senior criminal lawyers to monitor the quality of NLAF lawyers by observing them in court. If the audit team determines that the quality of a NLAF lawyer is unsatisfactory, the latter is either asked to improve or sent for further training.[74]

[62] Malaysia, Bar Council Legal Aid Centre (Kuala Lumpur), 'Overview of YBGK', online: www.kllac.com/ybgk-program/.

[63] *Interview with Nekoo*, *supra* note 57.

[64] *Hone Their Skills*, *supra* note 15.

[65] *Legal Aid Shrinking*, *supra* note 59.

[66] Tuan is the Malay term that means sir; it is used to address a person as a mark of respect.

[67] Ida Lim, 'Malaysian Bar: Delayed Payment for Legal Aid Scheme Not Due to Funding Issues', *The Malay Mail Online* (18 March 2017), online: www.malaymail.com/news/malaysia/2017/03/18/malaysian-bar-delayed-payment-for-legal-aid-scheme-not-due-to-funding-issue/1337937.

[68] *Interview with Varughese*, *supra* note 61.

[69] *Annual Report 2016/17*, *supra* note 16, at 266.

[70] Malaysia, National Legal Aid Foundation, 'Services Provided' (copy on file with author).

[71] Ibid.

[72] *Revised Rates of Payment to Lawyers* (Selangor Bar, 1 May 2014), online: www.selangorbar.org/Revised%20Rates%20of%20Payment%20to%20Lawyers%20(1%20May%202014).pdf.

[73] *Annual Report 2016/17*, *supra* note 16, at 268.

[74] *Interview with Nekoo*, *supra* note 57.

4. Lawyer-Funded Legal Services: The Malaysian Bar

A. CULTURE, TRADITION, AND STATUTORY DUTY. The triune concepts of culture, tradition, and statutory duty are key to understanding how the Malaysian Bar sees and implements its role in access to justice. The Legal Profession Act 1976 ('LPA 1976')[75] sets out the statutory duty of the Bar to 'uphold the cause of justice without regard to its own interests or that of its members, uninfluenced by fear or favour'[76] and provides that the Bar should 'make provision for or assist in the promotion of a scheme whereby impecunious persons may be represented by advocates and solicitors'.[77] However, as of 1965, the Bar had already put in place a pro bono scheme, for persons detained under the now repealed Internal Security Act 1960 ('ISA').[78] A number of senior lawyers interviewed for this chapter,[79] including the former President of the Malaysian Bar as well as the former Chairperson of the National Legal Aid Committee, explained that the principles identified above were prevalent within members of the Bar Council[80] at that time, and founding members of the Bar who contributed to the provisions of LPA 1976 merely ensured that it expressly included these principles. Also, according to YA Varughese, since then it has been a tradition for past Bar Council members to pass on to their successors the principles of rule of law, access to justice, and human rights. Over a span of six decades, these values, embedded in statutory duty and passed on through tradition, have nurtured a culture of access to justice, particularly amongst members of the Bar Council.

However, it appears that this convention of culture, tradition, and statutory duty is strongest amongst a small number of lawyers, who do most of the pro bono work. Due to media attention and the wide promotion of their work, the impression has arisen that the entire Malaysian Bar is involved in activism or pro bono work, but one lawyer interviewed for the chapter pointed out that most lawyers are unconcerned about such matters.[81]

B. SEMI-MANDATORY SCHEME. Over the past four decades, Bar Council members have ensured that its Bar Council Legal Aid Scheme ('BCLAS') gives meaning to Section 42(1)(h) and promotes a culture of access to justice. BCLAS was launched in 1983 with the objectives of providing free legal advice and assistance to indigent persons and promoting legal literacy and awareness.[82] To ensure that BCLAS is self-funding, the Bar Council infused semi-mandatory support by making it compulsory for every member of the Bar to contribute MYR100 (US$24.1) per year to BCLAS. This payment is a prerequisite to the renewal of one's practising certificate. The compulsory payment was introduced in 1983 following the establishment of the first official Legal Aid Clinic in Kuala Lumpur in 1982.[83]

75 *Legal Profession Act 1976*, Malaysia, Act 166 (as amended 1 August 2018) [*LPA 1976*].

76 *LPA 1976*, *supra* note 75, s 42(1)(a).

77 *LPA 1976*, *supra* note 75, s 42(1)(h).

78 *Internal Security Act 1960*, Malaysia, Act 82 (as amended 1 January 2006), repealed by the *Security Offences (Special Measures) Act 2012*, Malaysia, Act 747 (as amended 1 August 2015).

79 *Interview with 12J*, *supra* note 20; *Interview with 12M*, *supra* note 20; *Interview with 473WB*, *supra* note 20; *Interview with 682TR*, *supra* note 20.

80 Bar Council members are elected and are responsible for proper management of the affairs and the proper performance of the statutory functions of the Malaysian Bar, *LPA 1976*, *supra* note 75, s 47.

81 *Interview with 12J*, *supra* note 20.

82 Malaysian Bar, 'Mandatory Legal Aid Service by Lawyers to be Considered' (2002), online: www.malaysianbar.org.my/article/news/press-statements/press-statements/mandatory-legal-aid-service-by-lawyers-to-be-considered.

83 *Thematic Study*, *supra* note 50, at 83.

In 1983, the Bar also passed a resolution making it compulsory for every pupil-in-chambers to participate in BCLAS for a minimum period of 14 days.[84] Completion of BCLAS is a prerequisite of admittance to the Bar. However, after a person is admitted to the Bar, it is not compulsory for lawyers to take up pro bono cases.

In 1995, due to the high number of unassigned criminal files at the time,[85] the Bar passed a resolution requiring all members of the Bar to take up at least one BCLAS case/matter per year.[86] However, many lawyers turned down or ignored cases that were forwarded to them by the Legal Aid Clinics.[87] One explanation offered by Ravi Nekoo, Chairperson of the National Legal Aid Committee 2013–17, was that the Legal Aid Clinic files were mostly criminal files, and non-criminal lawyers felt ill-equipped to handle criminal cases. As such, the Bar did not pursue strict implementation of the resolution. According to YA Varughese, there are no immediate plans to revisit the idea of mandatory pro bono.

BCLAS provides legal advice and representation through various platforms, including 15 Legal Aid Clinics throughout Peninsula Malaysia, prison visits, a dock-brief programme where pupils-in-chambers represent unrepresented accused persons in bail applications or plea mitigation, an urgent arrest team, and law awareness events.[88] BCLAS is supervised by the Bar's National Legal Aid Committee. The scope of services provided by BCLAS includes for example criminal offences, including guilty pleas and criminal trials, public interest cases, housing/tenancy issues, family law, Syariah law, and immigration issues such as passports and identity cards.

The means test for BCLAS is a nett monthly income of less than MYR650 (US$160) for a single person and MYR900 (US$217) for a married person. In addition, a person should not own property worth more than MYR45,000 (US$10,864) for a house, MYR20,000 (US$4,828) for a car, or MYR4,500 (US$1,086) for a motorcycle, and should not have more than MYR5,000 (US$1,207) in savings. Those qualified for legal assistance are required to pay an administrative fee of MYR20 (US$4.82).[89] According to Ravi Nekoo, the means test varies to take into account the different costs of living in different Malaysian states. In 2016, BCLAS provided 19,629 clients with legal assistance, a 20 per cent decrease compared to five years before, as in 2011, it served 24,562 clients.[90] BCLAS volunteer lawyers are not paid any legal fees for their services.

Whilst BCLAS volunteer lawyers do not go through such rigorous training as NLAF lawyers, YA Varughese stated that the Bar's National Legal Aid Committee monitors the work of their volunteer lawyers. Ravi Nekoo added that since almost the same lawyers volunteer for both NLAF and BCLAS, the quality of BCLAS lawyers is indirectly ensured through the NLAF training process.

Whilst BCLAS strives to provide legal assistance to the poor, the reach of BCLAS is limited by its budget, which is a mere fraction of the budget of the Legal Aid Department (Table 6.3 opposite).[91]

[84] *The Role of Bar Associations in Supporting Pro Bono – The Malaysian Bar Experience* (Christopher Leong, Malaysia Bar, 2 October 2014).

[85] *Interview with Nekoo, supra* note 57.

[86] *49th AGM of the Malaysian Bar* (Malaysia Bar, 18 March 1995), online: www.malaysianbar.org.my/article/news/agms-and-egms/resolutions/the-49th-agm-of-the-malaysian-bar-held-at-the-shangri-la-hotel-kuala-lumpur—saturday-18-march-1995.

[87] Ibid.

[88] *Annual Report* 2016/17, *supra* note 16, at 263–4.

[89] Malaysia, Bar Council Legal Aid Centre, 'Bar Council Legal Aid Scheme', online: pdfslide.net/documents/malaysia-bar-council-legal-aid-centre.html.

[90] *Annual Report* 2016/17, *supra* note 16, at 268.

[91] For the budget of the Legal Aid Department, see *Legal Aid Shrinking, supra* note 59; for the budget of the BCLAS, this is calculated at MYR100.00 (US$24.63) collected per member, with 18,004 members in 2017.

TABLE 6.3. *Comparison of allocation and number of cases: Bar Council Legal Aid Scheme vs Legal Aid Department*

	2017 Allocation (approx.)	No. of Cases in 2015/16 (approx.)
BCLAS	MYR1.8 million (US$434,595)	20,000 cases
Legal Aid Department	MYR23.0 million (US$5.56 million)	64,000 cases

5. Public Interest Pro Bono Work

The Bar Council has historically incorporated public interest as a fundamental aspect of its pro bono repertoire, one of its first pro bono efforts being the provision of legal representation to those detained under the ISA in the 1960s. Today, public interest work continues to inspire BCLAS in three ways. First, the Bar mobilizes lawyers for its rapid response and urgent arrest teams. YA George Varughese, Bar President 2018–19, and Ravi Nekoo, the Chairperson of the Bar's National Legal Aid Committee 2013–17, were particularly proud of the different teams, consisting mostly of young lawyers, who are deployed at every peaceful assembly to manage hotlines for protestors to call in case of an arrest, to be on standby to provide urgent legal representation in the event of mass arrests of protesters, and to monitor the assembly itself.[92]

Second, not necessarily motivated by the need to help clients characterized as indigent or poor, a small section of Bar members take up public interest cases for free or at a lower cost because of their personal interest in the subject matter and/or their desire to change the legal landscape to be more receptive to human rights.[93] For example, BCLAS provided pro bono legal representation during the *Reformasi* movement in 1998, in which the former Deputy Prime Minister Anwar Ibrahim was detained and tried under the now repealed ISA. In the last few years, some lawyers have worked closely with NGOs such as MCCHR and Lawyers for Liberty to take up strategic litigation cases.

Third, the Malaysian Bar is perceived to be vocal about the defence of fundamental rights guaranteed by the Constitution. Apart from regular press statements speaking out against injustices, most senior lawyers cite the Walk for Justice in 2007 as an emblematic event that showcases the Bar's activism,[94] an event where about 2,000 lawyers marched from the Palace of Justice to the Prime Minister's office to peacefully protest the allegations of corruption in the appointments of judges.

V. SNAPSHOT OF PRO BONO LAWYERING

A. *Pro Bono Service*

To provide some data regarding pro bono among lawyers in Malaysia, the author conducted an online survey under the auspices of MCCHR (Figure 6.1 on p. 110).

The results of the survey suggest that women (57%) were slightly more inclined to carry out pro bono work than men (43%), and those in their early years of legal practice (59% of respondents) contributed the most to pro bono work.

[92] *Interview with Varughese, supra* note 61; *Interview with Nekoo, supra* note 57.
[93] *Interviews with Lawyers, supra* note 14.
[94] Ibid.

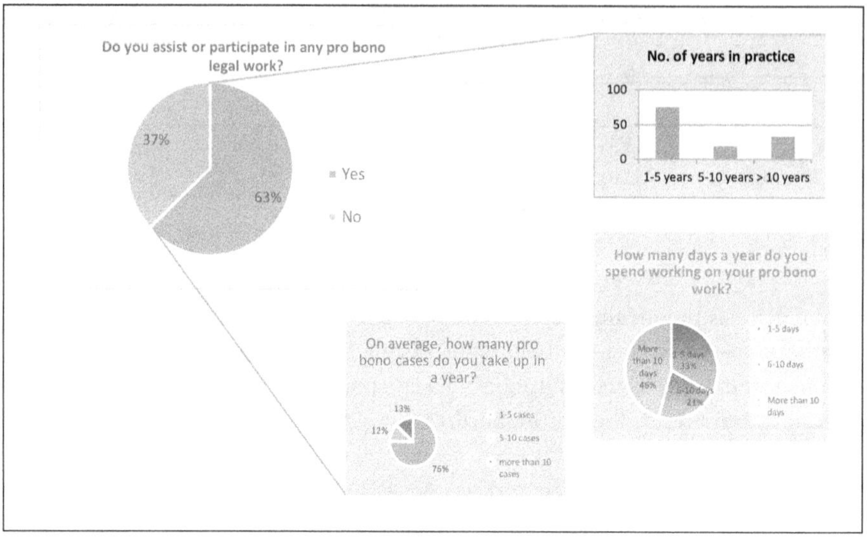

FIGURE 6.1. Participation in pro bono work

As to how they acquired pro bono work, 66% stated that pro bono work was referred to them by a friend, family, or an organization. Only 26% actively sought out pro bono cases or actively volunteered their legal services at an NGO. Interviews with lawyers revealed the same conclusion; here only one lawyer proactively asked the Legal Aid Clinics for files, whilst others obtained their pro bono cases through referrals.

The typical pro bono work undertaken by lawyers included cases taken up by their firms (57%), volunteering time at an NGO (44%), NLAF (39%), and BCLAS (34%).[95] Pro bono services were provided mostly in civil matters (73%), and frequently performed legal tasks included providing advice, interviewing or meeting clients, and representing clients in court.

Most of the lawyers began pro bono work in their first two years of practice. They felt equipped to handle the pro bono work, either because they received training from NLAF or they benefited from the guidance of senior lawyers or their employers.[96]

B. *Motivation*

1. Helping People in Need

For 85 per cent of respondents and almost half of the lawyers interviewed, the topmost reason for doing pro bono work was helping others (Figure 6.2 opposite). It was observed that the sense of helping others alleviate their legal predicaments was a common feature of memorable pro bono cases:[97]

> It was my first employment matter ... the client was retrenched after working more than two decades with the company ... the client did not have much money. We won the case and got around two years of back wages.

95 Respondents were allowed to select more than one answer.

96 *Interviews with Lawyers*, *supra* note 14.

97 Interview with 100S (7 August 2017, Kuala Lumpur) [*Interview with 100S*]; *Interview with 473WB*, *supra* note 20; Interview with 830K (26 July 2020, Kuala Lumpur).

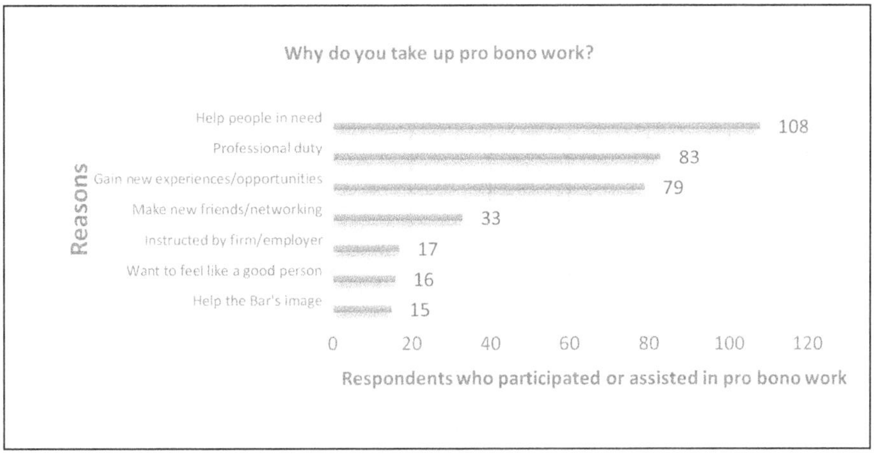

FIGURE 6.2. Reasons for taking up pro bono work

> I remember it was a construction claim where we successfully obtained the client's money … the money was not much but it was enough for the client to move on to the next project and it also meant that the client's company stayed afloat.

> It was a death penalty case and it was memorable because at the last stage of appeal, the client was found not guilty … it was one person's last chance of living.

2. Professional Duty

The survey showed that a professional duty to provide pro bono services is associated with being a lawyer generally and not because of the statutory duty set out in Section 42(1)(h) of the LPA 1976. All lawyers interviewed except one were unfamiliar with the access to justice provision in Section 42(1)(h), only 60 per cent of lawyers surveyed were aware of Section 42(1)(h), and 35 per cent of respondents who stated that they do pro bono work were not aware of Section 42(1)(h).

3. Professional Development

A large proportion of lawyers surveyed (77%) stated that pro bono provided them with experience and/or exposure, networking opportunities particularly with senior lawyers, court experience, advocacy skills and techniques, and the opportunity to learn about new areas of the law. Young lawyers benefited the most from the experience/exposure and networking opportunities of pro bono work.

C. *Weak Pro Bono Culture*

1. Only a Small Fraction of Lawyers Do Pro Bono Work

The Malaysian lawyers interviewed generally appreciated that they play a pivotal role in ensuring access to justice for the poor (90%). Lawyers surveyed stated that pro bono work was important to them (82%) because they felt that lawyers should help the less fortunate, that a lawyer's role is to serve the public, and that lawyers are the only people that can appear in court and therefore are in a position to help (Figure 6.3 on p. 112).

Despite this and contrary to the findings of the survey, which showed that 63 per cent of respondents did pro bono work, the number of volunteer lawyers with NLAF is merely 2,358, of

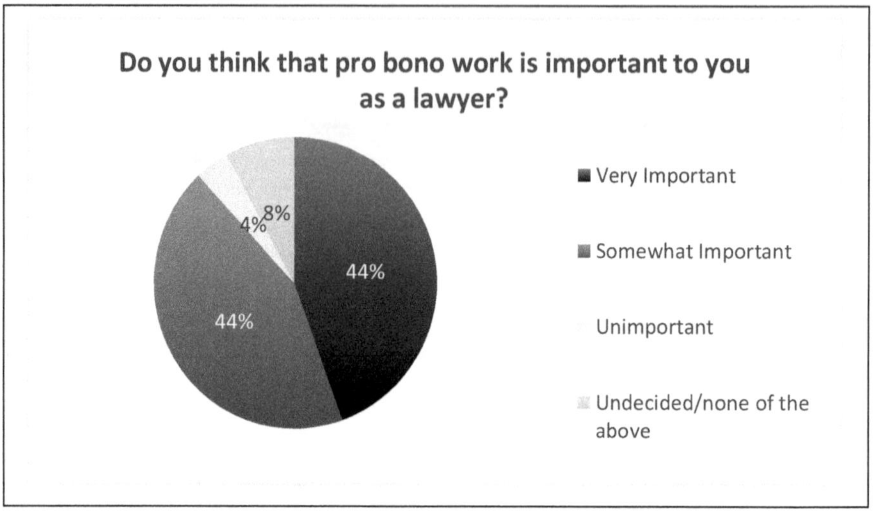

FIGURE 6.3. The importance of pro bono work to a lawyer

which only 1,706 are active volunteer lawyers.[98] Since most of NLAF lawyers are also volunteer lawyers for BCLAS,[99] it would be safe to assume the number of NLAF volunteer lawyers as the average. This number is a mere 12 per cent of the total number of qualified lawyers in Peninsular Malaysia.[100] There could be lawyers who may not work with NLAF or BCLAS, and instead provide pro bono legal services to the poor in their own way, but the data suggests that a relatively small percentage of lawyers actively engage in this role. As one lawyer put it, the role of a lawyer in access to justice is important, 'but it doesn't feel important'.[101]

2. Lack of Firm Support

Per 44 per cent of respondents, some law firms or employers encourage their lawyers to take up pro bono work, although only 11 lawyers out of 202 respondents reported that it was mandatory in their firm to participate in pro bono work, with no penalty imposed if their lawyers do not take up any pro bono cases.

Per 94 per cent of respondents, most law firms do not fix an allocated budget solely for the purpose of pro bono work, or the lawyers did not know about this. Per 98 per cent of respondents, almost all law firms did not credit pro bono hours toward the minimum billing requirement for lawyers, or the latter were unaware of this. Almost all the young lawyers expressed negative views about their firms or employers regarding pro bono work. Either their employers did not encourage them to take up pro bono work or they did not know their supervisor's views on pro bono, and their employers were less interested in pro bono work or accorded less priority to such work. One young lawyer stated that taking up pro bono work would not be looked upon favourably by the firm.

98 *Annual Report 2016/17*, *supra* note 16, at 316.

99 *Interview with Nekoo*, *supra* note 57.

100 This figure is based on the number of volunteer lawyers with NLAF (2,358) compared with the number of lawyers in 2019 (19,305): *General Statistics*, *supra* note 22.

101 *Interview with 133P* (28 August 2017, Kuala Lumpur).

Among mid-level lawyers, most of the lawyers interviewed stated that their employers or partners were supportive of their pro bono work or they assumed that they were supportive. This ability to engage in pro bono correlated with the greater overall amount of freedom these lawyers enjoyed in determining their work balance, including the proportion of paid and pro bono work. However, these lawyers worked in mid-sized law firms, and some lawyers expressed the view that in larger law firms, even mid-level and senior lawyers might enjoy less freedom to determine the amount of pro bono work they take up.[102]

Admittedly, a law firm is a business and generating income is a natural and reasonable goal for it to have. However, when founding partners and sole proprietors were asked how they balanced sustaining their firms and doing pro bono work, they stated that 'it is just a matter of doing more or less' pro bono work, and that it was possible to maintain profitability whilst helping the less fortunate.[103]

VI. IDENTIFYING AREAS FOR IMPROVEMENT IN MALAYSIA

In addition to the points analysed above, there are a number of areas within access to justice requiring improvement.

A. *An Incomplete Shift in Mindset*

Addressing the state of access to justice in Malaysia must begin with the degree to which the constitutional right to legal counsel and legal representation is respected by the police and the courts. Support for these rights by the police and the courts vacillates in two areas. First, despite the introduction of Section 28A of the CPC in 2006,[104] the police continue to view the participation of lawyers with apprehension. For example, in May 2009, a number of lawyers who were outside a police station providing legal advice to their clients via their mobile phones were arrested by the police. Also, the Human Rights Commission of Malaysia ('SUHAKAM') received complaints of arrested persons being denied access to lawyers, although no specific number of complaints was reported.[105] Similar concerns were raised during the United Nations Human Rights Council's Universal Periodic Review Second Cycle for Malaysia.[106]

The courts on the other hand have been robust in their application of Section 28A of the CPC. In *Fadiah Nadwa Fikri* v. *Konstable Fauziah Mustafa*,[107] the police arrested the plaintiffs, who were lawyers. The High Court held that the plaintiffs' wrongful arrest amounted to an unreasonable denial of access to legal advice and representation.[108]

102 *Interview with 473WB*, *supra* note 20.

103 *Interview with 12J*, *supra* note 20; *Interview with 12M*, *supra* note 20.

104 *Criminal Procedure Code*, *supra* note 27.

105 *SUHAKAM Annual Report 2013* (The Human Rights Commission of Malaysia ('SUHAKAM'), 2013) at 44; *SUHAKAM Annual Report 2015* (SUHAKAM, 2015) at 27; *SUHAKAM Annual Report 2016* (SUHAKAM, 2016) at 51.

106 *Summary Prepared by the Office of the High Commissioner for Human Rights in Accordance with Para. 15(b) of the Annex to Human Rights Council Resolution 5/1 and Para. 5 of the Annex to Council Resolution 16/21 – Malaysia* (United Nations Human Rights Council, 17th Session, Working Group on the Universal Periodic Review, 25 July 2013, A/HRC/WG.6/17/MYS/3) at para. 46.

107 [2015] 10 CLJ 259.

108 Ibid.; see also *Mohammad Shafiq Dollah* v. *Sarjan Mejar Abdul Manaf Jusoh & Yang Lain Dan Satu Kes Lagi* [2013] 2 CLJ 1096.

Second, the right to legal counsel has been weakened by its express exclusion from laws such as SOSMA, POTA, and the PCA, a development which is particularly troubling because the authorities have resorted to these laws to arrest and intimidate human rights defenders and political dissenters. When Maria Chin Abdullah, activist and former chair of Bersih, a coalition for clean and fair elections, and currently a Member of Parliament, was arrested and detained in 2016 pursuant to SOSMA for allegedly receiving funds from the Open Society Foundation to topple the government,[109] she was denied her right to legal counsel until her *habeas corpus* hearing, 10 days after her arrest.[110]

B. Lack of Access to Justice for Women and Non-Malaysians

There are two main areas of concern regarding unmet legal needs among marginalized communities in Malaysia. First, the majority of civil legal aid cases received by the Legal Aid Department consist of Syariah and civil family cases sought by women,[111] and concerns have been raised about the lack of information regarding enforcement of such rulings in the civil courts, and the lack of relevant legal officers to deal with the large number of Syariah family cases received by the Legal Aid Department.[112] Also, indigenous women have limited access to justice due to social and cultural constraints, and they are disadvantaged by native customary law; in an extreme example, for sexual offences, both parties are liable to pay a fine even though the woman was raped.[113] Overall there is generally a lack of publicly available gender-disaggregated data, and this statistical gap impacts the capacity to evaluate and reform women's access to justice.[114]

Second, the Legal Aid Act 1971 was amended in December 2017 to expressly exclude non-Malaysians from receiving free legal advice, with the exception of children accused of offences.[115] This amendment has been criticized as regressive, since the right to legal representation is a right, not a privilege.[116] Although the Bar has been working with embassies to provide their nationals in Malaysia with pro bono services,[117] the state of affairs is far from optimum. BCLAS is the main avenue for foreigners seeking legal assistance, but there are 3.3 million non-citizens currently residing in Malaysia,[118] and the majority are unskilled workers in the construction and plantation sectors[119] and domestic helpers, who are vulnerable to mistreatment and exploitation.

[109] Zurairi AR, 'IGP: Sosma Used on Maria to Counter OSF', *The Malay Mail Online* (23 November 2016), online: www.malaymail.com/news/malaysia/2016/11/23/igp-sosma-used-on-maria-to-counter-osf/1256727.

[110] Surach Gunasekaran, 'Maria Chin Abdullah Detained Under Sosma, 4-Day Remand for Jamal Yunos', *The Sun Daily* (19 November 2016), online: www.thesundaily.my/archive/2066049-NTARCH409350; see also Kamles Kumar, 'Ahead of Tomorrow's Trial, Maria Chin Still Denied Access to Lawyers', *The Malay Mail Online* (28 November 2016), online: www.malaymail.com/news/malaysia/2016/11/28/ahead-of-tomorrows-trial-maria-chin-still-denied-access-to-lawyers/1259983.

[111] About 56 per cent of the legal services for advice and litigation are Syariah civil cases, with divorce cases being the highest, followed by maintenance cases (*kes nafkah*), *Malaysia Millennium Development Goals Report 2015* (United Nations Malaysia, 2016), online: www.my.undp.org/content/malaysia/en/home/library/mdg/malaysia-millennium-development-goals-2015-report-.html#:~:text=The%20Millennium%20Development%20Goals%20Report,over%20the%20past%2015%20years [*MDG Report 2015*]; see also Sisters in Islam, 'Delays in Divorce Cases' (2001), online: https://sistersinislam.org/delays-in-divorce-cases/ [*Delays in Divorce Cases*].

[112] *MDG Report 2015*, *supra* note 111; see also *Delays in Divorce Cases*, *supra* note 111.

[113] *Washing the Tigers – Addressing Discrimination and Inequality* (London: Equal Rights Trust Country Report Series, 2 November 2012) at 95.

[114] *MDG Report 2015*, *supra* note 111, at n 100.

[115] *Legal Aid (Amendment) Act 2017*, *supra* note 56.

[116] Ho Kit Yen, 'We Can't Deny Foreigners Right to Legal Aid, Says Lawyer', *Free Malaysia Today* (12 August 2017).

[117] *Interview with Nekoo*, *supra* note 57.

[118] Department of Statistics Malaysia, *Current Population Estimates, Malaysia, 2016–2017* (2017) at 1.

[119] A. Jalil Hamid, 'Policy Poser Over Foreign Workers', *The New Straits Times* (3 July 2017).

VII. THE WAY FORWARD

A. *A Baseline Study on Criminal Legal Aid*

Many lawyers hail the establishment of NLAF as a success. Some lawyers[120] remarked that since NLAF came into operation, almost 80 per cent of those remanded are now legally represented, particularly those charged in the lower courts. Also, some lawyers observed that magistrates are postponing cases if accused persons do not have legal representation and advising unrepresented accused persons to contact NLAF for legal representation.[121]

Apart from such anecdotal evidence and the general statistics enumerated above, there are no available empirical data on the degree of representation from entities such as the Legal Aid Department, NLAF, the Court-assigned Counsel scheme, or BCLAS. This gap in empirical data presents a concern, as it would be difficult to measure whether these schemes have helped accused persons to access the court system for legal remedies and whether NLAF has improved criminal legal aid, or if there continue to be barriers faced by indigent clients in accessing available criminal legal aid and pro bono schemes. The dearth of empirical data means that any recommendation for improvement lacks thorough analysis and could be misdirected. A baseline study of criminal legal aid in Malaysia could provide a disaggregated data and information base, which multiple stakeholders could use to better understand, monitor, and assess the effectiveness of criminal legal aid and pro bono services, and to identify areas where Malaysia can do better in terms of the constitutional right to legal counsel. It may be that the data needed for this baseline already exist, and if this is the case, such data and information should be made public, to assess whether it requires supplementation.

B. *Reform Civil Legal Aid*

The *Orang Asli*, indigenous peoples in Peninsula Malaysia, and the *Bumiputeras* in Sabah and Sarawak have the highest poverty rates amongst all the ethnic groups in Malaysia, at 34%, 20.2%, and 7.3%, respectively.[122] If Malaysia is serious about meeting the legal needs of marginalized communities in Malaysia, it is important not only for civil legal aid to undergo a thorough reform but also to ensure that the reform process is open and participatory. Therefore, it is recommended that an ad hoc committee composed of cross-sectional representatives should be established, including the government, members of the Bar, and the judiciary. Feedback from the legal community and the public should also be sought. The desired outcomes of the committee should be first, to ensure that civil legal assistance is provided to the lower-income sectors of society including non-Malaysians so that they are able to gain access to justice, including exploration of whether legal fees are too onerous for middle-class Malaysians. Second, this committee should ensure that funding for civil legal aid corresponds to social injustices faced by Malaysians, which could mean increased funding for Syariah divorce matters and enlarging legal services to domestic violence cases, human trafficking, and the like.

[120] *Interview with Varughese*, *supra* note 61; Boo Su-Lyn, 'Ex-AG Gani Now a Private Lawyer', *The Malay Mail Online* (23 December 2016).

[121] Samantha Chong, 'Pro Bono Culture Development in Malaysia: The Historical Foundation, Current Diverse Climate' (Speech delivered at the 6th Pro Bono Conference, Kuala Lumpur, 30 September 2017).

[122] Malaysia, Economic Planning Unit, *Eleventh Malaysia Plan (2016–2020), Strategy Paper 2: Elevating B40 Households Towards a Middle-Class Society*, at Exhibit 2-7, Incidence of Poverty Amongst Ethnic Groups, 2009 and 2014.

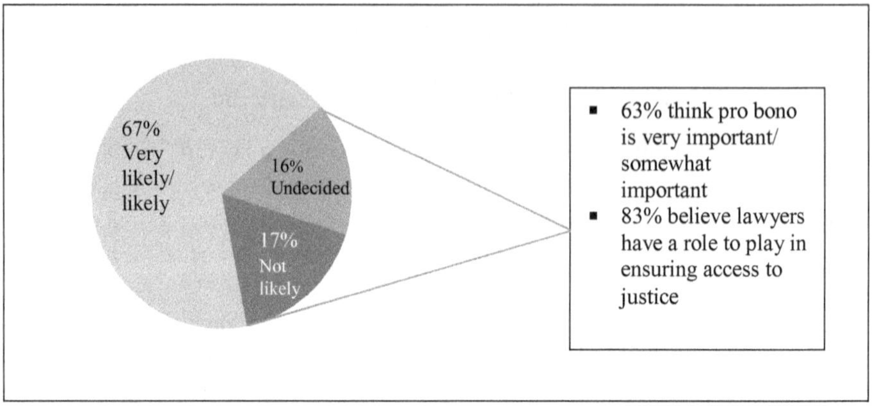

FIGURE 6.4. Likelihood of providing pro bono

C. *Strengthen Pro Bono Culture Amongst Lawyers*

Pro bono culture amongst Malaysian lawyers is relatively unimpressive, and most lawyers assert that lawyering is foremost a business.[123] Nonetheless, it is believed that most lawyers genuinely would like to give back to society (Figure 6.4 above).[124]

Also, although most lawyers who responded to the survey cited the lack of time as a discouraging factor, 61 per cent still found time to do it. For lawyers who reported not having done any pro bono work, the discouraging factors they identified, such as the lack of skills or experience, lack of time, scheduling conflicts, and lack of support by their firm or employer, could be remedied. Although the impetus to take up pro bono work could start from the individual lawyer, the Malaysian Bar could help to create an enabling environment so that more lawyers come forward to help the less fortunate. Possible schemes include the following.

1. Structured Mentorship

One of the top three factors that lawyers identified as something that could encourage them to be more involved in pro bono work was mentorship and/or supervision (63%). Many lawyers believed that guidance from senior lawyers would make pro bono work less daunting. Training for NLAF and BCLAS already exists, and the Bar could consider expanding these programmes. One mentorship programme that the Bar could look at is the structured and institutionalized mentoring and training[125] system that was implemented in the Enhanced Criminal Legal Aid Scheme ('CLAS') in Singapore. Apart from the usual team of a junior lawyer and a senior lawyer, Enhanced CLAS allows law firms to pay their legal associates a salary and second them to the Pro Bono Services Office on a full-time basis for one year, to work exclusively on CLAS cases and receive extensive training and mentorship.[126]

[123] *Interview with 100S*, *supra* note 97; *Interview with 1592S* (7 August 2017, Kuala Lumpur); *Interview with 594P* (24 July 2017, Kuala Lumpur); Interview with 395EV (20 September 2017, Kuala Lumpur); *Interview with 70J* (27 July 2017, Kuala Lumpur); *Interview with 12J*, *supra* note 20.

[124] *Interviews with Lawyers*, *supra* note 14.

[125] This recommendation is inspired by feedback from some lawyers who stated that they felt equipped to handle the pro bono work because they received training from NLAF or because they benefited from the guidance of senior lawyers or their employers.

[126] Singapore, Ministry of Law, *Enhanced Criminal Legal Aid Scheme Set to Provide Greater Access to Justice* (19 May 2015), online: www.mlaw.gov.sg/news/press-releases/enhanced-clas-to-provide-greater-access-to-justice.

2. Continuing Professional Development ('CPD') Points for NLAF and Other Pro Bono Work

One way to get more lawyers on board is mandatory pro bono. The findings of the survey showed that about half (52%) felt that it was time for the Bar to make pro bono compulsory, and younger lawyers who had just begun practice (57%) and women (59%) were most in favour of this proposition. Interviews produced similar findings, and young lawyers were more in favour of mandatory pro bono.

Senior lawyers believed that making pro bono mandatory would be ineffective for a number of reasons. Many felt that pro bono work should be driven by a genuine desire to help the less fortunate, that a resolution making it mandatory might not be well received by members of the Bar, and that compelling lawyers could negatively affect pro bono clients and access to justice. These senior lawyers felt that instead of mandatory pro bono, providing incentives such as awarding CPD points would be a more pragmatic solution. At the moment, one CPD point is awarded per completed LAC file (limited to one file per lawyer) and lawyers can accumulate a total of seven CPD points per CPD cycle (24 months) from BCLAS work.[127] No CPD points are awarded for NLAF files.

For now and until the Bar is able to obtain more feedback from its members regarding whether they are ready to accept mandatory pro bono or incentivize pro bono work, it is recommended that the Bar award CPD points to lawyers who volunteer with NLAF, any BCLAS activity such as law awareness week, or any pro bono work that entails active legal intervention. It is also recommended that more CPD points be awarded per LAC file, without any limit for CPD cycle.

3. Compulsory Reporting for Law Firms

The influence and control that employers and law firms wield over their lawyers' pro bono work is undeniable. Both the survey and the interviews suggested that employer or law firm support was a contributing factor in a lawyer's participation in pro bono, and that one of the top three factors that encourages all lawyers to take up pro bono work regardless of seniority was more support from their employers and/or firms. The type of support lawyers desired included express and clear encouragement that lawyers are allowed to do pro bono work, and talking more about pro bono.[128] It was also observed that for lawyers engaged in pro bono work, most of their employers or firms expressly encouraged pro bono work or assigned pro bono work to these lawyers. Firm support is imperative to lawyer engagement with access to justice, and it is timely that law firms lend their support in shaping a supportive culture in Malaysia. A number of jurisdictions have implemented a mandatory pro bono reporting requirement,[129] and in view of the impact that law firms have on pro bono, it is suggested that the Bar impose mandatory reporting for all law firms for:

- The number of pro bono hours carried out per year, with no penalties for law firms which do not carry out any pro bono work; and
- The ways in which pro bono is encouraged by law firms.

[127] *CPD Guidelines: Computation Table for the CPD Scheme* (Malaysian Bar, 2014), online: www.malaysianbar.org.my/cpd/wp-content/uploads/2013/08/CPD-Scheme-CPD-Guidelines_V4-20-06-2014.pdf.

[128] *Interviews with Lawyers, supra* note 14.

[129] See e.g. the *Legal Profession Act* (2009 Rev. Edn), Singapore 2009 (as amended 30 July 2020); *Legal Profession (Mandatory Reporting of Specified Pro Bono Services) Rules 2015*, Singapore 2015 (1 March 2015); and see *Pro Bono Reporting* (American Bar Association, 2020), online: www.americanbar.org/groups/probono_public_service/policy/arguments/.

4. Introspection of BCLAS

With a large proportion of criminal legal aid work being embraced by NLAF, an area that used to be the domain of BCLAS, there is an opportunity for BCLAS to expand to civil pro bono matters. It is recommended that the Bar undertake research on the civil legal needs of low and middle-income Malaysians. The scope of this research should identify the civil legal needs of Malaysians, assess whether these needs are being met by BCLAS, and consider how to redesign BCLAS to meet any gaps.

In addition to these longer-term goals, there are some quicker solutions in the form of countering a number of assumptions made by lawyers about BCLAS that appear to hinder participation in their pro bono projects. These assumptions include the view that, compared to other matters, criminal legal aid/pro bono cases are more challenging, unsafe, or unsuitable for women lawyers, or that BCLAS is the domain of criminal lawyers or litigators only. It is recommended that the Bar implement outreach programmes in the following areas:

- Equality and non-discrimination, including how to litigate non-discrimination cases;
- The exact work involved in urgent arrest and monitoring teams, so that lawyers know what is expected of them and that the work involved is not intimidating;
- How to deal with any safety or harassment issues in criminal legal aid or pro bono work, particularly for female lawyers;
- The opportunities available for civil lawyers to contribute their time and expertise, including participation in Law Awareness Week initiatives organized by BCLAS, where booths are set up in malls for lawyers to provide free legal advice on civil matters, as lawyers may find these smaller commitments more acceptable;
- The role of lawyers in access to justice, the impact of pro bono work, and the professional benefits of pro bono work.

VIII. CONCLUSION

Malaysia has had the foundation for legal aid and pro bono in place for a while, and it has resulted in participation in access to justice by different actors via different schemes. However, it is evident that there is a great deal more that Malaysia should and can achieve. The time is apt for more dynamic improvements in this area to institutionalize access to justice, requiring the maximum effort from the government, the Bar, law firms, and employers, and leadership at every level. First, as a start, there must be a change of attitudes and conduct in terms of pro bono and legal aid. As much as legal aid is the primary responsibility of the government, pro bono work should also be an integral part of being a lawyer. Second, legal professionals must not be lulled into convincing themselves that the current schemes are adequate. Instead, they must be willing to be their own biggest critics, so that the most vulnerable sectors of society are able to seek justice. Finally, Malaysia must not settle for mere middling changes – a progressive approach toward reforming legal aid and pro bono requires reconfiguration of current norms and processes. Malaysia should grow accustomed to a reform process that is based on thorough analysis of the legal aid and pro bono schemes, the use of disaggregated data, having open and transparent consultation with the public and stakeholders, and the commitment to listen to those currently excluded from access to justice.

APPENDIX 6.1 SURVEY: 'LAWYERS AND ACCESS TO JUSTICE: CHALLENGING PRO BONO IN MALAYSIA'

1. Please note that this survey is only for lawyers who are members of the Malaysian Bar. Your participation in this Research Project is voluntary and you are free to withdraw from this survey at any time without giving any reason. Please note that because your data is anonymous, once you complete this survey and submit your questionnaire, we are not able to identify your data so the data cannot be withdrawn. However, we will protect your anonymity. Please also note that the non-identifiable data from this survey will be used for the Research Project and will be published. By clicking the 'agree' button below, you indicate that you understand the above and agree to take part in this survey. You understand that once you click 'submit' at the end of the questionnaire, it will not be possible to withdraw the data. * *Mark only one oval.*
   - Agree
   - Disagree

Member of the Bar

2. Have you been called to the Bar? * *Mark only one oval.*
   - No
   - Yes *Skip to question 3*

Thank you for your time. This survey is only for members of the Bar

Personal Background

3. Gender * *Mark only one oval.*
   - Female
   - Male
   - Other
4. Age range * *Mark only one oval.*
   - 21–30 years old
   - 31–40 years old
   - 41–50 years old
   - 51–60 years old
   - 61–70 years old
   - 70 years old and above
5. Number of years in practice * *Mark only one oval.*
   - 1–3 years
   - 3–5 years
   - 5–7 years
   - 7–10 years
   - Above 10 years
6. Which state bar are you from? * *Mark only one oval.*
   - Johor
   - Kedah
   - Kelantan

- Kuala Lumpur
- Malacca
- Negeri Sembilan
- Pahang
- Penang
- Perak
- Perlis
- Selangor
- Terengganu

7. Did your university promote/encourage you to participate in pro bono work? **Mark only one oval.*
   - Yes
   - No
   - I don't know
   - Other:

Participation in pro bono work

For the purposes of Questions in this section, 'you' refers to both your personal capacity and/or your capacity working on pro bono cases of your firm/employer/team.

8. Do you assist or participate in any pro bono legal work (for example, Bar's legal aid clinic, Yayasan Bantuan Guaman Kebangsaan ('YBGK'), Court-appointed counsel, your firm's/ employer's pro bono cases, or volunteering at NGOs involved in social/human rights causes)? **Mark only one oval.*
   - Yes
   - No *Skip to question 16*
9. How do you get your pro bono work? (You can select more than one answer) * *Check all that apply.*
   - Actively seek out legal aid cases
   - Cases referred to by friend/family/organization/etc.
   - Actively seek out volunteer work at an NGO
   - Friend introduced me to NGO volunteer work
   - Other:
10. Why do you take up pro bono work? (You can select more than one answer) * *Check all that apply.*
    - Help people in need
    - Professional duty
    - Want to feel like a good person
    - Help the Bar's public image
    - Gain new professional experience/opportunities
    - Make new friends/networking
    - Instructed by firm/employer
    - Other:

11. Which pro bono work are you involved in? (You can select more than one answer) * *Check all that apply.*
    - Court-appointed counsel
    - YBGK (Yayasan Bantuan Guaman Kebangsaan)
    - Bar's Legal Aid centre
    - Pro bono cases taken up by my firm
    - Volunteering my time at an NGO involved in social/human rights causes
    - None of the above
    - Other:
12. On average, how many pro bono cases do you take up in a year? * *Mark only one oval.*
    - 1–5
    - 5–10
    - More than 10
13. How many days a year do you spend working on your pro bono cases or pro bono work? * *Mark only one oval.*
    - 1–5 days
    - 6–10 days
    - More than 10 days
14. What area of law are your pro bono cases? (You can select more than one answer) **Check all that apply.*
    - Civil matters
    - Criminal matters
    - Syariah civil matters
    - Syariah criminal matters
    - Capital cases
    - Other:
15. What type of legal tasks do you perform in your pro bono cases? (You can select more than one answer) * *Check all that apply.*
    - Provide advice
    - Review/draft documents
    - Interview/meet with the client
    - Write a letter/communicate with the other party's lawyer/relevant parties
    - Represent the client in court
    - Refer to other organization(s)
    - Represent the client in administrative proceedings
    - Other:

Views on pro bono

16. Do you know that there is a legal aid centre in every State Bar? * *Mark only one oval.*
    - Yes
    - No
    - I just found out

17. Which of the following best describes the term 'pro bono' to you? (You can select more than one answer) * *Check all that apply.*
    - YBGK
    - Bar's Legal Aid Clinic
    - Volunteering time at an NGO
    - Court-appointed counsel
    - Providing free legal advice to a friend/relative
    - Conducting research for an NGO
    - Providing funding for a case
    - Other:
18. Are you aware that the Legal Profession Act 1976 obligates the Bar to ensure that poor persons are represented by lawyers? **Mark only one oval.*
    - Yes
    - No
19. Do you personally believe that as a lawyer, you have a role to play in ensuring access to justice for all including the poor? * *Mark only one oval.*
    - Yes
    - No
20. Do you think that pro bono work is important to you as a lawyer? * *Mark only one oval.*
    - Very important
    - Somewhat important
    - Unimportant
    - Undecided
    - None of the above
21. What factors (if any) discourage you from participating in pro bono work? (You can select more than one answer) **Check all that apply.*
    - Lack of time
    - Not interested
    - Not aware of where to get pro bono work
    - Lack of skills or experience
    - Firm does not support
    - Scheduling conflicts
    - Need to complete billable hours at firm
    - Discouragement from employer
    - Personal/philosophical objections
    - Other:
22. Does your law firm/employer actively encourage their lawyers to take up pro bono work? * *Mark only one oval.*
    - Yes
    - No
23. Is it mandatory in your law firm for you to participate in pro bono work? * *Mark only one oval.*
    - Yes
    - No

24. If yes, how, in what ways?

---

25. Does your law firm fix an allocated budget or targets solely for the purpose of pro bono work? * *Mark only one oval.*
    - Yes
    - No
    - I don't know
26. Does your law firm credit your pro bono hours toward your minimum billing requirement? * *Mark only one oval.*
    - Yes
    - No
    - I don't know

The future of pro bono work in Malaysia

27. Should it be mandatory for lawyers to take up pro bono work? * *Mark only one oval.*
    - Yes
    - No
28. If it is mandatory to do pro bono work, in your opinion, how many days per year should a lawyer spend on pro bono work? * *Mark only one oval.*
    - 1–5 days
    - 6–10 days
    - More than 10 days
29. If pro bono work was made mandatory, but you could satisfy your obligations by donating either your time or money, what would you choose to contribute? * *Mark only one oval.*
    - Time
    - Money
    - Other:
30. Why?

---

31. What do you think would encourage you to take up pro bono cases? (You can select more than one answer) * *Check all that apply.*
    - Formal recognition of my efforts
    - More support from my employer
    - Mentorship/supervision by another lawyer
    - More monetary compensation
    - Administrative support
    - Online description of cases from which I could choose
    - CPD points for doing pro bono work
    - Personal recommendation by my friends/family
    - Making it mandatory

32. Would you like to see a more diverse legal aid programme, besides what is already available? **Mark only one oval.*
    - Yes
    - No
33. How?

---

34. Does pro bono work benefit your career in any way? * *Mark only one oval.*
    - Yes
    - No
35. If yes, how so?

---

36. What is the likelihood of you taking up pro bono cases next year? * *Mark only one oval.*
    - Very likely
    - Likely
    - Not Likely
    - Undecided

    Thank you for your time!
37. Please enter your email address if you would like to us to interview you for the Research Project as part of its qualitative survey.

7

Political Lawyers and the Legal Occupation in Myanmar

Alice Dawkins and Nick Cheesman*

Abstract

Following a coup in 1962, the legal sector in Myanmar, then Burma, went into a protracted and steep decline. The practice of law fell from its earlier high status to that of a hobby or amateurish pursuit. The legal profession transformed into what this chapter characterizes as a legal occupation: legal education degenerated, the national bar association lost autonomy, and lawyers daring to challenge state power were met with strict sanctions. Myanmar's opening up in the 2010s has brought international attention to its legal occupation as well as questions of access to justice and the rule of law. Drawing on in-depth cumulative research of almost a decade from 2008 to 2017, in this chapter we present findings which suggest that having weathered decades of military dictatorship under which even the assertion of minimal legal rights brought parties into conflict with the state, lawyers in the 2010s found both the wherewithal and the desire to refashion the legal sector in Myanmar. Following the work of Lucien Karpik and his co-authors, we class our subjects of inquiry as 'political lawyers', insofar as they mobilize for basic legal freedoms as well as civil and political rights by drawing on an array of material and social resources.

I. INTRODUCTION

Following a coup in 1962, the legal sector in Myanmar, then Burma, went into a protracted and steep decline. The practice of law fell from its earlier high status to that of a hobby or amateurish pursuit. Under successive military and military-controlled governments, legal education degenerated. The national bar association lost its autonomy. Lawyers who dared to challenge state power met with sanctions ranging from suspension of licence to imprisonment.

* The first author's fieldwork in Myanmar was funded by the Australian Government's New Colombo Plan scholarships. The author would like to thank the Tharthi Myay Foundation for generous assistance in locating interlocutors and providing insights from which this chapter has greatly benefited. Special thanks to Zunetta Herbert, Melissa Crouch, and Nyi Nyi Kyaw for their generosity of time and spirit, reading and commenting on this chapter; and to Helena Whalen-Bridge for inviting this contribution and for her work as editor of the volume. Readers should note that this chapter was written prior to the military coup in February 2021 that removed from office the government of the National League for Democracy, and it addresses the experiences of lawyers and lawyering in the period of the two semi-civilian legislatures of the 2010s. The chapter does not address those practices subsequent to the coup, which occurred as this book was going to press and that will call for further research in years to come.

In the mid-2000s, and especially in the 2010s, the situation changed rapidly. Myanmar's political opening up brought with it an influx of international donors and their hired hands, with broad goals 'to increase legal literacy, access to justice, and the participation of marginalized populations' in legal processes.[1] New studies documented conditions in increasing detail, and recommended a variety of changes in the delivery of legal services and management of courts.[2]

Some consultants and legal experts from abroad characterize Myanmar lawyers as lacking 'basic skills, tools to do their jobs, and capacity to absorb outside help', and conclude that the state of legal practice in Myanmar is 'truly dismal'.[3] Others concur that lawyers' 'legal skills are minimal; their substantive legal knowledge woefully deficient'.[4] Still others presume that lawyers are working in conditions that are devoid of law, where neither lawyers nor judges have the knowledge or aptitude to build coherent legal institutions, and that only the integration of international standards and experiences, as in other parts of South East Asia, will allow the legal sector to evolve.[5]

Undoubtedly, lawyering in Myanmar has seen better days. But contra these rather pessimistic and sometimes self-absorbed readings of the situation, the findings we present in this chapter, based on in-depth cumulative research of almost a decade, from 2008 to 2017, reveal that having weathered decades of military dictatorship, under which even the assertion of minimal legal rights brought parties into conflict with the state, lawyers in the 2010s found both the wherewithal and desire to refashion the legal sector in Myanmar. The findings are consistent with Frank Munger's observation of Thailand, based on a review of scholarship into forces that draw lawyers into different kinds of activism around the world, that 'the seemingly limited overall prospects for law in opposing the state may not tell the whole story of the production of legal advocacy'.[6] Bemoaning inadequate legal education or evoking the absence of law does not get us very far in assessing lawyers' part in access to justice in Myanmar. Deeper inquiry into what motivates these lawyers to act and why just might. This chapter is one step, among others, in that direction.

Following the work of Lucien Karpik and his co-authors, we propose to class our subjects of inquiry, Myanmar lawyers working in different contexts, as political lawyers, insofar as they

[1] United States Agency for International Development, *Promoting the Rule of Law Project* (Quarterly Report No. 13, 2016) at 8.

[2] Some recommended studies include: *Behind Closed Doors: Obstacles and Opportunities for Public Access to Myanmar's Courts* (Justice Base, June 2017), online: www.myjusticemyanmar.org/sites/default/files/Justice-Base-Behind-Closed-Doors.compressed-1.pdf; *Monitoring in Myanmar: An Analysis of Myanmar's Compliance with Fair Trial Rights* (Justice Base, October 2017), online: www.myjusticemyanmar.org/monitoring-myanmar-analysis-myanmar%E2%80%99s-compliance-fair-trial-rights; *Right to Counsel: The Independence of Lawyers in Myanmar* (International Commission of Jurists, November 2013), online: www.refworld.org/docid/530f07694.html. All three reports, and most others cited in this chapter, are available on the Online Burma Library website, online: www.burmalibrary.org.

[3] *Myanmar Rule of Law Assessment* (DLA Piper New Perimeter, Perseus Strategies, and Jacob Blaustein Institute for the Advancement of Human Rights, 2013) at 35.

[4] *Emerging Faces: Lawyers in Myanmar* (International Legal Assistance Consortium, and the Central and Eastern European Law Initiative Institute, 2014) at 5.

[5] Arm Tungnirun, 'Practising on the Moon: Globalization and Legal Consciousness of Foreign Corporate Lawyers in Myanmar' (2017) 5 *Asian Journal of Legal Studies* 49 at 51. Tungnirun distinguishes newcomers from 'old hands', namely, a small cohort of foreign legal advisors who have worked in the country since the 1990s. The latter's views are closer to our own, as they recognize the contingency and density of legal practice in Myanmar.

[6] Frank W. Munger, 'Globalization, Investing in Law, and the Careers of Lawyers for Social Causes: Taking on Rights in Thailand' (2008–9) 53 *New York Law School Review* 745 at 756.

mobilize for civil and political rights and basic legal freedoms by drawing on an array of material and social resources.[7] The members of this category concentrate on political issues that relate 'to the central and old conflict between the state and civil society where basic freedoms have to be established, defended or restored'.[8] Political lawyers are, like cause lawyers, activists. But in contrast to cause lawyers, who frequently need to advocate for the moral urgency of their issues and lobby for public support, political lawyers' defence of fundamental individual rights is taken to be self-evident. It is not niche work. They do not need to convince people of its merits. They are there 'because basic freedoms have to be established'.[9]

Myanmar is certainly a country where this statement holds. And yet, while political lawyering is at one level a useful category for our inquiry, it quickly encounters empirical obstacles when applied to our observations of lawyering there. Lawyers in contemporary Myanmar are neither as bounded nor as clearly identifiable, in our view, as the category of political lawyering would have them be. For historical and contextual reasons that we spell out in the pages that follow, political lawyering in Myanmar strikes us as being more nebulous, more inchoate, than the extant literature suggests. Does this make its practitioners more akin to cause lawyers than political lawyers? Or does it make them less 'political' lawyers than Karpik would have it? We do not think so. Rather, we think that one of the things about Myanmar that makes it an interesting case study is how lawyering there forces us to rethink established categories of access to justice and legal activism, in particular, the categories of both political and cause lawyering.

Whereas Karpik and his co-authors envisage the professional bar as influencing political lawyers' collective identity and activism, in Myanmar we find that while political lawyers do have, like their counterparts elsewhere, a shared sense of collective *identity*, and that cumulatively their work contributes to institution building for legal and judicial autonomy in response to public demands,[10] they locate resources and build identities in more fragmented location- and politics-specific communities. They do so as a consequence of the conditions in which they work, as they confront heavy residual structural constraints following decades of military dictatorship. Consistent with Melissa Crouch's observations of activist lawyers in Indonesia, we find that political lawyers in Myanmar have been motivated to mobilize for basic freedoms during or subsequent to critical junctures *despite* their lacking a unified and universal legal professional body or bar association.[11]

For these reasons, rather than talk of the community of legal practitioners in Myanmar today as a *profession*, we designate it an *occupation*. According to Sida Liu, an occupation becomes a profession 'only if it goes through a series of structural changes, such as the establishment of licensing, professional education, professional association, and code of ethics'.[12] Military

7 Lucien Karpik, 'Postscript: Political Lawyers' in Terence C. Halliday, Lucien Karpik, and Malcolm M. Feeley, eds., *Fighting for Political Freedom: Comparative Studies of the Legal Complex and Political Liberalism* (Oxford: Hart Publishing, 2007) [*Political Lawyers*].

8 *Political Lawyers*, *supra* note 7, at 491.

9 *Political Lawyers*, *supra* note 7, at 493.

10 See Terence C. Halliday and Lucien Karpik, 'Political Lawyering' in Neil Smelser and Paul Baltes, eds., *International Encyclopedia of the Social and Behavioral Sciences* (Amsterdam: Elsevier, 2001) at 11673 [*Political Lawyering*].

11 Melissa Crouch, 'Cause Lawyering, the Legal Profession and the Courts in Indonesia: The Bar Association Controversy' (2011) *LawASIA Journal* 63.

12 Sida Liu, 'Professional Ecologies' in William C. Cockerham et al., eds., *The Wiley Blackwell Encyclopedia of Health, Illness, Behaviour and Society* (New Jersey: Wiley-Blackwell, 2014) at 1892–5.

dictatorship stripped many of these characteristics from lawyering in Myanmar, and it co-opted those aspects of the profession it did not destroy.

By designating lawyering in Myanmar as occupational rather than professional, we are pointing to important differences in the conditions in which lawyers work there. These give rise to different logics of practice. The purpose of the designation is not to imply relations of inferiority. Rather, it is to help us explain how and why lawyers in Myanmar mobilize in ways that differ from their counterparts discussed in most other chapters in this volume. Occupational conditions call for different kinds of practices to establish basic freedoms compared to professional conditions. Indeed, among the most fundamental concerns of lawyers in Myanmar is that they obtain autonomy through growing professionalism – in our interpretation, by collectively moving the practice of law, or rather, the status of practice, from occupation to profession.

The chapter is organized in two sections, as follows. Section I provides an overview of the legal occupation in Myanmar. In three subsections, it briefly sets the scene for the changes of the 2010s, sketching conditions of legal education and training, and further explicating the category of the political lawyer in Myanmar. This section of the chapter is informed by research undertaken by each of the authors, the second author from 2008 to 2015, and the first author in 2016 and 2017.

Section II of the chapter introduces new empirical data on lawyering in Myanmar, from research by the first author from December 2016 until September 2017, across three field sites: Yangon, the commercial hub and former capital, adjacent to the Bay of Bengal; Pyay, a provincial capital in the agricultural heartland; and Myitkyina, the capital of restive Kachin State, in the north of the country near the border with China. The core of the data comprises material generated from semi-structured interviews in Burmese and English with 15 qualified lawyers.[13] The interviews ran for a minimum of 30 minutes to sometimes several hours.[14] Material generated in discussions with approximately 30 other lawyers, and participant observation in 12 law offices and at Yangon University, supplements the interview data.

Data generation followed a purposive method of targeted interview participant recruitment through chains of contacts from the Tharthi Myay Foundation as well as associates of the Myanmar Lawyers Network. Because of the manner in which the data were generated, and because of the smallness of the interview set, we do not intend it to be read as a representative sample of political lawyering in Myanmar.[15] Nevertheless, we do think that it casts light on some salient features of lawyering relevant to our discussion of how lawyers pursue access to justice there. Furthermore, some of these features are more brightly illuminated through this method of sampling than through other modes of inquiry, since the manner of data generation is heavily dependent on, and partakes in, the dynamics of the very participants' networks in which we are interested.[16] Among those features that recurred in conversations and observations are the influence of family support and legal mentorship, collective if diverse responses to critical junctures, and boundary blurring and crossing. We address each one of these features in turn

[13] See Appendix for tabulated details of the interviewees.

[14] Interviews were conducted in accordance with an Australian National University Human Research Ethics Committee Protocol (2016/640). All participants gave oral consent for use of their comments.

[15] We are grateful to Melissa Crouch for prompting us to clarify this aspect of our project.

[16] Chaim Noy, 'Sampling Knowledge: The Hermeneutics of Snowball Sampling in Qualitative Research' (2008) 11:4 *International Journal of Social Research Methodology* 327.

before concluding the chapter by revisiting the occupational character of lawyering in Myanmar over the 2000s and 2010s, and the logics of political lawyering in the conditions we describe.

A. *The Legal Occupation in Myanmar*

1. From Profession to Occupation

The legal profession had considerable status in the late colonial period, prior to Burma's independence in 1948, much of which carried over into the early postcolonial period.[17] As in other British postcolonies, legal practice not only brought with it opportunities for a good living but also carried a high degree of political and social capital.[18] Despite the country's calamitous economic conditions, fractious politics, and civil war, lawyers, as well as politicians, bureaucrats, and businesspeople with legal training, continued to situate themselves at the forefront of Burma's national affairs throughout the 1950s.

Things changed after a definitive military takeover in 1962, which followed an earlier period of interim military rule. A junta headed by the army commander, General Ne Win, detained the chief justice and consolidated the two superior courts into a single apex court. Ne Win subsequently catapulted his civilian right-hand man and legal ideologue, Dr Maung Maung, into the court.[19] The new justice, subsequently chief justice, reoriented the courts toward regime policy objectives, and began work on a new assemblage of courts that would implement rather than question executive prerogatives.

In 1972, panels of lay judges began to replace the professional judiciary. From the establishment of a one-party legislature in 1974 until regime collapse under the weight of nationwide protests in 1988, judicial and executive functions were formally integrated in a horizontal fashion at all levels of government. Party policy overrode legal considerations.

Although private lawyering was not prohibited, as in some other one-party states, the fortunes of Burma's lawyers plummeted.[20] By the 1970s the pursuit of law lacked the cachet it had once had. A licence to practise law no longer carried the promise of prosperous living, nor did it accrue any special respect. Senior lawyers retired or were pressured out, taking with them the professional habits and knowledge of earlier periods.

[17] The scholarship on law and lawyers in this period is well established and we do not retread its ground here. Some recommended English-language sources include: Nick Cheesman, *Opposing the Rule of Law: How Myanmar's Courts Make Law and Order* (Cambridge: Cambridge University Press, 2015) [*Rule of Law*] at ch 2–3; Melissa Crouch, 'The Layers of Legal Development in Myanmar' in Melissa Crouch and Tim Lindsey, eds., *Law, Society and Transition in Myanmar* (Oxford: Hart Publishing, 2014); Maung Maung, *Law and Custom in Burma and the Burmese Family* (Dordrecht: Springer Netherlands, 1963); Myint Zan, 'Judicial Independence in Burma: No March Backwards Towards the Past' (2000) 1:5 *Asian-Pacific Law & Policy Journal* 1; Jonathan Saha, *Law, Disorder and the Colonial State: Corruption in Burma, c. 1900* (London: Palgrave Macmillan, 2013). For a range of available sources on law and legality in Myanmar, past and present, see Melissa Crouch, 'Rediscovering "Law" in Myanmar: A Review of Scholarship on the Legal System of Myanmar' (2014) 23:3 *Pacific Rim Law & Policy Journal* 543; Melissa Crouch and Nick Cheesman, 'A Short Research Guide to Myanmar's Legal System' in Melissa Crouch and Tim Lindsey, eds., *Law, Society and Transition in Myanmar* (Oxford: Hart Publishing, 2014).

[18] For a general comparative discussion of elite lawyers in colonial and postcolonial Asia see Yves Dezalay and Bryant G. Garth, *Asian Legal Revivals: Lawyers in the Shadow of Empire* (Chicago: University of Chicago Press, 2010).

[19] For a lengthier discussion of events in this period see Nick Cheesman, 'How an Authoritarian Regime in Burma Used Special Courts to Defeat Judicial Independence' (2011) 45:4 *Law & Society Review* 801.

[20] See Nick Cheesman and Kyaw Min San, 'Not Just Defending; Advocating for Law in Myanmar' (2014) 31:3 *Wisconsin International Law Journal* 702 [*Not Just Defending*].

After the one-party government collapsed and a new junta massacred protestors and forced its way into power in 1988, it shut down the people's courts and replaced them with a new judiciary drawn from the numbers of judicial bureaucrats. Courts were now again arrayed hierarchically under the apex court, itself answerable to the military. The junta amended the Bar Council Act to remove from lawyers the remnants of their autonomy, putting the Bar Council under the authority of the Attorney General and the Supreme Court.[21]

The military's aggrandizement of power created the terrain on which Myanmar's lawyers practised, and the boundaries between legal and political action became increasingly blurred. In some areas, such as the defence of alleged public enemies,[22] they disappeared entirely. However, the blurring and erasure of boundaries did not immediately foster a generation of lawyers ready to advocate for basic freedoms in their working lives. It was not until limited economic and social changes in the 2000s, followed by more significant events in the late 2000s, that more talented youth entered the occupation, and more lawyers mobilized in an increasingly concerted effort for the defence of basic freedoms.

B. *Legal Education, Training, and Licensing*

University students have been key participants in every step of Myanmar's turbulent political history. Rangoon – now Yangon – University was a hub for the nationalist movement during the late British colonial period.[23] Students shot to political prominence with a strike in 1936. They participated actively in national affairs throughout the 1940s and 50s, launched major strikes against the government in 1953–4,[24] and were the first to protest against the military takeover in 1962. In 1974, students abducted the body of the deceased former secretary general of the United Nations, U Thant, from where it had been put on display, and built a temporary mausoleum in the Rangoon University campus. The standoff with state security forces lasted for days until it was again put down with violence.[25] In 1988, students took the lead in the nationwide protests that precipitated the downfall of one-party government.[26] And they were at the centre of protests against the military coup in 2021 as well.

From the colonial period onwards, successive governments sought to contain student protests through structural changes to campuses, classes, and pedagogy. Nevertheless, throughout the 1950s, legal curricula and postgraduate training bore a strong resemblance to colonial antecedents. Students at Rangoon University studied core legal subjects that were similar to those of their counterparts in other former British colonial jurisdictions. They completed a chamber student period taken after graduation but prior to admission, like the articled clerk process in British postcolonial and late settler colonial jurisdictions elsewhere.[27]

[21] *SLORC Law 22/1989 – The Law Amending the Bar Council Act*, Myanmar (31 August 1989).

[22] See *Rule of Law*, *supra* note 17, at ch 4.

[23] See Josef Silverstein and Julian Wohl, 'University Students and Politics in Burma' (1964) 37:1 *Pacific Affairs* 50.

[24] See Nick Cheesman, 'Las Cuatro Décadas de Lucha Interna en Birmania' (Burma's Four Decades of Struggle Within) in Pedro Iacobelli, Robert Cribb, and Juan Luis Perelló, eds., *Asia y el Pacífico Durante la Guerra Fría* (Mexico City: Fondo de Cultura Económica, 2017) 209 at 209.

[25] For an eyewitness account of these events see Andrew Selth, *Death of a Hero: The U Thant Disturbances in Burma, December 1974* (Queensland: Griffith University, 1989).

[26] See generally, Bertil Lintner, *Outrage: Burma's Struggle for Democracy*, 2nd edn (Banglamung: White Lotus, 1990).

[27] See Maung Maung, 'Lawyers and Legal Education in Burma' (1962) 11:1 *International and Comparative Law Quarterly* 285.

Beginning in 1964 and again after the protests of 1988, military juntas split up campuses into smaller and smaller units, dispersing students so as to prevent gatherings that could quickly swell to a point at which they might pose a political threat. Both in the mid-1970s and early 1990s – and now again in the early 2020s – the university campuses were subject to constant, arbitrary closures.[28] Staff could not plan for classes. During short periods when the campuses opened, instructors were forced to teach at double-speed, completing a year's work in half the time.[29] Even then, due to shutdowns and political instability, students took many years longer than necessary to complete their degrees. They knew not when they would graduate.

From the mid-1960s, law was a third-rate discipline. Bright students entering tertiary education aimed for careers in medicine first, and engineering and science second. People who already had careers took up law on the side. Civil servants, schoolteachers, and small goods traders found in it a way to earn some extra cash and spend their spare time. Many studied at night classes and through correspondence courses. Some did so out of idealistic feelings about social injustice, but others wanted to get some skills that they could use on behalf of family and friends, by working as notaries or on divorce and inheritance cases.

Despite lawyers' low status, the number of law degrees awarded surged upwards by 2000. As the military government continued to adopt methods to keep students dispersed, it established more universities in provincial areas, and encouraged a rise in correspondence courses through the University of Distance Education, which it had established in 1992. Myint Zan estimated that the University of Distance Education, Yangon had over 25,000 law students enrolled in 2005.[30] According to him, cheating on examinations was rife, and anecdotally, the level of legal knowledge among then-recent graduates was low.

After decades of not offering on-campus legal education, a major change occurred in 2000. As part of a range of reforms ostensibly to modernize higher education in Myanmar, universities began to offer a bachelor degree in law on selected campuses.[31] As of 2018, a bachelor degree in law was available not only at Yangon University, but also at Dagon University, to the north of Yangon, and in the provincial and state universities, such as at Myitkyina, Pyay, Magway, and Mandalay. However, pedagogically not much had changed from the 1990s and 2000s, and distance education remained a popular choice. Students were taught to memorize codified laws but were offered little guidance by their teachers on matters of interpretation. Responsibility for these aspects of training fell to the students' seniors, or chamber masters, during their chamber-student period after graduation.

Following a year as a chamber student, a budding lawyer can apply to be a higher-grade pleader, which is the lower of two strata for qualified lawyers. The higher stratum is for the title of advocate. Higher-grade pleaders can appear in all courts except the Supreme Court, which is reserved for advocates. In 2012, Myanmar had 39,682 people qualified as higher-grade pleaders

28 See generally, Christina Fink, *Living Silence: Burma under Military Rule* (London: Zed Books, 2001) at ch 9.

29 Interview with Interviewee 1 (21 February 2017, Yangon) [*Interviewee 1*]; Interview with Interviewee 2 (27 February 2017, Yangon) [*Interviewee 2*]. The first-named author conducted all interviews with interviewees enumerated in the Appendix.

30 Myint Zan, 'Legal Education in Burma since the Mid-1960s' (2008) 12 *Journal of Burma Studies* 63 at 78. Yangon covers lower Myanmar, and the University of Distance Education, Mandalay, upper Myanmar.

31 Rozilini M. Fernandez-Chung and Tim Gore, 'Higher Education in Myanmar: The Potential Impact of TNE in the Adaptation of its National Higher Education for a Globalised World' in Christopher Hill and Rozilini M. Fernandez-Chung, eds., *Higher Education in the Asian Century: The European Legacy and the Future of Transnational Education in the ASEAN Region* (Abingdon: Routledge, 2017) 134 at 138.

and 8,272 advocates.[32] As of 2014, the United Nations Development Programme reported that Myanmar had roughly 40,000 higher-grade pleaders and 9,000 advocates, of which only some 15,000 and 2,000 respectively were in active practice.[33]

The government discontinued higher-grade pleader examinations in the early 1990s. It left it to the Bar Council to scrutinize applications and grant or deny licences, under the auspices of the Supreme Court, which was also assigned responsibility for matters pertaining to the suspension and revocation of lawyers' licences. Consequently, admission to and progression through the legal occupation has become essentially an administrative process that government departments oversee and regulate.

Although newly minted lawyers need only stay with their chamber masters for a year to obtain their licences, some continue working with them in the longer term.[34] Those who go their own way sometimes return to chamber masters for advice and mentorship.[35] It is through these close and often enduring relationships, rather than formal education, that young graduates and early career lawyers develop skills for legal practice. Certain pedagogical lineages are maintained in this way despite poor formal education.

In addition to the resources accrued from the accumulated knowledge and experience of senior lawyers passed down to juniors, the rapid proliferation of increasingly affordable mobile phones in Myanmar has allowed younger lawyers and law students to turn to Facebook pages and groups for the latest happenings in the legal sector. Users upload the texts of new laws, share inspirational quotes, and post news about court cases. Anyone can join these groups, and in 2018 the numbers of members in some groups exceeded the estimated number of active lawyers in Myanmar.[36]

Offline, new organizations like the Myanmar Lawyers Network in the 2010s ran regular legal English training in their downtown Yangon offices, and hosted senior lawyers to lecture on issues such as contract, maritime, and telecommunications law. The Yangon University law department had since 2013 introduced early morning and night classes for diploma courses, which were suspended after the 2021 coup. Lawyers who studied in the 1990s were in the 2010s also returning to campus to upgrade their skills in fast-moving, increasingly fashionable areas like intellectual property law.[37]

In sum, lawyers' lives in Myanmar differ significantly from jurisdictions with established and autonomous legal professions. The turbulent interjections of successive military-dominated governments into the legal sector in post-independence Myanmar have deeply influenced all lawyers' trajectories, although not all have reacted by engaging in political activity, or by actively defending basic freedoms in the manner of political lawyers. It is to that category that we now again turn our attention, before going to the case studies in the second part of the chapter.

[32] *The Rule of Law in Myanmar: Challenges and Prospects* (International Bar Association, 2012) at 62; data provided by staff of the Office of the Attorney General.

[33] *Bridges to Justice: Rule of Law Centres for Myanmar* (UNDP Myanmar, 2014) at 5. The UNDP did not define 'active practice', but we take it to mean that the licences of lawyers in active practice were being renewed. Of those renewing licences so as to take cases, those practising law as a primary occupation would be fewer again.

[34] *Interviewee 1, supra* note 29; *Interviewee 2, supra* note 29.

[35] Interview with Interviewee 6 (14 May 2017, Pyay) [*Interviewee* 6]; Interview with Interviewee 7 (8 October 2017, Yangon) [*Interviewee* 7]; Interview with Interviewee 12 (24 March 2017, Myitkyina) [*Interviewee 12*].

[36] As of 15 January 2018, Myanmar Legal Buffet had 26,822 members, and its closed Myanmar Online Lawyer Group had 26,669 members; *Ubade agyozaungmya* (Legal Services) had 50,791 members.

[37] Based on observations and encounters of the first-named author at Yangon University during fieldwork in 2016 and 2017.

C. *Access to Justice Amid Political Change*

There are many ways to describe lawyers with social or political goals who provide legal services to others. These include pro bono lawyers, human rights lawyers, legal aid lawyers, public interest lawyers, social justice lawyers, and, to address two particular categories, political and cause lawyers. In Myanmar, where legal aid has only very recently entered the text of policy,[38] and where legal work has for decades not been accompanied by a strong financial incentive, none of these terms map neatly onto local usage.

The misalignment between these various usages and our observations in Myanmar is not especially surprising or problematic. Empirical inquiry always entails a distancing move of some sort between what is documented and how it is analysed. With Munger and his co-authors, our interest lies not in insisting upon a precise match between nomenclature and the lawyers' practices that we have observed, but in asking how law is mobilized for justice and toward what contingent ends.[39] While we find the category of political lawyers congenial for heuristic purposes, we recognize that the lawyers who are the subjects of our inquiry in this chapter sometimes exhibit characteristics that align also with the category of cause lawyering, inasmuch as they frequently aim to alter some aspect of the social, economic, and political conditions through their practice by giving priority to morally imbued commitments that alter the relationship with the client, such that client service is only one component of serving the cause.[40]

One reason for the ambiguity we encounter in bringing our findings on Myanmar into contact with categories of lawyering is that Burmese phraseology does not map neatly onto them and carries with it its own peculiar connotations. Commonly used Burmese terms themselves do not capture the full sweep of what lawyers in Myanmar do in and around the courts. Lawyers there tend to describe legal services to indigent persons as lawyering that is free (*alaga*) or without-fee (*agamè*), terms that approximate the idea of pro bono in English.[41] More cosmopolitan types code switch with English and drop the phrase legal aid into their vernacular, a term that has no precise Burmese equivalent. Previously, lawyers referred to the idea of voluntaristic lawyering in the public interest or public good (*agyozaung*), but this phrase, which was associated with practice after 1962, has fallen out of fashion.[42] None of these terms work for us analytically all that well, which is also why we have preferred to work, albeit imperfectly, with the 'experience-distant' category of political lawyering, rather than attempting to communicate our observations on lawyering and access to justice in Myanmar through vernacular usages that invite us to look at things 'from the native's point of view'.[43]

38 See *Pyidaungsu Hluttaw Law No. 10/2016 – The Legal Aid Law*, Myanmar (28 January 2016) [*Legal Aid Law*].

39 Frank W. Munger, Scott L. Cummings, and Louise G. Trubek, 'Mobilizing Law for Justice in Asia: A Comparative Approach' (2014) 31:3 *Wisconsin International Law Journal* 353.

40 See Austin Sarat and Stuart Scheingold, 'Cause Lawyering and the Reproduction of Professional Authority: An Introduction' in Austin Sarat and Stuart Scheingold, eds., *Cause Lawyering: Political Commitments and Professional Responsibilities* (Oxford: Oxford University Press, 1998) at 4.

41 Some lawyers joke about the double meaning of the first usage, which can imply that something is useless, since it has come at no cost. Others express frustration that clients have little understanding of the time and opportunity cost involved in taking cases for no charge, and that the term 'without-fee' implies to the client that it costs nothing at all to run the case.

42 A young lawyer with whom the second author spoke in Yangon during March 2018 went so far as to say that at a recent hearing he had objected to a judge referring to him as *agyozaung*, which he took to imply a diminished status in the courtroom, and had insisted that the judge refer to him correctly as the 'lawyer' (*shene*) for the defendant.

43 Clifford Geertz, *Local Knowledge: Further Essays in Interpretive Anthropology* (New York: Basic Books, 1983) at ch 3.

Although in making a case for the category of political lawyering in Myanmar, we aim to identify certain shared characteristics among lawyers who work for basic freedoms, it is important to recognize that the specific issues that motivate them to act vary greatly from one part of the country to the next, as do the kinds of cases they pursue. In Yangon, an urban centre facing the challenges of rapid development and profound economic and social inequalities, lawyers with whom the first author spoke represented unaccompanied minors, vulnerable women, and evicted squatters. In Pyay, lawyers represented farmers seeking redress for lands taken by the military and military associates.[44] In Myitkyina, against the backdrop of ongoing ethno-nationalist conflict, lawyers insisted on their rights to defend ethnic minorities embroiled in cases under the colonial-era Unlawful Associations Act (1908),[45] for alleged contact with the insurgent Kachin Independence Army and its affiliates.

Each of these communities of lawyers associated with particular causes, which might be variously classed as coming under the ambit of women's and children's rights, farmers' rights, and minority rights. Yet it does not follow, in our view, that they be bracketed as cause lawyers. The remarkable character of Myanmar lawyering is that despite their divergent upbringings and career trajectories, lawyers have converged on certain core ideas about the practice of law and the defence of basic freedoms through legal practice. In short, what brings them together despite their tremendous differences and the structural obstacles to collective struggle is in many respects more integral to a Myanmar lawyer's role in access to justice than their pursuit of particular causes, causes that may align with where they were born, or their religious beliefs, or the stipulations of an international donor.

As such, we adopt the political lawyers rubric as an instrument with which to guide our inquiry, rather than as a category into which we would insert all the lawyers that we have observed. The notion of political lawyering assists us in sorting through some of the shared, elementary features of these lawyers, who are dispersed across Myanmar and varied in their purposes, but who in one way or another mobilize with a common sense of purpose to defend juridical rights, foundational political freedoms, and the property rights of people in Myanmar.[46] Central to the success of this mobilization also is the fight for the autonomy of the bar – a fight that was still very much underway in Myanmar during the successive periods in which we did our research, and one that occupies the threshold between lawyering as occupation and as profession.

Two salient features of the legal occupation in Myanmar that distinguish it from the conditions of professional practice spelled out in most other chapters in this volume, perhaps with the notable exception of China, have implications for how we identify political lawyers and interpret their relations with one another, and with state institutions. The first, already noted, is the high level of state control over lawyering, exerted administratively via the offices of the Attorney General and the Supreme Court.

[44] On land reclamation cases generally see SiuSue Mark, 'Are the Odds of Justice "Stacked" Against Them? Challenges and Opportunities for Securing Land Claims by Smallholder Farmers in Myanmar' (2016) 48:3 *Critical Asian Studies* 443, and *Land and Law in Myanmar: A Practitioners' Perspective* (Myanmar Lawyers Network and Asian Human Rights Commission, 2015).

[45] Unlawful Associations Act, Myanmar (India Act XIV, 1908) (11 December 1908).

[46] See Terence C. Halliday, Lucien Karpik, and Malcolm M. Feeley, 'Introduction: The Legal Complex in Struggles for Political Liberalism' in Terence C. Halliday, Lucien Karpik, and Malcolm M. Feeley, eds., *Fighting for Political Freedom: Comparative Studies of the Legal Complex and Political Liberalism* (Oxford: Hart Publishing, 2007).

The second, a corollary of the first, is that for want of an autonomous nationwide professional legal body to represent their interests, lawyers lack opportunities and therefore also incentives to manage their own practices, maintain ethical standards, and police the lawyering community. Absent a national professional body, lawyers in Myanmar not only work geographically dispersed, but also organizationally dispersed. At the time of writing, the multiple groups that represented lawyers' interests included the Myanmar Lawyers Network, the Independent Lawyers' Association of Myanmar, and the Myanmar Legal Aid Network. All of these groups had sizeable constituencies of lawyers in Myanmar, but none of them could claim to represent the legal occupation as a whole.

Although lawyers have no autonomous national body through which to mobilize, the Legal Aid Law (2016)[47] put the onus on them to give access to justice for people who need lawyers' services, albeit ostensibly under a coordinated, universal scheme. Despite the wording of the 2008 Constitution, that 'the Union shall guarantee any person to enjoy equal rights before the law and shall equally provide legal protection',[48] the Legal Aid Law excises the government from fiscal responsibility to provide legal aid services, and instead anticipates funding from the United Nations, and other international and domestic organizations and individuals.[49]

A growing reliance on foreign donors in the 2010s meant that access to justice projects were frequently single-issue-oriented. In contrast to earlier years, when most lawyers were generalists, local lawyers increasingly were being trained on-the-job in discrete fields. Consequently, far from the occupation becoming more cohesive as political change occurred, it has encountered tensions between certain imperatives toward collective action for judicial and legal autonomy and the defence of basic freedoms, and others that made it more fractionalized, by pushing lawyers toward specific causes that they might not otherwise have taken up.

An example of the specialization trend of this period was the donor funding of land cases in rural Myanmar. These cases very often fall under Section 447 of the Penal Code,[50] which concerns the law of trespass. Namati, an international non-governmental organization ('NGO'), in conjunction with the Civil and Political Rights Campaign Group ('CPRCG') in Pyay, a local firm, engaged with an extensive network of paralegals, which operated throughout central Myanmar. These paralegals were trained to record complaints, mostly from farmers with land rights issues, and subsequently assist clients with resolution, or connect them with a practising lawyer. One of the programme's talented lawyers remarked to the first author of her fatigue in handling so many similarly styled trespass cases, since she was keen to gain legal experience across a broader spectrum of matters, such as civil cases, but was unable to do so.[51]

[47] *Legal Aid Law*, *supra* note 38.

[48] *Constitution of the Republic of the Union of Myanmar* (29 May 2008), s 347.

[49] *Legal Aid Law*, *supra* note 38, s 32. In this regard, the law indicates the persistence since 2015 of what Gerard McCarthy refers to as 'authoritarian welfare capitalism' in Myanmar, such that the responsibility for welfare provision is shifted from state agencies to private benefactors, large and small: see *For Whose Benefit? Distributive Politics, Inequality and Informal Institutions in Myanmar's Transition* (Department of Political and Social Change Seminar Series, The Australian National University, 2017).

[50] Penal Code, Myanmar (India Act XLV 1860) (1 May 1861) (as amended 7 January 2016) ('Whoever commits criminal trespass shall be punished with imprisonment of either description for a term which may extend to three months, or with fine which may extend to fifty thousand kyats, or with both.').

[51] *Interviewee 6*, *supra* note 35.

Another example was the Blessing Law Firm, based in Insein, in the northern suburbs of Yangon. Female lawyers with strong connections in the Kayin, or Karen, an ethnic minority, and a network of Christian churches in Myanmar, established Blessing in 2007 through the Myanmar Council of Churches. UNICEF gave support for them to pursue women's and children's cases, as per Myanmar's commitments under the UN Convention on the Rights of the Child and the Convention on the Elimination of Discrimination against Women.[52] As of 2018, the Tharthi Myay Foundation was the firm's sole donor. It also provided ongoing technical assistance with case documentation training and practice management.

While at first glance increasingly specialized firms like the CPRCG and Blessing in Yangon may seem worlds apart in their orientations and objectives, common themes emerged in interviews and conversations with the lawyers at each, as well as those fighting overtly political cases in Myitkyina. All of the interviewees in 2016 and 2017 were motivated to work for social justice because of connections with politically active family members, committed senior lawyers, and friends. Some explicitly drew attention to events in Myanmar's recent past, be they the anti-government protests of 1988 or 2007, the 2008 referendum process, or the novelty of the 2010 and 2015 general elections. At these points, interviewees made key decisions to take the practice of law seriously. For some, the choice was to return to law after years of disenchantment or disinterest. For others, it was to make a career of law.

The second part of the chapter is taken up with these narratives, collected from interviews. It addresses the lawyers' experiences through three recurrent themes in the data generated during 2016 and 2017: family support and legal mentorship, responses to critical junctures, and lawyers' boundary blurring and crossing.

II. CHARACTERISTICS OF POLITICAL LAWYERING IN MYANMAR

A. *Family Support and Mentorship*

Many lawyers in Myanmar today attribute their political consciousness and motivation to practise law to the influence and support of family members and mentors – chamber masters especially. Two young women, Interviewees 9 and 13, said that their fathers had urged them into law during the early 2000s because they could use law to interpret and debate politics, and use it to seek out pathways into politics. Both interviewees were raised in the agricultural heartland of the country, in townships that lie along the Ayeyawady or Irrawaddy River: one in Padaung, Bago Region, the other in Minbu, Magway Region.

Interviewee 13's father was a senior figure in the local National League for Democracy ('NLD') chapter who lived on land gifted to the family by farmers whom he assisted in a land reclamation matter. He was imprisoned multiple times during her childhood for his political work. The family has three sons and two daughters. The sons all became bus drivers to support the family financially during their father's incarceration. The two daughters, as per their father's wishes, went into politics; Interviewee 13, in addition to working as a lawyer, was at the time a

[52] At the time, these were the only two international human rights treaties the government of Myanmar had ratified. It has since ratified the International Covenant on Economic, Social and Cultural Rights and the Convention on the Rights of Persons with Disabilities, but none of the conventions on civil and political rights, torture, enforced disappearances, or racial discrimination.

member of the Bago state-level legislature. When asked about law and politics, her tone became passionate:[53]

> My father was arrested twice for politics, and put in prison twice, six months and then the next time, another six months. I thought to myself, how does the law do this? How is it connected with politics? Because it's unjust, and the police know it's unjust . . . one person after another . . . there's no rule of law . . . this is connected to why I am a political lawyer.

Family members with legal backgrounds also set examples to follow. One of the lawyers who established the women's and children's legal aid centre in Insein said: 'I grew up in Insein and could see the courthouse from my schoolyard. I watched the lawyers go about their business in their black jackets. I wanted to be like them. I knew about what they did because my grandfather had been a judge.'[54]

Similarly, Interviewee 8, now based in the activist community in Pyay, also had a grandfather who had been a judge. She began working as a teacher in Sagaing Division, but felt the need to 'follow my father's wishes',[55] as she put it, and become a lawyer to continue the family tradition.

The majority of the interviewees came from families with some kind of connection to the pro-democracy movement, in particular to the NLD led by Daw Aung San Suu Kyi,[56] and to parties or groups affiliated with the political goals of linguistic and cultural minorities. But not all the interviewees who said they had gone into law with the encouragement of family members had prior connections or explicit political motivations. Interviewee 9's father, a village carpenter, encouraged her to use the emerging opportunities in the country to study and have the kind of career that he could not. He pushed her to read voraciously during high school, and he remained keenly involved in her career, asking about current cases and accompanying both her and her old chamber master to court matters when they were not too distant from the village.

Another lawyer began practising out of a concern to defend her brother and his friends, but soon aspired to build a country grounded in liberal values: 'In my country there is a lot of administrative power but only a very small space for judicial power; we need checks and balances otherwise the judicial power is more and more reduced . . . My dream is to set up a precedent system for land issues, and then also other things like investment and extractive resources.'[57]

For those lawyers who are the first in their families to take to the law, the mentorship of chamber masters is critical. The calibre of mentorship these lawyers can offer to juniors partly offsets the deficiencies in formal legal education. Some interview participants chambered with the country's top senior lawyers. These men – and a few women – in the 2010s cultivated a sizeable number of chamber students over time, appeared regularly in the media to speak on high-profile court cases, and provided commentary on legal and political issues. They included Robert Sann Aung, a political prisoner many times over and self-described human rights defender;[58] U Aung Thane, a well-known criminal defence lawyer and then-member of the

[53] Interview with Interviewee 13 (12 May 2017, Padaung) [*Interviewee* 13]. Quote translated from Burmese. Here the interviewee uses the notion of being a political lawyer, in the Burmese vernacular, *naingnganye shene*, with somewhat different albeit overlapping connotations to those that come with our sociologically informed notion.

[54] Interview with Interviewee 5 (8 April 2017, Yangon). Quote translated from Burmese.

[55] Interview with Interviewee 8 (29 March 2017, Pyay) [*Interviewee* 8]. Quote translated from Burmese.

[56] *Interviewee* 1, *supra* note 29; *Interviewee* 2, *supra* note 29; Interview with Interviewee 3 (5 April 2017, Yangon); *Interviewee* 6, *supra* note 35; *Interviewee* 7, *supra* note 35; *Interviewee* 8, *supra* note 55; *Interviewee* 13, *supra* note 53.

[57] *Interviewee* 7, *supra* note 35. Quote from the original English.

[58] A short biography of Robert Sann Aung is available at 'Martin Ennals Award for Human Rights Defenders: Robert Sann Aung 2015 Finalist', *Martin Ennals Foundation*, online: www.martinennalsaward.org/hrd/robert-sann-aung-2.

national legislature, who was jailed for declining to instruct his clients to stop a protest mid-hearing;[59] and the late U Ko Ni, a constitutional and civil law expert whom an assassin, apparently acting on orders of ex-military personnel, shot dead at the international airport terminal in January 2017.[60]

That some chamber masters' careers were themselves marked by periods of imprisonment or suspension or licence revocation has had consequences for the careers of their juniors, particularly those who graduated in the 1990s. Two interviewees had their career prospects diminished not only by the tremendously difficult political and social conditions at that time but also because their chamber masters went to prison, denying them the mentorship they sought and reducing their law firm's business.[61] For Interviewee 2 this was especially unfortunate, as a prominent Yangon-based lawyer had handpicked her to be his junior after her academic success at Yangon University, where she topped the Military Law subject. However, both this lawyer and the other interviewee expressed a sentiment that it would be improper to break from their chamber masters and work in other firms.

For some junior lawyers, interruptions to seniors' careers also presented unexpected opportunities. When Robert Sann Aung and U Aung Thane had their licences to practise revoked, they did not withdraw from practice but instead changed their business card titles from 'advocate' to 'legal advisor', and continued to handle cases, instructing their juniors on how to argue them in court. Whereas a legal profession might have acted collectively to prevent this kind of continued relationship after a senior lawyer had been struck from the register, the fluidity and ambiguity of the legal occupation in Myanmar allowed for these partnerships to continue, and with them, perhaps somewhat ironically, for the fight for basic freedoms undertaken by these legal offices to continue.

B. Critical Junctures

Critical junctures are relatively short periods of heightened contingency when dramatic transformation is possible.[62] These are turning points in history when the status quo is interrupted and new political and social relations are fought over and negotiated, which Terence Halliday and Lucien Karpik label *événements*.[63]

Whereas in some British postcolonies, such as Pakistan and Hong Kong, these moments have brought with them significant legal mobilization, structural constraints on lawyering in Myanmar mean that lawyers have lacked collective institutional bases from which to initiate and sustain collective action for basic freedoms in response to such moments.[64] But we should

[59] A short biography of U Aung Thane is contained in *Not Just Defending*, *supra* note 20, at 710.

[60] For an obituary reflecting on U Ko Ni's life and work see Melissa Crouch, 'In Memoriam: "Saya" U Ko Ni, Myanmar's Advocate for Constitutional Reform' (2016) 17:2 *Australian Journal of Asian Law* 1.

[61] *Interviewee 1*, *supra* note 29; *Interviewee 2*, *supra* note 29.

[62] Nora Fisher Onar, James H. Liu, and Mark Woodward, 'Critical Junctures? Complexity and the Post-colonial Nation-State' (2014) 43 *International Journal of Intercultural Relations* 22 at 25; see also, Giovanni Capoccia and R. Daniel Kelemen, 'The Study of Critical Junctures: Theory, Narrative, and Counterfactuals in Historical Institutionalism' (2007) 59:3 *World Politics* 341.

[63] Terence C. Halliday and Lucien Karpik, 'Political Liberalism in the British Post-Colony: A Theme with Three Variations' in Terence C. Halliday, Lucien Karpik, and Malcom M. Feeley, eds., *Fates of Political Liberalism in the British Post-colony: The Politics of the Legal Complex* (Cambridge: Cambridge University Press, 2012).

[64] See Sadaf Aziz, 'Liberal Protagonists? The Lawyers' Movement in Pakistan' in Terence C. Halliday, Lucien Karpik, and Malcom M. Feeley, eds., *Fates of Political Liberalism in the British Post-colony: The Politics of the Legal Complex*

not infer from this that lawyers in Myanmar have failed to act in response to critical junctures. Lawyers there have responded to critical junctures by engaging more deeply and deliberately in legal action for basic freedoms, but in ways that are not so easily discerned from afar or so immediately obvious.

For lawyers who graduated in the 2000s, the antigovernment uprising of 2007, and synchronously the lead-up to the 2008 constitutional referendum, gave impetus to new politically oriented projects. These two seemingly contrariwise events – the monk-led anti-government protests in 2007 that went by the moniker of the Saffron Revolution, and the preparations for the military-run constitutional referendum in 2008 – variously pushed otherwise part-time lawyers to engage with the legal occupation full time and encouraged a new generation of recent graduates into practice.

The effects of events like these on lawyers have not been even. Some interviewees indicated that it was the protests that had brought them into the fight for basic freedoms and motivated them to develop or use their legal knowledge to effect political change. Other interviewees said that it was the referendum process that had done so. For the latter, practising law was a way to comprehend the constitutional process and advocate for the rights of their communities;[65] and for the former, to defend the rights of friends and family members accused of criminal offences for participating in the protests.[66]

The 2008 referendum also meant different things in different political contexts. For the lawyers in conflict-ridden Kachin State, where opportunities for organizing through the language of law had been severely limited, the referendum was a call to action and an invitation to speak with people throughout the state about the defence of basic freedoms. One lawyer decided to leave her job at a jade company to work with fellow law graduates from Myitkyina University so as to advocate for their community: 'In 2007 when the Constitution was in the drafting process, people talked about it a lot. Together with groups of friends we read it together, considered it, decided we should think about it together. There were sections that would relate to Kachin people – we realized we needed to stand for our rights.'[67]

Back in Yangon, a land rights lawyer recalled how as a recent graduate she had accompanied her brother, then an underground political activist, from Pyay to Yangon, approximately six hours away, to organize the protests:[68]

> How do I remember the Saffron Revolution? Well . . . I was standing right over there, watching my brother and his friends [from a distance]. When people started getting arrested, I began organizing the documents, going to the [International Labour Organization] office, the UN office. I wasn't yet a practising lawyer but I could do those things . . . At that time I was going back and forth from Pyay and Yangon, so many times.

Until this point, her decision to study law was one made with few strong feelings about entering practice, other than an appreciation that 'in other countries, many of the leaders were

(Cambridge: Cambridge University Press, 2012); Shoaib A. Ghias, 'Miscarriage of Chief Justice: Judicial Power and the Legal Complex in Pakistan under Musharraf' (2010) 35:4 *Law & Social Inquiry* 985; Waikeung Tam, *Legal Mobilization under Authoritarianism: The Case of Post-colonial Hong Kong* (Cambridge: Cambridge University Press, 2012).

65 *Interviewee 12*, *supra* note 35.

66 *Interviewee 7*, *supra* note 35.

67 *Interviewee 12*, *supra* note 35. Quote translated from the original Jinghpaw.

68 *Interviewee 7*, *supra* note 35. Quote from the original English.

lawyers: Lincoln, and Gandhi'. The poor standard of education on offer at Pyay University meant that she had not assigned to law any special political significance. It was only during her chamber student period, which she decided to undertake after the Saffron Revolution, that she realized that being a lawyer would give her opportunities to defend basic freedoms, including those of her brother and friends.

Lawyers also benefited from a suite of novel activities run in the early years of the political transition period, beginning with the general election in late 2010 and then increasing with the re-entry of the NLD into institutional party politics following the release from detention of its leadership in 2012.[69] These activities included programmes like the ASEAN People's Forum in Yangon, where like-minded activists could connect with each other, which led in some cases to the formation of civil and political campaign groups;[70] events offered or hosted by groups like the NLD-affiliated Bayda Institute, to which people travelled for training in the rule of law; and election monitoring. It was on one of these occasions that two interviewees from the agricultural heartland met: 'In 2010 there was the referendum. I finished my chamber student period and left Minbu to go to Yangon and join the Bayda Institute where I was a trainer in the rule of law. I continued there and worked in the library. That was where I met [current colleagues] and then we went to Pyay to set up our office together.'[71]

Those who chose a legal career before the 2000s had different reasons for entering practice, and different experiences in their training and career development, although their life stories were no less marked by disruption. After matriculating in 1988, two lawyers of this generation had to wait several years for Yangon University to reopen, only to face multiple instances where semesters would be cancelled and they received only a few days' notice that they had to return to their native towns in the north, to wait again for notification that they could return.[72] These two women, who are both from upland minority groups, became friends in university partly because of a sense of shared minority identity vis-à-vis the dominant Burman student population,[73] and more particularly, because they both had ties to upland elites.[74] Like Interviewee 2, Interviewee 1's career was affected by political turbulence in Yangon and back in her home in Kachin State. In the wake of declining business at her chamber master's firm following his imprisonment in the 1990s, she returned to Myitkyina, where she used her high-level English skills to succeed in the NGO world. However, this success was short-lived. The ceasefire between the Kachin Independence Army and state military broke down in 2011. Many projects were no longer feasible. Yet as things took a turn for the worse in Kachin State, the ill-fated political transition in the lowlands was gathering pace. She returned to Yangon, where at the time of interview she was spending most of her time, travelling to Kachin State two or three times per year.

Interviewee 1 remained attached to her old law firm but lamented her lack of confidence in working as a lawyer from years of lost opportunities. Together with Interviewee 2 and a third

[69] On this period see generally, Nick Cheesman, Monique Skidmore, and Trevor Wilson, eds., *Myanmar's Transition: Openings, Obstacles and Opportunities* (Singapore: Institute of Southeast Asian Studies, 2012); Nick Cheesman, Nicholas Farrelly, and Trevor Wilson, eds., *Debating Democratization in Myanmar* (Singapore: Institute of Southeast Asian Studies, 2014).

[70] For example, the organization of Interviewees 8 and 9, which doubles as a law firm and as a political campaign group.

[71] *Interviewee 6*, *supra* note 35. Quote translated from Burmese.

[72] *Interviewee 1*, *supra* note 29; *Interviewee 2*, *supra* note 29.

[73] See generally, Matthew J. Walton, 'The "Wages of Burman-ness": Ethnicity and Burman Privilege in Contemporary Myanmar' (2013) 43:1 *Journal of Contemporary Asia* 1.

[74] Interviewee 1's grandfather was a *duwa*, a hereditary ruler, in Bhamo, Kachin State. Interviewee 2, from a prominent family in Lashio, later married into Shan royal lineage, her husband being one of the grandchildren of the last *sawbwa*, a hereditary ruler of the Kengtung principality in Shan State.

friend from student days, she attended workshops offered by the Myanmar Lawyers Network. They also returned to their alma mater, Yangon University, to take diploma-level classes in specialized topics. Both interviewees also ran in the 2015 national election for minor parties, but they were defeated in the NLD landslide.[75] Interviewee 1 wanted to return to Kachin State to run for a seat in the state legislature, but felt she needed to build up her legal skills first, with a view to using her legal credentials and experience to enter politics. Driving past the legislature in Myitkyina with the first author in early 2017, she pointed, laughed, and said – in hindsight, poignantly – 'next time you come here, you can visit me in there'.[76]

1. Boundary Blurring and Crossing

The physical and associational locations where lawyers congregate in Myanmar are loosely bounded sites for action in defence of basic freedoms. They are not sites demarcated as the exclusive or privileged territory of the lawyerly community, like law schools or law societies in other countries, either because such sites do not exist or because they prohibit or discourage the kinds of conversation and organization necessary for political lawyering. Rather, these are porous sites, where lawyers working for basic legal freedoms can meet and strategize with political activists.

Physically, lawyers gather in firms' chambers, political training centres, and at private homes – many of which also contain lawyers' individual offices. Teashops and restaurants near to courthouses are places of constant, lively discussion too. There, lawyers are constantly bumping into one another, exchanging ideas, and in the 2010s, cards with activists and donors as well as with their clients.

In Yangon, the law offices downtown are concentrated around 39th and 40th Streets, particularly in the middle block that runs from Anawrahta Road to Merchant Road, near the old court complex. Many senior chamber masters' offices are found here. So too was the office of the Myanmar Lawyers Network. It served as a weekly meeting place for politically inclined lawyers as well as others. Anyone was welcome to attend meetings and workshops, whether trained as a lawyer or not.

Outside the downtown area, and in provincial centres, lawyers gather in scattered suburban offices, and congregate in houses. In many locations, the boundaries between the home and office are blurred. Away from the city centres, individual lawyers typically work out of their own homes. NGO offices in the 2010s doubled as accommodation for their staff and clients.[77]

One reason why Myanmar's lawyers make do without specific institutional practice sites and are at ease in conducting their affairs pretty much anywhere is that they are accustomed to travelling long distances to handle cases, and to doing things en route. If the legal occupation in Myanmar is dispersed, then so too is its work. This physical dispersal applies to political lawyers, who bring expertise and clout to cases in courts scattered around the country when their local counterparts might not otherwise get an adequate hearing. These lawyers are constantly on the move. Myanmar's paper-based courts put a heavy burden on them to appear in person to lodge forms and complete basic formalities.[78]

[75] On the election and the ongoing war in Kachin State, as well as other political developments in this period, see generally, Nick Cheesman and Nicholas Farrelly, eds., *Conflict in Myanmar: War, Politics, Religion* (Singapore: Institute of Southeast Asian Studies, 2016).

[76] *Interviewee 1, supra* note 29. Quote from the original English.

[77] In Pyay the first author stayed in the office of an active law and campaign group for several weeks. Not only she but also staff and colleagues slept downstairs. Rollout sleeping mats were swiftly stowed away in the morning to provide floor space for visitors, only to come back out at nightfall.

[78] During her research, the first author accompanied one Pyay-based lawyer on a six-hour journey in a van with no air-conditioning at the height of the hot season to visit the district court in the neighbouring region, Magway. The

Long-distance travel imposes a heavy burden on lawyers in Myanmar, but it also presents unplanned opportunities for more boundary crossings and dialogue. Lawyers and activists run into each other all the time without intending to do so, such as on the busy Yangon–Pyay bus line, at the roadhouse where the bus stops halfway – and on board the bus itself. On one trip in 2017 the first author was surprised to be seated on the bus next to a judge, who it transpired presided over a case that she observed the next day. Serendipity is as much a part of a lawyer's practice in Myanmar as design.

Lawyers' firms that pursue particular kinds of cases blur their boundaries with other groups that have shared causes. It is here that we note most obviously the slippage between the work that these lawyers undertake for core political goals and those that align more closely with the particular interests of certain segments of the population. The legal aid networks in Myitkyina, for instance, are closely aligned with the Kachin ethno-nationalist struggle. Kachin graduates from an early batch of law students at Myitkyina University, which commenced offering law degrees in 2000, during the 2010s ran the two main legal aid projects in town. Both began working on cases together with friends, outside their commitments to senior lawyers. Personal connections brought them to clients. Friends and relatives or their contacts approached the firms with news of Kachin political and criminal accused. Both lawyers were able to take on these cases full-time and hire staff thanks to the extensive domestic and transnational donor networks pledging funds to the struggle for Kachin self-determination.

In Pyay the town's two prominent legal aid centres had their origins in the democracy movement. In both offices, lawyers worked alongside political activists and former political prisoners, who provided direction on campaigning and outreach, and engaged with foreign donors. As lawyers took matters through the courts, their activist partners collaborated with campaign groups working on closely aligned issues such as farmers' rights to land, and against environmental degradation.[79] They connected with the local media. Occasionally they presented at workshops in Yangon's then well-populated rule-of-law community.

Lawyer agility in negotiating physical and associational boundaries, moving between legal duties, social worlds, and political roles, became an increasingly important skill as political conditions in Myanmar got more fluid. Interviewee 13 oscillated between being a sitting member of a legislature to acting as a lawyer for farmers in her local town. She marked her shifting of roles by donning a black jacket and white shirt to be a lawyer, and the beige blouse of the NLD to be a politician.

Changes in occupation and dress underscore the difficulties that presented themselves to us in classifying political lawyers in Myanmar, but they were also difficulties that some lawyers themselves felt. Interviewee 1, the Kachin lawyer whose career has been caught between the NGO world in Myitkyina and the activist centres in Yangon, felt divided about herself and her career objectives. She expressed worries that she was perhaps less adept at boundary crossings than her counterparts:[80]

> I'm split in how I think about law and about my career ... if we are speaking in Myitkyina, what I think, how I answer your questions would be very different. In Yangon, I just do ordinary and

purpose of this trip was simply to lodge a power of attorney application to represent their client. Trips of this sort are commonplace for lawyers working on cases throughout the agricultural regions around Pyay.

79 For a case study of an alliance between urban lawyers, regional activists, and motivated farmers, see *Not Just Defending*, *supra* note 20, at 702.

80 *Interviewee 1*, *supra* note 29. Quote translated from Burmese.

uneventful cases, none of those sensitive cases, political cases. But in Myitkyina, yes, there I am interested in Kachin livelihoods and politics.

Yangon was a hub for the politically ambitious, but this lawyer's political commitments were elsewhere. Her sense of the political, of what it meant to be a political lawyer, differed from many of those around her, even if she shared many goals and values with them. One reason for her difficulties was that the physical and associational distances between her hometown and the busy commercial capital were formidable. For her, legal practice entailed a choice between what she would like to be doing and what the situation allowed. For others, like the lawyers in Pyay and Yangon, a greater consonance then existed between aspiration and action.

III. CONCLUSION

Lawyers in Myanmar draw on accrued knowledge and skills in their fight for basic legal freedoms on a daily basis. Our findings reveal that structural barriers to action and the paucity of opportunities for formal legal education and training notwithstanding, a committed subsection of the country's thousands-strong community of qualified lawyers has dedicated itself to activism for political and social change in Myanmar – and will continue to do so in the 2020s under resurgent military dictatorship. These lawyers have accumulated abilities and knowhow, most of it through on-the-job training and involvement in larger alliances with non-lawyers.

We are not overstating the case for political lawyering as a feature of the legal sector in Myanmar. We recognize that for every lawyer whose experiences are described in this chapter, there are many more who have not been lucky enough to get the family support they need to progress, or who have not been talented or dedicated enough to secure a place with a prominent chamber master or mentor. A great many junior lawyers in Myanmar spend their days, weeks, and years filling out forms, doing photocopies, and lodging documents for seniors rather than developing the skills they need to fight for basic freedoms.

Furthermore, there are some places where even the most hardened political lawyers fear, or refuse, to tread. None of the lawyers interviewed in 2016 and 2017, and only a handful of those with whom the second author has had ongoing contact since his earlier research, had spoken out or represented clients in cases following communal violence that swept the country from 2012 to 2014, overwhelmingly targeting the Muslim population.[81] Nor had any lawyers mobilized strongly in response to the state violence wrought upon the Rohingya population on the border of Bangladesh that followed in 2016, and swelled to a massive and unprecedented scale in 2017. Some cited safety concerns, describing Rakhine State in particular, where the army and police force launched an all-out assault on an entire population, as a no-go zone for non-local lawyers.[82] Others clearly are unsympathetic to Muslims generally and Rohingya especially, and tacitly, if not explicitly, support the project to expel them from Myanmar.

The failure of political lawyers to engage with some pressing issues might in part be due to individual limitations or prejudices, but insofar as this is the case it is consistent with the distinction that we have been drawing throughout this chapter between political lawyering

[81] See generally, Nick Cheesman, 'Introduction: Interpreting Communal Violence in Myanmar' (2017) 47:3 *Journal of Contemporary Asia* 335; some key elders of the profession who have represented Muslim clients include U Aung Thane and Robert Sann Aung, who is himself from the Muslim community, in Yangon and U Thein Than Oo in Mandalay.

[82] Second author field notes, July 2015, August 2016, and February–March 2018.

and cause lawyering. As Halliday and Karpik point out, political lawyering does *not* extend to fights against racism or xenophobia.[83] That lawyers did not mobilize more actively and collectively in defence of the rights of Muslims affected by violence in Myanmar might be morally deplorable, but their failure to do so does not make them any less political. On the contrary, it reflects their principally reactive role, in response to public authority, and concerns for the fundamental rights of citizens.[84]

The failure to intervene in such cases is also consistent with the distinction we have been making between legal occupation and profession. No single autonomous lawyering association as yet exists in Myanmar to take responsibility for a failure on the part of its members to act, so it falls to smaller, informal networks and individual cause-oriented lawyers and their firms to intercede. If nobody does so, no one is any more or less to blame. The fluidity of the legal occupation is such that it is easier to pass the buck than to accept collective responsibility for manifest and gross injustices.

But if the activism of lawyers in Myanmar, and their political progressiveness, should not be overstated, then nor should it be underestimated. Lawyers in Myanmar do use law with dexterity in rapidly changing political conditions. Enough of them use it often enough, in response to shared concerns, as to amount to something more than just the sum of their parts. The occupational tendencies we describe, of reliance on family engagement and legal mentorship, collective identification despite dispersed responses to political changes, and boundary blurring and crossings, are all indicative of the lawyers' responses to the structurally challenging conditions in which they have taken up the task of fighting for basic freedoms.

That political lawyers have emerged in Myanmar, not by coming together under a nationwide autonomous professional body but in a more disparate manner, across multiple physical and associational locations, and in spite of an atrophied legal education system and a complacent judiciary that remains at the bidding of the executive, is noteworthy and inspiring. These lawyers are not working in the manner of their professional counterparts elsewhere, but it would be foolish to infer from this difference that they want for skills and knowledge to effect change or that they are unaware of what needs to be done to enhance the structures of the legal occupation.

If we have privileged the voices of younger lawyers in this chapter, it is because their stories are the stories of the 2010s, a time between dictatorships when a new generation took shape and prepared itself for a renewed struggle against military rule to come – one that is still gathering pace as this book goes to press. They are the overwhelming majority of lawyers in the country. Some will become important actors in years to come, as legal campaigners, political activists, or even as revolutionary leaders. Do they constitute a nascent legal profession in Myanmar? The coup of 2021 makes an answer to this question in the affirmative all the much harder. Professionalization is not only far from inevitable, but far less likely now than it was a few years back. If it does eventually happen, it will not be because foreign consultants have willed it, or because globalization made it so, or not only for those reasons, but because Myanmar's political lawyers have fought for it.

[83] *Political Lawyering*, *supra* note 10, at 11676.

[84] On the part that a diminished conception of citizenship plays in the conflict over the status of the Rohingya in particular, see Nick Cheesman, 'How in Myanmar "National Races" Came to Surpass Citizenship and Exclude Rohingya' (2017) 47:3 *Journal of Contemporary Asia* 461.

APPENDIX 7.1 INTERVIEWEE DETAILS

TABLE 7.1. *Details of interviewees*

No.	Age in 2017	University	Years of Study	Salient Features
1	47 (Approx.)	Yangon	1991–7	Kachin, Christian. Father a senior member of NLD. Ran in the 2015 election.
2	47	Yangon	1991–7	Shan, born in Lashio. Previously assisted with political cases concerning Shan defendants. Ran in the 2015 election.
3	50	Yangon	1990–3	Former schoolteacher. Studied law by correspondence. Eventually took to practice full time. Peasants Union and NLD affiliations.
4	49	Yangon	1989–2001	Kayin, Christian. Acts for children and women. Supported by husband financially. Law firm established initially with UNICEF support.
5	59	Yangon	1979–82	Kayin, Christian. Grandfather was a judge. Key interest is fairness, seeing justice for those harmed, but also a fair defence for the accused.
6	36	Magway	2001–5	Focus is on criminal cases/land cases due to NGO funding but prefers civil cases.
7	35	Pyay	2001–7	Took an interest in law to help her brother and friends, who were targeted for political activism in the 1990s.
8	37	Distance Education	2001–4	Went to teachers' college first. Father a headmaster at a school. Studied LLB by distance, influenced by father's wishes for her to become a lawyer.
9	35	Magway	2007–11	Studied business first. Changed career to law. Thought earnings as a lawyer would be good. Met activist network in Pyay via wife.
10	37	Myitkyina	2000–3	First batch of the law programme at Myitkyina University. Started in business but moved back to practising law after Saffron Revolution. Spent about 20 per cent of time on legal aid cases.
11	33	Myitkyina	2007–10	Kachin, Christian. Set up legal aid firm with fellow lawyers after wave of arrests in 2011.
12	33	Myitkyina	2007–10	Kachin, Christian. First worked for a jade company but felt need to practise law during referendum process.
13	32	Pyay	2002–6	Always wanted to enter politics. Encouraged by father to study law for the training and experience. At the time of research, sitting member in the Bago Region legislature. Represented clients in land rights cases.
14	35	Distance Education	2001–5	From a small village on the road between Bago and Rakhine State. Initially wanted to be a teacher. Studied law to help with village matters.
15	36	Pyay	2002–6	Originally wanted to be a police officer. Decided to study law because interested in investigations. Chamber master introduced her to defence work and from then she committed to lawyering.

8

Alternative Lawyering versus Pro Bono in the Philippines: From Challenging an Authoritarian Government to Working with the State

*George Radics and Alpha Pontanal**

Abstract

The Philippines currently has an impressive set of guidelines and regulations concerning pro bono service, including a 60-hour annual service requirement for all licensed attorneys, and a 100-hour service requirement for all new attorneys. Although the government implemented pro bono requirements as a means to address ongoing problems with public access to justice, the state is plagued by the historical understanding that it is an elite institution that only uses the law to disenfranchise, exploit, and disempower citizens. Historically, a number of public interest law non-governmental organizations ('NGOs') emerged to address the access to justice issue and to challenge the state. Over time some of these left-leaning NGOs were taken over by younger attorneys born after martial law, who began working with the state. The question in the Philippines is whether this blurring of NGO alternative lawyering and state-led pro bono lawyering will continue and produce a new access to justice identity for lawyers as well as the state. The chapter argues that over time, the lawyers that provided free legal services went from providing such services for the purpose of addressing crimes by the state, to eventually working with the state as a result of pro bono service requirements.

I. INTRODUCTION

As a developing nation, the Philippines has over the past few decades struggled to find its footing politically and economically. Ferdinand Marcos' dictatorship from 1972 to 1986 was marked by a negative economic growth rate, a rise in political persecution, and the deterioration of political institutions and civil rights. The nation continues to endure an active communist insurgency, while it also attempts to address Islamic separatist demands. High rates of poverty, a grossly unequal distribution of wealth, and continuing violence have marginalized a large proportion of

* The authors would like to express their gratitude to all those willing to be interviewed for this chapter. Additional thanks should be made to Teresita Cruz-Del Rosario and Sarasu Esther Thomas for their useful comments during the Lawyers and Access to Justice: Challenging Pro Bono Symposium held at the National University of Singapore Faculty of Law from 7 to 8 June 2017. The authors are especially grateful to Helena Whalen-Bridge and her excellent team of support staff and editors for making this chapter possible.

the population from access to justice. To expand access to justice, the government developed and expanded public agencies, such as the Public Attorney's Office, to provide publicly funded legal services to the poor. In 2009, the Supreme Court took the step of enacting a resolution to mandate that the Integrated Bar of the Philippines ('IBP'), a government-established bar association for lawyers in the Philippines, require all of its members to engage in 60 hours of pro bono work annually to remain in good standing and avoid penalties.[1] In 2017, the Supreme Court passed another resolution, requiring all new attorneys to provide 100 hours of pro bono work within the first year of passing the bar exam.[2] To operationalize the resolution, the Philippine House of Representatives passed Republic Act No. 9999, or the 'Free Legal Assistance Act of 2010'. Can the government ease the burden of those marginalized from justice by forcing lawyers to take on cases pro bono?

In the past few years, studies regarding pro bono have begun to examine how a lawyer's role in access to justice is conceptualized in different jurisdictions.[3] While scholarship in primarily western countries has identified a main variable in access to justice as pro bono legal service, this phrase takes on a completely different meaning in the Philippines. As a former colony of Spain, the Philippines embodies many Catholic cultural values which are deeply embedded in its codified laws.[4] Enhancing the civil law traditions of a dominant judge and a sovereign court, the American colonial government elevated the relevance of the law, making it even more powerful and elitist. Post-independence, Marcos' use of the law to concentrate power led to the declaration of martial law, which politicized many attorneys and drove them into public service against the state. The chapter argues that the development of the law under two colonial regimes in conjunction with martial law has therefore created a complicated environment in which many are marginalized from justice, a strong perception of an elitist and exploitative state prevails, and pro bono service has become a political act. To some, pro bono is traditional and antithetical to social progress, especially when pro bono initiatives are state-led. In contrast, public interest law or alternative law is practised by those outside the state to protect citizens from human violations – violations that are many times conducted by state actors.

This background provides the context in which the topics of access to justice and pro bono in the Philippines will be explored. The chapter examines public access to justice by first examining the legal infrastructure of courts and the right to an attorney, particularly for the indigent, and the historical development of this infrastructure in the Philippines. Next, the chapter

[1] *Proposed Rule on Mandatory Legal Aid Service for Practising Lawyers*, Philippines February 2009, B.M. No. 2012 [*MLAS*].

[2] *Rule on Community Legal Aid Service*, Philippines October 2017, A.M. No. 17-03-09-SC [*Rule on Community Legal Aid Service*].

[3] *See* Daniel Bonilla Maldonado, 'The Mandarins of the Law: Pro Bono Legal Work from a Comparative Perspective' (2020) 27:1 *Indiana Journal of Global Legal Studies* at 131–88; Fabio de Sa e Silva Fabio, '"A Little More Complex": Pro Bono Commitment in São Paulo Corporate Law Firms' (2020) *International Journal of the Legal Profession* 1; Vivien Holmes, 'Pro Bono and Ethics Build a Noble Profession' (2015) 18:2 *Legal Ethics* at 182–4; and see footnotes 25–31.

[4] *See* Attorney Rosario T. Setias-Reyes, 'The IBP National Center for Legal Aid: A Revitalized and Reinvigorated Enterprise' (2012) *The Bar Tribune: The Official Publication of the IBP* [*The Bar Tribune*] at 3; in this piece, Attorney Setias-Reyes starts off her discussion on the IBP's responsibility to honour the Supreme Court's mandate with the biblical story of Elijah and the widow (1 Kings 17: 7–16) in which the Bible states, 'We should be ready to suffer inconveniences, to suffer pains and to be hurt for the sake of helping other people. We should learn to give until it no longer hurts. Give until giving becomes so much a part of us. Give until giving becomes something like breathing. Give until giving becomes like food that will sustain our life. Give until giving becomes so much a part of us that we cannot survive without it.'

explores efforts to shift some of the state's responsibility for ensuring access to justice onto all practising lawyers in the Philippines by creating mandatory pro bono requirements. This section will include interviews with representatives of the IBP, representatives from the Supreme Court, and practising attorneys.[5] Lastly, the chapter provides a brief glimpse into the work being done by NGOs to address the gap left by government agencies and private lawyers working with the IBP. A biographical sketch of two non-governmental legal aid[6] organizations, the Free Legal Assistance Group ('FLAG') and the Alternative Law Groups ('ALG'), will be provided in the final section.

II. PHILIPPINE HISTORY AND LEGAL INFRASTRUCTURE

This section briefly discusses the development of law in the Philippines and how it impacted access to justice. Each phase of history played an important role in shaping the practice of law and how a lawyer understands his or her obligations to society at large. Although the Philippines has a rich pre-Hispanic history, this section begins with the Spanish colonial period since many of the pre-colonial laws were codified at this time. The section will then discuss the impact of American colonization on the expansion and entrenchment of Anglo-American legal traditions, and how the law gained currency as an elitist enterprise. Lastly, the section will look at how politics during post-independence shaped not only the current institutions providing pro bono services, but also how the practice of law is perceived by lawyers and society-at-large.

A. *Spanish Period*

The Philippines is a democratic nation with strong legal influences from its Spanish and American colonial history.[7] The death of Ferdinand Magellan off the coast of modern-day Cebu in 1521, and Miguel López de Legazpi's arrival in the Philippines in 1561, marked the beginning of nearly 333 years of Spanish colonial rule over the Philippines and the subsequent imposition of Spanish culture, religion, and political institutions. To establish a legal infrastructure, the Spanish relied on the *Audiencia*, or local tribunals, to adjudicate over grievances. In 1599, Franciscan Friar Juan de Plasencia codified customary laws that did not contradict basic precepts of Spanish-Christian morality, and tribunals applied these customary laws in all cases. When issues emerged that could not be resolved by customary laws, Roman jurisprudence was used.[8] These laws were again codified in the *Recopilación de las Leyes de las Indias* and

[5] For this section, six attorneys were interviewed to get their views on the reforms. All interviews were conducted in the Philippines, either over the phone or in person. Those interviewed were informed of their rights to privacy and confidentiality. While all interviews helped with the drafting of this chapter, only those who agreed to be named were cited in this chapter. Institutional Review Board approval for these interviews was obtained from the National University of Singapore.

[6] In the Philippines, 'legal aid' refers to the legal assistance to poor individuals as provided by a variety of organizations, not just government-funded assistance.

[7] Elizabeth Aguiling-Pangalangan, 'The Philippines: Native Culture, Transplanted Institutions and Women's Rights' in Gary Bell, ed., *Law and Legal Institutions of Asia* (Cambridge: Cambridge University Press, 2011) 372 [*Native Culture*] at 374.

[8] John Leddy Phelan, *The Hispanization of the Philippines: Spanish Aims and Filipino Responses 1565–1700* (Madison: University of Wisconsin Press, 1967) [*Hispanization of the Philippines*] at 129.

promulgated by Charles II in 1680.[9] By the 1880s, customary laws and Roman laws were combined and formally codified in the *Código Penal* (1886) and the *Código Civil* (1889).

Under the Spanish, the law was seen as an administrative necessity, handled by bureaucrats. It was also seen as obligatory, with the Spanish providing free services to natives and the Chinese. The government appointed interpreters, as well as a 'crown attorney' to represent the natives and Chinese immigrants in their cases, although these appointed attorneys functioned more as bureaucrats appointed by the government.[10] This approach is an early example of the government provision of access to justice, but it has been argued that the Spanish clergy believed that Filipinos were overly litigious, and that they were prone to abuse the system to further personal interests, for example by antagonizing enemies in family feuds. These sceptics expressed nothing but 'contempt for the veracity of a Filipino's testimony' and questioned the desirability of applying Spanish judicial procedures to cases involving Filipinos.[11]

B. American Period

Frustration over what was perceived as the growing excesses of the Spanish clergy, and the ineptitude and arrogance of the king's official administrators in the Philippines, prompted a revolution that ended with the entrance into Philippine history of the Americans, who purchased the recalcitrant colony from Spain in 1898.[12] After forcibly subduing the Filipinos, the Americans began one of the largest infrastructure development projects the nation had ever seen, building roads, schools, post offices, and telegraphic services. American lawyers flooded the country and became influential in the early decades of American colonial rule. By 1917, 20 per cent of the lawyers practising in Manila were Americans.[13] Many American lawyers were appointed to important judicial roles, and nearly half of the seven Supreme Court justices were American from 1901 to 1935. Regarding the written law, a series of commissions were established to update and revise the Spanish codes, and the Revised Penal Code (1930) and the Civil Code of the Philippines (1950) were promulgated. While these codes retained many of the Spanish principles, they also instituted new concepts and ideas that facilitated American business and enterprise in the country. By the 1930s, citations to American legal authority by the Philippine Supreme Court overwhelmingly prevailed.[14] The decay of the civil law continued, and access to civil law materials decreased. Some court opinions were still written in Spanish in the 1930s, but eventually such use disappeared completely. The Americans had however always insisted that their colonial rule of the Philippines was temporary, and by the mid-1930s, many of the

[9] Ruperto Martin, *Introduction to Philippine Laws* (Manila: Premium Book Store, 1986) at 17; Melquiades Gamboa, *An Introduction to Philippine Law* (Quezon City: Central Law Pub. Co., 1955) at 82.

[10] The term 'crown attorney' is the term used in the texts cited above. Sometimes 'crown attorney' is a translation of the term *fiscales*: *see* Lyle McAlister, *Spain and Portugal in the New World, 1492–1700*, Vol. III (Minneapolis: University of Minnesota Press, 1984) at 190. Regardless of the manner in which the term is translated, many 'crown attorneys' were trained in canonical and civil law, given that the *letrado* system in Spain required a combination of credentials and connections to be appointed to serve the crown: *see* Richard L. Kagan, *Students and Society in Early Modern Spain* (Baltimore: Johns Hopkins University Press, 1974) at 82–7; and Charles R. Cutter, *The Legal Culture of Northern New Spain, 1700–1810* (Albuquerque: University of New Mexico Press, 2011) at 53.

[11] *Hispanization of the Philippines*, *supra* note 8, at 129.

[12] *Native Culture*, *supra* note 7, at 374.

[13] Jose Trias Monge, 'Salience and Unity in the Mixed Jurisdiction Experience: Traits, Patterns, Culture, Commonalities' (2003) 78:1/2 *Tulane Law Review* 333 [*Salience and Unity*] at 338.

[14] *Salience and Unity*, *supra* note 13, at 333.

institutions established by the Americans became 'Filipinized'; ultimately all of the Supreme Court justices were Filipino from 1935 onwards. The Philippines gained independence from the United States in 1946. At this point, although American law introduced a certain guarantee of rights under the constitution, particularly in the areas of criminal law and criminal procedure, the law itself had become increasingly more powerful. Common law practices allowed judges to sign off on their own opinions, and the ability to understand and draft law became progressively more elitist.

C. *Post-Colonial Philippines*

By the mid-1960s and 1970s, political instability in the South East Asian region, along with strong American influence on the country, created a period of political volatility. The communist insurgency that had mobilized Filipinos to resist the Japanese during World War II continued to wage war, except this time it fought against the Philippine government, which was described as a 'neocolony in crisis' with 'fascist puppet Marcos' at the helm.[15] On other fronts, many Muslims in the country became frustrated with their marginalized position in the nation, and the same student movements that swept much of the world at this time to protest the Vietnam War were also present in the Philippines, particularly in Manila.[16] The law had become a tool of power and control under the Americans, and now Filipino politicians used this same tool to consolidate and aggrandize their power over the newly independent nation. Ferdinand Marcos, the Philippines' democratically elected president in 1965 and again in 1969, used the law to his advantage by declaring martial law in 1972 to suspend democratic protections, such as the writ of *habeas corpus* and due process guarantees. Although Marcos argued that martial law was necessary to restore order during this tumultuous time, his actions were more successful in temporarily thwarting the political ambition of his rivals.[17] Marcos also altered the constitution to entrench his position, transforming the Philippine government into a parliamentary democracy, with himself as prime minister, to circumvent the presidential two-term limit.[18] Thus, by the 1980s the law began to lose currency as an instrument of justice, and instead was seen as a tool used by brilliant lawyers and technocrats to justify their authority. On the bright side, because Marcos himself was a lawyer who attempted to present his reign as legal to the outside world, progressive lawyering reached its peak at this time. Some of the most important NGOs in the Philippines today were established during the martial law period, such as FLAG, which provided legal representation to detainees. Although providing legal assistance may have seemed like a fruitless endeavour, these progressive lawyers were successful in gaining release for political detainees, although mainly on highly technical and jurisdictional, not substantive grounds.[19]

[15] Jose F. Lacaba, *Days of Disquiet, Nights of Rage: The First Quarter Storm and Related Events* (Manila: Salinlahi Pub., 1982) [*Days of Disquiet*] at 15.

[16] Lela Noble, 'The Philippines: Muslims Fight for an Independent State' *Southeast Asia Chronicle* No. 75 at 12–17; *see Days of Disquiet, supra* note 15, at 15.

[17] H. W. Brands, *Bound to Empire: The United States and the Philippines* (Oxford: Oxford University Press, 1992) at 298.

[18] Mark Thompson, *The Anti-Marcos Struggle* (New Haven: Yale University Press, 1995) at 45.

[19] Gill Boehringer, 'A Perspective on Human Rights Lawyering in the Philippines: A Conversation with Attorney Romeo Capulong' (2013) 25:2 *Philippine Law & Society Review* 45 [*Human Rights Lawyering*] at 51.

After the fall of Ferdinand Marcos in 1986, the Philippines enacted a new constitution that affirmed the nation's commitment to rule of law. Article III of the 1987 Constitution, entitled the 'Philippine Bill of Rights', enshrined the ideals of progressive lawyering by providing that 'free access to the courts and quasi-judicial bodies and adequate legal assistance shall not be denied to any person by reason of poverty'.[20] Although a similar provision had existed in the 1973 Constitution under Marcos, it was found at the bottom of the Bill of Rights in Section 23, the last section of the article. In 1987, it was moved up to Section 11, and broadened with the language 'and quasi-judicial bodies and adequate legal assistance', ensuring that indigent litigants had access to a larger range of judicial bodies and a lawyer. To support this initiative, the government established the Public Attorney's Office ('PAO'), an agency under the Department of Justice, to provide free legal representation to individuals with either no income or income below certain thresholds, in civil, criminal, and administrative cases.[21] While this was a continuation of the Citizen's Legal Assistance Office established by Marcos in 1972,[22] the PAO effectuated the broader mandate of the 1987 constitution, and arguably received greater freedom from politics through its recognition as an 'independent and autonomous office attached to the Department of Justice'.[23] The PAO's expanded mandate was meant to complement the work already being done by the IBP, a mandatory bar association for Philippine lawyers established by the Supreme Court in 1971. According to the by-laws of the IBP, '[i]t shall be the duty of the committee on legal aid to establish legal aid bureaus for deserving poor litigants and set up lawyer referral services'.[24]

III. THE PRACTICE OF PRO BONO IN THE PHILIPPINES

Pro bono is commonly understood in the North American context as the provision of free legal services by a lawyer to benefit persons of limited means.[25] The history of pro bono practice however is complex, emerging as a topic of study predominantly in the last 20 years.[26] In the United States, for instance, there is a long history of legal activism, from facilitating the process of Americanization for white immigrants in the first half of the twentieth century, to the internationalization of public interest law and human rights advocacy in the latter half of the twentieth century.[27] The civil rights movement in the 1950s and 1960s, and the rise of new public interest lawyers from the 1970s onwards, were periods of US history in which domestic lawyers took advantage of expanded constitutional protections.[28] This trajectory of expanded

[20] *The 1987 Philippine Constitution* (ratified on 2 February 1987 by a plebiscite, proclaimed in force on 11 February 1987) [*1987 Philippine Constitution*], Article III, s 11, online: www.lawphil.net/consti/cons1987.html.

[21] Public Attorney's Office, Department of Justice, online: www.pao.gov.ph/.

[22] Manila, Department of Justice, *Letter of Implementation Relative to Part XXI on Administration of Justice and other pertinent provisions of the Integrated Reorganization Plan*, No. 20, 31 December 1972, s 1972.

[23] *Republic Act No.* 9406, An Act Reorganizing and Strengthening the Public Attorney's Office (PAO), Amending for the Purpose Pertinent Provisions of Executive Order No. 292, 23 March 2007, Thirteenth Congress Third Regular Session, s 2.

[24] *By-Laws of the Integrated Bar of the Philippines*, 1974, Article IV [*IBP By-Laws*], s 29, ss 11.

[25] Helena Whalen-Bridge, 'The Conceptualisation of Pro Bono in Singapore' (2014) 9:1 *Asian Journal of Comparative Law* [*Pro Bono in Singapore*] at 97.

[26] Robert Granfield, 'The Meaning of Pro Bono: Institutional Variations in the Professional Obligations Among Lawyers' (2007) 41:1 *Law & Society Review* at 113.

[27] Scott L. Cummings, 'The Internationalization of Public Interest Law' (2008) 57:4 *Duke Law Journal* 891 at 898.

[28] Comment, 'The New Public Interest Lawyers' (1970) 79:6 *Yale Law Journal* 1069 at 1079, n 19.

rights enforced by lawyers has not been uniform throughout the world, and pro bono work has only recently begun to expand in the South East Asian region,[29] particularly in the context of Singapore, where it has been argued that pro bono law has gone from being recognized as a charitable donation to a professional obligation.[30] How lawyers identify pro bono obligations as an aspect of their professional obligation is also a recent area of research.[31]

Aspects of pro bono practice in the Philippines can be traced to the aforementioned early Spanish trials, in which the natives and the Chinese received free legal representation from the government. It can also be seen in the early 1900s, with lawyers representing the poor in land claims or cases against the American government.[32] In the early 1900s, for instance, Ramon Diokno and Felipe Buencamino represented Filipino general Macario Sakay in his trial for treason, after Sakay refused to plead guilty in exchange for the promise of a later pardon. Legal activism, however, ironically reached its zenith under the Marcos regime. As a lawyer, Marcos attempted to justify all of his actions as legal, altering the constitution, issuing decrees, and establishing legal bodies aimed at enhancing the status of the law. These institutions were controlled by Marcos and his cronies, but at the same time they provided opportunities for lawyers to push boundaries and test the new institutions. This section will therefore discuss government initiatives that began under Marcos, and how these initiatives became the foundation for the mandatory pro bono requirements later introduced by the government. It will then discuss the emergence of NGOs during the Marcos period, and how these NGOs have reacted and responded to government initiatives over the years. This section will focus on two NGOs, FLAG, founded by Ramon Diokno's son, Jose Diokno, in 1974, and a consortium of public interest law organizations called ALG. Both the government section and the NGO section will briefly discuss how lawyers in these sectors perceive their obligation to provide access to justice for marginalized individuals and groups.

A. *Government Initiatives*

The IBP is the official organization of all Philippine lawyers. The IBP was created by the Supreme Court on 5 October 1970.[33] In deciding whether it had the constitutional power to integrate the bar, the Supreme Court found that integration was imperative, in part because of the fundamental reason that 'the practice of law is not a vested right but a privilege; a privilege, moreover, clothed with public interest . . .'.[34] As a result, 'the Supreme Court may adopt rules of

[29] *See* Daniel Lev, 'Lawyers' Causes in Indonesia and Malaysia' in Austin Sarat et al., eds., *Cause Lawyering: Political Commitments and Professional Responsibilities* (Oxford: Oxford University Press, 1998); Stephen Ellmann, 'Cause Lawyering in the Third World' in Austin Sarat et al., eds., *Cause Lawyering: Political Commitments and Professional Responsibilities* (Oxford: Oxford University Press, 1998).

[30] *Pro Bono in Singapore, supra* note 25, at 142; *also see* Helena Whalen-Bridge, ed., *Pro Bono in Singapore: The PBG Story* (Singapore: National University of Singapore Faculty of Law, 2016).

[31] *See* Robert Granfield et al., *Private Lawyers and the Public Interest: The Evolving Role of Pro Bono in the Legal Profession* (Oxford: Oxford University Press, 2009), and Austin Sarat et al., eds., *The Worlds Cause Lawyers Make: Structure and Agency in Legal Practice* (Stanford: Stanford Law and Politics, 2005).

[32] *Human Rights Lawyering, supra* note 19, at 56.

[33] Prior to the establishment of the IBP, a number of voluntary bar associations existed. S 17 of *Republic Act No. 6397 / Presidential Decree No. 181*, 4 May 1971 [*Republic Act No. 6397*], which established the IBP, states, 'All voluntary Bar associations now existing or which may hereafter be formed may co-exist with the Integrated Bar but shall not operate at cross-purposes therewith.'

[34] *Per Curiam* Resolution of the Supreme Court of the Philippines, 9 January 1973.

court to effect the integration of the Philippine Bar under such conditions as it shall see fit'.[35] The creation of the IBP therefore reflects the authority and prestige of the Supreme Court. Prior to martial law in 1973, the Supreme Court was considered 'one of the most powerful and highly respected courts in the world'.[36] Even after the declaration of martial law, although Marcos had disbanded Congress, detained oppositionists, suspended the rights of *habeas corpus*, speech, press, and assembly, and imposed strict censorship requirements, the courts were left intact and free to review all of Marcos' directives.[37] Under Marcos then, and due in part to the Supreme Court, the strength of the legal profession was enhanced.

The history of IBP's support for access to justice began in 1974, when by-laws explicitly provided for a Committee on Legal Aid, stating that 'this committee shall promote the establishment and efficient maintenance of Chapter legal aid organizations suited to provide free legal service'.[38] Since then, the IBP has allocated parts of its budget to providing legal services,[39] has developed several programmes over the years to coordinate the provision of free legal services across the chapters, and has developed niche areas of free legal service specialization, such as programmes for OFWs, human trafficking, and jail decongestion. The Committee on Legal Aid has been described as the 'flagship project of the IBP since its integration in 1973' and has been institutionalized in most of its 85 chapters nationwide.[40] However, although the national IBP has funds for legal services, some local IBP chapters receive no support from the national IBP at all. The national budget of the IBP is not readily made available to the public. The more lucrative local chapters, such as the Makati IBP chapter situated in the country's premier financial district, have funds from the chapter's members to carry on successful pro bono programmes. Other IBP chapters may not have the local funds to carry out such programmes.[41]

In 2009, the Supreme Court placed additional pressure on the IBP to become even more active in providing free legal services. The Supreme Court decided that the IBP must mandate its members to provide free legal services to the indigent. On 10 February 2009, the Supreme Court released the 'Proposed Rule on Mandatory Legal Aid Service for Practising Lawyers', otherwise known as 'Bar Matter No 2012: Mandatory Legal Aid Service' ('MLAS'). The resolution required all lawyers in the Philippines to provide 60 hours of pro bono legal services, at five hours a month, with mandatory reporting every quarter under threat of losing the licence to practise law and accruing a PHP4,000 fine (US$79).[42]

[35] *Republic Act No. 6397*, *supra* note 33, s 1.

[36] Imelda Deinla, 'Public Support and Judicial Empowerment of the Philippine Supreme Court' (2014) 36:1 *Contemporary Southeast Asia* 128 at 134.

[37] Stacia Haynie, 'Paradise Lost: Politicisation of the Philippine Supreme Court in the Post Marcos Era' (1998) 22:4 *Asian Studies Review* at 460.

[38] *IBP By-Laws*, *supra* note 24, s 55.

[39] *See* Interview with Attorney Jovian Dumalo, Senior Associate, Platon Martinez Flores San Pedro Leaño Law Offices (conducted by Alpha Pontanal, Manila, March 2017) [*Interview with Attorney Dumalo*].

[40] *The Bar Tribune*, *supra* note 4, at 3. Today, the IBP manages bar exams, oversees professional responsibility and ethical standards for all lawyers and judges, promotes legal education and continuing legal education centres, and expands legal aid throughout the country by providing free legal services and referral services to indigent Filipinos. To practise law in the Philippines, attorneys must pay a lifetime membership fee of PHP25,000 (US$489) and an annual fee of PHP2,000 (US$39). IBP Memorandum Circular (2018), online: www.ibp.ph/pdf/announcement/MD%20GUIDELINES.pdf.

[41] *Interview with Attorney Dumalo*, *supra* note 39.

[42] MLAS, *supra* note 1; XE Currency converter, online: www.xe.com/currencyconverter/convert/?Amount=4000&From=PHP&To=USD. Unless another reference was cited, US$ denominations in the chapter were derived from

Initially, the Supreme Court's MLAS was met with great suspicion and hostility. According to Attorney Ted Te, former law professor at the University of the Philippines and long-time volunteer attorney, 'I'm afraid that [the Supreme Court] proposing a Rule on Mandatory Legal Aid Service for practicing lawyers will only serve to do the reverse – get everyone so pissed off at the rule that all possible loopholes will be scoured and exploited.'[43] Attorney Te entitled his blog piece on the issue, 'you can't legislate compassion' and he argued that 'it is the height of disservice for indigent and poor litigants to be given the ultimate dole out, i.e. petulant, unwilling, coerced, and even downright hostile lawyers who will not only drag their feet under this rule, but perhaps even ... drag their clients down'.[44] In fact, many of the private lawyers of the IBP believed that MLAS seemed excessive and represented the shifting of responsibility of providing legal representation for the indigent from the government to private attorneys. According to a heated comment online from one attorney, 'wtf???? i have nothing against rendering services for free ... except i dont even have enuf time to finish my work, where the freak will i find time to do this????'.[45] The attorney stated that it was 'easy for those SC dude siguro ksi light na yng load nila [probably because their load is light] ... pero [but] what about newbie lawyers who have to put in the hours to clinb [*sic*] the corporate/firm ladder???'.[46] Another attorney added, '[t]his rule is pathetic. What this country needs the most, are decent court rooms, competent court staff, support technology and facilities. We have already our hands full ...'[47]

Other attorneys were frustrated with the IBP. According to Attorney Marlon Manuel, '[w]e were informed that the draft that eventually became the rules came from the IBP ... apparently the national office was the one [that signed off on the rule] ... the chapters did not know about it'.[48] Manuel went on to add that after the Supreme Court inquired into the existing state of the Legal Aid programme of the IBP, including its use of funds, it was unclear if the IBP had complied with its own obligations, and he asked, 'why are you going to require the lawyers to render [free] legal aid when the IBP has funds [to pay for legal services]?'.

Efforts to compel pro bono service were not limited to the Supreme Court or the IBP. In 2010, the Philippine House of Congress passed Republic Act No. 9999, or the Free Legal Assistance Act of 2010 ('Free Legal Assistance Act').[49] Supplementing the right to an attorney in the Philippine Constitution,[50] the Free Legal Assistance Act stated, 'the State shall guarantee free legal assistance to the poor and ensure that every person who cannot afford the services of a counsel is provided with a competent and independent counsel preferably of his/her own choice, if upon determination it appears that the party cannot afford the services of a counsel,

www.xe.com at the time of publication; they are intended for general reference and may have been rounded up or down for ease of reference.

43 Attorney Ted Te, 'You Can't Legislate Passion' (17 February 2009) [*You Can't Legislate Passion*] (copy on file with authors).

44 Ibid.

45 Comment by Rosa, Bar Matter 2012: Rule on Mandatory Legal Aid Service, *Everybody Loves Raymund* (25 February 2009), online: therainman96.wordpress.com/2009/02/25/bar-matter-2012-rule-on-mandatory-legal-aid-service/.

46 Ibid.

47 Ponente, 'Rule on Mandatory Legal Aid Service Issued by Supreme Court', *Atty at Work* (20 February 2009), online: attyatwork.com/rule-on-mandatory-legal-aid-service-issued-by-supreme-court/comment-page-1/#comments.

48 Interview with Attorney Marlon Manuel, National Coordinator, Alternative Law Groups (conducted by Alpha Pontanal, March 2017, Manila) [*Interview with Attorney Manuel*].

49 *Republic Act No.* 9999, 'Free Legal Assistance Act of 2010', February 2010 [*Free Legal Assistance Act*].

50 1987 *Philippine Constitution*, *supra* note 20, s 12(1).

and that services of a counsel are necessary to secure the ends of justice and protect[ion] of the party'.[51] This document implemented the Supreme Court's MLAS by requiring various governmental bodies to coordinate in the reporting requirements, including the Bureau of Internal Revenue, which would allow attorneys to deduct the value of services rendered over the 60-hours requirement from their annual taxable income.[52] Senator Manuel 'Lito' Lapid said he felt a sense of urgency to draft the bill after he witnessed the wrongful conviction of a poor litigant in his home province of Pampanga.[53] He thanked his colleagues for 'recognizing the need to encourage more private lawyers to do pro bono work so they can help unburden the Public Attorney's Office'.[54] Former Speaker of the House of Representatives Prospero Nograles lauded then-President Gloria Macapagal Arroyo's signing the legislation, stating that '[w]e should never underestimate the President's sincerity and determination to strengthen social justice in the country'.[55]

Immediately after the passing of the bill, former president Arroyo became embroiled in controversy, with her successor Benigno Aquino III and many of her political enemies seeking her arrest for alleged graft and corruption during her presidency. Aquino also began impeachment proceedings against the Chief Justice of the Supreme Court, for the court's alleged bias against Aquino's policies and the court's perceived allegiance to Arroyo. After these developments, Senator Lapid, the proponent of the legislation who also had a controversial record, was met with sardonic headlines such as '[f]inally, a law from Senator Lito Lapid: Legal Assistance'.[56] It was even suggested that his law would provide anti-crime advocates with new ammunition in their attempts to reinstate capital punishment.[57] Senator Lapid's Free Legal Assistance Act, therefore, faded into the background. The Free Legal Assistance Act ultimately did not generate as much attention or ire as MLAS. According to Attorney Ben, 'I remember reading this years ago and I felt positive about it. But . . . I haven't seen any implementing rules and regulation of it, even from Public Attorney's Office or the Bureau of Internal Revenue. No one knows what happened to it. No one is pushing it.'[58] Attorney Ben added, '[t]he law is good, but it has a "snare" or a trap for lawyers. You have to present your income to be able to take advantage of the privilege in that law.'[59] Attorney Manuel was even more critical. When asked about the 'Free Legal Assistance Act of 2010', he characterized it as useless, observing that:[60]

> Senator Lapid rested his election campaign on being the author of this legal aid law, 'you now have a free lawyer!' So many people ask about it. I explain that it is not effective, there is no funds for it, and that all it is, is a tax incentive for lawyers to render legal aid on top of what is required. But again, even attaining the required is hard already how can you expect to have the excess?

In June 2012, the IBP responded to these developments by preparing a document entitled, 'Implementing Regulations on the Rule on Community Legal Aid Service' ('CLAS'). The

[51] *Free Legal Assistance Act*, *supra* note 49, s 2.

[52] *Free Legal Assistance Act*, *supra* note 49, s 5.

[53] Paolo Romero, 'GMA Signs Law Giving Free Legal Assistance to Poor Clients', *PhilStar* (25 February 2010).

[54] Philippine Senate Press Release, 'Senate Approves Lapid Bill on Free Legal Services to the Poor' (28 January 2010).

[55] 'Philippines: Nograles Lauds Enactment of Free Legal Assistance Act', *Thai News Service* (1 March 2010).

[56] Aurea Calica, 'Finally, a Law from Senator Lito Lapid: Legal Assistance', *PhilStar* (30 January 2010).

[57] 'Solon Sees Stronger Bid to Re-impose Capital Punishment', *Manila Bulletin* (22 March 2010).

[58] Interview with Attorney Noel Ben, Vice Chair, Lawyers Beyond Borders (conducted by Alpha Pontanal, Manila, April 2017) [*Interview with Attorney Ben*].

[59] Ibid.

[60] *Interview with Attorney Manuel*, *supra* note 48.

document reduced the 60-hour requirement to 20 hours, with reporting only taking place once a year. Furthermore, pro bono legal service was broadened to include legal advice, preparation of legal documents, and counselling, in addition to legal representation before the courts, initially the only activity the MLAS counted toward the pro bono requirement. Finally, whereas non-compliance under the MLAS would lead to the PHP4,000 (US$80) penalty, CLAS imposed a PHP200 penalty (US$3.97) for every hour of deficiency. Some attorneys were supportive of these new regulations. According to Atty Noel Ben, from Lawyers Beyond Borders, '[u]nder the CLAS, it would be very easy to comply. For example, in the course of doing our jobs when people know that you are a lawyer people ask legal questions and that could be counted as legal aid. So it is not very taxing. We look at the IBP legal aid guidelines (CLAS), it includes counseling even through phone or Skype.'[61] Although Ben's views may have been influenced by the fact that he served as president of the IBP chapter in Cotabato City, he stated that, 'for the five of us who are active in the [Lawyers Beyond Borders], they find no issue. Other members are more for "wait and see" and are open to paying the penalty.'[62]

In October 2017, the Supreme Court tried again, passing another resolution entitled 'Rule on Community Legal Aid Service'.[63] This new document required young lawyers who successfully passed the annual bar examination to provide 120 hours of pro bono legal aid within the first year of admission to the bar.[64] There were several exemptions, such as lawyers in government service, lawyers who completed clinical legal education in their final year of law school, or lawyers who worked for one year with a law firm that provided pro bono services or with an accredited legal aid service provider.[65] It also required the IBP Chapter Legal Aid Committee and the accredited legal aid service provider to submit annual reports to the Office of the Bar Confidant, the office in charge of the bar examination and lawyer discipline.[66]

Expenses for the new requirements were to be borne by the IBP with subsidies from the Philippine judiciary, or an accredited legal aid service, which could also ask the judiciary for support.[67] Such reliance on the Supreme Court's budget may cause alarm, but its budget has been fairly stable; for example, even though President Rodrigo Duterte filed impeachment papers against the Chief Justice of the Philippine Supreme Court Maria Lourdes P. A. Sereno in October 2017, this did not affect the budget of the judiciary, which experienced a modest increase for 2018.[68] Some of the legal aid burden may also be shifted from the Supreme Court to other government bodies. According to the Department of Budget and Management, an executive body under the Office of the President, the Public Attorney's

[61] *Interview with Attorney Ben*, *supra* note 58.
[62] Ibid.
[63] *Rule on Community Legal Aid Service*, *supra* note 2.
[64] *Rule on Community Legal Aid Service*, *supra* note 2, s 5(a).
[65] *Rule on Community Legal Aid Service*, *supra* note 2, s 5(c).
[66] *Rule on Community Legal Aid Service*, *supra* note 2, s 12.
[67] *Rule on Community Legal Aid Service*, *supra* note 2, s 13. The IBP received PHP100,000,000 (US$2.08 million) from the Supreme Court in 2019 to support court-mandated activities. This amount was reduced to PHP30,900,000 (US$641,718.45) in 2020, similar to what was received in 2017 and 2018. *See* General Appropriations Act, Vol. IB, XXX (A) 'Supreme Court of the Philippines and the Lower Courts', online: www.dbm.gov.ph/index.php/dbm-publications/general-appropriations-act-gaa/.
[68] Leila B. Salaverria, 'Duterte to File Impeachment Complaints vs Sereno, Morales', *Philippine Daily Inquirer* (5 October 2017). Although the judiciary requested PHP46.85 billion (US$926.88 million) for 2018, only PHP34.36 billion (US$679.78 million) was approved in November 2017. This was an increase from PHP32.8 billion (US$648.87 million) in 2017.

Office, the executive body discussed above, was scheduled to receive a total amount of PHP3.2 billion (US$63.3 million), 18.5 per cent higher than in 2017, 'to provide the poor and other qualified persons with free and accessible legal services'.[69] Thus in spite of political turmoil with President Duterte, access to justice is still seen as an important issue warranting state funding.

Overall, interviews and a review of the comments of lawyers online convey a distinct scepticism over whether attempts by the Supreme Court or the House of Congress are effective or sincere. At one end of the spectrum, mild criticisms of the law portray the government as out of touch, or pushing extra work onto lawyers to lessen the government's burden. At the other end, these laws are seen as traps used to peer into the bank accounts of unsuspecting lawyers. There is also the view that mandatory pro bono regulation is temporarily on hold because the IBP is refusing to reveal to the Supreme Court how funds earmarked for legal services are actually being used. With the new Rule on Community Legal Aid Service applying only to attorneys who passed the Philippine bar exam in 2017 and were admitted to practice in 2018, very few new attorneys have been subject to the rule. Furthermore, in September 2019, the law was formally suspended while new rules on law student practice were rolled out in 2020–1.[70] Thus, at least from the perspectives of lawyers, government initiatives to promote or mandate pro bono services are seen as empty, poorly thought-out gestures that cause more harm than good. According to Attorney Manuel, 'every time we have a discussion about legal aid, even foreigners will say, "oh you have this legal aid law ..." but that is a useless law'.[71] So, if according to Attorney Te 'you cannot legislate compassion', who will provide pro bono services? This chapter will conclude with a discussion on the legal non-governmental organization sector in the Philippines.

B. *Non-Governmental Organizations*

Following political changes in Eastern Europe from 1989 onwards, NGOs emerged as a powerful influence in Philippine national politics.[72] However, the nation has a rich and deep history of civil society organizations and private voluntary organizations that go as far back as the 1890s, when Filipinos organized to resist Spanish colonial rule.[73] Americans attempted to organize and regulate charities and other service organizations that arose between 1898 and 1946.[74] These organizations have played an important role in ushering in social change and providing essential services for Philippine society. By the 1970s, with the confluence of authoritarian rule, support from the Catholic Church, and the emergence of overseas development

[69] Philippines, Department of Budget and Management, *Technical Notes on the Proposed 2018 Budget* (September 2017) at 55.

[70] Notice of Resolution, Supreme Court of the Philippines (3 September 2019), sc.judiciary.gov.ph/wp-content/uploads/2019/09/A.M.-No.-17-03-SC-Re-Rule-on-Community-Legal-Aid-Service.pdf. The revised law student practice rule in the Rules of Court was promulgated on 25 June 2019 and was rolled out in the 2020–1 academic year. *Law Student Practice* (Supreme Court of the Philippines), Philippines 2019, Rule 138-A, A.M. No.19-03-24-SC, online: sc.judiciary.gov.ph/4808/.

[71] *Interview with Attorney Manuel*, *supra* note 48.

[72] Isagani R. Serrano, 'Civil Society in the Philippines: Struggling for Sustainability' in David C. Schak and Wayne Hudson, eds., *Civil Society in Asia* (Burlington: Ashgate, 2003) 103 at 104.

[73] *See* Teodoro C. Agoncillo, *History of the Filipino People*, 5th edn (Quezon City: Garotech Publishing, 1977) at 73–279.

[74] Virginia A. Miralao and Ma. Cynthia B. Bautista, 'The Growth and Changing Roles of NGOs and the Voluntary Sector' (1993) 41:1/4 *Philippine Sociological Review* 19 at 21.

assistance, a massive proliferation of these organizations was able to bypass the limited, and many times corrupt, government agencies, making substantial progress.[75] It was during this time that some of the most prominent legal aid organizations currently in existence in the Philippines emerged. According to human rights lawyer Attorney Romeo Capulong, 'the peak of progressive lawyering was in the Marcos period, especially after the Martial Law declaration in September 1972'.[76] Free Legal Assistance Group, for instance, was founded in 1974 to represent political detainees under martial law. Its emergence led to the growth of other organizations, such as the Alternative Law Groups. These two organizations and their approaches to providing free legal services are discussed in the next sections.

1. Free Legal Assistance Group

FLAG is a national human rights lawyer organization committed to the protection and promotion of human rights and civil liberties in the Philippines. Founded in 1974 by Jose W. Diokno, Lorenzo Tanada Sr, and Joker Arroyo, the organization pioneered a strategy of training and deploying paralegals for 'first aid legal aid'.[77] Martial law was a transformative period for civil society and particularly for lawyers. According to Jose Diokno, 'by spreading a chilling climate of fear over the nation and by steadily militarizing social institutions, martial law has led lawyers and laymen to question not only the political system of martial rule, but even the social, economic, military and cultural structures ... As a consequence, martial law added a new dimension to legal aid: by politicizing lawyers and laymen, it politicalized legal aid.'[78] In response to this condition, FLAG saw the role of lawyers and the use of law as an instrument of societal transformation called 'Developmental Legal Advocacy' or 'DLA'. This concept of DLA emphasizes that lawyers should attack injustice in ways that address underlying issues and reach beyond individual cases.[79] FLAG also gave rise to a law student group, the University of the Philippines Paralegal Volunteer Organization, which became an incubator for many budding attorneys who went on to found and staff public-service-oriented law organizations.[80] Moreover, many prominent legal aid lawyers, such as Attorney Romeo Capulong, founder of the Public Interest Law Center, and Attorney Ted Te, former Assistant Court Administrator and Chief of the Public Information Office at the Supreme Court of the Philippines, volunteered with FLAG. The emergence of FLAG also facilitated the 'radicalization' of middle-class politics, allowing a budding group of educated youth to channel their frustration against the increasingly hostile and oppressive military regime.[81]

[75] Gerrard Clarke, 'People Power? Non-Governmental Organisations and Philippine Politics Since 1986' (1993) 21:3 *Philippine Quarterly of Culture and Society* 231 at 238.

[76] *Human Rights Lawyering, supra* note 19, at 59.

[77] Jennifer Franco, Hector Soliman, and Maria R. Cisnero, *Community Based Paralegalism in the Philippines: From Social Movements to Democratization* (Justice and Development Working Paper Series: World Bank, 2014) [*Paralegalism*] at 5.

[78] Jose W. Diokno, 'Legal Aid and Development' in Florangel Rosario-Braid et al., eds., *Crimes and Unpunishment – The Killing of Filipino Journalists* (Asian Institute of Journalism and Communication, 2012) at 90.

[79] Stephan Golub, 'Participatory Justice in the Philippines' in Mary McClymont et al., eds., *Many Roads to Justice: The Law Related Work of Ford Foundation Grantees Around the World* (The Ford Foundation, 2000) 197 [*Many Roads*] at 203.

[80] Ibid.

[81] Temario Rivera, 'The Middle Class in Philippine Politics' in Teresa Tadem et al., eds., *Philippine Politics and Governance: Challenges to Democratization and Development* (Quezon City: University of the Philippines, 2006) at 186.

The work of FLAG was profound, and although legal aid had existed in the past, the day-to-day violation of human rights under Marcos and the role of lawyers in ameliorating these conditions left an indelible impression on volunteer attorneys. According to Attorney Romeo Capulong, a volunteer attorney with FLAG in the 1970s:[82]

> At the level of where ordinary people experienced the regime of Martial Law, there were countless, now nameless, faceless lawyers who continued to work for their communities all over the country. They did what they could in different small tactics and techniques to fight the oppression of the Marcos regime. And all of this has contributed to the cumulative experience of Filipino people's lawyers.

As a result of his political orientation and work with FLAG, Attorney Capulong's office was raided three times, he was placed under house arrest and went into hiding, and eventually escaped to the United States in 1975, only to return after the fall of Marcos in 1986. When Attorney Capulong returned to the Philippines, inspired by his work with FLAG, he started the Public Interest Law Center to help litigate human rights claims against Marcos. Reflecting on his work, Attorney Capulong stated, '[lawyers] are miseducated. They are not taught that they have a duty, a calling, especially in view of their important position in the social-political structure, to use their knowledge and skills to help others in a common struggle for social justice.'[83] To him, the political situation in the Philippines contributes to an inequality and desecration of justice that must be rectified. He added that the Public Interest Law Center 'tries to show the people that the present conditions, in which exploitation is massive – the rich growing richer, and the poor growing poorer – call[ ] forth repression. And that leads to many of the incidents such as extra-judicial killings and disappearances, in which we are asked to lead the legal challenge against what are largely government operations.'[84]

Attorney Ted Te also seemed sceptical of legal education and the capacity of lawyers to serve in pro bono capacities. Volunteering with FLAG as a paralegal, and then later as an attorney after passing the Philippine Bar exam in 1991, he continued to serve FLAG for close on two decades. In his experience, however, providing 'free legal aid is not for everyone'. Commenting on government attempts to mandate pro bono service, Attorney Te stated that, 'Before my tax and corporate friends get all [heated] up, I am not proposing to include you in this rule. I think you would be more dangerous in the court room simply because of lack of practice and/or interest and I would prefer you stay in the board room.'[85] Attorney Te concluded that, 'you cannot legislate compassion for another, nor passion to serve others. This comes from the heart; if one's heart is incapable of compassion, then a change of heart must be encouraged. But forcing lawyers to render free legal aid will ensure most certainly resentment, anger, hostility and the indigent and poor are not better served by this.'[86]

FLAG continues to take the government to task, challenging President Duterte's plans to restore the death penalty and what they perceive as his 'shoot-to-kill' orders for organized criminals or those who violently resist arrest.[87] FLAG lawyer Jose Diokno in October

[82] *Human Rights Lawyering*, *supra* note 19, at 61.
[83] *Human Rights Lawyering*, *supra* note 19, at 47.
[84] *Human Rights Lawyering*, *supra* note 19, at 49.
[85] *You Can't Legislate Passion*, *supra* note 43.
[86] Ibid.
[87] Jee Y. Geronimo, 'Lawyers' Group Opposes Death Penalty, "Shoot-to-Kill" Policy', *Rappler.com* (21 May 2016).

2017 petitioned the Supreme Court for an injunction and prohibition against Philippine National Police Command Memorandum Circular (CMC) No. 16-2016[88] and the Department of Interior and Local Government CMC No. 2017-112,[89] two circulars that provided general guidelines, procedures, and tasks for police officers and local government units in Duterte's controversial 'Project Double Barrel' anti-illegal drug campaign. Attorney Diokno argued that the CMCs 'expressly authorize the police to kill suspected drug pushers, users or "illegal drug personalities" in the guise of "neutralizing" or "negating" them'.[90]

2. Alternative Law Groups

ALG is a coalition of 23 legal resource NGOs that adhere to the principles and values of alternative or developmental law, as developed by Jose Diokno of FLAG, and they are regarded as effective contributors in the creation of a political environment that solicits civil society involvement.[91] The first batch of ALGs was founded in the early 1980s, and they served mostly as groups providing legal resources to the indigent.[92] By the early 1990s, ALG organizations became staffed by lawyers who specialized in distinct areas of practice.[93] Areas of practice were primarily concerned with the pursuit of public interest, respect for human rights, and promotion of social justice, and they addressed areas such as the environment, women's rights, agrarian reform, and children.[94] By 1987, an ALG that started off as an apprenticeship programme training public interest lawyers by the name of Structural Alternative Legal Assistance for Grassroots, or 'SALAG', began a linkage programme with peoples' organizations ('POs'), other NGOs, and governmental organizations ('GOs'), for a coordinated approach in assisting the disadvantaged.[95] In 1990, Attorney Hector Soliman from SALAG drafted the piece, 'The Practice, Problems and Prospects of Alternative Lawyering in the Philippines' for the First Alternative/Developmental Law Workshop held in the municipality of Subic. This document became the primer for the formal launch of the ALG coalition in 1992.[96] Today, as a coalition of several organizations, each group works on a diverse range of issues, but the 'alternative' in their coalition's name flows from the several ways in which their perspectives and operations differ from private legal practice and traditional legal aid in the Philippines.[97]

According to Attorney Marlon Manuel, national coordinator of ALG, although he was a 'late bloomer', becoming a lawyer for him was about social change. Starting off at one of the most prestigious law firms in the Philippines, early on he knew that private practice was not for him.

[88] Philippine National Police Command Memorandum Circular No. 16-2016 (1 July 2016), online: https://didm.pnp.gov.ph/images/Command%20Memorandum%20Circulars/CMC%202016-16%20PNP%20ANTI-ILLEGAL%20DRUGS%20CAMPAIGN%20PLAN%20%20PROJECT%20DOUBLE%20BARREL.pdf.

[89] Ibid.

[90] Lian Buan, 'Lawyers File Petition to Declare Drug War Circulars Unconstitutional', *Rappler.com* (11 October 2017).

[91] 'History' ALG Website [*History: ALG Website*], online: alternativelawgroups.ph/index.php/about-us/history; 'Achievements in Building and Maintaining the Rule of Law' (USAID *Occasional Paper Series*, 2012), online: https://pdf.usaid.gov/pdf_docs/pnacr220.pdf.

[92] Ibid.

[93] *Paralegalism*, *supra* note 77, at 3.

[94] *History: ALG Website*, *supra* note 91.

[95] Arneldo S. Valera et al., 'An Integrated Approach in Providing Legal Services to the Rural Poor and Other Disadvantaged Groups: SALAG (Structural Alternative Legal Assistance for Grassroots)' in *Report of Seminars on Legal Services for the Rural Poor and Other Disadvantaged Group* (International Commission of Jurists, 1987) at 55–6.

[96] *History: ALG Website*, *supra* note 91.

[97] *Many Roads*, *supra* note 79, at 203.

Attorney Manuel stayed in private practice for close to two years and ultimately left to join SALIGAN, an ALG organization that engaged in developmental legal work with women, farmers, workers, the urban poor, the indigenous peoples, and local communities. At SALIGAN, he worked his way up to Executive Director, ultimately becoming the National Coordinator for all 23 ALGs. Given his trajectory, his position seems to indicate that ALG has a more open and tolerant attitude toward lawyers compared to FLAG. For instance, Attorney Manuel did not agree with Attorney Ted Te's idea that lawyers who have not already developed a pro bono practice are incapable of serving the poor. He argued, 'it doesn't mean that a lawyer who does not engage in legal aid can no longer be trusted [to help] . . . given the dearth of lawyers, having more lawyers (for the poor) is already good in itself'.[98] In fact, having been a participant in many of the consultation sessions with the IBP, he reported that the IBP was 'surprised and pleased' that ALG supported the proposal to mandate all lawyers in the Philippines to provide pro bono service, and that the IBP saw ALG's agreement as making the position of mandatory legal aid stronger.

One barrier to pro bono legal practice identified by Attorney Manuel is the supposed sufficiency of the PAO. He stated, 'the existence of the PAO . . . minimizes the perceived need for legal aid'.[99] He explained that in 'other ASEAN countries, there is a very high recognized need for legal aid, for pro bono lawyers, there are no lawyers even handling for defense of criminal cases. Here there is the PAO, so in a way, the lawyers see that as addressing the issue.'[100] A second barrier to pro bono legal practice is the lack of incentives for pro bono. On this issue, he noted that 'we do not have any system for incentivizing pro bono work. In other countries, there is a requirement and law firms have their pro bono offices within the firm.'[101] On a brighter note, Attorney Manuel added that legal education provides students with internships, apprenticeships, and clinical legal education. Even though students are not required to work for NGOs, according to Attorney Manuel, 'I think it is a good opportunity in itself that law students know that there are NGOs that do this type of legal aid work . . . the opportunity is provided and some students take it.'[102] He concluded by reflecting on his own experience as a student: 'I did half of my internship in SALIGAN and the other half in a law office. So eventually that SALIGAN experience helped me decide when I was deciding to go into this line of work. Without that exposure, I might not be here.'[103]

What can be discerned from the experiences of these two NGOs who provide legal aid is that many actors in the access to justice space share the same root desire to provide legal services in a highly stratified and unequal society. Free legal services emerged at a time of political repression, thus doing legal work pro bono often involved political issues. Those who worked with FLAG, such as Attorney Romeo Capulong or Attorney Ted Te, felt a strong need to use the law as a means to change the structure of society, with the government as the enemy. Perhaps given that the Marcos dictatorship ended in 1987, ALG now takes a more collaborative approach with the IBP, the Supreme Court, and the current government. Their view is that a government mandate for lawyers to serve the poor is not problematic, but rather a welcomed relief from the burden of servicing such a large need.

98 *Interview with Attorney Manuel, supra* note 48.
99 Ibid.
100 Ibid.
101 Ibid.
102 Ibid.
103 Ibid.

IV. CONCLUSION

Colonized by the Spanish, and then by the Americans, the legal infrastructure of the Philippines is dominated by the perception that the law is mainly used by those in power to aggrandize their position. Ferdinand Marcos' use of the law to extend his rule over the Philippines for 15 years serves as a perfect case in point. So while the government has attempted to step in and address ongoing issues of economic and political displacement, the state is plagued by the impression that it is an elite institution that uses the law to disenfranchise, exploit, and disempower citizens. Lawyers themselves are sceptical of government moves to implement pro bono requirements, and they question the IBP's motivations and whether the IBP has truly represented the beliefs and values of the members of the bar, even though most lawyers *do* believe that it is their duty to use the law to help others. Also active in access to justice is a complex tapestry of NGOs which use the law as an essential tool. Many of these NGOs remember the oppressive days under Marcos, and they take a hardline approach to the law and pro bono practice, making a clear distinction between traditional pro bono lawyers and true public interest lawyers. According to Attorney Romeo Capulong, '[u]nlike the typical pro bono lawyer, the people's lawyers do not limit themselves to the generally accepted interpretation and use of the law to uphold and protect their clients' interest. They know that in an elite-dominated society, the law is merely the expression of elite interests.'[104] In contrast, those who have emerged in the last 30 years take a more conciliatory approach to pro bono practice. Attorney Manuel notes that given the dearth of pro bono attorneys, and the massive need, any help, including from private attorneys, is welcomed.

The fact that a significant number of people in the Philippines lack affordable legal representation prompted the Supreme Court to use its regulatory power over the IBP to mandate pro bono legal services. Yet, because of adverse reactions from lawyers and the inability to provide acceptable guidelines for implementation, the Supreme Court suspended this scheme indefinitely.[105] Moreover, the legislation regarding mandatory pro bono, Republic Act No. 9999, or the 'Free Legal Assistance Act of 2010', while well received by some, was generally seen as a political performance, and not necessarily in the best interest of lawyers. Mandating pro bono legal service in the Philippines, therefore, remains a controversial issue, given the perception of the government as elitist and ineffectual, and the history of struggle against the state. The future of pro bono lawyers thus partially rests in the hands of young lawyers, who like Attorney Manuel may have been exposed to the practice of public interest law through internships and apprenticeships. Given the deeply embedded class stratification, and the ongoing marginalization from justice for many segments of the population, Filipino lawyers who feel a strong sense of responsibility will continue to render their services pro bono. Whether these voluntary acts will remain disparate and under-organized will depend on whether the IBP, the government, and the non-governmental sector can devise a mutually beneficial and accepted method of giving credit to such work.

[104] Romeo Capulong, 'Public Interest Litigation in the Philippines: Challenges, Problems, and Prospects' (18 September 2010), online: romycapulongnymemorial.wordpress.com/2012/10/14/public-interest-lawyering/.

[105] *Access to Justice: Human Rights Abuses Involving Corporations – Philippines* (International Commission of Jurists, 2010) at 38.

9

Access to Justice in Singapore: A Government and Lawyer Dynamic

Helena Whalen-Bridge

Abstract

The government in Singapore is highly centralized and powerful. In this environment, access to justice would seemingly be determined by the government. But while the government does play a major role in access to justice, e.g. by funding legal aid and supporting pro bono schemes, other actors impact access to justice. The chapter examines how access to justice developed between lawyers and the government, starting from the initial government position of implementing civil but not criminal legal aid, to the Law Society's creation of the Criminal Legal Aid Scheme in 1985 and its 2006 Legal Aid Review Report that prompted many improvements, to the government's 2013 decision to fund broad-based criminal legal aid. The chapter argues that access to justice in Singapore should be viewed primarily as a government and lawyer dynamic, and that although the government exercises more power over a variety of decisions, these two actors have negotiated a changing relationship over the years that continues to offer new possibilities.

I. INTRODUCTION: THE SINGAPORE CONTEXT

Singapore is a common law city-state in South East Asia. It has received praise for an efficient legal system and low crime rate.[1] A thriving metropolis, its population in 2020 was 5.69 million,[2] and in 2019 its GDP per capita was US$65,640.[3] Singapore's legal profession in 2020 comprised 5,955 lawyers;[4] this translates into one lawyer for every 955 residents.[5] The legal profession is regulated by the Legal Profession Act[6] and relevant subsidiary regulation. The Law Society of

1 Cheah Wui Ling, 'Developing a People-Centered Justice in Singapore: In Support of Pro Bono and Innocence Work' (2012) 80 *University of Cincinnati Law Review* 1429 [*People-Centered Justice*] at 1431.
2 Department of Singapore Statistics, 'Singapore Population', online: www.singstat.gov.sg/modules/infographics/population.
3 World Bank, 'GDP Per Capita (current US$) – Singapore', data.worldbank.org/indicator/NY.GDP.PCAP.CD?locations=SG&most_recent_value_desc=true.
4 Law Society of Singapore, 'Statistics of Legal Practitioners in Singapore', online: www.lawsociety.org.sg/news-media/statistics/.
5 Singapore Department of Statistics, 'Population and Population Structure', online: www.singstat.gov.sg/find-data/search-by-theme/population/population-and-population-structure/latest-data.
6 *Legal Profession Act*, Singapore (Cap. 161, 2009 Rev. Edn Sing.) (as amended 2 January 2021) [*Legal Profession Act*].

Singapore ('Law Society') represents the interests of lawyers and the legal profession, and carries out statutory duties including maintaining and improving standards of conduct and learning, and assisting the public in matters related to law.[7] The Singapore Academy of Law functions as the promotion and development agency for Singapore's legal industry, and is active in law reform.[8]

The main political party in Singapore, the People's Action Party ('PAP'), has been in power since independence in 1965.[9] The government is highly centralized and powerful, and it makes 'all key political, social and economic decisions'.[10] The long-standing political majority also renders the government a dominant force in the law landscape.[11] In this environment, access to justice would seemingly be determined solely by the government. But while the government plays a major role in access to justice, by funding legal aid and supporting pro bono schemes, other actors impact access to justice. In the context of penal prohibitions on male sodomy, Chen has observed that the Singapore government's position reflected a compromise of relevant interests,[12] and in the access to justice field, actors such as Singapore lawyers and the Law Society,[13] and more recently the Law Society Pro Bono Services ('LSPBS'),[14] play an important role. The courts and the judiciary have contributed to access to justice in many respects,[15] for example by sharing court statistics regarding the percentage of unrepresented parties in criminal, maintenance, and family violence cases.[16] But the Singapore courts do not impose policy, and they see themselves not 'as natural adversaries of the executive, waiting to pounce on the government at the slightest prompting', but as 'an impartial referee, to ensure that the government stays on the correct side of the law'.[17] The chapter therefore examines how access to justice developed between lawyers and the

7 See Law Society of Singapore, 'What We Do', online: www.lawsociety.org.sg/the-law-society/what-we-do/.

8 See Singapore Academy of Law, 'Introduction', online: www.sal.org.sg/About-Us/Introduction; and Singapore Academy of Law, 'Law Reform', online: www.sal.org.sg/Resources-Tools/Law-Reform/.

9 Po Jen Yap, 'The Supreme Court of Singapore and the Promise of Enforceable Constitutional Conventions', in Po Jen Yap, ed., *Courts and Democracies in Asia* (Cambridge: Cambridge University Press, 2017) 19 at 19.

10 Kevin Y. L. Tan, *The Constitution of Singapore: A Contextual Analysis* (Oxford: Bloomsbury, 2015) at 238, and see 2–9.

11 See Jothie Rajah, *Authoritarian Rule of Law: Legislation, Discourse and Legitimacy in Singapore* (Cambridge: Cambridge University Press, 2012) [*Authoritarian Rule of Law*].

12 Jianlin Chen, 'Singapore's Culture War over Section 377A: Through the Lens of Public Choice and Multilingual Research' (2013) 38:1 *Law & Social Inquiry* 106.

13 Regarding the Law Society of Singapore, see Jothie Rajah and Arun Thiruvengadam, 'Of Absences, Masks and Exceptions: Cause Lawyering in Singapore' (2014) 31:3 *Wisconsin International Law Journal* 646 [*Cause Lawyering in Singapore*] at 654–60; and see *Authoritarian Rule of Law*, *supra* note 11, at 165.

14 The 'Pro Bono Services Office of the Law Society of Singapore' was first established as an Institution of a Public Character, on 10 September 2007, and was later incorporated as a Company Limited by Guarantee on 1 April 2017, when it commenced operations as 'Law Society Pro Bono Services', a registered charity and Institution of a Public Character: see Law Society Pro Bono Services, 'Home', online: www.lawsocprobono.org/Pages/default.aspx. After initial historical references to the Pro Bono Services Office, this chapter will primarily use the organization's current name, Law Society Pro Bono Services ('LSPBS').

15 See Gary Chan Kok Yew, 'Access to Justice for the Poor: The Singapore Judiciary at Work' (2008) 17:3 *Pacific Rim Law & Policy Journal* 595; and Helena Whalen-Bridge, 'Court Backlogs: Balancing Efficiency and Justice in Singapore' (2017) 7:4 *Oñati Socio-Legal Series* 879; Kevin Y. L. Tan, 'As Efficient as the Best Businesses: Singapore's Judicial System' in Jiunn-rong Yeh and Wen-Chen Chang, eds., *Asian Courts in Context* (Cambridge: Cambridge University Press, 2014) [*Singapore's Judicial System*] 228, at 244–6; and *Thematic Study on Legal Aid* (ASEAN Intergovernmental Commission on Human Rights, 2019) at 133–4 and 136.

16 Chief Justice Chan Sek Keong, 'Access to Quality Justice for All' (Keynote Address delivered at the Subordinate Courts Workplan 2010, 26 February 2010) at para. 6.

17 *Singapore's Judicial System*, *supra* note 15, at 258.

government, starting from the initial government position of implementing civil but not criminal legal aid, to the Law Society's creation of the Criminal Legal Aid Scheme in 1985 and its 2006 Legal Aid Review Report that prompted many improvements, to the government's 2013 decision to fund broad-based criminal legal aid. This chapter argues that access to justice in Singapore should be viewed primarily as a government and lawyer dynamic,[18] and although the government has exercised more power over a variety of decisions, these two actors have negotiated a changing relationship regarding access to justice over the years that continues to offer new possibilities.

II. ACCESS TO JUSTICE DEVELOPMENT IN SINGAPORE

A. *Early Approaches to Civil and Criminal Legal Aid*

Legal aid was formally adopted in 1956 by the Legal Aid and Advice Ordinance.[19] The Ordinance provided for legal aid in civil cases and criminal cases, as well as legal advice,[20] a structure carried over into the Legal Aid and Advice Act by independent Singapore.[21] Broad-based criminal legal aid had been included when legal aid legislation was first enacted, but unlike civil legal aid, provisions regarding criminal representation were never implemented. Other issues took precedence in the early years of Singapore's history, and government policy opposed the simultaneous representation of an accused person it was prosecuting.[22] The government did provide criminal defence for capital crimes, which since the 1990s has been organized under the Assigned Counsel Scheme for Capital Cases, currently the Legal Assistance Scheme for Capital Offences ('LASCO').[23] Under this Scheme, defendants charged with capital offences are assigned free legal counsel, and there is 'no means test to pass or eligibility criteria to satisfy'.[24]

[18] While analysis of legal education and access to justice is beyond the scope of the chapter, it can be noted that Singapore has made a strong connection between the two; for example, the need to produce lawyers interested in practising areas of community law such as criminal and family law ultimately translated into a third law school, the Singapore University of Social Sciences (SUSS), that focuses on preparing professionals for these areas (see Singapore University of Social Sciences, 'SIM University to Start Full-time Programmes in 2014 and to Set Up Third Law School in Singapore', online: www.suss.edu.sg/news-and-events/news/sim-university-to-start-full-time-programmes-in-2014-and-to-set-up-third-law-school-in-singapore#:~:text=Share%3A,ceremony%20on%20October%2016%20morning), and a mandatory pro bono programme for law students has been implemented (see Singapore Institute of Legal Education, 'Pro Bono Programme', online: www.sile.edu.sg/pro-bono-programme).

[19] *Legal Aid and Advice Ordinance*, Singapore 1956 [*Legal Aid Ordinance*].

[20] *Legal Aid Ordinance*, *supra* note 19, Parts III, II, and VI, respectively.

[21] The *Revised Edition of the Laws Act*, Singapore 1966, s 4(q), allowed appointed Law Revision Commissioners to restyle Ordinances as Acts, resulting in the *Legal Aid and Advice Act* (Cap. 9) in the 1970 Revised Edition of the Laws of Singapore.

[22] Helena Whalen-Bridge, 'The Conceptualisation of Pro Bono in Singapore' (2014) 9 *Asian Journal of Comparative Law* 97 at 110–12; and see Christine Sim and Tan Zhi Feng, 'The Paradox of Legal Aid in Singapore: Civil Legal Aid Without Criminal Legal Aid' (2012) 30 *Singapore Law Review* 165 [*Paradox of Legal Aid*] at 169–70.

[23] *Legal Aid Review Committee Report* (Legal Aid Review Committee of the Law Society of Singapore, 2006) [*LAR Report*] at 14, and Singapore Supreme Courts, 'Join the Legal Assistance Scheme for Capital Offences Counsel', www.judiciary.gov.sg/join-us/join-legal-assistance-scheme-capital-offences-counsel.

[24] Supreme Court of Singapore, 'Legal Assistance Scheme for Capital Offences (LASCO)', online: www.judiciary.gov.sg/legal-help-support/criminal-case.

The lack of broad-based criminal legal aid funded by the government ultimately led to the formation of a volunteer scheme of criminal representation in 1985.[25] As observed by Kevin Tan in his history of the Law Society:[26]

> [b]y the mid-1980s, there was a sense of restlessness at the Bar, especially among the younger lawyers, most of whom had been called to the Bar in [the] 1970s. Many young lawyers . . . wanted a more vibrant and energetic Bar who did more to serve the public . . . this desire . . . manifested itself in the establishment of the Criminal Legal Aid Scheme in 1985. But this activism within the Bar was beginning to worry the PAP government who viewed with grave suspicion any kind of political mobilisation.

A study done in 1981 by Stanley Yeo, a law lecturer at the National University of Singapore, also contributed to the creation of the scheme, as it demonstrated that accused persons had a greater likelihood of acquittal and a lesser sentence if they had representation.[27] A number of lawyers urged the Law Society to do something, and in 1983, the Law Society's Council established a two-person Legal Aid Sub-Committee to investigate.[28] In January 1984, the Law Society announced the intention to make free legal assistance available to poor accused persons in criminal cases,[29] and in 1985, the Criminal Legal Aid Scheme ('CLAS') was launched with volunteer lawyers.[30]

For many years CLAS did not receive direct funding from the government.[31] Charitable donations to CLAS were supported by then Minister for Law S. Jayakumar, e.g. in 1998 when over S$200,000 was raised in a charity golf tournament.[32] Volunteer CLAS lawyers did not receive payment for the legal services they provided, and they frequently waived disbursements that they would have been entitled to.[33] These funding arrangements greatly limited indigent criminal defence. It was noted in 2006 that, given the financial constraints since the scheme's inception, only 2,230 applicants out of a total of 10,323, or 20 per cent, were successful in getting legal services.[34] Together with the Association of Criminal Lawyers of Singapore ('ACLS'),[35] which was formally founded in 2004,[36] CLAS provided the bulk of indigent criminal defence via this pro bono arrangement for many years. Criminal legal aid remained on the statute books, but during the 1995 amendments to the Legal Aid and Advice Act, provisions regarding criminal legal aid were deleted, effectively abolishing 'any hopes of a state-run scheme' similar to the government-run Legal Aid Bureau ('LAB') for civil matters.[37]

[25] *LAR Report*, *supra* note 23, at 11.

[26] Kevin Y. L. Tan, *Fiat Justitia: A History of the Law Society of Singapore* (Singapore: Straits Time Press, 2017) [*Fiat Justitia*] at 64.

[27] Stanley Yeo Meng Heong, 'Unrepresented Defendants in the Subordinate Criminal Courts of Singapore' (1981) 23 *Malaya Law Review* 41 at 46–9; see also Stanley Yeo Meng Heong, 'Re-opening the Case for Criminal Legal Aid in Singapore' (1983) 2 *Malayan Law Journal* cxxiv.

[28] *Fiat Justitia*, *supra* note 26, at 66.

[29] Ibid.

[30] *LAR Report*, *supra* note 23, at 11.

[31] *LAR Report*, *supra* note 23, at 12.

[32] *Fiat Justitia*, *supra* note 26, at 140.

[33] *LAR Report*, *supra* note 23, at 12.

[34] *LAR Report*, *supra* note 23, at 13.

[35] *Paradox of Legal Aid*, *supra* note 22, at 167.

[36] Association of Criminal Lawyers of Singapore, 'About', online: www.facebook.com/pg/ACLS-802897269743245/about/.

[37] Yeo Hwee Ying, 'Provision of Legal Aid in Singapore' in Kevin Y. L. Tan, ed., *The Singapore Legal System*, 2nd edn (Singapore: Singapore University Press, 1999) 446 at 463.

B. *Law Society Deliberations Regarding Access to Justice*

The report issued by the Law Society's Legal Aid Review Committee ('Committee') in October 2006 arguably marked the beginning of a wider shift[38] in Singapore's attitudes toward access to justice. In 2006, the Law Society established the Committee to review legal aid and pro bono in Singapore as part of its mission to promote access to justice.[39] The Committee's Legal Aid Review Report ('LAR Report') constituted what appears to be the first comprehensive review of legal services for the poor in Singapore. The LAR Report is not raised in current discussions of access to justice, but many important developments followed its lead, and when viewed together with CLAS it illustrates the role that the Law Society can play.

The LAR Report evaluated the state of civil and criminal legal assistance. Regarding civil legal aid, the Committee noted that although the bottom 10 per cent of the population were covered by the means test then in use, some of these applicants were not able to access services because they could not afford the obligatory co-payment.[40] Significant portions of the population, including the lower middle class or 'sandwich' class, were excluded from legal aid but still could not afford legal services.[41]

The Committee reviewed how different sources of civil legal aid were funded. LAB was the main provider of civil legal services for the poor,[42] pursuant to the Legal Aid and Advice Act, and it was funded primarily by the government.[43] LAB handled 75 per cent of its cases with its legal services office and support staff, while the remaining 25 per cent were handled by a panel of volunteer lawyers,[44] paid by honorarium.[45] The Committee also reviewed the system for defence in capital cases, LASCO. LASCO did not administer a means test, and volunteer lawyers on the scheme were paid an honorarium.[46] Unlike civil legal aid, there were no government employees providing defence services; the entire structure of indigent capital defence was based on the honorarium model, in which the government provided a minimum payment to the lawyer and the lawyer essentially donated a portion of the legal services.

The LAR Report recommended that the Law Society address the needs of the population via an increased means test and other financial adjustments.[47] To implement the suggestions, the LAR Report recommended that each law firm pledge 25 pro bono hours per lawyer per year, and that starter funding from the government and other resources be provided for a new office of Pro Bono Services.[48] The office would function within the Law Society, allocating and administering pro bono work.[49] In 2007, the Law Society adopted the recommendations of its Committee, and on 10 September 2007 the Pro Bono Services Office was launched to manage and develop all of the Law Society's pro bono programmes.[50]

[38] See *People-Centered Justice*, *supra* note 1.
[39] *LAR Report*, *supra* note 23, at 1–2.
[40] *LAR Report*, *supra* note 23, at 27.
[41] *LAR Report*, *supra* note 23, at 28–9.
[42] *LAR Report*, *supra* note 23, at 5.
[43] *LAR Report*, *supra* note 23, at 6.
[44] Ibid.
[45] *LAR Report*, *supra* note 23, at 10.
[46] *LAR Report*, *supra* note 23, at 15.
[47] *LAR Report*, *supra* note 23, at 54–6.
[48] *LAR Report*, *supra* note 23, at 53.
[49] Ibid.
[50] Law Society Pro Bono Services, 'Who Are We?', www.lawsocprobono.org/Pages/default.aspx.

LAR Report recommendations were directed at voluntary legal services by lawyers, but there were subsequent discussions in Parliament regarding legal aid. On 2 March 2007,[51] Dr Teo Ho Pin noted that many low-wage earners would not meet the legal aid criteria but could not afford the services of a private lawyer.[52] In criminal matters, they did not know how to make representations in court and would have no choice but to plead guilty without mitigating their cases, an unfair situation.[53] Then Deputy Prime Minister and Minister for Law Prof. S. Jayakumar noted that LAB would improve the situation in three ways: adjustments to the means test, giving discretion to the Legal Aid Director to grant aid, and a partnership with the Law Society.[54]

Proposing a partnership between the Ministry of Law and the Law Society signalled a sea change. The Law Society and the government had clashed, for example regarding the Law Society's ability to comment on pending legislation.[55] In 1986, the Law Society issued a press statement querying the terms of proposed legislation 'designed to give the state control over what the "foreign press" published on Singapore'.[56] The press statement was consistent with the Legal Profession Act as it was then framed, which stated that the Law Society had the ability to 'examine and if it thinks fit to report upon current or proposed legislation and other any legal matters'.[57] The government however objected, because per Jothie Rajah, 'the Law Society had, by making a public statement, breached state–Law Society relations'.[58] The relevant provision was amended[59] to read that the Law Society had the power 'to examine and if it thinks fit to report upon current or proposed legislation submitted to it and any other legal matters',[60] understood to mean that the Law Society could only comment 'when requested by the government'.[61] For almost 20 years after hearings regarding this matter, 'the Law Society of Singapore stayed out of the public domain'.[62] Proposing in 2007 that the government and Law Society work together meant that a different relationship was being suggested, one in which more progress on access to justice could be made.

The creation of a pro bono office, first as the Pro Bono Services Office, an arm of the Law Society, and then as Law Society Pro Bono Services ('LSPBS'), a separate charity under the direction of a Board of Directors with Law Society representation,[63] had a catalysing effect on pro bono in Singapore.[64] As reviewed by then Law Society Vice President Lok Vi Ming in 2012,

[51] *Singapore Parliamentary Debates, Official Report*, vol. 82 (2 March 2007) [*Debates 2 March 2007*] at cols. 2338–40 (Teo Ho Pin).

[52] *Debates 2 March 2007*, *supra* note 51, at col. 2338 (Teo Ho Pin).

[53] *Debates 2 March 2007*, *supra* note 51, at cols. 2338–9 (Teo Ho Pin).

[54] *Debates 2 March 2007*, *supra* note 51, at col. 2352 (S. Jayakumar).

[55] See *Authoritarian Rule of Law*, *supra* note 11, at 161–218; and Gillian Koh and Ooi Giok Ling, 'Relationship between State and Civil Society in Singapore: Clarifying the Concepts, Assessing the Grounds' in Lee Hock Guan, ed., *Civil Society in Southeast Asia* (Singapore: Institute of Southeast Asian Studies, 2004) at 181.

[56] *Cause Lawyering in Singapore*, *supra* note 13, at 658.

[57] *Legal Profession Act*, Singapore 1982 (Cap. 217), s 61(1)(d).

[58] *Cause Lawyering in Singapore*, *supra* note 13, at 659.

[59] *Legal Profession (Amendment) Act*, Singapore 1986, s 6.

[60] *Legal Profession Act*, Singapore 1987 (Cap. 161, 1985 Rev. Edn Sing.) (as amended 30 March 1987), s 56(1)(d).

[61] Alvin Yeo, 'Law and Politics: Should Law Society Speak Up Only When Asked?', *The Straits Times* (19 July 2008).

[62] *Cause Lawyering in Singapore*, *supra* note 13, at 659.

[63] See *Annual Report 2019–20* (Law Society Pro Bono Services, 2020) [*Annual Report 2019–20*] at 9–12.

[64] See Thio Shen Yi, 'President's Message' (*Singapore Law Gazette*, March 2016) at 1 and 4, online: v1.lawgazette.com.sg/2016-03/; 'Pro Bono Special' (*Singapore Law Gazette*, March 2016) at 16–40, online: v1.lawgazette.com.sg/2016-03/; Ng Shi Yang and Sadhana Rai, '2017 Pro Bono Highlights' (*Singapore Law Gazette*, February 2017), online: v1

LSPBS concentrated on three areas: '(1) creation of programmes; (2) volunteer recruitment and mobilisation to sustain the programmes; and (3) coordination with other agencies in the legal landscape to ensure an integrated approach'.[65] Different programmes were launched or augmented for individuals, community-serving organizations, and the community at large.[66] To better coordinate pro bono in Singapore, LSPBS created formal collaborations in which the Law Society supported the initiatives of other organizations with manpower and institutional resources.[67] They also shared expertise with others who wished to start or develop a programme and helped to channel volunteers to assist those programmes.[68] To support volunteers, LSPBS offered schemes such as a 'Mentor/Specialist Resource programme' which provided 'mentorship to fresh volunteers and a specialist resource scheme for queries by volunteers on practice areas', and a 'Knowledge Database Contributor' scheme which provided paralegal support and information resources.[69] LSPBS also launched and supported Community Legal Clinics, which in 2019 served 1,689 persons, and expanded into additional specialized clinics.[70]

Under LSPBS' lead, pro bono hours increased considerably. Respondents to LSPBS surveys indicated that the number of pro bono hours grew from 35,634 hours in 2009 (10 hours/lawyer) to almost double that amount in 2014, 68,256 hours (13 hours/lawyer).[71] The government has provided support and necessary resources,[72] but the main impetus for LSPBS was the Law Society and its LAR Report.

C. Considering Mandatory Pro Bono

The first recorded references to mandatory pro bono in Singapore appear to be in the Law Society's 2006 LAR Report.[73] Consideration of this issue indicates how far-reaching the LAR Report was, because at that time Singapore did not even have a recommended number of pro bono hours for lawyers. The Committee did not make any recommendations regarding mandatory pro bono, but it noted that lawyers had these obligations in other jurisdictions.[74] The report suggested that Singapore could consider whether lawyers should be required to 'contribute a yearly sum towards legal aid, if they cannot contribute in services and time'.[75]

The LAR Report's consideration of mandatory pro bono was followed by discussion in Parliament in 2007.[76] Ms Ellen Lee asked whether the 25 hours of pro bono services would

.lawgazette.com.sg/2017-02/; and Law Society of Singapore, 'Annual Reports', online: www.lawsociety.org.sg/About-Us/Annual-Reports.

65 Lok Vi Ming, 'Growing a Pro Bono Culture in Singapore's Legal Profession: An Update from the Law Society of Singapore', *Law Society of Singapore* (10 February 2012) [*Law Society Update 2012*] at 3 (copy on file with author).

66 Ibid.

67 *Law Society Update 2012*, *supra* note 65, at 4.

68 Ibid.

69 *Law Society Update 2012*, *supra* note 65, at 5.

70 *Annual Report 2019–20*, *supra* note 63, at 38.

71 *Annual Report 2015* (Law Society of Singapore, 2015) at 56.

72 See Amir Hussain and Amanda Lee, 'Govt Will Provide Direct Legal Aid to Defendants In Criminal Cases', *Today* (6 December 2013) [*Direct Legal Aid*], and see *Paradox of Legal Aid*, *supra* note 22, at 166.

73 *LAR Report*, *supra* note 23, at 47–50.

74 *LAR Report*, *supra* note 23, at 48 and 50.

75 *LAR Report*, *supra* note 23, at 49–50; although the LAR Report does not refer to Malaysia, the Bar Council had already instituted its mandatory contribution in 1983: see Chapter 6.

76 *Debates 2 March 2007*, *supra* note 51, at col. 2369.

be compulsory.[77] Then Minister of Law, S. Jayakumar, clarified that the Ministry of Law would not prescribe that lawyers do compulsory pro bono, as that would be up to the Law Society.[78] The understanding was that the Law Society was not going to do that, but rather 'exhort' members to provide the annual 25 hours.[79] In response to a question about whether the 25 pro bono hours would be tracked, for example in connection with and dependent upon renewal of the Practising Certificate required for practice, the Minister stated that it was the Law Society's proposal and the Ministry was merely assisting to facilitate it, but that the understanding was that the pro bono was not compulsory.[80] The government statement that compulsory pro bono would be up to the Law Society provides additional support for the significance of the Law Society's role in access to justice.

Discussions of mandatory pro bono wound down, and deliberation regarding pro bono focused on voluntary pro bono and measures to increase it. For example, there were parliamentary discussions about the pro bono spirit amongst lawyers.[81] Then Senior Minister of State for Law, Associate Professor Ho Peng Kee, noted that to the Bar's credit, the rate of volunteerism had grown.[82] Associate Professor Ho also stated that 'support from employers is a key factor', and that the Pro Bono Services Office was raising awareness among law firms of the value of pro bono and corporate social responsibility, via seminars and articles.[83]

A year later, on 14 February 2011, the discussion in Parliament started to take a different turn. In discussions regarding the amendment of the Legal Profession Act, Mr Michael Palmer addressed the pending subject of mandatory continuing professional development, asking whether the Minister for Law could 'provide some indication of the form he envisages the continuing professional development of advocates and solicitors will take? ... And whether the Minister will consider including in continuing professional development a certain minimum number of hours of pro bono legal work?'[84] In response, Minister for Law Mr Shanmugam noted that 'Mr Palmer's suggestion of a mandatory minimum of pro bono hours as part of CPD is an interesting one. We have many avenues for lawyers to contribute pro bono now, and their work in this area is important to the community.'[85]

On 9 March 2011, Palmer raised the subject again, noting that the reaction of lawyers to mandatory pro bono was varied:[86]

> ... the majority of lawyers interviewed felt that pro bono legal work ought not to be mandated as it should come from the heart. Other lawyers who spoke to me directly felt that it was a good idea. What was heartening to note was that most of the profession felt that lawyers ought to do some pro bono legal work. What we disagreed on was how to accomplish that ...

77 Ibid.

78 *Debates 2 March 2007*, *supra* note 51, at col. 2370 (S. Jayakumar).

79 Ibid.

80 *Debates 2 March 2007*, *supra* note 51, at cols. 2371–2 (S. Jayakumar).

81 *Singapore Parliamentary Debates, Official Report*, vol. 86 (11 March 2010) [*Debates 11 March 2010*] at cols. 4052–3, 4064–5.

82 *Debates 11 March 2010*, *supra* note 81, at col. 4064 (Ho Peng Kee).

83 *Debates 11 March 2010*, *supra* note 81, at col. 4065 (Ho Peng Kee).

84 *Singapore Parliamentary Debates, Official Report*, vol. 87 (14 February 2011) [*Debates 14 February 2011*] at col. 2592 (Michael Palmer).

85 *Debates 14 February 2011*, *supra* note 84, at col. 2597 (Michael Palmer).

86 *Singapore Parliamentary Debates, Official Report*, vol. 87 (9 March 2011) [*Debates 9 March 2011*] at cols. 4373–4 (Michael Palmer).

> The Law Society of Singapore has approximately 3,500 members. In 2006, a collaborative commitment by the Singapore legal profession was made to donate at least 25 hours per lawyer per year towards *pro bono* work. That works out to about 80,000 hours of free legal services for the community ... Regrettably ... figures provided by the Law Society show that approximately 3,500 lawyers declared only some 35,000 hours of pro bono work. That is less than 50% of the target.
>
> I feel that something needs to be done and if it is not to be mandated, then perhaps an alternative proposition might be to allow pro bono legal services to be credited within the professional development framework.

When raised initially in February 2011, the suggestion regarding mandatory pro bono had been somewhat general, but these remarks indicate that by March 2011 the suggestion had become more pointed. In response, then Senior Minister of State for Law, Associate Professor Ho Peng Kee, stated that:[87]

> while all in the legal fraternity agreed that *pro bono* work is important, not all are of the view that it should be made mandatory. There are really different perspectives on the issue. The CPD scheme is intended to help lawyers keep abreast of legal, regulatory and practice related developments, so that they are better equipped to handle their work ...
>
> Mr Palmer's alternative suggestion, that of giving credit for pro bono work within the framework of the CPD by allowing lawyers who do pro bono work to do fewer hours of CPD, appears to be one that is carefully thought through. This could be a means of recognising the value of pro bono work, incentivising lawyers to do more. I understand from SILE [Singapore Institute of Legal Education] that it is already considering this possibility.

Mandatory pro bono had been identified and discussed, but it did not seem to be going anywhere. Then in October 2012, the Singapore Academy of Law, via the Committee to Study Community Legal Services Initiatives ('CLS Committee'), circulated a discussion paper ('First Paper') suggesting mandatory pro bono legal services for lawyers holding a practising certificate.[88] The CLS Committee was chaired by Justice V. K. Rajah, Judge of Appeal of the Singapore Supreme Court, and included representatives from the Singapore judiciary, the Ministry of Law, the Singapore Academy of Law, and the Singapore Bar.[89] The composition of the CLS Committee indicates that it was a joint endeavour involving the judiciary, the government, and the bar.

On 31 October 2012, members of the community were invited to provide feedback on the First Paper's proposal for mandatory Community Legal Services ('CLS') to low-income and disadvantaged Singaporeans.[90] The phrase 'mandatory pro bono' was not used at all. The scheme would apply to all lawyers holding practising certificates, including those working in foreign law firms,[91] but not to foreign lawyers, 'Legal Service Officers ("LSOs"), academics working in tertiary

87 *Debates 9 March 2011*, *supra* note 86, at col. 4384 (Ho Peng Kee).

88 Singapore Academy of Law, 'Proposed Framework for Community Legal Services', online: www.sal.org.sg/Newsroom/News-Releases/NewsDetails/id/47 [*News Release*]; Singapore, Committee to Study Community Legal Services Initiatives, *Discussion Paper on Community Legal Services* (2012), online: www.sal.org.sg/sites/default/files/PDF%20Files/Newsroom/CLS%20discussion%20paper.pdf [*First Paper*].

89 *First Paper*, *supra* note 88, at Annex 1.

90 *News Release*, *supra* note 88.

91 *First Paper*, *supra* note 88, at para. B.1.1.

institutions, paralegals, in-house counsel, arbitrators, and legal counsel in government departments or ministries who are not LSOs' in order to avoid potential conflicts of interest.[92] The requirement would be 16 hours a year, with carryover of 8 hours per year.[93] The CLS Committee recommended that consideration be given to permitting contributions-in-lieu of hours, and that hours and contributions need not be mutually exclusive.[94]

Consistent with 'the core objective of serving the community', only CLS would satisfy the requirement, which would comprise four main areas: criminal legal aid; civil legal aid; '[c]ommunity mediation, legal clinics and various other voluntary services in the Subordinate Courts'; and '[l]egal advisory work to approved institutions and charities which provide assistance to the community'.[95] The CLS Committee noted that the mandatory nature of the requirement would 'provide a much needed push for the profession to become more involved in serving the community', and that 'a significant proportion of the litigants in the Subordinate Courts are unrepresented'.[96] The CLS Committee hoped that CLS would perhaps 'cultivate an ethos of service as well as a shared responsibility, and remind lawyers that the profession is a noble one with much to contribute to society'.[97]

There was some support for the proposal. One lawyer, Gloria James, said that 'some defendants are advised that their offences are minor and they do not need a lawyer as they would only be fined. But they are not told of the consequences of having a criminal record ...'; she suggested that 'pro bono work should be made compulsory for junior lawyers with up to three years in practice'.[98] However, the majority of lawyers who attended a town hall meeting on 27 November 2012, while acknowledging that approximately half of criminal defendants were unrepresented in court, 'were against making free legal work compulsory'.[99] Lawyer Barry Delaney, in his 60s, stated that it 'seems to be an oxymoron when one is forced to do charity',[100] and one newspaper article noted that the proposal 'faced opposition from some quarters who felt it ran contrary to the spirit of volunteerism'.[101] Another lawyer, Mr Andrew Goh, stated that he was 'against the idea of making it compulsory for a sector in Singapore to solve a wider social problem'.[102]

On 2 April 2013, the CLS Committee circulated a second consultation paper ('Second Paper').[103] It was noted that:[104]

[92] *First Paper, supra* note 88, at para. B.1.2.
[93] *First Paper, supra* note 88, at para. C.1.1–C.1.2.
[94] *First Paper, supra* note 88, at para. C.3.1.
[95] *First Paper, supra* note 88, at para. C.2.1.
[96] *First Paper, supra* note 88, at paras. A.2, A.3.
[97] *First Paper, supra* note 88, at para. A.2.
[98] Joyce Lim, 'Compulsory Pro Bono Work? Some Reject Idea', *The Straits Times* (15 December 2012) [*Compulsory Pro Bono Work?*].
[99] Ibid.
[100] Ibid.
[101] Neo Chai Chin, 'Debate on Probono Legal Work Continues', *Today* (23 July 2013).
[102] *Compulsory Pro Bono Work?, supra* note 98.
[103] Singapore Academy of Law, 'Second Consultation on Proposed Framework for Community Legal Services' (2 April 2013), online: www.sal.org.sg/Newsroom/News-Releases/NewsDetails/id/4 [*Second Paper News Release*]; Singapore, Committee to Study Community Legal Services Initiatives, *Second Consultation on Proposed Framework for Community Legal Services* (2013) [*Second Paper*].
[104] *Second Paper News Release, supra* note 103.

respondents were overwhelmingly of the view that pro bono work was an integral part of legal practice. Respondents also felt that the driving idea behind CLS to facilitate access to justice for those that could not afford aid was laudable. However, the majority felt that the legal profession was not ready to make pro bono legal work compulsory and that there should be phased implementation of CLS.

The Second Paper offered a refined proposal in two stages.[105] The first stage would establish an aspirational target of pro bono hours, paired with a mandatory reporting requirement of pro bono hours completed in a calendar year.[106] Under this scheme, lawyers could report zero hours, and only a failure to report would merit a sanction.[107] It was hoped that 'the act of reporting in itself will act as a catalyst in creating awareness and galvanizing interest within the profession in pro bono work'.[108] The second stage would involve a 'mandatory minimum number of pro bono hours as detailed in the first consultation paper', but the scope of CLS would depend on the data obtained through the first stage's mandatory reporting.[109] Prior to the implementation of the second stage, there would be consultations to determine who would be covered, the number of hours, and the definition of pro bono, which would depend on 'the needs of the pro bono landscape'.[110]

The Second Paper expounded on the reasoning behind the proposal. Regarding the need for community legal services, the paper noted that 'one-third of the criminal cases in the Subordinate Courts involve litigants-in-person and more than 90% of the litigants are not represented in maintenance and family violence cases'.[111] The Second Paper also reiterated other reasons for the proposal, of cultivating an ethos of service,[112] breaking down the silos created by expertise demands and cultivating the expertise needed to provide CLS,[113] and improving the public's perception of the profession.[114] The CLS Committee shared the comparative research it had done,[115] noting that the American Bar Association in the US established an aspirational target of 50 hours,[116] compared to Singapore's 25 hours.[117] The paper referenced schemes for lawyers in Japan and South Korea, both of which had mandatory pro bono requirements to some degree.[118]

The Second Paper also communicated the relationship envisioned between the government and lawyers, noting that the government was 'expanding the coverage of legal aid. It is hoped that CLS will further enhance access to justice for this section of society and plug the gap for legal assistance required by the community.'[119] However, while the general need for more pro bono was known, 'exactly how much is needed to plug the justice gap is not known. There is little empirical data on the total number of pro bono hours required and how this is, or should

[105] *Second Paper*, *supra* note 103, Section C.1.
[106] *Second Paper*, *supra* note 103, Section C.2.
[107] *Second Paper*, *supra* note 103, at para. A.3.
[108] *Second Paper*, *supra* note 103, at para. C.3.4.
[109] *Second Paper*, *supra* note 103, at para. A.4.
[110] Ibid.
[111] *Second Paper*, *supra* note 103, at para. B.1.3.
[112] *Second Paper*, *supra* note 103, at para. B.1.4.
[113] *Second Paper*, *supra* note 103, at para. B.1.5.
[114] *Second Paper*, *supra* note 103, at para. B.1.6.
[115] *Second Paper*, *supra* note 103, at Annex 3.
[116] *Second Paper*, *supra* note 103, at para. E.1.4.
[117] *Second Paper*, *supra* note 103, at para. C.3.1.
[118] *Second Paper*, *supra* note 103, at para. E.1.5 and E.1.6.
[119] *Second Paper*, *supra* note 103, at para. B.1.3.

be, split among all 4000 members of the profession. Therefore, CLS will first roll out the mandatory reporting system in order to facilitate data collection.'[120]

The CLS Committee collected feedback, with responses due May 2013.[121] On 28 November 2013, the CLS Committee submitted its report and recommendations ('Final Report') to the Ministry of Law and the Law Society.[122] As summarized in the Final Report, feedback suggested that there were still concerns about the mandatory nature of CLS, and that for some, 'this concern stemmed from the view that the State was in the best position to help lower-income Singaporeans and that the responsibility should rest with the Legal Aid Bureau'.[123]

Feedback summarized in the Final Report also noted drawbacks to a mandatory system, such as a negative impact on the essential nature of volunteerism and the ethos of service, which 'should be cultivated by encouragement and education instead of compulsion'.[124] It was felt that making pro bono mandatory would have a double-edged negative effect on the pro bono client relationship, in that it would 'reduce the emotional well-being from the giver's point of view, and breed a sense of entitlement on the part of the recipients'.[125] Finally, it was noted that 'a culture of pro bono must begin with senior lawyers within the firms',[126] the ones responsible for articulating the value of public service within the firm and implementing relevant practices such as assigning cases and crediting hours.

As summarized by the Ministry of Law, the Final Report made four recommendations: (1) all Singapore advocates and solicitors applying for a practising certificate would be required to report their preceding year's pro bono hours; (2) the reporting would be done on an individual basis, although firms could declare on a firm-wide basis; (3) pro bono work would include legal work for organizations and societies as well as other law-related work, if there was no remuneration or only an honorarium; and (4) there would be no adverse consequences to reporting zero hours.[127] The recommendations were adopted, and the relevant rules regarding mandatory reporting are now provided in subsidiary legislation.[128]

D. *Funding and Implementing Broad-based Criminal Legal Aid*

One theme running through the feedback on mandatory pro bono was the respective roles of the government and lawyers in access to justice. As noted above, for some, the concern regarding mandatory pro bono 'stemmed from the view that the State was in the best position to help lower-income Singaporeans and that the responsibility should rest with the Legal Aid Bureau'.[129]

120 Ibid.

121 *Second Paper*, *supra* note 103, at para. F.1–F.2.

122 Ministry of Law, 'Mandatory Reporting for Legal Pro Bono Work Done' (24 March 2014), online: www.mlaw.gov.sg/news/press-releases/mandatory-reporting-for-legal-pro-bono-work-done [*Mandatory Reporting*].

123 Singapore, Committee to Study Community Legal Services Initiatives, *Report of the Committee to Study Community Legal Services Initiatives* (2013), online: www.mlaw.gov.sg/files/news/press-releases/2014/03/Annex%20B%20-%20Report%20of%20the%20Committee%20to%20Study%20Community%20Legal%20Services%20Initiative.pdf [*Final Report*], at para. 9.

124 Ibid.

125 Ibid.

126 Ibid.

127 *Mandatory Reporting*, *supra* note 122, at para. 2.

128 *Legal Profession Act*, *supra* note 6, Legal Profession (Mandatory Reporting of Specified Pro Bono Services) Rules 2015, Singapore (with effect from 1 March 2015) [*Mandatory Reporting Rules*].

129 *Final Report*, *supra* note 123, at para 9.

The feedback appears to reflect the view that mandatory pro bono was being suggested in part to cover the criminal legal aid that was not funded by the government. In the Address by then President of the Law Society Mr Lok Vi Ming, at the Opening of Legal Year in January 2013, it was noted that 'providing access to justice is, however, not the sole responsibility of the Bar but one shared with the government. We are encouraged that the Ministry of Law has been in discussion with the Law Society on this. I am, however, particularly concerned with the issue of funding which will become more pressing as we enlarge our pro bono footprint.'[130] The possibility of change was mentioned in Parliament on 11 November 2013, when then Second Minister for Home Affairs Mr S. Iswaran stated that he understood that 'the Ministry of Law has been generally looking at enhancing criminal legal aid and I think it will be able to announce its position on this soon'.[131]

These discussions hinted that a major transformation was coming. On 6 December 2013, in 'a significant departure from its long-held stance towards legal aid for those accused of non-capital crimes', the Singapore government announced it would provide direct legal assistance and support to defendants in criminal cases.[132] At the Association of Muslim Lawyers' Inaugural Lecture, the Minister for Foreign Affairs and Law, Mr K. Shanmugam, noted that the government had expanded civil legal aid and given LAB more discretion to grant assistance in certain matrimonial cases.[133] However, he shared that the main focus of the speech would be criminal legal aid, to which the government was taking a new approach,[134] which represented 'a clear shift in policy and philosophy for the Government'.[135] Legal assistance for all capital cases was provided by the government via LASCO, and the government provided indirect funding for criminal legal aid via annual funding to the Law Society's Pro Bono Services Office,[136] but lawyers did 'a bulk of the heavy lifting, volunteering their services through 'CLAS', and various Community Legal Clinics'.[137] The government's position had been that 'providing criminal legal aid would put the State in the position of using public funds to both prosecute and defend the same accused persons, after significant resources had been allocated to the careful and meticulous investigation, assessment and conduct of prosecutions',[138] but the Ministry had been 'reviewing this position for quite some time now', and they had 'decided to give direct assistance and support in criminal cases to Defendants – through Criminal Legal Aid'.[139]

The envisioned programme was large. Estimates suggested that there were 'about 12,000 accused persons annually, of whom at least half, we think, or about 6,000, could benefit from some form of legal representation'.[140] In terms of structure, the Minister stated that criminal legal

[130] Lok Vi Ming, 'Speech for the Opening of the Legal Year 2013 and Welcome Reference for Chief Justice Sundaresh Menon' (*Singapore Law Gazette*, January 2013), online: https://v1.lawgazette.com.sg/2013-01/644.htm.

[131] *Singapore Parliamentary Debates, Official Report*, vol. 90 (11 November 2013).

[132] *Direct Legal Aid, supra* note 72; see also Thian Yee Sze, 'The Four Principles that Anchor Singapore's Criminal Justice System' (*Singapore Law Gazette*, February 2014), online: v1.lawgazette.com.sg/2014-02/964.htm.

[133] K. Shanmugam, 'Inaugural Lecture' (Speech delivered at the Association of Muslim Lawyers), online: www.mlaw.gov.sg/news/speeches/speech-by-min-at-aml-lecture [*Expanding Criminal Legal Aid*], at paras. 11 and 13.

[134] *Expanding Criminal Legal Aid, supra* note 133, at para. 16.

[135] *Expanding Criminal Legal Aid, supra* note 133, at para. 33.

[136] The government provided S$400,000 in public funding for its Pro Bono Services Office: see *Direct Legal Aid, supra* note 72.

[137] *Expanding Criminal Legal Aid, supra* note 133, at para. 16.

[138] *Expanding Criminal Legal Aid, supra* note 133, at para. 18.

[139] *Expanding Criminal Legal Aid, supra* note 133, at para. 20.

[140] *Expanding Criminal Legal Aid, supra* note 133, at para. 21.

aid would require 'statutory intervention; we'll put through the legislation'.[141] Extensive statutory changes would have been required to offer criminal legal aid through LAB, and as the Minister noted, 'provisions from the Legal Aid and Advice Ordinance relating to criminal legal aid were in fact deleted in 1995'.[142] A government-run criminal legal aid scheme however was not the plan. The Minister stated that they believed 'the Law Society should continue with these pro bono services in running CLAS'.[143] The government would increase the funding, and CLAS 'will be able to enhance its capacity to support the processing and granting of aid to a larger group of accused persons. Funds will be used towards honoraria or disbursements for lawyers as well.'[144] In terms of sustainability, the Minister noted that the intention was to form an independent Criminal Legal Assistance Steering Committee[145] to oversee the policies governing the disbursement of funds, to ensure that Singapore was not writing a blank cheque with public funds.[146]

The decision to fund broad-based criminal legal aid could only have been made by the government, but the Minister stated that the 'move to substantially support criminal legal aid is not a move that the Government can do alone'.[147] The Minister acknowledged that they were 'building on the substantial efforts that lawyers have already put in',[148] and that moving forward, 'the legal profession will have to take on a crucial role of ensuring that on the ground, aid is allocated with care, and legal representation is of high standard and high quality'.[149] In view of the Law Society's estimate that they would need 'about 200 lawyers who regularly contribute their time, for the proposed enhanced criminal legal aid structure to be successful', the criminal legal aid scheme 'has to be done in partnership between the Government and the Bar'.[150]

The system ultimately adopted is referred to as Enhanced CLAS,[151] in recognition of the non-paid work by CLAS lawyers that had provided the majority of non-capital criminal defence since 1985. The scheme received substantial funding from the government, although day-to-day operations were run by the Law Society. The Steering Committee, with diverse representatives from the Law Society, the criminal bar, the courts, Singapore Academy of Law, and the Ministry of Law,[152] formulated the policy framework for Enhanced CLAS, in consultation with the criminal bar.[153] The payment structure envisioned was essentially a low bono or honorarium approach; LSPBS would continue to run Enhanced CLAS, and the legal service was still done

141 *Expanding Criminal Legal Aid, supra* note 133, at para. 20.
142 *Expanding Criminal Legal Aid, supra* note 133, at para. 18.
143 *Expanding Criminal Legal Aid, supra* note 133, at para. 25.
144 *Expanding Criminal Legal Aid, supra* note 133, at para. 26.
145 *Expanding Criminal Legal Aid, supra* note 133, at para. 27.
146 *Expanding Criminal Legal Aid, supra* note 133, at paras. 28, 29.
147 *Expanding Criminal Legal Aid, supra* note 133, at para. 37.
148 Ibid.
149 *Expanding Criminal Legal Aid, supra* note 133, at para. 39.
150 *Expanding Criminal Legal Aid, supra* note 133, at para. 40.
151 See the Singapore Ministry of Law's brochure 'Enhanced Criminal Legal Aid Scheme' (*Singapore Ministry of Law*) www.mlaw.gov.sg/files/news/press-releases/2015/05/Enhanced%20CLAS_Infographic%201_for%20Media_FINAL.pdf.
152 On 19 May 2015, it was reported that the Committee included Senior Minister of State for Education and Law Indranee Rajah, as advisor to the Steering Committee, along with Judge of Appeal Justice Chao Hick Tin, and that the Chairman of the Committee was Presiding Judge of the State Courts, Judicial Commissioner See Kee Oon, and the Vice Chairman was then President of the Law Society, Mr Thio Shen Yi, SC: see Ministry of Law, 'Enhanced Criminal Legal Aid Scheme Set to Provide Greater Access to Justice', online: www.mlaw.gov.sg/news/press-releases/enhanced-clas-to-provide-greater-access-to-justice [*Enhanced Criminal Legal Aid Scheme*] at para. 7.
153 *Enhanced Criminal Legal Aid Scheme, supra* note 152, at para. 8.

primarily by volunteer lawyers, but funding would cover 'operational costs, honoraria and disbursements' to lawyers.[154]

Enhanced CLAS was officially launched on 18 May 2015,[155] and government funding since then has allowed a considerable expansion of CLAS services. A relaxed means test, of disposable income of not more than S$10,000 per annum and a disposable capital of not more than S$10,000, allowed more applicants to qualify for criminal legal aid.[156] CLAS assistance was also extended to the Moneylenders Act, resulting in coverage for offences under 16 statutes.[157] Finally, under the previous scheme only defendants claiming trial were allowed full representation, with the exception of young offenders and those with mental illnesses; Enhanced CLAS meant that criminal defendants pleading guilty to charges could also be covered,[158] and legal assistance with mitigation provided. A co-payment was required 'to ensure that applicants also contribute towards their defence, and do not abuse the system'.[159]

Statistics confirm that criminal legal aid has been expanded considerably. Prior to Enhanced CLAS, 431 applicants out of 1,780 applications[160] were assisted in 2014 and 427 in 2013.[161] In 2015, 2,433 applicants were assisted under the new scheme, more than five times the 2014 figure.[162] In 2016, Enhanced CLAS received 2,308 applications, compared to 1,780 applications in 2014 prior to government funding, and all 2,308 accused persons who applied received basic legal advice, while 1,373 'also received full representation or legal services not involving court attendance'.[163] The LSPBS 2019–20 Annual Report indicated that 1,947 applicants received advice, of which 930 were granted aid in the form of representation.[164]

III. CONCLUSION

This chapter has argued that access to justice in Singapore should be understood primarily as a government and lawyer dynamic. The government is the main actor, a point well illustrated by legal aid: in civil legal aid, the government funds and sets application cut-offs via regulation, and in criminal legal aid, broad-based criminal legal aid was not implemented after Singapore gained independence, but it was funded in the 2010s. The decision to provide funds for non-capital criminal legal aid could only have been made by the government, but it was accomplished via a partnership with lawyers and the Law Society, and the resulting scheme has had a major, positive impact on access to justice.

[154] *Enhanced Criminal Legal Aid Scheme*, *supra* note 152, at paras. 3 and 5(iii).

[155] Lim Yi Han and Amos Lee, 'Enhanced Criminal Legal Aid Scheme Officially Launched', *The Straits Times* (19 May 2015).

[156] Sara Grosse, 'Enhanced Criminal Legal Aid Scheme to Benefit Up to 6,000 People Yearly', *Channel News Asia* (18 May 2015).

[157] Ibid.

[158] Ibid.

[159] *Enhanced Criminal Legal Aid Scheme*, *supra* note 152, at para 5(ii).

[160] Lim Yi Han, 'Government to Help Fund Enhanced Criminal Legal Aid Scheme', *The Straits Times* (18 May 2015).

[161] Lim Yi Han, 'Criminal Legal Aid Scheme Helping More Accused People', *The Straits Times* (29 February 2016).

[162] Ibid.

[163] Senior Minister of State for Law, Indranee Rajah (Speech delivered during the Committee of Supply Debate 2017) at para. 13(a)(ii), online: www.mlaw.gov.sg/news/parliamentary-speeches/speech-by-senior-minister-of-state-for-law–indranee-rajah–durio.

[164] *Annual Report 2019–20*, *supra* note 63, at 42.

Mandatory pro bono has an interesting half-life in access to justice, not necessarily coming to fruition, but never quite going away. When it was first mentioned in 2006, by the Law Society, the Minister for Law indicated that the government would not impose a mandatory requirement, as that would be up to the Law Society.[165] When the issue was considered more seriously in 2012–13, the proposal was raised by the Singapore Academy of Law via a committee with diverse representation. Following negative feedback and queries regarding the state's role in supporting access to justice, mandatory pro bono was put on hold, and currently Singapore only imposes mandatory reporting requirements. The CLS Committee's Final Report suggested that a review of compulsory community legal services would occur after three to five years of mandatory reporting, or approximately in 2020.[166] This did not occur, and conditions do not appear conducive to a resurrected mandatory pro bono scheme. Singapore has liberalized its legal sector and allowed foreign lawyers to practise commercial aspects of Singapore law, and there has been a perceived need for parity in the treatment of domestic and foreign lawyers to the extent possible.[167] Foreign lawyers are not allowed to practise the areas targeted by CLS, including family and criminal law,[168] so imposition of a mandatory contribution of hours or payment-in-lieu would function as a tax that could make domestic legal services less competitive. The relationship between the government and the bar is also relevant. It has moved from mistrust to a working relationship, one that attempts to take respective concerns into account. In this context, the fact that the bar does not have a consensus in favour of mandatory pro bono will continue to play a role in whether such a scheme would be adopted.

Overall Singapore has made impressive improvements in access to justice. It is considering schemes of lower fees for legal services, i.e. low bono,[169] and could explore the deployment of paralegals beyond current limits.[170] These programmes will however need to accommodate the government and lawyer dynamic. The announcement that the government was studying the setting up of a public defenders' office for accused persons who cannot afford a lawyer,[171] after the Law Society's supervision of CLAS for more than 35 years, confirms that this dynamic is central, and still subject to change.

165 *Debates 2 March 2007*, *supra* note 51, at col. 2370 (S. Jayakumar).

166 *Final Report*, *supra* note 123, at para. 30, and *Mandatory Reporting Rules*, *supra* note 128, r 1.

167 See Committee to Review the Regulatory Framework of the Singapore Legal Services Sector, *Final Report* (2014) at para. 30, online: www.mlaw.gov.sg/files/Final-Report-of-the-Committee-to-Review-the-Reg-Framework-of-the-Spore-Legal-Sector.pdf/.

168 *Legal Profession Act*, *supra* note 6, Legal Profession (Law Practice Entities) Rules 2015, Singapore, r 50(1); and see Ministry of Law, 'Oral Answer by Minister for Law, K. Shanmugam, to Parliamentary Question on Foreign Law Firms' (21 October 2013), online: www.mlaw.gov.sg/news/parliamentary-speeches/oral-answer-by-minister-for-law-on-foreign-law-firm.

169 See 'New Law Society Scheme Offers Cheaper Family Law Help for the Lower-Income', *Channel News Asia* (24 January 2021) (video); and see Covenant Chambers LLC, online: www.covenantchambers.com/access-to-justice/; and Eden Law Corporation, online: edenlaw.com.sg/low-bono/.

170 See Lim Hui Min et al., 'Soaring Paralegal Eagles – The Specialist Legal Executives of the Legal Aid Bureau', *Singapore Law Gazette* (May 2021).

171 Fabian Koh, 'Parliament: Govt Studying Setting Up of Public Defenders' Office for Accused Who Can't Afford Lawyer, says Shanmugam', *The Straits Times* (5 November 2020).

10

Public Interest Lawyering in South Korea: Standing on the Shoulders of Giants

Takgon Lee and JaeWon Kim*

Abstract

A salient feature of legal aid in South Korea is the presence of the state-subsidized legal aid institution, the Korea Legal Aid Corporation. It is large in comparison to private sector involvement in access to justice, although there are concerns that state-subsidized legal aid still falls short of providing sufficient legal services to the public. Private lawyer involvement in access to justice began with the tradition of human rights lawyers during the democracy movement in the 1970s and 80s, and grew into the current practice of public interest lawyering. While the number of public interest lawyers is not big enough, they have made significant progress in advancing public interest agendas. The more recent voluntary pro bono initiatives led by major law firms arose in part to address increasing scrutiny from civil society, and they have also been the site of considerable growth. A different kind of scrutiny led South Korea to adopt a mandatory pro bono requirement by the Attorney-at-Law Act of 2000. Even though the mandatory requirement scheme has been criticized for its vague scope of public interest activities and lack of penalties for non-compliance, the requirement has positively impacted law firm pro bono and access to justice.

I. INTRODUCTION

In South Korea[1] there exist two interesting features concerning a lawyer's role in access to justice. One is the presence of a sizeable state-subsidized programme; the other, a mandatory pro bono requirement. While a fairly large percentage of the population is potentially eligible for government-funded legal aid, a much smaller percentage receives aid, and the number of unrepresented civil litigants is substantial. This state-subsidized legal aid appears to have impeded the growth of pro bono activities of the non-public sector; legal aid functions separately from private lawyer activity, and interactions between legal aid and pro bono are relatively scarce. Private lawyers who provide lawyer-funded legal services to indigent or vulnerable

* The author would like to thank Julie Kum and Jiyoung Lee for their diligent proofreading of the chapter. The views expressed in this chapter are those of the author and do not necessarily represent the views of, and should not be attributed to, UNHCR.

[1] 'Korea' shall refer to 'South Korea' unless otherwise noted in this chapter.

persons in Korean society are understood to engage in public interest activities. Public interest lawyers present themselves as defenders of social minorities, and they have defined public interest law within this context. The pro bono activities of major law firms, a much more recent phenomenon associated with the rise of big corporate law firms in Korea, arose in response to demands by Korean society that law firms should fulfil their social responsibility to provide legal assistance to various socio-economic minorities.

This chapter first outlines the current state of state-subsidized legal aid and points out its shortcomings. The chapter begins with the legal aid system because it currently represents the bulk of legal services to poor or vulnerable individuals. While state-subsidized legal aid has grown in recent years and receives significant amounts of funding, it still faces criticism for not adequately addressing the unmet legal needs of the Korean people. The chapter then goes further back in time and surveys the history of public interest law in Korean society and the development of public interest lawyers. There was a strong tradition of human rights lawyers during the democracy movement in the 1960s–1980s, and public interest lawyering built upon this tradition. The chapter follows the development of this type of lawyering, which has seen considerable growth. The more recent development of law firm pro bono in part also grew out of the success of public interest lawyering, and from civil society's ever-growing demands. While the mandatory pro bono requirement in Korea initially arose for reasons other than access to justice, and it is easily satisfied and lacks an effective enforcement mechanism, the requirement has encouraged law firm pro bono practice and improved access to justice. To analyse the recent developments of public interest law and mandatory pro bono, the authors conducted interviews in Korean, with practitioners and staff who were directly involved with the recent developments, who were working at law firms and their pro bono entities, as well as the Seoul Bar Association. The interviews were conducted by phone or in person in April and May 2017. All interviewees gave their informed consent for inclusion in the study.

II. OVERVIEW OF STATE-SUBSIDIZED LEGAL AID

There exist two major cornerstones of state-subsidized legal aid: one is the Korea Legal Aid Corporation, and the other, court-ordered legal assistance. The former is provided by a state-funded organization and encompasses legal consultations and representations in court. The latter is funded and ordered by the court, in the form of providing a public defender in criminal matters or financing litigation expenses in civil matters.

A. *Korea Legal Aid Corporation*

The Korea Legal Aid Corporation ('KLAC') was established in 1987. Article 8 of the Legal Aid Act[2] declares the purpose of KLAC to be 'efficient promotion of legal aid'. Legal aid is provided to indigents and those ignorant of the law, in order to protect fundamental human rights and contribute to the promotion of legal welfare.[3] As provided by KLAC, legal aid encompasses 'all support concerning legal consultation' and includes legal representation in court proceedings.[4] Brief legal consultations are given free of charge to everyone, while legal representation in court proceedings is provided to indigents and social minorities as specified in KLAC regulations, for

[2] 법률구조법 (Legal Aid Act), Law No. 14102, South Korea (enacted on 23 December 1986, as amended in March 2016) [*Legal Aid Act*].

[3] *Legal Aid Act*, *supra* note 2, Article 2.

[4] Ibid.

nominal fees.[5] With 120 offices nationwide, KLAC provided representation in 154,585 civil cases (including administrative and family court cases) and 3,052 criminal cases in 2018.[6] On average, approximately 50 per cent of civil lawsuits pertain to unpaid wage claims.[7]

KLAC's annual budget in 2019 amounted to 152 billion KRW[8] (US$125 million),[9] and it received approximately 49 per cent of its budget from the government. The rest of the budget is mostly funded by government ministries and trade associations that support KLAC when it provides legal aid to people represented or supported by that organization.[10] For instance, the National Agricultural Cooperative Federation provides annual funding to KLAC for legal aid for farmers,[11] and the Ministry of Employment and Labour supports KLAC for legal aid for workers with wage claims.[12] The personnel resources of KLAC are also largely state-subsidized. In an interesting variation on mandatory pro bono, the Ministry of Justice assigns 'public-service advocates' to KLAC. Public-service advocates are bar exam passers who are performing mandatory military service through employment by the Ministry of Justice for three years.[13] They have not yet received their licence from a bar association, but they can act as legal representatives within their scope of employment. In 2017, the number of public-service advocates was 130, while the number of licensed lawyers working for KLAC was 100.[14]

Unlike the situation in many countries, the definition of indigents eligible to receive KLAC's legal aid has been criticized as being too broad and unrealistic.[15] Currently, KLAC provides legal aid for those 'whose income is below 125% of the "median income"' as established by the Ministry of Health and Welfare.[16] The median income is tied to the number of dependent family members and is annually revised to reflect current income levels. This standard was amended from a previous one that was even more generous, in order to 'suppress unnecessary legal aid demand and focus on social minorities who must depend upon legal aid services',[17] but even now, an impressive 67.3 per cent of the Korean people fall under this criterion.[18] KLAC

5 The recipients, if given court representation, need to pay administrative costs including filing fees and a small portion of the attorney costs predetermined by the value of the claims: see 법률구조사건처리규칙 (KLAC Regulations for Legal Aid Cases), South Korea (enacted on 5 October 1987, as amended 17 January 2020) [*KLAC Regulations*], Articles 36–40.

6 법률구조현황통계 (Legal Aid Statistics), online: Korea Legal Aid Corporation, www.klac.or.kr/disclosure/countryStatistic.do.

7 Assembly Research Service, 임금체불 피해근로자를 위한 무료법률구조 사업의 현황과 과제 (Current State and Theme of Free Legal Aid for Victims of Unpaid Wages) (2016) 47 NARS Situation Report 38.

8 Korea Legal Aid Corporation, 연간출연 및 증여 (Annual Budget Report), online: Korean Legal Aid Corporation, www.alio.go.kr/popReportTerm.do?apbaId=C0055&reportFormRootNo=32001.

9 XE Currency Converter, online: www.xe.com/currencyconverter/convert/?Amount=152&From=KRW&To=USD. Unless another reference was cited, US$ denominations in the chapter were derived from www.xe.com at the time of publication; they are intended for general reference and may have been rounded up or down for ease of reference.

10 Kookmin University Industry-Academic Cooperation Foundation, 대한법률구조공단 법률구조사업의 활성화 방안 (Measures to Vitalize Legal Aid Programmes of the KLAC) (2016) Research Report [*Legal Aid Programmes*] at 19

11 In 2015, it provided 1.3 billion KRW (US$1.19 million) to KLAC; see *Legal Aid Programmes*, *supra* note 10, at 23.

12 As of 2015, it provided 19 billion KRW (US$17.4 million) to KLAC; see *Legal Aid Programmes*, *supra* note 10.

13 공익법무관에 관한 법률 (Act on Public-Service Advocates), Law No. 14102, South Korea (enacted on 31 December 1994, as amended on 29 March 2016), Articles 3 and 8.

14 Kim Minhee, 박주민 '양질 법률서비스 위해 인력충원·업무량 조정해야' (Legislator Park Joomin, 'More Officials and Less Workload Necessary for Quality Legal Service'), *Financial Today* (20 October 2018), online: www.ftoday.co.kr/news/articleView.html?idxno=103616.

15 *Legal Aid Programmes*, *supra* note 10, at 65.

16 *KLAC Regulations*, *supra* note 5, Article 5.

17 KLAC, 2 회 정기이사회 회의록 (Minutes of 2nd Regular Board of Directors) (2015).

18 *Legal Aid Programmes*, *supra* note 10, at 69.

also provides legal aid to various social minorities, including, among other categories, persons with disabilities, farmers, fishers, North Korean defectors, and single-parent families.[19]

Internal regulations of KLAC provide that it may refuse to provide legal aid for various reasons, including, among other things, if the case is deemed to be unwinnable, or legal aid is deemed to be impractical.[20] This practice has been criticized for limiting people's right to access to justice based on criteria provided only by internal regulations, without input from the public.[21] There is also a widespread belief that KLAC tends to accept only cases likely to win.[22] Recently another kind of criticism raised by young lawyers is that KLAC's scope for recipients of legal aid is too broad and takes away potential paying clients from lawyers. Relevant to this criticism are the agreements between KLAC and trade associations, most notably the National Agricultural Cooperative Federation and the National Federation of Fisheries Cooperative, which allow all members of such trade associations to rely on KLAC for free legal service[23] in return for the trade associations providing annual funding to KLAC. This practice is criticized by lawyers in that KLAC effectively acts 'as a dedicated law firm for the trade associations' on a 'fixed fee billing'.[24] The surge in the number of lawyers in the last few years and the increasing pressure on young lawyers to find work within the legal market is believed to be a significant contributing factor to the recently pronounced tension between lawyers and KLAC.

B. Court-Ordered Litigation Aid

Courts may provide 'litigation aid' to parties in civil proceedings, either *ex officio* or upon request of the party, if s/he cannot pay for litigation costs, provided, however, that the case passes a merits test, which requires that it is not obvious that the lawsuit shall fail.[25] Litigation aid includes administrative costs, attorney fees, and other costs.[26] The provisions on litigation aid had been obsolete for several decades, but following a Supreme Court decision in 2001 giving a broad interpretation of the provisions, and subsequent policy change in 2002, the number of parties receiving litigation aid began to increase rapidly.[27] The provisions also apply *mutatis mutandis* to administrative and family court proceedings.[28] In 2018, out of

[19] *Legal Aid Act*, *supra* note 2, Article 7.

[20] *KLAC Regulations*, *supra* note 5, Article 19. While criminal cases are not subject to these criteria, KLAC may still refuse legal aid if the case is deemed to be impractical, etc.: see *KLAC Regulations*, *supra* note 5, Article 45(2).

[21] See, for example, Kim Do-Hoon, 법률구조법상 법률구조에 관한 소고 (A Few Thoughts on Legal Aid in the Legal Aid Act) (2012) 22 *Yonsei Law Review* 93 at 120.

[22] See, for example, Ahn Hyesung, 법률구조공단, 변호사 생계 위협하는 황소개구리? (KLAC, a Bullfrog Threatening the Local Ecosystem of Lawyers?), *The Law Journal* (15 December 2017), online: www.lec.co.kr/news/articleView.html?idxno=46289.

[23] They are exempted from administrative fees per *Legal Aid Act*, *supra* note 2, Article 7(2).

[24] Kim Jin Woo, 대한법률구조공단 운영의 문제점과 개선방안 (Problems and Improvement Proposals for the KLAC) in *Forum on Improving Problems of the Management of the KLAC* (2017) Korean Bar Association at 15.

[25] 민사소송법 (Civil Procedure Act), Law No. 13952, South Korea (enacted on 4 April 1960, as amended on 3 February 2016) [*Civil Procedure Act*], Article 128.

[26] *Civil Procedure Act*, *supra* note 25, Article 129. The extent of the attorney's fee provided by the court is limited to a nominal amount.

[27] Kim Yong-duk, 주석 민사소송법 (Annotated Civil Procedure Act) 7th edn, Vol. II (Korean Academy of Law and Administration, 2012) at 243.

[28] 행정소송법 (Administrative Litigation Act), Law No. 12844, South Korea (enacted on 24 August 1951, as amended on 19 November 2014), Article 8(2); 가사소송법 (Family Litigation Act), Law No. 14278, South Korea (enacted on 31 December 1990, as amended on 2 December 2016), Article 12.

approximately 6,000 applications for litigation aid in civil proceedings, approximately 50 per cent were granted.[29]

C. *Legal Aid for Criminal Defence*

Article 12(4) of the Constitution provides for the right to state-appointed counsel for criminal defendants unable to secure counsel by their own efforts. The court will appoint counsel *ex officio* if the defendant is placed under arrest, is a minor, is 70 years of age or older, is a person with hearing and speaking impairments, is suspected of having mental disabilities, or is indicted for a case with potential punishments of the death penalty, life imprisonment, or imprisonment for longer than three years.[30] If a defendant is unable to appoint a defence counsel for reasons other than the above, such as poverty, the court will appoint a counsel if the defendant so requests.[31]

State-appointed counsel were traditionally private lawyers occasionally assigned as state-appointed criminal counsel, and they represented defendants in a considerable proportion of criminal proceedings.[32] In response to criticisms that the state-appointed counsel lacked expertise,[33] a system of full-time state-appointed defence counsel has been implemented since 2006.[34] The new system of full-time state-appointed defence counsel now supplements the existing system of state-appointed counsel, and it is generally well received by the public and the legal profession.[35]

D. *Shortcomings of State-Subsidized Legal Aid*

There has been no comprehensive study conducted on the legal needs of the people in Korea, and whether or to what extent the existing state-subsidized legal aid fulfils legal needs is not clear.[36] However, a comparison between the annual budget allotted for KLAC in Korea and that of other advanced countries suggests that there is still a significant gap between the legal needs of the people and legal aid.[37] For the fiscal year 2007–8, the annual legal aid budget per person in Korea was 1.1 per cent of that of the United Kingdom and 9.2 per cent of that of Germany.[38]

29 The Supreme Court, 사법연감 (2019 Legal Yearbook) [2019 *Legal Yearbook*] at 846. The total number of civil proceedings amounts to approximately 4,750,000 as of 2018: at 568.

30 형사소송법 (Criminal Procedure Act), Law No. 14179, South Korea (enacted on 23 September 1954, as amended on 29 May 2016) [*Criminal Procedure Act*], Article 33(1).

31 *Criminal Procedure Act*, *supra* note 30, Article 33(2).

32 As of 2018, 127,027 defendants were appointed defence counsel by the court, the vast majority of which were upon request by the defendants. Approximately 35 per cent of the total number of criminal proceedings are represented by state-appointed counsel: see 2019 *Legal Yearbook*, *supra* note 29, at 618.

33 Kookmin University Industry-Academic Cooperation Foundation, 변호사 공익활동 활성화를 위한 지원방안에 관한 연구 (Measures to Support Lawyer Pro Bono) (2012) Research Report 6 [*Lawyer Pro Bono*].

34 As of 2017, there were approximately 200 lawyers appointed as full-time state-appointed defence counsel: see Ko Yoonsang, 국선변호인 선정 작년 12 만건 넘어…'빈곤 이유'가 80% (Cases with state-appointed defence counsel number more than 120,000 last year … 'reason of poverty' more than 80%), *The Korea Economic Daily* (24 October 2017), online: www.hankyung.com/society/article/201710248150l.

35 Judicial Policy Research Institute, 국선전담변호사제도의 개선 방안에 관한 연구 (Research on the Improvement of the Indigent Defence System) (Judicial Policy Research Institute, 2014) at 31.

36 Hwang Seung Heum, 법률구조 서비스의 전달체계의 재구성 (Reconstitution of the Delivery System of Legal Aid Service) (2012) 43 *Korean Law & Society Association* 71 at 77; Hwang Pil Kyu, 공익법운동의 활성화를 위한 소고 (A Study on Vitalizing the Public Interest Law Movement) (2014) 5 *Yonsei Journal of Public Governance & Law* 27 at 34.

37 Chong Jong-Sup, 21 세기 법치국가의 법률복지 방향과 제도 설계 (Suggesting New Directions in Designing Legal Welfare System) (2012) 43 *Korean Law & Society Association* 19 at 38.

38 Ibid.

With only a few hundred lawyers and public interest advocates working at KLAC, inadequate quality legal consultations and/or representations are often observed.[39] The sufficiency of the court-ordered litigation aid in meeting access to justice needs is also questionable. In the years 2015–19, more than 50 per cent of civil lawsuits in the lower courts were conducted without legal representation of either plantiffs or defendants.[40]

The low ratio of legal representation should also be partially attributed to the small lawyer population in Korea. Among developed countries, Korea has had one of the highest ratios of civil lawsuits per lawyer, resulting from an insufficient number of lawyers and a relatively high number of legal disputes.[41] The strictly state-controlled number of lawyers and its homogeneous composition has often been regarded as the primary reason for blocking access to justice for individuals.[42] Bar Associations have argued that the size of the Korean legal profession is large enough,[43] and they caution that the recent increase in the number of lawyers has saturated the market for lawyers. Nonetheless, 21 per cent of Korean persons surveyed in 2016 still cite a lack of affordability as the main reason for not attempting to obtain legal assistance.[44] This percentage is the highest among member states of the Organization for Economic Co-operation and Development ('OECD').[45]

III. PRIVATE LAWYERS AND ACCESS TO JUSTICE

A. *The Korean 'Human Rights Lawyers' Legacy*

The Attorney-at-Law Act of Korea provides that the attorneys shall 'protect fundamental human rights and . . . realize social justice'.[46] In this context, the term 'human rights lawyer', widely used in Korea, may seem redundant, as all lawyers are seemingly entrusted with the task of protecting human rights.[47] However, as used in Korean society, the term 'human rights lawyer' denotes a very particular group of lawyers, those who fought against authoritarian military regimes and defended political prisoners indicted for their participation in democracy movements from the 1960s to the 1980s.[48] Many of these lawyers began their career as a human rights lawyer in 1974, when they collectively defended 180 students who were indicted for alleged participation in the 'National Federation of Democratic Young Students'.[49] This federation was a fictional

39 Kim Sungho, 법률구조공단 변호사, 일반보다 30 배 이상 사건 처리..서비스 부실 우려 (KLAC Lawyers Handle 30 Times More Cases than Other Lawyers . . . Decrease in Service Quality Feared), *Financial News* (4 September 2016), online: www.fnnews.com/news/201609041009162805.

40 The Supreme Court, 사법연감 (2020 Legal Yearbook) (2020) at 586 .

41 Han Sang Hie, 우리 변호사체계의 문제점 — 법치와 경쟁력 확보를 위한 실태분석 (Why do the Korean People Want More Lawyers?) (2010) 43 *Democratic Legal Studies* 271 at 286.

42 Kim JaeWon, 'The Ideal and the Reality of the Korean Legal Profession' (2001) 2 *Asian-Pacific Law & Policy Journal* 45 [*Korean Legal Profession*] at 68.

43 *Korean Legal Profession*, *supra* note 42, at 46.

44 OECD, 'Access to Legal and Justice Services', in *Government at a Glance 2017* (Paris: OECD Publishing, 2017) [*Government at a Glance*], Table 14.15 at 239, online: www.oecd-ilibrary.org/docserver/gov_glance-2017-85-en.pdf?expires=1583110119&id=id&accname=guest&checksum=4129A80C3C18BACA03E48EA3C2BBC871.

45 *Government at a Glance*, *supra* note 44, at 238.

46 변호사법 (Attorney-at-Law Act), Law No. 17366, South Korea (enacted on 7 November 1949, as amended on 9 June 2020) [*Attorney-at-Law Act*], Article 1(1).

47 Kim JaeWon, 'Legal Profession and Legal Culture during Korea's Transition to Democracy and a Market Economy' in William P. Alford, ed., *Raising the Bar: The Emerging Legal Profession in East Asia* (Cambridge, MA: Harvard Law School East Asian Legal Studies, 2007) at 60.

48 Ibid.

49 Kim Jung-nam, 진실, 광장에 서다: 민주화운동 30 년의 역정 (Truth, Stands on the Plaza: 30 Years of Hardship of Democracy Movement) (Changbi Publishers, 2005) [*Hardship of Democracy*] at 63.

organization fabricated by the military regime to condemn the opposition movement for conspiring with North Korea. The incident gained international renown as the first lawsuit that imprisoned an attorney for his defence of defendants during trial.[50] The human rights lawyers continued their zealous defence of political prisoners through the 1970s and 1980s, but they refrained from forming a dedicated organization, fearing that the military regime would target such an organization for persecution.[51] At this time, the number of human rights lawyers remained small and thus they were easily controlled and harassed by the military regime,[52] but a second generation of human rights lawyers arose later, adding numbers and strength.

The first and second generations of human rights lawyers had their first opportunity to cooperate in a civil lawsuit of 1984, representing the collective victims of flood damage in claims against the government and a construction company for negligence in the prevention of flooding.[53] That lawsuit, widely recognized as the prototype for public interest lawsuits in Korea,[54] prompted active discussions about the need for an organization of human rights lawyers.[55] Consequently, in 1986, the Lawyers for the Realization of Justice, known as *Chongbophoe*, was formed. Lawyers belonging to *Chongbophoe* participated in several significant criminal cases that involved democracy movement activists, but the organization itself operated covertly. The public face of *Chongbophoe* was the Human Rights Committee of the Korean Bar Association, which was gradually taken over by members of *Chongbophoe*.[56] In the late 1980s, lawyers who were influenced by the radical student movement in the 1980s formed the Young Lawyers Association, known as *Chongbyon*.[57] This organization was formed to take a more proactive role in social reform.[58] *Chongbyon* never entirely took off but eventually merged with *Chongbophoe*, as the members of *Chongbyon* deemed that a separate organization would be premature. Nonetheless, the initial objective of *Chongbyon* influenced how some of the early members of a new organization of human rights lawyers, the Lawyers for a Democratic Society, known as *Minbyeon*, opted for a more proactive role in social reform.[59]

Minbyeon was formed in 1988, after the massive democracy movement in June 1987 that pressed the military regime to promise and then later implement general presidential elections. With 51 lawyers as founding members,[60] *Minbyeon* was the first independent lawyers' association for democracy that operated openly and legally.[61] Initially, *Minbyeon* focused on defending political cases,[62] in which

[50] *Hardship of Democracy*, *supra* note 49, at 64.

[51] Minbyeon, 민변백서 (Minbyeon White Paper) (1998) [*Minbyeon White Paper*] at 23.

[52] Patricia Goedde, 'Lawyers for a Democratic Society (Minbyun): The Evolution of its Legal Mobilization Process since 1988' in Gi-Wook Shin and Paul Y. Chang, eds., *South Korean Social Movements: From Democracy to Civil Society* (Abingdon: Routledge, 2011) at 225.

[53] *Minbyeon White Paper*, *supra* note 51, at 21.

[54] Hwang Seung Heum, 우리 나라 공익소송의 현황과 과제 (Current State and Theme of Korea's Public Interest Litigation) (Symposium Commemorating Yeong-nae Cho: Public Interest Litigation Yesterday and Today, 1998), at 8.

[55] *Minbyeon White Paper*, *supra* note 51, at 22.

[56] *Minbyeon White Paper*, *supra* note 51, at 42.

[57] *Minbyeon White Paper*, *supra* note 51, at 60.

[58] *Minbyeon White Paper*, *supra* note 51, at 65.

[59] *Minbyeon White Paper*, *supra* note 51, at 72.

[60] *Minbyeon White Paper*, *supra* note 51, at 73. Members currently number more than 1,000: see Seo Young-ji, 인권 품어온 27 살 민변, 1000 명이 함께 한다 (27 Years Old, Minbyeon that Protected Human Rights Now has 1,000 People), *The Hankyoreh* (31 May 2015), online: hani.co.kr/arti/society/society_general/693620.html.

[61] Patricia Goedde, 'The Making of Public Interest Law in South Korea via the Institutional Discourses of Minbyeon, PSPD and Gonggam' in Hyunah Yang, ed., *Law and Society in Korea* (Cheltenham: Elgar Korean Law, 2013) [*Public Interest Law*] at 133.

[62] *Minbyeon White Paper*, *supra* note 51, at 80.

defendants were usually charged with violations of the Criminal Act or the National Security Act.[63] Many of the human rights lawyers in *Minbyeon* also increasingly represented workers. Such lawyers, who focused on workers' rights in their legal representations, were eventually referred to as labour lawyers.[64] At the time, these groups of human rights lawyers and labour lawyers were not yet widely understood as working in public interest law. However, considering the modus operandi of *Minbyeon* and its focus on vulnerable and disadvantaged social groups, its work may be viewed as an early form of what is now referred to as public interest law.[65] *Minbyeon* operated as a network of its members, who usually worked as solo practitioners or in small private law firms.[66] They volunteered in various causes beginning with political cases and workers' rights, later expanding to other causes such as women, the environment, and consumer rights.

B. *The Advent of Public Interest Law and 'Public Interest Lawyers'*

The concept of public interest law (*gongik beob*) entered public discourse in the mid-1990s with the efforts of the People's Solidarity for Participatory Democracy ('PSPD'). PSPD was the forerunner of the NGOs that emerged in Korea in the late 1980s and early 1990s after the 1980s democracy movement and which paved the way for the growth of civil society. PSPD was the first NGO to utilize law in strategic litigation and legislative petitions. By conducting several pieces of high-profile public interest litigation and labelling them as such, PSPD popularized the concept of public interest law along with the public interest law movement.[67] At this point the media began to refer to the lawyers working at NGOs and labour unions, a novel phenomenon, as public interest lawyers.[68] In 2004, the first explicit public interest lawyers' group, *Gonggam*,[69] was established. Unlike *Minbyeon* or PSPD, *Gonggam* did not rely on the voluntary services of lawyers who had other jobs, and it was instead staffed with eight paid lawyers working full time. Its work included public interest litigation and policy reform, education of NGO activists, research, cooperation with other NGOs, and pro bono coordination.[70] *Gonggam*'s work distinctively focused on social minorities, initially sex trafficking victims, migrants, the homeless, and persons with disabilities, and later expanding to refugees, LGBTs, vulnerable children, precarious workers, and overseas victims of Korean companies' human rights violations. While the term 'public interest lawyer' was introduced into Korean discourse before the emergence of *Gonggam*, the term gained prominence through the activities of *Gonggam* lawyers. They also labelled their work as public interest law, and in turn they actively helped to focus public interest

63 국가보안법 (National Security Act), Law No. 13722, South Korea (enacted on 1 December 1948, as amended on 6 January 2016); this act punishes alleged pro-North Korean acts, and has been used to oppress anti-government activists.

64 Hwang Seung Heum, 한국사회에서 노동변호사의 성장 (Growth of Labour Lawyers in Korean Society) (1997) 14 *Law and Society* 301.

65 *Public Interest Law, supra* note 61, at 134.

66 The advent of big law firms is relatively recent in Korea, and law firms with more than 50 lawyers were first established in the mid-1990s: see Hong Sung Soo, 로펌의 성장과 변호사윤리의 변화: 개인윤리에서 조직윤리로, 공익활동에서 사회적 책임으로 (Growth of Law Firms in Korea and Change of Lawyer's Ethics) (2011) 41 *Law and Society* [*Growth of Law Firms*] at 145.

67 *Public Interest Law, supra* note 61, at 136.

68 Lee Je Hoon, 시민단체로 출근하는 변호사들 (Lawyers Who Go to Work at NGOs), *The Hankyoreh* (29 September 1999).

69 The Korean word 공감 *Gonggam* means 'empathy' in English.

70 Youm Hyung-kuk, 한국의 공익변호사 현황과 전망 (The Public Interest Lawyer's Present Condition and Prospect in Korea) (2013) 13 *Public Interest and Human Rights* [*Public Interest Lawyer*] at 5.

law on the human rights of social minorities, democracy, and expansion of access to justice.[71] In short, through its existence and priorities, *Gonggam* defined what Korean people, in general, recognize as public interest law.[72]

Gonggam also paved the way for other public interest lawyer groups. In 2011, the Advocates for Public Interest Law ('APIL') was established, building upon previous work of the Christian Lawyers' Fellowship ('CLF') of Korea.[73] APIL focuses on migrants in detention, refugees, stateless persons, victims of human trafficking, and overseas victims of Korean companies' human rights violations. In 2012, the Korean Lawyers for Public Interest and Human Rights was established, with a focus upon legal assistance to civil society groups, business and human rights, rights of persons with disabilities, and the rights of sexual minorities.[74] In 2014, the Immigrants Advocacy Centre (*Gamdong*), which provides legal assistance to migrants and refugees, was established.[75] The group Companion Lawyers for Public Interest, or *Donghaeng*, was established in 2015, the first public interest lawyer group to be located outside Seoul.[76] Along with four lawyers staffing *Minbyeon*, the total number of public interest lawyers working at these organizations as of 2016 was approximately 30.[77] The groups all follow *Gonggam*'s precedent in the sense that they engage in public interest litigation, policy reforms, and research, and they focus on the fundamental rights of social minorities, labelling themselves and their work as public interest lawyers and public interest law. They mostly rely on funding by individual donors, other lawyers, and in some cases churches.

Other lawyers identify themselves as public interest lawyers as well. Currently, lawyers are employed by approximately 20 NGOs working in various areas such as corporate monitoring, children, refugees, migrants, educational reform, environment, and disabilities.[78] While the term 'human rights lawyers' seems to have been almost replaced by public interest lawyers in public discourse, labour lawyers, who work at labour unions or small law firms specializing in the representation of workers, are still deemed to be a distinct group.[79]

C. *The Emergence of Law Firm Pro Bono Activities*

Recent pro bono initiatives led by major law firms are another notable trend in access to justice in Korea. As noted above, lawyers who had *Minbyeon* membership usually worked at small law firms or as solo practitioners. They provided their services voluntarily, and their work was usually not conducted or viewed as a coordinated law firm effort. In fact, the law firm structure has had a relatively short history in Korea. Sizeable law firms only appeared in the mid-1990s, and their growth accelerated after the financial crisis in 1999. Law firm growth to a level more

71 *Public Interest Lawyer, supra* note 70, at 9; Hwang Pil Kyu, 공익법 운동의 성과와 도전 (Achievements and Challenges for Korean Public Interest Law Movement) (Seminar delivered at the Commemoration of five years of Gonggam, 2009) at 12.

72 *Public Interest Law, supra* note 61, at 143.

73 APIL, 'About Us' (APIL, 2017), online: www.apil.or.kr.

74 Korean Lawyers for Public Interest and Human Rights, 'About Us' (Korean Lawyers for Public Interest and Human Rights, 2012), online: www.hopeandlaw.org.

75 Gamdong, 'About Us' (Gamdong, 2013), online: www.gamdonglove.org.

76 Donghaeng, 'About Us' (Donghaeng, 2016), online: www.companion-lfpi.org.

77 Ibid.

78 Kang Jung Eun, 공익변호사의 관점에서 본 로펌 공익활동 활성화 방안 (How to Promote Law Firm Pro Bono, seen from a Public Interest Lawyer's Perspective) in *Promoting Law Firm Public Interest Activities* (Law Firm Public Interest Network, 2016), at 109.

79 As such, they are usually not counted toward the total number of public interest lawyers.

conducive to organized, systematic pro bono activities only occurred after the mid-2000s.[80] In tandem with the swift growth of law firms in the 2000s, civil society also became more vocal, demanding more ethical and socially responsible activity from law firms. Initially, the sharpest point of criticism by NGOs was the fact that big law firms competitively hired former judges, reinforcing the widespread concern that former-judges-turned-lawyers enjoyed special treatment from the courts. Criticisms from NGOs and the media first focused on the Kim & Chang Law Office, the most prominent law firm in Korea, culminating in 2006 with the publication of several articles and books criticizing the law firm for only representing the interests of multinational corporations.[81] Since then, other law firms have been subject to various criticisms, including high-handed sales of their services and monopoly of the legal market, as well as the employment of former judges, prosecutors, and other high-ranking public officials.[82]

Until the mid-2000s, the majority of law firms paid little attention to the pro bono activities of their members.[83] Law firm corporate social responsibility ('CSR') activities focused more on donations and volunteer work,[84] similar to the early stages of business CSR[85] and matching the general trend of Korean company CSR practices at the time.[86] Some attorneys at law firms, many of them members of *Minbyeon*, conducted pro bono activities in their individual capacity. A survey by PSPD in 2003 showed that out of eight law firms that responded to the survey, only four firms financially supported the pro bono activities of their attorneys.[87] While most of the responding law firms stated that pro bono work was counted toward billable hours, only two firms had internal pro bono policies. Another telling aspect of the survey was that PSPD contacted twenty-five law firms having over ten lawyers, but only eight of them responded. In 2005, *Gonggam* contacted ten major law firms, based on the number of law firm attorneys, for focus interviews. Out of five firms that were interviewed, three firms had a pro bono committee to coordinate pro bono activities, and three firms had internal pro bono policies.[88] The responses to these interviews indicated that the firms did not systematically coordinate the pro bono activities of the attorneys, and instead depended on the will and capacity of individual attorneys; firm-level pro bono activities focused more on legal assistance to government agencies.[89]

The first effort to institutionalize pro bono activity at the law firm level was made by Bae, Kim, and Lee, LLC ('BKL'). BKL initially set up an internal pro bono committee, and later a

80 Han Chang Wan, 한국 로펌 공익활동의 과거와 현재, 성과와 과제 (Past and Present, Achievement and Challenges of Korean Law Firm Public Interest Activities) (Seminar delivered at the Commemoration of five years of Dongcheon Foundation – Current Situation and Challenges for Public Interest Law Movement, 2014) [*Past and Present*], at 48.

81 *Growth of Law Firms*, *supra* note 66, at 160.

82 Ibid.

83 *Past and Present*, *supra* note 80, at 47.

84 Yang Dong Soo, 로펌 프로보노 그리고, 새로운 공익법 운동 상상하기 (Law Firm Pro Bono and Imagining New Public Interest Law Movement) (Seminar delivered at the Commemoration of five years of Dongcheon Foundation – Current Situation and Challenges for Public Interest Law Movement, 2014) at 26.

85 Ibid.

86 Ye Jong Seok, 우리나라 기업의 사회공헌활동에 관한 연구 (Study on Korean Companies' Corporate Social Responsibility) (Beautiful Foundation, 2003) at 28.

87 PSPD Media Comments, 국내 로펌들 변호사 공익활동 이행 미흡 (Korean Law Firms Fall Behind in Public Interest Activities) (PSPD Media Comments, 2003).

88 Gonggam, NGO 의 법률수요 실태 및 로펌의 프로 보노 활동에 대한 조사 (Research on NGO's Legal Demand and Law Firm Pro Bono) (Gonggam, 2005) at 85.

89 *Past and Present*, *supra* note 80, at 47.

foundation, which was staffed by non-law-firm employees and handled exclusively pro bono work. This effort was followed by Jipyong, LLC ('Jipyong'), a smaller law firm widely recognized as another forerunner of active pro bono work in terms of the number of dedicated pro bono attorneys as well as the extent of funding and support. Within BKL and Jipyong, and to some extent other law firms, the leading advocates for robust law firm pro bono organization came from what is commonly referred to as the 86 generation, people who were born in the 1960s and were university students in the 1980s. Without a doubt, they were part of, or were heavily influenced by, the democratic student movement of the 1980s.

BKL's efforts were matched and followed by other large law firms, and in view of BKL's influence, it is examined here in detail. In 2001, BKL established a pro bono committee. At that time, it conducted pro bono work as it came by, referred by different sources including individual attorneys, bar associations, and *Minbyeon*, among others. The firm discovered that, due to the complex and evolving nature of different areas of public law, law firm attorneys were not fully equipped to handle pro bono cases without specialized knowledge and experience. In 2009, the pro bono committee was divided into different subcommittees, so that each subcommittee could accumulate relevant expertise through experience and study.[90] Also in 2009, BKL founded the Dongcheon Foundation. The establishment of the Dongcheon Foundation was followed by the employment of a full-time pro bono attorney for the Foundation, the first to be hired by a law firm. A newspaper interview held at the time stated that the mission of the Dongcheon Foundation was 'to promote pro bono activities of BKL lawyers, support and nurture non-profit activists and pro bono lawyers, as well as provide legal assistance to minorities through public law research, litigation, and policy reforms'.[91] The former managing partner of BKL has cited the 'founding spirit of the firm to focus on values, not money', and the need to maintain 'society's respect for the legal profession', as the reasons for the pro bono initiatives of the firm.[92]

At the outset, the pro bono work of the Dongcheon Foundation was organized into five categories: social enterprises, refugees, migrants, persons with disabilities, and North Korean defectors.[93] This categorization reflects the way subcommittees within the BKL pro bono committee were initially organized. The work has since expanded to seven categories, including social welfare and female/youth. Within these categories, the Dongcheon Foundation acts as a pro bono coordinator, doing intake and conducting a preliminary review of cases. If it deems the cases to be acceptable, it refers the cases to the BKL pro bono committee. Sometimes the Foundation handles cases by itself, and sometimes law firm attorneys handle the matter. Each case is judged on its own merits, and evaluation takes into account matters such as the situation of clients and the underlying social problem. Within its seven areas of focus, the Dongcheon Foundation also independently participates in civil society movements for advocacy and policy reform. Other law firms, notably Jipyong, follow a similar model of structuring pro bono, although the exact area of focus and details of the organization's relationship with the mother firm vary by firm.

In 2016, the Law Firm Public Interest Network was formed, with eleven member law firms, comprising ten major law firms in terms of number of attorneys, and one mid-level law firm with

90 Interview with senior BKL attorney (14 April 2017, Seoul) [*BKL Interview*].

91 Kim Jong-tae, 양동수 재단법인 동천상임변호사 (Yang, Dong-soo, The Dongcheon Foundation's Standing Attorney), *Monthly Labor Law* (July 2011), online: www.worklaw.co.kr/view/view.asp?in_cate=104&gopage=1&bi_pidx=18316 [*Dongcheon Foundation*].

92 Kwon Yong-tae, [인터뷰] 공익재단법인 '동천' 이사장 이정훈 변호사 (Interview: The President of the Public Interest Foundation Dongcheon, Attorney Lee Jung-Hoon), *The Law Times* (24 June 2011), online: www.lawtimes.co.kr/Legal-News/Legal-News-View?serial=58105.

93 *Dongcheon Foundation*, *supra* note 91.

high interest in pro bono activities,[94] to 'invigorate public interest activities of law firms in order to fulfil the lawyer's mission and to implement law firms' corporate social responsibility'.[95] The Network was initially formed to share member firms' best practices and to conduct joint pro bono activities. While the latter have been limited to a few roundtables and joint forums, the sharing of best practices within the Network has had a significant impact on the member firms, as discussed in more detail below.

A 2016 survey of the member firms of the Network provides an overview of law firm pro bono policies and practices.[96] The survey indicates that the landscape for law firm pro bono has changed considerably in the last few years, with more pro bono activities and more structures supporting that work. As appears from Table 10.1, most of these major law firms now either have pro bono committees or separate entities dedicated to pro bono work. Many of them now hire full-time lawyers and allocate a separate budget for pro bono. Most firms also tend to focus on a few specific areas of public interest law, rather than providing general legal aid to indigents. Relevant parts of the survey are provided in Table 10.1 (see p. 191).[97]

Establishing separate institutions such as a foundation for law firm pro bono work is not unheard of in other jurisdictions, but this approach is widely used in Korea. Considerations regarding hiring full-time pro bono coordinators within separate institutions, who can be completely detached from the firm's work, as well as concerns for conflict of interest, seem to have been the primary force behind this approach. When pro bono work is conducted within a law firm, conflicts of interest may arise between such work and the firm's clients, many of whom are *chaebols* and government entities in Korea, which would deter the law firm from actively pursuing pro bono work.[98] Another factor has been that law firm donations of money to its pro bono organization, rather than spending the money as its internal expenses, is regarded as a tax-wise practice.[99]

Despite the recent rush to engage in pro bono activities, there are criticisms that many law firms still place too much emphasis on social contribution which does not fulfil their corporate social responsibility.[100] Civil society is demanding that law firms give due consideration to human rights and social justice, in addition to their representation of the government and *chaebols*, but law firms are criticized as responding to this demand with charity work and pro bono activities in a manner which is separate from their legal services business.[101] This law firm orientation is evidenced by annual reports published by the law firms associated with the Law Firm Public Interest Network, which mostly pertain to explanations of pro bono activities and charity and volunteer work.[102]

94 Law Firm Public Interest Network, 로펌공익네트워크 출범취지문 (Declaration for Founding the Law Firm Public Interest Network) in *Promoting Law Firm Public Interest Activities* (Law Firm Public Interest Network, 2016) [*Declaration for Founding*], at 154.

95 *Declaration for Founding*, *supra* note 94, at 153. It also declares its intention to share information in regard to public interest activities and to seek opportunities for collaborative work.

96 Yoo Wook, 로펌 공익활동의 현황과 과제 (Current Situation and Challenges for Law Firm Public Interest Activities) in *Promoting Law Firm Public Interest Activities* (Law Firm Public Interest Network, 2016) [*Current Situation and Challenges*].

97 *Current Situation and Challenges*, *supra* note 96, at 12.

98 Kim Sung Jin, 로펌 프로보노 활성화 방안 (How to Promote Law Firm Pro Bono) (Seminar delivered at the Commemoration of five years of Dongcheon Foundation – Current Situation and Challenges for Public Interest Law Movement, 2014), at 194.

99 *BKL Interview*, *supra* note 90.

100 *Growth of Law Firms*, *supra* note 66, at 65.

101 *Growth of Law Firms*, *supra* note 66, at 66.

102 A notable exception is the Jipyong law firm, which for the first time in 2017 published a CSR report examining its policy and practice relating to diversity, non-discrimination, ethics, etc.: see Jipyong, 'CSR Policy', online: www.jipyong.com/en/csr/csr_policy.php.

TABLE 10.1. *Survey on Law Firm Public Interest Network*

	Answer					
Question		Yes			No	
1. Does the firm have a pro bono committee?		9			2	
2. Does the firm have a separate pro bono entity?		7			4	
3. Does the firm count pro bono work toward billable hours?		6			2	
4. Is pro bono work reflected in lawyer evaluations		7			2	
	5 or more		3–4	1–2		None
5. How many full-time pro bono lawyers does the firm have?	1		2	4		4[103]
	>1 bil KRW (US$0.85 mil)	500 mil–1 bil KRW (US$0.43–0.85 mil)	200–500 mil KRW (US$0.17–0.43 mil)	100–200 mil KRW (US$0.085–0.17 mil)	<100 mil KRW (US$0.085)	Undisclosed
6. How much is the law firm's budget for pro bono?	1	1	2	2	2	3
7. Area of Focus?						
Persons with disabilities					6	
Children and youth					6	
Migrants					5	
Welfare and poverty					4	
North Korean refugees					4	
Environment					3	
Social economy					3	
Refugees					2	
International human rights					2	
Female					2	
Single parent family					2	
Prisoners					2	
NPO support					2	
Homeless					1	
Solitary elder					1	
Adult guardianship					1	
Hansen's disease victims					1	
Legal assistance for developing countries					1	
Others					3	

[103] As at the end of 2017, two of the law firms who answered 'None' in the survey had hired or were in the process of hiring a full-time pro bono attorney.

D. Mandatory Public Interest Activities

The 2000 Amendment of the Attorney-at-Law Act provides that all Korean lawyers should devote a certain number of hours per year to public interest activities, referred to here as the 'mandatory public interest activities requirement'.[104] Public service of lawyers mandated by law, as opposed to a requirement of bar association membership, is a rare instance from the perspective of comparative law.[105] It is, however, worth noting that the pro bono and public interest law in Korea, as reviewed above, evolved separately from these mandatory public interest activities requirements. This development does not mean that the mandatory public interest activities requirement has not influenced pro bono and public interest law. The requirement has been, and is, a contributing factor to overall progress in access to justice, especially for the growth of law firm pro bono.

1. History

The historical background to the introduction of the mandatory public interest activities requirement has been studied in the most detail by Seung Heum Hwang.[106] According to Hwang, a series of legal scandals in 1998 and 1999 severely eroded the public's trust in the legal profession. In 1998, it was reported that a former-judge-turned-lawyer had been providing money and other gifts to several judges. A prosecutor later announced that 15 judges had received the money. In 1999, another former-judge-turned-lawyer was alleged to have bribed 300 judges, prosecutors, and police officers.[107] The former scandal was the first in the history of Korea to see judges being investigated for criminal allegations, and the latter scandal was infamous for members of legal professions being implicated in large numbers.

During this time, the Ministry of Justice ('MOJ') announced its plan to abolish the mandatory bar system, granting freedom to join and establish different bar associations. This plan would have also transferred the Korean Bar Association's disciplinary power over its members to the government. While the MOJ's plan was devised and introduced separately from the series of legal scandals noted above, the legal scandals and the public's disaffection with the legal profession were driving factors behind the MOJ's plan. The Korean Bar Association ('KBA') objected strongly to the plan, claiming, among other things, that the KBA was not merely a professional organization, but also existed to serve the public interest. In his article, Hwang defined the struggle between the MOJ and KBA as 'power politics', in which the MOJ wanted to dismantle or weaken KBA, and KBA fought to hold on to its monopoly power.[108] On the verge of losing its power, the KBA chose to emphasize its public nature, and it petitioned to amend the

104 While a 'mandatory pro bono requirement' would be a more recognized term in other jurisdictions such as the US, the authors will use a more direct translation of the Korean term, 'public interest activities'. As examined below, its scope is distinctive from 'pro bono activities' in other jurisdictions.

105 South Africa introduced a bill in 2014 that requires similar mandatory pro bono activities of lawyers: see Na Ji Won, 변호사 공익활동 의무제도의 개선방안 연구 (A Study on Improvement of Obligatory Pro Bono in Korea) (2013) 48 *Lawyer* at 204, although the extent of enforcement is unclear.

106 Hwang Seung Heum, 변호사의 공익활동의무 (The Mandatory Pro Bono Service of Lawyers) (2004) 26 *Law and Society* [*Mandatory Pro Bono*] at 237.

107 PSPD, 의정부 법조비리사건 대응 – 무너 진 법조윤리, 변호사징계정보자료실 구축으로 이어지다 (Our Activities Addressing the Uijeongbu Legal Scandal – the Shattered Legal Ethics Lead to the Establishment of Database of Disciplinary Actions against Lawyers) (*PSPD*, 2017), online: www.peoplepower21.org/pspd100/1338974.

108 *Mandatory Pro Bono*, *supra* note 106, at 242.

Attorney-at-Law Act to include a mandatory public interest activities requirement in April 1999. The amendment eventually passed the National Assembly in December 1999, and it was promulgated on 28 January 2000.

2. The Public Interest Activities Requirement

Article 27 of the Attorney-at-Law Act prescribes the duty to perform public interest activities in very abstract terms.[109] Paragraphs 1 and 2 of the Article do not state how many hours an attorney should devote to public interest activity, nor does the Article provide details of what types of work constitute public interest activity. Article 27(3) delegates these details to the Korean Bar Association. The current provision, reproduced below, is almost unchanged from the original version introduced in 2000:

> Article 27 (Duty to Perform Designated Services, such as Public Interest Activities)
>
> (1) Each attorney-at-law shall engage in public interest activities for not less than a specified number of hours a year.
> (2) Each attorney-at-law shall handle affairs designated by public agencies, the Korean Bar Association, or the local bar association with which he/she is affiliated under Acts and subordinate statutes.
> (3) Necessary matters concerning the scope of public interest activities and the method of performing such activities shall be determined by the Korean Bar Association.

In September 2000, KBA promulgated its 'Regulation for Public Interest Activities, etc.' ('KBA Regulation').[110] Under the KBA Regulation, the scope of public interest activities was defined as (1) providing for free or at significantly low cost legal service to, or working at positions of board members or committee members of, public interest organizations, such as charity organizations, religious organizations, social organizations, educational organizations that are operated for citizens' rights and freedoms or public interest, or for indigents; provided that such provision of legal service or holding positions shall be accepted by KBA or local bar associations to be public interest activities; (2) working at KBA or local bar associations; (3) working as a legal advisor as designated by KBA or local bar associations; (4) working at public interest programmes as designated by KBA or local bar associations; (5) working as a state-appointed counsel; (6) working in a capacity appointed by the government in accordance with law; provided however that cases where significant remuneration is paid shall be excepted; or (7) providing legal service to individuals, as defined by KBA or local bar associations.[111]

While this Regulation was being drafted, there were debates regarding whether to follow the Japanese precedent of defining 'public interest activities' with more precision. For example, the Daini Tokyo Bar Association limited public interest activities to activities and programmes run

[109] *Attorney-at-Law Act*, *supra* note 46, Article 27 (Duty to Perform Designated Services, such as Public Interest Activities).

[110] 공익활동 등에 관한 규정 (Regulation for Public Interest Activities, etc.), South Korea (enacted on 26 June 2000, as amended on 5 February 2018) [*KBA Regulation*]; see Appendix 10.1 for a translation of the current version of these regulations as at the time of publication.

[111] *KBA Regulation*, *supra* note 110, Article 2.

or designated by the bar association.[112] After a series of discussions, it was decided to follow what was understood as the American approach to pro bono and define public interest activities broadly, but to limit the scope of the activities by requiring acceptance by KBA or local bar associations.[113]

The KBA Regulation requires attorneys to devote 30 hours of their time annually to such public interest activities, but the requirement may be reduced to 20 hours as determined by local bar associations.[114] If an attorney cannot fulfil his/her requirement, that lawyer must pay the local bar association 20,000–30,000 KRW (US$17–26) per hour for each hour that he/she was unable to fulfil.[115] The money goes toward a separate fund used for public interest activities.[116]

The 2003 revision of the Regulation introduced the concept of 'designated public interest lawyer'.[117] According to Article 4, the public interest activities of a designated lawyer may be distributed to other lawyers in the same law firm in fulfilment of the mandatory hours. In effect, this allows any lawyer who has exceeded her 20 or 30 hours to distribute the surplus to her colleagues. Many law firms are known to utilize this provision actively. Some law firms choose to rely extensively on a few members to satisfy the mandatory hours of hundreds of their colleagues.[118]

In 2010, Article 2 was amended to include 'donations to public interest foundations that KBA or local bar associations have established'.[119] This revision was intended to benefit the Korean Bar Association Human Rights Foundation, launched in 2010. The Foundation was founded by the KBA to promote new human rights agendas such as North Korean human rights, international human rights, and environmental human rights. However, the Foundation faltered from lack of donors and support from KBA; the homepage of the Foundation shows only five individual donors since its establishment.[120] In 2016, KBA petitioned the MOJ for the dismantlement of the Foundation.[121]

The KBA Regulation allows local bar associations to provide additional standards on what qualifies as public interest activities for the mandatory requirement. Since the Seoul Bar Association holds a large majority of attorney members of the KBA,[122] its regulation on public interest activities merits a short examination. The Seoul Bar Association's Regulation for Public

[112] Daini Tokyo Bar Association, Rules Regarding Public Interest Activities of Members, Article 2 (in Japanese); see Chapter 5, 'Access to Justice and Lawyer Independence in Japan', Appendix 5.2, for an English translation of these rules.

[113] Ha Chang Woo, 변호사 공익활동 의무화의 의의와 시행방안 (Meaning and Implementation of Lawyer Pro Bono Requirement) (Seminar delivered at the PSPD on How to Conduct Public Interest Activities, 2000), at 7.

[114] *KBA Regulation*, *supra* note 110, Article 3(1).

[115] *KBA Regulation*, *supra* note 110, Article 3(2).

[116] *KBA Regulation*, *supra* note 110, Article 6.

[117] *KBA Regulation*, *supra* note 110, Article 4.

[118] Park Ji-yeon, 수억들인 로펌 공익법인... 활동은 아직 실험단계 (Several Hundred Millions of KRW Spent for Law Firm Public Interest Entities ... Their Work Still at Experimental Stage), *The Law Times* (9 January 2015), online: www.lawtimes.co.kr/Legal-News/Legal-News-View?serial=89986.

[119] *KBA Regulation*, *supra* note 110, Article 2(8).

[120] 지난 기부·모금 (Past Donations) (KBA Human Rights Foundation, 2010), online: www.kba-humanrights.or.kr/bbs/board.php?bo_table=old_donation (no donor information after 2017 displayed).

[121] 대한변협인권재단에 대한 면밀한 점검 필요하다 (A Close Scrutiny of Korean Bar Association Human Rights Foundation Required), *The Law Times* (21 November 2016), online: www.lawtimes.co.kr/Legal-Opinion/Legal-Opinion-View.aspx?serial=105885.

[122] A vast majority of sizeable law firms and all major law firms are based in Seoul as well.

Interest Activities[123] provides a much broader definition of public interest activities compared to the KBA. The Seoul Bar Association allows public interest activities to include:

- legal assistance to help the rights and freedom of an individual who belongs to a social or economic minority;[124]
- state-appointed counsel;
- legal assistance to government agencies;
- participation in public interest activities of public organizations;
- legal assistance to public interest organizations;
- participation in public interest activities of public interest organizations;
- working at public interest organizations;
- working at bar associations;
- participating in public interest programmes of bar associations;
- working in a capacity appointed by public organizations, public interest organizations, or bar associations;
- providing for free or for significantly low cost legal assistance in drafting or amending laws, or drafting or changing policies; and
- other activities as may be provided by Seoul Bar Association's Directive for Evaluation of Public Interest Activity.

The Seoul Bar Association's Directive for Evaluation of Public Interest Activity[125] added the following activities within the scope of public interest activities:

- donations to legal organizations whose primary purpose is to provide legal assistance to social minorities; and
- free legal consultations that an in-house counsel provides to his/her colleagues.

3. Criticism of the Mandatory Requirement

The KBA and the Seoul Bar Association's regulations define the parameters of 'public interest activity' broadly, and some of the activities listed as 'public interest activities' do not appear related to access to justice. Considering donations as pro bono activities seems to defeat the purpose of the Attorney-at-Law Act, which obligates each lawyer to *engage* in public interest activities.[126] Working at a bar association or as a state-appointed counsel is paid work. The Seoul Bar Association's Directive includes answering surveys performed by the Seoul Bar Association or participating in its events as public interest activities.[127] While the mandatory public interest activities requirement may be fulfilled by paying 30,000 or 20,000 KRW (US$26 or 17) per hour, there do not seem to be many lawyers who need to rely on this option. In 2008, only 29 out of 20,169 lawyers paid any money to the pro bono fund, in the amount of approximately 15 million KRW (US$12,842). More recently, in 2016, the amount donated to

[123] See Appendix 10.2 for a translation of the current version of these regulations as at the time of publication.

[124] Seoul Bar Association's Directive for Evaluation of Public Interest Activity (Article 3) clarifies that for-profit legal assistance is not included.

[125] Seoul Bar Association, 공익활동심사지침 (Directive for Evaluation of Public Interest Activity), South Korea (as amended 12 November 2019) [*Directive for Evaluation*].

[126] *Attorney-at-Law Act, supra* note 46, Article 27 (emphasis supplied).

[127] *Directive for Evaluation, supra* note 125, Article 4(9).

the pro bono fund was similar.[128] There seem to be two reasons for a small number of lawyers paying the penalty in lieu of service. The requirement's broad scope allows for various ways to fulfil the requirement, and there is virtually no bar association vetting of the lawyer's report of their public interest activities hours. Lawyers simply need to fill in a simple form on the Internet for their report without supporting documents. Bar associations cite the lack of resources to review individual reports.[129]

While the regulations provide for possible disciplinary action by the bar associations if their members do not comply with the requirement, such actions are rare.[130] In the only known instance, a request for disciplinary action was submitted to KBA by the Seoul Bar Association in 2015 for eight members' refusal to report public interest activities, which was executed by the KBA in 2016. However, the KBA's actions were overturned in the administrative court.[131] The court cited a lack of regulations to punish the act of non-reporting. Consequently, Seoul Bar Association does not plan to commence similar disciplinary proceedings in the future, preferring to give repeated notice to its members to report their annual public interest activities.[132] Sensing the lacklustre enforcement from bar associations, many lawyers opt to ignore the regulations and do not report their activities.[133] Whether the employers take due consideration of the mandatory public interest activities requirement is also questionable. As examined above, major law firms tend to have some form of policies on pro bono work of their attorneys, but smaller firms, as well as corporations hiring in-house counsel, are less likely to pay attention to the requirements.

Comprehensive data on the quantity and quality of legal services provided under the mandatory requirement are not available. While state-appointed counsel have been subject to continuing criticisms for not enthusiastically defending their clients,[134] no empirical data exist on the level of legal services provided through mandatory requirements. Since bar associations do not actively review the reported public interest activities, members' public interest activities are also challenging to classify. The KBA made the only attempt of statistical analysis in 2010, using the reports from 2008. According to the analysis, (a) working within the bar, or working for the government, accounted for 17.1% of the total public interest activity hours; (b) working as state-appointed counsel accounted for 27.7%; (c) participating in 'public interest activity programmes' provided by bar associations took up 11%; (d) participating in public interest organizations accounted for 18.8% of the total hours; and (e) 25.4% of the hours were not classified.[135]

The increasing number of lawyers in Korea may also play a role in the non-enforcement of the mandatory requirement. Due to the transition from the old judicial examination system to

[128] Seoul Bar Association, 2017 년도 일반회계 및 특별회계 결산 (2017 General Accounts and Special Accounts) (Seoul Bar Association, 2017) at 4.

[129] Shin Ji-min, 변호사 공익활동 의무제 실효성 논란으로 확산 (The Mandatory Public Interest Activity Requirement Sparks Debate on its Effectiveness), *The Law Times* (18 September 2014), online: www.lawtimes.co.kr/Legal-News/Legal-News-View?serial=87359.

[130] This is especially because, rather than being subject to disciplinary actions, the lawyer may simply opt to pay toward the pro bono fund.

[131] 2016 구합 84849 (2016KuHap84849), 17 November 2017 (Seoul Administrative Court).

[132] Phone interview with Seoul Bar Association staff (10 May 2017, Seoul).

[133] As of 2017, a sizeable number of Seoul Bar Association members failed to report their public interest activities, despite repeated notices from the Bar. Interviews with multiple officers of the Seoul Bar Association (10 and 24 May 2017, Seoul).

[134] *Lawyer Pro Bono*, *supra* note 33.

[135] Korean Bar Association, 한국변호사백서 2010 (2010 Korean Lawyer White Paper) (Korean Bar Association, 2010) at 115.

the new law school system, the number of students becoming lawyers each year increased by at least 50 per cent.[136] This recent surge in the number of lawyers has likely decreased the percentage of hours of categories (a) and (b) mentioned above, as the number of bar association officials and state-appointed counsel have not increased correspondingly. Lawyers often complain that it is difficult for them to fulfil their mandatory 20 or 30 hours when bar associations do not provide them with enough meaningful cases for them to take on a pro bono basis,[137] although the number of unrepresented litigants noted earlier suggests that opportunities to assist are available.

4. Impact of the Mandatory Requirement

Despite the significant loopholes and lax enforcement of the mandatory public interest activities requirement, it has acted as a decisive factor in the development of law firm pro bono. The authors believe that the introduction of the concept of designated public interest lawyer has incentivized a few law firms to hire full-time pro bono lawyers, so that their work can help fulfil the requirement of the law firm as a whole. While some may question the desirability of such an approach, the presence of full-time pro bono lawyers has enabled law firms to engage better with non-profit organizations and public interest law organizations. Although it does not indicate a counter-trend, the Seoul Bar Association amended its Directive in 2015 to limit the number of hours that a designated public interest lawyer can provide to his/her colleagues at the same law firm.[138] By this amendment, an attorney can only receive ten hours from the designated public interest lawyer; therefore, each attorney must fulfil ten hours annually by him/herself. A Seoul Bar Association officer involved with this amendment believes that the restriction was possible because of the relatively progressive stance of the President and the executives of the Seoul Bar Association at the time, and that there was a general consensus that each member of the Bar Association should be obligated to conduct at least some public interest activities annually.[139]

Perhaps more importantly, in terms of impact, the annual mandatory 20 hours has become the benchmark for major law firms to fulfil or even exceed. The Law Firm's Public Interest Activity Index, created and announced by KBA in 2013,[140] includes a criterion evaluating the percentage of attorneys that have conducted more than 20 hours of public interest activity. Out of eleven member firms of the Law Firm Public Interest Network, nine firms use the Index, and eight firms publish the results.[141] Seven firms indicated that their attorneys conduct more than

[136] In 2017, 1,581 students passed the bar exam, an increase from 1,000 students who passed the judicial exam before the introduction of the law school system: see Lee Sang Yeon , 제 5 회 변호사시험 1581 명 합격… 총점 862.37 점 (1,581 People Passed the 5th Bar Exam, Ministry of Justice, Total Score of 862.37), *The Law Journal* (21 April 2016), online: www.lec.co.kr/news/articleView.html?idxno=40218, and see Ministry of Justice, 2012년 기준 최근 10년간 사법시험 합격인원 및 합격점수 현황 (Number of People who Passed the Bar Exam and Their Passing Scores for the Last 10 Years as of 2012), *Ministry of Justice* (3 December 2012), online: www.moj.go.kr/moj/403/subview.do.

[137] Youm, Hyung-kuk, 프로보노지원센터를 통한 변호사 공익활동 활성화 (Vitalization of Lawyer's Public Interest Activities through Seoul Bar Association Pro Bono Support Centre) (Symposium for Vitalization of Lawyer's Public Interest Activites, 2018), at 24.

[138] *Directive for Evaluation*, *supra* note 125, Article 7(5).

[139] Phone interview with a senior Seoul Bar Association officer (24 May 2017, Seoul).

[140] The index measures how the firm is structured for pro bono work (whether the firm has a pro bono committee, has hired pro bono coordinators or full-time pro bono lawyers, etc.); and how the firm conducts its pro bono activities (total number of pro bono hours, ratio of pro bono hours to total billable hours, average pro bono hours of an attorney, ratio of attorneys who have contributed more than 20 hours to pro bono, etc.).

[141] *Current Situation and Challenges*, *supra* note 96, at 13.

20 pro bono hours on average.[142] Some of the firms that have exceeded the average of 20 hours emphasize this achievement in the law firm's pro bono report, by graphically comparing the 'Seoul Bar Association's requirement of 20 hours' with their achievement of more than 20 hours.[143] Other law firms report that their internal pro bono policies for recommended minimum pro bono hours reflect the 20 hour requirement. Some law firms' pro bono lawyers leverage the mandatory requirement by contacting the firm's lawyers who have not yet fulfilled the 20 hour requirement and suggesting participation in pro bono activities.[144]

IV. THE WAY AHEAD

The recent increase in the lawyer population has overall positively influenced access to justice in Korea. It seems quite apparent that the recent development in public interest lawyering has benefited from this growth. New public interest lawyers now fill up the positions at NGOs and law firm pro bono coordinators. Another positive aspect is the fact that law schools are mandated by law to run public interest legal clinics.[145] The experiences law school students gain from legal clinics are expected to influence their career choices.[146]

Law firms will increasingly find themselves in need of responding to heightened scrutiny from civil society regarding their compliance with corporate social responsibility. The Law Firm Public Interest Network provides a peer pressure effect, where each member firm strives not to fall too far behind its competitors in pro bono efforts. Despite the positive impact the mandatory public interest activity requirement has had on the law firm pro bono scene, there is no denying that the legal profession views the requirement with cynicism, and the President of the Seoul Bar Association, who was elected in 2017, conducted his campaign on the platform that he would abolish the requirement.[147] It is, however, also correct that there exist many lawyers in need of viable public interest activities, and to date, there has been no earnest effort to tap into this potential pool of pro bono resources. One possibility is the recent creation of pro bono coordination/referral organizations that connect non-profit organizations with pro bono demands to law firms and individual lawyers. Of particular note is the Seoul Bar Association Pro Bono Support Centre,[148] the first full-fledged pro bono clearinghouse in Korea that aims to connect legal services of law firms/lawyers with non-profits who need legal assistance. The Dongcheon Legal Centre for Non-profit Organizations has been taking a slightly different approach.[149] It attempts to match lawyers with non-profit organizations one on one for an extended time, rather than

[142] *Current Situation and Challenges*, *supra* note 96, at 14.

[143] For instance, see 2017 율촌 온율 공익활동보고서 (2017 Yulchon Onyul Pro Bono Report) (2017) at 27.

[144] Interviews with three law firm pro bono coordinators (24 May 2017, Seoul).

[145] 법학전문대학원 설치・운영에 관한 법률 시행령 (Enforcement Decree of the Act on the Establishment and Operation of Law School), Presidential Decree No. 27866, South Korea (enacted on 28 September 2007, as amended on 22 February 2017), Article 13, provides for the establishment of an 'actual practice programme' in order to provide students with 'opportunity to serve society'.

[146] Some studies show that law school graduates tend to put more focus on values rather than monetary compensation when choosing jobs, perhaps due to more diversity in the student pool and professors: see Lee Joon Woong, Lee Jae Hyub, and Hwang Hyun Jung, 법학전문대학원과 사법연수원 교육이 직장선택 고려사항과 법조현실 평가에 미치는 영향 (Influence of Law School Education and JRTI Education on Choosing Jobs and Evaluating the Current Situation of the Legal Profession) in Lee Jae Hyub, ed., *Legal Professions of Korea* (Pakyoungsa, 2016) at 116.

[147] Sohn Hyun-soo, 이찬희 변호사, 제 94 대 서울지방변호사회장 당선 (Lee Chan-hee Elected as the 94th President of the Seoul Bar Association), *Law Times* (23 January 2017), online: https://m.lawtimes.co.kr/Content/Article?serial=107564.

[148] Established in April 2016.

[149] Established in December 2016.

connecting lawyers to individual cases. These referral organizations may develop into full-blown clearinghouses that leverage the mandatory pro bono requirement and mobilize a potentially significant number of lawyers toward pro bono work.

Many improvements to access to justice are needed, but there is a strong foundation to build on in Korea. The military regime that preceded the democracy movement spurred human rights lawyers to develop access to justice, allowing contemporary lawyers to stand on their shoulders and see future possibilities.

APPENDIX 10.1 KOREAN BAR ASSOCIATION REGULATION FOR PUBLIC INTEREST ACTIVITIES, ETC. (**REGULATION NO. 54**)

Enacted on 26 June 2000
Revised on 10 February 2003; 13 February 2006; 25 January 2010; 2 June, 2014; 5 February 2018

Article 1 (Purpose)

This Regulation purports to stipulate such matters that are necessary for the public interest activities of members of the KBA, in accordance with Article 9-2 of the KBA's Member Regulations.

Article 2 (Contents of Public Interest Activities)

Public interest activities shall be such activities as defined below:

1. Providing for free or at significantly low cost legal service to, or working at positions of board members or committee members of, public interest organizations, such as charity organizations, religious organizations, social organizations, educational organizations that are operated for citizens' rights and freedoms or public interest, or for indigents; provided that such provision of legal service or holding positions shall be accepted by KBA or local bar associations to be public interest activities;
2. Working as officers at KBA or local bar associations, or their committees;
3. Working as a legal advisor as designated by KBA or local bar associations;
4. Working at public interest programmes as designated by KBA or local bar associations;
5. Working as a state-appointed counsel;
6. Working in a capacity appointed by the government in accordance with law; provided however that cases where significant remuneration is paid shall be excepted;
7. Providing legal service to individuals including free representation in court, or activities of legal assistance that have public interest characteristics such as legislative research, as defined by KBA or local bar associations; or
8. Donations to public interest foundations that are founded by KBA or local bar associations.

Article 3 (Execution of Public Interest Activities, etc.)

(1) Individual members shall conduct annually more than 30 hours of more than one of public interest activities provided in Article 2. Provided however, that local bar associations under special circumstances may reduce the 30 hour requirement above to 20 hours.

(2) Members who, due to extenuating circumstances, have not fulfilled the annual hours of public interest activities in accordance with para. 1 above shall pay 20,000 KRW or 30,000 KRW per hour to the local bar association that he or she is a member of.

(3) Members who have practised for less than 2 years, are older than 60, cannot continue normal practice due to illness, etc., or have other rational reasons for not conducting public interest activities shall be exempted from the obligations as provided in para. 1.

Article 4 (Substitution for public interest activities, etc.)

(1) Hours of public interest activities that law firms, limited liability law firms, and law firm partnerships have conducted for all of their partners and associates in accordance with the following paragraphs may be deemed to be conducted by all of the individual partners and associates belonging to such law firms, limited liability law firms, and law firm partnerships, and distributed to individual partners and associates which shall be accepted as hours of public interest activities of each individual member.

1. Public interest activities that law firms, limited liability law firms, and law firm partnerships have conducted for all of their partners and associates;
2. Public interest activities of a lawyer(s) who has been designated by law firms, limited liability law firms, or law firm partnerships to conduct public interest activities on behalf of all of their partners and associates.

(2) For the designated public interest activity lawyer provided in para. 1 subpara. 2, his or her public interest activity hours shall be considered to be his or her own public interest activity hours only for the hours that have been distributed to him or her.

(3) Provisions in para. 1 and para. 2 shall apply *mutatis mutandis* to the joint law office authorized as notary public and other joint law office partnership.

(4) Acceptance of distribution of public interest activity hours as provided in para. 1 and para. 2 shall be subject to the approval of the local bar association, upon application by the representative of the law firm, limited liability law firm, law firm partnership, joint law office authorized as notary public, and other joint law office partnership.

(5) The law firm, limited liability law firm, law firm partnership, joint law office authorized as notary public, and other joint law office partnership may designate an individual member who has practised for less than 2 years or is older than 60 as the designated public interest activity lawyer.

Article 5 (Establishment of public interest activity evaluation committee)

The local bar association shall establish a public interest activity evaluation committee to evaluate and determine such matters necessary for public interest activities, etc. of its members.

Article 6 (Management of fund)

(1) The local bar association shall establish and manage a special fund for stable execution of public interest activities.

(2) Payment in accordance with Article 3 para. 2 shall be deposited into the special fund as provided in para. 1 above.

Article 7 (Duty to cooperate)

Law firm members that employ individual members, or individual members, shall cooperate to ensure that individual members participate in public interest activities, etc.

Article 8 (Reporting of public interest activities, etc.)

(1) Individual members shall report no later than the end of February of each year the result of his or her public interest activities, etc. during the previous year to the local bar association that he or she is a member of.
(2) The local bar association shall report no later than the end of May of each year the result of public interest activities, etc. of its members to the KBA.

Article 9 (Disciplinary actions)

The president of the local bar association may apply for disciplinary action to the president of KBA for individual members who have not conducted public interest activities, etc. in accordance with this Regulation or have not paid payment in accordance with Article 3 para. 2.

Article 10 (Delegation)

The local bar association may enact necessary regulations, rules, and by-laws under the scope of this Regulation.

APPENDIX 10.2 SEOUL BAR ASSOCIATION REGULATION FOR PUBLIC INTEREST ACTIVITIES, ETC.

Enacted on 21 July 2000
Revised on 28 May 2001
Partly revised on 13 December 2004; 16 June 2005; 16 January 2008; 18 January 2010; 23 July 2012, 15 January 2012; 13 November 2014; 1 September 2015; 15 May 2018; 31 May 2019; 6 August 2019; 26 November 2019

Article 1 (Purpose)

This Regulation purports to stipulate, in accordance with para. 3, Article 12-4 of the Member Regulations, the scope and the manner of execution of public interest activities, etc.

Article 2 (Definition)

The definition of the terms used herein shall be as follows:

1. Legal Aid shall refer to activities of lawyers in their capacity as lawyers for free or for a considerably low cost, including representation, legal aid, and volunteer work.

2. Public Organization shall refer to organizations or facilities established and run for the government, regional governments, or other public interest purposes.
3. Public Interest Organization shall refer to social organizations, charity organizations, civil movement organizations, educational organizations, religious organizations, etc., the purposes of which are public interest of the nation and society, and assistance and support for economic and social minorities.
4. Bar Association shall refer to Korea Bar Association and each local bar association.
5. Evaluation Committee shall refer to the Public Interest Activity Evaluation Committee established in accordance with Article 11 of this Regulation.
6. Directive shall refer to the Directive for Evaluation of Public Interest Activities which is drafted by the President of this bar association, upon evaluation of the Public Interest Activity Evaluation Committee.
7. President shall refer to the President of this bar association.

Article 3 (Scope and contents of public interest activities)

(1) The following activities that individual members have conducted for the purpose of defending basic human rights and realization of social justice shall be deemed to be public interest activities.
   1. Legal aid for individuals: legal aid for realization of rights and freedom of an individual who is a social or economic minority;
   2. State-appointed legal representation and counsel as provided by law;
   3. Legal aid for Public Organizations: legal aid conducted toward Public Organizations;
   4. Public interest activities through participation of public interest activities of Public Organizations: participation in or support for public interest activities or public interest projects conducted by Public Interest Organizations;
   5. Public interest activities for Public Interest Organizations: legal aid activities toward Public Interest Organizations for realization of their rights and purpose;
   6. Public interest activities for Public Interest Organizations: participation in or support for public interest activities or public interest projects conducted by Public Interest Organizations;
   7. Work at Public Interest Organizations: working as board members, staff, or permanent staff in Public Interest Organizations for no reimbursement or significantly low reimbursement to participate in or support such projects and activities the Public Interest Organizations are conducting for public interest purposes for the nation and the society;
   8. Work at Bar Association: conducting activities and work in the capacity of an official or committee member of the Bar Association;
   9. Public interest activities through participation in public interest activities of the Bar Association: participating, conducting, executing, or supporting public interest activities conducted by the Bar Association, including legal consultation, legal aid, disaster relief, social welfare;
   10. Public interest activities through conducting work appointed by Public Organizations, etc.: conducting work appointed by Public Organizations, Public Interest Organizations, and Bar Association;

11. Public interest activities in regard to legislation, etc.: providing for free or for significantly low cost legal assistance in drafting or amending laws, or drafting or changing policies;
12. Other activities recognized as public interest activities by the Directive.

(2) The President, after deliberation by the Evaluation Committee for Public Interest Activities, may render a decision to deny approval of public interest activities for activities provided in subparas. 1, 3, 4, 5, 6, 7, 10, 11, 12 of para. 1 above which have considerable reasons not to be recognized as public interest activities or which fall under one of the reasons for non-approval of public interest activities as provided in the Directive.

(3) Individual members may, within ten (10) days upon the receipt of the non-approval of public interest activities provided above, apply for re-evaluation of the President, and the President shall render a decision of re-evaluation within twenty (20) days from the application for re-evaluation, after deliberation by the Evaluation Committee for Public Interest Activities, and shall without delay give notice of the decision to the applicant.

Article 4 (Members for public interest activities)

(1) Public interest activities shall be conducted by individual members as provided in para. 2, Article 7 of the Member Regulations.

(2) The following individual members shall be exempted from their obligations of public interest activities:
1. Individual members with less than 2 accumulated years of legal practice;
2. Individual members older than 60;
3. Individual members who are unable to or have difficulties in conducting public interest activities for reasons of physical disabilities, disease, pregnancy, birth, child-raising and other reasons, and have been recognized by the President after deliberation by the Evaluation Committee to be members exempted from public interest activities.

(3) The recognition of exemption from public interest activities shall be made by this bar association *ex officio* or upon application.

(4) Applications for exemption from public interest activities submitted by individual female members for reasons of pregnancy or birth as provided by subpara. 3, para. 2 above shall be granted for 1 year as applied by the member.

(5) Applications for exemption from public interest activities submitted by individual members having a child of less than 8 years of age for reasons of child-raising as provided by subpara. 3, para. 2 above shall be granted for 3 years as applied by the member.

Article 5 (Hours of public interest activities)

Hours of public interest activities shall be 20 hours for each individual member annually.

Article 6 (Collective public interest activities, etc.)

(1) For public interest activities conducted collectively by individual members, actual hours that each individual member has conducted shall be considered to be his or her public interest activities.

(2) Hours of public interest activities that law firms, limited liability law firms, and law firm partnerships have conducted for all of their partners and associates in accordance with the following paragraphs may be distributed to partners and associates of such law firms, limited liability law firms, and law firm partnerships, which shall be accepted as hours of public interest activities of each individual member. Provided, however, that public interest activities of a lawyer(s) who has been designated by law firms, limited liability law firms, or law firm partnerships to conduct public interest activities on behalf of all of their partners and associates in accordance with subpara. 2 may be limited by the Directive.
  1. Public interest activities that law firms, limited liability law firms, and law firm partnerships have conducted for all of their partners and associates.
  2. Public interest activities of a lawyer(s) who has been designated by law firms, limited liability law firms, or law firm partnerships to conduct public interest activities on behalf of all of their partners and associates.

(3) For the designated public interest activity lawyer provided in para. 1 subpara. 2, his or her public interest activity hours shall be considered to be his or her own public interest activity hours only for the hours that have been distributed to him or her.

(4) Provisions in para. 2 and para. 3 shall apply *mutatis mutandis* to joint law offices authorized as notary public and joint law offices.

(5) Acceptance of distribution of public interest activity hours as provided in para. 2 and para. 4 shall be subject to the approval of the President, upon application by the representative of the law firm, limited liability law firm, law firm partnership, joint law office authorized as notary public, and joint law offices. The President shall render a decision on the approval or non-approval upon deliberation by the Evaluation Committee.

(6) The law firm, limited liability law firm, law firm partnership, joint law office authorized as notary public, and joint law office may designate an individual member falling under the scope of subparas. 1 and 2, para. 2 Article 4 above as the designated public interest activity lawyer.

Article 7 (Provision of opportunities for public interest activities, etc.)

(1) This bar association shall survey policies and measures to voluntarily conduct public interest activities and inform all individuals thereon.

(2) This bar association shall study and identify opportunities and instruments to allow participation of all individual members in public interest activities, and allow participation therein.

(3) The law firm, limited liability law firm, law firm partnership, joint law office authorized as notary public, and joint law office shall encourage and provide opportunities and time for public interest activities of its partners and associates.

Article 8 (Reporting and evaluation of public interest activities)

(1) Individual members who have conducted public interest activities shall report his/her public interest activities, conducted from the start through the end of each year, by the end of February of the following year to the President.

(2) The President, with reasonable doubt on the verity of the whole or the part of the report as provided in para. 1 above, shall order the Evaluation Committee to evaluate the report.
(3) The Evaluation Committee, for evaluations as provided in para. 2 above, may demand clarification on the contents of the report to the reporting individual member, and the member shall respond to the demand without delay.
(4) This bar association may grant appropriate benefits to the member in their activities and training if he/she has dutifully fulfilled the reporting obligations.

Article 9 (Notice of public interest activities, etc.)

(1) The President may give notice to individual members to participate in public interest activities in the following circumstances.
   1. If he or she has not performed public interest activities;
   2. If his or her hours of public interest activities do not fulfil the requirement provided in Article 5; or
   3. If he or she has not reported his or her public interest activities in accordance with para. 1, Article 8.
(2) Individual members who have received such notice as provided in subpara. 1, para. 1 above shall without delay perform public interest activities for hours exceeding the hours provided in Article 5, and individual members who have received such notice as provided in subpara. 2, para. 1 shall perform public interest activities to supplement the unfulfilled public interest hours, and report it to the President.
(3) Individual members who have received such notice as provided in subpara. 3, para. 1 above shall without delay report his or her public interest activities to the President.
(4) [deleted]
(5) The President may, upon deliberation by the Evaluation Committee, render such decisions that correspond to the failure of individual members to respond to notice provided in paras. 2 and 3.

Article 10 (Payment of legal aid support fund and conditions for recognition as public interest activities)

In the case where individual members who have not performed public interest activities due to unavoidable circumstances or have performed less than the minimum hours as provided in Article 5, and have paid as legal aid support fund in the amount of 30,000 KRW per hour, the President may, after deliberation by the Evaluation Committee, render a decision to recognize the payment as public interest activities.

Article 11 (Committee for Evaluation of Public Interest Activities)

In accordance with this Regulation, deliberations and other matters on the public interest activities shall be conducted by the Evaluation Committee which is established in accordance with Regulations for Establishment of the Evaluation Committee.

Article 12 (Usage of legal aid support fund)

The legal aid support fund as provided in Article 10 shall be used by this bar association for public interest activities such as performing legal aid projects.

Article 12-2 (Social welfare support fund)

Social welfare projects such as helping teenagers responsible for providing for their family, helping children of prisoners, sponsorship of children of low-income families, and fundraising for disaster relief shall be conducted through special accounts.

Article 13 (Directive for Evaluation of Public Interest Activities)

Matters necessary for execution of this Regulation or evaluation of public interest activities shall be separately stipulated in the Directive.

Article 14 (Scope of the Regulation)

This Regulation and the Directive as provided in Article 13 shall be in effect retroactively from 29 July 2000.

11

A Hub, a Knot, and a Powerhouse: The Legal Aid Foundation and Access to Justice in Taiwan

*Ching-Fang Hsu and Yong-Ching Tsai**

Abstract

The main legal force for access to justice in Taiwan is the Legal Aid Foundation, a state-subsidized but independent agency. The institutionalization of legal aid was a crucial part of judicial reform during democratization in Taiwan, in which lawyers aimed to advance access to justice for the general public and the judiciary agreed to take up responsibility as supervising agency. Over time the Legal Aid Foundation has moved beyond court representation of indigent persons, and it now plays a critical role in legal mobilization, coordinating public interest lawyers, social minorities, and other actors in the Taiwanese civil society, and allowing them to bring cases to court and lobby for social justice legislation in the parliament. The Legal Aid Foundation's expanded role has however exposed its organizational weakness as a hybrid model of access to justice, creating tension with the state regarding accountability and conflict with the bar over quality control.

I. INTRODUCTION

The Taiwan Legal Aid Foundation ('LAF'), which started operations in 2004, is the official organization authorized to administer legal aid with public funds, providing pre-trial legal counsel, formal representation in litigation, and other legal services. LAF also plays a critical role in legal mobilization in Taiwan, coordinating public interest lawyers, social minorities, and other actors in the Taiwanese civil society, and allowing them to bring cases to court as well as lobby for social justice legislation in the parliament. The expanded reliance on LAF has however exposed its organizational weakness as a hybrid model of access to justice, and LAF has experienced tension with the state and conflicts with the bar.

In Taiwan, *falu fuchu* or 法律扶助 refers to legal aid: *falu* is law, and *fuchu* means aid, or assistance. The abbreviation *fafu or* 法扶 (law-aid) refers to the legal service provided by LAF to indigent persons. Pro bono is a widely accepted foreign concept among Taiwanese legal professionals, who often use the Latin phrase to refer to the practice of free legal representation

* The authors wish to thank Professor Helena Whalen-Bridge and Dr Yun-chien Chang for their kind support. The first author would also like to thank Professor Dan Puchniak and Weitseng Cheng at the Centre for Asian Legal Studies, National University of Singapore for being generous hosts.

in public interest litigation, usually by large law firms. The common understanding of a pro bono case is a dispute of great public interest in which ideologically driven lawyers are willing to assist. There are no expectations of monetary reward for these legal services, but the necessary costs (such as court fees, transportation, and/or other administrative costs) might be reimbursed by their firms or civic organizations that mobilize support. Because pro bono cases usually involve mid- to large-scale mobilization and have a longer civic tradition in the Taiwanese context, the concept of pro bono has great moral importance. Pro bono lawyers have represented victims of serial labour disputes, and sometimes more controversial cases, such as rescuing allegedly innocent convicts from death row.[1] In contrast, *fafu* (legal aid) has neutral cultural connotations, and the term only appeared after 2004, specifically referring to services assigned and supported by LAF.

Currently, LAF is the primary provider of legal services involving indigent persons, and given these responsibilities and its expanded role in access to justice, this chapter focuses not on individual lawyer pro bono but rather on this major player in the Taiwan context. We first introduce the background of LAF, providing the context of relevant legislation and the policy goals of the institutionalization of access to justice in Taiwan. Next, using official data from LAF, including public annual reports as well as internal records provided to the authors in connection with this research, we present three important trends of the past decade: the growing need for legal assistance, ensuring fair quality legal services, and diversification of legal aid. In the third section, we use two instances of legal mobilization in Taiwan, a class-action lawsuit regarding recovery for injuries caused by toxic chemicals in manufacturing, and legislation regarding consumer credit card debt, to argue that LAF functions as a hub and a powerhouse in Taiwanese civil society. The fourth section presents an analysis of the embedded tension between LAF and the state, and conflicts between LAF and the Taiwanese Bar. A final discussion situating Taiwan in a comparative context concludes the chapter.

II. BACKGROUND: LAWYERS, DEMOCRATIZATION, AND THE LEGAL AID FOUNDATION

Taiwan is a civil law jurisdiction. The Judicial Yuan, one of the five main branches of the Taiwanese government, is a civil administrative body that governs the judiciary. Regarding admission to the bar, students with an undergraduate or graduate law degree, or those who have taken more than 20 credits of given law subjects in a recognized institution, may take the bar exam.[2] A national Taiwan Bar Association and 16 local bar associations carry out lawyer disciplinary functions, while the Minister of Justice ('MOJ') issues a practising licence.[3] Taiwanese lawyers are required to register at (a) any Taiwanese court, and (b) the local bar association where s/he wishes to litigate in order to represent clients in proceedings.[4]

Currently, there are roughly 9,000 to 10,000 lawyers in the country of roughly 23 million people, per official statistics from the MOJ (Table 11.1 on p. 209).[5]

[1] A prototypical example is the pro bono lawyer group for the *Xhizi Trio* case, where Lawyer Su Yo-chen led a team of six lawyers and fought side by side with the three defendants for over a decade. They were eventually declared innocent in 2012. For the lawyers' role, see Chang Chuang-fen, 無彩青春 (Colourless Youth) (Taipei: Flâneur Culture Lab, 2013).

[2] 專門職業及技術人員高等考試律師考試規則 (Regulations of Bar Examination), Taiwan 2001 (as amended 12 April 2019), s 5.

[3] 律師法 (Attorney Regulation Act), Taiwan 1941 (as amended 15 January 2020) [*Attorney Regulation Act*], s 6.

[4] *Attorney Regulation Act*, *supra* note 3, s 11.

[5] Taiwan, Ministry of Justice, 本國律師人數 (Numbers of Domestic Lawyers) (2019), online: www.rjsd.moj.gov.tw/RJSDWeb/common/WebList3_Report.aspx?list_id=1527.

TABLE 11.1. *Number of lawyers in Taiwan*

Year	Number of licences issued by MOJ (accumulated)	Number of lawyers registered in bar associations	Number of lawyers registered in courts
2017	16,451	9,153	10,007
2018	17,288	9,768	10,625
2019	18,028	10,305	11,217

Bar fees vary from region to region. For example, one-time registration fees range from TWD23,000 (US$779.65)[6] in the Taipei Bar Association to TWD50,000 (US$1,694.89) in the Taitung Bar Association, and monthly fees range from TWD300 (US$10.17) in the Keelung Bar Association to TWD700 (US$23.73) in the Taipei Bar Association.[7]

LAF in Taiwan is a state-subsidized but independent agency that provides free legal aid to the 'socially disadvantaged and minorities'.[8] LAF is in charge of registering lawyers who want to provide legal services in legal aid cases and assigning cases to them. Practising lawyers are not obligated to provide legal aid, but they can sign up with local LAF offices and request cases after three years of practice. Each lawyer can register with up to three branch offices in different regional jurisdictions and take up to 24 cases per year.[9]

LAF was first advocated by a group of liberal-minded lawyers in the late 1990s,[10] and was subsequently enacted in 2004.[11] The institutionalization of legal aid was a crucial part of judicial reform during democratization in Taiwan, in which lawyers aimed to advance access to justice for the general public, and the judiciary agreed to take up responsibility as the supervising agency.[12]

[6] XE Currency Converter, online: www.xe.com/currencyconverter/convert/?Amount=50%2C000&From=TWD&To=USD. Unless another reference was cited, US$ denominations in the chapter were derived from www.xe.com at the time of publication; they are intended for general reference and may have been rounded up or down for ease of reference.

[7] You Po Hsiang, 請將權利還給律師－論律師權益、公會存續與執業區域限制 (Please Return the Rights Back to Lawyers: On the Lawyers' Rights and Benefits, Survivals of Bar Associations, and Limitation on Practice Locations) (2016) 20 *National Lawyers* 9 at 54.

[8] 法律扶助法 (Legal Aid Act), Taiwan 2004 (as amended 1 July 2015) [*Legal Aid Act*], ss 1, 5, 37.

[9] The authors acquired information regarding the limited number of registrations in interviews. The 24-case limitation is an internal regulation but it is referred to in many documents by LAF. For example, one of the former board members explained why he set the limitation, first at 36, then at 24, in Hua Jin-Ding, 'An Interview of Lawyer Lin Chun-Rong on Quality of Legal Aid', Special Issue on the Fifteenth Anniversary of Legal Aid Foundation, 31 July 2019, online: Legal Aid Foundation, https://reurl.cc/1gxoNG.

[10] Taiwan, Legislative Yuen, 立法院第五屆第四會期第 16 次會議記錄 (Conference Minutes of Session 5-4), Book 92, Issue 60 (Taiwan: 2003) [*Conference Minutes*] at 485: 'Today, in order to substantiate the constitutional protection of equality and right to litigate, the Taipei Bar Association, Judicial Reform Foundation and the Taiwan Association for Human Rights collaborated to form an action group in 1998, calling monthly meetings to gather scholars and lawyers to study comparative institutions. In July 1999, the National Judicial Reform Forum also resolved to "institute a legal aid institution" which shows consistent goals, reaffirming our resolution.'

[11] *Legal Aid Act*, *supra* note 8, Preamble.

[12] *Conference Minutes*, *supra* note 10, at 380. The Judicial Yuan put forward a statement to advocate for the pressing need of the legal aid legislation. In the statement, the Yuan justifies its support of the legislation by referring to the 1999 National Judicial Reform Forum, which resolved to institute a system to defend financially disadvantaged defendants. In the National Judicial Reform Forum, the Judicial Yuan was asked to fund a legal organization by the 2002 budget year, and gradually stopped the original public defendant system. In fact, at the time, there were only 51 public defenders nationally, and on average, each of them had to defend 26.4 cases every month, while courts in all jurisdictions in Taiwan had 11,750 cases to address annually. This showed the urgent need: without a new legal aid institution, no proper legal representation could be afforded to these defendants, especially when the Yuan was also implementing a new criminal litigation policy of cross-examination in the early 2000s.

Before LAF was founded, disadvantaged litigants in need of legal services usually sought assistance from individual volunteer lawyers, or from civic organizations on specific social justice issues such as women's rights or labour rights. In 1999, it was reported that only 4.6 per cent of all civil lawsuits had representation for both parties, whereas in criminal cases, 'only 12.5% of defendants were represented at the district court level, and less than one-third were represented at or above the High Court level'.[13]

The legislation to create legal aid and LAF was initiated in 1999 at the National Forum of Judicial Reform, where the concept was accepted unanimously by government officials, lawyers, judges, prosecutors, and academics. Heeding this consensus to reform, the Judicial Yuan put forth a draft bill in 2002.[14] The then newly elected government had strong incentives to follow through and legislate a bill for two reasons. First, liberal lawyers were major supporters of the new ruling party, and some prominent leaders of the bar actually took up positions in the judiciary to commence a series of judicial reforms. Second, the bill to institutionalize legal aid was lobbied as non-partisan legislation that enhanced social justice. In fact, 'help the poor in court', the slogan publicized by lawyer-led NGOs at the time, was such a strong mandate that even the opposition party could not say no. LAF was therefore a collaborative project, supported by all stakeholders and driven by the democratization momentum: the new government needed a gesture of reform, the judiciary was pressured to transform, and the bar pushed for more comprehensive representation in court on behalf of their clients. Access to justice was therefore a shared purpose in the Taiwanese context in the early 2000s, and the LAF became the way to realize this shared policy goal via the Legal Aid Act.[15]

III. LEGAL AID IN ACTION

LAF is an independent organization, legally authorized to administer legal aid. At the time of writing, LAF had 22 branch offices with 4,352 lawyers registered to provide service, and as of 2019 it had provided assistance in approximately 60,000 cases.[16] See Table 11.2 on p. 211 for information on the number of registered lawyers in legal aid offices.

LAF provides legal representation in both civil and criminal cases to disadvantaged citizens.[17] Disadvantaged status is determined by: (1) property and disposable income, depending on the number of in the household and the place of residence;[18] or (2) legal status as a low-income household, defined by the Public Assistance Act;[19] or (3) legal status as a family in need, defined by the Act of Assistance for Family in Hardship.[20] The applicant is also deemed disadvantaged, if s/he is: (1) aboriginal; (2) mentally challenged; (3) a juvenile; (4) a debtor defined in the Consumer Debt Clearance Act;[21] or (5) a criminal defendant whose offence is legally prescribed

[13] *A Survey of Pro Bono Practices and Opportunities in 84 Jurisdictions* (Latham & Watkins LLP, 2016) at 640.

[14] Taiwan, Legislative Yuen 法律扶助基本法草案 (Legal Aid Fundamental Act Draft), Volume 91, Issue 32 (Taiwan: Legislative Yuan Gazette, 2002) [*Legal Aid Fundamental Act Draft*] at 173–217.

[15] *Legal Aid Act*, *supra* note 8, s 38.

[16] 2019 *Legal Aid Foundation Annual Report* (Legal Aid Foundation, 2020) [2019 *LAF Report*] at 6, online: Legal Aid Foundation, www.laf.org.tw/index.php?action=report.

[17] *Legal Aid Act*, *supra* note 8, ss 4, 5.

[18] For the regulations on the Means Test for the Recipient, please see the LAF website, online: https://ppt.cc/fbYL3x.

[19] *Legal Aid Act*, *supra* note 8, s 5.

[20] Ibid.

[21] Ibid.

TABLE 11.2. *Number of registered lawyers in legal aid offices (2017)*[22]

Branch office	Number of registered legal aid lawyers
Keelung	370
Taipei	1,890
Shilin	1,325
New Taipei	1,780
Taoyuan	845
Hsinchu	205
Miaoli	211
Taichung	634
Nantou	281
Changhua	343
Yunlin	133
Chiayi	120
Tainan	191
Kaohsiung	465
Pingtung	240
Taitung	28
Hualien	56
Yilan	61
Kinmen	201
Matsu	119
Penghu	74
Total number of registrations	9,572
Number of lawyers after removal of repeated appointments	3,722

no less than three years of imprisonment, or whose case is tried in the first instance by the Taiwan High Court.[23]

LAF also has detailed regulations regarding eligible case types. In criminal cases, LAF does not provide assistance for the following matters: (1) complaints or reports of an offence, with the exception of mentally challenged clients and victims of sexual offences and human trafficking; (2) private prosecutions; (3) defence in retrials and extraordinary appeals, with the exception of death penalty cases; (4) applications for setting the case for trial; or (5) complaints in trademark infringements.[24] In civil cases, LAF does not provide assistance in: (1) election lawsuits; (2) small-claims procedures and compulsory executions; (3) retrials; or (4) trademark and patent cases.[25] Finally, LAF does provide non-citizens with legal assistance, such as legal migrant workers in certain trades, or spouses of Taiwanese citizens who are economically underprivileged.[26]

In the following section, we present three important trends regarding LAF and access to justice that have emerged in the past decade: the growing need for legal assistance, measures undertaken to maintain the quality of legal aid services, and diversification of legal aid services. Drawing on LAF's annual reports[27] as well as internal data provided to the authors by LAF in

[22] Interview with TWO201702 (29 January 2018, Taipei) [*Interview with TWO201702*].
[23] Ibid.
[24] 法律扶助施行範圍辦法 (Regulation of the Extent of Legal Aid), Taiwan 1993 (as amended 12 November 2013) [*Regulation of the Extent of Legal Aid*], s 3.
[25] *Regulation of the Extent of Legal Aid*, *supra* note 24, s 4.
[26] *Legal Aid Act*, *supra* note 8, s 14.
[27] All annual reports can be found on the official website of LAF, online: www.laf.org.tw/index.php?action=report.

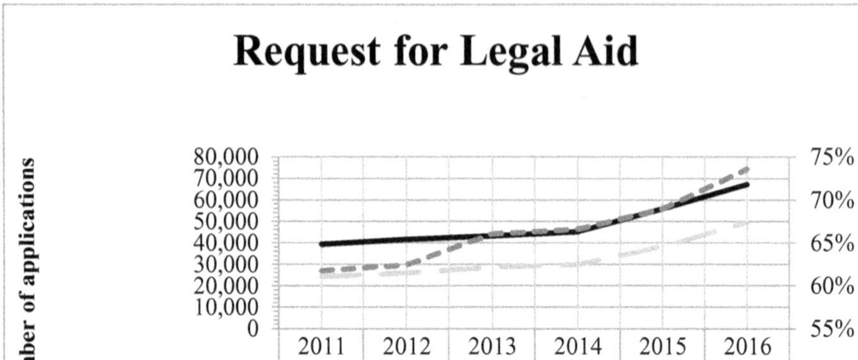

	2011	2012	2013	2014	2015	2016
Applications	39,393	41,641	43,277	45,133	55,679	67,116
Approved applications	24,334	26,005	28,584	30,047	38,380	49,365
Approval rates	62%	62%	66%	67%	69%	74%

FIGURE 11.1. Growth of legal aid applications (2017)[28]

connection with this research, we argue that LAF takes a holistic approach to promoting access to justice in Taiwan. LAF not only offers a wide variety of services to the general public and disadvantaged groups, but also initiates systematic remedies and legal mobilization, to provide protection from the very beginning of legal disputes to their final resolution.

A. *Growing Needs*

Undoubtedly, there is a growing need for legal aid, and data from LAF corroborates this consistent trend. First, the number of applications for legal aid has grown steadily since 2011. Second, the application approval rates, which are consistently higher than 60 per cent, also increased in the same time period (Figure 11.1 above).

The LAF has provided aid to three special types of applicants through separate schemes since 2014: labourers, aboriginal persons, and credit card debtors. Statistics also show an increasing trend in the number of these types of filed and approved applications, although the approval rate for credit card debtors dropped in 2015 (Figures 11.2–11.4 on pp. 213–14).

B. *The Quality of Legal Representation in Legal Aid*

As LAF is an independent organization, and the only organization legally authorized to administer legal aid, bar associations in Taiwan have no power to oversee the conduct of lawyers providing legal aid services. LAF is therefore concerned with the quality of legal service that lawyers provide, and it takes steps to ensure that indigent clients receive quality services. First, LAF provides legal aid recipients primarily with experienced lawyers. Statistics provided by LAF show, as presented in the pie charts in Figure 11.5 on p. 215, that 72–79% of lawyers registered with LAF have over six years of practice (2013: 79%; 2012: 75%; 2011: 73%; 2010: 72%; 2009: 75%). Admittedly, more experienced lawyers do not necessarily translate into better quality legal

[28] Compiled by the authors from LAF Annual Reports.

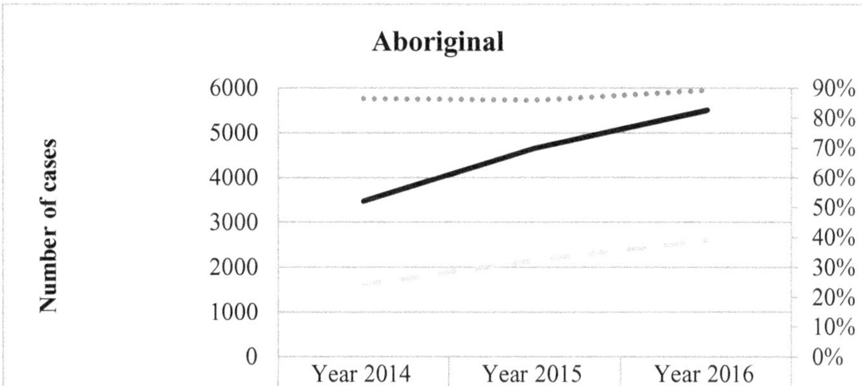

	Year 2014	Year 2015	Year 2016
Application	1859	2503	2908
Approved application	1607	2150	2594
Approval rates	86%	86%	89%

FIGURE 11.2. Growth of legal aid applications (aboriginal cases) (2017)[29]

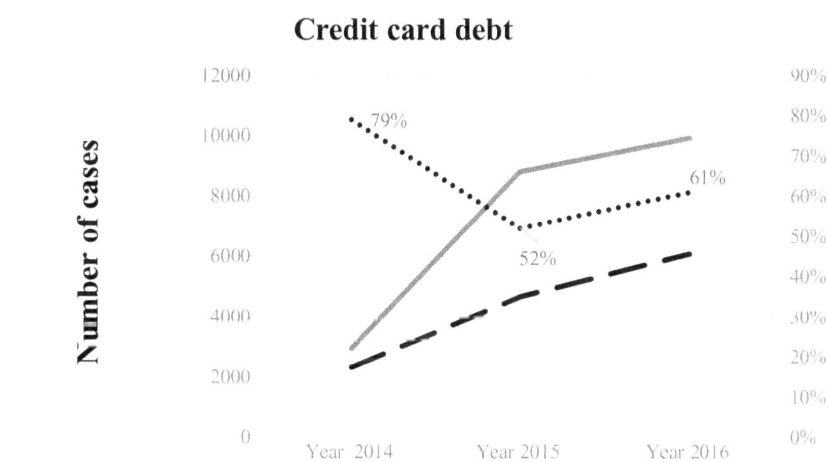

	Year 2014	Year 2015	Year 2016
Application	2947	8817	9933
Approved application	2318	4663	6087
Approval rates	79%	52%	61%

FIGURE 11.3. Growth of legal aid applications (credit card debtor cases) (2017)[30]

services, but this practice does allow legal aid recipients in Taiwan to avoid the legal services of inexperienced lawyers.

Viewed from the client's perspective, legal aid recipients generally report positive experiences with their lawyers. According to surveys conducted by LAF (Figure 11.6 on p. 217), approximately 50 per cent of the respondents believed that the legal aid lawyer's assistance brought about a

[29] Compiled by the authors from LAF Annual Reports.
[30] Compiled by the authors from LAF Annual Reports.

	Year 2014	Year 2015	Year 2016
Approved application	1613	2431	3264
Application	2050	2865	3785
Approval rates	79%	85%	86%

FIGURE 11.4. Growth of legal aid applications (labour cases) (2017)[31]

favourable outcome in criminal cases from 2005 to 2013. In a 2012 survey, 87.7 per cent of legal aid recipients were satisfied with the quality of legal services provided by LAF in litigation.[32] In fact, not just legal aid recipients, but presiding judges and groups that refer applicants to legal aid, such as social workers, recognized the quality of LAF legal services: 76.3% of the recipient respondents, 78.8% of referral groups, and 51.4% of judges provided positive feedback.

LAF also tracks outcomes in legal aid cases. LAF reported that in 2005–13, LAF clients prevailed or partially prevailed in around 35–52% of civil cases, and that 20–39% of LAF cases settled with LAF's assistance, while fewer than 20% of LAF cases did not prevail at all (Figure 11.7 on p. 217). Admittedly, LAF's application review system, which excludes cases 'with clearly no chance of winning', likely produces a pool of cases with relatively fair chances of prevailing. However, the data suggest that legal services delivered via LAF had consistently fair quality, as reflected by stable distributions of case outcomes with no tendency toward negative results in the past decade. It can be argued that LAF-registered lawyers render a quality of legal service that is either no different from or better than average lawyers in the legal services market.

C. *Diversification of Aid Services*

Along with litigation-focused legal aid assistance, LAF also carries out a wide variety of legal activities for poor or vulnerable persons, such as free legal consultation, community and public education, and legislative counsel or lobbying. A distinct feature of LAF in the Taiwanese context is that the focus of LAF has expanded, from legal representation in court to various public services. LAF can be said to take a holistic approach to facilitating access to justice in Taiwan.

LAF has overseen a rise in the number of clients who received free legal consultation, a figure which increased by a factor of 23 from 2005 to 2016 (Figure 11.8 on p. 218). These increases are a

[31] Compiled by the authors from LAF Annual Reports.

[32] 法扶律師服務品質評鑑調查結果報告 (The Report of the Survey of the Quality of the Services Provided by Legal Aid Lawyers) (Apollo Survey & Research Co. Ltd, 2012) at 26.

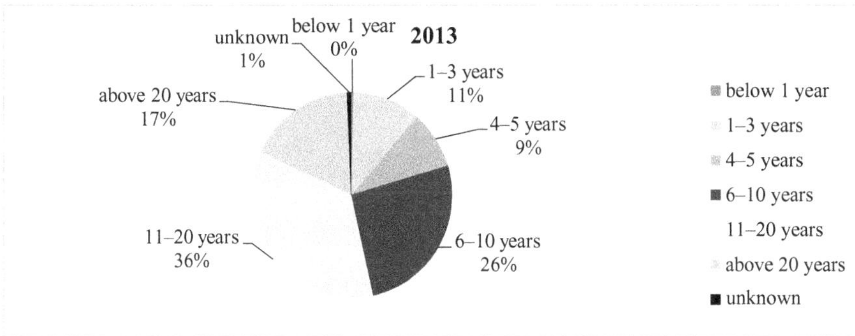

(i) Years of practice: legal aid lawyers' seniority distribution in 2013

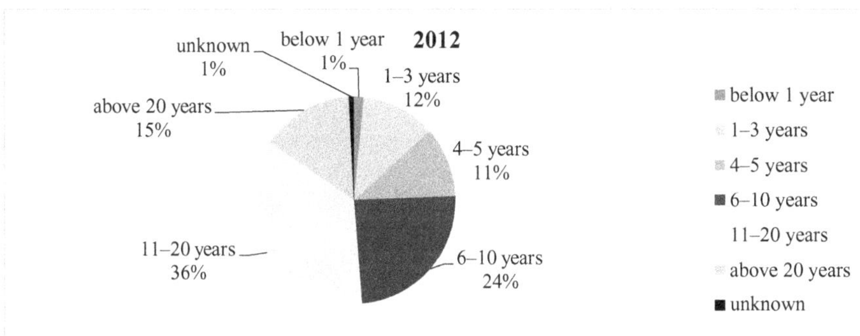

(ii) Years of practice: legal aid lawyers' seniority distribution in 2012

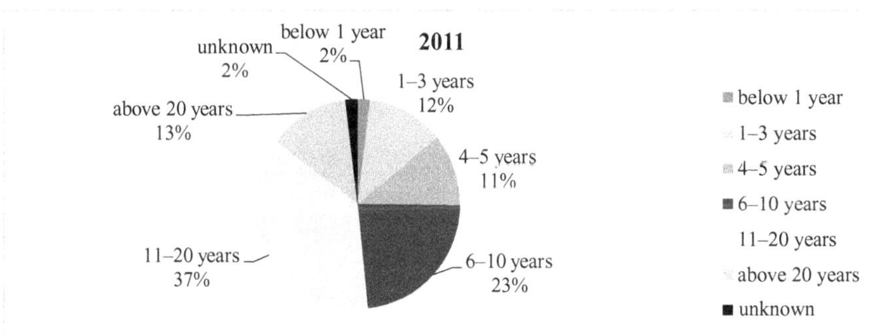

(iii) Years of practice: legal aid lawyers' seniority distribution in 2011

FIGURE 11.5. Legal aid lawyers' qualification: seniority by years of practice (2017)[33]

direct result of LAF loosening up the means test. Particularly notable is 2009, when the number of consultation cases quintupled from 6,446 to 35,852, due to a new policy LAF instituted to promote better access to legal advice through the Internet, hotlines, and over 60 local community centres across Taiwan, e.g. at household registration offices and district offices. Figure 11.9 on p. 218 shows further details on the approval rates for free consultation applications; here, the overall number of applications as well as approval rates are increasing. In 2009, the application approval rate rose sharply from about 16% to 43%, and it has remained high at over 50% ever

[33] Compiled by the authors from LAF Annual Reports.

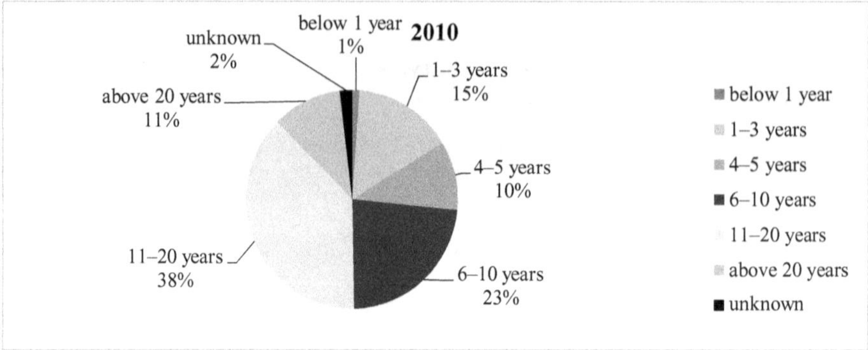

(iv) Years of practice: legal aid lawyers' seniority distribution in 2010

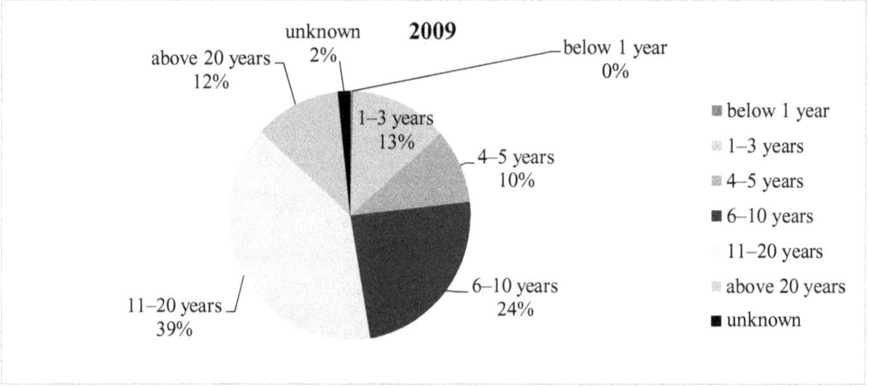

(v) Years of practice: legal aid lawyers' seniority distribution in 2009

FIGURE 11.5. *(cont.)*

since. Evidently, by increasing the provision of free legal consultation, LAF stepped into the earlier stages of dispute resolution and effectively broadened public access to justice.

In addition, LAF put in considerable effort to raise legal consciousness across the country. Evidence shows positive results from LAF's early efforts to publicize its services. As illustrated in Figure 11.10 on p. 219, most respondents in 2005, one year after LAF was founded, reported that they came for legal aid because of advertisement and promotion materials. After the first successful wave of promotion, LAF promoted its services by word of mouth and by recommendation of courts, as indicated in the 2006 and 2007 survey results. The data corroborates the LAF's active role, not only as a legal aid services provider, but as a promoter of access to justice recognized by its users, legal aid recipients, and its collaborator, the court.

In 2015, in order to provide general legal education and publicize LAF services, LAF held 578 events in schools, churches, temples, prisons, aboriginal communities, and many other local agencies across the country, indicating wide coverage.

Finally, LAF is deeply involved in the legislative process in Taiwan. The Consumer Debt Clearance Act[34] provides a good example. In 2005, Taiwan suffered from the worst credit card debt crisis in its history, in which over 500,000 card debtors went bankrupt and became

[34] 消費者債務清理條例 (Consumer Debt Clearance Act), Taiwan (11 July 2007).

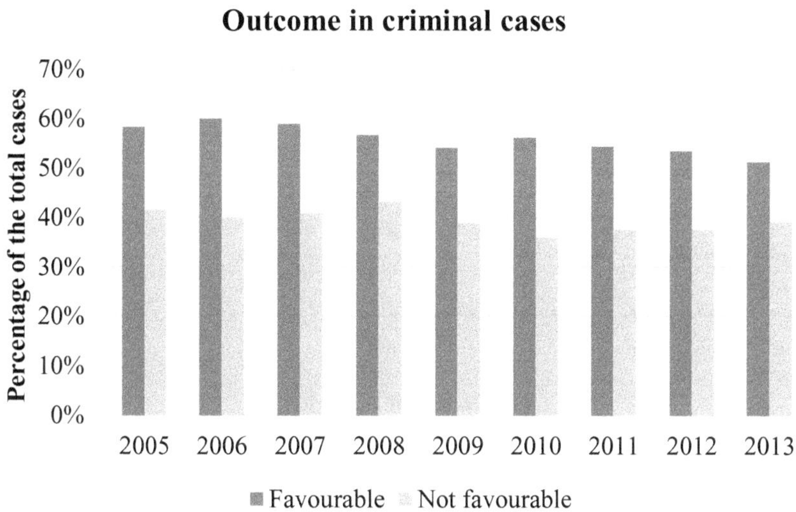

FIGURE 11.6. Legal aid case outcome: criminal case (2017)[35]

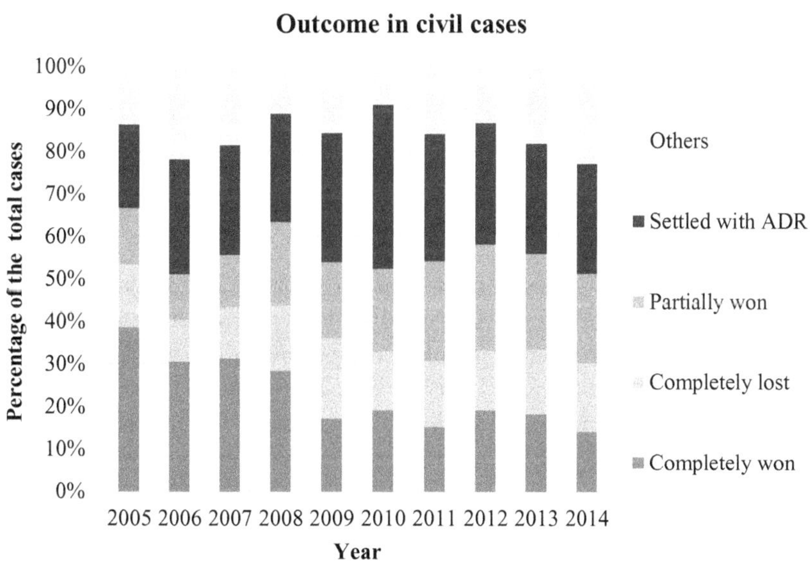

FIGURE 11.7. Legal aid case outcome: civil case (2017)[36]

insolvent.[37] The government authorities launched a relief measure to help the debtors, and LAF played a critical role in this policy-making process. After representing a number of credit card debtors suffering from high interest rates, LAF took the initiative with other NGOs to lobby for legislation to

[35] Compiled by the authors from LAF Annual Reports.

[36] Compiled by the authors from LAF Annual Reports.

[37] 回顧 2005 年 -2006 年之台灣卡債風暴 (Reflection on the 2005–2006 Credit Card Debt Crisis in Taiwan) (National Policy Foundation, 2007), online: www.npf.org.tw/2/3558.

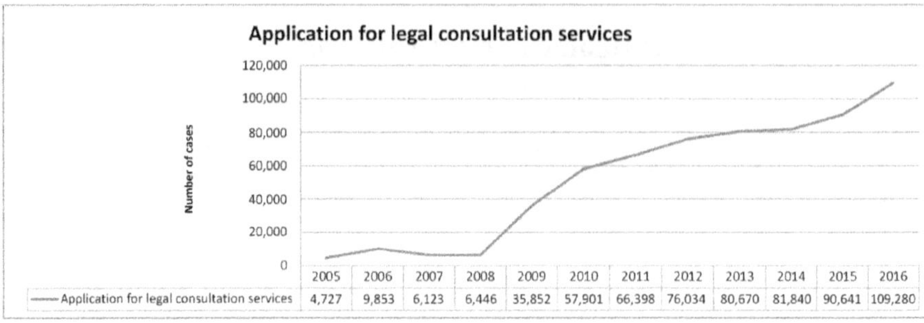

FIGURE 11.8. Number of applications requesting legal advice (2017)[38]

FIGURE 11.9. Approval rate of legal consultation applications (2017)[39]

balance the asymmetrical bargaining power between banks and individual consumers. The Consumer Debt Clearance Act was quickly passed, and it remains a powerful instrument today. Other examples of LAF's legislative prowess include the revisions to Taiwan labour law in 2013. LAF found that the discrepancy between the high rate of occupational accidents and the low rate of labour insurance coverage indicated that legal protection for employees was insufficient. Consequently, LAF cooperated with other concerned groups to lobby for a revision to the Labour Standards Act.[40] LAF also played a vital role in drafting a number of bills concerning social welfare and environmental protection,[41] including the Water Pollution Control Act (2013),[42] the maintenance chapter in the family law in the Civil Code (2009),[43] and decriminalization of shotgun possession by aboriginals in the Act for Controlling Guns, Ammunition and Knives (2015).[44]

38 Compiled by the authors from LAF Annual Reports.

39 Compiled by the authors from LAF Annual Reports.

40 勞動基準法 (Labour Standards Act), Taiwan 1984 (as amended 10 June 2020).

41 Zhan Shun-Gui and Chen Pin-An, 法律人如何捍衛環境–從水汙法修法談起 (How Do Attorneys Protect Environment? From the Perspective of the Modification of Water Pollution Control Regulation) (2013) 43 *Legal Aid Quarterly* 33 at 33–8.

42 水汙染防治法 (Water Pollution Control Act), Taiwan 1983 (as amended 13 June 2018).

43 民法 (Civil Code), Taiwan 1929 (as amended 19 June 2019).

44 槍砲彈藥刀械管制條例 (Controlling Guns, Ammunition and Knives Act), Taiwan 1983 (as amended 14 June 2017).

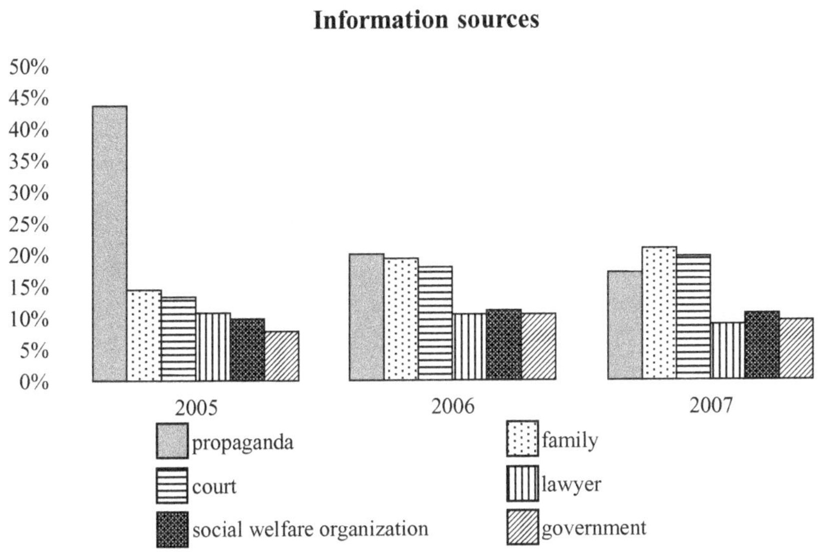

FIGURE 11.10. Information source of Legal Aid Foundation (2017)[45]

To conclude, LAF takes a holistic approach to promoting access to justice in Taiwan. Moving from individual representation to systemic problems, and taking up roles both in the legislature and on the street to advance legal consciousness and legal protection for the public, LAF visibly supports access to justice on a wide variety of platforms.

IV. A POWERHOUSE AND A HUB OF THE TAIWANESE CIVIL SOCIETY

Evolving from a service provider to an organizer, LAF has moved from a passive agency, set up to fulfil a semi-governmental function, to an active player, mobilizing resources and connecting with social groups. Simply put, LAF functions as a hub and a powerhouse in Taiwanese civil society. In the following section, we use two cases, a class-action lawsuit and a piece of consumer legislation, both well known in Taiwan in the late 2000s and 2010s, to argue that LAF has grown to be a focal point of public interest legal mobilization in the jurisdiction.

A. *A Powerhouse of Legal Mobilization:* The Civil Society in Taiwan *v.* Radio Corporation of America

The Radio Corporation of America ('RCA') set up production lines for televisions and other electronics in Taoyuan City, Taiwan, in 1970. During its two decades of operation, RCA manufacturing continuously released unprocessed toxic chemicals, mainly trichloroethene and tetrachloroethene, first directly onto land and later into illegally dug wells.[46] The waste contaminated both the soil and the groundwater in the region. This manufacturing caused unprecedented environmental

[45] Compiled by the authors from LAF Annual Reports.
[46] Indy Liu and Chu Fangchun, 'RCA Taiwan and Its Victims', *New Bloom* (24 September 2015), online: https://newbloommag.net/2015/09/24/rca-taiwan-and-its-victims/.

pollution as well as large-scale occupational injury amongst its employees. Without proper protection, RCA employees had direct exposure to, and even intake of, organic solvents used in the manufacturing process. The RCA plant closed in 1992, but in 1998 former employees organized a self-help association. Their records show that in 2001, at least 1,375 people had been diagnosed with various types of cancer, 221 of them terminal.[47] Another report from the Council of Labour Affairs of the Taiwanese government indicated an even higher number of 829 deaths recorded among former RCA employees.[48] These numbers could still be underestimated, as the insurance record at the time shows that RCA once employed more than 50,000 people, whose offspring might also be affected.

For the victims, holding RCA accountable was a long and difficult journey. The manufacturing had taken place three decades ago, and RCA formally closed the plants in 1992. Many employees had left the region or even died, extinguishing their right to claim damages. Bringing these cases to court in Taiwan also raised considerable procedural and substantive legal barriers. First, collective redress in Taiwan requires that claimants meet strict standing requirements. Victims filed a lawsuit as early as in 2004, but it took the courts three years to grant standing to the self-help association to carry out litigation. Second, the substantive legal issues in this case were complex and challenging. As the plaintiffs in a civil case, the victims had the burden of proving the claims, but the victims and their lawyers encountered a massive volume of evidence requiring extensive knowledge of epidemiology and public health – if they were lucky enough to acquire the needed decades-old data. Attributing legal responsibility was also difficult, as RCA Taiwan was first bought by General Electric Company ('GEC') and then Thomson Consumer,[49] both multinational technology companies. Lastly, victims had to fight a legal battle regarding the criterion for damage and the amount of compensation, and little property was left in Taiwan to satisfy a judgment.

With several ongoing lawsuits, the initial class action filed in 2007 reached its first victory in 2018. The Taiwanese Supreme Court finalized compensation of roughly TWD$510 million (US$17.29 million) to 262 workers, while the remaining 246 victims in the case were sent back to the High Court. In the decade-long process, however, the Taiwanese courts have largely supported the workers' claims: in 2015, the Taipei District Court ordered the now-defunct RCA, and its current owner Thomson, to pay TWD$564.45 million (US$19.13 million). In October 2017, the Taiwan High Court confirmed judgment in favour of the workers, raising the amount to TWD$718.4 million (US$24.35 million) and further ordering GEC to jointly compensate.[50] With a partial victory in the Supreme Court, a separate group of RCA victims filed a second class action for further compensation and greeted their first victory in the Taipei District Court on 27 December 2019. In the second lawsuit, the court ordered the four companies to compensate TWD$2.3 billion (US$82 million) to 1,120 workers.[51]

[47] 工作傷害受害人協會 (Association for Victims of Occupational Injury), RCA 工人職業性癌症答客問 (Q&A: Occupational Cancer of the RCA Employees) (2001) 33 *Judicial Reform Magazine* 49 at 49–51.

[48] Liu Tsui-jung, 近二十年來 1986–2006 臺灣河川污染的防治 (River Pollution Prevention in Taiwan in the Recent Two Decades (1986–2006)) in Fu-san Huang, ed., 海、河與台灣聚落變遷 (Ocean, River and Urban Change in Taiwan) (Taipei: Institute of Taiwan History, Academia Sinica, 2009) 229 at 247.

[49] A year after the takeover of RCA by General Electric ('GE') in 1986, the firm was sold to Thomson Consumer Electronics, the US subsidiary of France-based Thomson Multimedia, which is now called Technicolor SA: see Apple Daily, RCA 案判賠確定無良商相應不理 律師團出大絕讓奇異吐還 7 億 (Ignoring the RCA Decision, GE was Cornered by Lawyers to Compensate 700 million), *Apple Daily* (5 December 2019), online: https://reurl.cc/OqZKAy.

[50] Lin Yu-yo, 沒有盡頭的抗爭—RCA 污染案不只爭官司勝利，還有世代的覺醒 (The Endless Fight: They are Fighting Not Only for a Victory in Court, but a Generational Awakening), *The Reporter* (27 December 2019), online: https://reurl.cc/L03mZ9.

[51] Lin Chang-shun, RCA 二軍求償判賠逾 23 億元，創工傷賠償紀錄 (The Second Group of RCA Victims Received Over $2.3 billion, Marking a Historical Record for Vocational Injury), *Central News Agency* (27 December 2019), online: www.cna.com.tw/news/firstnews/201912275004.aspx.

The volunteer lawyers received the Supreme Court verdict positively, and they welcomed LAF's expanded approach to legal mobilization. Organized by LAF, volunteer lawyers played an essential role in this monumental class action in Taiwan. The most important role LAF played was coordination, thereby substantially reducing communication costs. In 2007, when the case first entered the substantive review procedure, there were over 400 plaintiffs involved. The supporting network was composed of dozens of experts from law, public health, and environmental engineering, several governmental agencies such as the Ministry of Labour and the Environmental Protection Administration, multiple NGOs, and a movie documentary team. LAF not only helped victims establish common grounds for standing in litigation, but also incorporated and translated the expert knowledge into comprehensible legal arguments. The size of the team reflected this extensive professional manpower: LAF solicited help from its own in-house lawyers, hired lawyers through legal aid schemes, and mobilized yet another group of volunteer lawyers to provide legal support. The entire team, composed of 50 lawyers, was led by the charismatic and high-profile human rights lawyer Joseph Lin. Another crucial role that LAF played was supplying stable administrative resources for RCA victims and a support network to prevent clients from dropping out of the prolonged litigation process. As pointed out by an evaluation report, a private law firm in Taiwan 'would not have had the manpower, money, and time to coordinate hundreds of plaintiffs for over 10 years'.[52]

Judging from the RCA experience, LAF, with its stable governmental funding, provided an indispensable link between disadvantaged labourers and their rightful claims. This landmark case between Taiwanese civil society and American/international corporations demonstrates LAF's role in empowering the disadvantaged to secure access to justice in court.

B. *A Hub of Law-Making: Legislating the Consumer Debt Clearance Act*

In addition to acting as a powerhouse in dispute resolution, LAF acts as a hub in legislation. It has played a vital role in coordinating social groups, raising awareness for a concrete goal of legislation, and framing social issues in a legal way that can be addressed by law and policy

Lobbying for credit card debtors began in 2007. The Taipei branch of the Legal Aid Foundation ('TLAF') was approached by the Antipoverty Coalition, an NGO network working on a wide range of social justice issues, including youth labour, poverty, social housing, tax and judicial reform, disability, and other social economic rights.[53] Many credit card debtors were in great debt not because they were luxurious consumers; rather, they were usually financially unstable small-wage earners, and credit cards gave them a quick loan with unreasonably high interest rates (usually 20% annual interest), which dragged them into a vicious circle. As stated by a labour union activist, the 'issue of credit card debtors is a common issue that all of us [different NGOs] encountered when helping different groups of socially disadvantaged, such as labourers and the homeless'.[54] This activist also clearly identified the then president of TLAF,

[52] Liang Chia-ying and Lee Bin-hung, 法扶作為重大集體訴訟之平台：從 RCA 公害及職災集體訴訟案談起 (The Legal Aid Foundation as Platform for Critical Class Action Lawsuits: The RCA Case), online: Legal Aid Foundation, www.laf.org.tw/index.php?action=media_detail&p=1&id=120.

[53] These groups and NGOs include: 卡債受害人自救會 (Victims of Debtor Self-Help Association), 當代漂泊協會 (The Contemporary Homeless Alliance), 社會住宅推動聯盟 (Alliance of Social Housing Promotion), 台灣國際醫學聯盟 (Taiwan International Medical Alliance), 台灣人權促進會 (Taiwan Association for Human Rights), 勞工陣線 (Alliance of Labour), 稅改聯盟 (Alliance of Taxation Reform), 殘障聯盟 (Disability Alliance), 民間司法改革基金會 (Judicial Reform Foundation).

[54] *Interview with TWO201702, supra* note 22.

Joseph Lin, as the key person who took up coordination responsibilities to push for the 2007 legislation: 'We NGOs went to Joseph Lin for volunteer legal counsel very often. We know each other from social movements via long-term cooperation and with firm mutual trust. The 2007 legislation was lobbied by several key figures, such as Joseph Lin (lawyer) and Chien Hsi-chieh (politician), who coordinated multiple NGOs.'[55]

Similar to the role LAF played in the RCA case, TLAF provided critical support in the making of the Consumer Debt Clearance Act on three fronts. First, there was strong and consistent administrative assistance for NGOs, such as space for meetings and events, and press correspondence and other logistical support. Second, TLAF mobilized legal knowledge to effectively frame the issue in a rights discourse, which elevated the debate to a systematic level that called for state intervention via legislation. Lawyers at TLAF also provided essential knowledge to credit card debtors, allowing them to commence negotiation with banks or initiate necessary legal procedures to restructure their debts. Third, TLAF organized a lobbying team with NGO workers to visit different stakeholders, including the banks, financial institutions, legislators, and the Judicial Yuan.

TLAF's role in pushing for legislation attracted attention, and in fact TLAF faced pressure from the government, namely the Judicial Yuan, to defer their involvement in this lobbying process with social movement organizations.[56] Facing concerns from the Judicial Yuan, the TLAF originally halted the lobbying efforts but eventually joined other NGOs to push for the legislation, because:[57]

> after completing 300 cases of debt negotiation, we felt so strongly that these negotiations were unfair and unreasonable. The banks had in-house counsels but did not allow the debtors to have lawyer[s] as representatives. The negotiation deals were set by the banks, where the debtors and lawyers had no room to negotiate. It's meaningless to the debtors. . . . if the bill did not pass in the first half of 2007, elections would come . . . and every bill restarts in the new term . . . therefore, the Legal Aid Foundation and all the concerned organizations aligned to push for the Consumer Debt Clearance Act.

TLAF encountered disagreement with other LAF branch offices. The main objection, that the credit card debtors are fully responsible for their debts, overlooked the high interest rates, the unfair payment structure, and the unbalanced negotiation power between the bank and the debtors. The public stigma debtors suffered was exactly the target that the TLAF and NGO alliance sought to tackle: 'We repeatedly explained and emphasized that these credit card debtors are victims. They are the disadvantaged group that the Legal Aid Act ought to protect; this is the right thing to do to realize the policy goal of the Act. Also NGOs kept mobilizing, and the Judicial Yuan gradually conceded to the public opinion.'[58]

Essentially, TLAF and the NGOs formed a team to overcome multiple challenges from different collective actors: the government (including the Judicial Yuan and the legislature), the private sector (including the bank and other financial stakeholders), and the public.

More specifically, TLAF played two roles in law-making. It was a coordinator, constituting a hub for NGOs and lawyers to transform legal expertise and practical experience into policy statements and problem resolution. It was also a gatekeeper, especially in subsequent rounds of

[55] Ibid.

[56] Joseph Yong-Song Lin, 從日本之經驗看台灣律師在「消費者債務清理條例」立法與施行的功能及角色 (Taiwan Attorneys in the Legislation and the Enforcement of the Consumer Debt Clearance Act – From the Japanese Experience Perspectives) (2008) 344 *Taipei Bar* 78.

[57] Xia Chuan-Wei, 塑膠鴉片 (Plastic Opium) (Taipei: Pedestrian, 2008) at 10–11.

[58] *Interview with TWO201702*, *supra* note 22.

legislation revision in the 2010s, when LAF, together with TLAF and the Judicial Reform Foundation, took active roles in the legal debates, but with the NGOs 'consciously waiting for their signals to take combat positions to mobilize'.[59] In sum, the process of legislating the Consumer Debt Clearance Act demonstrates the deep involvement of LAF in policy-making and its reciprocal relationship with Taiwanese NGOs.

V. EMBEDDED TENSION WITH THE STATE AND THE BAR

Having taken up more responsibilities to advance access to justice, both as an actor in civil society and as a public agency, LAF occupies a pivotal position in the legal community, but its embeddedness within a monolithic governmental system creates tension with the state and with the normally autonomous lawyering of the bar. LAF constitutes a quasi-governmental agency yet functions without direct democratic supervision. To address this potential accountability issue, LAF developed two organizational strategies to sustain its legitimacy, bureaucratization and power delegation. In this section, we argue that the embedded tension between state and bar is a development of the growth of LAF's role. It is not only empirically intriguing but suggests an inherent contradiction in the institutionalization of access to justice.

A. *Hybrid Model: A Quasi-Governmental Agency*

LAF is a quasi-governmental agency that is fully resourced and well run, but its recent development means that it runs the risk of outgrowing its original goals. Because it administers public legal aid, LAF undoubtedly has the organizational nature of a governmental agency, and its legally guaranteed status affords LAF ample resources that flow directly from the government. The scale of monetary support differentiates LAF from other similar public organizations in Taiwan, such as the Consumers' Foundation and the Association for Victim Support, which are also legally regulated and publicly funded. Budget figures illustrate these differences. In 2018, the annual spending of LAF was over TWD1.49 billion (US$50.51 million),[60] while the Association for Victim Support operated with TWD152 million (US$5.15 million).[61] Compared to the Association for Victim Support, the Consumers' Foundation had an even smaller amount of initial funding when it was set up in 1980, only TWD 1 million (US$33,897.26), and their budget growth has been limited.[62] LAF also has a higher proportion of governmental funds. In 2020, 87.6 per cent of LAF's income came directly from the government,[63] while the Association for Victim Support, for example, received only 71.8 per cent of its funding from the government.[64] The source of LAF's funding within the government appears critical to its expansion and success in different roles, as the Judicial Yuan is an independent judiciary immune to shifting political and financial winds.

59 Ibid.

60 *2018 Legal Aid Foundation Annual Report* (Legal Aid Foundation, 2019) at 8, online: www.laf.org.tw/upload/2019/05/20190524132457.pdf.

61 財團法人犯罪被害人保護協會 107 年度決算書 (Association for Victim Support 2018 Annual Financial Statement) (Association for Victim Support, 2018) at 12.

62 關於我們 (About the Consumers' Foundation), Consumers' Foundation, online: www.consumers.org.tw/contents/text?id=11.

63 財團法人法律扶助基金會 109 年度預算 (The Legal Aid Foundation 2020 Annual Budget) (Legal Aid Foundation, 2020) at 82.

64 財團法人犯罪被害人保護協會 109 年度預算 (Association for Victim Support 2020 Annual Budget) (Association for Victim Support, 2020) [*Victim Support*] at 31.

LAF is also equipped with substantial human resources. According to LAF's 2019 Financial Report, LAF has 288 employees (including 21 in-house lawyers), with another 30 staff members on special projects, and it operates with yet another 4,352 registered lawyers across the country to take on legal aid cases.[65] The coverage of LAF branch offices is extensive, and almost every court jurisdiction in Taiwan has a corresponding LAF office. By contrast, the Consumers' Foundation has 2 managers and only 12 employees in the main office, with 52 full-time staff members in 22 branch offices across the country, according to the 2020 annual budget.[66]

With steady funds and sufficient manpower, LAF has engaged in an expanding cycle of activities. Resources enlarge the LAF's capacity to take on more tasks and provide more and diverse services. As business grows, LAF needs more resources to deal with various tasks. Two indicators signal the degree of growth. First, legal aid recipients have increased quantitatively and qualitatively. The vulnerable groups entitled to legal services have shifted, from the original target of low-income individuals, to broadly defined social minorities, depending on their ethnicity, occupation, and legal status, e.g. labourers, aboriginals, and felony defendants. Because of these separate tracks for specific groups, current legal aid recipients are not necessarily financially disadvantaged, leaving the means test a less effective filter. Second, LAF is moving beyond the strict confines of the official policy goal legislated in the act,[67] which is protection of the 'right to litigate'.[68] LAF started with legal aid for formal legal representation, then moved to informal consultation, and later began to provide counsel assistance in pre-trial investigations. The right to litigate no longer manifests only in courtrooms, but constitutes an umbrella concept that offers citizens protection via various legal means.

LAF is in a tough position. The scale and practice of legal aid in large part defines what access to justice is in Taiwan, but LAF's hybrid model raises tensions which are difficult to resolve. It operates with autonomy and flexibility, like a civic association, but it has stable funding from the state. It is essentially a quasi-governmental agency, but with the strengths of a non-governmental organization. The outcome is positive, as LAF has grown to be an able and indispensable organizational actor in the Taiwanese justice system. However, this model faces two serious issues: first, how much authority and discretion in policy development does LAF have, and what are the normative bases for that? Second, how will LAF respond to rising expectations from the state to take up more responsibilities in access to justice, and at the same time maintain a balanced budget with growing operational costs? LAF's continual growth and record of success have created risks to its current authority and further development.

B. Organization Strategies: Bureaucratization and Delegation

In response to its organizational weakness as a hybrid agency, LAF uses two strategies that regularize and disperse responsibility. First, its administration of legal aid has become a highly bureaucratic process. Second, it delegated the authority of approving legal aid provision to a separate committee, composed of external experts to enhance its legitimacy.

The Legal Aid Act includes a set of detailed regulations that assign roles and responsibilities at the management and decision-making level of legal aid. According to Chapter 5, 'The Organization and Supervision of the Foundation', LAF is required to set up the Board of Directors as the highest

[65] 2019 *LAF Report*, *supra* note 16, at 6 and 42.
[66] *Victim Support*, *supra* note 64, at 1–2.
[67] *Legal Aid Fundamental Act Draft*, *supra* note 14.
[68] *Legal Aid Fundamental Act Draft*, *supra* note 14, at 173.

decision-making body, comprising 13 directors who have a three-year term.[69] The President of the Judicial Yuan appoints the directors, and discharges them when requested by LAF. In addition to the Board of Directors, the Legal Aid Act also assigns a Chief Executive Officer to oversee the daily operation, as well as a Deputy Chief Executive Officer, various specialized Committees handling matters relating to legal aid, presidents of branch offices, and executive secretaries. The Legal Aid Act also lays out a detailed structure for policy implementation.

In practice, LAF not only adheres to the Legal Aid Act but develops further standard operating procedures to carry out daily operations. A good example is the legal aid application process. A potential recipient first files standardized application forms, and then the applicant is interviewed by the Review Committee in person. Next, if the applicant passes the means test and merits test, a lawyer will be assigned or other legal services will be provided in a timely manner. If the applicant is denied, s/he may submit a request for reconsideration, and a Reconsideration Committee then reviews the case. Finally, after the legal recipient's case is complete, LAF will follow up to review the performance of the assigned lawyer. The recipient is also able to file a complaint against the lawyer with LAF at this stage. The entire process involves a lot of paperwork, is well structured, and is supervised by different agencies, which altogether makes it a highly bureaucratic operation. By developing a standard operating procedure and strictly following it, LAF reduces uncertainty and limits personal discretion in the process of providing aid. This approach helps them to maintain their legitimacy as a quasi-governmental agency by acting like a bureaucracy.

Another organizational strategy, authority delegation, complements this detailed bureaucratic structure. LAF does not approve individual applications, but only administers the process. The Review Committee and the Reconsideration Committee are the entities that have the authority to approve and deny legal aid, but they are composed of external lawyers, judges, and/or prosecutors in the jurisdiction, who serve on a committee independent from LAF. This separation decentralizes LAF's power over resource distribution, which in fact protects LAF from challenges to its legitimacy. Using the example of a case he handled, a lawyer working at the management level in LAF explained the dynamics:[70]

> We once aided a case of a runaway migrant worker. The district prosecutor's office sent a letter to the Judicial Yuan, questioning why a runaway migrant worker could get legal aid. And they attached a document showing that the worker was not residing in Taiwan [so was indeed not eligible for legal aid], but the LAF Review Committee did not have access to this type of information when they reviewed the case. Later the Judicial Yuan asked us to send the application documents to the Yuan for supervision. The director said, sure, let them have it, it is a decision made by the external Review Committee, not us [LAF].

LAF is aware of the need for supervision and accountability. As a hybrid organization that has strong governmental funding but the flexible autonomy of a civic association, LAF practises its prerogatives with conscious strategies.

C. *Tension With the Bar: Who is Responsible for Ensuring Quality Service?*

Tension between LAF and the lawyer community has become aggravated in recent years, because LAF has taken steps to control quality in legal aid cases, which in turn puts pressure

[69] *Legal Aid Act*, *supra* note 8, s 38.
[70] Interview with TWL201718 (14 August 2017, Taipei).

on the bar. LAF's bureaucratic evaluation process sometimes fails to comprehensively capture lawyers' input in legal aid cases, resulting in grievances among lawyers providing legal services.

Both LAF and the general lawyer community agree that in order to better support access to justice, the monetary reward for legal aid service can and should be a minimum amount. However, LAF and legal service providers are at odds regarding the ways in which legal aid service is delivered. LAF applies a hands-on approach, closely recording and evaluating lawyers' performance in legal aid cases. LAF has developed various standard operating procedures and guidelines of reward and sanction for quality control. This supervision creates inevitable tension with lawyers. A disagreement demonstrating this tension occurred in September 2017, when a renowned human rights lawyer, Leon Huang, publicly announced that he would no longer take legal aid cases. Leon Huang stated that, despite his effort acquiring extralegal evidence and presenting oral defence in court for his client, LAF withdrew payment simply because he did not offer a written statement for the defendant. This provoked a fierce discussion among legal professionals, some disappointed by the bureaucratic and formal paperwork at LAF, especially when the remuneration of legal aid cases is disproportionately low compared to the time spent. A sympathetic judge commented, 'Those who work their butts off do not get their full payment, and those who sleep through it get the pay cheques comfortably. This is the kind of legal aid we have.'[71]

This debate points to a profound tension. LAF is the only association that actively holds lawyers accountable for their performance in individual cases. Although the bar associations are the regulatory agencies with official disciplinary authority, they take cases passively via complaints. The Taiwanese bar associations assume an unassertive role in overseeing the quality of legal service in Taiwan, whereas LAF, based on the separate market it has created for lawyers via legal aid cases, challenges lawyer autonomy by supervising and evaluating their performances. LAF has done its own comprehensive lawyer evaluations biannually since 2007, and as of December 2016, LAF had identified 101 incompetent lawyers subject to sanctions, e.g. removal from the legal aid registry, official admonishment, suspension, decreased assignments for a certain time period, or formal notification of the need for improvement. The general lawyer community feels pressured by LAF, to the extent they take on legal aid cases. Arguably, the ways in which legal aid agencies promote access to justice can and will affect the autonomy of lawyers' legal practices. The institutionalization of access to justice inevitably involves mobilization and reshaping of the lawyer community, and the Taiwanese experience suggests that the legal profession's individual autonomy might be at odds with a more extensive and meticulous administration of access to justice.

VI. CONCLUSION: SITUATING TAIWAN IN COMPARATIVE CONTEXT

An evaluation of LAF's performance indisputably establishes it as a strong, dominant presence in the administration and promotion of access to justice in Taiwan. Two developments stand out. On the one hand, the legal services that LAF provides have expanded exponentially, in volume and in kind. Starting from litigation services, LAF continuously added new schemes to serve more clients, sometimes in collaboration with other governmental agencies, and added new types of legal services, to raise legal consciousness and intercept disputes early. On the other hand, LAF grew to be a major actor with dynamic relationships with civil society and the state. However, an issue with the current model also stands out. To guarantee quality service and equal distribution of legal aid, LAF is in need of the government's resources and centralized

[71] Interview with TWJ201710 (14 August 2017, Taipei).

authority, yet its organizational nature as a quasi-autonomous agency creates the risk of over-reaching and invites criticisms based on lack of accountability and legitimacy.

The role of Taiwanese lawyers and NGOs in the ascendency of civil rights and liberties has been diligently recorded and studied in the legal mobilization literature.[72] The partnership of lawyers and NGOs advances public interests and rights protection via judicial means in many Asian jurisdictions. In fact, Asian experiences show that legal mobilization evolves to adapt to various political and social contexts. For example, in Singapore, Chua[73] presents an unexpected story of gay rights mobilization in an authoritarian state. In Thailand and Nepal, where resources are scarce for marginalized women, cause lawyers and NGOs play a role in helping individuals to engage with the legal system.[74] Tactics also move across borders; for example, to win compensation for Korean leprosy survivors, Korean lawyers took a template from Japan.[75]

However, what is missing in the current literature is the entangled relationship between state and lawyers serving a public interest. Studies on pro bono lawyers, coming first from common law jurisdictions, naturally label lawyers as representatives of normative values, supported by a professional community with ample material means. A strong image arising out of American pro bono programmes is the private practice lawyer, able and independent, volunteering outside the state.[76] In contrast, studies on legal aid identify the state as the major actor that determines service delivery. In the context of state-provided legal aid, good governance is at the core of discussions, regarding the amount of the budget, the appropriate means and merits tests, the quality of legal service provision, and other accountability issues.[77] The role of lawyers is either active, autonomous from the state, or passive, employed by the state.

LAF in Taiwan restructures the access to justice debate by altering the relationship between lawyers, the state, civil society, and the legal profession. All are autonomous actors with a 'two-way street' relationship with one another that evolved over time. First, a group of reformist lawyers pressured the newly democratized state to institutionalize a state-funded organization to provide legal aid to people in need. Over time, LAF developed and expanded, and it hosted and then mobilized lawyers in Taiwan. In public interest litigation, LAF organized various types of resources and capital to challenge the state, but it also helped the state achieve better governance, sometimes even filling gaps that state agents were unable to reach. In many ways, the Taiwan LAF markedly reduced costs in legal mobilization, between indigent clients and lawyers, between different civic associations with common goals in advancing public interests, and between the state bureaucracy and its constituency. Its practices changed the state–society

72 Ching-fang Hsu, 'The Currency Exchanger: Taiwanese Public Interest Lawyers in the 21st Century' (2019) 36 *UCLA Pacific Basin Law Journal* 33 at 36.

73 See Lynette J. Chua, *Mobilizing Gay Singapore: Rights and Resistance in an Authoritarian State* (Philadelphia: Temple University Press, 2014) at 25; Lynette J. Chua, 'Collective Litigation and the Constitutional Challenges to Decriminalizing Homosexuality in Singapore' (2017) 44 *Journal of Law and Society* 433.

74 See Margaret Becker, 'Constructing SSLM: Insights from Struggles over Women's Rights in Nepal' (2015) 39 *Law, Support Structures and the Realisation of Human Rights in Asia* 247; Frank W. Munger, 'Trafficking in Law: Cause Lawyer, Bureaucratic State and Rights of Human Trafficking Victims in Thailand' (2015) 39:1 *Asian Studies Review* 69.

75 See Celeste L. Arrington, 'Leprosy, Legal Mobilization, and the Public Sphere in Japan and South Korea' (2014) 48:3 *Law & Society Review* 563.

76 Rebecca L. Sandefur, 'Lawyers' Pro Bono Service and American-Style Civil Legal Assistance' (2007) 41:1 *Law & Society Review* 79 at 84–5.

77 Steve Hynes and Jon Robins, *The Justice Gap: Whatever Happened to Legal Aid?* (London: Legal Action Group, 2009) at 8–11; Don Fleming and Francis Regan, 'Evatt's Bastard Child: The Commonwealth Legal Service Bureaux 1942–51' (2003) 7:2 *Australian Journal of Legal History* 255 at 272–7.

dynamic, by changing the interactions among lawyers, the rights-supporting community, and the state. In its daily practice, LAF is substantially successful in rendering service to the public, yet individual lawyers have diverse relationships with LAF, both positive and negative, and LAF quality control practices have created tension and even grievances within the legal profession.

Our findings, which substantiate LAF's success in delivering legal aid and identify LAF's growing importance as a hub and powerhouse in Taiwan, suggest that the Taiwanese experience is an example of positive access to justice development with several intriguing empirical characteristics. Ruptures between LAF and the state and the bar warrant special attention in understanding the embedded tensions between different stakeholders acting to advance access to justice. Initial indications though are that LAF will continue its expanded role in Taiwan, and that while skirmishes and sporadic disagreements will arise, the tensions between different actors appear to have created a new equilibrium.

APPENDIX 11.1 INTERVIEWEE DETAILS

To keep the interviewees anonymous in accordance with the ethical guidelines for the research project conducted by one of the authors, the following system is used to assign IDs, with numbers to indicate the order of the interviewee. For example, if the interviewee is the fourteenth judge in Taiwan the author(s) interviewed in 2016, the ID will be TWJ2016014.

TABLE 11.3. *Interviewee's occupation and location*

Jurisdiction	Abbreviation	Profession	Abbreviation
Taiwan	TW	Lawyer	L
		Judge	J
		Other professionals	O

Interviews quoted in this article include:

TABLE 11.4. *Basic information on interviewees*

Identifier of interviewee	Location of the interview	Format	Full date	Notes
TWO201702[78]	Taipei, Taiwan	Personal interview	29-01-2018	20 years' experience as a major Taiwanese labour union staff member
TWL201718	Taipei, Taiwan	Personal interview	14-08-2017	Lawyer in admin. position at LAF, superior to TWL201719
TWL201719	Taipei, Taiwan	Personal interview	14-08-2017	Lawyer in admin. position at LAF
TWJ201710	Yunlin, Taiwan	Personal interview	19-06-2017	About eight years' experience on the bench at a rural district court

[78] Identified in 2017 and interviewed in 2018.

12

Lawyers and Democratic Centralism in Vietnam

*Nguyen Hung Quang**

Abstract

This chapter discusses the challenges that lawyers face in promoting justice and the rule of law in Vietnam. The chapter argues that these challenges currently stem primarily from the principle of democratic centralism, the backbone of the Vietnamese government, which in some ways contradicts the state's aspiration to be a 'rule of law state'. Democratic centralism subordinates the role of courts and the government to that of the National Assembly by giving the latter power to make the final decision with absolute obedience from the former, notwithstanding the 'democratic' discussion before the decision is made. Although changes have been introduced, this orientation continues to shape the role of courts and lawyers in Vietnam. Legal aid has been implemented, but it focuses primarily on law dissemination, and legal aid to persons in court is hampered by the small number of legal aid staff. Practising lawyers face a number of difficulties and challenges in supporting access to justice, particularly when providing criminal defence, as lawyers' services are still considered obstacles to the operation of state agencies. However, in the Vietnamese system, lawyers could accelerate the assurance of equality before the laws and access to justice.

I. INTRODUCTION: DEMOCRATIC CENTRALISM AND LAWYERS IN VIETNAM

Before lawyers developed into a profession in Vietnam, the people who helped the poor and ordinary people to make a complaint before the mandarins were called 'thầy cãi' (defending master), 'thầy cò' (exciter), or 'thầy kiện' (litigator). There is no historical evidence regarding the difference between these terms, but lawyers were considered to be 'opponents' or 'provokers' against the government, and the profession was, from time to time, prohibited or limited in its areas of practice.[1] The legal profession was introduced to the country when France imposed colonial rules through its

* The author greatly appreciates the assistance of the dispute resolution team at NH Quang & Associates in searching for documents, interviewing, and giving helpful comments on this chapter. The author would also like to convey gratitude to Tran Bao Tran and Tran Ngoc Anh for editing assistance, and to Bui Ngoc Son for feedback and assistance on an earlier draft of the chapter. Regarding references in Vietnamese, the author has provided the title in Vietnamese if it was deemed to be of assistance to readers; other references in Vietnamese are identified with the notation 'in Vietnamese'.

[1] Linguistics Institute, Từ điển Tiếng Việt (Vietnamese Dictionary) (Da Nang: Da Nang Publishing House, 2000) at 929; Nguyễn Văn Tuân, Sự hình thành và phát triển nghề luật sư tại Việt Nam (Formation and Development of the Lawyer Profession in Vietnam) (2001) *Law and Democracy Magazine* (Special Issue on Ordinance for Lawyers) at 30;

court system in the late nineteenth century.[2] Today, 'Luật sư' is commonly translated as 'lawyer', and the terms 'thầy cãi', 'thầy cò', or 'thầy kiện' indicate someone who specializes in filing a complaint or seeking legal action in a society.[3]

When the Communist Party came to power and declared independence from France in 1945, the right to counsel was not clearly recognized in criminal procedural laws.[4] The role of defence counsel in criminal hearings was mentioned in legal statutes in the first months of this administration, however it was not fully respected in practice. As Vietnam focused on fighting wars in the period from 1946 to 1958, i.e. the First Indochina War from 1946 to 1954 and then the first phase of the Vietnam War from 1954 to 1958, and conducting social reforms based on communist ideals, the courts mostly focused on activities aimed at punishment and class renovation. Persons involved in court adjudication, such as judges, people's jurors, and defenders such as lawyers or 'bào chữa viên nhân dân' (people's defenders), did not receive professional training in interpreting and applying laws. This practice restricted the quality of adjudication and the role of lawyers in assisting people to access justice.[5]

The principle of democratic centralism was a fundamental concept in the government of the Democratic Republic of Vietnam, and it has significantly impacted later concepts of rule of law and access to justice. Originally, Lenin introduced this principle in Russia to guide the activities of the members of the Communist Party, but the principle was later applied to the design of socialist state institutions and their daily activities. Stated simply, this Leninist principle focuses on 'democratic discussion', followed by centralized actions. After democratic discussion, superiors issue a conclusion or order which requires unquestioning obedience from inferiors.[6] The principle was introduced in Vietnam's 1959 Constitution,[7] and the current Constitution of Vietnam confirms this principle in Article 8: 'The State is organized and operates in concordance with the Constitution and the law, manages society by the Constitution and the law and practises the principle of democratic centralism.'[8] This principle leads to the supreme position of the National Assembly, and the subordinate positions of the government and the courts. These subordinate institutions must report to and are subject to the supervision of the National Assembly, and they cannot question what the National Assembly has decided or challenge its laws.

Lê Kim Quế, 'Origin of the Lawyer Profession' (in Vietnamese) (2003) *Lawyer Today Magazine* of Hanoi Bar Association at 3–5.

[2] Phan Đăng Thanh and Trương Thị Hòa, Lịch sử nghề luật sư ở Việt Nam (History of Legal Profession in Vietnam) (Ho Chi Minh City: Ho Chi Minh City General Publishing House, 2015) [*History of Legal Profession*] at 25; Nguyễn Đình Tư, Chế độ thực dân Pháp trên đất Nam Kỳ 1859–1954 (French Colonial Rule on Cochinchina Land 1859–1954, Vol. I) (Ho Chi Minh City: Ho Chi Minh City General Publishing House, 2016) at 501; Đỗ Ngọc Thịnh, Vị trí, vai trò và chức năng xã hội của luật sư (Status, Role, and Social Function of Lawyers in Vietnam Bar Federation–JICA Legal 2020), in *Lawyer Handbook – Vol. I: Lawyer and Practice* (Hanoi: Su That – National Political Publishing House, 2017) [*Social Function of Lawyers*] at 20.

[3] Tạ Văn Tài, Pháp quyền trong pháp luật truyền thống của Việt Nam và Trung Quốc cổ (Tập tục pháp lý Đông Á truyền thống dưới ánh sáng của các chuẩn mực pháp quyền hiện đại) (The Rule of Law in Ancient Vietnam and China – Traditional Legal Customs of East Asia in Light of Modern Rule of Law Standards, Vol. II) (Hanoi: The Gioi Publishing House, 2002) at 437–8.

[4] *History of Legal Profession*, *supra* note 2, at 25; John Stanley Gillespie, *Transplanting Commercial Law Reform: Developing a 'Rule of Law' in Vietnam* (Aldershot: Ashgate, 2006) at 50.

[5] *Comprehensive Report on Reforming Judicial Agencies, Completing Procedural Laws, and Improving the Efficiency and the Effectiveness of the Court System in a Socialist Rule of Law State of the People, by the People and for the People* (in Vietnamese) (Vietnam, State Social Scientific Research Programme (2001–5), KX04 (Vietnam: 2006) [*Reforming Judicial Agencies*] at 95–7.

[6] John Gillespie, 'Changing Concepts of Socialist Law in Vietnam' in John Gillespie and Pip Nicholson, eds., *Asian Socialism & Legal Change: The Dynamics of Vietnamese and Chinese Reform* (Canberra: ANU Press, 2005) [*Asian Socialism & Legal Change*] at 47.

[7] *The Constitution of the Socialist Republic of Vietnam* (in Vietnamese) 1959, Article 4.

[8] *The Constitution of the Socialist Republic of Vietnam* (in Vietnamese) 2013, Article 8.1.

This arrangement has had a profound influence on the role of courts as well as lawyers in Vietnam. Consistent with democratic centralism, Vietnam reformed its judiciary by organizing judicial bodies according to the Soviet model of institutions entrusted with protection of the law.[9] The resulting Supreme People's Court and the Supreme People's Procuracy were part of the government and subordinate to the National Assembly.[10] These agencies concentrated their work on suppressing those opposed to the government, protecting state assets, and maintaining social order.[11] In this period of Vietnam's history, lawyer organizations did not exist, and people who defended the accused before the courts were only public defenders (*bào chữa viên nhân dân*) in local areas, who were not required to have any professional training.[12] The Supreme People's Court directly managed all defence activities from 1959 to 1974,[13] and many of the individuals acting as defenders were also state officials. In the years 1987–2001, lawyers who were also officials of state bodies accounted for about 40 per cent of the total number of lawyers nationwide, and the remaining lawyers were mostly retired state officials.[14] In fact, due to the lack of defenders in criminal cases and the need to comply with the 1988 requirement of mandatory counsel, discussed below,[15] some courts had to request court officials or other persons with legal knowledge to participate in hearings.[16]

In 1986, the Communist Party of Vietnam conducted political reform of state management to improve economic development, and introduced '*Doi Moi*' (Revolution), a series of economic reforms aimed at transforming the centrally planned economy into a market-oriented economy.[17] However, this far-reaching reform did not interfere with the political structure. The mechanism of democratic centralism was maintained, with no separation of powers.[18] The continued role of democratic centralism limited the role of courts, as well as the role of lawyers in protecting human rights or improving access to justice.[19]

In 1991, a new concept, the 'socialist rule of law state', was introduced by the Party.[20] This Vietnamese concept was arguably inspired by the Soviet doctrine of '*pravovoe gosudarstvo*'

[9] *Reforming Judicial Agencies*, *supra* note 5, at 360; on the borrowing of the Soviet court system in Vietnam, see Penelope (Pip) Nicholson, *Borrowing Court Systems: The Experience of Socialist Vietnam* (Leiden: Martinus Nijhoff Publishers, 2007).

[10] *Decree No. 381-TTg of the Prime Minister, Mandates and Powers of the Supreme People's Court* (in Vietnamese), Vietnam (20 October 1959); *Decree No. 321-TTg of the Prime Minister, Establishment of Appeal Prosecution and Other Prosecutions* (in Vietnamese), Vietnam (27 August 1959).

[11] *Reforming Judicial Agencies*, *supra* note 5, at 95–7.

[12] *Reforming Judicial Agencies*, *supra* note 5, at 101.

[13] Ibid.; Ministry of Justice, Tổ chức hoạt động luật sư ở Việt Nam hình thành và phát triển (Organization of Lawyer Activities in Vietnam: Process of Formation and Development) (31 May 2010), online: moj.gov.vn/qt/cacchuyenmuc/70TuPhapVietNam/Pages/tu-lieu-nganh.aspx?ItemID=27 [*Organization of Lawyer Activities*].

[14] *Reforming Judicial Agencies*, *supra* note 5, at 177; *Organization of Lawyer Activities*, *supra* note 13.

[15] See Section II.E of this chapter.

[16] Ministry of Justice, *Organization of People's Advocates* (in Vietnamese), Circular No. 101/HCTP (Vietnam: 29 August 1957); *Law on People's Court Organization* (in Vietnamese), Vietnam (14 July 1960), Article 8; *Organization of Lawyer Activities*, *supra* note 13.

[17] *Reforming Judicial Agencies*, *supra* note 5, at 104.

[18] *The Constitution of the Socialist Republic of Vietnam* (in Vietnamese), Vietnam (15 April 1992), Article 6.

[19] For discussions on the role of lawyers in human rights protection in Vietnam, see John Gillespie, 'The Juridification of Cause Advocacy in Socialist Asia: Vietnam as a Case Study' (2013) 31 *Wisconsin International Law Journal* 672; John Gillespie, 'Human Rights as a Larger Loyalty: The Evolution of Religious Freedom in Vietnam' (2014) 27 *Harvard Human Rights Journal* 107 at 145.

[20] Nguyễn Thanh Tuấn, Nhà nước pháp quyền xã hội chủ nghĩa Việt Nam trong việc bảo đảm quyền con người, quyền công dân (The Rule of Law Socialist State of Vietnam in the Guarantee of Human Rights and Citizenship), *Communist Party Journal* (5 September 2016), online: www.tapchicongsan.org.vn/web/guest/xay-dung-ang2/-/2018/40653/nha-nuoc-phap-quyen-xa-hoi-chu-nghia-viet-nam-trong-viec-bao-dam-quyen-con-nguoi%2C-quyen-cong-dan.aspx.

TABLE 12.1. *Lawyer development in Vietnam*

Year	Lawyers	Population[21]	Lawyers per capita
1989	186[22]	64,774,000	1:348,247
2001	2,100[23]	78,620,500	1:37,438
2009	5,700[24]	86,025,000	1:15,092
2011	6,250[25]	87,860,300	1:14,058
2015	10,000[26]	91,713,300	1:9,171
2019	13,563[27]	96,462,106	1:7,094

(law-based state), as well as the idea of the rule of law as a critical governance value in western liberal discourse.[28] With the adoption of the new concept of a socialist rule of law state, reforms began to focus on the judicial agencies and improving the quality of adjudication. The state apparatus maintained democratic centralism but enacted minor modifications to promote control at grassroots levels.[29]

In 1997, Vietnam began to reform its approach to lawyers. It initiated the policy of 'reforming the state administration over lawyers' practice, law consultancy, judicial appraisal … [t]raining, developing the contingency of lawyers with moral virtue, professional competency; promoting their roles in law consulting in proceedings … [and] [f]acilitating the poor's enjoyment of free legal advice services'.[30] This policy provided the basis for amending legal instruments on lawyers.[31] The Ordinance on Lawyers, promulgated in 2001, set forth specific conditions and criteria for those wishing to become lawyers, prohibited state officials and public servants from being lawyers, and permitted lawyers to freely establish a practice organization.[32] Thanks to these changes, the number of lawyers experienced a sudden increase in 1989–2001, and there has been continuous growth from 2001 to the present, as the sample years in Table 12.1 above show.[33]

Although the quantity of lawyers increased quickly, numbers are still rather low compared to some Asian countries, such as Thailand (1:1,526), Singapore (1:1,000), and Japan (1:4,546).[34] Moreover, the number of lawyers is still insufficient to meet the public demand. From 2007

[21] Việt Nam (World Bank Group, 2019), online: data.worldbank.org/indicator/SP.POP.TOTL?locations=VN.

[22] *Reforming Judicial Agencies, supra* note 5, at 177; *Organization of Lawyer Activities, supra* note 13.

[23] *Reforming Judicial Agencies, supra* note 5, at 177; *Organization of Lawyer Activities, supra* note 13.

[24] Ministry of Justice, *Report No. 23/BC-BTP of the Ministry of Justice on Summary of Judicial Works in 2009 and Orientation and Tasks of* 2010 (in Vietnamese) (Vietnam: 5 February 2010).

[25] *Approving the Strategy for Development of the Lawyer Profession through 2020* (in Vietnamese), Decision No. 1072/ QĐ-TTg of the Prime Minister (Vietnam: 5 July 2011) [*Decision No. 1072*].

[26] *History of the Legal Profession, supra* note 2.

[27] Phát huy vai trò của luật sư trong công cuộc cải cách tư pháp (Promoting the Role of Lawyers in Judicial Reformation), *Communist Party of Vietnam Online Newspaper* (10 October 2019), online: dangcongsan.vn/thoi-su/phat-huy-vai-tro-cua-luat-su-trong-cong-cuoc-cai-cach-tu-phap-538822.html.

[28] Thiem Bui, 'Deconstructing the 'Socialist' Rule of Law in Vietnam: The Changing Discourse on Human Rights in Vietnam's Constitutional Reform Process' (2014) 36:1 *Contemporary Southeast Asia* 77 at 82.

[29] *Reforming Judicial Agencies, supra* note 5, at 107–12.

[30] Communist Party Central, *'The Third Meeting of the Party Central Committee (VIII) on the Promotion of the Autonomy of the People and Continuing to Build the Clean and Strong State of the Socialist Republic of Vietnam'* (in Vietnamese), Resolution No. 03-NQ/HNTW (Vietnam, 1997); *Reforming Judicial Agencies*, supra note 5, at 177.

[31] *Reforming Judicial Agencies, supra* note 5, at 180.

[32] *Reforming Judicial Agencies, supra* note 5, at 183.

[33] *Reforming Judicial Agencies, supra* note 5, at 177–86.

[34] *Decision No. 1072, supra* note 25.

to 2010, only 10–20 per cent of criminal cases were adjudicated with representation of legal counsel.[35]

Lawyers criticized a number of aspects of the system that prevented them from providing effective representation of parties.[36] Per the law in effect previously under Criminal Procedure Code 2003 and the Law on Lawyers 2006, if a lawyer wanted to defend a case, he/she had to obtain a Certificate of Defender issued by the body conducting the proceedings.[37] In order to obtain this certificate, the lawyer had to satisfy certain conditions, including presentation of a lawyer card, a reference letter from the law firm where the lawyer was practising or from the provincial bar association if the lawyer was practising independently, and most importantly, a 'request for lawyer by the accused'.[38] The request for lawyer by the accused was a document written by the accused, or his/her family or representative, to formally request a specific law firm/ lawyer to defend the accused.[39] The requirement for the request for lawyer was an almost insurmountable challenge, because it had to be provided by the accused, who was usually kept in a detention camp without access to information allowing them to select a lawyer.[40] While the law allowed the accused to ask their family to request a lawyer, this alternative was equally challenging, as the investigation bodies rarely supported the accused's attempts to contact their family.[41] In other cases, it was impossible for lawyers to meet their client to get confirmation that they had been chosen by the client as their legal representative.[42] The requirement for the request for lawyer of the accused has been considered the biggest challenge to the ability of criminal lawyers to operate.[43]

35 Nguyễn Văn Hiển, Thực trang vai trò của luật sư trong tranh tụng tại các phiên toà hình sự ở nước ta thời gian qua (Actual Situation of the Role of Lawyers in Criminal Litigation in Vietnam Up To Now) (2010) *State and Law Review* 64 [*Role of Lawyers in Criminal Litigation*] at 65; Ministry of Justice, *Five-year Implementation of the Law on the Lawyer* (in Vietnamese), Report No. 46/BC-BTP (Vietnam: 6 March 2012) at 5; Vân Anh, Bộ trưởng Bộ Tư pháp: Chỉ có 20% vụ án có luật sư (Minister of Justice: Only 20% of Cases have Lawyers), *Vietnamnet* (5 November 2007), online: vnn.vietnamnet.vn/chinhtri/2007/11/753203/. According to *Appointed Counsels in Vietnamese Criminal Laws and Practice* (United Nations Development Programme, 2012) (in Vietnamese and English, references are to the English version) [*UNDP Report on Appointed Counsels*] at 33, 10 per cent of the criminal cases had defence counsel.

36 United Nations Development Programme, *Report on the Survey of Needs of District People's Courts Nationwide* (Hanoi: Justice Publishing House, 2007) (in Vietnamese and English, references are to the English version) [*Needs of District People's Courts*] at 256–60; Phạm Hồng Hải, Mô hình lý luận Bộ luật tố tụng hình sự Việt Nam (Analytical Framework for the Criminal Procedure Code of Vietnam) (Hanoi: Public Security Publishing House, 2003) at 57; Trần Danh, Vai trò của luật sư đã thực sự được phát huy? (Has the Role of Lawyers Been Enhanced?), *Dong Nai* (9 October 2011), online: baodongnai.com.vn/phapluat/201110/Vai-tro-cua-luat-su-da-thuc-su-duoc-phat-huy-2101393/; Một số ý kiến trong hoạt động hành nghề luật sư (Some Opinions on the Legal Profession) (Ho Chi Minh City Bar Association, 23 March 2009, online: www.hcmcbar.org/NewsDetail.aspx?CatPK=4&NewsPK=105; *Role of Lawyers in Criminal Litigation*, *supra* note 35, at 64; *UNDP Report on Appointed Counsels*, *supra* note 35, at 42–50.

37 *Law on Lawyers* (in Vietnamese), Vietnam 2006 (as amended 2012) [*Law on Lawyers 2006*], Article 27; *Criminal Procedure Code* (in Vietnamese), Vietnam 2003 (as amended 26 November 2003) [*CPC 2003*], Article 56.

38 *Law on Lawyers 2006*, *supra* note 37, Article 27; *CPC 2003*, *supra* note 37, Article 56; Ministry of Public Security, *Guiding the Criminal Procedure Code 2003 on Ensuring the Right to Counsel in the Investigation Phase of the Criminal Case* (in Vietnamese), Circular No. 70/2011/TT-BCA (Vietnam, 2011) [*Circular No. 70/2011*], Article 5.

39 *Circular No. 70/2011*, *supra* note 38, Article 4.

40 Phan Trung Hoài, Những điểm mới về chế định bào chữa trong Bộ luật tố tụng hình sự năm 2015 (New Features of the Regulations on Access to Counsel in Criminal Procedure Code 2015) (Hanoi: National Politics Publishing House, 2016) [*New Features*] at 197–259.

41 *Report on the Right to Counsel in Criminal Law and Practice in Vietnam* (United Nations Development Programme, 2012) [*UNDP Report on the Right to Counsel*] at 35–6.

42 *UNDP Report on the Right to Counsel*, *supra* note 41, at 49; *UNDP Report on Appointed Counsels*, *supra* note 35, at 48.

43 *UNDP Report on the Right to Counsel*, *supra* note 41, at 39; *UNDP Report on Appointed Counsels*, *supra* note 35, at 48–9.

In addition to the difficulty of obtaining the Certificate of Defender, lawyers also faced difficulties in the litigation process. They were not given the assistance needed to attend interrogation sessions or site examinations in the investigation stage of proceedings.[44] Lawyers also had difficulty accessing case files once the case had been transferred to the people's procuracy or the courts.[45] Finally, during the litigation process in the courts, lawyers were not encouraged to present their views to the adjudication panel or allowed to have their opinions written in hearing minutes and judgments.[46]

Another issue is that as a result of the continued relevance of the principle of democratic centralism, judges adjudicating criminal cases often obtain opinions from court leaders, senior courts, or other agencies before hearings are held.[47] This practice means that many judgments are already decided before adjudication, and therefore even though litigants are represented by a lawyer, there is little opportunity for litigants to effectively exercise their right to counsel.[48] The practice of consultation with others prior to hearings is maintained to the present day,[49] and some lawyers even characterize their presence at a hearing as just a '*dien vien*' (actor or actress) for a '*vo kich*' (drama).[50]

These limitations on the practice of law reflect a long-lasting understanding that lawyer activities and organizations are not independent of the government, similar to institutional arrangements for the oversight of the practice of law. The Supreme People's Court administered defence activities in the years 1959–74.[51] This practice impacted the independence of lawyers' activities for many reasons, including the fact that the judge could select defence counsel for the case without any clear criteria.[52] As noted above, up until 2004, a defence counsel could also be a civil servant if they were qualified or instructed.[53] After the period of administration by the Supreme People's Court, the practice of law was managed by the Law Committee of the Government, then renamed the Ministry of Justice ('MOJ'), and its provincial department of justice ('DOJ') until 1987.[54] From 1987 to 2009, lawyers were managed by both state authorities, the MOJ and the DOJ, as well as provincial bar associations. Management committees of the bar associations had the right to select lawyer candidates.[55] The provincial bar associations began to gain their independence via their authority to grant and cancel lawyer certificates (*thẻ luật sư*).[56]

44 *UNDP Report on the Right to Counsel, supra* note 41, at 40; *UNDP Report on Appointed Counsels, supra* note 35, at 44.

45 *UNDP Report on the Right to Counsel, supra* note 41, at 42.

46 *UNDP Report on the Right to Counsel, supra* note 41, at 92.

47 *Report on the Survey of the Reality of Local Court Governance in Vietnam* (United Nations Development Programme, 2014) [*Reality of Court Governance*] at 30; *Needs of District People's Courts, supra* note 36, at 249–53.

48 Nguyễn Hưng Quang, 'Lawyers and Prosecutors under Legal Reform in Vietnam: The Problem of Equality' in Stephanie Balme and Mark Sidel, eds., *Vietnam's New Order: International Perspectives on the State and Reform in Vietnam* (New York: Palgrave MacMillan Publishing House, 2007) [*Lawyers and Prosecutors*] at 166–7.

49 Nguyễn Như Phong, Lạm bàn về án 'bỏ túi' (Breakdown of 'Pocket Convictions'), *PetroTimes* (15 November 2013), online: petrotimes.vn/lam-ban-ve-an-bo-tui-143681.html; *Reality of Court Governance, supra* note 47, at 69–76; *Needs of District People's Courts, supra* note 36, at 249–53.

50 *Lawyers and Prosecutors, supra* note 48, at 172; and *Social Function of Lawyers, supra* note 2, at 20.

51 *Lawyers and Prosecutors, supra* note 48, at 165.

52 *UNDP Report on Appointed Counsels, supra* note 35, at 29–30, 40, and 55.

53 *Lawyers and Prosecutors, supra* note 48, at 166–7.

54 *Ordinance on Lawyer Organization* (in Vietnamese), Vietnam 1987 [*Ordinance on Lawyer Organization* 1987], Article 11; *Lawyers and Prosecutors, supra* note 48, at 165.

55 *Ordinance on Lawyer Organization* 1987, *supra* note 54, Article 11.

56 Kim Phụng, Đúng sai vụ tranh cãi giữa Đoàn Luật sư Tp. Hồ Chí Minh và Bộ Tư pháp ('Right or Wrong' Argument between Ho Chi Minh Bar Association with the Ministry of Justice), *Ho Chi Minh City Legal Newspaper* (13 August 2019), online: plo.vn/phap-luat/dung-sai-vu-tranh-cai-giua-doan-luat-su-tphcm-va-bo-tu-phap-851730.html.

In 2001, the Ordinance on Lawyers gave the MOJ the authority to grant and cancel a new certificate of legal practice for lawyers (*chứng chỉ hành nghề luật sư*),[57] while the provincial bars continued their management of lawyer certificates.[58] The bars were also given a new responsibility to encourage lawyers to provide legal aid services.[59]

In 2008, the Vietnam Bar Federation was established.[60] The Vietnam Bar Federation is considered a 'self-governance' (*tu quan*) organization managed by the lawyers themselves.[61] The Federation is mainly funded by contributions of its members, which are the provincial bar associations and lawyers.[62] The provincial bar associations are in charge of collecting fees from lawyers, including fees for trainee lawyers (not exceeding VND5 million (US$214.89)),[63] fees for joining the bar (not exceeding VND10 million (US$429.87)), and membership fees (VND200,000 (US$8.60) per month). The exact amount of fees for a lawyer to join a bar association varies from province to province. Depending on the number of lawyers enrolled, a bar association must send from 10 to 50 per cent of such fees to the Vietnam Bar Federation.[64]

A lawyer must join a bar association to practise,[65] thus all practising lawyers are members of the Vietnam Bar Federation and subject to its management.[66] The Federation has a division to provide legal aid to the poor, as well as a department for lawyer protection effective while they are practising law. At present, the Federation's activities are considered to have significantly improved lawyers' independence in their practice compared to the previous period when lawyers were governed by state agencies,[67] although lawyers continue to face considerable challenges.

II. LEGAL AID AND FREE-OF-CHARGE OR PRO BONO LEGAL SERVICES IN VIETNAM

Vietnam does not have a term in Vietnamese for pro bono lawyer services, defined as legal services provided by the lawyer free of charge to poor or vulnerable clients. Vietnamese lawyers who can speak English use the English term 'pro bono service', meaning a free-of-charge legal service, rather than translate pro bono into Vietnamese as '*dịch vụ pháp lý miễn phí*'. Lawyers do

[57] *Decree No. 15-HĐBT of the Ministerial Council, Regulation of the Provincial Bar Association* (in Vietnamese), Vietnam (21 February 1989); Official Letter No. 1060 of the Ministry of Justice sent to all provinces relating to implementation of *Ordinance on Lawyer Organization*, Vietnam 1987 (11 July 1996); *Ordinance on Lawyers* (in Vietnamese), Vietnam (25 July 2001) [*Ordinance on Lawyers 2001*], Article 13.

[58] *Ordinance on Lawyers 2001, supra* note 57, Article 10.

[59] *Ordinance on Lawyers 2001, supra* note 57, Article 6.

[60] *Approving the Proposal for 'Establishing National Lawyer Organization'* (in Vietnamese), Decision No. 76/QĐ-TTg of the Prime Minister (Vietnam: 16 July 2008) [*Decision No. 76/QĐ-TTg*]; *Reforming Judicial Agencies, supra* note 5, at 177.

[61] *Decision No. 76/QĐ-TTg, supra* note 60, Article 1; Ministry of Justice, Liên đoàn luật sư Việt Nam – Triển vọng và thách thức (Vietnam Bar Federation – Prospects and Challenges), by Đỗ Hoàng Yến (6 July 2009), online: moj.gov.vn/qt/tintuc/Pages/thong-tin-khac.aspx?ItemID=1222.

[62] *Law on Lawyers 2006, supra* note 37, Article 64.

[63] XE Currency Converter, online: www.xe.com/currencyconverter/convert/?Amount=5%2C000%2C000&From=VND&To=USD. Unless another reference was cited, US$ denominations in the chapter were derived from www.xe.com at the time of publication; they are intended for general reference and may have been rounded up or down for ease of reference.

[64] *Frame of Probationary Fees, Admitting Fee, Membership Fee and Exemption and Reduction of Membership Fee* (in Vietnamese), Resolution 05/NQ-HĐLSTQ of the National Assembly of Lawyers of Vietnam Bar Federation (Vietnam: 14 December 2015), Article 4.

[65] *Law on Lawyers 2006, supra* note 37, Article 11.

[66] *Charter of Vietnam Bar Federation* (in Vietnamese), Article 26.

[67] *New Features, supra* note 40, at 197–259.

not want to use the term *'dịch vụ pháp lý miễn phí'* because 'free' implies low-quality service. Vietnamese lawyers also use the term 'legal aid' (*trợ giúp pháp lý*) to mean the provision of a free-of-charge legal service, as the Vietnamese phrase *'trợ giúp pháp lý'* comprises two words: '*pháp lý*' (legal) and '*trợ giúp*' (aid). However, this usage is practical and unofficial. The first Law on Legal Aid in 2006 provided an official definition of legal aid:[68]

> Legal aid means the provisions of free of charge legal services to legal aid beneficiaries in accordance with this Law to help them to protect legitimate rights and interests and improve their legal understanding as well as their sense of respect for and observance of law; to contribute to the legal propaganda and education, to protect justice, to ensure social equity and prevent and restrict disputes and violations of law.

The current Law on Legal Aid 2017 revised the definition of legal aid to the following:

> Legal aid means the provisions of free of charge legal services to legal aid beneficiaries in a legal aid-related case in accordance with this Law, contributing to the assurance of human rights and citizenship in the access to justice and equality before the law.[69]

The Law on Legal Aid 2006 also confirmed that legal aid was the state's responsibility,[70] a point affirmed in the Law on Legal Aid 2017.[71] In Vietnam then, 'legal aid' in English or '*trợ giúp pháp lý*' in Vietnamese is used primarily for state-funded legal services within the framework of the Law on Legal Aid. Other free-of-charge legal services normally use different terms, including the occasional 'pro bono', and they are conducted pursuant to different regulations.

A. *Legal Aid*

Legal aid (*trợ giúp pháp lý*) activities, initiated by a decision of the Prime Minister, began in the late 1990s.[72] After nine years of implementation, the 2006 Law on Legal Aid ('LLA') consolidated and organized relevant activities.[73] The state is responsible for legal aid activities, and it 'plays a key role in providing, and organizing the provision of, legal aid; encourages and facilitates the Vietnam Fatherland Front and its member organizations, law-practising organizations and lawyers, other agencies, organizations, and individuals in participating in, making contributions to, and supporting legal aid services'.[74] Legal aid beneficiaries include 'the poor, people with meritorious services to the revolution, lonely elderly people, disabled people, helpless children, and ethnic minority people permanently residing in areas with exceptionally difficult socio-economic conditions'.[75] In 2019, the number of legal aid cases accepted and conducted by legal aid centres was 47,027, of which 36,310 cases were resolved.[76]

[68] *Law on Legal Aid* (in Vietnamese), Vietnam 2006 (as amended 2012) [*Law on Legal Aid 2006*], Article 3.

[69] *Law on Legal Aid* (in Vietnamese), Vietnam 2017 (1 January 2018) [*Law on Legal Aid 2017*], Article 2.

[70] *Law on Legal Aid 2006*, *supra* note 68, Article 6.

[71] *Law on Legal Aid 2017*, *supra* note 69, Article 4.

[72] *Establishment of Legal Aid Agencies for Supporting the Poor and Other Vulnerable Peoples* (in Vietnamese), Decision No. 734-TTg of the Prime Minister (Vietnam: 1997).

[73] *Law on Legal Aid 2006*, *supra* note 68.

[74] *Law on Legal Aid 2006*, *supra* note 68, Article 6.

[75] *Law on Legal Aid 2006*, *supra* note 68, Article 10.

[76] Số vụ trợ giúp pháp lý trong hoạt động tố tụng tăng cao (The Number of Legal Aid Cases in Litigation Significantly Increased), *The Communist Party Online Newspaper* (8 January 2020), online: dangcongsan.vn/phap-luat/so-vu-tro-giup-phap-ly-trong-hoat-dong-to-tung-tang-cao-546389.html.

The definition of legal aid in the LLA is rather broad and includes a focus on protecting state laws.[77] When implementing these regulations, state agencies focus more on education of the law, such as printing leaflets to disseminate legal provisions, making noticeboards for legal news, and distributing legal materials to people in rural and mountainous areas, detainees, or imprisoned persons.[78] Legal advice largely concentrates on answering people's questions about law upon request as opposed to legal representation. Socio-political organizations, such as the Vietnam Lawyers Association (*Hội Luật gia Việt Nam*), Vietnam Women's Union, Vietnam Veterans' Association, and provincial bar associations, also support this practice. Legal advice accounts for 95 per cent of the total number of legal aid cases, while legal aid in proceedings only accounts for 5 per cent.[79] Although the MOJ is of the view that legal aid effectively enhances people's legal awareness and helps state agencies, officials, and civil servants to perform their statutory functions and tasks properly,[80] there is criticism that legal aid activities are formal in nature with little actual effectiveness, because they have not yet focused on criminal defence and human rights protection.[81]

The small number of legal aid staff nationwide is one of the biggest challenges for legal aid activities in court cases. In the whole country, there were only 572 law graduates employed in 2016 for 63 legal aid centres in 63 provinces. On average, each centre had five to ten officials with legal qualification, and eight centres had fewer than five qualified officials. Consequently, legal aid counsel must rely for representation in court cases on lawyers,[82] who are either appointed by law firms/legal advisory organizations participating in the state's legal aid programme, or directly sign legal aid service contracts with the provincial legal aid centre.[83]

The second challenge for legal aid is the difficulty people have in accessing legal aid services, especially legal consulting and litigation services, due to the procedures required of applicants to demonstrate they are entitled to legal aid. Under relevant regulation, applicants must present personal papers to prove that they are eligible. For example, the poor must present the Poor Household Book, people with meritorious services to the revolution must present their certificate, etc.[84] Furthermore, there is normally only one legal aid centre in each province, usually located in an urban area, while the applicants entitled to legal aid mostly live in remote and mountainous areas under difficult economic conditions.[85]

Legal aid beneficiaries could request legal aid services to make claims against state agencies, e.g. in land-taking disputes. However, legal aid centres are requested to support local state

77 *Law on Legal Aid 2006*, *supra* note 68, Article 3.

78 Ministry of Justice, *Summary of Eight Years of Implementation of the Law on Legal Aid* (in Vietnamese), Report No. 158/BC-BTP (Vietnam: 1 October 2016) [*Summary of Implementation*] at 4–6.

79 *Summary of Implementation*, supra note 78, at 3–6; Đặng Thị Loan, Nâng cao hiệu quả hoạt động trợ giúp pháp lý bảo đảm quyền con người ở Việt Nam (Improving the Effectiveness of Legal Aid for Human Rights in Vietnam), *Political Theory Journal* (31 May 2016), online: lyluanchinhtri.vn/home/index.php/thuc-tien/item/1485-nang-cao-hieu-qua-hoat-dong-tro-giup-phap-ly-bao-dam-quyen-con-nguoi-o-viet-nam.html [*Effectiveness of Legal Aid*]; *New Law on Legal Aid* (in Vietnamese), Proposal No. 335/TTr-CP (Vietnam: 23 September 2016) at 1.

80 *Summary of Implementation*, *supra* note 78, at 12.

81 *Effectiveness of Legal Aid*, *supra* note 79.

82 *Summary of Implementation*, *supra* note 78, at 12.

83 *Law on Legal Aid 2006*, *supra* note 68, Articles 14 and 17.

84 *UNDP Report on the Right to Counsel*, *supra* note 41, at 57, 60; Tạ Thị Minh Lý – Chairwoman of Vietnam Judicial Support Association for the Poor, Trợ giúp pháp lý: Các hình thức và phương pháp thực hiện (Legal Aid: Performance Modes and Methods) (Delivered at the National Conference on Free Legal Assistance to the Public, Hanoi, Vietnam, 31 May to 1 June 2013) [*Performance Modes and Methods*] at 11–14.

85 Ministry of Justice, Nhìn lại 7 năm thực hiện trợ giúp pháp lý miễn phí cho người nghèo, đối tượng chính sách (Overview of Seven Years of Free Legal Aid for the Poor and Policy Beneficiaries), by Trần Huy Liệu (28 May 2015), online: moj.gov.vn/qt/cacchuyenmuc/70TuPhapVietNam/Pages/tu-lieu-nganh.aspx?ItemID=14.

authorities in land-taking disputes through legal dissemination or dispute mediation,[86] and staff or lawyers of legal aid centres usually mediate these disputes rather than represent people against state authorities. Practically speaking, people rarely seek legal aid centres' support for land disputes with the state.[87]

A 2012 survey conducted by the UNDP indicated that there were several reasons why lawyers accepted legal aid court cases, such as social responsibility, the fee, getting more experience in court work, or enhancing their reputation. Some lawyers accepted legal aid court cases because it helped them to connect closely with the officials in state agencies.[88] In this survey, 59 per cent of lawyers 'thought that there was no difference in working attitude … nor any difference between the spirit of appointed counsel and normal counsel'.[89] Some lawyers however disclosed that they did not defend the legal aid court cases seriously because they were advised to maintain good relationships between the legal aid centres or provincial departments of justice with courts, procuracies, and investigation bodies.[90] MOJ has stated that the quality of the legal aid services provided by lawyers was problematic and needed to be improved.[91]

Due to the deep-seated nature of principles such as democratic centralism, the overall ability of lawyers to do their work is affected by the organization through which they offer legal services and the connection that organization has to the state, sometimes to their benefit. Lawyers working for state legal aid centres are regarded as 'public lawyers', and when practising these lawyers are usually better supported by the government and court institutions, particularly when compared to lawyers who practise independently,[92] discussed below.[93]

B. *Legal Assistance from Social Organizations*

In addition to state legal aid activities, social organizations or Vietnamese style-NGOs are also permitted to provide legal assistance.[94] They include for instance the Vietnam Lawyers Association,[95] the Vietnam Women's Union, the Vietnam Farmers' Union, and the Vietnam

86 *Summary of Implementation*, *supra* note 78, at 12; Đỗ Văn Nhân, Điểm nóng khiếu kiện: Cần tăng cường trợ giúp pháp lý (Hot Disputes Should be Strengthened Legal Aid Activities), *Giao Duc va Thoi Dai* (6 July 2017), online: giaoducthoidai.vn/thoi-su/diem-nong-khieu-kien-can-tang-cuong-tro-giup-phap-ly-3504065-c.html.

87 *2015 Justice Index: Toward a Justice System for the People* (United Nations Development Programme, 2016) at 25.

88 *UNDP Report on Appointed Counsels*, *supra* note 35, at 61.

89 *UNDP Report on Appointed Counsels*, *supra* note 35, at 37.

90 Interview with Lawyer Nguyen A (2012, Vietnam) [*Interview with Lawyer Nguyen A*]; Interview with Lawyer Nguyen B (2012, Vietnam) [*Interview with Lawyer Nguyen B*]; Interview with Lawyer Ngo B (2017, Vietnam) [*Interview with Lawyer Ngo B*]; Interview with Lawyer Nguyen C (2019, Vietnam) [*Interview with Lawyer Nguyen C*]; Interview with Lawyer Pham (2019, Vietnam) [*Interview with Lawyer Pham*]; Ministry of Justice, Một số suy nghĩ về nâng cao chất lượng hoạt động trợ giúp pháp lý (Some Opinions on Strengthening Quality of Legal Aid Services) (3 February 2019), online: legalaid.gov.vn/node/1277 [*Strengthening Quality*].

91 *Summary of Implementation*, *supra* note 78, at 12; Ministry of Justice, Tổng kết hoạt động tham gia trợ giúp pháp lý của luật sư theo Chỉ thị số 03-CT/TW ngày 30/03/2009 của Ban Bí Thư (Summary of Legal Aid Services of Lawyers According to Instruction 03-CT/TW of Party Secretariate Dated 30 March 2009) (11 December 2019), online: trogiupphaply.gov.vn/nghien-cuu-trao-doi/tong-ket-hoat-dong-tham-gia-tro-giup-phap-ly-cua-luat-su-theo-chi-thi-so-03-cttw.

92 *UNDP Report on Appointed Counsels*, *supra* note 35, at 64.

93 See Section II.D of this chapter.

94 *Decree No. 77/2008/ND-CP of 16 July 2008, on Legal Consultancy* (in Vietnamese), Vietnam 2008 [*Decree No. 77/2008/ND-CP*], Article 1.

95 The Vietnam Lawyers Association ('VLA') was established in 1955 and is different from the Vietnam Bar Federation ('VBF'), which is the national association of practising lawyers. VLA's members are broader than those of VBF. A citizen who has worked in the legal sector for three or more years can be a VLA member (*VLA Charter*, Article 7, Decision No. 770/QD-Ttg dated 5 June 2020 of the Prime Minister).

General Confederation of Labour. Legal assistance provided by these organizations includes legal consulting activities and appointing 'lawyers to participate in proceedings for defending, representing, and protecting legitimate rights and interests of individuals and organizations'.[96] These activities can be free-of-charge for members of the relevant organization or subject to some fees for non-members.[97] Social organizations wishing to provide legal consultancy must establish a legal consulting centre under their organization via an operation permit granted by the provincial Department of Justice.[98]

Only large socio-political organizations, such as the Vietnam Lawyers Association, Vietnam Women's Union, Vietnam Farmers' Union, and Vietnam General Confederation of Labour, receive state funding for their legal dissemination and propaganda activities.[99] For legal consultancy or participation in proceedings, these organizations mainly rely on contributions from members, sponsorship by domestic organizations and individuals, or support from permitted development assistance activities from international donors. Normally, those legal consulting centres handle cases for their intended beneficiaries, such as the poor, the disabled, women, and minority people.[100] The legal consulting centres run by social organizations provide free or chargeable services, depending on the objectives of each centre.[101] The fee paid by legal consulting centres to lawyers is usually based on a mutual agreement between the centres and lawyers.[102] Lawyers acting in proceedings for clients gained through legal consulting centres encounter practice conditions similar to lawyers practising independently, and they are not considered 'public lawyers' like those working for legal aid centres.[103]

C. Lawyer Legal Aid

Under the Law on Lawyers 2006, lawyers are obligated to provide *'trợ giúp pháp lý'* (legal aid or pro bono services). These services are different from the state legal aid discussed above,[104] although according to guidance of the Vietnam Bar Federation, the beneficiaries, scope of support, and methods of pro bono services are quite similar to state legal aid as provided in the Law on Legal Aid.[105] Lawyers therefore perform dissemination of legal information, provide legal advice, and represent beneficiaries before the courts or other state agencies.[106] Some bars organize the service provision at their offices, while other bars organize legal aid service tours to rural and remote areas.[107] However, lawyers are primarily requested to perform legal

96 *Decree No. 77/2008/ND-CP, supra* note 94, Article 7.
97 *Decree No. 77/2008/ND-CP, supra* note 94, Articles 10 and 11.
98 *Decree No. 77/2008/ND-CP, supra* note 94, Articles 12 and 13.
99 *Summary of Implementation, supra* note 78, at 3–6.
100 Hoàng Bình Nguyên, Policy Law and Development Institute, Xây dựng năng lực trợ giúp pháp lý cho các tổ chức xã hội tại Việt Nam (Building Legal Aid Capacity for Social Organizations in Vietnam) (Delivered at the National Conference on Free Legal Assistance to the Public, Policy Law and Development Institute, 2013) at 5–6.
101 *Performance Modes and Methods, supra* note 84, at 2.
102 *Decree No. 77/2008/ND-CP, supra* note 94, Articles 18, 21, and 22.
103 *UNDP Report on Appointed Counsels, supra* note 35, at 65.
104 *Law on Lawyers 2006, supra* note 37, Articles 21, 65, and 67.
105 *Decision No. 93/BTV of Standing Committee of Vietnam Bar Federation, Regulations on Legal Aid Obligation of Lawyers* (in Vietnamese) (9 October 2014) [*Decision No. 93/BTV of the Vietnam Bar Federation*], Article 6. This regulation was replaced by *Decision No. 112/BTV of Standing Committee of Vietnam Bar Federation, Regulations on Free-of-Charge Legal Aid Obligation of Lawyers* (in Vietnamese) (18 October 2018) [*Decision No. 112/BTV of the Vietnam Bar Federation*].
106 *Decision No. 112/BTV of the Vietnam Bar Federation, supra* note 105, Articles 1, 4, and 5.
107 *Report No. 176//BC-DLS of Ho Chi Minh City Bar Association, 2018 Operation of Ho Chi Minh City Bar Association* (in Vietnamese) (17 December 2019) at 5 and 6; Nguyễn Đăng Tùng, Đoàn luật sư thành phố Hà Nội tổ chức

dissemination and help the state to settle protests.[108] The legal aid services provided by a number of local bars are mostly legal dissemination and legal advice rather than free litigation services.[109] The legal aid services rendered by lawyers have been assessed as 'formalistic'.[110]

The Vietnam Bar Federation as well as local bars are responsible for guiding and monitoring legal aid activities provided by lawyers.[111] Instruction from the Vietnam Bar Federation regarding legal aid previously stated that each lawyer had to provide eight hours per year of legal aid work. If the lawyer could not render legal aid services, he or she was obligated to contribute the cash equivalent of 40 per cent of a monthly basic salary, approximately US$20 per year, into the Legal Aid Fund of the provincial bar where he or she was admitted.[112] After the Law on Legal Aid 2017 was enacted, the Vietnam Bar Federation issued new instructions. These instructions expanded the scope of beneficiaries, the support for legal aid, and the methods of delivery, and commercial matters were excluded from the scope of legal aid services. However, the legal aid obligation of lawyers was also reduced, from eight hours per year to four hours per year. Lawyers were also no longer obligated to contribute cash if their obligation was not fulfilled, so the Legal Aid Fund of the provincial bar was removed. The current sanction for unfulfilment is only that the lawyer will not qualify for any award from the provincial bar and the Vietnam Bar Federation.[113] There were two main reasons for these changes. First, there were an insufficient number of lawyers to fully satisfy the requirements, and second, the cash contribution was considered to be a financial burden for lawyers.[114]

D. *Independent Lawyers and the Chuong My Dust Case*

Apart from the state legal aid system, NGOs, and lawyer legal aid, independent lawyers provide pro bono legal services across the country. The modes for providing these services are diverse. Some lawyers are willing to accept 'hot' cases (*vụ án nóng*), while some lawyers take cases from vulnerable clients, and others prefer mandatory cases. Hot cases (*vụ án nóng*) attract considerable attention from the public, both on social media and state-driven media. These cases frequently contain suggestions of wrongful conviction, torture, or abuse of state power, or they involve protests relating to land disputes and environmental pollution. The lawyers in the

chương trình Trợ giúp pháp lý và trao quà cho đồng bào vùng cao xã Y Tý, huyện Bát Xát, tỉnh Lào Cai (Hanoi Bar Association Organized a Legal Aid Programme and Presented Gifts to Highland People in Y Ty Commune, Bat Xat District, Lao Cai Province), *Hanoi Bar Association* (2 October 2018), online: luatsuhanoi.vn/tin-hoat-dong/doan-luat-su-thanh-pho-ha-noi-to-chuc-chuong-trinh-tro-giup-phap-ly-va-trao-qua-cho-dong-bao-vung-cao-xa-y-ty-huyen-bat-xat-tinh-lao-cai.html [*Hanoi Bar Association*].

[108] *Decision No. 93/BTV of the Vietnam Bar Federation, supra* note 105, Articles 1, 3, and 4. This regulation was replaced by *Decision No. 112/BTV of the Vietnam Bar Federation, supra* note 105, Article 4; Trung Anh, Sự tham gia hỗ trợ pháp lý của các luật sư giúp giảm tình trạng khiếu nại tố cáo (Participation of Lawyers in Legal Assistance Will Reduce Complaints and Denunciation), *Communist Party* (14 May 2018), online: dangcongsan.vn/xay-dung-dang/su-tham-gia-ho-tro-phap-ly-cua-cac-luat-su-giup-giam-tinh-trang-khieu-nai-to-cao-483552.html.

[109] *Hanoi Bar Association, supra* note 107; Đoàn luật sư tỉnh Nghệ An trợ giúp pháp lý miễn phí (Nghe An Bar Association Holds Legal Aid Activities), *Vietnam Bar Federation* (19 July 2019), online: www.liendoanluatsu.org.vn/post/%C4%91o%C3%A0n-lu%E1%BA%ADt-s%C6%B0-t%E1%BB%89nh-ngh%E1%BB%87-an-t%E1%BB%95-ch%E1%BB%A9c-ho%E1%BA%A1t-%C4%91%E1%BB%99ng-tr%E1%BB%A3-gi%C3%BAp-ph%C3%A1p-l%C3%BD.

[110] Proposal No. 335/TTr-CP for the New Law on Legal Aid (in Vietnamese), 23 September 2016; *Interview with Lawyer Nguyen A, supra* note 90; *Interview with Lawyer Nguyen B, supra* note 90; *Interview with Lawyer Ngo B, supra* note 90; *Interview with Lawyer Nguyen C, supra* note 90; *Interview with Lawyer Pham, supra* note 90; *Strengthening Quality, supra* note 90.

[111] *Decree No. 123/2013/ND-CP, Detailing a Number of Articles and Measures to Implement the Law on Lawyers* (in Vietnamese), Vietnam 2013 (as amended 14 October 2014), Article 3.

[112] *Decision No. 93/BTV of the Vietnam Bar Federation, supra* note 105, Article 6.

[113] *Decision No. 112/BTV of the Vietnam Bar Federation, supra* note 105, Article 7.

[114] Interview with Lawyer Tien (2020, Vietnam).

Chuong My incident discussed below followed this mode. Lawyers who shy away from hot cases may still take cases from vulnerable clients, clients who are poor, children, people with disabilities, domestic violence victims, or other persons not qualified for legal aid under the Law on Legal Aid. These lawyers rarely participate in hot cases and do not report their pro bono work to local bars, the Vietnam Bar Federation, or the media, because they want to keep the cases confidential to protect themselves. It is difficult to research this mode of practice or count the number of lawyers who do it, because they do not want to be considered 'troublemakers'. Some lawyers following this mode also cooperate with legal aid agencies.[115]

Lawyers participating in hot cases do so because the hot nature of the case offers opportunities to protect victims in difficult cases.[116] Lawyers who engage in these activities measure the risks that may impact their career or create unfavourable conditions for their practice in the future, such as state officials who may be averse to them. This mode of representation began in the early 2000s, when the National Assembly enacted a Resolution on State Compensation to wrongfully convicted people in litigation processes, referred to as 'Resolution 388'.[117] Some lawyers founded a group for helping people who were victims of wrongful convictions within the scope of Resolution 388, named the 'For Justice Initiative Group' (*Nhóm Sáng kiến Vì Công lý*). However, the founders were refused permission to establish by Hanoi Bar and state authorities,[118] and they were considered troublemakers (*kẻ chống đối*).

After this incident, the formation of independent lawyer groups providing pro bono services became more difficult. However, the development of social media has in the last decade enabled lawyers to connect with each other via social networks such as Facebook. They get together to provide pro bono services and use both social media and state-driven media to advocate for their cases. There have been some successful cases in which state agencies committed wrongful convictions and accepted the obligation to compensate, such as *Hàn Đức Long* v. *Bắc Giang Investigation Body*[119] and *Huỳnh Văn Nén* v. *Bình Thuận Provincial Court*.[120] These lawyers are characterized by social media as 'brave' (*dũng cảm*) and 'for justice' (*vì công lý*), but state-driven media continue to characterize them as troublemakers.

Compared to legal practice in legal aid services, lawyer representation in pro bono criminal cases encounters difficulties because, with the exception of mandatory cases, there is no connection between these legal services and state activities. Lawyers' services in these cases are still considered obstacles to the operation of state agencies, particularly investigation bodies. The Chuong My dust case study, discussed immediately below, is considered typical of practices interfering with lawyer representation in criminal proceedings.

Do Dang Du, a 17-year-old boy, resided in Dong Cuu hamlet, Dong Phuong Yen Commune, Chuong My District, Hanoi. He was caught for theft red-handed by the Police of Chuong My District. Du was detained in the chamber for juveniles with three other defendants of the same

[115] *Interview with Lawyer Nguyen A*, *supra* note 90; *Interview with Lawyer Nguyen B*, *supra* note 90.

[116] *Interview with Lawyer Ngo B*, *supra* note 90; *Interview with Lawyer Nguyen C*, *supra* note 90.

[117] *Compensation to Wrongfully Convicted People in Litigation Process* (in Vietnamese), Resolution No. 388/2003/NQ-UBTVQH11 of the Standing Committee of National Assembly (Vietnam: 17 March 2003). This Resolution was replaced by the *Law on State Compensation* (in Vietnamese), Vietnam 2009, and then replaced by the *Law on State Compensation* (in Vietnamese), Vietnam 2017.

[118] Anh Thư, Việc ra đời nhóm sáng kiến 'Vì công lý' có vi phạm pháp luật? (Does Establishment of 'For Justice' Initiative Group Break the Laws?), *VnExpress* (7 May 2004), online: vnexpress.net/phap-luat/viec-ra-doi-nhom-sang-kien-vi-cong-ly-co-vi-pham-phap-luat-2005157.html.

[119] Ngô Ngọc Trai, Hành trình minh oan cho tử tù Hàn Đức Long (The Journey for Exonerating the Innocence of Han Duc Long, Death Row Prisoner) (Hanoi: Domino Books and Writers Publishing House, 2018) at 13.

[120] Hoàng Trường-Hải Hà, 'Người tù lịch sử' Huỳnh Văn Nén được tự do ('Historic Prisoner' Huynh Van Nen is Exonerated), *VnExpress* (28 November 2018), online: vnexpress.net/phap-luat/nguoi-tu-lich-su-huynh-van-nen-duoc-tu-do-3319474.html.

age. After nearly two months of temporary detention, Du's relatives were informed that Du had died as a result of beating by his roommates.[121]

Immediately after the death of Do Dang Du, some lawyers sent a request to the Minister of Public Security, the Supreme People's Procuracy, and the Director of Hanoi Police, asking for an investigation into the reason for his death.[122] Two lawyers, Mr Tran Thu Nam and Mr Le Van Luan, agreed to act as counsel for the victim's family free-of-charge during investigation and adjudication of the case. However, when they went to the relevant investigation body to apply for the then required Certificate of Defender to do their job, they were refused because the victim's mother had not requested the participation of lawyers.[123] The two lawyers then visited the victim's mother's house at Chuong My District, Hanoi to learn more about the case. However, on their way back home, they were 'assaulted and hit' by eight masked men. Learning about this development, the Vietnam Bar Federation and the Hanoi Bar Association promptly contacted the local police and the people's procuracy, and requested that they take necessary measures to protect the lawyers and investigate the attack. According to the lawyers, the attack showed signs of the involvement of organized criminals as well as local police.[124]

One week after the incident, Hanoi police issued a press release stating that the incident occurred suddenly and was not an organized crime, and that the identity of the assaulters had been detected. The police also affirmed that no policeman was engaged in the case, contrary to what the lawyers asserted. According to the police, the suspects declared that on the way to visit a sick patient, they were splashed with dust generated from a car driven too fast by two lawyers, became annoyed, and picked a quarrel.[125] On 12 November 2015, seven persons in the case were prosecuted for deliberate infliction of bodily harm on other persons.[126] However, the lawyers

[121] Yêu cầu điều tra bổ sung vụ Đỗ Đăng Dư bị đánh chết (Request for Further Investigation of Do Dang Du's Death), *Tuoi tre* (15 May 2016), online: tuoitre.vn/tin/phap-luat/20160525/yeu-cau-dieu-tra-bo-sung-vu-do-dang-du-bi-danh-chet/1107082.html; Mẹ Đỗ Đăng Dư: công an ngăn gia đình thăm (Do Dang Du's Mother: Police Prevented Family from Visit), *BBC News Vietnam* (14 October 2015), online: www.bbc.com/vietnamese/vietnam/2015/10/151014_do_dang_du_journo [*Do Dang Du's Mother*].

[122] Bộ trưởng Công an: Điều tra khách quan vụ bị can tử vong vì bị đánh trong trại giam (Minister of Public Security: Investigates Death of Accused from Being Beaten in Prison), *Nguoi lao dong* (14 October 2015), online: nld.com.vn/phap-luat/bo-truong-cong-an-dieu-tra-khach-quan-vu-bi-can-tu-vong-vi-bi-danh-trong-trai-giam-2015101408451511.htm; Vụ Đỗ Đăng Dư: Thư gửi Bộ trưởng Công an (Do Dang Du: Letter to the Minister of Public Security), *BBC News Vietnam* (13 October 2015), online: www.bbc.com/vietnamese/vietnam/2015/10/151012_do_dang_du_update; *Do Dang Du's Mother*, *supra* note 121.

[123] Về việc 2 luật sư bị hành hung tại xã Đông Phương Yên, huyện Chương Mỹ (Regarding the Case of Two Lawyers Being Beaten at Dong Phuong Yen Commune, Chuong My District), *An Ninh Thu Do* (11 October 2015), online: anninhthudo.vn/chinh-tri-xa-hoi/ve-viec-2-luat-su-bi-hanh-hung-tai-xa-dong-phuong-yen-huyen-chuong-my/643701.antd.

[124] Vụ 2 luật sư bị hành hung: 'chúng tôi nhận ra kẻ đánh mình' (Two Lawyers were Assaulted: 'We Recognise the Attackers'), *Vietnamnet* (6 November 2015), online: vietnamnet.vn/vn/thoi-su/vu-2-luat-su-bi-hanh-hung-chung-toi-nhan-ra-ke-danh-minh-271596.html.

[125] Luật sư vụ Đỗ Đăng Dư bị đánh vì phóng xe gây bụi? (Lawyers of Do Dang Du Case were Beaten Because Driving Caused Dust), *Vietnamnet* (10 November 2015), online: vietnamnet.vn/vn/thoi-su/lua-t-su-vu-do-dang-du-bi-da-nh-vi-pho-ng-xe-gay-bu-i-272430.html; Mai Chi and Võ Hải, Đại biểu Quốc hội: 'Vì bắn bụi mà hành hung luật sư, xã hội sẽ loạn' (Member of Parliament: 'Because of Shooting Dust and Assaulting Lawyers, Society will be Upset'), *VnExpress* (11 November 2015), online: vnexpress.net/tin-tuc/phap-luat/dai-bieu-quoc-hoi-vi-ban-bui-ma-hanh-hung-luat-su-xa-hoi-se-loan-3310334.html; Luật sư bị hành hung vì 'bắn bụi bẩn' muốn rút đề nghị khởi tố (Lawyers Assaulted for 'Shooting Dirt' Want to Withdraw the Prosecution), *VnExpress* (1 December 2016), online: vnexpress.net/tin-tuc/phap-luat/luat-su-bi-hanh-hung-vi-ban-bui-ban-muon-rut-de-nghi-khoi-to-3341267.html.

[126] Cao Nguyên, Khởi tố vụ hai luật sư bị hành hung (Prosecuting the Case of Two Beaten Lawyers), *Lao Dong* (13 November 2015), online: laodong.com.vn/phap-luat/khoi-to-vu-hai-luat-su-bi-hanh-hung-396632.bld.

then withdrew their application asking for prosecution, for unknown reasons.[127] This case led 200 lawyers to sign a nationwide petition requesting that the legal provision compelling lawyers to obtain a Certificate of Defender from the body conducting proceedings be done away with.[128] The requirement for a Certificate of Defender was ultimately replaced by a simpler requirement for registering the defender of the case.[129]

E. Mandatory Defence Counsel

After Vietnam agreed to the International Covenant on Civil and Political Rights ('ICCPR'), it promulgated the Criminal Procedure Code ('CPC') 1988, which required a defence counsel in some cases called 'mandatory cases', including:[130]

- Cases in which the punishment is the death penalty; or
- Cases in which the accused persons are juveniles, or persons with physical or mental disabilities.

As required by criminal procedure, defence counsel must be present at all stages of mandatory cases, from investigation to prosecution and trial. Without participation of counsel, the case could be reversed.[131]

When the mandatory defence counsel requirement was enacted, lawyers practised as part of a bar association, and they were not allowed to establish their own firms per the Ordinance on the Organization of Lawyers 1987.[132] Therefore, to meet the requirement, investigation bodies, procuracies, or courts had to request the local bar association to appoint defence counsel in the relevant case.[133] The mechanism of the local bar association appointing a defence counsel, instead of direct selection of a lawyer by the body in charge of proceedings, helped to support the independence of lawyers from the courts in appointed counsel activities.[134]

Due to an insufficient number of lawyers in some provinces, the CPC 2003 expanded the type of organizations entitled to appoint lawyers in mandatory cases. For example, the Fatherland Front and its member social organizations had the right to appoint 'people's defenders' to protect its members.[135]

[127] Lương Kết, Luật sư bị đánh ở Chương Mỹ xem xét rút đơn yêu cầu khởi tố (The Attorney Who was Beaten in Chuong My Considered Withdrawing the Request for Prosecution), *Dân Việt* (10 January 2016), online: danviet.vn/phap-luat/luat-su-bi-danh-o-chuong-my-xem-xet-rut-don-yeu-cau-khoi-to-653756.html; LS rút đơn yêu cầu khởi tố vụ 'Bụi Chương Mỹ' (The Lawyers Withdrew Their Request to Prosecute the Case of 'Chuong My Dust'), *BBC News Vietnam* (8 January 2016), online: www.bbc.com/vietnamese/vietnam/2016/01/160108_lawyers_beaten_withdraw.

[128] Đơn Kiến nghị (góp ý sửa đổi Bộ luật tố tụng hình sự, đề nghị bãi bỏ thủ tục cấp giấy chứng nhận người bào chữa) (Petition – Suggestions for Modification of the Criminal Procedure Code, Requesting the Abolition of Procedures for the Granting of Certificates of Defence), *Ngô Ngọc Trai* (1 November 2015), online: ngongoctrai.com/kien-nghi-cua-221-luat-su-ve-bo-thu-tuc-cap-giay-bao-chua/.

[129] *Criminal Procedure Code* (in Vietnamese), Vietnam 2015 [*CPC 2015*], Article 78; Phương Thảo, Một số điểm mới trong phần chung của Bộ luật tố tụng hình sự (sửa đổi) năm 2015 (New Regulations in General Section of the Criminal Procedure Code (Amendment) 2015), *Nội Chính* (11 October 2017), online: noichinh.vn/ho-so-tu-lieu/201710/mot-so-diem-moi-trong-phan-chung-cua-bo-luat-to-tung-hinh-su-sua-doi-nam-2015-303041/.

[130] *Criminal Procedure Code* (in Vietnamese), Vietnam 1988 [*CPC 1988*], Article 37.

[131] *UNDP Report on Appointed Counsels*, *supra* note 35, at 52.

[132] Nguyễn Hưng Quang and Kerstin Steiner, 'Ideology and Professionalism: The Resurgence of the Vietnamese Bar' in *Asian Socialism & Legal Change*, *supra* note 6, at 196, and *Social Function of Lawyers*, *supra* note 2, at 22.

[133] *CPC 1988*, *supra* note 130, Article 37.

[134] Ibid.

[135] *CPC 2003*, *supra* note 37, Article 57.

In the CPC 2015, provisions on mandatory defence counsel were reinforced further. The CPC 2015 expanded the scope of mandatory defence counsel to include lawyers, representatives of an accused person, people's defenders, and legal aid officers.[136] The CPC 2015 also extended the scope of mandatory cases to include:[137]

- Cases in which the punishment is 20 years' imprisonment, life imprisonment, or death; or
- Cases in which the accused is a person with physical or mental disabilities, or under 18 years old.

Because the law now requires bodies to have defence counsel in mandatory cases, state agencies usually facilitate representation by defence counsel, at least more than in other cases. According to a 2012 UNDP survey, it was easier and quicker for mandatory lawyers to be granted with the Certificates of Defence, access to case files, and other assistance from the authorities.[138]

However, the goal of the mandatory counsel scheme in Vietnam, especially the assertion that 'the right to counsel is an act of protecting the accused's interests', still encounters significant challenges because of defence quality and a lack of independence of lawyers. Under the CPC 2003 and CPC 2015, authorized agencies must rely on provincial bar associations and organizations such as the Fatherland Front to appoint the defence counsel in mandatory cases. The agencies conducting proceedings therefore do not directly appoint lawyers.[139] In reality, however, many agency officials invite lawyers with whom they have a personal relationship.[140]

The effectiveness of defence counsel in mandatory cases is also diminished because CPC 2013 allows state agencies to use persons who are not qualified lawyers as counsel. In many localities, defence counsel may be state officials who are members of the local subsidiary of the Vietnam Lawyers Association, Vietnam Women's Union, Vietnam Farmers' Union, or Vietnam Veterans' Association.[141] The use of persons who are not lawyers, including those who have no court experience or legal training, raises serious concerns about the quality of defence in mandatory cases.[142]

Another factor negatively impacting the mandatory defence scheme is remuneration. Under Inter-Circular No. 66/2007/TTLT-BTC-BTP of the Ministries of Finance and Justice, payment for mandatory defence services was made by state agencies in accordance with specified standards.[143] The remuneration level from 2007 to 2014 was VND120,000 (US$5.16) for one working day. If the work takes only half a day, the lawyer is only paid 50 per cent of the value of such working day.[144] According to the 2012 UNDP survey, lawyers said that this reimbursement was too low, as it did not even meet the travelling expenses of lawyers to the court or detention centre to learn about their client's case.[145] The payment procedures under provisions of Inter-Circular No. 66/2007/TTLT-BTC-BTP were also flawed. State officials or judges directly in charge of the investigation, prosecution, or trial were the persons who decided the number of pay days for the defence counsel.

[136] *CPC 2015*, *supra* note 129, Article 72.
[137] *CPC 2015*, *supra* note 129, Article 76.
[138] *UNDP Report on Appointed Counsels*, *supra* note 35, at 53–4.
[139] *CPC 2003*, *supra* note 37, Article 57; *CPC 2015*, *supra* note 129, Article 72.
[140] *UNDP Report on Appointed Counsels*, *supra* note 35, at 40.
[141] *UNDP Report on Appointed Counsels*, *supra* note 35, at 67.
[142] *UNDP Report on Appointed Counsels*, *supra* note 35, at 38.
[143] Ministry of Finance and Ministry of Justice, *Guide to Remuneration and Payment of Lawyers' Expenses in Cases Where Lawyers Participate in Legal Proceedings at the Request of Agencies Conducting the Proceedings* (in Vietnamese), Joint Circular No. 66/2007/TTLT-BTC-BTP (Vietnam: 19 June 2007) [*Joint Circular No. 66/2007*], Section II, paras. 1–3; *UNDP Report on Appointed Counsels*, *supra* note 35, at 90.
[144] *Joint Circular No. 66/2007*, *supra* note 143, Article 2, para. 2.
[145] *UNDP Report on Appointed Counsels*, *supra* note 35, at 70.

The Inter-Circular did not provide details on the methods and formulas used to calculate pay days, which left this determination to the discretion of the officials or judges.[146]

In early 2015, the remuneration paid to mandatory defence counsel changed in accordance with Inter-Circular No. 191/2014/TTLT-BTC-BTP.[147] The remuneration paid for one working day in a mandatory case was established to be 0.4 times the 'basic salary'.[148] According to this calculation, a defence counsel receives approximately VND484,000 per working day (about US$20.81 at present). Inter-Circular No. 191 also provided details on how to calculate the working time of lawyers as a basis for payment.[149] Compared with the former regulation, this remuneration is higher.[150] However, the agencies and persons in charge of calculating the number of working days and directly paying the remuneration remain unchanged,[151] and challenges to the independence and quality of lawyers in mandatory defence still exist.

Why do lawyers take these cases in view of all the difficulties? According to a 2012 UNDP survey, the majority of lawyers stated that they took mandatory cases because of their social responsibility. Only a few lawyers said that their purpose was remuneration. Some lawyers wished to build relationships with the state officials, get more experience, or build a reputation. Some lawyers said that their cases were appointed by the provincial bars, which manage their practice, and they felt obligated to accept the cases.[152]

III. CONCLUSION

The CPC 2015 contains several new features on access to defence counsel that have created more favourable conditions for lawyers in criminal proceedings, such as the removal of the requirement of the Certificate of Defender, early participation in the investigation process, the right to participate in interviews with clients, and the right to collect and assess evidence.[153] The CPC 2015 also extends access to justice via more effective participation in mandatory cases. These changes are remarkable advances in the history of legal reform in Vietnam. But are these and other new features sufficient to encourage state agencies and courts to recognize the legitimate role of lawyers in supporting people's access to justice, in a state where such activity appears to contradict the democratic centralism of a socialist state? It is likely that additional judicial reform is needed in Vietnam for this change to be realized. The independence of the courts must be assured, and the quality of court operations enhanced, in order to create a sustainable basis to prohibit state agency intervention in lawyers' professional practice and more fully recognize and appreciate the role of lawyers in supporting access to justice.

146 *Joint Circular No. 66/2007*, *supra* note 143, Article 2, paras. 2 and 4; *UNDP Report on Appointed Counsels*, *supra* note 35, at 29.

147 Ministry of Justice and Ministry of Finance, *Guiding the Remuneration and Payment of Expenses to Lawyers in Cases Where Lawyers Participate in Legal Proceedings at the Request of Agencies Conducting the Proceedings* (in Vietnamese), Joint Circular No. 191/2014/TTLT-BTC-BTP (Vietnam: 12 December 2014) [*Joint Circular No. 191/2014*], Article 2.

148 Ibid.

149 *Government Decree No. 47/2016/ND-CP, Determining the Base Salary Level for Officials, Public Employees, and the Armed Forces* (in Vietnamese), Vietnam 2016 [*Decree No. 47/2016*], Article 2.

150 *Decree No. 47/2016*, *supra* note 149, Article 3.

151 *Joint Circular No. 191/2014*, *supra* note 147, Article 2.

152 *UNDP Report on Appointed Counsels*, *supra* note 35, at 36–7.

153 *New Features*, *supra* note 40, at 197–259.

PART II

Comparative Perspectives on Access to Justice

13

Access to Justice and an Islamic Ethic of Justice

*Arif A. Jamal**

'Indeed, Allah loves those who act justly.' (Qur'an, 60:8)

Abstract

The theme of justice is central in Islam. Among the 99 'beautiful names' (asma al-husna) *of God is* 'al-Adl' *– the Just or Fair. The Qur'an is replete with references to the ideals and pursuit of justice, and justice was also linked with the actions and outlook of the Prophet Muhammad. This chapter elaborates on the importance of the theme of justice in different sources of Islamic normativity. It proposes that in contemporary times the salience of the ideal of justice must also be linked to access to justice. The idea of access to justice, particularly in its contemporary register, was not part of previous Islamic understandings. However, since it was important to realize justice among people and in the world, this chapter argues that access to justice, understood as the capacity for individuals or groups to reach justice-providing venues, is implicit in the Islamic emphasis on justice and may be seen as one part of an Islamic ethic of justice. The emphasis on the ideal of justice (or of acting justly), as a reflection of the justice of the divine, also suggests another facet of an Islamic ethic of justice, namely a concern with substantive fairness.*

I. INTRODUCTION

The theme of justice is central in Islam.[1] For instance, among the 99 beautiful names (*asma al-husna*) of God is *al-Adl* (the Just or Fair) and *al-Muqsit* (the Upholder of Equity (or Fairness)).

* Significant work on this chapter was done during a sabbatical visit to Auckland Law School, University of Auckland, in early 2019. My thanks, in particular, go to Nicole Roughan, Janet McLean, and Arie Rosen for their stimulating fellowship and warm hospitality during my visit, and to the staff of the Davis Law Library/Te Herenga Ture for facilitating access to materials.

[1] Regarding the words 'Muslim', 'Islam', and 'Islamic', some use these terms interchangeably and, effectively, synonymously. Others would distinguish between 'Islam' and the adjective 'Islamic' and 'Muslim'. In this distinction, the term Muslim highlights human agency and activity – that is the responses of adherents of Islam to the faith. In addition to agency, this view also highlights that these responses have been plural and diverse over time and geography formed by a range of contextual factors, including historical, political, cultural, economic, and other social forces. The differentiation is well expressed in an observation made by Carl Ernst: '[a]lthough it is common to hear people say, for example, "Christianity says that . . ." or "according to Islam . . ." the only thing that can be observed is that individual people who

In addition, the Qur'an is replete with references to the ideals and pursuit of justice. In a similar vein, justice was also linked with the actions and outlook of the Prophet Muhammad. Thus, justice is conceived of in association with both the divine and the human or worldly.

This chapter begins with elaborating on the importance of the theme of justice in different sources of Islamic normativity. From this basis, it will propose that in contemporary times the salience of the ideal of justice must also be linked to access to justice. Of course, the idea of access to justice, particularly in its contemporary register, was not part of previous Islamic understandings. However, since it was important to realize justice among people and in the world, this chapter will argue that access to justice, here understood as the capacity for individuals or groups to reach justice-providing venues, is implicit in the Islamic emphasis on justice and thus may be seen as one part of an Islamic ethic of justice.

In addition, the emphasis on the ideal of justice (or of acting justly) as a reflection of the justice of the divine, also suggests another facet of an Islamic ethic of justice, namely a concern with fairness (not being biased or prejudiced, being balanced in consideration).

Thus, this chapter will try to develop an understanding of an Islamic ethic of justice that has access to two justice touchstones: a sense of being able to utilize venues of justice and the requirement that those venues act fairly.

II. THE ETHOS OF JUSTICE: QUR'AN AND SUNNA

The significance of the concept, or perhaps better the ideal, of justice in Muslim thinking and the message of Islam is clear. Starting with the scriptural sources, at least two terms for justice are used in the Qur'anic text:[2] *qist* and *adl*. *Adl* can be rendered simply as justice, though it also has the cognate meaning of rectilinear or well balanced. In this sense *adl* has a moral quality which one might say is about 'uprightness', both in a religious and in a moral sense. For instance, witnesses must be *adl* for their testimony to have weight. *Adl* is related to *adala*, i.e. having the quality of acting with *adl*, which has also been described as a state of moral and religious perfection, or at least conformity with moral and religious propriety.[3] *Qist* as justice conveys similar senses of fairness and equity, fair distribution, and balance.

Different variants of both *adl* and *qist* in are used repeatedly in the Qur'an, sometimes together. For example, in Sura 5, verse 8 (Q5:8), the Qur'an says: 'O you who have believed, be persistently standing firm for Allah, witnesses in justice, and do not let the hatred of a people prevent you from being just. Be just; that is nearer to righteousness. And fear Allah; indeed, Allah

call themselves Christians or Muslims have particular positions and practices that they observe and defend. No one, however, has ever seen Christianity or Islam do anything. They are abstractions, not actors comparable to human beings.' (Carl W. Ernst, *Following Muhammad: Rethinking Islam in the Contemporary World* (Chapel Hill: UNC Chapel Hill Press, 2003) at 51.) In sum, one option is to distinguish between the use of 'Muslim' and 'Islam/Islamic' and use Muslim when one wants to make a point about the fact that definitions, interpretations, and articulations of Islam, qua abstraction, are not inherent – because Islam is always expressed through what Muslims do or say. However, this is by no means a general, or generally adopted, position and one routinely sees reference to, for example, 'Islamic architecture' or 'Islamic philosophy' instead of architecture by Muslims or philosophy by Muslims.

2 I say at least two terms because in addition to the two identified here – *adl* and *qist* – it may be suggested that there are other justice-connoting terms in the Qur'an such as *ihsan* (doing good) and *maruf* (knowing good or right). Doing good and knowing good would be allied concepts to justice, and particularly relevant in some contexts.

3 Emile Tyan, 'Adl', in Bearman Peri et al., eds., *Encyclopaedia of Islam*, 2nd edn (Leiden: Koninklije Brill NV, 2012). As the article notes in footnote 2: 'In numismatics '*adl* means "of full weight", and therefore this word is stamped on coins to show that they have the just weight and are current ('*adlī*).' Thus, a sense of 'rightness' is part of *adl*.

is acquainted with what you do.' In this verse, it is a derivative of *qist* that provides the sense of justice in the 'witnesses in justice', but in 'Be just' and 'prevent you from being just', the sense of justice comes from derivatives of *adl*.[4]

Other verses use one or the other words, or both (or their homologues), to express justice. So, Q49:9 says: 'And if it returns, then make settlement between them in justice [from *qist*] and act justly [from *adl*]. Indeed, Allah loves those who act justly [from *qist*].'

One of the notable senses of justice in the Qur'anic text, whether expressed via *adl* or *qist*, is the emphasis on justice being done; that is, of justice as something to be acted out and applied. Consider the following Qur'anic verses: 'Indeed, Allah commands you to render trusts to whom they are due and when you judge between people to judge with justice' (Q4:58) and 'O you who have believed, be persistently standing firm in justice, witnesses for Allah, even if it be against yourselves or parents and relatives' (Q4:135). The second of these verses is thematically aligned to Q5:8, quoted above.

The theme of justice and acting justly is also present in the Sunna – that is, the collection of traditions of the Prophet Muhammad, which constitute a source of religious and legally weighty normativity for Muslims. The 'canonical' collections are referred to as '*sahih*' or reliable collections, and these *sahih* are referred to widely. In the *Sahih* Muslim (i.e. the *Sahih* of Muslim) is found the following:[5]

> It has been narrated on the authority of 'Abdullah b. 'Umar that the Messenger of Allah said:
>
> > Behold! the Dispensers of justice will be seated on the pulpits of light beside God, on the right side of the Merciful, Exalted and Glorious. Either side of the Being is the right side both being equally meritorious. [The Dispensers of justice are] those who do justice in their rules, in matters relating to their families and in all that they undertake to do.

The idea of dispensing justice in the sense of being fair and avoiding oppressiveness is also in the following two hadith: 'Abu Dharr (May Allah be pleased with him) said: The Prophet, Allah, the Exalted, and Glorious, said: "O My slaves, I have prohibited Myself injustice; and have made oppression unlawful for you, so do not oppress one another."'[6] And:[7]

> Jabir b. Abdullah reported that Allah's Messenger said:
>
> > Be on your guard against committing oppression, for oppression is a darkness on the Day of Resurrection, and be on your guard against stinginess for stinginess destroyed those who were before you, as it incited them to shed blood and make lawful what was unlawful for them.

The Qur'anic text and the Sunna materials constitute key normative textual sources for Muslims. As the above excerpts suggest, and to reiterate, not only is the ideal of justice expressed in these sources but it is also expressed as what one might call an applied value. That is to say, while justice is associated with the divine, as a divine attribute – hence the names of God

[4] Arabic, like Hebrew, generally operates on a trilateral root structure, with words with connected ranges of meaning derived from the different roots. For instance *a-l-m* is 'to learn' and an *aalim* (the active participle) is a teacher or scholar (or one who makes learning); *a-r-f* is 'to know' and *aarif* (active participle) is one who knows. Thus, both *qist* (*q-s-t*) and *adl* ('*a-d-l*) are connected to words with related meanings deriving from their respective roots.

[5] Sahih Muslim, 1827; In-book reference: Book 33, Hadith 21; USC-MSA web (English) reference: Book 20, Hadith 4493.

[6] Riyad al-Salihin, In-book reference, Introduction, Hadith 111.

[7] Sahih Muslim 2578, In-book reference, Book 4, Hadith 74; USC-MSA web (English) reference Book 32, Hadith 6248.

including al-Adl and al-Muqsit – it is not just confined to the realm of the divine. Justice is also human and practical, and can be exhibited and lived in the world by people. This applies to officials like judges, governors etc., as well as to ordinary individuals, for instance in the way one conducts one's daily life and treats those who are one's dependants, such as children. Moreover, there is the suggestion that the justice that is done (or not done as the case may be) in the material world is part of a spiritual, other worldly, reckoning. In short, it counts. This point has implications for the importance of access to justice that will be developed further below.

III. THE ETHOS OF JUSTICE: SHARIʿA

Given this analysis of justice in the Qur'an and Sunna, which are foundational sources for the development of Shariʿa norms, it is not surprising that commentators have identified an ethic of justice infusing the Shariʿa. Thus, Khaeld Abou el-Fadl posits, evocatively, that: 'the shariʿa ought to stand in an Islamic polity as a symbolic construct for the divine perfection that is unreachable by human effort – a concept summed up in the Islamic tradition by the word *husn*, or beauty. It is the epitome of justice, goodness and beauty as conceived and retained by God.'[8] On this understanding, the Shariʿa is an attempted homage to the divine, perfect justice. This makes the Shariʿa a living meditation attempting to understand and give effect to divine justice in different aspects. There are the ritual aspects and norms governing the relationship of the individual to the divine, as well as its 'material' aspects, namely the relationship of people *inter se*. Shahab Ahmed notes the 'centrality of the values of *justice* and *human welfare* to the constitution of the excellent or virtuous [Muslim] state and society' and cites Fazlur Rahman's observation that from '[*Nasr al-din*] Tusi onwards, the Muslim ethical writers began to stress the virtue of justice'.[9] One of Ahmed's conclusions is '. . . the value that emerges as pre-eminent in this conceptualization of Islamic law is the value of *justice* which requires, for its constitution, the Muslim to draw on sources for Truth beyond the Text'.[10]

These interpretations of the ethic of justice in Islamic law are reinforced by an understanding of the practice of Islamic law provided from anthropological studies. Lawrence Rosen, for instance, writing about Arab societies, notes that 'in the Arab world the concept of justice is absolutely central. But whereas Westerns tend to frame matters in terms of rights, Arabs emphasize a language of justice.' He goes on to suggest that, therefore, 'it may be necessary to think as much in terms of a rule of justice as of a rule of law'.[11] Rosen also adds that justice (here in its '*adl*' formulation) is more an attribute of a person than a disembodied idea, with an emphasis on persons rather than institutions.[12] Thus, justice has a strong element of being active, social, and lived.

These anthropological observations about Islamic law in practice are reinforced by a rather famous historical instruction from the Caliph Ali b. Abi Talib (cousin and son-in-law to the

[8] Khaled Abou el-Fadl, 'Foundations' in Amyn B. Sajoo, ed., *The Shariʿa: History, Ethics and Law* (London: IB Tauris, 2018) 19 at 21–2.

[9] Ahmad Shahab, *What is Islam: The Importance of being Islamic* (Princeton: Princeton University Press, 2016) [*What is Islam*] at 478.

[10] *What is Islam, supra* note 9, at 481–2 (emphasis in original).

[11] Lawrence Rosen, *Islam and the Rule of Justice: Image and Reality in Muslim Law and Culture* (Chicago: University of Chicago Press, 2018) [*Islam and the Rule of Justice*] at 166.

[12] *Islam and the Rule of Justice, supra* note 11, at 167.

Prophet Muhammad, and the fourth and final of what are referred to as the 'Rightly Guided (or "*Rashidun*")' Caliphs) to Malik al-Ashtar, upon the latter's appointment, by Ali, as Governor of Egypt. In this famous letter, Ali writes:[13]

> Then, know, O Malik, that I have sent you to an area where there have been governments before you, both just as well as oppressive. People will now watch your dealings as you used to watch the dealings of the rulers before you, and they [people] will criticise you as you criticised them [rulers]. Surely, the virtuous are known by the reputation that Allah circulates for them through the tongues of His creatures. Therefore, the best collection with you should be the collection of good deeds. So, control your passions and check your heart from doing what is not lawful for you, because checking the heart means detaining it just half-way between what it likes and dislikes.
>
> Habituate your heart to mercy for the subjects and to affection and kindness for them. Do not stand over them like greedy beasts who feel it is enough to devour them, since they are of two kinds, either your brother in religion or one like you in creation. They will commit slips and encounter mistakes. They may act wrongly, wilfully or by neglect. So, extend to them your forgiveness and pardon, in the same way as you would like Allah to extend His forgiveness and pardon to you, because you are over them and your responsible Commander [*Imam*] is over you while Allah is over him who has appointed you. He [Allah] has sought you to manage their affairs and has tried you through them.[14]

Perhaps even more important for our purposes is the counsel that Ali gives to Malik regarding judges and judicial appointments:[15]

> For the settlement of disputes among people select him who is the most distinguished of your subjects in your view. The cases [coming before him] should not vex him, disputation should not enrage him, he should not insist on any wrong point, and should not grudge accepting the truth when he perceives it; he should not lean towards greed and should not content himself with a cursory understanding (of a matter) without going thoroughly into it.
>
> He should be most ready to stop [to ponder] on doubtful points, most regardful of arguments, least disgusted at the quarrel of litigants, most patient at probing into matters and most fearless at the time of passing judgement. Praise should not make him vain and elation should not make him lean [to any side]. Such people are very few.

These extracts from Ali's letter lend more evidence to several points already raised. First, they reiterate the salience of the ethos of justice within the legal tradition. Second, in combination with Rosen's observations about contemporary practice, they show the continuity of this ethic in practice from the past into contemporary times. Third, they show how the ethic was, and is, not just thought of in theoretical or abstract terms but is (and has been) referred to in applied terms,

[13] Sharif Razi, *Nahjul Balagha Part 2, Letters and Sayings*, Ahlul Bayt Digital Islamic Library Project 1995–2019 [*Letters and Sayings*], at Letter 53, online: Al-Islam.org, www.al-islam.org/nahjul-balagha-part-2-letters-and-sayings/letter-53-order-malik-al-ashtar#2-chief-judge.

[14] Similar language is found in Ali's letter to al-Aswad ibn Qutbah, the Governor of Hulwan: *Letters and Sayings*, *supra* note 13, at Letter 59, online: www.al-islam.org/nahjul-balagha-part-2-letters-and-sayings/letter-59-al-aswad-ibn-qutbah-governor-hulwan, which says the following (including a rendition of the 'golden rule'): 'Now, if the actions of a governor follow the passions he will be greatly hampered in justice. All the people should be equal in right before you, because injustice cannot be a substitute for justice. Avoid that thing the like of which you would not like for yourself. Exert yourself in what Allah has made obligatory on you, hoping for His reward and fearing His chastisement.'

[15] Ibid.

encompassing institutions and individuals that engage in the practical work of judging and governing. Rosen also points out another aspect of Islamic law that complements this practical and applied aspect we have been discussing, and this is the focus on procedure. As Rosen suggests, this focus allows 'difference to flourish, settlements to be varied and the ability to negotiate relationships', and thus that the (Islamic) rule of law is more a 'rule of justice', with justice being constructed in terms of the particular relationships in play.[16] This, too, speaks to justice as being a thing 'to be done'. Additionally, the fundamental point that Rosen seems to be driving at is that the concern is not with a formalistic understanding of the rule of law, but with achieving justice in the context of the particular dispute and particular disputants.

In this same vein, Abou El Fadl remarks on man's special status as God's 'vicegerent' in the Qur'an. He notes that 'a fundamental Qur'anic idea is that God vested all of humanity with a kind of divinity by making every person the viceroy of God on this earth'.[17] This posits that human beings were created with a special dignity that cannot be violated, as well as the responsibility for protection of the earth, such that each human being is capable of discharging his or her duty as God's vicegerent.[18] As Elizabeth Barre notes, it is on this basis that Abou El Fadl makes an argument for individual rights in Islamic law. Rights, of course, particularly make sense when they are justiciable – when they count in an enforceable way – and so Abou El Fadl's argument can be seen as affirming what other analysts also suggest as the applied tenor of the Islamic legal tradition.

Indeed, the ethos of justice, and its references in the Qur'an, Sunna, and other textual sources, as well as legal practice, can be seen as a motif that provided a juristic capacity to deal with the inevitable and unavoidable multiplicity of issues that emerge in society. Anver Emon notes that 'Pre-modern Muslim jurists knew that lived experience presents an infinite number of questions that no finite body of source-text can be expected to answer. Consequently, they recognized the necessity to grant reason ontological authority for Shari'a analysis.'[19] What I am suggesting here is that the salience of the references to justice and to doing justice, along with the allied concepts of fairness, equity, balance, etc. – ideas captured within the terms '*adl*' and '*qist*' – provided the animating spirit for understanding the textual meaning as well as furnishing a framework for how to address legal questions. In short, the prominence of the theme of justice – conceptually as well as in practice – operates as a normative architecture for Muslim legal traditions.[20]

[16] *Islam and the Rule of Justice*, *supra* note 11, at 184.

[17] Khaled Abou El Fadl, 'Islam and the Challenge of Democracy' in Joshua Cohen and Deborah Chasman, eds., *Islam and the Challenge of Democracy* (Princeton: Princeton University Press, 2004) 1 at 6.

[18] Elizabeth Barre, 'Review of Khaled Abou El Fadl (with Jeremy Waldron, John L. Esposito, Noah Feldman, et al.); Joshua Cohen and Deborah Chasman eds., Islam and the Challenge of Democracy (Princeton: Princeton University Press, 2004)' (2008) 9:1 *Political Theology* 121 at 122–3.

[19] Anver Emon, *Islamic Natural Law Theories* (Oxford: Oxford University Press, 2010) at 201.

[20] It is necessary to note possible objections to this characterization. In his article, John Makdisi, 'Legal Logic and Equity in Islamic Law' (1985) 33 *American Journal of Comparative Law* 63 at 67, John Makdisi says: 'This latter interpretation suggests that, despite the primacy of reasoning by analogy in developing the law from the Koran and the sunna, a legal solution derived by such reasoning may be rejected by the Islamic jurist in favor of one based on and justified by "equity". Yet, the concept of equity as we know it in the West is the antithesis of the Islamic view that all law is derived from God through the Koran and the sunna. Equity is grounded in the precepts of the conscience, a preconceived set of norms existing apart from positive law ... [and] derives its legitimacy from the belief in a natural right or justice beyond positive law. This concept contradicts one of the basic premises of Islamic law, the total reliance on the revealed Word of God in the Koran and sunna as the only primary source of law.' I say this may be a potential objection because what I am saying here about the ethos of justice might be seen to be making the type of equity argument with which Makdisi is taking issue. I do not feel there is a real conflict that emerges here, however, because what I am suggesting is that an ethos of justice is within the textual materials and indeed contained within the

All of these observations allow us to segue from an elaboration of the ethos of justice to a discussion about access to justice.

IV. JUSTICE IN ROLES

In their study of the role of *muftis*, that is scholars who give (non-binding) legal opinions, and of the opinions themselves, known as fatwas, Masud, Messik, and Powers help to clarify and distinguish different legal roles and the way these roles have worked.

In the course of their discussion, Masud, Messik, and Powers usefully point out that the efforts of the *muftis* (which is what their study focuses on) were by no means the only legal work done. Specifically, they mention the role of the judges (*qadis*) and contrast this with that of the *muftis*. They point out straightforwardly that: 'The *domain* of legal procedure, including adversarial cases, rules of evidence, binding judgments, and state enforcement, belongs to the judge (*qadi*); the issuance of non-binding advisory opinions (*fatawa* or *fatwas*) to an individual questioner (*mustafti*), whether in connection with litigation or not, is the separate domain of the jurisconsult (*mufti*).'[21] While the analogy is not exact, the *qadi*'s role as thus described is closely comparable to the role of (trial) court judges, while the *muftis* we might say are more akin to law professors. Thus, the basis of the legal engagement was different. As Masud et al. characterize it, the *mufti*'s interpretive work followed indications in textual sources, while the work of the *qadi* was grounded in evidentiary materials including testimony, oaths, and admissions:[22]

> As a consequence, fatwas and judgments represent different orientations to the relationship of law and fact. In a fatwa, the factual description . . . is taken as given, as the point of departure for an interpretive solution that engages the sources of law . . . In a judgment, competing factual versions put forward by the litigants are themselves the crux of the problem, and sorting them out is the judge's central task.

The significant point for our purposes is that the pursuit of justice applies to both of these roles, though in different ways. For the judge, as Rosen's work has pointed out and as articulated in Ali's letter, justice was particular and, appropriately, related to the case before them. For the *mufti*, justice could also be said to be particular inasmuch as it was in response to a specific question, but this question was not answered in the context of the need to render a decision in a 'real life' case at hand. The example of the *mufti* raises the issue of whether we can find that, in fact, there has been an emphasis on the provision of forums for justice. I believe that the answer to this question is yes.

The reason for my giving this answer is because, as scholars have noted, from almost its outset the Muslim community was not only a religious community but also a political and administrative community, a pre-modern state. In this context, Muslim legal traditions and thinking were harnessed to practical needs from early on. Thus, Bernard Weiss states that 'Islam developed in a polity of its own making' and further that 'Muslim history places the revelation of Islam's law in the context of a polity based in Medina and portrays Muhammad as, like Moses,

Qur'anic terms. Perhaps, as I believe it to be, Makdisi's reference to equity is to the common-law sense of 'equity' which he finds antithetical to Islamic law, not to a sense of equity-in-*adl* or equity-in-*qist*.

[21] Muhammad Khalid Masud, Brinkley Messik, and David S. Powers, *Islamic Legal Interpretation: Muftis and their Fatwas* (Cambridge, MA: Harvard University Press, 1996) [*Islamic Legal Interpretation*] at 3.

[22] *Islamic Legal Interpretation*, *supra* note 21, at 18.

both prophet and ruler.'[23] Muhammad died in 632CE and the last of his 'rightly guided' successors, Ali b. Abi Talib, died in 661CE. Thereafter, the first of the early empires, the Umayyad Empire (661–750CE), was founded, with a caliph at its head. Weiss notes that one of the major contributions of the Umayyads was their establishment of a system of caliphal justice with judges (*qadis*) operating under caliphal authority.[24] This developed into the dual system of legal authority and legal roles we have discussed, namely the law of the jurisconsults and the law of the judges.

So, an important point to note is that from the early days Islamic law became applied by virtue of its use within the polities of the time. These early structures of application were of course about doing the necessary work of the government – settling disputes, enforcing criminal law, etc. – and as such forced Islamic law to articulate itself as a set of practically enforceable norms and not just theoretical constructs. Abdulaziz Sachedina puts this pithily when he says: 'Islamic law has been regarded as the embodiment of Divine Justice. In order for Muslims to attain that divine scale of justice they must implement these norms of justice in their everyday life.'[25] Of course, Sachedina is here primarily speaking, as he says, about what the individual does in her or his individual life, but his observations reinforce the applied aspect of Islamic law.

This enforceable law also 'is embedded in a moral hermeneutic'.[26] Within this hermeneutic, I am suggesting, a sense of justice, whether through *adl* or *qist*, plays an important role as a pervading, even if amorphous, theme. One institution that developed and may be seen to have helped to give concrete expression to this theme was the *mazalim* courts. These were courts that dealt with the conduct of officials, such as judges or other governmental functionaries, and in which complaints about official action could be made. Thus, the *mazalim* courts were different from the normal Shari'a, *qadi*, courts that would have dealt with routine matters. The development of the *mazalim* courts may be read as a concern for ensuring the norms of propriety, fairness, balance, etc. – that is, ethos of justice norms – were part of the lived administrative and judicial practice. Moreover, the very existence of the *mazalim* courts can also be seen as having an important access to justice aspect. Inasmuch as the *mazalim* courts could hold judges or officials to account for failing to act with fairness or propriety, they helped to ensure that when the people interfaced with officials or judges, these functionaries would know that if they failed to act appropriately and thereby corrupted access to justice with unfairness or bias they could be sanctioned. Even when, later, the Ottomans did away with the *mazalim* courts, the principle of review of official action continued, but this was done within the purview of the *qadis* in the regular Shari'a courts.[27]

In addition to the *mazalim* courts, mention can also be made of the *muhtasib*. The *muhtasib* were officials that had a supervisory function over several activities concerning public morality, overseeing the public welfare, and supervising the markets, including prayers, mosque maintenance, community matters, and market dealings.[28] With respect to the market, the *muhtasib* are

[23] Bernard G. Weiss, *The Spirit of Islamic Law* (Athens, GA: University of Georgia Press, 1998) [*Spirit of Islamic Law*] at 3.

[24] *Spirit of Islamic Law*, *supra* note 23, at 6.

[25] Abdulaziz Sachedina, 'The Ideal and the Real in Islamic Law' in Ravindra S. Khare, ed., *Perspectives of Islamic Law, Justice and Society* (London: Rowman & Littlefield Publishers Inc., 1999) 15 at 29.

[26] Roy P. Mottahedeh, 'Introduction' in Muhammad Baqir As-Sadr, ed., *Lessons in Islamic Jurisprudence* (trans. and intro. by Roy P. Mottahedeh) (Oxford: Oneworld, 2003) 1 at 3.

[27] Wael Hallaq, *Shari'a: Theory, Practice and Transformations* (Cambridge: Cambridge University Press, 2009) [*Shari'a*] at 209.

[28] The *Oxford Dictionary of Islam*, 'Muhtasib' (*Oxford Islamic Studies Online*, 2019), online: www.oxfordislamicstudies.com/article/opr/t125/e1589; see also Kristen Stilt, *Islamic Law in Action: Authority, Discretion and Everyday Experiences in Mamluk Egypt* (Oxford: Oxford University Press, 2011) [*Law in Action*] at 42.

sometimes referred to as 'market inspectors' since they were empowered to deal with foul play with respect to weights and measures; fraud in sale and pricing of merchandise; and refusal to pay back debts.[29] The *muhtasib* operated under the authority of '*hisba*' (which might be literally rendered as 'accountability')[30] based on the Qur'anic injunctions 'commanding the right and forbidding the wrong'.[31] Wael Hallaq talks about how the work of the *qadi*, the *mazalim* courts, and the *muhtasibs* can all be seen as part of a 'Circle of Justice' in which justice was required to sustain the conditions for a prosperous society.[32] I wish to draw out two points from considering these institutions. First, I note the different offices through which justice was supposed to be effectuated and the emphasis that this gave to the practical and applied aspects of the ethos of justice. Second, the values associated with *adl* and *qist* – such as fairness, balance, and integrity – would have been a key component of the orientation of the justice-providing officials. The Qur'anic and Shari'a norms thus provided 'an unwavering standard of justice'[33] for the legal tradition and legal activity.

Indeed, one can find similar concerns operating today. John Bowen describes the settlements of an inheritance case in the Shari'a courts in Indonesia. To simplify, these cases involved the distribution of land between male and female heirs on the basis that the heirs had come to a mutual agreement between themselves on who would get what parcels of land. In one case it transpired that the male heir (a son) had been given a vastly larger piece of land as compared to the female heirs (daughters) under the 'agreement'. In looking at this distribution, the court found that the disparity in distribution meant that there really could not have been agreement between the heirs because the distribution was just too unequal for that to make sense.[34] In commenting on these three basically similar fact pattern cases and the approach of the Indonesian courts toward them, Bowen notes that the judges drew on two social norms: 'their own ideas of equality and fairness and their assumptions about the ideas held by daughters at the time of the earlier division'. He further notes that the judges might have reasoned otherwise 'within an Islamic framework', but the fact that they chose to decide the way they did is illustrative of the capacity to reach different decisions within the same framework. Most importantly for our purposes is the matter of where the judges were getting their ideas: from where did the judges derive these ideas of equality and fairness? The answer is that one can find such ideas in the traditions of Islamic jurisprudence, in norms of Gayo adat (local customary norms), and in the general values of gender equality that have served as a ground for a number of Indonesian reinterpretations of Islamic law.[35] Bowen concludes his chapter by noting that this style of reasoning 'has much in common with a style of reasoning about Islamic law that I frequently encounter in Takengen and Jakarta'.[36]

[29] *Shari'a, supra* note 27, at 210. See also *Law in Action, supra* note 28, for a more detailed account of the several activities that muhtasibs would undertake.

[30] Sami Zubaida, *Law and Power in the Islamic World* (London: IB Tauris, 2005) at 58–60.

[31] For a detailed discussion of the literature on this concept see Michael Cook, *Commanding Right and Forbidding Wrong in Islamic Thought* (Cambridge: Cambridge University Press, 2000).

[32] *Shari'a, supra* note 27, at 199 and 211.

[33] *Shari'a, supra* note 27, at 211.

[34] John R. Bowen, 'Fairness and Law in an Indonesian Court' in Muhammad Khalid Masud, Rudolph Peters, and David S. Powers, eds., *Dispensing Justice in Islam: Qadis and their Judgments* (Leiden: Brill, 2006) 139 [*Fairness and Law*] at 140.

[35] Ibid.

[36] *Fairness and Law, supra* note 34, at 141.

Bowen's description is interesting because, like Rosen's observations in Arab societies, he notes the mix of values and considerations that are at play, and how these are undergirded by a practical sense of fairness and equality that has at least partial rooting in the classical Islamic tradition. In this respect, we can see how the tradition furnishes 'ethos of justice' normativity that can be called upon. In addition, Bowen's observations of the way in which resolutions based on equity and fairness are present in contemporary Indonesian Shari'a court practice resonate with the historical practices of justice we have looked at and the importance of the ethos of justice discussed earlier.

To this may be added the observations in this volume from Euis Nurlaelawati's chapter, which begins by noting that '[a]ccess to justice has been a central concern of Indonesia' but then details the structural and other challenges confronting those engaged in Islamic lawyering in the Indonesian system. Nurlaelawati's chapter thus highlights the issues in Indonesia that inhibit the realization of an Islamically grounded ethos of justice in practice but also its normative presence.

V. FROM ETHOS OF JUSTICE TO ACCESS TO JUSTICE

If I am correct in reading the importance of the pursuit of justice in both a theoretical as well as an applied sense as part of the Muslim legal traditions, this surely must lead to the importance of access to justice, here understood as the availability to seek out justice-rendering institutions, whether these are courts or other forums.

Again, we can begin with history. Hallaq elaborates on the type of procedure used in *qadi* courts and states that 'equity was of the essence'. Furthermore, he describes the modes to ensure that fairness and decorum were maintained. These included a prohibition on gifts and bribes, the capacity to charge appropriate court fees, recusal of the judge in cases involving relatives or friends, the presence of legal scholars (jurisconsults) in the court presumably to ensure normative integrity, the capacity to review a predecessor's decisions and to have the judge's decisions reviewed by his (since the judge would almost always have been male) successors, as well as, once out of office, for the judge to have to account for any misconduct and face justice as a normal defendant in such an instance.[37] In addition, emphasis was placed on the quality and reliability of testimony and, within the overarching moral hermeneutic, oaths were used to attest to truth where other evidence was not producible.[38] These practices and values speak to a concern with ensuring that fair procedure was followed in formal court processes and that the courts and judges operated with integrity, providing access to justice rather than working as unprincipled tools of control.

Courts, however, were not the only forums for the resolution of disputes. Muslim legal traditions have long recognized mediation and the use of arbitrators.

With the advent of Islam, the values of mediated and amicable settlement that were familiar in the pre-Islamic milieu were not just validated, but enhanced and reinforced by receiving Qur'anic sanction. Both the use of amicable settlement involving mediation (*sulh*) and the use of arbitration (*takhim*) are noted in the Qur'an. The Qur'an makes reference to the concept of *sulh*, saying: 'And if a woman fears cruelty or desertion on her husband's part, there is no sin on them both if they make terms of peace between themselves; and making peace [*sulh*] is better'

[37] *Shari'a, supra* note 27, at 343.

[38] *Shari'a, supra* note 27, at 348–53.

(Q4:128). And also, 'The believers are nothing else than brothers [in the Islamic religion]. So make reconciliation [*sulh*] between your brothers, and fear Allah, that you may receive mercy' (Q49:10).

Sulh therefore is presented as both a legitimate and even a desirable form of settlement, and indeed the maxim 'amicable settlement is best' (*al-sulh khayr*)[39] or that amicable settlement is the best verdict (*al-sulh sayyid al-ahkam*) captures the notion that, as Ann Black et al. have put it, 'Sulh is not only regarded as an accepted method of dispute resolution within the Islamic justice system, but for some is seen as the "ethically and religiously superior" means of settling disputes.'[40] So, too, the use of arbitrators and arbitration [*takhim*] is mentioned in the Qur'an: 'If you fear breach between them [husband and wife] appoint two arbiters, one from his family, and the other from hers. If they wish for peace, Allah will cause their conciliation. For Allah has full knowledge and is acquainted with all things' (Q4:35).

It is important to note, as one can see in the verse above, that arbitration was not conceived, as it seems to be in the contemporary context, as distinct and independent from attempts at conciliation. Rather these processes could work simultaneously and in a complementary fashion.

The Qur'anic ethos of amicable settlement was complemented by early practice, including of the Prophet Muhammad himself, of mediation or mediation-cum-arbitration of disputes. Indeed, this too has a Qur'anic grounding from Qur'an 4:59, which says: 'O you who believe, obey Allah and obey the Messenger and those charged in authority from amongst you. If you differ in anything among yourselves, refer it to Allah and His Messenger, if you do believe in Allah and the Last Day. This is best and most suitable for final determination.' The Prophet as well as early leaders of the Muslim community after him served as mediators for private and public disputes and spoke of the virtue of *sulh*. The limits of amicable settlement were also identified in this early period with the Caliph Umar (the second caliph after the Prophet) and his view that amicable settlement was fine but it could not be agreed to make licit the illicit, or illicit the licit.[41]

Mediation, conciliation, and arbitration have thus been a fundamental part – and not just a recent addition – of the pre-Islamic and Islamic systems of dispute settlement. They have been sanctioned by past and continuing practice and by the Qur'anic text and are thus considered virtuous parts of the ethos of the Islamic system of justice.

This said, we should not be anachronistic. We have seen an emphasis in the Islamic legal tradition on having courts operating with appropriate procedure and integrity and within the ethos of justice, and, in addition, outside the courts, the encouragement of fair and amicable settlement or arbitration. It would be too much of a stretch, however, to see these emphases as expressive of a norm of access to justice as this phrase is understood in contemporary thinking. However, what the tradition does seem to tell us is that forums for justice – *qadi* courts, *mazalim* courts, mediation, or arbitration – were indeed recognized as important. Justice was not just a

[39] From the above-referenced Qur'anic verse 4:128 but differently translated as: 'And if a woman fears from her husband contempt or evasion, there is no sin upon them if they make terms of settlement between them – and settlement (*sulh*) is best.'

[40] Ann Black, Hossein Esmail, and Nadirsyah Hosen, *Modern Perspectives on Islamic Law* (Cheltenham: Edward Elgar, 2013) at 15.

[41] Frank Vogel, *Islamic Law and Legal System: Studies of Saudi Arabia* (Leiden: Brill, 2000) at 153.

theoretical (or indeed theological) concern, but rather had to be applied – and here access was significant. This is borne out by other chapters in the volume.

For instance, Kerstin Steiner's chapter on Malaysia speaks about how the judge in the Shari'a system acts in a more facilitative/mediator role when compared to what one would expect of a 'regular' common law judge. She also highlights how the provision of legal aid is employed in the country, including in the Shari'a (Malaysian rendering 'Syariah') system, and the challenges posed by legal aid limitations. Of course, it cannot be suggested that legal aid provisions in Malaysia, which is a Muslim majority country with Islam as the religion of the federation, have emerged solely out of Islamic concerns or motivations. However, these provisions can at least be viewed as not inconsistent with, and perhaps even facilitative of, the Islamic ethos of justice. In the case of Singapore, where there is no Muslim majority population, the Administration of Muslim Law Act[42] establishes a Shari'a court system and, as Ahmad Nizam explains in his chapter, cases can involve the use of arbitrators (*hakams*).

At one level, these examples show how certain institutional forms, such as the use of arbitration and the way in which judges operate in Shari'a courts, have continued over time as part of the Islamic legal tradition. I would argue that they also demonstrate the concern within this tradition to make sure that there are forums for the redress of claims. In any system which is influenced by Islamic legal traditions – and the ethos of justice – whether this is Malaysia, Indonesia, or Singapore, the doing of justice and the manifestation of fairness and equity will be an important normative value, even if it is not always realized in practice. It is here that we can develop the importance of access to justice as this is understood in contemporary terms.

This Islamic access to justice would have two dimensions. First, it would be about having the appropriate institutions and offices established, whether these are courts with judges-cum-mediators or the use of arbitrators, etc. These 'formal' institutions have been part of the historical experience of Muslim societies and, in common with other contexts, are basically necessary as venues for claims and disputes.

Second, and perhaps more distinctively, an Islamic understanding of access to justice would place emphasis on the normative values of fairness and equality that are ingrained in the Qur'anic terminology of *adl* and *qist* (and their homologues). Thus, access to justice will, of course, need institutions and procedures, but these will be overshadowed in importance by achieving the appropriate manifestation of *adl/qist*. Therefore, an Islamic understanding of access to justice may be less formalistic, or at least less concerned to see justice as essentially a procedural matter, and more concerned to get fair outcomes based on the particular situation and particular relations at play. This orientation can explain the observations of both Rosen and Bowen about how they have seen judges actually work. Rather than seeing the judges acting haphazardly or informally, however, we can say that their work is fundamentally motivated by the normative values that are part and parcel of the *adl/qist* understanding of justice in its Islamic articulation.

Another set of issues regards practice before the Shari'a courts and specifically whether this is open to non-Muslims. Relevant practices will vary across different jurisdictions. The case of the three South East Asian neighbouring countries of Singapore, Malaysia, and Indonesia, each of which has Shari'a or religious courts and two of which have Muslim majorities, illustrates this national variation. While the Shari'a courts are there to deal with Muslim parties, non-Muslim

[42] *Administration of Muslim Law Act*, Singapore 1966, Chapter 3, as amended 31 October 2009.

counsel may appear before these courts in Singapore and Indonesia – the world's most populous Muslim majority nation – but may not appear before the Shari'a courts in Malaysia.[43] Of course, representation has an impact on access to justice so this point is germane to the contents of this volume.

VI. CONCLUSION

Justice is a key concept and value in Islam. Its salience is grounded in the Qur'anic text, in the 'beautiful names' and in accounts of the practice of the Prophet Muhammad and some of his successors. Through these normative sources, we see justice elaborated as an emphasis on fairness, equity, and integrity. As Majid Khadduri has noted, 'despite diversity of standards, the believers maintain that a higher standard of justice must be found, consisting of a higher order of norms and virtues which mankind aspires to realize on Earth'.[44] History tells us that justice was also to be an applied value, something practical and lived, and hence that attention was paid to the delivery of justice via institutions like courts, to the use of mediation or, failing this, arbitration, and to the articulation of norms of conduct for judges and administrators, and, if the need arose, to establishing institutional means by which to hold officials accountable for their actions. These institutional forms have not been fixed but have, to quote Khadduri again, accommodated to 'changing conditions which enabled its [Islam's] standard of justice to endure up to the modern age'.[45]

Implicit in all of the above has been the importance of access to justice. After all, if justice is supposed to be lived then it must be applied and there must be ways and places for its application. Access to justice by means of ensuring there are venues where people can go to seek justice and that these operate fairly and with integrity is thus not novel for Islamic legal traditions. Indeed, this continues today through a variety of means in contexts in which Islamic law is present. Examples include Shari'a courts in Malaysia and Singapore, the still-present use of arbitrators, the mediating role of judges, as well as very modern structures such as the provision of legal aid to help litigants have their day in court. However, it is the ethos of justice and the normative values of fairness and equity – values that reach far back to the beginning of the story of Islam and that come out of its most sacred sources – that fundamentally define access to justice in Islam. For institutions as well as for individuals (whether officials or not) it is the pursuit of these ends that ultimately grounds access to justice in Islam.

[43] In Malaysia this was established by *Majlis Agama Islam Wilayah Persekutuan* v. *Victoria Jayaseele Martin* [2016] 2 MLJ 309.

[44] Majid Khadduri, *The Islamic Conception of Justice* (Baltimore: Johns Hopkins University Press, 1984) at 227.

[45] Ibid.

14

Lawyering in Indonesia's Religious Courts: Legal Aid, Procedural Justice, and Pragmatism

*Euis Nurlaelawati**

Abstract

This chapter analyses the practice of lawyering in Indonesia's religious courts and focuses on the role that lawyers play in the creation of justice. The chapter also seeks to explore the extent to which the state's programme of providing legal aid has contributed to the realization of justice for litigants, particularly poor people. The chapter argues that while some litigants in Indonesian religious courts appear to benefit from lawyer strategies tailored to particular disputes, there is evidence that lawyer pragmatism, in which lawyers are more concerned with fees for their legal assistance to litigants than with respect for law and justice, interferes with the accomplishment of justice for the client. The bureaucratic orientation of first instance religious courts, one that prioritizes procedural justice, also acts as a barrier to justice, because it limits lawyers' contributions to a well-informed legal decision. Bureaucratization also poses obstacles to access to justice for poor persons in the context of legal aid, because undue demands for documentation from legal aid applicants creates opportunities for corruption and cuts off the most vulnerable applicants.

I. INTRODUCTION

Access to justice has been a central concern of Indonesia, one reflected in the Indonesian Constitution since the state was founded.[1] In addition to other actors, lawyers play an important role in providing access to justice, in non-religious and religious courts.[2]

There is little research on Islamic lawyering in Indonesia, particularly on the role of lawyers in creating justice for Muslim litigants in religious courts. Many bachelor theses have been written

* The author would like to thank Helena Whalen-Bridge for her invaluable remarks and reviews on the chapter draft. The author would also like to thank the staff and lawyers of 'Afta and Bothers' law firm, all the other lawyers interviewed for this chapter, for their interviews, and my assistant researchers, Kholifatun Nur Mustofa and M. Fahmi Ahmadi, for their assistance and help during the fieldwork.

[1] *Constitution of the Republic of Indonesia of 1945* (as amended 19–21 October 2019) (the Second Amendment), Article 28 (D), which states that 'every person has the right to recognition, guarantees, protection, and fair legal certainty and equal treatment before the law'.

[2] I use the term 'religious court' as the English translation of the Indonesian term 'Pengadilan Agama', in which 'Pengadilan' indicates Muslims.

on the practice of Islamic lawyering, but they have not discussed the actual practices in place. In an academic article, Lukito addressed the recruitment process of Islamic lawyers, the education provided for the lawyer profession, the development of lawyers' careers, and the organization of Islamic lawyers, but he did not consider their contribution to the creation of justice.[3] In other research, Lukito discussed the struggle of Islamic lawyers for recognition equal to their colleagues practising in civil courts. Regarding the establishment of the Indonesian Association of Islamic Advocates (*Asosiasi Pengacara Syariah Indonesia*), Lukito argued that Islamic lawyers have been recognized in Indonesia as entitled to normative equal footing with civil lawyers, and this is why they have been allowed to practise in civil courts, just as civil lawyers are allowed to practise in religious courts.[4] This research discussed the attempt of the association to create justice for Islamic lawyers, but it did not discuss the sort of justice lawyers are responsible for or tend to bring about.

Focusing on cause lawyers, Lindsey and Crouch have discussed the fluid and dynamic nature of cause lawyering in Indonesia. They observed that cause lawyers pursued a long-standing and elusive objective of a united and disciplined bar, but that their efforts failed to unite lawyers and remake them as a single profession. They also argue that cause lawyers confronted reform fatigue and political disappointment, as illustrated by Munarman, who transformed from being a supporter of pluralism and tolerance to becoming an outspoken opponent of pluralism and tolerance, reflecting a broader rupture in wider legal and political reform movements.[5] This research is not directly concerned with access to justice, although it highlights the relevance of the practice of lawyering to the realization of social legal justice in Indonesia.

To analyse the degree to which women's rights to property were protected in religious courts, Amalia observed the communication of litigants with their lawyers. Taking four examples of inheritance cases involving lawyers, she argued that lawyers have different attitudes and motivation in becoming a lawyer. As these cases concerned property with obvious economic value, many lawyers exercised their roles in ways that brought themselves an economic profit which might disadvantage their clients, by for example negotiating with the lawyers of the other side to benefit the lawyers on both sides.[6] Amalia's work, although it does not use the term access to justice, is more relevant to this chapter's focus on how lawyers contribute to or undermine access to justice, and it will be addressed further.

This chapter aims to examine the role of Islamic lawyers in providing access to justice for Muslims within religious courts. Analysis is based on a literature review, legal analysis, and data gathered from field investigation via: interviews with Islamic lawyers, judges, and litigants; observation of case hearings involving lawyers; and analysis of decisions in cases assisted by lawyers. Eleven Islamic lawyers and four judges, in the religious courts of Jogjakarta, Jakarta, and the cities surrounding Jakarta, were interviewed.[7] Twenty-two decisions in which litigants were assisted by lawyers were analysed.

The chapter identifies the kind of cases that are mostly assisted by lawyers in religious courts, i.e. those of divorce and property (whether jointly owned or inherited), and investigates

[3] Ratno Lukito, 'The Training, Appointment and Supervision of Islamic Lawyers in Indonesia' (2012) 21:1 *Pacific Rim Law & Policy Journal* 65 [*Training, Appointment and Supervision*] at 65–83.

[4] Ratno Lukito, 'Leveling the Unleveled? Syariah Advocates' Struggle for Equality in Indonesian Legal Pluralism' (2011) 49:1 *Al-Jami'ah Journal of Islamic Studies* 87 at 102–3.

[5] Tim Lindsey and Melissa Crouch, 'Cause Lawyers in Indonesia: A House Divided' (2013) 31:3 *Wisconsin International Law Journal* 620 at 622.

[6] Nanda Amalia, 'Inheritance for Women: The Role of Lawyers in Women's Access and Rights' in John R. Bowen and Arskal Salim, eds., *Women and Property Rights in Indonesian Islamic Legal Contexts* (Leiden: Brill, 2019) [*Inheritance for Women*] at 69–78, 82.

[7] The interviews were done with the consent of the interviewees and were conducted under a formal letter of permission issued by Al Jami'ah State Islamic University Research Centre.

contributions by lawyers and the sort of justice they help to create. The chapter also identifies some challenges faced by lawyers when they help justice seekers secure their legal rights. The chapter argues that while litigants in Indonesian religious courts appear to benefit from lawyer strategies tailored to particular disputes, there is evidence that lawyer pragmatism, in which lawyer concern for fees is elevated above respect for the law, interferes with the accomplishment of justice for the client. The bureaucratic orientation of first instance religious courts that prioritizes procedural justice also acts as a major barrier to reaching the best, most well-informed decisions. Bureaucratization poses further obstacles to access to justice for poor persons in the context of legal aid, because undue demands for documentation from legal aid applicants create opportunities for corruption and cut off the most vulnerable applicants.

II. ISLAMIC LAWYERING IN INDONESIA

The practice of lawyering in Indonesia began in the colonial period, and western traditions of lawyering have helped shape the practice of law in Indonesia. In the Dutch colonial period, lawyers practising in the courts for Dutch people were Dutchmen with a master's degree in law, while in *Landraad*, the civil court for Indonesians, representatives were Indonesian people with no academic degree in law, called *Pokrol Bambu*.[8] The practice of *Pokrol Bambu* was also seen in religious courts, *Priesterraad*.

After Indonesia started to adopt modern systems of lawyering, legally trained persons were recruited to become lawyers, and litigants started to turn to representatives who were formally educated. The practice of *Pokrol Bambu* in *Landraad* disappeared in the 1960s, although *Priesterraad* or religious courts continued this practice until the 1970s.[9] More modern lawyering practices became established in the religious courts only after the Religious Judicature Act was promulgated in 1989.[10] While the Act does not clearly govern the matter of lawyering, it nevertheless marked a turning point in the development of advocacy in the religious courts, because the Act, which was amended in 2009 through the Religious Judicature Act No. 50,[11] put the religious courts on an equal footing with the civil courts. For example, Articles 60B and 60C state that every justice seeker has the right to legal assistance, and Article 12B states that religious courts as other domains of the judiciary are under the auspices of the Supreme Court.

In the years preceding 2003, there were serious debates regarding the training and requirements for advocates, particularly regarding Islamic law schools as opposed to law schools in general. It was determined that law school graduates could become advocates and practise in both civil and religious courts,[12] but the reverse was not true.[13] Graduates from Islamic law

[8] Daniel S. Lev, 'Colonial Law and the Genesis of the Indonesian State' (1985) 4 *Indonesia* 57 at 68; Daniel S. Lev, *Bush-Lawyers in Indonesia: Stratification, Representation, and Brokerage* (Berkeley: Law and Society Program Working Paper No. 1 1973); and *Training, Appointment and Supervision*, *supra* note 3, at 67.

[9] Daniel S. Lev, *Legal Evolution and Political Authority in Indonesia: Selected Essays* (The Hague: Kluwer Law International, 2000) at 143.

[10] *Religious Judicature Act*, Indonesia, Law No. 7/1989 (as amended 29 October 2009) [*Religious Judicature Act*].

[11] Second Amendment to Act No. 7 of 1989 on Religious Judicature, Indonesia, No. 50/2009 (29 October 2009).

[12] See Regulation of the Supreme Court, PMA No. 33/2016, regarding the Academic Titles for Graduates of Islamic Universities.

[13] One of the Supreme Court's Circular Letters for the recruitment of clerk positions in 2017 stated that there were 100 positions to be filled in both Islamic and civil courts, and that while the position of clerk in the civil court could only be filled by alumni with the title of *Sarjana Hukum* (Bachelor of (Civil) Law), those positions to be filled in Islamic courts could be filled by alumni of both schools of laws, with either the title of *Sarjana Hukum* or *Sarjana Hukum Islam* (Bachelor of Islamic Law).

schools could only become an advocate and practise in religious courts. Criticism of this position arose from graduates and members of Islamic law schools. They complained about the restricted opportunities given to Islamic law school graduates flowing from the inability to practise in civil courts. In 2003, the government issued a rule which made it possible for graduates from Islamic law schools to apply for the position of advocate.[14] In the same year, an organization for advocates practising in religious courts was established, the Indonesian Association of Islamic Advocates ('APSI'). APSI became the first, and the only officially recognized, association or bar for advocates practising in religious courts. It charges its members IDR350,000 (US$25.07)[15] for three years.[16] In practice, client opportunities for these advocates are more limited, but the ability to practise in other courts has opened up more prospects for them. In terms of restricting rights of access to the religious courts, there have not been any arguments that only lawyers graduating from Islamic law faculties should be allowed to practise in religious courts. Lawyers graduating from Islamic law faculties have been fighting for a right of access to the civil courts equal to their colleagues from civil law faculties. In their fight to get into the civil courts, they could not say that the lawyers graduating from civil faculties were not allowed to practise in the religious courts.

Currently, lawyers and advocates in Indonesia must be law school graduates. The degree in law must be from one of the following institutions: a faculty of law, a faculty of Sharia, an Institute of Military Law, or an Institution of Police.[17] In order to be admitted to practise law, graduates must first join the Special Education for Advocate Profession (*Pendidikan Khusus Profesi Advokat*). A number of rules apply to trainees, including the requirement to attend 80 per cent of the training sessions. After the sessions, applicants take the test of advocate profession (*Ujian Profesi Advokat*). When they pass the test, they are required to do an internship for a minimum of two years with an advocate or law firm. The requirements do not end there, as the successful trainee must pass an exam given by a bar association to be named an advocate. The oath that advocates take says that lawyers shall be just, responsible, reliable, and shall not give rewards to judges to win cases.[18]

Membership in a bar association is obligatory for all advocates. After being sworn, applicants must apply for a bar association membership, for which they pay IDR500,000 (US$35.82). Besides the fee for the membership application, applicants must also pay IDR50,000 (US$3.58) per month for membership. The payment should be made for the coming two years, and is therefore equivalent to IDR600,000 (US$43) per year, or IDR1,200,000 (US$86.01) for two years.[19] It has been reported that, as the payment was not that well thought out by senior

[14] See *Law on Advocate Profession*, Indonesia, Law No. 18/2003 [*Law on Advocate Profession*], Article 2(1), which states that an applicant can be appointed as an advocate if they graduated from law school and have been trained in an institute of advocate profession; see also *Training, Appointment and Supervision, supra* note 3, at 68

[15] XE Currency Converter, online: www.xe.com/currencyconverter/convert/?Amount=350000&From=IDR&To=USD. Unless another reference was cited, US$ denominations in the chapter were derived from www.xe.com at the time of publication; they are intended for general reference and may have been rounded up or down for ease of reference.

[16] Interview with CHA (1 July 2020, Jakarta) (via phone) [*Interview with CHA*], and interview with FLH (3 July 2020, Yogyakarta). FLH mentioned that the fees charged by APSI are less than those of PERADI, and that the small amount charged is to accommodate the burden to be borne by the junior advocates who have just started practising.

[17] *Law on Advocate Profession, supra* note 14, Article 2(1) of Clarification to the Law.

[18] *Law on Advocate Profession, supra* note 14, Article 4(1).

[19] *Interview with CHA, supra* note 16; see also Himpunan Konsultan Hukum Pasar Modal, Persyaratan Anggota (Membership Qualifications), online: https://hkhpm.com/persyaratan-anggota/, and PERADI, Pendaftaran Online dan Formulir Manual (Application by Online and Manual Forms), online: www.peradi.co/pendaftaran.

lawyers, the fee will be reduced to IDR25,000 (US$1.79) per month or even to IDR500,000 (US$35.82) for two years.[20]

As of 2019, there were about 50,000 registered lawyers or advocates in Indonesia.[21] There are more lawyers than judges in Indonesia,[22] in part because, while judges are recruited based on the number of cases to be resolved, the number of courts, and the budget, lawyers are recruited based on community demand and interest from law students. The number of lawyers is not considered to be adequate for the huge number of Indonesian citizens, i.e. 269 million.[23] In 2016, the Chief of the Department of Law and Legal Drafting of the advocate association PERADI, Simanjuntak, said that Indonesia needs 500,000 lawyers for the existing number of Indonesian citizens,[24] and with the number being 50,000 in 2019, more lawyers are still needed.

III. STATE-SUBSIDIZED LEGAL AID: POSBAKUM AT RELIGIOUS COURTS

Legal assistance for litigants has long been the subject of legal guarantees in Indonesia, indicating that legal assistance is necessary for those seeking justice. In fact, the very early law on the judiciary, Law No. 14 on Judicial Authority,[25] states that legal aid must be provided to individuals in the legal process. The point is revisited in the Criminal Procedure Code,[26] which enumerates the rights and obligations of advocates to provide legal assistance to individuals in both the investigation and trial process.

Under the new Law on Legal Aid enacted in 2011, legal aid is defined as 'legal assistance that is given by a legal aid provider free of charge to the recipient of legal aid'.[27] Legal aid is provided to 'poor' persons in criminal, civil, and administrative matters, and it applies to all courts, including religious courts.[28] Legal aid services are provided by a legal aid provider, who must be accredited

[20] See Aji Prasetyo, Polemik Iuran Anggota DPC Peradi (Polemics on Fee of PERADI Membership), *Hukumonline.com* (14 December 2018), online: www.hukumonline.com/berita/baca/lt5c1363918e7e9/polemik-iuran-anggota-dpc-peradi/.

[21] See Elias Sumardi Dabur, Tantangan Baru bagi Advokat Baru (New Challenges for Newly Sworn Advocates), *JPNN .com* (19 February 2020), online: www.jpnn.com/news/tantangan-bagi-advokat-baru; see also Fuadi, Peradi: Jumlah Advokat di Indonesia Belum Ideal (PERADI: the Number of Advocates is Not Yet Ideal), *Waspada Aceh* (23 July 2019), online: https://waspadaaceh.com/2019/07/23/peradi-jumlah-advokat-di-indonesia-belum-ideal/ [*Number of Advocates*].

[22] As of 2018 and 2019, there were about 7,000 judges in both first instance Islamic courts and civil courts; the number had once reached 11,000: see Mahkamah Agung: Indonesia Kekurangan 4.000 Hakim (Supreme Court: Indonesia Still Needs about 4,000 Judges), *CNN Indonesia* (19 July 2018), online: www.cnnindonesia.com/nasional/20180719065206-12-315260/mahkamah-agung-indonesia-kekurangan-4000-hakim. See also Mohammad Bernie, Ketua MA Curhat Masih Kurangnya Hakim di Indonesia (The Chief of Supreme Court is Worried about the Numerical Lack of Judges in Indonesia), *Tirto.id* (27 December 2019), online: https://tirto.id/ketua-ma-curhat-masih-kurangnya-jumlah-hakim-di-indonesia-ephz; and Jumlah Hakim di Indonesia tak Sebanding Jumlah Kasus (The Number of Judges in Indonesia is Not Equal to or Proportional to the Number of Cases), *IMCNews.ID* (27 February 2019), online: https://imcnews.id/jumlah-hakim-di-indonesia-tak-sebanding-dengan-jumlah-kasus.

[23] See *Number of Advocates*, *supra* note 21.

[24] Ibid. See also Boy Yendra Tamin, Idealnya Indonesia Punya 500 Ribu Advokat (The Ideal is that Indonesia has 500,000 Advocates), *Dunia Hukum*, online: www.boyyendratamin.com/2011/07/idealnya-indonesia-punya-500-ribu .html.

[25] *Law on Judicial Authority*, Indonesia, Law No. 14/1970 (as amended 29 October 2009) [*Law on Judicial Authority*].

[26] *Law on Criminal Procedure*, Indonesia, Law No. 8/1981.

[27] *Law on Legal Aid*, Indonesia, Law No. 16/2011 [*Law on Legal Aid*], Article 1(1).

[28] Government Regulation No. 83 of 2008, Requirements and Procedures for Free Legal Aid Provision; see also the series of four laws on courts: *Law on Judicial Authority*, *supra* note 25; *Law on the Anti-Corruption Court*, Indonesia, Law No. 49/2009; *Religious Judicature Act*, *supra* note 10; and *Law on State Administrative Courts*, Indonesia, Law No. 51/2009.

every three years.[29] Accreditation is awarded if the provider meets certain requirements; for example, it must be a legal entity (*badan hukum*) and have an office.[30]

To help realize access to justice, *Posbakum* (Legal Aid Posts) were established in 2010.[31] *Posbakum* were established to provide free access to a range of court services to poor people, including representation by a court-appointed lawyer. *Posbakum* are run by the government. They were established in both the general courts and religious courts, and they are a significant and influential presence in access to justice. *Posbakum* are accompanied by other legal aid posts, such as PEKKA (*Perempuan Kepala Keluarga*, or Female Heads of Households), run by an NGO supporting the empowerment of female households to secure their legal rights.[32]

As an example of *Posbakum* within the religious courts, the town of Cianjur's legal aid post provided legal assistance to more than 220 people, the majority of whom were women, within the first four months of operation in 2012.[33] This example is consistent with the general increase in the provision of legal aid to poor litigants after the Law on Legal Aid was introduced in 2011. In 2016, national statistics from Suyogi, based on *Kompas*, a national newspaper,[34] indicated that the total number of applications for legal aid was 6,695, comprising 5,592 litigation applications and 1,103 non-litigation applications.[35] Not all applications were approved. Only 4,132 out of the 6,695 applications were accepted for evaluation, with 3,335 approved and 797 rejected. The remaining 2,563 applications were not evaluated as they lacked some documents, and therefore, like the 797 rejected applications, these matters were tried by courts without legal assistance.[36] The rejection of applications is linked to strict regulations about who has the right to free legal aid assistance and the procedures required to get legal aid. For example, the Law on Legal Aid states that 'a person who receives legal aid has certain rights and obligations and must prove that he or she is poor by providing evidence of poverty from the *lurah*, the head of his or her village, or other local official.'[37]

Posbakum runs two different schemes of legal aid in religious courts. One scheme is run by the Supreme Court and the religious courts, and the second scheme is run by the Ministry of Law and Human Rights and the religious courts, with the help of law firms accredited by the government. The first scheme provides assistance only in appeals, while the second scheme assists litigants in litigation and appeals.

There are only a few law firms accredited by the government to participate in the second scheme. The Ministry of Law and Human Rights, acting under the Law on Legal Aid,

29 See *Regulation of Ministry of Law and Human Rights*, Indonesia, Law No. 3/2013 [*Regulation of Ministry of Law and Human Rights*], Article 2, Procedure of Verification and Accreditation of Legal Aid Institution.

30 *Law on Legal Aid*, *supra* note 27, Article 8(2), and *Regulation of Ministry of Law and Human Rights*, *supra* note 29, Article 12.

31 See *Guidelines for Provision of Legal Aid* (Supreme Court Circular Letter (SEMA), No. 10/2010).

32 Cate Sumner and Tim Lindsey, *Courting Reform: Indonesia's Islamic Courts and Justice for the Poor* (Lowy Institute for International Policy, 2010) [*Courting Reform*] at 42–4.

33 Pengadilan Agama Cianjur (Religious Court of Cianjur), Laporan Pelaksanaan Sidang Keliling, Prodeo dan Posbakum Tahun 2012 Bulan Januari s/d April 2012 (A Report on the Realization of Circuit Court, Prodeo (Fee Waiver Cases) and Legal Aid) (Pengadilan Agama Cianjur, 8 May 2012).

34 Irma Tambunan, Bantuan Hukum Gratis bagi Kaum Miskin (Free Legal Aid for Poor) *Kompas* (16 January 2017).

35 Suyogi Imam Fauzi and Inge Puspita Ningtyas, 'Optimalisasi Pemberian Bantuan Hukum Demi Terwujudnya Access to Law and Justice Bagi Rakyat Miskin' (Optimalization of Legal Aid for the Realization of Access to Law and Justice) (2018) 15:1 *Jurnal Konstitusi* 50 at 53.

36 Ibid.

37 *Law on Legal Aid*, *supra* note 27, Article 14.

established the standards that must be satisfied by legal aid providers. To be involved in the service of legal aid or to receive state funding from the Ministry of Justice and Human Rights and private sources, organizations are required to meet the standards and be accredited by a committee.[38] Based on the verification and accreditation process in 2013, only 310 organizations were selected to receive funds for legal aid services in Indonesia to practise in all domains of the judiciary, including religious courts. This number was considered small, particularly as the approved providers were concentrated in Java, with little to no coverage in areas such as Papua, Bali, Nusa Tenggara Timur, and Nusa Tenggara Barat. Even with a limited number of accredited organizations, the resources to support the approved providers are stretched thin. The Ministry of Law and Human Rights allocated IDR53 billion (US$3.7 million) to the 524 accredited legal aid organizations between 2019 and 2021.[39] This means that, on average, the state can only reimburse about six cases per organization per year. One of the most prominent local legal aid organizations, the Jakarta Legal Aid Institute (LBH Jakarta), receives and handles more than 1,000 cases per year,[40] which are covered by funding from legal aid as well as other sources.

The 'Afta and Brothers' Law Firm ('AFTA') is one of the few organizations approved to be a legal aid provider. In 2018, AFTA was approved by the Supreme Court to provide legal assistance to two religious courts in Jogjakarta and Sleman. A year before, in 2017, it was entrusted to deal with over 12 religious courts, including East and North Java, Kalimantan, and Sumatera. In 2018, AFTA provided legal aid services in 805 cases in Jogjakarta. Of these cases, 414 were wives petitioning to divorce their husbands, 162 were husbands petitioning to divorce their wives, 29 were parents requesting dispensation for their underaged children to marry, and the remaining 200 were various litigation matters such as inheritance and economic disputes.[41]

IV. WHAT TYPES OF CASES HAVE LAWYERS AND WHICH PARTIES USE THEM?

A. *Women's Fight for Divorce and Custody*

In Indonesia's religious courts, most cases are divorces, and divorce cases are mostly brought by women. As the most numerous kind of cases in religious courts, divorce presents an important example of how cases are processed and presented at court, and the extent to which women are able to access justice.

38 The Committee comprises: (i) members of government departments that govern affairs in the field of law and human rights; (ii) academics; (iii) community leaders; and (iv) members of institutions that provide legal aid: see National Law Development Agency, Petunjuk Pelaksanaan tentang Tata Cara Verifikasi dan Akreditasi Pemberi Bantuan Hukun serta Perpanjangan Sertifikasi (The Guidelines of the Procedures of Verification and Accreditation of Legal Aid Institution and of Extension of its Certification) (Nomor: PHN-HN.04.03-09 Tahun, 2018), and Cegah Organisasi Bantuan Hukum Abal-abal, BPHN Bentuk Tim Khusus (Anticipating Unqualified Legal Aid Institutions, BPHN Formed Exclusive Team), *Hukumonline* (14 July 2018), online: www.hukumonline.com/berita/baca/lt5b498a0eee3e9/cegah-organisasi-bantuan-hukum-abal-abal–bphn-bentuk-tim-khusus/.

39 Norman Edwin Elnizar, Pemerintah Sediakan 53 Miliar untuk Bantuan Hukum Masyarakat Marginal 2019–2021 (Government Allocates 53 Billion for Legal Aid Granted to Marginalized or Poor Society 2019–2021), *Hukumonline* (7 January 2019), online: www.hukumonline.com/berita/baca/lt5c33123bb3929/pemerintah-sediakan-53-miliar-untuk-bantuan-hukum-masyarakat-marginal-2019–2021.

40 See Demokrasi di Persimpangan: Catatan Akhir Tahun LBH Jakarta 2018 (Democracy at the Crossroads: Final Report Year 2018 LBH Jakarta) (LBH Jakarta, 2018) at 19–20, online: https://docplayer.info/122591947-Demokrasi-di-persimpangan-catatan-akhir-tahun-lbh-jakarta-2018.html.

41 Interview with TNC (30 January 2019, Yogyakarta) [*Interview with TNC*].

In 1974, a significant legal reform regarding divorce was introduced. Following the example of other Muslim countries, Indonesia passed a national Marriage Law in 1974[42] intending to improve women's access to the legal system and promote fair and equitable treatment in divorce. Both a husband who wants to divorce his wife, and a wife who wants to initiate a divorce, are required to appear in court and convince the judges in the panel that one or more of the grounds for divorce set out in the statute[43] are present. Judges who are satisfied that a valid ground exists may order a husband to utter the divorce formula or grant a wife's request for a *khul*ʿ (irrevocable divorce).[44]

Due to these changes, women began to make increased use of the courts, particularly for divorce. Earlier research by the author demonstrates that although the percentage differs from court to court, and changes from one year to another, this upward trend remains the same.[45] This data however does not mean that women are responsible for divorces, as the statistics merely tell us that most divorce petitions are brought by women.

In addition to presenting grounds for their divorce petition, women also deploy strategies to persuade judges to approve their petitions.[46] One strategy is to ask lawyers to help them with the procedure of divorce. Women who involve lawyers are not necessarily from the middle class, and they can include poor litigants, a trend that began when the state started to provide legal aid and also waived court fees which were otherwise payable. The author's investigation of hearings by Yogyakarta Religious Court on wife-petitioned divorces in 2016 demonstrated that four out of twelve petitions involved lawyers.[47] For this chapter, the author collected data on the involvement of lawyers in divorce cases petitioned by women via hearing observations in Bantul, Indonesia. In October 2018, the author attended a half day of hearings at the Bantul Islamic courtrooms, which dealt with thirteen divorce cases, seven of which were divorces petitioned by wives. Of these seven cases, three involved lawyers. The author was not able to confirm the financial condition of these three female litigants, but the portion of the decision which included a job description and the joint property to be divided suggests that they were middle class.

The involvement of lawyers is also evident in divorce petitions by men. In all six cases observed by the author in Bantul, lawyers were involved. The involvement of lawyers by male litigants in divorce cases can also be seen in Jogjakarta in 2016; out of eleven cases, three

[42] *Law on Marriage*, Indonesia, Law No. 1/1974 [*Law on Marriage*].

[43] The grounds for divorce specified in the Presidential Instruction No. 1/1991 on *Kompilasi Hukum Islam* [*Presidential Instruction on Kompilasi*] include: (1) illicit sexual relations by the wife or husband, intoxication, drug addiction, gambling, or the like; (2) the absence or disappearance of a spouse; (3) the imprisonment of a spouse; (4) cruelty by a spouse; (5) an acute illness that prevents a spouse from performing his or her duties as a husband or a wife; (6) a protracted dispute between spouses; (7) the husband's violation of a conditional *talak* (*taʿliq talaq*); and (8) the conversion of one spouse from Islam to another religion; see also *Presidential Instruction on Kompilasi*, Article 116.

[44] See *Presidential Instruction on Kompilasi*, *supra* note 43, Article 131.

[45] Euis Nurlaelawati, *Modernization, Tradition and Identity: The Kompilasi Hukum Islam and Legal Practice in the Indonesian Religious Courts* (Amsterdam: Amsterdam University Press, 2010) [*Modernization, Tradition and Identity*] at 34.

[46] Euis Nurlaelawati, 'Muslim Women in Indonesian Religious Courts: Reform, Strategies, and Pronouncement of Divorce' (2013) 20:3 *Islamic Law and Society* 242 at 261–8.

[47] See Euis Nurlaelawati and Stijn van Huis, 'The Status of Children Born Out of Wedlock and Adopted Children in Indonesia: Interactions between Islamic, Adat and Human Rights Norms' (2019) 34:3 *Journal of Law and Religion* 354 at 359. Regarding the involvement of lawyers in research conducted in Tangerang and Serang in 2009 and 2012, see Euis Nurlaelawati, 'Women's Financial Rights after Divorce', in John R. Bowen and Arskal Salim, *Women and Property in Indonesian Islamic Legal Context* (Leiden: Brill, 2019) 89 [*Women's Financial Rights*] at 91.

involved lawyers. Therefore, in divorce cases petitioned by both male and female litigants, lawyers appear to be involved.

In cases regarding the custody of children, the involvement of lawyers is also evident, particularly when custody is considered separately from divorce. In religious courts, custody cases can be resolved in separate proceedings or as part of the divorce proceedings.[48] Custody cases can be brought by either women or men.[49]

Custody of children is the responsibility of both parents.[50] Fathers are obliged to provide financial support for their children, and women have a right to receive financial maintenance from their ex-husbands.[51] Regulations on post-divorce rights are expanded further in the *Kompilasi*,[52] a legal reference provided by the state for Muslims, which follows the classical Islamic doctrine of giving mothers priority in the custody of minors. It grants children younger than 12 to their mothers, but gives freedom to children aged 12 or older to choose one of their parents to be their custodian.[53] The *Kompilasi* also states, however, that the right to custody can be transferred from one party to another to achieve the best interests of the children.[54]

In custody cases, women often face two kinds of problems at court. First, they run the risk of losing the right to be custodian, even though according to the law they have the right to custody of children under 12 years old, and they have equal rights as fathers to the custody of children over 12 years old following the children's choice. Problems arise particularly when the husband argues that the divorce is a result of the wife's alleged misbehaviour, and the judges agree with the husband and deny the wives custody. The second problem arises from the difficulty of executing the court decisions that grant wives custody.[55] Due to both problems, women ask lawyers to assist them.

The involvement of lawyers by women in custody cases heard separately from divorce cases is illustrated by two examples. The first case from Semarang involved a woman who sought custody of her two children under two years old, in which she, referring to the relevant law, argued that she had the right to the custody of the children. The matter was heard in the first instance court without a lawyer and dismissed. The case was then filed in the appellate court with a lawyer, and the decision was corrected by the appellate court judges in the woman's favour. In the second case, *Freederika* v. *Rudy*,[56] a man who had divorced his wife two years earlier petitioned for custody of his eight-year-old daughter in the religious court on the basis that the mother was not a religiously qualified custodian. The husband convinced the judges that his ex-wife was no longer Muslim as she had been close to a Christian man. The mother objected to the ruling and filed an appeal to the religious high court. In order to file the correct documents

48 *Religious Judicature Act*, *supra* note 10, Article 66(5).

49 See *Law on Marriage*, *supra* note 42, a national law to be referred to all Indonesian citizens, and the *Presidential Instruction on Kompilasi*, *supra* note 43, a special reference for Muslims.

50 *Law on Marriage*, *supra* note 42, Article 41(a).

51 *Law on Marriage*, *supra* note 42, Article 41(b).

52 *Presidential Instruction on Kompilasi*, *supra* note 43, Article 136.

53 *Presidential Instruction on Kompilasi*, *supra* note 43, Article 105.

54 Euis Nurlaelawati, 'Indonesia', in Nadjma Yassari, Lena-Maria Möller, and Imen Gallala-Arndt, eds., *Parental Care and the Best Interest of the Child in Muslim Countries* (The Hague: TMC Asser Press, 2017) [*Nurlaelawati on Indonesia*] at 68.

55 Euis Nurlaelawati, 'The Legal Fate of the Indonesian Muslim Women at Court: Divorce and Child Custody' in Tim Lindsey and Helen Pausacker, eds., *Law, Religion, and Intolerance in Indonesia* (London: Routledge, 2016) at 359.

56 Supreme Court Decision No. 382/K.AG/2012; the decisions of the lower courts in this case are No. 0936/Pdt.G/2011/PA.JS and No. 135/Pdt.G/2011/PTA.JK.

and convince the judges about her legal position, she paid a lawyer. Unfortunately, although the lawyers provided strong legal arguments, i.e. the award of custody should avoid discrimination and be based on the best interests of the child, the appeal was not approved. The mother did not give up, and she filed an appeal to the Supreme Court, which however affirmed the decisions of the lower courts, that the religion of the custodian is relevant and determinative in custodial issues. So, while the lawyer's arguments provided strong support for the mother's petitions, the ruling suggests, as I have argued elsewhere,[57] that great priority is given to religious protection.

B. *Complicated Disputes: Inheritance*

There are two types of inheritance cases in the religious courts, volunteer cases and contentious cases. Volunteer cases are matters of inheritance in which all the parties constitute petitioners and there are no disputes. The petitioners present the case to the court to receive a ruling confirming who the heirs are and what each of them is entitled to. Contentious cases involve petitioners and defendants who dispute a matter in the case. Lawyers are usually involved in contentious cases.

Inheritance cases are not numerous, but they have a consistent presence in religious courts. In the years 2002 to 2005, each court recorded the registration of from nine to twelve inheritance cases in their jurisdiction.[58] In 2018, one court in East Java recorded seven cases of inheritance.[59] The AFTA legal aid firm stated that they provided legal aid assistance to three contentious cases in 2018 within the Jogjakarta region. While the contentious cases are not numerous, they stand out because almost all of them involved lawyers.

One example of the kind of complexity these cases involve arose during the author's fieldwork for her PhD thesis in Cianjur. The deceased in the case was a husband. The case involved the husband's second wife and five children from two wives. Three children, one daughter and two sons, were from the first wife, who had died after the husband, and two children were from the second wife, who was still alive. In this case, the individual shares of the three children of the first wife, which included the inheritance shares of the three children as well as their mother, together with their mother's portion of the joint property, were each greater than the individual shares of the two children of the second wife. The two children, who received the smaller shares and who did not comprehend the Islamic law of the issue debated, were very upset with the result, and they regretted involving lawyers and even judges.[60]

A second case observed for this chapter involved a wife and two sons of the deceased. The first son had moved away from the family house, and he was worried about his share of the inherited wealth. The first son asked his mother and brother about the distribution of the wealth, and the mother replied that the entire wealth would be distributed only when the other son had a house to stay in. Years passed but the distribution had not been completed, and the first son became more worried, ultimately going to the court. Before he filed court papers, he went to a lawyer for assistance. The case was heard, and with the help of the lawyer, the first son insisted that the court issue a ruling stating the names of the heirs and the share of each heir, so that the first son knew he would be granted his share.[61]

[57] *Nurlaelawati on Indonesia*, *supra* note 54.
[58] *Modernization, Tradition and Identity*, *supra* note 45, at 203.
[59] Court of Purworejo, 2018 Statistical Data (copy on file with author).
[60] *Modernization, Tradition and Identity*, *supra* note 45, at 205.
[61] Interview with AS (30 January 2019, Jogjakarta); see also Decision No. 1450/Pdt.G/2016/PA.Smn.

V. DO LAWYERS HELP CREATE JUSTICE?

A. *Legal Arguments in Appeals*

Research for this chapter included analysis of court decisions, to assess whether lawyers made significant differences in legal arguments in the cases they were involved with compared to cases with no lawyer. This research indicated that lawyers did have an impact, particularly in cases of divorce, custody, and inheritance, and that although the lawyer's arguments did not necessarily influence the court's ruling, they made legal arguments stronger and helped litigants to understand legal rules better.

Two decisions are discussed here. The first was a divorce case,[62] a published matter available to the public, and it involved a number of laws rarely cited by litigants or judges, including the Law on the Elimination of Domestic Violence[63] and the Convention on the Elimination of All Forms of Discrimination against Women ('CEDAW').[64] The lawyer in this case elaborated the types of violence prohibited in the Law on the Elimination of Domestic Violence, including physical, sexual, mental, and economic violence. The lawyer argued that the woman had received mental violence through her husband's having a relationship with another woman, which then led her to petition for divorce. The lawyer stressed that the husband's attitude had also brought about neglect of his obligation to provide financial support for the wife.

A number of custody cases also support the value of lawyers' legal arguments. In one case, lawyers made the unusual argument that the difference of religion between a mother and her daughter was not grounds for the mother to be denied her right to custody, and that it constituted discrimination to rob the mother of her right due to her religiosity. While most lawyers practising at the Islamic courts tend to agree with the 1996 Supreme Court ruling that religion constitutes a determinative factor regarding custody,[65] this lawyer challenged it. Referring to the Law on the Protection of Children's Rights[66] and the Convention on the Rights of the Child ('CRC'),[67] he also questioned the nature of the justice provided by all the courts involved in custody decisions.

This small sample of divorce and custody cases illustrates that lawyers in religious courts can play a role in contributing to a just result. The lawyers in these cases cited a number of laws that have often been neglected by the judges,[68] such as the Law on the Protection of Children's Rights[69] and CEDAW.[70] These laws were issued to implement Indonesia's ratification of the CRC and CEDAW,[71] but they were overlooked by judges because, following ratification of the

[62] Case No. 0149/Pdt.G/2012/PA.YK; see also a decision from the appellate court of Semarang, Decision No. 273/Pdt.G/2017/PTA. Smg, where lawyers who helped a wife divorce her husband provided strong legal arguments and won the case.

[63] *Law on the Elimination of Domestic Violence*, Indonesia, Law No. 23/2004 [*Law on Domestic Violence*].

[64] *Convention on the Elimination of All Forms of Discrimination against Women* (CEDAW), Indonesia, Law No. 7/1984.

[65] See Decision 210/K.AG/1996.

[66] *Law on Child Protection*, Indonesia, Law No. 23/2002 [*Law on Child Protection*].

[67] *Convention on the Rights of the Child* (CRC), Indonesia, Law No. 44/25/1989, with effect from 20 November 1989.

[68] See Hotnida and Dewi Sukarti, 'Law in Action: Analisis Implementasi UU No. 23 Tahun 2002 pada Putusan Hakim dalam Perkara Hadhanah di Pengadilan Agama' (Law in Action: Analysis of the Implementation of Law No. 23 of 2002 in the Islamic Court Decisions on the Cases of Custody) (2010) 27:2 *Jurnal Alqalam: Jurnal Keagamaan dan Kemasyarakatan* 264, at 276–80.

[69] *Law on Child Protection*, *supra* note 66.

[70] *Law on Domestic Violence*, *supra* note 63.

[71] Interview with judges of Serang (September 2012, Tangerang and Depok).

two international covenants, unlike other Muslim countries such as Morocco,[72] Indonesia issued new laws rather than amending existing laws. Lawyers were required to point out the laws that the judges had not considered.

B. Lawyering Strategies Tailored to Religious Courts

In addition to strengthening legal arguments, lawyers have assisted parties in the religious courts by using strategies which are tailored to particular kinds of cases. Lawyers interviewed for the chapter stressed three strategies. First, lawyers simplify cases. Second, lawyers pair down the grounds of appeal. Third, lawyers attempt to mediate between the parties, particularly in inheritance and joint property cases, before submitting the cases to the court.[73]

1. Simplification of Cases

The first strategy of case simplification is most relevant in divorce petitions by wives. The law states that wives do not have rights to financial support as *mut'ah* (compensation or consolatory right) or as *nafkah* during the waiting period after divorce (*iddah*), but they may appeal for those rights, particularly when the basis giving rise to the divorce petition does not arise from the woman's side. Although judges will consider this plea, the relatively poor financial condition of the husband may prompt lawyers to advise wives to either decrease the amount of money requested or forgo the request altogether. In the lawyers' experience, demanding higher amounts of money interferes with the effectiveness of the petition. Another simplification strategy is that lawyers advise wives not to integrate the issue of children's custody into the case of divorce, particularly if the issue of custody is complicated.[74]

2. Lessening the Documentary Burden by Asserting Simple Grounds for Appeal

The second strategy, also relevant in cases of divorce petitions by wives, is a variation of the simplification strategy. When filing for divorce, both women and men have to state the grounds for their divorce petitions as specified in the 1974 Marriage Law[75] and the *Kompilasi*.[76] Many women relate several reasons for their divorce proposal, e.g., husbands having relationships with other women, extra-marital sexual intercourse, drug addiction, and cruel behaviour. Although all these grounds are listed in the law and could be presented as the basis of the petition, lawyers prefer to group them into the category of continuous dispute. This strategy lessens both the need to provide elaborate documents and the necessary procedures, which may not prevail. For example, extra-marital sexual intercourse is a valid reason for a divorce petition in religious courts, but it requires valid documents or proof, which may not exist. An important aspect of the applicable law is that if an accusation of *zina* (extra-marital sexual intercourse) as a basis for a petition of divorce is not proved, and the petition is

[72] See John Hursh, 'Advancing Women's Rights through Islamic Law: The Example of Morocco' (2012) *Berkeley Journal of Gender Law and Justice* 252 at 283; see also Euis Nurlaelawati and Muhrisun, 'Islam and Children's Rights: The Implementation of the Best Interest of the Child in Indonesia and Morocco' (Unpublished Research Report, Centre for Research, State Islamic University, Yogyakarta) (copy on file with author).

[73] *Interview with TNC, supra* note 41, and Interview with NZW (14 October 2018, Jakarta).

[74] *Interview with TNC, supra* note 41.

[75] *Law on Marriage, supra* note 42, Article 39.

[76] *Presidential Instruction on Kompilasi, supra* note 43, Article 116.

processed with the husband and wife condemning each other under God's words, the judges would decide the case under the category of *li'an*. This decision would bring the marriage to an end forever and leave the parties with no possibility to return to any marriage, even to remarry each other. Moreover, if an alleged but unproven allegation of *zina* resulted in a pregnancy, the allegation brings about the loss of the legal status of the child. Therefore, rather than asserting that reason in the divorce petition, lawyers prefer to assert continuous dispute as the ground for the divorce petition.[77]

3. Initial Mediation by Lawyers before Litigation

In addition to simplification strategies, lawyers take on another role to provide litigants with access to justice, that of mediator on behalf of their client. Mediation is a significant phase in trials in religious courts. Its significance can be traced from the establishment in 1954 of *Badan Penasihatan Pembinaan dan Pelestarian Perkawinan* (BP4) or the Institution of Consultation, Development, and Resolution of Marriages, in which couples wanting to dissolve a marriage were required to visit the Institution for a consultation.[78] Although the Institution continues to exist, its role has lessened as mediation has been formally integrated into trial. Since 2008, the mediation process has been regulated in detail, regarding, for example, the schedule of mediation and qualifications of mediators.[79] However, lawyers in religious courts do not so much try to mediate the entire dispute between the parties, although that may result, as attempt to lay the groundwork for a peaceful and conflict-free procedure in trial. This strategy was often used where joint property was being addressed in divorce cases. Lawyers usually advised both spouses to be lenient and agree to the amount of money to be shared, which would then be told to the judge. It appears that this strategy is consistent with the discretion exercised by judges to adapt to the economic situation of the husband.[80]

In this mediatory capacity, some lawyers may even appear to represent the opposing litigant. For example, when a divorce is initiated by a husband, but the wife has already agreed, lawyers sometimes ask the wife to act as the petitioner. This strategy is based on the lawyers' estimation of the judges' sensitivity to gender.[81] In the lawyers' view, it is much easier to process divorces petitioned by wives than petitions brought by husbands. So as not to negatively impact the wife who then serves as the petitioner, this agreement is coupled with the important stipulation that the fees of litigation will be paid by the husband.[82] In this context, lawyers served as initial mediators between the spouses and tried to contribute to what is called 'peaceful divorce', the approach desired by the formal mediators.[83]

77 *Interview with TNC*, *supra* note 41.

78 See Hisako Nakamura, *Divorce in Java: A Study of the Dissolution of Marriage among Javanese Muslims* (Gadjah Mada University Press, 1983) at 60–2; see also *Modernization, Tradition and Identity*, *supra* note 45, at 185; Rita Pranawati, 'Changes in Muslim Divorce Mediation in Indonesia: A Case Study of the Yogyakarta Religious Court' (2017) 4 *International Journal of Indonesian Studies* 31.

79 See Supreme Court Regulation No. 1/2008 on Mediation, Indonesia, Articles 5, 7, and 13.

80 See *Women's Financial Rights*, *supra* note 47, at 96–9.

81 See *Courting Reform*, *supra* note 32, at 18–35.

82 Interview with AS (16 October 2018, Jakarta) [*Interview with AS*].

83 See Rita Pranawati, 'Changes in Muslim Divorce Mediation in Indonesia: A Case Study of the Yogyakarta Religious Court' (2017) 4 *International Journal of Indonesian Studies* 31 at 41–2.

VI. SYSTEMIC CHALLENGES: BUREAUCRATIZATION AND LAWYER PRAGMATISM

Although lawyers play a significant role in access to justice in religious courts, by providing legal arguments and clearing procedural pathways, one major limitation of the justice lawyers can achieve for clients is that they are not allowed to debate or argue against the rulings and legal bases issued by judges.[84] All the lawyers interviewed for this chapter said that in court they play the role of the litigant's consultant, and they are not authorized to debate in trial. This point was confirmed by the judges interviewed for the chapter. They said that the issue at stake regarding legal assistance by lawyers is a formal one, and that any points regarding the material issue should be addressed in writing, not orally in court.[85] Disappointed lawyers are required to go to appellate courts to debate the ruling and fight for the result they think is just. Both lawyers and judges distinguish between *keadilan formil* (formal justice), understood as procedural requirements, and *keadilan materiil* (material justice), understood as actual justice in the case itself; the litigant's right to formal justice is met when the lawyer is present to help the case proceed and provide a legal basis in the appeal text, but he or she is not allowed to debate points of law or fact at the hearing itself in order to obtain material justice.[86]

Freederika v. *Rudy*, discussed above, is a good example of this difficulty. The lawyers in this case provided strong legal arguments that a mother who was an apostate, a convert from Islam to Christianity, should be awarded custody of her children. But although the argument was based on the concept of religious freedom mandated in the constitution and was put clearly in the appeal text, the mother failed at trial, and both the appellate and the Supreme Court held that a mother who was an apostate was not to be awarded the right to custody. The lawyers referred to a number of international legal standards, but the judges relied only on a decision issued by the Supreme Court which held that religion is determinative in awarding the right of child custody, and that a parent of a different religion from their child is prevented from receiving that right. In this case, the lawyer desired to raise questions and give arguments regarding the court's position. Nevertheless, he understood that in the vast majority of cases, a lawyer is viewed as a procedural consultant to the client, one not entitled to speak to the judge in court, or given chances to debate and argue against the ruling decided by the judges. This approach to lawyers in religious courts greatly weakens realization of access to justice, as it prohibits lawyers from engaging in the role they are expected to play.

This limitation of a lawyer's role in religious courts arises in part from the fact that the Indonesian legal system's method of resolving all disputes tends to be bureaucratic. Judges make substantive decisions on the law in pending cases, but in Indonesia bureaucracy often tends to dominate the process of dispute resolution. In the management of religious disputes, Sezgin and Kunkler argue that unlike India, which 'largely delegated the resolution of divisive religious questions to the courts, thereby contributing to the judicialization of religion', Indonesia opted for bureaucratization of religion and 'allocates the authority to a specialized agency to delineate what constitutes "religion" or "the religious"'.[87] Kunkler's characterizations are supported by this

[84] Interview with TNC and SP (30 January 2019, Jogjakarta), and Interview with NZW and AS (18 October 2018, Jakarta).

[85] Interview with MIW (12 December 2018, Jogjakarta) [*Interview with MIW*], and Interview with MN (18 October 2018, Jakarta) [*Interview with MN*].

[86] See Elisabeth Nurhaini Butarbutar, 'Konsep Keadilan dalam Sistem Peradilan Perdata' (Justice Concept in Personal Legal System) (2009) 21:2 *Mimbar Hukum* 203 at 365–7.

[87] Yuksel Sezgin and Mirjam Kunkler, 'Regulation of "Religion" and the "Religious": The Politics of Judicialization and Bureaucratization in India and Indonesia' (2014) 56:2 *Comparative Studies in Society and History* 448.

chapter's investigation of family issues in religious courts, where judges seem bound by the bureaucratic system, and which in turn decreases the effectiveness of their substantive decisions. One judge interviewed for the chapter said that as long as the lawyers met all the procedural requirements, the case would be well resolved.[88]

In addition to obscuring the basis of judicial decisions, the bureaucratization of justice in religious courts also lessens access to justice because it impedes effective usage of the government programme of free legal aid for poor people. Many applicants have found that the mechanism required to prove one is poor is overly bureaucratic, with burdensome procedural requirements and inflexible demands for papers and documents. Unrealistic eligibility requirements for clients means that many people who need legal aid continue to miss out. For example, as noted above, the poor must have an identity card and obtain approval from low-level government officials, such as the village head or equivalent official at the applicant's place of residence, to support their application and prove the costs of transportation and documents. While this procedure is intended to ensure that free legal aid is only provided to deserving applicants, the requirements have in some cases excluded undocumented poor persons and some of the most vulnerable members of Indonesian society – just the individuals the Law on Legal Aid was supposed to assist.[89] To some extent this administration process also exposes vulnerable applicants to bribery demands from the local offices dealing with the required letter of low-income status, which of course would hinder the creation of justice.

A different kind of challenge to access to justice is identified here as lawyer pragmatism, which some lawyers say applies to most lawyers. One lawyer interviewed for the chapter stated, 'there are two types of lawyers in Indonesia, idealist and pragmatist. Most of the lawyers have a pragmatic way of thinking.'[90] For example, most lawyers would take a case even if it conflicts with the laws fairly understood. In one case, the lawyer NZ helped a husband convince the court that he had sufficient reason to enter into a polygamous marriage and met the requirements set out in the laws, i.e. the husband had adequate financial resources, and he could treat his co-wives fairly. The lawyer knew the actual reason for polygamy, that the prospective wife was pregnant, and he also was aware that it was not a legal reason specified in the laws for the basis of the application, which include first, that the first wife had not given birth to a child, second, that she was seriously unhealthy, and third, that she could be regarded as not being able to perform her task as a wife.[91]

Judges interviewed for this chapter agreed with this characterization of lawyers. A judge from Jakarta said that lawyers act as a hired gun, and that most of the lawyers in the religious courts were money-oriented. In his view, most lawyers did not want to see the parties reconcile and settle their cases in a harmonious way. He supported his view by saying that many lawyers were not interested in the mediation process.[92] Although this characterization might not always be true, this view is consistent with what lawyers themselves said, that lawyering is a professional career, and that although they understand their duties as legal provider and justice helper, they needed to see their work be valued by the payment of fees.

These findings corroborate Amalia's observations in Aceh. Amalia observed three cases of inheritance in Aceh, and she argued that legal representation has not always guaranteed the

[88] *Interview with MIW, supra* note 85.

[89] See Aulya Rochman, 'Legal Aid Institutions as a State Solution for the Poor in Getting Legal Protection' (2020) 2:2 *Indonesian Journal of Advocacy and Legal Services* 214.

[90] *Interview with MN, supra* note 85.

[91] Interview with NZ (17 October 2018, Jakarta).

[92] *Interview with AS, supra* note 82.

litigants access to their rightful share of the inheritance. She suggested that some lawyers 'stand on two feet': the feet of the litigant they represent and the feet of the opposing litigant. She also described how in one case, both of the opposing parties 'were deeply dissatisfied with the attitude of the lawyer they had chosen. The plaintiff considered the lawyer to be purely profit oriented, seeking profit not only from his own client but also from the defendants, through collaboration with the lawyer of the defendant, who was actually his colleague.'[93] These lawyers, who were colleagues, understood that to allow one party to win would take more time in litigation, and that when one party wins it is only the lawyer of the winning litigant that would benefit financially. They therefore resolved the case more quickly and bargained for a result that benefited them both.

VII. CONCLUSION

Although Islamic lawyering was practised in the colonial period, it started to gain strength only after 1989, when religious courts were put on an equal footing with civil courts. Access to justice in the religious courts witnessed an important advance when legal assistance for the poor was acknowledged to be the government's responsibility and the government provided some funding. Legal aid is provided in civil and religious courts, and legal aid has increased access to justice in the religious courts. However, while legal aid has helped poor people gain better access to justice, it has quite significant flaws, e.g., the complicated mechanism required to obtain documents proving the applicant's poverty. A second barrier to access to justice is that in cases where a litigant has a lawyer, the bureaucratic nature of the religious court system is concerned more with *formiil* justice. In fact, although litigants benefited from the lawyers' legal assistance on procedural matters, litigants were often powerless on issues of substantive law, as lawyers are not able to engage in the advocacy role they were expected to play. Beyond these challenges, lawyers themselves display pragmatic attitudes toward the practice of law, which leads them to prioritize financial concerns over others. To improve access to justice in religious courts, therefore, a few reforms need to be undertaken. While the nature of justice realized in religious courts may hinder lawyers trying to obtain *materiil* (substantive) justice for their clients, and this barrier would be hard to overcome, mechanisms and procedures for legal aid access, particularly those regarding documents required for poor and vulnerable applicants, offer modifications which are necessary and more readily achievable.

[93] *Inheritance for Women*, *supra* note 6, at 81–2.

15

Access to Justice and Legal Aid in the Syariah Courts in Malaysia: A Colourful but Threadbare Patchwork System

*Kerstin Steiner**

Abstract

Malaysia has a plural legal system in which civil non-religious law[1] *and Islamic/ Syariah*[2] *law coexist and are adjudicated in different court systems. Indigent litigants with Syariah legal issues have some legal aid*[3] *available, but the legal aid system is a colourful patchwork of limited assistance, with the different coloured threads being the different programmes offered by numerous organizations linked to government, professional associations, and civil society. While there is this colourful patchwork system in place, it is threadbare in the sense that it offers quite limited assistance with different prerequisites for eligibility, with the result that some people in need of legal advice and representation will not receive it. This chapter critically examines the different schemes of financial legal aid that provide access to justice, with a focus on Malaysia's Syariah legal system. The chapter also reflects on how some structural aspects of the legal system, that is its plural and federal nature as well as the sentencing power, impact access to justice. It touches upon the contributions by lawyers as well as their professional associations to overcome these structural issues. It also reflects upon the legal and moral issues for lawyers representing criminal defendants in the Syariah criminal jurisdiction.*

I. SETTING THE SCENE: ISSUES OF LEGAL AID IN A PLURAL LEGAL SYSTEM

Malaysia's legal system consists of British common law inherited from the British colonial period and Syariah or Islamic law for Muslims in limited civil and criminal matters. As such there are numerous challenges to establish legal aid, including:

* The author is extremely grateful for the assistance of Zainah Anwar, Executive Director of Musawah, Shareena Sheriff, SIS Legal Manager, and Nik Shazarina, Advocacy, Legal Services & Research (ALSR), in helping me to access the Sisters in Islam material. I would also like to thank the Malaysian Bar for granting me access to some of their materials.

1 I use the term 'civil' non-religious legal system to describe the non-religious legal system in Malaysia. Sometimes this part of the Malaysian legal system is referred to as the secular legal system, but I prefer to avoid those terms given the dispute over the nature of Malaysia and whether it is an Islamic or a secular state: see Kerstin Steiner, 'Islamisierung des Rechtes in Malaysian' in Susanne Schröter, ed., *Normative Konflikte in Pluralen Gesellschaften* (Frankfurt: Campus Verlag, 2017) 255; and Kerstin Steiner, 'Malaysia at the Crossroads? The Never-Ending Discourse between Islam, Law, and Politics' (2018) 4:3 *Journal of Religious and Political Practice* 256.

2 In Malaysia, there are numerous local variations of spelling *syariah*, including *shari'a*, *syrie*, *syaria*, etc. The most common variant *syariah* is used throughout the chapter unless otherwise indicated.

3 Per usage in Malaysia, 'legal aid' refers to legal advice and legal representation for poor individuals, whether it is funded by the government or another source, and the chapter adopts this usage.

(1) the plural legal system, i.e. the necessity to offer aid in the civil non-religious and Syariah legal systems;
(2) the fact that consequentially, different organizations focus on different legal systems, such as civil non-religious or religious, and/or jurisdictions, i.e. civil and criminal, with the result that there is no dedicated comprehensive scheme for the Syariah legal system as such; and
(3) the use of different rules to determine eligibility, including different means and even some different merits tests, by the organizations that provide indigent legal aid.

This section will provide the backdrop for the following discussions of the different schemes. It will address the first issue, that of the plural legal system, as pertaining to the provision of legal aid.

Malaysia's society is multi-racial and multi-religious in nature. In terms of population percentages, the different religions comprise 61.3% Muslims, 19.8% Buddhists, 9.2% Christians, and 6.3% Hindus.[4] This diversity is also reflected in its legal system. Malaysia has a plural legal system in which civil non-religious law and Syariah law coexist.

Like the Syariah legal system, the civil non-religious legal system comprises both civil and criminal jurisdiction. In both systems, civil cases involve private disputes between persons or institutions, while criminal cases are initiated through the state and concern behaviour that can be considered harmful to the public, society, or the state.

The coexistence of different normative standards is a result of the colonial history of Malaysia and is still reflected in the current legal framework. Islam reached the Malay Peninsula by the fourteenth century and spread with the territorial expansion of the Malacca Sultanate during the fifteenth century.[5] In pre-colonial Malaysia, the Sultans of their respective states were the political leaders but also the heads of religion. In this sense, there was no separation between politics, Islam, and law.[6]

This relationship changed during the British colonial period. In the Federated Malay States, the Unfederated Malay States, and Brunei, the Sultans lost their political power to various degrees, depending on the colonial status of their respective territories, but they retained their religious power.[7] In all these colonial territories, the basic manner in which Islamic law was administered was the same; the British colonial administration saw Muslim law as a separate body of law, religious in nature, and thus left it to the prerogatives of the rulers of different states. The turn of the twentieth century then saw the codification and bureaucratization of the administration of Islam in the various Malay territories. The rationales for the process are varied. Milner, for example, argues that the rulers, having lost their 'real power' to colonial power, turned to the only field open to them, religion and custom.[8] These developments were the historical roots of the current plural legal system.[9]

4 See the 2010 Census, Population Distribution and Basic Demographic Characteristics, online: www.mycensus.gov.my/banci/www/index.php?&id=3&page_id=35.

5 K. G. Tregonning, *A History of Modern Malaysia and Singapore* (Washington: Eastern University Press, 1972) at 16–21.

6 For an account of this relationship, see for instance A. C. Milner, 'Islam and Malay Kingship' in Ahmad Ibrahim, Sharon Siddique, and Yasmin Hussain, eds., *Readings on Islam in Southeast Asia* (Singapore: ISEAS, 1985) 25.

7 See Gordon P. Means, 'The Role of Islam in the Political Development of Malaysia' (1969) 1:2 *Comparative Politics* 264 at 274, where he quotes from the first of these relevant agreements, the Pangkor Engagement, which stated that the Ruler shall 'receive and provide a suitable residence for a British Officer … whose advice must be asked and acted upon on all questions other than those touching Malay Religion and Custom'.

8 Anthony Milner, *The Invention of Politics in Colonial Malaya* (New York: Cambridge University Press, 2001) at 217.

9 See Tim Lindsey and Kerstin Steiner, *Islam, Law and the State in Southeast Asia: Malaysia and Brunei* (London: IB Tauris, 2012) [*Islam, Law and the State*].

The post-independence Malaysian Syariah system is still strongly influenced by its colonial history.[10] The 1957 Federal Constitution[11] retained certain key points from the colonial past intact. The new federal structure allowed individual states to keep the legislative and executive prerogative over Islam, and as such the scope and structure of the Syariah legal system is still in the purview of the individual states.[12] Therefore the current Syariah legal system only operates at the state level in post-independence Malaysia, which means that the rules governing this legal system are state enactments. There are no overarching federal standards or structures regarding (1) the qualification of Syariah lawyers, (2) professional associations of Syariah lawyers, or (3) higher Syariah courts at federal level, such as the Court of Appeal or the Federal Court in the civil non-religious legal system.

Despite Islam being an individual state matter, there are usually two or three 'models' of Syariah legislation.[13] Most states have the same or at least similar requirements to register and then practise as a Syariah lawyer. For example, in the Federal Territories, the applicant has to be a Malaysian citizen, Muslim, aged at least 21 years, academically qualified, not bankrupt, and not have any civil or Syariah criminal offence.[14] In recent years, states have enacted restrictions that only allow Muslims to practise as Syariah lawyers. In Selangor, a non-Muslim lawyer who had qualified and been registered in the Syariah courts since 1991 lost his licence in 2011.[15] In another case, that of *Victoria Jayaseele Martin*, the Federal Court ruled in 2016 that faith-based restrictions were indeed legal.[16] After the decision was handed down in 2017, the state *mufti*[17] of Perlis stated that he would support this non-Muslim lawyer's application if she were to apply for registration.[18] At the time of writing, this lawyer was not registered in the e-syariah list for registered Syariah lawyers in Perlis, so it is unclear whether she accepted the offer.[19] Syariah lawyers practising in Malaysia's Syariah courts are obviously limited to matters within Syariah court jurisdiction, including civil law and criminal law, and criminal law is limited to certain crimes for Muslims as stipulated in the different state enactments.

Syariah courts are also supposed to only adjudicate over matters involving Muslims. The delineation between the jurisdiction of the civil non-religious and Islamic courts is however not clear-cut. In recent years, the Syariah courts have been adjudicating on non-Muslim marriages and subsequent divorce after one spouse converts to Islam and then effects a unilateral

10 Compare *Islam, Law and the State*, *supra* note 9.

11 *Federal Constitution*, Malaysia 1957 (as amended 1 November 2010) [*Federal Constitution Malaysia*].

12 Ibid., List II, Ninth Schedule.

13 Discussing this in specific contexts, for zakat see for instance Kerstin Steiner, 'Variations of "Unpacking" a Global Norm in a Local Context: An Historical Overview of the Epistemic Communities that are shaping Zakat Practice in Malaysia' in John Gillespie and Pip Nicholson, eds., *Law and Development and the Global Discourses of Legal Transfers* (Cambridge: Cambridge University Press, 2011), and in the context of Islamic family law see Kerstin Steiner, 'Islam, Law and Human Rights of Women in Malaysia' in Niamh Reilly, ed., *International Human Rights: Human Rights of Women* (Singapore: Springer, 2019) [*Law and Human Rights*].

14 See Department of Syariah Judiciary Malaysia, 'Information of Syarie Lawyer', *E-Syariah Official Portal*, online: www.esyariah.gov.my/portal/page/portal/Portal%20E-Syariah%20BI/Portal%20E-Syariah%20Permohonan%20Peguam/Portal%20E-Syariah%20Peguam%20Syarie%20WP#j [*Syarie Lawyer*].

15 Amanda Whiting, 'The Training, Appointment, and Supervision of Islamic Lawyers in the Federal Territories of Malaysia' (2012) 21:1 *Pacific Rim Law & Policy Journal* 133 at 142 [*Training of Islamic Lawyers*].

16 *Victoria Jayaseele Martin* v. *Majilis Agama Islam Wilayah Persekutuan & Anor* [2016] 1 LNS 131.

17 A *mufti* is a Muslim jurist capable of giving an authoritative legal opinion or fatwa.

18 'Perlis Mufti Backs Non-Muslim's Application to Be Shariah Lawyer', *Malay Mail* (23 May 2017), online: www.malaymail.com/news/malaysia/2017/05/23/perlis-mufti-backs-non-muslims-application-to-be-shariah-lawyer/1382677.

19 *Syarie Lawyer*, *supra* note 14.

conversion of minor children.[20] This appropriation of jurisdiction used to be at least partially sanctioned by the civil non-religious courts, who have been reluctant to accept jurisdiction in those matters.[21] This situation illustrates how difficult it can be to negotiate the jurisdictional jungle that is the plural legal system of Malaysia, and how access to justice can arguably be denied by not having recourse to a specific legal system.

There are significant differences between the features of the civil non-religious legal system of Malaysia and the Islamic legal system in the context of access to justice. As mentioned briefly above, Malaysia was colonized by the British and the civil non-religious legal system stands in the British common law tradition. Certain elements of the Malaysian Syariah legal system are a hybrid of Islamic law and British common law influences, while other elements are uniquely Islamic in origin and nature.[22] For example, under Islamic law, the role of judges differs significantly. Historically, judges (*kadi* or *kathi*) in Islamic law were more a facilitator or mediator akin to the role of judges in an inquisitorial/civil legal system. Thus legal representation was therefore not deemed necessary.[23] This approach is in contrast to the common law tradition which is adversarial in nature and in which judges arguably have a less active role. This judicial orientation raises the question of whether legal representation in the Syariah courts in modern Malaysia is perceived as necessary or not. In 2009, it was estimated that about 70 per cent of litigants were unrepresented in the Syariah courts for various reasons.[24] The lack of representation is of course not unique to Malaysia, as other chapters in this collection will show. Nor is it unique to the Syariah courts, as a similar percentage of people were unrepresented in the Malaysian (civil non-religious) criminal courts in 2008, resulting in the creation of the National Legal Aid Foundation (*Yayasan Bantuan Guaman Kebangsaan*) ('YBGK'),[25] discussed below. The difference between the legal systems is that a lack of representation in the Syariah courts has received less attention, probably in part because of the historical role of and perspectives on Syariah court judges and their limited sentencing powers. The sentences by Syariah criminal courts are limited to a maximum three years in jail, six lashes with the cane, and a fine of no more than MYR5,000 (US$1,200[26]).[27]

The rates of unrepresented litigants pose the question of why there is such a lack of legal representation in Malaysia in general. Economic challenges are frequently cited as being an obstacle to participate in and access the legal system. Yet Malaysia has been doing relatively well economically. Its GDP ratio has averaged 140% since 2010, with an average annual growth of

[20] For a discussion of some of those cases, including the *Shamala*, *Subashini* and the more recent cases of *Indira Gandhi*, see Kerstin Steiner, 'The Case Continues? The High Courts in Malaysia and Unilateral Conversion of a Child to Islam by One Parent' (2013) 14:2 *Australian Journal of Asian Law* 1–15 [*The Case Continues*].

[21] See for instance the case of *Subashini Rajasingham* v. *Saravanan Thangathoray & Ors* [2007] 2 MLJ 705.

[22] See *The Case Continues*, *supra* note 20, and see Kerstin Steiner, 'Comparative Law in the Syariah Courts: A Case Study of Singapore, Malaysia, and Brunei' in Duncan Fairgrieve and Mads Adenas, eds., *Comparative Law before the Courts* (Oxford: Oxford University Press, 2015) 590 for a detailed analysis of Syariah court decisions and the methods used by Syariah judges in the context of comparative law.

[23] *Training of Islamic Lawyers*, *supra* note 15, at 144.

[24] Sonia Ramachandran, 'No Justice without Legal Aid', *New Straits Times* (3 May 2009).

[25] The National Legal Aid Foundation ('NLAF') or *Yayasan Bantuan Guaman Kebangsaan* ('YBGK') in Bahasa Melayu. Please note that the chapter usually uses the more commonly used abbreviations in Malaysia.

[26] XE Currency Converter, online: www.xe.com/currencyconverter/convert/?Amount=10&From=MYR&To=USD. Unless another reference is cited, US$ denominations in the chapter were derived from www.xe.com at the time of publication; they are intended for general reference and may have been rounded up or down for ease of reference.

[27] See *Syariah Court (Criminal Jurisdiction) Act* 1965, Malaysia, Act No. 355 (as amended 1 December 2014) [*Syariah Court (Criminal Jurisdiction) Act*], s 2.

about 5.4%. Fewer than 1% of Malaysian households are living below the poverty line. The poorest 40% of the population are however 'vulnerable to economic shocks as well as increases in the cost of living and mounting financial obligations'.[28] The economic disadvantages of the *bumiputra*,[29] as Malay Muslims are also referred to, have been well documented and have been a source of political concern. Over the last decades, a number of special economic and educational programmes have been designed and run for this group of Malaysians.[30] Those economic and educational challenges are also impacting participation in and access to the Syariah legal system. Yet, despite those known economic and educational issues for Muslims in general, legal aid in the Syariah court system has only started to draw attention in recent years.

In 2018, Professor Shad Saleem Faruqi, a frequent commentator on the legal system in Malaysia, made a comment in passing that 'legal aid is in its infancy',[31] presumably because of the difficulty of accessing legal aid and the high number of people unrepresented in court. This state of affairs exists despite the fact that there are legal aid schemes in the civil non-religious legal system that have been operating for about three decades. One reason why access to justice has not received more attention is that the Malaysian legal framework does not include a right to legal aid per se. As access to legal aid is not constitutionally enshrined in Malaysia, reference is usually made to the Malaysian Constitution Article 5(3), which provides that an arrested person 'shall be informed as soon as may be of the grounds of his arrest and shall be allowed to consult and be defended by a legal practitioner of his choice'.[32] This right to be represented by a lawyer in criminal cases is repeated in Section 28A(2) of the Criminal Procedure Code 2012.[33] The issue is that none of the provisions contain a right to legal aid as such, just legal representation. Indeed, the issue that legal aid is not guaranteed and that vulnerable groups, such as migrant workers, refugees, and asylum seekers, are often left without legal representation, has frequently been criticized.[34]

If legal aid is in its infancy in the civil non-religious legal system, then it is a premature newborn in the Syariah legal system. The next section will address the other two issues identified, namely the maze of different legal aid providers with different eligibility criteria. It will focus on access to justice in Syariah courts in Malaysia by analysing selective different legal service schemes and what they offer to indigent litigants. Legal aid is available through several initiatives, from government agencies, the legal profession, and non-governmental organizations.

II. LEGAL AID SCHEMES: A COLOURFUL PATCHWORK SYSTEM

In general, indigent persons who need legal advice and representation in Malaysia can consult three main organizations: the government Legal Aid Department ('LAD')[35], the Bar Council of

[28] Data taken from *The World Bank in Malaysia* (6 April 2021), online: World Bank, www.worldbank.org/en/country/malaysia/overview.

[29] *Bumiputra* literally means 'the people of the soil'; it does not have a fixed legal definition and is mostly used to refer to Malay Muslims as defined in Article 160(2) of the *Federal Constitution Malaysia, supra* note 11. It can also include Orang Asli and members of indigenous groups in Sabah and Sarawak.

[30] See for instance *Islam, Law and the State, supra* note 9, for an overview.

[31] Shad Saleem Faruqi, 'Fifth Raja Aziz Addruse Memorial Lecture' (Speech delivered at the Malaysian Bar's International Malaysia Law Conference, 15 August 2018).

[32] *Federal Constitution Malaysia, supra* note 11.

[33] *Criminal Procedure Code 2012*, Malaysia, Act 593 (as amended 1 October 2018).

[34] With further references, see Andika Ab. Wahab and Aizat Khairi, 'Right to Justice and Legal Aid Barriers to the Vulnerable Non-citizens in Malaysia' (2020) 16:1 *Malaysian Journal of Society and Space* 13 at 16.

[35] 'Legal Aid Department' ('LAD'), or *Jabatan Bantuan Guaman* in Bahasa Melayu. Please note that the chapter usually uses the most commonly used abbreviations in Malaysia which can be either in English or in Bahasa Melayu.

Malaysia, and the YBGK. However, while those three organizations provide legal aid in the civil non-religious legal system, they offer only limited assistance in the Islamic legal system. Moreover, the organizations apply very different tests to determine whether a person will receive legal aid, creating a complex formation of requirements which allows people to fall through the cracks. Various professional associations and civil society organizations are trying to fill in some of the gaps. Table 15.1 on p. 284 summarizes the main relevant legal aid schemes in the civil non-religious system and the Syariah legal system in Malaysia, indicating the type of services provided and the relevant legal system and jurisdiction.[36]

The following sections will review these different schemes, starting with the governmental assistance, followed by professional schemes, and then collaborations between the government and professional associations. These schemes provide legal aid in the civil non-religious system and limited assistance in the Syariah legal system. The final section will cover schemes that focus exclusively on the Syariah legal system, as provided by associations for Syariah lawyers as well as civil society initiatives.

A. *Legal Aid Department (LAD or* Jabatan Bantuan Guaman*)*

The Legal Aid Department ('LAD'),[37] originally called the Legal Aid Bureau, was established pursuant to the Legal Aid Act 1971 ('LAA').[38] It currently comes under the Prime Minister Department's Legal Affairs Division ('BHEUU').[39] It is funded solely by the government with a budget of MYR27.5 million (US$6.6 million) in 2016 and MYR23.5 million (US$5.6 million) in 2017.[40] It has been described as the 'biggest law firm' in Malaysia,[41] given its resources.

As reflected in Figure 15.1 on p. 285, the LAD provides assistance in a variety of cases.

According to Section 10(1) LAA, LAD provides legal aid in criminal cases only for the civil non-religious legal system, in the following circumstances: if an unrepresented accused pleads guilty to any criminal charge; in criminal proceedings under the Child Protection Act 1991,[42] later replaced by the Child Act 2001;[43] and in criminal proceedings under the Minor Offences Act 1955, Act 336.[44] As mentioned above, the scheme does not provide any legal aid in Syariah criminal cases. Given that the highest number of unrepresented litigants are in the Syariah jurisdiction, this is a significant gap.

According to Section 12(1) of the LAA, legal aid may only be granted in civil cases for matters set out in the Third Schedule to the LAA.[45] The Third Schedule was amended in 2011, with the

[36] There are of course numerous other legal aid schemes by academic institutions, such as higher education providers, and other civil society organizations for specific beneficiaries, e.g. consumers (Federation of Malaysian Consumers Associations ('FOMCA')), and Malaysian and migrant workers (Malaysian Trade Union Council ('MTUC') and 'TENAGANITA'). For a more comprehensive list, see *Thematic Study on Legal Aid* (ASEAN Intergovernmental Commission on Human Rights, 2019) at 86, 97, online: https://aichr.org/wp-content/uploads/2019/09/AICHR-Thematic-Study-on-Legal-Aid-for-web.pdf. They are, however, not relevant for this chapter as they do not provide services in the Syariah legal system and/or only legal advice but not legal representation in court.

[37] Data taken from the official website of the Legal Aid Department, 'Official Portal: Legal Aid Department Malaysia', online: www.jbg.gov.my/index.php/en/.

[38] *Legal Aid Act 1971*, Malaysia, Act 26 (as amended 1 January 2006) [*LAA*].

[39] As a result of the change of government in early 2018, the structure of the BHEUU under the purview of the Prime Minister has been questioned, with the Bar Council advocating for an independent Ministry of Law: see Vathani Panirchellvum, 'Malaysian Bar Supports Establishment of Independent Law Ministry', *The Sun Daily* (31 July 2018).

[40] Ida Lim, 'Legal Aid Shrinking Due to Delayed Payments, Malaysian Bar Report Says', *Malay Mail Online* (18 March 2017) [*Legal Aid Shrinking*].

[41] Sushma Veera, 'Malaysia's Biggest Law Firm', *Weekend Mail* (15 March 2008).

[42] *Child Protection Act 1991*, Malaysia, Act 468.

[43] *Child Act 2001*, Malaysia, Act 611 (as amended 1 February 2018).

[44] *Minor Offences Act 1955*, Malaysia, Act 336 (as amended 1 January 2006).

[45] *LAA*, *supra* note 38, Third Schedule.

TABLE 15.1. *Overview of main relevant legal aid schemes*

Overview of Legal Aid Schemes by Legal System and Jurisdiction						
Legal System	Jurisdiction	Legal Aid Department (LAD)	Malaysian Bar Council, Legal Aid Clinic (LAC)	National Legal Aid Foundation (YBGK)	(various) Syariah Lawyers' Associations	Sisters in Islam: Telenisa
Civil Non-religious Legal System	Civil Cases	Yes	Yes	No	No	No
	Criminal Cases	Yes	Yes	Yes		
Syariah Legal System	Civil Cases	Yes	Yes	No	Yes	No legal representation in court but advice
	Criminal Cases	No	No	Yes	Yes	

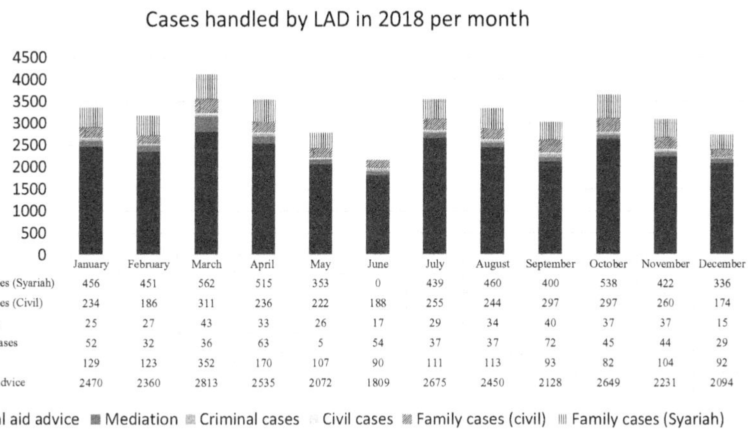

	January	February	March	April	May	June	July	August	September	October	November	December
Family cases (Syariah)	456	451	562	515	353	0	439	460	400	538	422	336
Family cases (Civil)	234	186	311	236	222	188	255	244	297	297	260	174
Civil cases	25	27	43	33	26	17	29	34	40	37	37	15
Criminal cases	52	32	36	63	5	54	37	37	72	45	44	29
Mediation	129	123	352	170	107	90	111	113	93	82	104	92
Legal aid advice	2470	2360	2813	2535	2072	1809	2675	2450	2128	2649	2231	2094

FIGURE 15.1. Number of Legal Aid Department cases in 2018 by type and month[46]

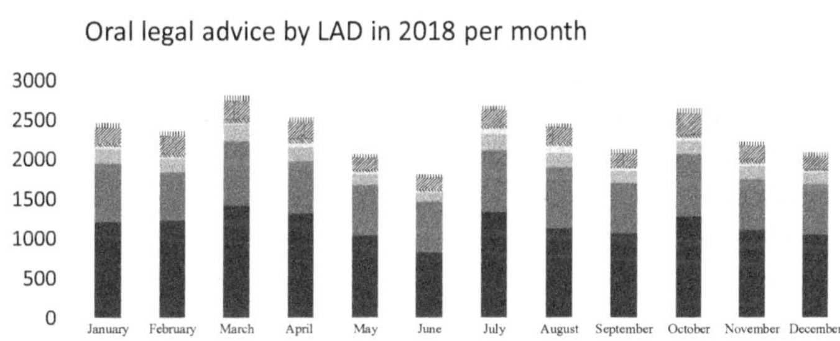

	January	February	March	April	May	June	July	August	September	October	November	December
Criminal (beyond jurisdiction)	59	55	66	63	45	35	47	43	51	71	56	52
Civil (beyond jurisdiction)	208	234	237	201	157	154	213	204	169	267	200	165
Criminal and civil (beyond jurisdiction)	35	39	41	55	22	25	25	31	14	28	22	17
Criminal cases	36	23	25	52	32	15	64	87	37	47	35	25
Civil cases	181	173	199	193	132	108	200	183	157	163	171	146
Family (civil)	733	596	820	652	639	637	792	768	626	786	636	639
Family (Syariah)	1218	1240	1425	1319	1045	835	1334	1134	1074	1287	1111	1050

FIGURE 15.2. Oral legal advice by Legal Aid Department in 2018 by area of law and month[47]

revised categories coming into force and effect on 1 January 2012. The revised categories include Syariah family law matters such as proceedings relating to betrothal (damages), maintenance, custody, divorce, marital debt, *mutaah*,[48] and *harta sepencarian*;[49] and Syariah court proceedings relating to gifts *inter vivos* (*hibah*) and wills.

Legal aid advice, that is oral legal advice for matters in any jurisdiction, is overall the most popular general service (Figure 15.2 above).

Within this category of legal advice, Syariah family law matters are the most popular service. This popularity however is not a reflection of the quality of the services provided. According to a

[46] Data taken from the official website of the Legal Aid Department, 'Legal Aid Department's Case Statistics for July 2018' [*LAD Case Statistics*] (copy on file with author).

[47] Data taken from the official website of the Legal Aid Department: see *LAD Case Statistics*, *supra* note 46.

[48] Also commonly spelt *mut'ah*. This is a consolatory gift that is given by a man who, having married a woman without specifying a dowry, then divorces her before having sexual relations.

[49] *Harta sepencarian*, jointly acquired property during a marriage, is conjugal property divided equally upon divorce.

study by Shariza Kamarudin observing women's experience in the Syariah courts in Penang, many of the respondents in the interviews were not satisfied with the court representation provided by the LAD lawyers, claiming that lawyers demonstrated a general lack of knowledge, were overburdened, or disinterested in the case.[50] In one extreme example, a woman who was suffering from domestic violence and had sought a divorce, had a recommendation made by her lawyer that she should reconcile with her husband.[51]

In order to qualify for LAD services, applicants have to meet two eligibility criteria, a merits and a means test. Regarding the merits test, Sections 15(2)(a), applicable to applicants with an income under MYR25,000 (US$6,040) per annum, and 16(1)(a) LAA, applicable to applicants with an income of MYR25,000 (US$6,040) to MYR30,000 (US$7,250) per annum, state that the Director General of Legal Aid has to be 'satisfied that the applicant has reasonable grounds for taking, defending, continuing or being party' to the proceedings. In addition, the Minister can authorize legal aid in the 'case of hardship' and in 'the interest of justice', regardless of whether the case falls within the general scope of the LAA.[52]

The means test requires that the Director General of Legal Aid must be 'satisfied that the applicant possessed financial resources which do not exceed (MYR30,000 or US$7,250) per annum'.[53] An exemption can be made if the applicant has a higher income but passes the merits test. The applicant would then have to contribute a certain amount. The Legal Aid (Fees and Contribution) Regulation 2017 establishes the contributions as shown in Table 15.2 opposite.[54]

The LAD website has an online test for applicants which allows them to self-check their eligibility under the means test, and it appears to be used frequently.[55] Indeed, establishing the financial need for free legal service appears to be an issue especially for women. In the NGO Shadow Report 2005, it was observed that many women could fail the means test, as they might be entitled to maintenance from their former spouse but the spouse fails to provide this. As such their theoretical financial resources could require them to make contributions which they cannot afford. The report referred to a survey in which 80 per cent of women whose husbands failed to make payments were not enforcing their entitlement to maintenance.[56]

In order to access legal aid, an onerous procedure has to be followed. In criminal cases, the applicant has to submit a written application to the court in which the applicant is being charged. The application is then referred to the Department of Social Welfare to assess the means of the applicant and whether the means test was passed. The court makes the final determination whether the applicant is without means and grants legal aid.[57]

50 The study included 30 women who were involved in family law litigation in the Syariah courts in Penang during 2004–11: see Shariza Kamarudin, *Access to Justice: Women's Experiences in Penang Syariah Courts* (Petaling Jaya: Malaysia Strategic Information and Research Development Centre, 2017) [*Penang Syariah Courts*].

51 Ibid. at 76–9.

52 See *LAA*, *supra* note 38, s 10(2A) (for criminal cases) or s 12(3) (for civil cases).

53 The amount is regulated in the *Legal Aid (Criteria and Means Test) Regulations* 2017, Malaysia, P.U. (A) 370. Section 15(2)(b) of the *LAA*, *supra* note 38, still refers to MYR25,000 (US$6,040) but has the provision that the Director can exercise his discretion for an applicant who has between MYR25,000 (US$6,040) and MYR30,000 (US$7,250).

54 *Legal Aid (Fees and Contribution) Regulation* 2017, Malaysia, Second Schedule.

55 Legal Aid Department, 'Online Application Usage Report Year 2018', online: www.jbg.gov.my/index.php/en/archive/online-application-usage-report/290-online-application-usage-report-year-2018.

56 NGO *Shadow Report on the Initial and Second Periodic Report of the Government of Malaysia: Reviewing the Government's Implementation of the Convention on the Elimination of All Forms of Discrimination against Women* (CEDAW) [NGO *Shadow Report* 2005] at Article 16.2.3.

57 Tsun Hang Tey, 'Malaysia' in E. A. Black and Gary F. Bell, eds., *Law and Legal Institutions of Asia: Traditions, Adaptations and Innovations* (Port Melbourne, Victoria: Cambridge University Press, 2011) 212 at 237.

TABLE 15.2. *Contributions by applicant according to the Legal Aid (Fees and Contribution) Regulation 2017*

	Contributions by applicant to legal aid services		
Financial resources per annum	Contributions according to s 16(2) LAA Legal aid granted by Director General	Contributions according to s 16A(2) LAA Legal aid granted by Director General as authorized by Minister	Contributions according to s 29H(3) LAA Legal companion service[58]
MYR0–30,000 (US$0–7,370)	None	None	None
MYR30,001-35,000 (US$7,371–8,599)	MYR500–2,000 (US$120–480)	MYR500–2,000 (US$120–480)	MYR500–2,000 (US$120–480)
MYR35,001–40,000 (US$8,599–9,827)	MYR2,001–3,000 (US$481–720)	MYR 2,001–3,000 (US$481–720)	MYR2,001–3,000 (US$481–720)
MYR40,001–50,000 (US$9,827–12,285)	MYR3,001–5,000 (US$721–1,200)	MYR 3,001–5,000 (US$721–1,200)	MYR3,001–5,000 (US$721–1,200)
MYR50,001 and above (US$12,285 and above)	NA	MYR5,001–50,000 (US$1,201–12,000)	MYR5,001–50,000 (US$1,201–12,000)

In general, there are numerous shortcomings in providing access to legal aid under this scheme: the prescriptive list of cases in which legal aid can be offered, even if the Minister can decide to broaden it on an ad hoc basis; the means test, which results in applicants being unable to qualify or having to pay a contribution; and the fact that Syariah criminal cases fall completely outside the scope of legal aid.

B. The Malaysian Bar's Legal Aid Scheme

The Malaysian Bar[59] was first established under the Advocates & Solicitor's Ordinance 1947,[60] and later replaced by the Legal Profession Act 1976 ('LPA').[61] The Malaysian Bar is thus an association created by statute, and all advocates and solicitors in private practice in the civil non-religious legal system are automatically members when they have a practising certificate.[62] Apart from representing and organizing its membership, the Malaysian Bar is grounded in ideas of civil society with a strong commitment to due process, separation of powers, judicial independence, and civil rights, as arguably can be seen in their sustained advocacy over the decades. In the area of access to justice, the Malaysian Bar Council, the governing body of the Malaysian Bar, has the power to 'make provisions of or assist in the promotion of a scheme whereby impecunious persons may be represented by advocates and solicitors'.[63]

58 Legal companions are a new service established in 2017. These are lawyers who act as a guide providing clarification in court proceedings, in particular for minor children in sexual misconduct cases.
59 The Malaysian Bar does not cover all territories in Malaysia, as the Borneo states of Sabah and Sarawak have their own legislation and scheme.
60 *Advocates & Solicitor's Ordinance* 1947, Malaysia, M.U. 4 of 1947.
61 *Legal Profession Act* 1976, Malaysia, Act 166 (as amended 1 August 2018) [*LPA*].
62 Ibid. at s 43.
63 Ibid. at s 42(1)(h).

The Malaysian Bar was one of the first private institutions to establish a self-funded legal aid programme in Malaysia.[64] Contributions became compulsory when in 1983, the Malaysian Bar passed a resolution requiring members to pay a levy to the Legal Aid Fund. The amount has been MYR100 (US$24) per annum.[65] Apart from the compulsory financial support, members are encouraged to take up cases with indigent persons after a resolution in that regard was passed in 1995. In addition to this voluntary work, the Bar requires chambering pupils[66] to assist in the running of the legal aid centres ('LAC') for at least two weeks.[67] During this period, pupils are supervised by LAC staff and a practising solicitor and advocate, who also act as mentors. LAC are located in the federal capital of Kuala Lumpur, and in every state capital city in peninsular Malaysia, thus excluding Sabah and Sarawak where the respective state bars have similar centres. This legal aid scheme aims to:[68]

- provide free legal advice, representation, and legal intervention for civil and criminal matters;
- offer assistance in mitigation of sentences, remand proceedings, and bail applications; and
- promote awareness and educate members of the public as to their legal rights.

The scheme assists in a wide array of matters, including civil and criminal law, but excluding cases that might carry a lifetime or death sentence, such as drug offences, murder, or armed robbery.

It also has a limited coverage of cases in the Syariah legal system. There are special Syariah Legal Clinics that provide services for:[69]

- divorce proceedings, including applications by the husband for divorce and *fasakh*[70] as well as divorce pronunciations;
- *kembali taat*;[71] and
- maintenance and matrimonial property claims.

In order to qualify for legal aid from the Malaysian Bar, applicants must pass a means test, one that differs significantly from the government scheme. First of all, income limits vary from state to state in Peninsular Malaysia, taking local circumstances and income disparities into account.[72] In addition, unlike the governmental LAD means test, the LAC test is based on net income, with different rates

[64] Shanmuga Kanesalingam, 'Monkey in a Wig: Loyarburok, Undimsia, Public Interest Litigation and Beyond' (2013) 31:3 *Wisconsin International Law Journal* 586 at 593.

[65] 2018 *Malaysian Bar Payments Required under the Legal Profession Act 1976* (Malaysia Bar Circular No. 109/2018, 2018), online: www.malaysianbar.org.my/notices_for_members/2018_malaysian_bar_payments_required_under_the_legal_profession_act_1976.html.

[66] Chambering pupils are law graduates who have completed their professional examination and undertake their nine months of professional apprenticeship prior to being called to the bar.

[67] *Compulsory attendance of pupil at a Legal Aid Centre* (Rulings of Bar Council, Malaysian Bar, 2014), Rules and Rulings of the Bar Council at Chapter 10, item 10.6 on pupillage, online: www.malaysianbar.org.my/bc_rulings/10.06._compulsory_attendance_of_pupil_at_a_legal_aid_centre.html.

[68] See, for example, details for the clinic in Kuala Lumpur: Malaysia Bar Council, 'LAC Program', online: www.kllac.com/lac-program/ [*LAC Program*]; for the clinic in Perak, see Perak Bar Log, '22 March 2010', online: perakbar.blogspot.com/2010/03/.

[69] See, for example, details for the clinic in Kuala Lumpur: *LAC Program*, *supra* note 68.

[70] *Fasakh* is a form of divorce initiated by the wife if the husband has not fulfilled certain obligations.

[71] *Kembali taat* literally means 'being loyal again'. This is a petition filed by a husband requesting his wife to be obedient again; if the wife does not fulfil the request, she can be declared *nusyuz* (which translates to 'disloyal' or 'disobedient') by the Syariah courts.

[72] Information Sheet 'Malaysia' provided by the Malaysian Bar for the Third Conference on *Access to Justice and the Role of the Bar Associations and Law Societies in Asia*, 30 November 2011 – 2 December 2011, Tokyo, Japan (copy on file with author).

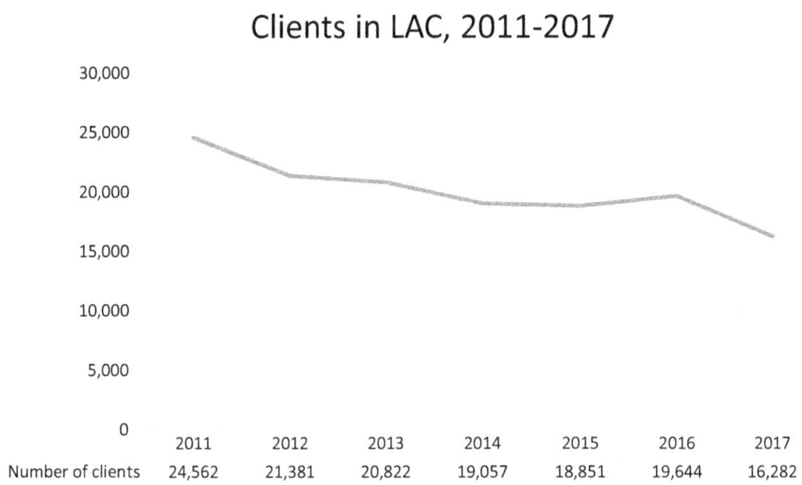

FIGURE 15.3. Number of clients in Malaysian Bar Council, Legal Aid Clinic, 2011–2017[73]

for married or unmarried people, thus potentially providing more assistance to people. This, however, is offset by the fact that the means test considers other assets as well as savings in the threshold. In order to be eligible, an applicant should have a monthly income of less than MYR650 (US$155) if single, or MYR900 (US$215) if married, net of all monthly expenses. This is a net yearly income of MYR7,800 (US$1,885) to MYR10,800 (US$2,609). In comparison, the governmental scheme has a gross income threshold of MYR25,000 (US$6,040). In addition, under the LAC scheme, the applicant is also prohibited from having a house or apartment worth more than MYR45,000 (US$10,870); a motorcar worth more than MYR20,000 (US$4,830); a motorcycle worth more than MYR4,500 (US$1,087); or savings of more than MYR5,000 (US$1,200).[74] Moreover, if an applicant does qualify for legal aid, they would have to pay for disbursements, e.g. transportation costs for lawyers and documentation fees, of between MYR300 (US$72) and MYR700 (US$165), which is about half the monthly net income for those clients. Comparative figures on the impact of the different qualification schemes, LAC and LAD, are not available, but the existence of different means tests and thresholds is highly likely to create confusion among applicants. Furthermore, it makes it more difficult to gauge how many indigent litigants are falling through the gaps.

Regarding use of the service, the number of clients receiving services through the LAC scheme has been decreasing slowly in recent years (Figure 15.3 above).

Currently the number of Syariah clients are not reported separately in the National Legal Aid Report by the Malaysian Bar. In general, they appear to be few; for example, in 2009 there were 19,328 clients in total, of which only 141 were Syariah clients.[75] This minute figure is not surprising. The Malaysian Bar is not the primary legal aid provider for the Syariah legal system, for very practical reasons. It is not the primary professional organization for Syariah practitioners, as Syariah lawyers belong to other professional organizations in far greater numbers. For

[73] Data taken from *Annual Report 2017: Report of the National Legal Aid Committee* (Malaysia Bar, 2017) (copy on file with author).

[74] For details in Selangor, see Selangor Bar, Legal Aid Centre Selangor (LACS), online: https://selangorbar.org/page_dtl.php?id=680.

[75] *Annual Report 2009* (Malaysia Bar, 2009), cited in *Training of Islamic Lawyers*, *supra* note 15, at 146.

example, in Johor in 2015–16, there were 206 Syariah practitioners and of those only 43 were also registered with the Malaysian Bar.[76] This means that the overall pool of qualified Syariah practitioners within the Malaysian Bar is very small, and combined with the ever-present challenge of getting lawyers to volunteer, the staffing challenges are significant.

The Malaysian Bar scheme also differs from the government scheme in terms of funding. In 2009, the scheme had a budget of MYR1.3 million (US$310,000), compared to the Legal Aid Department's annual budget of MYR9 million (US$2.15 million). Yet the Malaysian Bar's LAC shouldered all non-guilty-plea criminal cases for indigent persons in the civil non-religious legal system.[77] Given its budget, the Malaysian Bar's scheme is only supposed to complement the government-funded system of legal aid, and the restrictions it faces in terms of resources, staff, and finances mean that it is not able to provide extensive legal aid for the Syariah legal system.

C. *National Legal Aid Foundation* (Yayasan Bantuan Guaman Kebangsaan, *or YBGK)*

Launched in April 2012, YBGK is a joint programme between the government and the three civil non-religious legal system bar associations of Malaysia, that is the Malaysian Bar, the Sabah Law Association, and the Advocates' Association of Sarawak. YBGK was established as a result of findings that 84,376 out of 108,528 accused were unrepresented in criminal trials at magistrates' courts in 2008.[78] One of the reasons why people were unrepresented was financial hardship, and thus one of YBGK's objectives is to provide legal aid in criminal cases to Malaysians earning less that MYR36,000 (US$8,670) a year.[79] YBGK provides the following services and programmes for the civil non-religious and Syariah criminal jurisdictions:[80]

- the Prisons Programme, in which pupils visit prisons to conduct interviews, assist in needs in general, and refer inmates for further specific legal aid;
- the Walk-in Programme in Legal Aid Centres, in which pupils assist clients and refer them onwards for specific legal aid;
- the Arrest Programme, the Remand Programme, and the Bail Programme, offered during initial criminal investigations when a person is placed under arrest, or under remand when a person has been detained for a certain period. Detained individuals are given legal representation by a lawyer on duty. The lawyer will provide legal representation including explaining rights, argue remand applications, and assist in bail applications;
- the Trial Programme, where the YBGK lawyer will represent the client during the trial process, if the means test has been passed;
- the Mitigation Programme, where the YBGK lawyer assists in the mitigation process, in which a person has been found guilty but the sentence has not yet been passed; and
- the Appeal Programme and the Pardons Petition Programme, where after conviction at the initial trial, YBGK offers legal aid in the appeal process and pardons petitions.

[76] *Annual Report 2015/2016* (Malaysian Bar Johore, 2016), online: johorebar.org.my/wp-content/uploads/2015/03/Johore-Bar-Annual-Report-2015-16.pdf.

[77] *Legal Aid in Malaysia: The Need for Greater Government Commitment* (The Malaysian Bar: Members' Opinions and Comments, 23 November 2009).

[78] See the official YBGK website, 'YBGK Program: Overview of YBGK' (2020), online: www.kllac.com/ybgk-program/ [*Overview of YBGK*].

[79] V. Anbalagan, 'AG Wants Single Body to Offer Legal Aid, Says Bar Chief', *Free Malaysia Today* (11 June 2018), online: www.freemalaysiatoday.com/category/nation/2018/06/11/ag-wants-single-body-to-offer-legal-aid-says-bar-chief/ [*Single Body to Offer Legal Aid*].

[80] See the official YBGK website, *Overview of YBGK, supra* note 78.

FIGURE 15.4. Number of Yayasan Bantuan Guaman Kebangsaan (National Legal Aid Foundation) clients, 2012–2017[81]

The YBGK scheme has been plagued by two main issues from the outset, funding and staffing. There has been a lack of funding,[82] despite increases in the budget over the first few years. Originally MYR5 million (US$1.2 million) was allocated to launch the project. The 2012 budget allocated another MYR10 million (US$ 2.4 million). The 2013 budget confirmed MYR14 million (US$3.37 million) and another MYR20 million (US$4.81 million) to run the programme. As such, the YBGK annual budget was originally comparable to that of the LAD. However, there was no direct mention of this scheme by the Prime Minister in immediate subsequent budget speeches.[83] Disputes about adequate staffing numbers also accounted for delay in launching the programme. The Malaysian Bar and the Attorney General were in disagreement as to how many lawyers were needed and whether a sufficient number of lawyers had been trained for the programme.[84] The issue of not having sufficient lawyer participation in the scheme remains unresolved. For instance, in 2014 there were only 1,444 lawyers registered with YBGK nationwide, and only 25 lawyers in Sabah.[85] In 2017, 2,358 lawyers were accredited to provide legal aid under YBGK, yet only 1,706 lawyers were active.[86]

Still, the early years of the programme saw a steady increase in the numbers of clients, before significantly decreasing in 2016 and 2017 (Figure 15.4 above).

The decline in numbers coincides with increased criticism of the scheme and problems that have emerged over the last few years, including false claims by lawyers,[87] i.e. accusations of charging clients for the free service,[88] and delays in payment resulting in lawyers refusing to

[81] Data taken from *Annual Report 2017: Report of the National Legal Aid Committee* (Malaysian Bar, 2017).
[82] *Single Body to Offer Legal Aid, supra* note 79.
[83] *Legal Aid Shrinking, supra* note 40.
[84] Andrew Sagayam, 'Legal Aid Plan Put On Hold: Attorney General and Bar Council Have Conflicting Views Over Number of Lawyers', *Malay Mail* (7 February 2012).
[85] 'Only 25 Sabah Lawyers in National Legal Aid Foundation', *Borneo Post* (10 December 2014).
[86] *Legal Aid Shrinking, supra* note 40.
[87] *Single Body to Offer Legal Aid, supra* note 79.
[88] 'Former YBGK Lawyer Claims Trial to 15 Cheating Charges', *The Sun Daily* (5 August 2016), online: www.thesundaily.my/archive/1926492-LSARCH385642.

partake in the scheme.[89] In 2016, lawyers were owed MYR822,000 (US$196,700).[90] This issue continues to beset the system at the time of writing. In 2020, lawyers expressed concern that they had again not been paid for services rendered. The reason provided for the delay was that the YBGK had not received its entire 2020 budget from the Prime Minister's Department.[91]

One of the solutions to these problems, as suggested by the Malaysian Bar,[92] has been to merge this scheme with services provided by the Legal Aid Department.[93] This would create a 'super' legal aid organization, responsible for overseeing cases in all jurisdictions – civil and criminal – in both legal systems. However, both the LAD and the YBGK have been criticized for having significant shortcomings, and it is not clear how creating a super legal aid organization would address the issues these organizations have encountered separately. In criminal cases, the LAD only assists in cases where the accused has pleaded guilty, while the Malaysian Bar Council programme partially complements the service offered by the LAD. The YBGK was subsequently established in order to fill in more of those gaps, in particular in the criminal cases for both legal systems. It is not clear whether the service provided by this new super legal aid organization would cater to all needs. Moreover, all organizations face funding and staffing issues, and while reorganization may reduce some duplication, it is not clear where the funding and staff required by a combined organization would come from.

D. Legal Aid Schemes Solely for the Syariah Legal System

The above-mentioned legal aid schemes provide services, albeit in limited form, in both the civil non-religious system and the Syariah legal system. This section will cover initiatives that are solely dedicated to providing legal aid and assistance in the Syariah legal system. These initiatives are offered by either professional associations for Syariah lawyers or civil society organizations. This section will canvas the activities of associations for Syariah lawyers and civil society, taking the initiative by Sisters in Islam ('SIS') as an example of the latter.

There are some significant differences in the way the legal profession is organized in the civil non-religious system and the Syariah legal system which directly impact the availability of legal assistance. At the outset, unlike in the civil non-religious system and the Malaysian Bar, there is no overarching professional organization that Syariah lawyers have to be a member of. In order to practise law, they only have to register their service in the respective state, and there are currently about 4,930 registered Syariah lawyers in Malaysia (Figure 15.5 opposite).

These lawyers are then organized in various associations, including the Malaysian Syariah Lawyers Association (*Persatuan Peguam Syarie Malaysia*) ('PGSM'),[94] the Muslim Lawyers

[89] Kuthubul Zaman, 'Fundamental Right of Access to Justice', *Free Malaysia Today* (24 March 2017), online: www.freemalaysiatoday.com/category/opinion/2017/03/24/fundamental-right-of-access-to-justice/.

[90] 'Lawyers Not Keen to Help Needy Due to Late Payment', *New Straits Times* (14 September 2016).

[91] *YBGK and Payments to Lawyers* (Malaysian Bar Circular No 198/2020, 2020), online: www.malaysianbar.org.my/document/members/circulars/2020—2024/2020&rid=39683.

[92] Mohd Husni Mohd Noor, 'Bar Council Asked to Submit Proposal to Revamp Act', *New Straits Times* (12 June 2018), online: www.nst.com.my/news/nation/2018/06/378928/bar-council-asked-submit-proposals-revamp-legal-profession-act.

[93] *Single Body to Offer Legal Aid*, *supra* note 79.

[94] PGSM was established in 2001 and rebranded in 2015. It is one of the larger organizations, with ten registered branches in various states and about 600 members nationwide. Its focus is to foster and strengthen relationships among registered Syariah lawyers and to act as an intermediator with other legal institutions and associations. It aims to advance and promote Islamic law throughout Malaysia. See 'Home: PGSM Website' (2020), online: www.pgsm.org.my/.

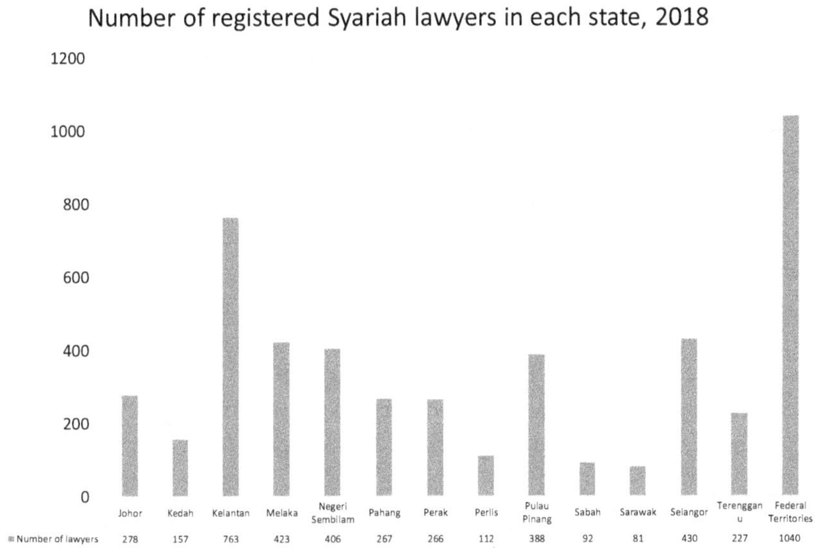

FIGURE 15.5. Number of registered Syariah lawyers per state[95]

Association (*Persatuan Peguam Muslim Malaysia*) ('PPMM'),[96] and Lawyers in Defence of Islam (*Peguam Pembela Islam*) ('PPI').[97] These associations are not state-based and operate throughout Malaysia, although they might only have branches in certain states.

Unlike the Malaysian Bar, there is no explicit mention of providing legal aid in the objectives and missions of these associations. Yet some of them offer legal aid. PGSM for instance runs a Syariah Law Clinic (KGS) and counselling services – not legal representation in court – which are free of charge, and which is staffed by PGSM volunteers who are also registered Syariah lawyers. A few years ago, PGSM floated the idea, following in the footsteps of the Malaysian Bar, of creating legal aid centres called BAGUS (*Pusat Bantuan Guaman Shariah*). It was envisioned that BAGUS would initially be dedicated to Syariah family law, and later expand to cover Syariah criminal law. Legal aid would be subject to a means test, limited to persons earning MYR30,000 (US$7,250) per annum or less, with some assistance provided to persons earning between MYR30,000 (US$7,250) and MYR50,000 (US$12,000).[98] This means test has a slightly higher threshold than the scheme set up by the LAD, although it appeared to function without a

[95] Data taken from Department of Syariah Judiciary Malaysia, 'Syariah Lawyer Search', *E-Syariah Official Portal*, online: www.esyariah.gov.my/portal/page/portal/Portal%20E-Syariah%20BI/Portal%20E-Syariah%20Carian/Portal%20E-Syariah%20Carian%20Peguam%20Syarie.

[96] PPMM was established in 1988 with the aim to advance Islam and Islamic law throughout Malaysia. Please note that the PPMM's official website is not available. For information, see PPMM Twitter Page (2020), online: Twitter, https://twitter.com/ppmm_official and PPMM Facebook Page (2020), online: Facebook, www.facebook.com/pg/Persatuan-Peguam-Peguam-Muslim-Malaysia-273403396465376/about/?ref=page_internal.

[97] PPI was formed in mid-2006 to 'defend Islam' against perceived attacks. It is led by a former President of the Bar Council, Zainur Zakaria. It was formed out of dissatisfaction with the Bar Council's 'partisan stand' on matters of apostasy and especially the *Lina Joy* case, and to counteract 'misconceptions' about Islam: see 'Muslim Lawyers Form Group to Defend Islam 'From Attacks'', *The Star* (14 July 2006).

[98] See Boo Su-Lyn, 'Why Muslims Accused of Shariah Offences Lack Access to Justice', *Malaysian Mail Online* (8 October 2018), online: www.malaymail.com/news/malaysia/2018/10/08/why-muslims-accused-of-shariah-offences-lack-access-to-justice/1680315 [*Lack of Access*].

merits test. Importantly, BAGUS would have addressed the limitation on criminal assistance under the LAD that the accused has to plead guilty in order to qualify for assistance, as under the BAGUS scheme this would not have been the case.

One question is how successful the scheme would have been. It appears that BAGUS would have followed the template of the Malaysian Bar's LAC, but as reviewed above, that scheme has not been able to fulfil all the needs in the civil legal system. More importantly, since BAGUS was raised in 2018, no further steps have been taken to advance such an idea. Indeed, it seems to have been engulfed or absorbed by the initiatives to establish a professional association for Syariah lawyers at the state level, as discussed below.

In addition to assistance from the previously mentioned main organizations, the Bar Council's services in Kuala Lumpur include a Legal Clinic in partnership with three organizations, All Women's Action Society ('AWAM'), Women's Aid Organization ('WAO'), and SIS. The scope of the project is much broader than legal aid and deals with various issues affecting women, such as domestic violence, divorce proceedings, gender discrimination, etc. While AWAM and WAO deal with issues affecting women of all religions, SIS focuses on issues affecting Muslim women and matters relating to Syariah law.[99]

SIS is one of most influential and effective women's advocacy groups focused on Islam in Malaysia.[100] It has been described as a group of 'Muslim feminists'.[101] Its focus is to advance women's rights within an Islamic legal framework, in order to ensure that Muslim women enjoy and are not denied 'the same legal rights and protections granted to their non-Muslim sisters'.[102] Originally established in the late 1980s as a group with the purpose to educate women about their legal rights under Islamic law, SIS did not offer legal services until 2002/2003, when they recognized the need to broaden their activities. Telenisa, as their free legal advice service is called, offers only advice, on both Syariah family and Syariah criminal law. It does not offer legal representation in court, instead operating a so-called court watch, where it monitors how judges and lawyers handle cases and observes the procedure followed in proceedings and judgments.

Telenisa is staffed by two legal officers from SIS, with assistance of two chambering students from the Malaysian Bar. No means or merits test is applied. SIS conducted a statistical survey in 2016 and found that the majority of their clients had a monthly income of between MYR2,501 (US$604) and MYR5,000 (US$1,200), although 85 per cent of clients did not want to disclose their income.[103] Financial assistance for filing is available through the Dr Nik Noriani Legal Aid Fund for clients who could not otherwise afford to file a case in court. However, clients have to apply for assistance and go through an interview before aid is granted.[104]

SIS has only one office in Kuala Lumpur, and due to limited resources, the number of clients served by this scheme is naturally relatively small (Figure 15.6 opposite).

99 The WAO provides legal aid through their Legal Aid Centre for Pupils. In 2017, they provided assistance to 428 cases, with nearly 350 of them being hotline calls. Less than 40 cases were court cases and there is no data as to how many of those cases were indeed in the Syariah legal system. Compare with their *Annual Report: Service Statistics 2017* (Women's Aid Organization, 2017), online: https://wao.org.my/wp-content/uploads/2019/04/Annual-Report-2017.pdf.

100 The information for this section is based on interviews, correspondence, and published material, including *Telenisa: Statistics and Findings 2016* (Sisters in Islam, 2017) [*Telenisa 2016*] (copy on file with author) and unpublished material by SIS.

101 *Islam, Law and the State*, *supra* note 9 at 8, 298.

102 Zainah Anwar, 'What Islam, Whose Islam? Sisters in Islam and the Struggle for Women's Rights' in Robert Hefner, ed., *The Politics of Multiculturalism: Pluralism and Citizenship in Malaysia, Singapore and Indonesia* (Honolulu: University of Hawai'i Press, 2001) 227 at 244.

103 *Telenisa 2016*, *supra* note 100, 3.

104 *Legal Aid Fund* (Sisters in Islam), online: sistersinislam.org.my.

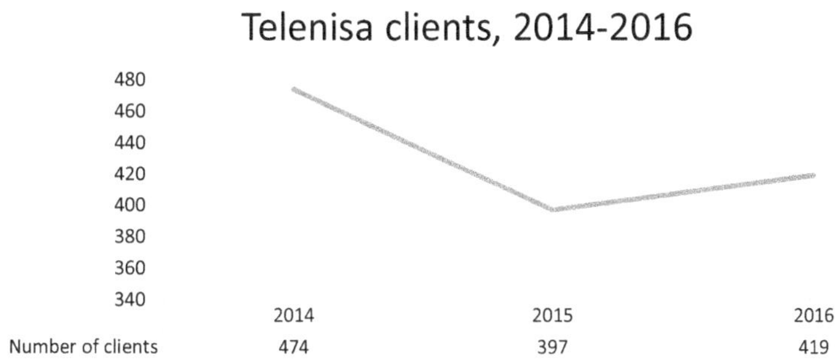

FIGURE 15.6. Number of Telenisa clients, 2014–2016[105]

The statistics regarding clients suggest relatively constant numbers of roughly 400 clients per annum. Given that legal advice is only one of a number of activities conducted by SIS, and is not one of their key activities, it is impressive that they have been able to provide this legal advice service, even though it does not include legal representation in court.

III. CONCLUSION: NAVIGATING A COLOURFUL THREADBARE PATCHWORK MAZE

In order to overcome the limitations of the colourful but threadbare patchwork system of legal aid in Malaysia, significant challenges need to be met, in the civil non-religious system but even more so in the Syariah legal system. At the outset, there are various organizations and associations that offer legal aid. Assuming that indigent clients are aware and have access to the different legal aid schemes, they are left on their own to navigate a labyrinth of various means and merits tests in order to ascertain whether they are eligible for assistance. Particular legal aid programmes might also not have a good reputation or not provide satisfactory service as especially the available governmental services have been criticized as being too slow and not committed to the clients.[106]

Legal aid providers do not comprehensively cover either the civil non-religious system or the Syariah legal system, let alone both systems. The two largest legal aid schemes, run by the Legal Aid Department and the Malaysian Bar, provide relatively little or limited assistance for Syariah matters.

There is currently no dedicated scheme that provides legal aid for legal representation in the whole Syariah legal system, apart from the sporadic initiatives by the professional associations and the legal advice given by non-governmental organizations such as Sisters in Islam and their Telenisa initiative. In general, legal aid in the Syariah civil jurisdiction is more readily available than in the Syariah criminal jurisdiction. A key issue for access to justice in Malaysia is the lack of access to legal representation in criminal cases generally, which occurs despite the Federal Constitution guarantee of legal representation. The lack of legal representation is blatant in Syariah criminal jurisdiction, a point that attracted significant, national and international, public attention in 2018, in the cases of three women sentenced to caning. The three women were all

[105] *Telenisa 2016*, *supra* note 100.
[106] *Penang Syariah Courts*, *supra* note 50, at 118–19.

not legally represented,[107] as is the case in many Syariah criminal cases. These cases were of concern particularly because from 2010 to 2017 there had not been a reported case of a woman being sentenced to caning.[108]

Apart from the patchwork nature of the legal aid provided, there are certain structural issues, some of which are a result of the legislative and bureaucratic framework of Syariah law. Unlike the civil non-religious system, there is no one overarching professional organization for Syariah lawyers, at the state or federal level. The Malaysian Bar and their LACs shoulder a heavy burden in providing legal aid as part of their services, and instituting such a professional association for Syariah lawyers could be a step toward closing the gap, especially if the professional association is required to take on matters of legal aid. A first step was taken in 2019, when the Federal Territories passed the Syarie[109] Legal Profession (Federal Territories) Act 2019 ('Syarie LPA (FT)'),[110] establishing a Syarie Legal Profession Qualifying Board,[111] *Badan Penguam Syarie*,[112] and *Majilis Penguam Syarie*,[113] with the purpose of regulating the practice of the Syariah legal profession in the Federal Territories. The *Badan Penguam Syarie*, of which every registered and admitted Syariah lawyer will be a member,[114] is authorized to 'uphold the cause of justice without regard to its own interests or that of its members, uninfluenced by fear or favour'.[115] This new professional association for Syariah lawyers in the Federal Territories does not explicitly mention the provision of legal aid in its statute, unlike its civil non-religious counterpart the Malaysian Bar which mentions a scheme providing representation for 'impecunious persons'.[116] This arguably indicates a lack of political will either to acknowledge or to address the problem of missing legal representation in the Syariah legal system. Yet the existing provisions, especially the above-cited Section 43(1)(b) Syaria LPA (FT), could, arguably, be used to establish a dedicated legal aid scheme at least in the Syariah legal system of the Federal Territories.

Creating an overarching professional body for Syariah lawyers at the federal level will be a different matter altogether as Islam is a matter for the states. Then Attorney General Tan Sri Tommy Thomas foreshadowed this possibility in his speech on the opening of the legal year in 2020, stating that:[117]

> It is our hope that this Act will be used as a model for other states so as [to] ultimately realise a uniform legal regime for Syarie lawyers throughout the country. The Syarie legal profession should, over time (like their brothers and sisters in the common law bar), have a national bar association.

[107] *Law and Human Rights*, *supra* note 13.

[108] Phelime Kine, 'Human Rights Watch: Indonesia's Aceh Authorities Lash Hundreds under Sharia Statutes: Repeal of Discriminatory, Brutal Bylaws Long Overdue', *Human Rights Watch* (8 February 2017), online: www.hrw.org/news/2017/02/08/indonesias-aceh-authorities-lash-hundreds-under-sharia-statutes.

[109] Please note that there are numerous local variations of the spelling of *syariah*, however here the Act itself uses the spelling *syarie*, which is adopted here.

[110] *Syarie Legal Profession (Federal Territories) Act 2019*, Malaysia, Act 814 [*Syarie LPA (FT)*].

[111] Ibid., Part II.

[112] *Badan Penguam Syarie* will be the professional association for lawyers in the Syariah legal system; see *Syarie LPA (FT)*, *supra* note 110, Part VII.

[113] *Majilis Penguam Syarie* will be the council of the *Badan Penguam Syarie*, similar to the Malaysian Bar Council: see *Syarie LPA (FT)*, *supra* note 110, Part VII.

[114] *Syarie LPA (FT)*, *supra* note 110, s 45.

[115] Ibid., s 43(1)(b).

[116] *LPA*, *supra* note 61, s 42(1)(h).

[117] Attorney General Thomas Tan Sri Tommy, 'Opening of Legal Year 2020 Speech' (Speech delivered at the opening of Legal Year 2020, Putrajaya, 10 January 2020).

Adding a professional Syariah lawyer association, whether at the state or, less likely, the federal level, with a legal aid scheme similar to the LAC of the Malaysian Bar, is no guarantee that legal aid will be on the agenda of a new federal professional body. Establishing a super legal aid organization by merging YBGK and the LAD would add one or two threads to Malaysia's patchwork of legal aid. These initiatives might make the tapestry more colourful, in the sense that each scheme has its own thread colour, but whether it will cover everyone in need remains to be seen.

Another obstacle is the historical traditional practice that legal representation is not necessarily required in Syariah courts. A shift in attitude for Syariah lawyers would be required for lawyers to donate their services. There is first the reluctance of lawyers in general to take on these cases. As noted above, only some of the accredited lawyers under the YBGK scheme are actively taking on cases, and that number accounts for both civil and criminal matters. Second, there is the difficulty that being a lawyer in a Syariah criminal case carries a stigma with it and creates a moral dilemma. Lawyers practising in non-religious criminal jurisdictions may experience qualms about representing criminal defendants, but Syariah criminal lawyers have to come to terms with defending people accused of acts that are not only legally wrong, but morally/religiously wrong. Syariah criminal lawyers are also subject to scrutiny from their fellow Muslims, or as one Syariah criminal lawyer put it, he was perceived as 'defending wrongdoers against Islam' and thus being 'with the enemies of Islam against Islam'.[118] The moral and religious dilemma could be, to a certain degree, overcome by allowing non-Muslims to practise in the Syariah courts, but that solution raises other potential problems. Non-Muslim practitioners might face increased scrutiny for being non-Muslims who are, even worse than Muslims, defending 'wrongdoers against Islam'. Given the recent developments of restricting Syariah legal practice to Muslims, this option appears to be even less likely in the near future.

Assuming that adequate legal services could be provided to parties in Syariah cases, there is a question of whether indigent litigants would avail themselves of the offered services, as navigation among the colourful threads of legal aid services is difficult, as mentioned above. Other litigants might choose not to be legally represented after doing a cost–benefit analysis. This is particularly the case in Syariah criminal cases. Syariah criminal courts are limited in their sentencing power by the 3–6–5 safeguards, three years in jail, six lashes with the cane, and a fine of no more than MYR5,000 (US$1,200).[119] The relatively low sentencing power means that sometimes clients balance the costs and benefits of hiring a lawyer and decide that, while they might desire representation, the costs to them would probably outweigh the benefits. In an interview with a daily newspaper, a Syariah court judge commented that 'one of the biggest reasons is the fine' as 'they have to pay more [to the lawyer] than the fine that will be imposed on them'.[120]

The initiatives considered here would add more threads to Malaysia's patchwork of legal aid, but they would not form a cohesive tapestry of legal aid. For that to happen much more needs to be unravelled and restitched together. The threads that are the different legal aid schemes need to be bought together and strengthened, and gaps need to be filled. Regarding the colourfulness provided by the different schemes, assistance needs to be provided so that indigent litigants know under which circumstances legal aid is available, i.e. means and merits tests, and what types of services are available in which jurisdiction. A more 'monochrome colour scheme' might make this navigation easier for indigent litigants, as well as be more efficient by pooling resources together to meet the existing need, which individual schemes are struggling to fulfil.

118 *Lack of Access*, *supra* note 98.

119 See *Syariah Court (Criminal Jurisdiction) Act*, *supra* note 27, s 2.

120 *Lack of Access*, *supra* note 98.

16

The Syariah Court of Singapore: Achieving a More Formal Access to Justice

Ahmad Nizam Abbas

Abstract

Singapore's Syariah Court has shifted over the years, from an informal court less reliant on written law to a more formal court with established law and procedure. This shift has in many ways supported access to justice, but challenges remain. Focusing on divorce in the Syariah Court, the chapter analyses illustrative examples of jurisdictional issues which impact access to justice. The chapter also critiques the resources available to improve the experiences of litigants navigating the process, which can be overwhelming for the uninitiated, and discusses the role and type of lawyers who practise at the Syariah Court, reflecting on the fact that most do not have any formal training in Muslim law. This chapter recommends methods of expanding access to justice in the Syariah Court further, including the need to incorporate technology to aid unrepresented litigants and lawyers alike.

I. INTRODUCTION

While Muslims had applied Muslim personal laws of marriage and divorce before and after Singapore came under British rule in 1819, it was not until 1880 that this situation was officially recognized with the enactment of the Mohammedan Marriage Ordinance 1880, which provided for the registration of Muslim marriages and divorces.[1] Under the Ordinance, the Governor of Singapore was given the power to appoint a *Kadi*, a Muslim judge who renders decisions according to Islamic law,[2] to solemnize or preside over marriages and divorces of Muslims in Singapore.

Prior to the creation of the Syariah[3] Court, Muslims would visit the *Kadi*'s office to obtain a divorce, and have the *Kadi* record the parties' consent on ancillary issues such as maintenance and property. If there was no agreement, the parties would end up at the civil courts, where English-trained judges would adjudicate and apply Muslim personal law.[4] The need for a proper divorce

[1] Taufik Abdullah and Sharon Siddique, eds., *Islam and Society in South East Asia* (Singapore: Institute of Southeast Asian Studies, 1986) at 321.

[2] There are several variations of the spelling, such as *Kathi* and *Qadi*; for consistency, *Kadi* shall be used throughout the chapter.

[3] This chapter adopts the Singapore spelling of *Syariah*, as opposed to *Shari'a*.

[4] *Hawah* v. *Dawood* [1868] SLP Leis 253, [1827–7] SLR Leicester's 253, cited in Leong Wai Kum, *Elements of Family Law in Singapore* (Singapore: LexisNexis, 2007) at 378.

court, to hear disputes on divorces and ancillary issues, was raised by community leaders who were concerned about the high rate of divorce and its impact on the Muslim community. In 1954, Ahmad Mohamed Ibrahim, a member of the Legislative Council, highlighted that 'there are *Kadi* courts in the Malay States but none in Singapore and at present, matters of Muslim marriage and divorce are dealt with by individual *kadis* who are, to a large extent, unfettered by any control or rules'.[5]

In 1958, the Syariah Court of Singapore was constituted pursuant to the Muslim Ordinance 1957,[6] the predecessor to the Administration of Muslim Law Act ('AMLA').[7] AMLA was enacted in 1966 and came into force in 1968,[8] soon after Singapore became independent in 1965. As the Syariah Court is a creature of statute,[9] it derives its jurisdiction and power from AMLA itself. The Syariah Court does not possess inherent jurisdiction or power, and any jurisdiction or power that it purports to have must be expressly provided for in AMLA or rules under this statute.[10]

Today *Kadi* no longer have the power to register divorces, and the Syariah Court is the only institution in Singapore with the legal powers to recognize divorces between Muslim couples.[11] The judicial officers at the Syariah Court are known as Presidents, and they are appointed by the President of Singapore.[12] Formerly under the purview of the Ministry of Social Affairs and then the Ministry of Community Development, the Syariah Court is currently under the Ministry of Culture, Community and Youth ('MCCY').[13] It is however commonly understood in Singapore that this arrangement is mainly administrative. In reality, the overall direction of the Syariah Court is the responsibility of the Minister-in-charge of Muslim Affairs, evident from the fact that every major amendment to AMLA has been presented to Parliament by the Minister-in-charge of Muslim Affairs at the time. The post of a minister in Cabinet who is entrusted with the additional responsibility of overseeing Muslim affairs in Singapore was announced in 1977, formalizing a de facto position present since self-government in 1959.[14]

Marriages and divorces in Singapore are registered and governed under the Women's Charter and AMLA. The former is applicable to all non-Muslims while the latter is exclusively for Muslims.[15] A Muslim cannot marry a non-Muslim under AMLA but may do so through the Women's Charter, subject to other eligibility conditions.[16] Under Section 35 of AMLA, the Syariah Court has jurisdiction regarding a divorce where both parties are Muslims or were married under Muslim law. While Muslims in Singapore have the option of having the civil courts adjudicate on matters ancillary to a divorce, they have no choice as to the forum for

[5] Noor Aisha Abdul Rahman and Azhar Ibrahim, *Singapore Chronicles: Malays* (Singapore: Straits Times Press, 2017) at 64.

[6] *Mohammedan Marriage Ordinance* (No. 5 of 1880), first enacted in 1880, went through several rounds of amendments in 1905, 1917, 1923, 1934, 1936, 1952, and 1957, including its renaming to the Muslim Ordinance.

[7] *Administration of Muslim Law Act* (Cap. 3, 1966 Rev. Edn Sing.) (as amended 31 October 2009) [*AMLA*].

[8] *Administration of Muslim Law Act (Commencement) Notification 1968* (S 166/1968 Sing.), n 2.

[9] *AMLA*, *supra* note 7, s 34, which provides that '[t]he President of Singapore may by notification in the Gazette constitute a Syariah Court of Singapore'.

[10] *Khamis Bin Haroon* v. *Norhamisah Binte Abdul Hamid*, Summons No. 14587 (Singapore Syariah Court, 29 November 1999, unreported), per Mr Shaiffudin Saruwan, who was formerly the Registrar of Syariah Court and now a member of the Appeal Board of MUIS.

[11] Roqiyah Begum, 'Muslim Divorce in Singapore', *Asia Law Network* (7 September 2017), online: learn.asialawnetwork.com/2017/09/07/muslim-divorce-in-singapore/.

[12] *AMLA*, *supra* note 7, s 34A.

[13] Ministry of Culture, Community and Youth website, online: www.mccy.gov.sg/sector/community.

[14] Zainul Abidin Rasheed and Norshahril Saat, *Majulah! 50 Years of Malay/Muslim Community in Singapore* (Singapore: World Scientific Publishing Co., 2016) at 100.

[15] *AMLA*, *supra* note 7, s 89.

[16] *Women's Charter* (Cap. 353, 1961 Rev. Edn Sing.) (as amended 31 October 2009), s 3(4).

divorce. Almost inevitably, from the start to the end of their divorce process, both local and foreign Muslims in Singapore find themselves enmeshed in the Syariah Court system.

The Syariah Court's jurisdiction and powers are highly relevant to access to justice, as they form the starting point of a person's contact with the entire court system. The interplay between the civil law and Syariah court systems however is not always well understood.[17] The root of the problem lies in determining exactly when the Syariah Court's jurisdiction and power comes into play and when it ends, and how these questions impact the parties and the justice achieved. For example, Syariah Court litigants currently have the right to resolve issues other than divorce, such as maintenance, in the civil courts. While some ponder aloud whether divorce and ancillary issues should be heard in two different legal systems in Singapore, any proposed amendment perceived to be a dilution of the standing of the Syariah Court will be robustly challenged.[18] The sometimes strong reaction of the Muslim community to any major amendments to AMLA gives a clue as to how the Muslim community regards the Syariah Court.

The first part of the chapter provides some examples of the issues regarding access to justice that arise out of the jurisdiction and powers of the Syariah Court. Focusing on divorce in the Syariah Court, the chapter analyses illustrative examples of jurisdictional issues which impact access to justice. The next parts consider the impact of resources, means of court navigation, and law awareness, and legal representation on access to justice. The chapter critiques the resources available to improve the experiences of litigants navigating the process, which can be overwhelming for the uninitiated, and discusses the role and type of lawyers who practise at the Syariah Court, reflecting on the fact that most do not have any formal training in Muslim law. The chapter argues that Singapore's Syariah Court has shifted over the years, from an informal court less reliant on written law to a more formal court with established law and procedure. This shift has in many ways supported access to justice, but challenges remain. This chapter recommends methods of expanding access to justice in the Syariah Court further, including the need to incorporate technology to aid unrepresented litigants and lawyers alike. The chapter concludes by observing that given the Syariah Court's importance in Singapore, the access to justice it provides should be supported in a manner similar to Singapore's other courts.

II. JURISDICTIONAL ISSUES AND ACCESS TO JUSTICE

Under AMLA, the Syariah Court hears and determines disputes on Muslim marriages, divorces, ancillary matters, e.g. division of assets, maintenance during the wife's *iddah* (period of three months when she is not allowed to remarry), and consolatory gift (*mutaah*).[19] While the Syariah Court hears cases at first instance, appeals from the Syariah Court are heard at the Appeal Board of MUIS (the Islamic Religious Council of Singapore).[20]

A. *Changing demographics*

Section 35 of AMLA provides that the Syariah Court of Singapore has jurisdiction over divorces where both parties are Muslims or were married under Muslim law. By and large, this criterion

[17] Mohamed Faizal Mohamed Abdul Kadir, 'Muslim Law' (2016) 17 *SAL Annual Review* 604 at para. 22.1.
[18] *Report of the Select Committee on AMLA Amendments (Bill No 18/98)* (10 February 1999).
[19] AMLA, *supra* note 7, s 35.
[20] AMLA, *supra* note 7, s 55.

seems straightforward enough for litigants to understand. So long as their marriage was registered at the Singapore Registry of Muslim Marriages, there is no issue at all on the Syariah Court being the forum for their divorce, and cases raising issues under Section 35 are rare.

Changing demographics and increasing cross-border relationships have however required the Syariah Court to deal with new issues. Over the course of the 50 years of the Syariah Court, the demographics of parties who appear at the Syariah Court have changed significantly. Between 1990 and 2016, the number of inter-ethnic marriages between Muslims rose from 16.5 to 33.9 per cent.[21] There are more Singaporeans who now live overseas yet maintain close links with Singapore. There are also more marriages between Singaporeans and persons of other nationalities. Lawyers have seen an increase in Singaporeans who have undergone divorces outside Singapore through non-court channels. This occurs in countries such as the United Kingdom, New Zealand, and Australia, where Muslims go through divorce proceedings conducted by local religious bodies. In the United Kingdom, parties initiate divorce proceedings through one of the Sharia Councils established across the country.[22] As these local councils do not have the power of a court, there is some uncertainty regarding how marital status will subsequently be treated in Singapore. The issue is complicated further when one party insists that the couple are already divorced but the other party refutes it.

B. *Different treatment for parties who have been divorced outside the Syariah Court of Singapore*

As the law currently stands, parties can be divorced in two different ways outside the Singapore Syariah Court. For parties who have been divorced by a *Kadi* and registered the same under Section 102, the Singapore Syariah Court has the power under Section 52(3) to make an order on the division of matrimonial assets.[23] For parties who are divorced overseas, the Singapore Syariah Court does not have the power to do so, and the parties must seek relief from the Family Justice Courts. Why is there a need for such a difference? It would be neater and legally sound to give the Syariah Court powers over ancillary matters where the parties had already been divorced.

One reason why it is practical for the Syariah Court to be granted this additional power is to cover situations where the validity of the foreign divorce is itself in dispute. How would the Family Justice Courts handle the situation if one of the parties disputes the validity of the divorce under Muslim law? As things stand, there is uncertainty whether the Syariah Court can make any Order on the validity of the divorce overseas, even though under AMLA Section 35(2)(b) the Syariah Court can determine disputes relating to divorces known in Muslim law as *fasakh* (divorce decreed by court based on specific incapacity or impossibility for parties to continue living together as a married couple),[24] *cerai taklik* (divorce based on a condition of marriage which the husband agreed to at the time of marriage),[25] *khuluk* (divorce where parties agree to a payment by the wife to the husband in return for his pronouncement of divorce),[26] and *talak* (pronouncement of divorce by the husband).[27] Past cases indicate that parties can only file an

[21] Department of Statistics Singapore, *Statistics on Marriages and Divorces, 2016*, at 8 (Chart 1.8), online: https://www.singstat.gov.sg/-/media/files/publications/population/smd2016.pdf>.
[22] Raffia Arshad, *Islamic Family Law* (London: Sweet & Maxwell, 2010) at 122.
[23] AMLA, *supra* note 7, s 52(3).
[24] AMLA, *supra* note 7, s 49.
[25] AMLA, *supra* note 7, s 48.
[26] AMLA, *supra* note 7, s 47(4).
[27] AMLA, *supra* note 7, s 47(3).

application for divorce at the Syariah Court if they are still married to each other. Any doubts could be erased if an additional line was inserted in Section 35(2), clarifying that the Singapore Syariah Court is entitled to make a determination on the issue of the validity of the foreign divorce itself.

The rise in Singaporeans marrying foreigners in the last 50 years since AMLA was enacted, together with the fact that more foreigners are settling in Singapore, may produce more complicated situations than were envisaged at the time AMLA was introduced. Practitioners have observed cases where one spouse has left Singapore and unilaterally obtained a divorce, in their country of origin or another country where they have set up a new home. In the Singapore Court of Appeal decision *TMO* v. *TMP*,[28] the parties were married in Singapore in 1998. In 2008, they moved to Johore in Malaysia. In mid-2012, the wife discovered that her husband had unilaterally obtained a divorce against her from the Johore Syariah Court in April 2012, and he had been granted interim custody of their two children as well. The wife was totally unaware that the husband had obtained the divorce, leaving her in the lurch.

It is however not always the wife who may be the victim. In the unreported case *Mohamed Saleem* v. *Jana Muna Fathima Dishad Parveen*,[29] a Singaporean husband was caught off guard when his Indian wife sent him a *Kazi* Certificate[30] confirming their divorce. To add insult to injury, the certificate cited that the divorce was on the ground of impotency. The husband then filed for divorce in the Singapore Syariah Court. The wife objected to the application on the basis that the parties were already divorced in India, and that a divorce by *Kazi* is legally valid as it is statutorily provided for under the Kazis Act.[31] The husband's position was that the wife had not obtained the divorce honestly as he was certainly not impotent and had the medical documents to prove this. While one way to resolve their dispute would have been to apply to an Indian court to set aside the *Kazi* divorce, the husband harboured grave concerns over the wife's family influence, and the resources required to mount a legal battle there would have been hefty. Fortunately, in this case the wife submitted to the jurisdiction of the Syariah Court, and the husband was granted a divorce by pronouncing the *talak* on his wife. The President then went on to make the order regarding the couple's matrimonial flat, resolving what could have potentially been yet another round of litigation at the Family Justice Courts.

C. *Jurisdiction in both Civil Court and Syariah Court*

While the Syariah Court has exclusive jurisdiction over Muslim marriages, both the Syariah Court and the Family Justice Courts have jurisdiction over issues regarding maintenance, custody, and property.[32] Parties in a Muslim marriage are often confused regarding which court to go to, and it is not uncommon for Muslims to find themselves straddling two court systems during and after divorce proceedings.

During the 1999 Select Committee Hearing on Administration of Muslim Law Amendment Bill, then Minister Abdullah Tarmugi acknowledged that there were calls for the Syariah Court to be a one-stop centre, but that feedback from the Syariah Court and practitioners indicated

[28] [2017] 1 SLR 585 (CA).

[29] *Saleem*, Summons No. 47116 (Singapore Syariah Court, 7 October 2015, unreported).

[30] Also spelled '*Qadi*' or '*Kadi*'.

[31] The Kazis Act, India, Act No. 12 of 1880 (as amended 25 February 2019).

[32] AMLA, *supra* note 7, s 52(3); *Supreme Court of Judicature Act* (Cap. 322, 1969 Rev. Edn Sing.) (as amended 31 July 2007), ss 17A(2)(a)–(c) [SCJA].

that this change would tax court resources, leading to a queue from the Syariah Court building all the way to Toa Payoh (a neighbouring housing estate). One reason why the dual system continues to exist can be seen in Minister Abdullah Tarmugi's speech in the Select Committee report of 1999, in the context of proposing a new Section 35A in AMLA that the civil courts could hear matters ancillary to divorces. He stated that 'Muslims, as citizens of this country, must be allowed the same right of access to the civil courts as non-Muslims.'[33]

The practice in Singapore is for Muslims to have maintenance matters adjudicated in the Family Justice Courts under the Women's Charter. This is not only because the Syariah Court lacks the enforcement machinery to take action against defaulters, a practice acknowledged by then Minister Abdullah Tarmugi at the reading of the AMLA (Amendment) Bill in April 1999.[34] It is also because under AMLA, the Syariah Court will have to stay proceedings for maintenance for a wife and child once it has notice that there are similar proceedings in the civil court.[35] For custody, care, and control of children, a Muslim party can apply to the Family Justice Courts prior to the commencement of divorce proceedings at the Syariah Court, whereupon the former will then stay proceedings pending the outcome of the Syariah Court application.

For matrimonial property, the High Court has held that if a party applies to the High Court for a determination on the assets prior to commencement of Syariah Court proceedings, the High Court case will proceed. In *Pereira Dennis John Sunny* v. *Faridah bte Abdul Latiff*,[36] the wife submitted the registration form to the Syariah Court on 28 July 2015, and it was only eight months later that the summons was issued. On 6 November 2015, the husband filed an application in the High Court for a declaration on the shares of parties in respect of four properties held in the parties' joint names. In effect, what he wanted to do was to have the properties disposed of based on property law, without invoking matrimonial law. As he had contributed more financially, his apparent objective was to secure a larger portion of the property than he would be entitled to under matrimonial law in the Syariah Court. The High Court held that as the Syariah Court proceedings only commenced upon the originating summons being issued and not at the time of the registration,[37] the High Court was earlier in time and thus had jurisdiction.[38] The law applied to the dispute was civil law and not matrimonial law, and certainly not Muslim law. The dual system can therefore be exploited by a party who is intent on frustrating the other, by delaying the divorce or getting a more advantageous outcome for him- or herself. This tactic exists because parties who intend to commence divorce action in the Syariah Court cannot do so immediately. The party will first have to submit a registration form, which will then be processed, and he or she will then be notified to attend counselling at a designated agency. It is only after the agency has certified that the parties have completed the counselling that they then receive a letter from the Syariah Court with an appointment date to file a Case Statement, and this can take several months.

The *Pereira* case exposed the unintended consequence on the wife of having the issue of the jointly held assets dealt with under property laws, where her non-financial contributions would

33 *Singapore Parliamentary Debates, Official Report* vol. 70 (15 April 1999) [*Parliamentary Debate 15 April 1999*] at col. 1249 (Abdullah Tarmugi, Acting Minister for Muslim Affairs).

34 *Parliamentary Debate 15 April 1999*, *supra* note 33, at col. 1264.

35 AMLA, *supra* note 7, ss 36(2)–(3).

36 [2016] SGHCR 9.

37 SCJA, *supra* note 32, s 17A(2) read with s 17A(3), indicates that what matters is whether the civil proceedings were 'commenced on or after the commencement of proceedings for divorce in the Syariah Court'.

38 *Pereira Dennis John Sunny* v. *Faridah bte* v. *Abdul Latiff* [2017] 5 SLR 529 (HC).

have little weight, if any, on the outcome. One cannot help feeling sympathy for the wife, as it was through no fault of her own that she could not prevent the husband from moving ahead with the action in the High Court. The irony however is that there was actually nothing in AMLA then that specified that one had to attend counselling first before being allowed to commence proceedings. The objective of ensuring parties have attempted reconciliation first is noble, but the way in which the Syariah Court implemented this practice had an adverse effect on the wife. After 2017 amendments to AMLA, a specific clause empowered the Syariah Court to mandate parties to attend counselling and other specified activities before and during divorce proceedings. Since August 2017, the Syariah Court has also modified its stance on issuing of summonses, and the rigid practice of only being allowed to file the Case Statement by appointment has been repealed. So long as a party has attended the counselling at the designated agency, he or she can commence action at any time during the prescribed hours. However, as long as the *Pereira* decision is the guiding principle regarding which actions may proceed, the party with greater financial muscle and resources will have an advantage over the other party.

III. RESOURCE FACTORS

A. *General Resources*

Another challenge the Syariah Court has faced is resources. A prime reason why some Muslims have gone to the civil courts in the past was because the Syariah Court did not have adequate resources to deal with their disputes.[39] While it is understandable that resources must be a factor in the running of any institution, one wonders how long this issue will continue, as it has already been 50 years since the Syariah Court was created.

Based on the statistics from the Singapore Department of Statistics, the number of Muslim divorces in Singapore was 1,667 in 2015, 1,702 in 2016, 1,637 in 2017, and 1,682 in 2018.[40] For marriages under the civil law, the figures were 5,450 in 2015, 5,505 in 2016, 5,570 in 2017, and 5,308 in 2018.[41] A direct comparison of the divorce figures alone does not give us a complete picture as to what each court does, as the caseloads of the Syariah Court and the Family Justice Courts go beyond divorce. For example, although there were 6,903 writs of divorce issued in 2017 from the Family Justice Courts, the total number of cases it handled for the year amounted to 27,538. As indicated in its annual report, more than 50 per cent of the total caseload was made up of divorces, maintenance, and probate cases.[42] As for the Syariah Court, the Presidents of the Syariah Court also issue Inheritance Certificates for estates of deceased Muslims, in addition to hearing divorce cases. This takes up valuable judicial time.

The Syariah Court has a heavy caseload, but in the eyes of practitioners, there is a huge difference in resources between the two courts. This view was reinforced by the different actions taken by the Family Justice Courts and Syariah Court in response to the measures imposed by the Singapore Government regarding COVID-19.[43] During the period from 7 April to 1 June

[39] *Parliamentary Debate 15 April 1999*, *supra* note 33, at col. 1249.

[40] Department of Statistics, Singapore, 'Divorces Under the Administration of Muslim Law Act', online: www.tablebuilder.singstat.gov.sg/publicfacing/createDataTable.action?refId=14107.

[41] Department of Statistics, Singapore, 'Divorces Under the Women's Charter', online: www.tablebuilder.singstat.gov.sg/publicfacing/createDataTable.action?refId=14107.

[42] Family Justice Courts, *Annual Report 2017 (Family Justice: Strengthening the Fundamentals)*.

[43] *COVID-19 (Temporary Measures) Act 2020* (No. 14 of 2020), Singapore (with effect from 19 November 2020).

2020, the Family Justice Courts continued with court hearings and filing of cases, albeit through online hearings and electronic hearings.[44] The Syariah Court was closed throughout,[45] with exceptions only for urgent matters, as the Syariah Court did not have an electronic filing system in place for divorce-related matters, and the manual filing system would have required contact between the public and lawyers seeking to file applications with the Syariah Court staff. During this period, the inability of litigants and lawyers to file any divorce-related application in court, and the lack of movement of live court matters, was frustrating, especially to parents who were denied access to their children by the other parent and could not get a hearing date from the Syariah Court for an order on child access.

B. *Judicial Strength*

Prior to 1999, there had never been more than two Presidents of the Syariah Court at any one time. When discussing the 1999 Select Committee Report on the Administration of Muslim Law (Amendment) Bill in Parliament, Minister Abdullah Tarmugi announced (i) the creation of a new post of Senior President to head and provide directions for the Court and lay down court procedures, (ii) the appointment of a panel of ad hoc Presidents of the Syariah Court to help cut down the backlog of cases, and (iii) the appointment of a Registrar to help relieve the Presidents of their non-substantive work, and explained that 'with these, the Syariah Court will be able to dispense justice to the community effectively and speedily. My ministry will also be looking separately at administrative measures, procedures and manpower needs to enhance the efficiency of the Court to dovetail the Committee's recommendations.'[46] The number of full-time Presidents, including the Senior President, has increased to three since 2017.[47] However, especially in the initial years, the ad hoc presidents contributed immensely to the clearing of a backlog of cases. The hearings presided by the ad hoc presidents typically took place in the evenings, and the term 'Night Court' became synonymous with ad hoc Presidents. Today, while there is still a panel of ad hoc Presidents, the cases are hardly ever held in the evenings, as there is no longer a clamour for available courtrooms and judicial time.[48]

The year 2017 saw the appointment of the first female President, Ustazah Raihanah Binte Halid,[49] and since 2008, the number of female members on the panel of the Appeal Board has risen from zero to six.[50] In a public statement which was published in the national newspaper

[44] Family Justice Court, *Family Justice Court Registrar Circular No. 2 of 2020* (5 April 2020), online: www.familyjusticecourts.gov.sg/news-and-events/news/view/registrar's-circular-no.-2-of-2020/.

[45] Syariah Court Singapore, *Syariah Court Registrar's Circulars No. 13* (6 April 2020), online: www.syariahcourt.gov.sg/syariah/front-end/Attachments/RC13of2020.pdf/; Syariah Court Singapore, *Syariah Court Registrar's Circulars No. 14* (23 April 2020), online: www.syariahcourt.gov.sg/syariah/front-end/Attachments/RC14of2020.pdf/.

[46] *Parliamentary Debate 15 April 1999*, *supra* note 33, at col. 1251.

[47] *Parliamentary Debate 15 April 1999*, *supra* note 33, at col. 1253.

[48] As of 1 July 2012, there were six members on the Ad Hoc Presidents panel; three of them were former Presidents of the Syariah Court. For details, see Ministry of Culture, Community and Youth, 'Leadership Renewal at the Syariah Court' (27 July 2020), online: www.mccy.gov.sg/about-us/news-and-resources/press-statements/2020/jul/-/media/A0B96198A20A4F10A4967D1708184CF0.ashx, particularly Annex B (Full List of Presidents and Ad Hoc Presidents of the Syariah Court).

[49] Press release by Ministry of Culture, Community and Youth (MCCY), online: www.mccy.gov.sg/about-us/news-and-resources/press-statements/2017/jan-jun/mccy-honours-two-syariah-court-presidents.

[50] Calvin Yang, 'More Women on MUIS Board of Appeal', *Straits Times* (6 February 2016), online: www.straitstimes.com/singapore/more-women-on-muis-board-of-appeal#:~:text=More%20women%20have%20been%20appointed,four%20in%20the%20previous%20term.last.

The Straits Times on 6 February 2016, MUIS announced that the appointment of women members to the Appeal Board 'ensures that the Appeal Board has the expertise needed from a female perspective, apart from their contributions in their own fields'.[51] This is a welcome move and it sends a strong message to the public on the progressive approach taken to the Syariah Court and Appeal Board appointments.

The first Registrar appointed to the Syariah Court in 1999 was a secondment from the then Subordinate Courts of Singapore. All four registrars since 1999, including the current one at the time of writing, have been at one time or the other, members of the Singapore Legal Service. Prior to her appointment in February 2018, the present Deputy Registrar was a District Judge in the Family Justice Courts.[52]

While the increase in the number of judicial officers did enhance the level of efficiency and quality of services at the Syariah Court, there still persists the perception of inadequate resources. A decade after the 1999 changes, a Member of Parliament stated:[53]

> It is important for the Syariah Court to seek ways to improve its administrative processes. To do this, the court needs to be adequately staffed. The appointment of a deputy registrar of the Syariah Court is to be welcomed, as it would lighten the existing administrative burden of the Syariah Court. However, it may not be enough to stop there. I would like to suggest that we investigate the workload of Syariah Court judges and consider whether there is a need to employ law clerks to assist the court with research and administrative matters. In addition, it is also important to plan for leadership renewal of the Syariah Court. I note that the key officers of the Syariah Court consist of officers who are retirees recalled for service or are close to retirement. It is imperative that we attract well-trained legal officers to serve the Syariah Court. As we all know, talent does not come cheap these days. In view of that, I think it is time we reviewed the compensation package of Syariah Court judges and other officers to ensure that we can attract promising young graduates to serve the Syariah Court.

More experienced practitioners at the Syariah Court remember the days when the Syariah Court President would be saddled with so many administrative matters that it led to the delegation of certain matters to the staff. As a result, the lines between judicial and non-judicial roles were sometimes blurred. An illustration of the manner in which some matters were conducted previously can be gleaned from the reported case of *Eddy Osman* v. *Yulita Ridowati Binti Sabar*,[54] in which a quarrelling couple went to the Syariah Court to get counselling and not to seek a divorce. On 13 September 1995, they met a clerk, M, who asked whether the appellant had pronounced the *talak*. Although the husband explained to the clerk that he had not used the word *cerai* (Malay for divorce) or *talak*, M confirmed before them that '*talak tiga*' (divorce by three *talaks*) had been pronounced and they had to wait for six months for an open court trial. This meeting at the Syariah Court took about five minutes. For one year there was no news from the Syariah Court. On 19 September 1996, they attended the Syariah Court where they met another clerk, S, who questioned them whether '*talak tiga*' had been pronounced, and the husband told her that the words '*cerai*' and '*talak*' were

[51] Ibid.

[52] Rahimah Rashith, 'Singapore's First Female Syariah Court Registrar Steps Down at Age 70', *Straits Times* (12 January 2018), online: www.straitstimes.com/singapore/singapores-first-female-syariah-court-registrar-steps-down-at-the-age-of-70.

[53] *Singapore Parliamentary Debates, Official Report* vol. 85 (17 November 2008) [*Parliamentary Debate* 17 *November* 2008] at cols. 750–1 (Hawazi Daipi, Senior Parliamentary Secretary to the Acting Minister for Manpower and Minister for Health).

[54] *Eddy Osman* v. *Yulita Ridowati Binti Sabar* [1999] SGMML 11; for readers unfamiliar with Singapore Syariah law reports, SGMML is the neutral citation for pre-SSAR decisions by the Syariah Appeal Board.

not used. She telephoned her colleagues and then confirmed with the parties that the '*talak tiga*' had been pronounced, and they were asked to sign some documents. They were then told to wait for a letter from the Syariah Court. On 19 February 1997, they appeared before the Syariah Court, where they presumed their individual case would be reviewed carefully, but there were three other couples whose cases were heard at the same time. At this hearing, the clerk merely asked them whether '*talak tiga*' had been confirmed. The husband recounted what he had said on the earlier occasions. They were shocked when the President duly recorded a Consent Order that the three *talaks* had been pronounced.

The Appeal Board chairman in his written judgment described the circumstances as related by the appellant and the respondent as 'somewhat bewildering'. The case was remitted back to the Syariah Court for the purpose of determining through evidence and a full trial whether in fact the three *talaks* were pronounced by the Appellant, and if they were not pronounced, then the Consent Order should be set aside.

The above case exposed various unfortunate elements of how certain cases were handled in the Syariah Court in the past, from the delegation of judicial functions to delays. In those days, the Presidents of the Syariah Court were religious scholars with a background in theology.[55] Matters of procedure and evidence were not as clear as today. The secondment of judiciary members from the civil courts has helped to streamline processes, which were loose and informal before amendments to AMLA in 1999. The Syariah Court also started to engage in consultations with lawyers to review the Muslim Marriage and Divorce Rules, and this resulted in a massive revamp of court forms in 1999. The Muslim Law Practice Committee ('MLPC') of the Law Society of Singapore held a conference with the Syariah Court in that same year, to educate the public and share with practitioners the reforms with the aim of improving the overall quality of the Syariah Court.[56]

IV. NAVIGATING THE COURT

A. *Forms and Procedures*

Almost every form in use at the Syariah Court today was drafted and introduced in 1999, including the Case Statement, which is absolutely necessary to kick off a divorce action.

The forms at the Syariah Court are relatively simple to fill in and are meant to get parties to focus on the core and key issues of their divorce. As illustrated by the *Eddy Osman* case discussed earlier, parties who entered the Syariah Court in the past may not even have had a basic grasp of what they were required to do. Although things have improved today, as the court provides instructional guides and checklists for the parties, even on details such as the court dress code, the court experience can still be an intimidating one, especially for the uninitiated.

Parties in the Singapore Syariah Court typically speak English and/or Malay. The forms at the Syariah Court meet this challenge, and they come in two languages, English and Malay. Proceedings in the hearing itself can also be in English or Malay.[57] Where the party is not competent in either English or Malay, he or she can use any language, so long as a competent interpreter is present to assist.

[55] Muhammad Haniff Hassan, 'The Training, Appointment and Supervision of Islamic Judges in Singapore' (1990) *Pacific Rim Law & Policy Journal* 190 at 191–3.

[56] Per the author, in his capacity as the Vice Chairman of the Organizing Committee of this conference.

[57] AMLA, *supra* note 7, s 38(1) provides that the languages of the Court shall be the national language and English.

B. *Electronic Litigation*

As the Family Justice Courts and other Singapore courts have already implemented electronic litigation, it is inevitable that the same will happen at the Syariah Court. The Syariah Court already has relevant experience in applications for Inheritance Certificates, which have utilized an online system for more than a decade.[58] To use this system, the applicant fills out an online form with details of the next-of-kin, and the Syariah Court will issue the Inheritance Certificate without the need for the applicant to attend physically. However, the applicant has to submit a Statutory Declaration that the information provided is true and accurate to the best of his knowledge, which must be affirmed before a Commissioner of Oaths, a service not available at the Court Registry. This online practice has saved valuable time and resources for both the Syariah Court and members of public who wish to obtain the relevant Inheritance Certificate.

Lawyers and litigants should be prepared for the eventual move to electronic litigation. At present, the Syariah Court has student volunteers from the local universities who assist members of the public in filling out paper forms. It will be necessary in the early stages to have more volunteers around at the computer terminals at the Syariah Court itself when electronic litigation is implemented. This is critical so that the litigants in person do not feel that they are at a disadvantage. While it is important that the Syariah Court not be seen as lagging behind, moving into electronic litigation is about more than presenting an updated image; it is about enhancing efficiency and performance. As seen by the COVID-19 experience in which the entire Syariah Court system had to be closed down, the implementation of an electronic litigation system is overdue.

V. LAW AWARENESS AND LEGAL REPRESENTATION

A. *Law Awareness*

It is hoped that over time there can be a more widespread understanding of the Syariah Court in Singapore. As espoused by then-Speaker of Parliament Madam Halimah Yaacob in her speech on 12 May 2017 at the Syariah Law Forum organized by students from the National University of Singapore ('NUS'), it is useful to have more 'open sharing'.[59] Kudos must be given to groups such as the NUS students who, together with the Syariah Law Forum Organizing Committee (a 16-member student organizing team in which 14 students were non-Muslims),[60] wrote a handbook titled 'Navigating Muslim Law in Singapore'.[61] It is a sad reality that there have been no authoritative textbooks on Muslim family law in Singapore since Professor Ahmad Ibrahim's *Islamic Law in Malaya* published in 1965.[62] Even materials like this are intended for lawyers, and are generally not accessible to unrepresented litigants.

58 Singapore Syariah Court, 'Online Application for Inheritance Certificate', online: www.syariahcourt.gov.sg/Syariah/front-end/ActualCal_Redirect.aspx.

59 Shaffiq Idris Alkhatib, 'Syariah Law Forum Fosters a Culture of Open Sharing: Halimah' *Straits Times* (13 May 2017), online: www.straitstimes.com/singapore/syariah-law-forum-fosters-a-culture-of-open-sharing-halimah.

60 Ibid.

61 Syariah Law Forum Organizing Committee, *Navigating Muslim Law in Singapore* (Singapore: Syariah Law Forum Organizing Committee, National University of Singapore, 2017).

62 Ahmad Ibrahim, edited by Shirle Gordon, *Islamic Law in Malaya* (Singapore: Malaysian Sociological Research Institute, 1965).

B. Legal Representation

As the Syariah Court moves ahead, there is a need to be mindful of ensuring that the stakeholders and parties who require its services move in tandem with it. While there are no published figures on the percentage of Syariah Court parties who are without lawyers, a visitor to the Syariah Court on any day can draw a conclusion that at least half of the cases are self-represented.

The Syariah Court does highlight to litigants that they can apply for assistance at the state-run Legal Aid Bureau ('LAB'),[63] where they will have to pass a financial means test and a merits assessment test. Those who fail to receive LAB assistance are usually referred to the Primary Justice Project ('PJP'), a settlement scheme jointly developed by the State Courts, the Law Society of Singapore, and the Community Justice Centre ('CJC') and implemented in 2014.[64] There are a number of legal clinics run by Muslim organizations and mosques where a member of the public can seek assistance in his legal issues.[65] In addition, litigants can also avail themselves of the clinics run at the respective Community Development Councils ('CDCs') in every district. The Syariah Court itself conducts a monthly briefing for those who are thinking about divorce, in collaboration with volunteer lawyers from the MLPC.

As not everyone qualifies for legal aid, there will continue to be many who are self-represented. As noted above, there are no statistics available on the percentage of persons who represent themselves at the Syariah Court. The only evidence is anecdotal, from the author's and fellow lawyers' observations at the Syariah Court. In the author's experience, it is a challenge for unrepresented litigants to navigate the system on their own. The available information on the Syariah Court website on court processes is very basic. For example, while there is a section on divorce on the website, most of the answers in the FAQ section are very brief and include court jargon. It is doubtful that litigants will find the answers to many of the questions they may need to ask in handling their own case. To illustrate, in response to the question, 'Where can I find details for a Muslim divorce in Singapore?', the answer is, 'For details on a Muslim divorce in Singapore, you can refer to the Administration of Muslim Law Act and Muslim Marriage and Divorce Rules.'[66] This may be baffling for litigants in person, who are unlikely to have ever had any experience in legal matters. To be fair, having a website with some details is a huge improvement from the days when parties had to physically attend the Syariah Court itself, just to enquire about the most basic questions regarding how to commence a divorce action.

While there are Malay translations of court forms on the website, practically all the other content is in English, including the guiding notes on the description and purposes of the forms.[67] This poses a potential problem for litigants who are not well versed in English, but it is not only a problem for those who are only conversant in Malay. With the rise of globalization,

[63] LAB offers representation in various fields of civil cases including divorces, adoption, personal injury, and estate matters: see *Legal Aid and Advice Act* (Cap. 160, 2014 Rev. Edn Sing.) (as amended on 30 April 2014), First Schedule. For Syariah Court cases, the LAB will assign such cases based on a list of lawyers who practise in this area.

[64] Community Justice Centre, 'Primary Justice Project', online: https://cjc.org.sg/services/legal-services/primary-justice-project/.

[65] Singapore Syariah Court, 'Community Centres/Clubs (CCs) Community Development Council (CDCs) that Provide Legal Counselling Services', online: www.syariahcourt.gov.sg/Syariah/front-end/Default.aspx?pid=M04.02.

[66] Singapore Syariah Court, 'Frequently Asked Questions', online: https://va.ecitizen.gov.sg/cfp/customerPages/syc/explorefaq.aspx.

[67] Singapore Syariah Court, 'Divorce Forms', online: www.syariahcourt.gov.sg/Syariah/front-end/Default.aspx?pid=M31.02.

there could be litigants from non-English-speaking countries who are not literate in either English or Malay. There is recourse during court hearings as arrangements can be made for interpreters to be utilized, but this would already be at the end of the case and litigants would be bound by the pleadings in their court forms.

C. *Proficiency of lawyers*

There is no special prerequisite to appear as a lawyer before the Syariah Court.[68] As alluded to by the Appeal Board in *Jamal Mahammath s/o T Musthafa* v. *Zarina bte Abdul Majid*,[69] the race or religion of the lawyer is not material. What matters is the proficiency of the lawyer on the Islamic law issues in the particular case. It thus becomes incumbent on the lawyer appearing at the Syariah Court to be equipped with the required knowledge and have a decent grasp of the procedures at the Syariah Court, so that he can represent the party adequately. The often-heard lament of lawyers is that there is a dearth of relevant local resource material available, and this impedes their preparation of cases, a matter considered immediately below.

It is encouraging that the newest law school in Singapore, the Singapore University of Social Sciences, has included Islamic Family Law in Singapore in its undergraduate law degree course from July 2020. This is a first-ever development in Singapore. As stated on its website, 'the family law practitioner needs to have knowledge of the Muslim law of marriages and divorces, and would also need to be aware of the jurisdictional issues between the Syariah Court and the civil courts'. The focus will be 'on the Syariah law as applied in the Singapore context'.[70]

At the Family Justice Courts Workplan 2020, Presiding Judge of the Family Justice Courts Justice Debbie Ong mentioned that the Family Specialist Accreditation Scheme for lawyers is targeted to be available in 2022.[71] It is envisaged that a family lawyer in Singapore would need to have at least a working knowledge of the Syariah Court system as there are occasions of overlap, for instance, maintenance, custody of children, and enforcement of Syariah Court orders. In the author's view, this knowledge would not only be useful but necessary.

D. *Publication of Decisions*

It was not until May 2011 that the *Singapore Syariah Appeal Reports* ('SSAR') were launched. This was long overdue. Many of the lawyers would go to the Syariah Court with hardly any case law, as they did not know where to obtain case reports. The lawyers who built up their personal libraries did so either through their own cases or by personally attending the Appeal Board. This state of affairs was certainly not conducive to the development of the law. And while lawyers had problems obtaining Appeal Board cases for their research, it was practically impossible for litigants in person.

Three years before the launch of the SSAR, a Member of Parliament made the call[72] for the written grounds of Syariah Court and Appeal Board decisions to be easily made available to the public, to enhance the transparency of the Court and facilitate teaching and research. While

[68] AMLA, *supra* note 7, s 39.
[69] [2008] 4 SSAR 165.
[70] Singapore University of Social Sciences, 'Islamic Family Law in Singapore', online: www.suss.edu.sg/courses/detail/law351.
[71] Justice Debbie Ong, 'Today is a New Day', *Family Justice Courts* (21 May 2020) at 18, online: www.familyjusticecourts.gov.sg/docs/default-source/news-and-events/2020_pj_address_workplan.pdf.
[72] *Parliamentary Debate 17 November 2008*, *supra* note 53, at col. 750.

the SSAR are obviously an improvement from the days when there were no decisions made publicly available, the general feeling amongst lawyers is still that even more can be done. As of June 2020, only the Appeal Board decisions up to 2015 had been published. It was not until July 2020 that a volume of decisions from 2015 to 2019 became available.[73] This situation is vastly different from other courts in Singapore, where updates of court cases and written judgments are uploaded to the court websites almost on a daily basis. It is an achievement that this latest volume contained selected Syariah Court decisions, and not just Appeal Board decisions. It is hoped that there will not be another wait of several years for the next volume to be published, especially if there are landmark judgments which impact on other cases. It is this author's wish that key written judgments could be posted on the Syariah Court website, in line with the practice of other courts in Singapore.

At the launch of the SSAR in 2011, Dr Yaacob Ibrahim highlighted that the main objective of the SSAR is to provide a source of authoritative references to Muslim law, as practitioners will be able to cite local cases of greater relevance to support their arguments instead of relying on cases decided in other jurisdictions.[74] On this note, there could be a scheme set up to assist the Presidents of the Syariah Court in the development of a body of law. Research assistants could be attached to the Presidents akin to the Justices' Law Clerk scheme at the Supreme Court.[75] There are multiple benefits in such a scheme, as the Presidents can issue the grounds of decision more quickly, saving time for parties awaiting appeal, and talented young minds can be exposed to the work of the Court, creating a pool of future judicial officers. Ultimately, such a scheme could lead to the development of a reservoir of knowledge of Singapore Syariah law, a valuable resource compared to relying on overseas publications which are likely to arise from a different social context.

Litigants, whether in-person or represented by lawyers, would benefit from being able to read for themselves on the issues that may be connected with their personal circumstances. Many misperceptions surrounding the Syariah Court may also be dispelled. A library should also be set up in the Syariah Court, to be made open to lawyers and the public.

VI. CONCLUSION

The Syariah Court holds an important position within Singapore's Muslim community, but it cannot be regarded as a key institution in the Muslim community simply by virtue of it being the exclusive body competent to adjudicate on divorces. Its reputation and standing rest on its capacity to dispense justice in a fair and just manner to all who go through its doors. To do this, it has to be on par with the standards set by other courts in Singapore. Given the resources and the cooperation of its stakeholders, the lawyers and the various agencies, there is every reason to believe that the Syariah Court can continue to expand access to justice to its litigants.

[73] Singapore Academy of Law, *Singapore Syariah Appeals Reports*, online: www.sal-e.org.sg/law-reports.

[74] Dr Yaacob Ibrahim, speech delivered at launch of SSAR, Suntec City, Singapore (21 May 2012), online: www.nas.gov.sg/archivesonline/data/pdfdoc/20120528003.htm.

[75] Singapore Legal Service, 'Justices' Law Clerk Programme', online: www.lsc.gov.sg/careers/who-are-we-looking-for/graduates-mid-career.

17

Access to Justice in Israel: Rights, Legal Aid, and Pro Bono in a Lawyer Dominant Environment

Michal Ofer-Tsfoni and Limor Zer-Gutman

Abstract

The last two decades have witnessed a delayed but growing awareness of the importance of access to justice. The change was led by courts and public interest lawyers, who identified obstacles blocking access for indigent people. To explain this delayed development, the chapter identifies the tension between the private legal sector who dominate the Israeli Bar and the public interest lawyer sector. Despite pressure from other stakeholders, the Israeli Bar has retained a self-regulatory scheme which primarily serves its professional and financial goals. Another major reason for late development is the lack of a statutory guarantee of the right of access to justice. Israel is a western democracy with no constitution but with a set of Basic Laws guaranteeing some rights, which do not include the right of access to justice; the right to access to justice was declared to be a constitutional right by the Supreme Court only in 2003. The chapter argues that access to justice in Israel is supported by courts and various schemes but has suffered in the lawyer dominant environment, and that serious access to justice reform will require a different balance of power among access participants.

I. INTRODUCTION

The State of Israel was established in 1948, following rule by the Ottoman Empire and subsequent British Mandatory administration in 1917. Since its establishment, Israel has developed into a liberal western democracy. It is devoid of a constitution but has a set of Basic Laws guaranteeing a series of constitutional rights. The Israeli economy is a mixed free-market economy subject to significant government intervention, operating alongside a developed private sector that includes a thriving high-tech industry, a security industry, and more. The economy is growing at an average rate of 5 per cent per year, and Israel enjoys a high GDP per capita of US$43,593 in 2019, higher than the average of OECD members, which is US$39,482.[1] Israeli society is multicultural, composed principally of Jewish immigrants who arrived in the immediate period following the establishment of the state, joined by large waves of Jewish

[1] *GDP Per Capita (current US$) – Israel, OECD Members* (World Bank), online: https://data.worldbank.org/indicator/NY.GDP.PCAP.CD?locations=IL-OE.

immigrants from Ethiopia and the former USSR in the 1990s. The country also contains an Arab-Moslem minority comprising about 20 per cent of the population.

Israel is governed as a parliamentary democracy. The legislative branch consists of a 120-member parliament. The majority party in parliament forms a coalition with other parties and establishes the government, which acts as the executive branch. The third branch is the judiciary.

The principle of the rule of law is fairly well established in Israel.[2] English law, introduced during the British Mandate and retained after Israel gained its independence, has most influenced the court system, as observed in its hierarchical structure and the status of judges. The court system integrates fundamental concepts of English law with original Israeli principles; for example, the concept of judicial independence is drawn from English common law, but the method of appointing judges, designed to ensure such independence, is unique to Israel.[3]

The courts are independent, although three facts severely weaken the judicial branch's institutional autonomy. The first is the absence of a statute declaring the judiciary's independence. A second, more important factor is structural. The judiciary is only one of many administrative units that make up the Ministry of Justice, and the law grants the Minister extensive power over the work of these units. Third, in recent years considerable pressure has been exerted by the legislature on the courts as part of a deepening rift between these two bodies, although in practice, the judiciary has remained steadfast in confrontations with the other two branches of government and operates in a fully independent manner.

There is no statute explicitly providing for the right of access to justice in the Israeli legal system, but a series of statutes establish various arrangements aimed at ensuring such a right. In addition, the right of access to justice has been recognized as possessing constitutional status in a series of judgments, so that its existence and applicability to every citizen is undisputed. When evaluating access to justice in Israel, one may ask whether this right is merely notional, or whether it has practical consequences. To address this question, the right of access to justice will be examined in terms of the weakest link in society – impoverished sectors of the population lacking the financial means to hire lawyers.

The availability of access to justice in Israel is influenced by three main actors. At the top of the hierarchy is the state. Through law, the state can determine when a person must be given due representation, in the absence of which, for example, a court hearing will not be held. The state can also invest resources in ensuring access to justice through government-sponsored programmes that guarantee legal representation for those who cannot afford it. Taking second place in the hierarchy is the legal profession, which in Israel controls the legal services market by virtue of the monopoly and professional autonomy granted by statute. Third in terms of influence are the civil society organizations and law school clinics that provide free legal services to indigent and vulnerable persons.

The state exerts the greatest influence on the exercise of the right of access to justice, but in Israel, mandatory representation by an attorney is only required in criminal matters. The first section of this chapter examines when this requirement applies and the scope of the state's obligation to provide criminal legal aid. The statutory arrangement in the criminal field is broad and comprehensive, and it stems from the perception that in criminal proceedings the right to representation is critical to ensuring the existence of due process. In the civil sphere, the state operates a programme that funds representation for those who cannot afford it, but there is no

[2] Suzie Navot, *The Constitution of Israel: A Contextual Analysis (Constitutional Systems of the World)* (Oxford: Hart Publishing, 2014) [*Contextual Analysis*] at 51.

[3] Shimon Shetreet, *Justice in Israel: A Study of the Israeli Judiciary* (Dordrecht: M. Nijhoff Publishers, 1994) at 62–6, 260.

mandatory obligation to ensure representation, and the relevant issue is whether the state has allocated an adequate budget.

The second group exerting influence over the exercise of the right of access to justice is the legal profession, which plays an especially dominant role, in the judicial system as well as Israeli society as a whole. The dominance of the legal profession stems from several factors. Law is central in Israeli society, politics, and public life, perhaps more so than in other countries, as will be considered below. Israel has the highest number of lawyers in the world per capita. Their impact is not merely numerical, but substantive. They have considerable public visibility and influence, and can be found in all spheres of society, including law, business, media, and politics. Another factor is the extensive professional autonomy enjoyed by the legal profession, a statutory state of affairs that has not changed for nearly 60 years. This professional autonomy allows lawyers to unite to promote their own interests, sometimes at the expense of the public interest in expanding access to justice. This autonomy also allows the legal profession continually to extend the types of cases in which a person requires legal services, but at the same time block the supply of services by anyone who is not an attorney through intensive implementation of unauthorized practice of law ('UPL') rules. In addition to prohibiting legal services viewed as competition, the Israel Bar Association ('IBA') has also fought state and non-governmental organization ('NGO') efforts to provide free legal representation for people in need.

A wide variety of NGOs operate in Israel, and although they exert the least influence on access to justice, they have a significant impact in the country. NGOs provide pro bono legal representation for poor persons and take on issues of public importance. Two decades ago, law schools began establishing legal clinics, and today clinics may be found in each of the 13 law schools operating in Israel.

This chapter analyses access to justice in Israel in the following order. Section II addresses the meaning of the right of access to justice and the manner in which that right has been formed indirectly by case law and legislation. Section III explores the state's role as the entity exerting the greatest influence on the right of access to justice, describing the legal aid provided by the state and numerical data relating to relevant budgets. Section IV deals with the second most influential group, the legal profession, describing how it affects the scope and ways of exercising the right of access to justice. Section V analyses the role of NGOs and law school legal clinics, and Section VI concludes. The chapter argues that there is a growing awareness of access to justice by indigent people who cannot afford legal services. In the past two decades, courts have recognized that right and the state has supported various programmes offering legal aid in criminal and civil cases together with NGOs and law school legal clinics. Yet, the dominance of the legal profession and its broad regulatory monopoly continue to influence access to justice, to the point that only a fundamental reform will be able to establish a different balance of power among access participants and optimally support access to justice.

II. THE RIGHT OF ACCESS TO JUSTICE IN THE ISRAELI LEGAL SYSTEM

It is only in the past two decades that Israeli law has recognized the importance of the right of access to justice. This recognition was led by two groups, the courts, and NGOs and public interest lawyers, who identified the barriers to accessing the legal system.[4] One of the reasons for

[4] Neta Ziv, *Who Will Guard the Guardians of Law? Lawyers in Israel between the State, Market and Civil Society* (Ramat Gan: Bar Ilan University Press and Hakibbutz Hameuchad, 2015) [*Guardians*] at 91–115 (in Hebrew); Elbashan Yuval,

tardy recognition was the absence of an express statutory provision establishing its parameters. Statutes protect various aspects of the right, such as exemptions from court fees or the right to legal aid, and a number of Basic Laws guarantee important basic rights,[5] but none explicitly refer to the right of access to the legal system. Despite this, the Supreme Court recognized the right of access to justice as a basic constitutional right of high importance.[6] This right is not absolute but relative, although it may only be restricted in limited circumstances. Any restriction of the right must be for a proper purpose and will only be allowed when such purpose cannot be achieved by a more limited infringement, balancing the benefit of the restriction against the violation.[7]

The right of access to justice depends, among other things, on the existence of the right to representation, which in turn consists of the right to professional legal advice and the right to representation by an attorney.[8] These rights are recognized in Israeli law, but are not absolute rights. The right to representation has two main aspects. The first is the individual freedom to choose an attorney, and the second is the obligation to provide representation to persons who cannot afford it. The right to representation prohibits infringement of either element of the right, and it incorporates the duty to act affirmatively in order to protect and realize it.[9] Realization of the right is not intended to protect the litigant's personal interest only, but also that of the general public in establishing the truth in disputes and maintaining due process.[10]

The first aspect of the right to representation is expressed in Section 22 of the Israel Bar Association Act, which states that '[a]nyone who has empowered an advocate is entitled to be represented by him before any State or local authority and any other body or person carrying out public functions by virtue of law . . . .'[11] The Supreme Court expanded this right, holding that the right of a person to be represented by an attorney of his choice is a basic right, the restriction of which impairs the autonomy of the private will.[12] Israel's adversarial legal system also contributes to the importance of the right in both criminal and civil proceedings.[13] The right is of particular importance when a lawyer represents the individual against the government, an aspect most

'The Smell of the Robe is Like the Scent of the Field – The Fundamental Principles of Clinical Legal Education' (2004) 34 *Mishpatim Law Review* 455 at 457–9 (in Hebrew).

5 Israel does not have a constitution, but a number of Basic Laws create the foundation for the establishment of a future constitution: see Israel, The Knesset, *Basic Law: Human Dignity and Liberty* (1992) (in Hebrew) (for an English translation, see online: www.knesset.gov.il/laws/special/eng/basic3_eng.htm) [*Dignity and Liberty*]; and Israel, The Knesset, *Basic Law: The Judiciary* (1984) (in Hebrew) (for an English translation, see online: www.knesset.gov.il/laws/special/eng/basic8_eng.htm); see also, *Contextual Analysis, supra* note 2, at 21.

6 See Barak Aharon, 'The Right to Access the Legal System' in Asher Grunis, Eliezer Rivlin, and Michael Karayanni, eds., *Shlomo Levin Book: Essays in Honour of Justice Shlomo Levin* (2013) 31 at 36, 38–41, 43–50 [*Right to Access*] (in Hebrew); see also Rabin Yoram, 'The Right of Access to Courts – from an Ordinary to a Constitutional Right' (2000) 5 *Hamishpat Law Review* 217 (in Hebrew) [*Right of Access to Courts*], and Orgad Liav and Rabin Yoram, 'Access to Courts for Enemy Aliens (following CAR 993/06 *State of Israel* v. *Dirani*)' (2014) 29:2 *Mechkarey-Mishpat Law Review* 469 at 472 6.

7 See *Right to Access, supra* note 6, at 52–3 (in Hebrew).

8 Porat Assaf, 'About the Right to Legal Representation in Disciplinary Procedures in the Military' (2014) 17 *Business-Law Law Review* 471 [*Legal Representation*] at 472 (in Hebrew).

9 Ibid.

10 CA 816/10 *Gold* v. *The State of Israel* (2012), at 9.

11 *Israel Bar Association Act*, Israel 1961, as amended 7 August 2017, s 22.

12 HCJ 1437/02 *The Association for Civil Rights in Israel* v. *The Minister of Public Security* (2004), at 759–60; HCJ 4330/93 *Ganem* v. *The Israeli Bar* (1996), at 223.

13 Iris Ilotovitch-Segal and Eli Bukspan, 'Legal Representation by Students in Academic Clinics, Through the Prism of the Right of Access to Justice and Education to Social Responsibility' (2005) 2 *Business-Law Law Review* 427 [*Legal Representation by Students*] at 434–6 (in Hebrew).

clearly arising in criminal proceedings, where it is acknowledged that the right plays a central role in the legal system in Israel.[14] In disciplinary proceedings, there are areas in which the right to legal representation is fully recognized, and other areas in which it is recognized in a partial or relatively limited manner;[15] for example, there is no right to representation by an attorney in military disciplinary proceedings.[16] The right to representation is significantly weaker in civil proceedings, but it is understood that there are cases in which representation is necessary to ensure fair proceedings, and the absence of representation may in many cases negate the possibility of such a process. In other words, the right to representation is part of the guarantee of due process.[17]

Israel's development of a right of access to justice is significant, but it is necessary to examine whether the right is exercised in practice. When the right to access the legal system cannot be exercised because the recipient lacks the means to hire an attorney, the right is deprived of any practical significance.[18] Using this test case, the chapter first considers the role played by the principal organization ensuring legal representation, the state.

III. THE STATE'S ROLE IN ACCESS TO JUSTICE

A. *State Funded Legal Aid: Overview and Numbers*

In 2016, the annual public budget allocated to the judicial system per inhabitant was €83 (US$97.77),[19] and the legal aid budget was €10.18 (US$11.99) per inhabitant.[20] These figures are on the low side, considering that in 2016, the GDP per capita (in €) in Israel was €35,323 (US$41,610), while the average figure in the OECD was €24,564 (US$28,936.05). Moreover, the average gross salary in Israel stood at €29,079 (US$34,254.66) per year, compared to an OECD average of €24,756 (US$29,162.22). The average expenditure on legal aid of the members of the OECD in 2016 was €6.50 (US$7.66) per inhabitant, and so the expenditure of €10.18 (US$11.99) brought Israel to the rank of eighth among the countries examined in the OECD report, although England and Wales spent three times as much, and Sweden 3.6 times as much as Israel.

[14] CA 8077/08 *Haifa University* v. *Ben-Harosh* (2012) at paras. 23–4, per Justice Rubinstein.

[15] See *Legal Representation, supra* note 8, at 487. See also Disciplinary Tribunal Appeal (Tel Aviv District Court) 43024-07-17 *Alkobi* v. *Ashdod Municipality* (2018) at paras. 7–13 (in Hebrew).

[16] See *Legal Representation, supra* note 8, at 496–501.

[17] See *Legal Representation, supra* note 8, at 480–3. See also Permitted Civil Appeal 6810/97 *Ben-Shushan* v. *Ben-Shushan* (1997) [*Ben-Shushan*] at para. 5, per Justice Turkel.

[18] Neta Ziv, 'Legal Education and Social Responsibility: Between the Law School and the Community' (2001) 25:2 *TAU Law Review* 385 at 390 (in Hebrew); *Legal Representation by Students, supra* note 13, at 437. Disadvantaged populations face many obstacles beyond the economic barriers that prevent them from accessing the legal system in general and the courts in particular, including limitation periods and psychological, language, and geographical barriers: see Yuval Elbashan, 'Access to Justice of Unempowered Communities in Israel' (2003) 3:2 *Aley-Mishpat Law Review* 497 (in Hebrew). Regarding other solutions adopted by the state of Israel to minimize economic barriers, such as granting exemptions from payment of court fees in certain circumstances as stipulated in Court Regulations (Fees), Israel 2007, as amended 1 January 2020, s 14, and the establishment of small claims courts, which allow professional and cheap dispute resolution, see Shmuel L. Becher and Avishai Klein, 'The Paradox of Power and Representation in Small Claims Court' (2010) 50 *Hapraklit Law Review* 327 at 334–5.

[19] XE Currency Converter, online: www.xe.com/currencyconverter/convert/?Amount=83&From=EUR&To=USD. Unless another reference was cited, US$ denominations in the chapter were derived from www.xe.com at the time of publication; they are intended for general reference and may have been rounded up or down for ease of reference.

[20] *European Judicial Systems – Efficiency and Quality of Justice – CEPEJ Studies No. 26* (European Commission for the Efficiency of Justice, 2018) [*European Judicial Systems*] at 12, 26, 78.

The OECD report indicates significant increases in Israel's legal aid budget. The legal aid budget increased from €39,771,572 (US$46.85 million) in 2012 to €55,055,454 (US$64.85 million) in 2014 and to €88,530,589 (US$104.29 million) in 2016.[21] The budget approved for legal aid in 2016 also constituted 12 per cent of the general budget of the entire Israeli legal system that year.[22] These figures indicate that the legal aid allocation in Israel has central importance in the budget, flowing from the understanding that the right to receive legal aid is a basic right and a necessary condition for a just and fair justice system.

B. State Funded Mandatory Legal Representation in Criminal Law Cases

Until 1996, mandatory representation of defendants and suspects was very limited, as was the state's funding for such representation, and the vast majority of defendants were tried without legal representation. There were cases in which a defence attorney from the private sector was appointed by the court, but there was no supervision of the quality of representation, and there were concerns that the courts appointed defence attorneys based on the attorney's convenience or his random presence in the courtroom.[23] This situation was criticized by the Supreme Court[24] and by NGOs, and in the 1980s the Minister of Justice appointed an investigative committee headed by a retired Supreme Court justice. This committee strongly criticized the lack of representation, called for change in the legal aid system in Israel, and proposed a transition to a public defence system.[25] In 1992, the Basic Law: Human Dignity and Liberty was enacted in Israel,[26] and the legal system began to place special emphasis on various aspects of human rights. In 1996, significant reform was implemented with the establishment of the Public Defender's Office ('PDO').[27] Initially, the PDO employed only a few lawyers, and its budget was negligible. Over the years, however, the budget increased dramatically, and relevant statutes were amended. Today, the obligation to appoint a defence attorney for suspects and defendants is very broad, with many defendants entitled to the appointment of a state-funded defence attorney without undergoing any means test.[28]

The PDO provides legal representation throughout the entirety of criminal proceedings, from consultation for suspects during police interrogation, to detention hearings, trials, and sentencing, to leave to appeal and appeal. The PDO represents prisoners and the mentally ill. The PDO also protects and preserves the interests of defendants and suspects through intensive intervention in legislative processes and by submitting expert legal opinions as *amicus curiae*.[29] In Israel today, cases where an accused wants representation but is unable to get it due to costs are rare. Correspondingly, the budget of the PDO has increased considerably. Initially, in 1998, the PDO's budget stood at ILS20 million (US$5.87 million), while in 2016 it exceeded

[21] *European Judicial Systems*, *supra* note 20, at 87.
[22] *European Judicial Systems*, *supra* note 20, at 77.
[23] Ministry of Justice, *The Public Defender Office – A Summary of 20 Years* (Israel: Ministry of Justice, 1 January 2016) at 1–4, online: www.justice.gov.il/Units/SanegoriaZiborit/DohotRishmi/dohot/The%20Public%20Defender%20Office%20-%20A%20summary%20of%2020%20Years.pdf.
[24] See for example RCA 134/89 *Shmuel Abergil* v. *The State of Israel* (1990).
[25] Ministry of Justice, *The Report of the Committee for Inspection the Issue of Legal Aid in Criminal Matters* (1985).
[26] *Dignity and Liberty*, *supra* note 5.
[27] *Public Defence Act*, Israel 1995, as amended 11 August 2016 [*Public Defence Act*].
[28] For a full list of those entitled to representation, see *Public Defence Act*, *supra* note 27, s 18.
[29] Ministry of Justice, 'About the Public Defense', online: www.justice.gov.il/En/Units/PublicDefense/About/Pages/default.aspx.

ILS249 million (US$73.09 million) and in the budget proposal for 2019, the figure rose to ILS264,100,000 (US$77.52 million).[30] The 2016 Ministry of Justice Report states that the PDO represents defendants in about 33 per cent of the criminal cases conducted in the district courts and about 57 per cent of the criminal cases conducted in the magistrates' courts.[31] In light of the PDO's extensive activity, only a few other bodies provide legal aid in the criminal field, apart from specialist associations and law school clinics,[32] such as the 'Association of Rape Crisis Centers in Israel',[33] and human rights organizations that deal with wider issues such as prison overcrowding.[34]

In terms of staffing, the PDO employs a relatively small number of 'internal' defence attorneys who work as civil servants, about 125 in 2018, and it provides the bulk of defence representation through outsourcing arrangements with a wide range of 'external' defence attorneys. These external lawyers manage cases from their private offices, and they numbered about 860 lawyers in 2018. The PDO handled 109,492 different procedures in 2018, of which 30,984 were criminal trials (out of about 59,000 criminal trials in the magistrates' and district courts in 2018); 1,461 were handled by the internal defence team, and the remainder by external lawyers.[35] In 2018, the amount paid by the PDO to external lawyers stood at ILS179,107,000 (US$52.57 million).[36] Compared to market rates, PDO external lawyers' fees, paid by the state, are lower.[37] Yet, many lawyers apply for these positions due to the high volume of cases that allows a considerable income.

PDO representation is not totally free, and recipients must pay fees in accordance with regulations.[38] The PDO's position is that a fee on some of the defendants is justified, as long as an exemption is granted to defendants who are unable to pay, and the regulations enable the PDO to exempt a defendant from paying the fee in exceptional cases.[39] The payments help the PDO finance its activities, and in the PDO's view, they have a positive effect on the relationship between the recipient and the service provider.[40]

The amount of the fee contributed by the defendant depends in part on the court in which the hearing is to be conducted; the higher the court, the higher the payment. In 2020, the

[30] Ministry of Finance, *Budget Proposal 2019* (Israel: Ministry of Finance, 2019) at 46, online: www.gov.il/BlobFolder/dynamiccollectorresultitem/ministry_of_justice_2019/he/state-budget_2019_government-ministries-budget_Mishpatim_Prop.pdf.pdf (in Hebrew]) [*Budget Proposal 2019*].

[31] *Budget Proposal 2019*, *supra* note 30, at 83.

[32] See for example, The Clinical Legal Education Center, 'The Criminal Justice Clinic', *Hebrew University of Jerusalem*, online: https://openscholar.huji.ac.il/clinicallecen/book/criminal-justice-clinic.

[33] The Association of Rape Crisis Centers in Israel, 'Home Page', online: www.1202.org.il/en/.

[34] See HCJ 1892/14 *The Association for Civil Rights in Israel* v. *The Minister for Public Security* (2017).

[35] Israel's Judiciary – Court Administration, *Annual Report 2018* at 18, 26, online: www.gov.il/BlobFolder/reports/statistics_annual_2018/he/2018.pdf (in Hebrew).

[36] Ministry of Justice, *Public Defender Annual Report 2018* at 7–8, 125, 131–2, online: www.justice.gov.il/Units/SanegoriaZiborit/DohotRishmi/dohot/annual%20report%202018.pdf (in Hebrew).

[37] David Zalmanovitsh, 'Economic Measures of the Legal Market in Israel', *GLawBAL* (2018) at 19, online: www.glawbal.com/upload/Finance%202018.pdf (in Hebrew).

[38] *Regulations of the Public Defender's Office (Duty of Payment of Persons Eligible to Representation) (Temporary Order)* 5772, Israel 2011, enacted 26 October 2011, as amended 1 January 2020 [*Public Defender's Office Regulations*].

[39] *Public Defender's Office Regulations*, *supra* note 38, Regulation 5. See Ministry of Justice, 'Information about Fees', online: www.justice.gov.il/En/Units/PublicDefense/PublicInfo/Pages/FeesInfo.aspx. In 2017, the total fees amounted to ILS9,457,724 (US$2.78 million), from which the defence granted an exemption of ILS1,351,328 (US$396,575.65) (Israel, Ministry of Justice, *Public Defender Annual Report 2017*, at 131–2, online: www.justice.gov.il/Units/SanegoriaZiborit/DohotRishmi/Pages/dohot.aspx (in Hebrew)).

[40] Ministry of Justice, *Public Defender Annual Report 2000*, at 27, online: www.justice.gov.il/Units/SanegoriaZiborit/DohotRishmi/Pages/dohot.aspx (in Hebrew).

maximum payment according to the regulations was ILS1,255 (US$363.56) and the minimum was ILS457 (US$132.39).[41] The amount of the fee is not high bearing in mind that the minimum wage in Israel in 2020 was ILS5,300 (US$1,535.34) per month and the average national wage was ILS10,887 (US$3,153.82) per month.[42] Failure to pay the fee by a defendant will not interfere with PDO representation. The Ministry of Justice and the PDO have recently begun to promote legislation aimed at allowing the full costs of the procedure to be collected from defendants in more complicated and expensive cases, although a full or partial exemption for individuals not able to finance costs is also proposed here.

Initially, the Israel Bar Association objected to the establishment of the PDO,[43] or was at the least ambivalent about its creation. While the IBA expressed concern about the fact that most defendants were not represented, it was 'anxious about the entry of State funded attorneys into a field that had been almost exclusively under the jurisdiction of the private bar'.[44] In response to a request from the first head of the PDO for assistance to increase the PDO's budget in 1996, absent which many poor defendants would not be represented at all, the chairman of the IBA stated that the Bar had no responsibility whatsoever for representing such defendants.[45]

Against this backdrop, it is not surprising that the broad scope of the representation provided by the PDO has provoked criticism from the IBA. On 20 June 2016, the Chairman of the IBA wrote to the Minister of Justice claiming that the representation given to defendants, suspects, and prisoners by the PDO was too widespread, and accordingly 'violate[d] the freedom of occupation of lawyers engaged in the criminal field'.[46] According to the Chairman of the Bar, the purpose of creating the PDO had been to allow impoverished sectors of the population to obtain representation; however, now, in most cases, eligibility was not being examined on the basis of a means test, either because of the broad statutory grounds creating a mandatory duty to appoint a defence attorney regardless of the means income test, or because judges frequently used the discretion conferred on them to appoint a defence attorney for those who were not represented.[47] In February 2017, the Chairman of the Bar informed the members of the Bar that in view of his request, the Minister of Justice was considering several legislative amendments that would reduce the scope of representation by the PDO.[48]

C. *State Funded Legal Representation in Private Law Cases*

In Israel, civil proceedings may take place without representation, and there is no overarching obligation for a person to be represented by an attorney. There are situations in which courts have recognized the importance of representation and the impact of the failure to conduct fair

[41] *Public Defender's Office Regulations*, *supra* note 38, Regulation 1; amounts are adjusted on 1 January in accordance with the index, the amounts reflected here were correct as of 1 January 2020.

[42] The wage data referred to here was correct as of April 2020. See Central Bureau of Statistics, 'Average Monthly Wages and Employee Jobs', online: www.cbs.gov.il/reader/cw_usr_view_SHTML?ID=329 (in Hebrew).

[43] Eli Salzberger, 'The Israeli Lawyers' Connection: On the Israel Bar Association and its Allies' (2002) 32 *Mishpatim Law Review* 43 [*Israeli Lawyers' Connection*] at 68, n 115 (in Hebrew).

[44] Neta Ziv, 'Combining Professionalism, Nation Building and Public Service: The Professional Project of the Israeli Bar 1928–2002' (2003) 71 *Fordham Law Review* 1621 [*Combining Professionalism*] at 1659.

[45] *Combining Professionalism*, *supra* note 44, at 1659, n 163.

[46] Israel Bar Association, *Re: Representation by Public Defender* (2016), online: www.israelbar.org.il/UpLoadFiles/public_defence_representation_attachments.pdf (in Hebrew).

[47] Ibid.

[48] Israel Bar Association, 'Update for Criminal Lawyers: Reducing the Scope of Representation by the Public Defender' (27 February 2017), online: www.israelbar.org.il/article_inner.asp?pgId=382433&catId=3082 (in Hebrew).

proceedings without it. Thus, the Supreme Court overturned a ruling by a lower court regarding the dissolution of a partnership in a residential apartment, noting that there was justification for recognizing the right of a litigant in a family dispute to be represented.[49] There are civil matters of negligible importance, but there are also civil disputes that influence a person's fate more significantly than do minor criminal charges, leading some to propose that the duty of representation should apply to any critical process that adversely affect an individual's rights and obligations.[50] While no such obligation has been established, it is widely recognized that the mere existence of the freedom to hire a lawyer is insufficient on its own, and that legal assistance in this category of civil cases must be provided to people with low incomes in order to achieve access to justice.

The Legal Aid Department of the Ministry of Justice provides legal aid in civil matters to eligible applicants of limited means,[51] which extends to all manner of legal advice and representation in legal forums.[52] For many years the Legal Aid Department's budget was low. In the early 2000s, the budget stood at about ILS40 million (US$11.74 million) annually. In light of the growing discourse on the importance of accessibility to justice and criticism that the Legal Aid Department was unable to provide a response to the public's needs, the Director General of the Ministry of Justice established a committee that was asked to examine the gap between public needs and the state resources available to the department. Following the committee's recommendations, the budget was raised significantly. In 2009, the utilized budget was ILS65,855,000 (US$19.33 million), while in 2013 this figure rose to a total of ILS115,042,000 (US$33.76 million), and in the budget proposal for 2019 was ILS187,356,000 (US$54.98 million).[53]

Currently, the Legal Aid Department operates six district offices, receiving applicants in accordance with their place of residence. In order to make it easier for people from distant geographical areas, there are also points for receiving members of the public outside the district offices. In 2018, the department employed some 271 workers, of whom about 128 were lawyers, with most of the representation performed by 1,111 external lawyers who contracted with the department for this purpose.[54] In 2018, 92,422 new cases were opened, with the majority of the representation being performed by external attorneys.[55]

Who is eligible for state-funded civil legal aid? Per the regulations, aid is to be provided only in specified areas, such as family matters, housing claims, various financial matters, labour laws, and social security matters.[56] Aid is given to those who meet the means and property test set out in the regulations. These are stringent tests, which confine the right to legal aid to the most underprivileged sector of the population. For example, if an applicant is one of a family of three, legal aid will be granted if the family's combined income does not exceed 67 per cent of the average national monthly wage, which was ILS10,499 (US$3,081.66) in November 2019.[57]

[49] See *Ben-Shushan*, *supra* note 17, at para. 5 per Justice Turkel.

[50] *Right of Access to Courts*, *supra* note 6, at 240–7.

[51] *Legal Aid Law*, Israel 1972, as amended 2 May 2004; *Legal Aid Regulations*, Israel 1973, as amended 15 January 2020 [*Legal Aid Regulations*].

[52] Ministry of Justice, 'Activity of the Legal Aid Department', online: www.justice.gov.il/En/Units/LegalAid/About/Pages/ACTIVITY-OF-THE-LEGAL-AID-DEPARTMENT-.aspx.

[53] *Budget Proposal* 2019, *supra* note 30, at 48.

[54] Ministry of Justice – Legal Aid, *Annual Report* 2018 at 53–4 online: www.gov.il/he/departments/publications/reports/legal-aid-2018 [*Annual Report* 2018].

[55] *Annual Report* 2018, *supra* note 54, at 40.

[56] *Legal Aid Regulations*, *supra* note 51, s 5.

[57] *Legal Aid Regulations*, *supra* note 51, s 2.

Additionally, if the applicant owns any property, such as savings, a vehicle, or an apartment, of a value three times the average national wage (ILS31,743) (US$9,317.18), he will not be eligible for legal aid. In cases such as forced hospitalization, human trafficking victims, and Holocaust survivors, the applicant's economic eligibility is not examined. Meeting the strict financial tests does not guarantee the grant of aid, since the Department of Legal Aid will also examine the likelihood of success of the proceedings before deciding whether or not to undertake the representation of the applicant.

Notwithstanding the low income cut-offs, a recipient of civil legal aid must pay a fee. The amount, which ranges from ILS68 (US$19.96) to ILS137 (US$40.21) (as of 2019), depends on the applicant's income, although the department supervisor can exempt the applicant from payment of the fee in view of his economic circumstances. There are also cases in which applicants are exempt from fees, for example, where the applicant is hospitalized in a psychiatric ward, imprisoned, or on remand.[58] Lastly, if a judgment grants the applicant monies or assets which allow him to bear all or part of his service expenses, the applicant, at the request of the supervisor, must pay the expenses to the Legal Aid Department.[59]

Apart from civil legal aid, free legal advice is provided by the 'Citizens Advice Service', an organization belonging to the volunteer branch of the Community Resources Division of the Ministry of Social Affairs and Social Services, which works in cooperation with the local authorities.[60] The service assists applicants with counselling and guidance regarding various rights, duties, and services. Assistance is provided by volunteer lawyers, and advice is given to every applicant regardless of income or economic situation. Free advice is provided as part of the service, but it does not include legal representation. The year 2013 was a turning point for the Citizens Advice Service, when the budget was increased from about ILS2 million (US$587,046.41), to about ILS15 million (US$4.40 million), most of it funded by the state with a small part from local authorities.[61] In 2013, approximately 240,000 inquiries were processed at stations operating in 62 localities spread throughout the country. About 500 volunteer lawyers provide legal advice within the framework of this service, alongside experts in other fields such as labour relations, mortgages, and cooperative housing. These lawyers are volunteers who work without pay. The state also supports a website called 'All Your Rights', a comprehensive site providing detailed information about the rights due to citizens according to various categories, such as health and illness, education, and senior citizens.[62]

IV. THE LEGAL PROFESSION

A. *The Monopoly and Self-Regulation of the Legal Profession*

The state is the central actor in access to justice in Israel, but the legal profession and its representative, the IBA, are extraordinarily influential regarding the degree to which the right to access justice is realized. To grasp the dimensions of this influence, it is necessary to understand how the Israeli

[58] *Legal Aid Regulations*, *supra* note 51, Regulation 3B.

[59] *Legal Aid Regulations*, *supra* note 51, Regulation 8.

[60] See Ministry of Labour, Social Affairs and Social Services, online: www.gov.il/he/Departments/Guides/molsa-shill-guide (in Hebrew).

[61] Research and Information Center, *Making the Legal System Accessible to Disadvantaged Population Groups* (30 March 2015), online: https://fs.knesset.gov.il/globaldocs/MMM/88c28d55-f7f7-e411-80c8-00155d010977/2_88c28d55-f7f7-e411-80c8-00155d010977_11_8608.pdf (in Hebrew).

[62] Kol Zchut, 'Main Page', online: www.kolzchut.org.il/en/Main_Page.

legal profession developed and gained monopoly status in the legal services market, in particular its broad regulatory autonomy. Professional autonomy is established by statute, and in the nearly 60 years since the conferral of this broad autonomy, no aspect of this self-regulation has changed.[63]

In the first two decades of the twentieth century, when the territory was still under Ottoman rule, fewer than ten lawyers were active.[64] The Ottoman Code of Civil Procedure declared that litigants could be represented by a lawyer, but most legal services were provided by groups lacking any legal training. Organization of the legal profession began during the British Mandate and resulted in the creation of two bodies. One was the Legal Board, established by law under the responsibility of the Ministry of Justice. This body was responsible for licensing lawyers and instituting disciplinary proceedings. The other body was a voluntary organization based on ethnicity, which included two associations – one comprising about 500 Arab lawyers and the other comprising about 800 Jewish lawyers. After the establishment of the State of Israel, only the organization of Jewish lawyers continued to operate. This organization aimed to establish a new regulatory regime, which would be independent of the state and wield its own broad powers. It became the IBA, and it accomplished its goals with the passage of the IBA Act of 1961, which is in force to this day.

This Act established the IBA as a statutory entity mandated to 'incorporate the advocates in Israel and [to] take good care to observe, supervise and ensure the standards and ethics of the legal profession'.[65] The law granted the IBA authority over lawyers via a wide range of powers. First, membership in the IBA is mandatory.[66] A lawyer may not practise if he is not a member of the Bar and does not pay its annual membership fees. The IBA's annual fees are not considered high; they start at ILS576 (US$169.16) a year for junior members and reach a maximum of ILS1,112 (US$326.58) for senior lawyers.[67]

Second, the law granted the IBA expansive autonomy to administer the affairs of the profession independently, with little external oversight by the Ministry of Justice and the Attorney General, an oversight which is rarely exercised. The Bar is responsible for overseeing every stage of professional licensing as well as the disciplinary system. It is authorized to promulgate rules governing the behaviour of all lawyers, and while the rules must be approved by the Ministry of Justice, in practice this always occurs after deliberations between the Bar and the Ministry. A comprehensive international comparison of similar laws indicates that the degree of self-regulation of lawyers in Israel is unprecedented in western democracies, in both the degree of autonomy enjoyed by the profession and the scope of its monopoly over the market for legal services.[68] Based on the indicators specified in the International Bar Association's task force report, it appears that the legal profession in Israel enjoys full independence.[69]

Third, the IBA fulfils the dual functions of representing the interests of lawyers together with the oversight functions of regulation and discipline, and the oversight functions are carried out solely by elected officials of the Bar without any outside representation. In other countries where

63 See Limor Zer-Gutman, 'Israel: Regulation of Lawyers and the Legal Services in Israel' in Andrew Boon, ed., *International Perspectives on the Regulation of Lawyers and Legal Services* (Oxford: Hart Publishing, 2017) 139 [*Regulation of Lawyers*] at 140–3.

64 Nathan Brun, *Judges and Lawyers in Eretz Israel: Between Constantinople and Jerusalem, 1900–1930* (Jerusalem: The Hebrew University Magnes Press, 2008) at 22 (in Hebrew).

65 *Israel Bar Association Act*, Israel 1961, as amended in 2016 [*IBA Act*], s 1.

66 *IBA Act*, *supra* note 65, ss 42, 46.

67 For the 2020 rates, see Israel Bar Association, online: www.israelbar.org.il/article_inner.asp?pgId=410685&catId=1138; lawyers after age 67 (retirement age) pay a lower amount.

68 *Israeli Lawyers' Connection*, *supra* note 43, at 62.

69 *The Independence of the Legal Profession: Threats to the Bastion of a Free and Democratic Society* (International Bar Association Task Force on the Independence of the Legal Profession, 2016) at 8–33.

the Bar performs these dual functions, care has been taken to reduce the built-in problem of conflict of interests by ensuring the participation of significant public representatives or creating genuine external oversight of the Bar bodies involved in regulation. A body representing lawyers, which seeks to promote their interests, cannot also have sole supervisory authority over lawyers, as such supervision often clashes with the interests of the lawyers.[70]

The IBA asserts that it can carry out the conflicting responsibilities of public trustee of democracy and the rule of law, and as advocate for the profession. A good example of how the IBA proceeds occurred in 2016, when as part of Amendment 38 to the IBA Act, the mandatory role of the IBA was amended to include an obligation 'to protect the rule of law, human rights and the basic values of the State of Israel', while at the same time, Amendment 38 and Amendment 39 extended the period of internship from 12 to 18 months and changed the structure of the licensing examination, in order to raise entry requirements for lawyers and limit the number of lawyers to protect the legal market.[71]

The legal profession has indicated that it is threatened by increases in the number of lawyers. In the mid-1990s, following the opening of a series of private law colleges, the number of lawyers increased dramatically, so that Israel now has the highest number of lawyers in the world.[72] In 2017, 62,960 active lawyers practised in Israel[73] out of a population of 8.6 million.[74] This constitutes one lawyer for every 140 residents, which outnumbers even the US, with one lawyer for every 243 residents.[75] Two and a half decades ago, it was almost impossible to find lawyers in towns located in Israel's southern and northern peripheries. Today there is a sizeable presence of lawyers and law firms in these areas, particularly in comparison to the size of the local population. For example, in 2010, 346 lawyers worked in Ashkelon, a southern city, whereas in the 1990s only 70 lawyers practised in this city; the number of lawyers in this city grew at a rate of approximately 500 per cent, while the city's general population grew by only 30 per cent.[76]

The acceleration in the number of lawyers has led to a sharp decline in lawyers' fees, albeit the decline mainly affects small and medium-sized firms serving small households.[77] However, despite the decline in fees, evidence indicates that the legal needs of the poor in Israel are not being met and access to justice has not improved.[78]

70 Deborah L. Rhode, *In the Interests of Justice: Reforming the Legal Profession* (Oxford: Oxford University Press, 2000) [*Interests of Justice*] at 143–4; David B. Wilkins, 'Who Should Regulate Lawyers?' (1992) 105 *Harvard Law Review* 799 at 863, n 286; Ministry of Justice, *Minority Opinion, Public Committee Report Regarding the Israel Bar Association* (2013) at 111 (in Hebrew).

71 For further discussion about the IBA's control over entry to the profession see *Regulation of Lawyers, supra* note 63, at 150–3.

72 Limor Zer-Gutman, 'Effects of the Acceleration in the Number of Lawyers in Israel' (2013) *International Journal of the Legal Profession* 247 [*Acceleration*] at 250.

73 Efrat Noieman, 'New Data: How Many Lawyers Really Practise in the Profession', *The Marker* (26 June 2017), online: www.themarker.com/law/1.4197017 (in Hebrew). According to this data, the number of registered and fee-paying lawyers is higher and reaches 77,000.

74 Central Bureau of Statistics, *Statistical Yearbook for Israel 2017*, online: www.cbs.gov.il/he/publications/DocLib/2017/shnaton68/shnaton68.pdf (in Hebrew).

75 The number of US lawyers in 2017 was 1,338,678: see 'Lawyer Population 15% Higher than 10 Years Ago, New ABA Data Shows', *ABAJOURNAL* (3 May 2018), online: www.abajournal.com/news/article/lawyer_population_15_higher_than_10_years_ago_new_aba_data_shows. The US population in 2017 was 325,923,198: see United States Census Bureau, *US and World Population Clock*, online: www.census.gov/popclock/.

76 *Acceleration, supra* note 72, at 251.

77 'Distribution of Specialization and Billing Income in the Legal Sector', *GLawBAL* (2011) at 4, online: www.glawbal.com/upload/Practices%202011(1).pdf (in Hebrew).

78 Neta Ziv, 'Unauthorized Practice of Law and the Production of Lawyers' (2012) 19:2 *International Journal of the Legal Profession* 175 [*Unauthorized Practice of Law*] at 178.

B. Expanding Legal Services while Blocking Competition

Scholars like Rhode and Parker have explained that it would be naive to think that an increase in the number of lawyers would result in the majority of the population being able to finance the legal services they need.[79] This proposition applies in Israel, and one of the reasons is the expansion of the type of cases in which people require the services of an attorney. Since the mid-1980s, the rise of the ideology of individualism and the market economy has allowed the 'discourse of rights' to become central to Israeli society.[80] The legalization process is expressed in ever-increasing appeals to the courts to solve personal, economic, social, and even political conflicts, leading the courts to expand their jurisdiction, and generating an increasing demand for legal services. In Israel, it is now difficult to cope with the bureaucratic system without the help of lawyers, and the Court Administration Report 2019 indicates that every seventh person finds himself involved in litigation necessitating representation by an attorney.[81] Some litigants who cannot afford an attorney appear in court without representation, and these numbers are high; in 2007, 80 per cent of defendants in civil cases appeared in first instance courts without legal representation, and in debt collection proceedings, 95 per cent of debtors were not represented compared to 94 per cent of creditors who were.[82]

The rising demand for legal services cannot be met in Israel by persons who are not licensed lawyers because of the unauthorized practice of law rules.[83] Far reaching compared to other countries,[84] the rules were established in the IBA Act 1961,[85] and since then the IBA has aggressively and successfully enforced them via civil lawsuits. The IBA argues that this activity trespasses upon lawyers' jurisdiction,[86] and it asserts the altruistic argument that the bar must protect the public by ensuring high-quality legal service, and that only lawyers who have undertaken studies, internships, certification examinations, and are subject to ethical and disciplinary rules, can ensure these goals. While maintenance of standards is a legitimate goal and it protects the reputation of the profession, the outcome is that self-interested lawyers completely control the market for legal services. In addition to enforcement against profit-making activities, the Bar has also used UPL rules in a way that impedes access to justice via action against social organizations and law school legal clinics who support underserved populations that do not have access to lawyers, discussed below in Section V.

Lawsuits against persons and bodies stem not only from complaints made by members of the public and lawyers, but also from investigations initiated by the Bar. In 2017 and 2018, 7 per cent of the annual IBA budget was invested in this struggle. In comparison, only 3 per cent was invested in disciplinary action, and only 2.5 per cent in the pro bono programme.[87]

79 Christine Parker, *Just Lawyers: Regulation and Access to Justice* (Oxford: Oxford University Press, 1999) at chapter 3; *Interests of Justice*, *supra* note 70, at 18.

80 Gad Barzilai, 'The Ambivalent Language of Lawyers in Israel: Liberal Politics, Economic Liberalism, Silence and Dissent' in Terence C. Halliday, Lucien Karpik, and Malcolm M. Feeley, eds., *Fighting for Political Freedom: Comparative Studies of the Legal Complex and Political Liberalism* (Oxford: Hart Publishing, 2007) 247 [*Ambivalent Language*] at 265–7.

81 The Judicial Authority, *Court Administration Annual Report 2019*, at 9, online: www.gov.il/BlobFolder/news/spokemen message150920/he/%D7%93%D7%95%D7%97%20%D7%A9%D7%A0%D7%AA%D7%99%202019.pdf (in Hebrew).

82 *Unauthorized Practice of Law*, *supra* note 78, at 178.

83 *IBA Act*, *supra* note 65, s 20.

84 *Policy Roundtables: Competitive Restrictions in Legal Professions* (OECD, 2007) at 32–3.

85 *IBA Act*, *supra* note 65, s 20.

86 *Unauthorized Practice of Law*, *supra* note 78, at 179.

87 Israel Bar Association, *Annual Budget 2017*, online: www.israelbar.org.il/UpLoadFiles/israelbar_budget_2017.pdf (in Hebrew); Israel Bar Association, *Annual Budget 2018*, online: www.israelbar.org.il/uploadfiles/israelbar_budget_2018.pdf (in Hebrew).

In recent years, the Bar has also blocked access to justice by launching a battle against technologies that provide legal services through algorithm-based websites and applications. Israel is known as a start-up nation, producing technological companies which are world leaders in their field, including legal-tech or technology in the service of lawyers. Such technology includes, for example, contract drafting, contract scanning and error detection, and examination of documents. However, if the technology is designed for use by the public, e.g. if a client uses an algorithm to produce a draft contract instead of a lawyer using the same technology, the Bar prohibits the activity under UPL rules.[88] The IBA sued companies providing legal technology to the general public, seeking permanent injunctions to prevent its use. However, here the Bar encountered a surprise; in the cases available at the time of writing, courts have not upheld the Bar's assertion that these technological companies are engaged in the unauthorized practice of law, and the claims have been dismissed.[89] The IBA appealed one of these cases to the Supreme Court but withdrew the appeal upon the advice of the court. Legal services technology appears likely to expand in the coming years, and this development has at least the potential to increase access to justice, particularly if there is a significant reduction in legal costs.

The IBA's use of UPL rules should be considered together with the Bar's fierce opposition over many years to the PDO and NGOs and legal clinics, pursued on the grounds that they harmed the livelihood of private lawyers. When seen together, they indicate a malfunctioning self-regulation that prioritizes self-interest over access to justice.

C. *Free Legal Assistance Offered by the Israel Bar Association*

While individual lawyers take part in the Citizens Advice Service and governmental legal aid bodies mentioned above, the IBA as an entity has not been involved. It was not until 2001, 40 years after its founding, that the IBA initiated a programme offering free legal assistance from volunteer lawyers to the public. What prompted the IBA to offer this programme was the newly elected president of the IBA, Shlomo Cohen, who entered office with a left-liberal agenda that supported civil rights and pro bono.

The name of the programme is *Schar Mitzvah*, which means the reward for a *mitzvah* or good deed, a concept taken from the Jewish religion. The purpose of the programme, as declared by the Bar, is to increase access to the legal system and protect the rights of those who cannot afford to hire an attorney. In 2009, at the initiative of the IBA, a legal provision was enacted requiring the IBA to provide legal assistance to persons with limited means, in accordance with criteria set forth in the rules.[90] The rules came into effect in 2014, and they regulate the duty of the Bar.[91] This national programme operates in about 65 locations spread throughout the country, including residential areas with disadvantaged populations. The programme provides assistance in civil matters, various monetary claims, labour laws, and family matters.[92] It provides legal assistance to those who are not entitled to legal aid from the state, creating another stratum

[88] Neta Ziv, 'Who Moved My Mouse? Technology, Online Legal Services and Professional Ethics' (2016) 39 *TAU Law Review* 189 at 215–20 (in Hebrew).

[89] Cf. (District Court, Jerusalem) 50926-10-15 *IBA* v. *Hasavim Ltd* (2017); (District Court, Tel Aviv) 28548-03-17 *IBA* v. *Abrahamov and Others* (2018).

[90] *IBA Act*, *supra* note 65, s 2(4).

[91] *Bar Association Rules (Providing Legal Aid to Persons of Limited Means)*, 5714, Israel 2014, with effect from 29 October 2014 [*Bar Association Rules*].

[92] For further details, see *Bar Association Rules*, *supra* note 91, Rule 10.

of protection for persons of limited means, those who earn up to 15 per cent more than persons entitled to assistance from the Legal Aid Department. However, if the applicant has realizable property worth six times the average national wage (compared to the legal aid test of three times the national average wage), the applicant is not entitled to assistance.[93] In exceptional cases, aid may also be approved for those whose income and property are slightly higher than allowed by the rules.[94] The recipient is not required to pay attorney's fees but must bear the costs of the proceedings, e.g. court fees and expert opinions. A donor's fund has been set up to assist those who cannot afford these costs, and according to the Bar's website, approximately ILS700,000 (US$205,556.23) was collected as donations to the fund by 2015.[95]

In the first years after the establishment of the programme, there were large annual increases in the number of applicants. In 2009,[96] 4,744 persons applied to the programme; in 2012, 14,637 persons applied;[97] and in 2014, 25,389 applied.[98] This trend has reversed in recent years. In 2016, 14,795 persons applied to the programme.[99] In 2017, the number of applications declined further, and only 10,497 applied.[100] The trend continued in 2018, and only 9,398 applied.[101] A sharp drop also occurred in the percentage of applicants receiving voluntary legal representation. In 2009, approximately 4% of the applicants received representation through the programme, and in 2012, approximately 8%. In 2014, about 4.4% of applicants received legal representation,[102] and in the years 2016–18, only about 1% of applicants received legal representation under the programme. The decline in activity, especially in cases involving representation, is enormous. Inquiries at the programme's offices suggested that the decrease is due 'to greater efficiency and budget reductions decided upon by the Bar'.[103] However, the overall IBA budget has increased in recent years, due to continued increases in the number of lawyers. Like the IBA's approach to UPL and its objections to legal aid, these policy decisions further reflect the Bar's inability to recognize and embrace a sustained obligation regarding access to justice.

V. NGOS AND LAW SCHOOL LEGAL CLINICS

The influence of NGOs and law school clinics on the realization of the right of access to justice has occurred on a number of levels. First, they spurred a growing recognition of the importance

[93] See *Bar Association Rules*, *supra* note 91, Rule 9.

[94] *Bar Association Rules*, *supra* note 91, Rule 14.

[95] Israel Bar Association, 'Pro Bono Donation Fund', online: www.israelbar.org.il/uploadFiles/pro-bono_donation_fund_info_march_2015.pdf (in Hebrew).

[96] The data reflects the period from September of one year to the end of August of the following year, i.e. the data for 2009 refers to the period between September 2008 and the end of August 2009. The same is true for the other years described. See Israel Bar Association, 2009 *Annual Report*, at 16, online: www.israelbar.org.il/UpLoadFiles/annual_activity_report_2009_site.pdf (in Hebrew).

[97] See Israel Bar Association, 2012 *Annual Report*, at 18, online: www.israelbar.org.il/UpLoadFiles/2012_site.pdf (in Hebrew).

[98] See Israel Bar Association, 2014 *Annual Report*, at 21, online: www.israelbar.org.il/UpLoadFiles/activity_report_2014_site.pdf [2014 *Annual Report*] (in Hebrew).

[99] See Israel Bar Association, 2016 *Annual Report*, at 10, online: www.israelbar.org.il/magazine/activity_report_2016 (in Hebrew).

[100] See Israel Bar Association, 2017 *Annual Report*, at 10, online: www.israelbar.org.il/magazine/activity_report_2017 (in Hebrew).

[101] See Israel Bar Association, 2018 *Annual Report*, at 9, online: www.israelbar.org.il/magazine/activity_report_2018/8/ (in Hebrew).

[102] 2014 *Annual Report*, *supra* note 98, at 21.

[103] Email and phone correspondence between the authors and the IBA officials (copy on file with author).

of the right of access to justice over the past two decades. Second, through their diverse activities, they have demonstrated a deep commitment to human rights which in turn has strengthened Israeli society; for example, the Association for Civil Rights in Israel is monitoring and involved in legislative initiatives that impact on human rights, civil liberties, and equality.[104] Third and most importantly, they have for years provided free legal representation to the weaker strata of society and engaged with cases that raised issues of public importance.

Since the mid-1980s, social organizations in Israel have developed rapidly, with some operating in the legal field. Lawyers in these organizations use several strategies to enable all strata of society to gain access to the legal system. They work to change existing legal norms, promote legislative initiatives to increase access, curb legislative initiatives that undermine access, and present or join claims and petitions of fundamental importance.[105] They have succeeded in influencing and improving accessibility.[106] There are now quite a few civil organizations that provide legal aid to disadvantaged populations through free consultation and representation. Gradually this assistance has become an important part of the legal services market, although the scope of the services cannot meet existing needs.[107] Prominent organizations include the Movement to Fight Poverty in Israel,[108] the Worker's Hotline,[109] WIZO,[110] and the Movement of Working Women and Volunteers (Na'amat).[111] Today, growing numbers of lawyers are becoming involved in full- or part-time public-social action,[112] albeit their numbers still pale in comparison to the total number of lawyers practising in Israel.[113]

In addition to the efforts of NGOs, since the beginning of the twenty-first century all 14 law schools in Israel have opened legal clinics. They offer free legal aid to various disadvantaged communities and deepen their law students' commitment to ensuring access to justice.[114] Clinics employ dozens of lawyers and encourage hundreds of students to participate every year, making a significant contribution to the implementation of their clients' rights.

In March 2008, these legal clinics as well as social organizations received a letter from the National Ethics Committee of the IBA, imposing a number of restrictions for alleged violations of UPL rules.[115] Previously, these rules were usually applied only to commercial entities established for profit, and the IBA's new approach applied the UPL rules in a technical manner which conflicted with access to justice. The decisions of the National Ethics Committee bind lawyers, and whoever fails to comply with them may expect to face disciplinary proceedings. Therefore, the legal clinics and social organizations were forced to change their activities, severely limiting their ability to open the legal system to weaker sectors of the population. Both bodies formed a joint coalition that began a dialogue with the Bar, which lasted for several years without result.[116] The restrictions remained in

[104] See the Association for Civil Rights in Israel, 'Homepage', online: www.english.acri.org.il/in-the-knesset.

[105] See CA 4223/12 *The Center for Medical Rights Ltd* v. *The Israel Bar Association* (2014).

[106] *Guardians, supra* note 4, at 106–8.

[107] Ibid.

[108] Halev Project, the Movement to Fight Poverty, online: www.halev.org.il/ (in Hebrew).

[109] Kav Laoved, 'Worker's Hotline', online www.kavlaoved.org.il/ (in Hebrew).

[110] WIZO, 'Home Page', online: www.wizo.org (in Hebrew).

[111] Na'amat, 'Home Page', online: www.naamat.org.il/english/.

[112] *Guardians, supra* note 4, at 106–17.

[113] *Ambivalent Language, supra* note 80, at 258.

[114] *Guardians, supra* note 4, at 107–8.

[115] See the decision in Issue No. 29 of the Ethics Committee of 11 February 2009 at 'Legal Representation by Associations, Non-profit Organizations, and Clinics in Schools and Law Faculties', *Israel Bar Association* (11 February 2009), online: www.israelbar.org.il/newspaper_innerData3.asp?pgId=76234&catId=60&path_catID=60&fatherId=76227 (in Hebrew).

[116] Limor Zer-Gutman, 'The Israeli Bar and the Legal Clinics: Anatomy of a Struggle' (2013) 17 *HaMishpat Law Review* 59 at 96–7.

effect until 2017, when in the wake of the appointment of a new head of the National Ethics Committee, a different and more lenient approach was initiated, which is now applied almost without restrictions, and which allows the organizations and clinics to operate.[117]

VI. CONCLUSION

The right of access to justice is not explicitly contained in Israeli law, but a series of statutory provisions and voluminous case law have transformed access to justice into a basic constitutional right. The chapter examined the strength of this right through a practical prism, the ability of a person of limited means to obtain legal representation. Three organizations have the greatest impact on the exercise of this right. The first organization is of course the state, which recognized, mandated, and funded legal representation in criminal cases. All forms of representation in criminal matters are supplied by the Public Defender's Office, which benefits from a government budget that has expanded over the years. The state also provides legal aid in civil matters through the Legal Aid Department in the Ministry of Justice, and although the means cut-off is stringent, this budget has also seen substantial increases.

The second organization that affects exercise of the right of access to justice is the legal profession, which benefits from a broad monopoly on the legal services market. The IBA protects that monopoly with UPL rules, blocking the entry of competing entities into the legal services market and extending UPL rules to those serving impoverished segments of society. Until recently, IBA's efforts were aimed primarily at NGOs and law school legal clinics, but today, IBA efforts are primarily directed against technologies that offer online low-cost legal services to the general public. While the influence of the third type of organization, NGOs and law clinics, is smaller than the state and the IBA, its contributions are important because of the nature of the consistent, no-cost, legal representation services offered over the years and ancillary commitment to human rights which have helped entrench the right of access to justice in Israel.

We expect the relative influence of the state, NGOs, and law school legal clinics to remain unchanged. The significant development that could lead to increased access to justice among disadvantaged and intermediate populations unable to afford lawyers' fees may follow from the current failure of the legal profession to prevent companies from offering legal technology services to the general public. Courts have rejected the IBA's assertion that these companies have breached UPL, usually with reference to the importance of increasing access to justice.[118] These online services and legal applications have the capacity to simplify many legal processes and offer a variety of legal services at cheap prices, which would increase access to justice but will also push lawyers away from particular legal areas, for example, drafting contracts and wills. However, even if legal technology accomplishes these goals, the IBA will remain a major actor that significantly limits exercise of the right of access to justice.

[117] See the decision in Issue No. 64 of the Ethics Committee of 17 January 2017 at 'Clarifying a Decision: Providing Non-profit Legal Services that Ease Restrictions', *Israel Bar Association* (17 January 2017), online: www.israelbar.org.il/newspaper_innerData3.asp?pgId=381509&catId=60&path_catID=60&fatherId=381230 (in Hebrew).

[118] CC (Jer) 50926-10-15 *Israel Bar Association* v. *Hasavim Ltd* (2017), Nevo Legal Database (by subscription) (in Hebrew); CC (TA) 28548-03-17 *Israel Bar Association* v. *Averamof* (2018), Nevo Legal Database (by subscription) (in Hebrew).

18

Vuk'uzenzele – Arise and Act: Lawyers and Access to Justice in South Africa

Helen Kruuse

Abstract

South Africa's context is one that has to deal with apartheid and its devastating legacies. The chapter traces the evolution of pro bono and related practices in this context, from a professional 'duty' or 'calling' to one founded in the South African Constitution. The chapter argues that it is this constitutional foundation that has led to the institutionalization of 'community service' as a mandatory feature of being a South African legal professional. The chapter then considers the contemplated community service regime and other recent legislative changes to the South African access to justice landscape. The drafters of the legislation clearly see the community service regime as a chance for improved access to justice for vulnerable persons. However, having erased enforcement mechanisms for pro bono in the process, and with no implementation of community service in sight, South Africa's new legislative scheme may not have its intended effect. The chapter argues that a complementary, multipronged approach is needed. This approach includes the provision of community service alongside state legal aid and pro bono, together with the caps on legal fees currently being considered by the government – all ideas worth serious consideration in a country where there is considerable unmet legal need.

I. INTRODUCTION

This chapter follows the development of ideas regarding lawyers and access to justice in South Africa, from their early history to current times. As pro bono was a relatively unknown phrase in South Africa until 30–40 years ago, I consider the equivalent practices of *pro deo* and *pro amico* as they functioned until the mid-1980s. I consider the justification for these practices, and trace their evolution from a professional foundation of so-called tradition, of a duty or calling, to one arguably founded in the South African Constitution. The chapter argues that it is this latter feature of a 'constitutional foundation' that has led to the recognition and institutionalization of pro bono, at least on some levels, as an inherent feature of being a South African legal professional. The interesting questions raised in this context are why has this happened, what does this mean for access to justice in South Africa, and whether anything can be learned from the South African experience. With its extremes of poverty and wealth, and its extensive constitutional guarantees, the South African experience is indeed a compelling environment for jurisdictions grappling with the relationship between lawyers and access to justice. South Africa's unique history of apartheid, and the devastation that apartheid left in its wake politically and socio-economically, provide the foundation for this chapter's discussion. This legacy, together with the country's adoption in 1996 of one of the most progressive, if not *the* most progressive, constitutions in the world,[1] prompts examination into the country's approach to access to justice, including the role of lawyers in a democratic state.

Before embarking on such an exercise, a few definitions and limitations to the study are useful. Access to justice has both wide and narrow definitions. In its broad sense, it should be understood as a way to enforce substantive equality rights and promote constitutional guarantees.[2] This broad definition covers a multitude of actions by the state, and includes actions by private entities and persons in order to recognize and address systemic barriers faced by different community members in achieving equality or redress for wrongs committed against them.[3] The broad definition of access to justice is also associated with the rule of law, in that justice should be achieved in an impartial and non-discriminatory way.[4] In its narrow sense, access to justice is understood as the right to a fair hearing, including the right of every person to use the system or have access to legal representation. It is access to justice in this narrower sense that is the subject of this chapter.[5]

If there is an obligation to provide legal representation to those who cannot afford it, who should provide these services? Where does the state's duty to fund and provide legal services end, and where does the duty of private lawyers to give up their time and render a service to the public begin?[6] While there is debate about whether history supports a pro bono requirement,[7] countries such as the US and the UK have accepted the view that access to justice, provided in part by pro bono legal services, is one of the core values of the profession. The chapter argues that it is the unique circumstances of the South African legal landscape, particularly the nature of its Constitution, that require lawyers to take positive steps to realize access to justice. This requirement is reflected in the title of the chapter, a call for lawyers to arise and act (*vuk'uzenzele*). However, the chapter also argues that the positive duty of legal professionals to provide pro bono work should not ease the pressure on the state to improve access to justice through state-sponsored legal aid.

The chapter first considers the more recent historical relationship between lawyers and access to justice in South Africa. I discuss the move from the concepts of '*pro deo*' and '*pro amico*', to the phrase 'pro bono', which mirrors changing expectations regarding a lawyer's obligation to

[1] Drucilla Cornell and Karin van Marle with Albie Sachs, *Albie Sachs and Transformation in South Africa: From Revolutionary Activist to Constitutional Court Judge* (UK: Birbeck Law Press, 2014) at 6.

[2] See Y. A. Vadwa, 'Access to Justice: From Legal Representation to Promotion of Equality and Social Justice – Addressing the Legal Isolation of the Poor' (2005) 26:2 *Obiter* 234.

[3] For broad definitions of access to justice, see in general Lawrence M. Friedman, 'Access to Justice: Some Historical Comments' (2010) 37:1 *Fordham Urban Law Journal* 3 and Estelle Hurter, 'Access to Justice: To Dream the Impossible Dream?' (2011) 44:3 *Comparative and International Law Journal of South Africa* 408.

[4] See United Nations, 'Access to Justice', online: www.un.org/ruleoflaw/thematic-areas/access-to-justice-and-rule-of-law-institutions/access-to-justice/.

[5] See Legal Aid South Africa, *Legal Aid Guide 2014*, 13th edn (Cape Town: Juta and Company, 2014) at 5 (the ability 'to claim rights and *enforce obligations* in our justice system') (emphasis in original).

[6] Mauro Cappelletti, 'Access to Justice as a Theoretical Approach to Law and a Practical Programme for Reform' (1992) 109 *South African Law Journal* 22 at 28–9.

[7] See Zino I. Macaluso, 'That's OK, This One's on Me: A Discussion of the Responsibilities and Duties Owed by the Profession to Do Pro Bono Publico Work' (1992) 26 *University of British Columbia Law Review* 65 at 67, n 10.

provide free or low-cost legal services to indigent persons. Second, I attempt to provide some insight into the current unmet need for legal services in the country. Third, I set out the constitutional guarantees of access to justice, as a way of grounding a duty to provide access to justice, a duty owed by the state but also by the legal profession. Finally, the chapter considers and critiques recent legislative initiatives designed to implement constitutional guarantees of access to courts and representation and address the country's unmet legal need.

II. ACCESS TO JUSTICE: HISTORICAL PRECURSORS

South Africa's legal system is best described as a hybrid or a mixed system, given its inheritance of a civil law system from its first colonizer, the Dutch, in the mid-1600s, and then a common law system from its second colonizer, the English, in the early 1800s. The current legal system, under the umbrella of a Constitution,[8] recognizes customary law systems belonging to the different ethnic indigenous groups.[9] While elements of the inquisitorial method existed from the 1600s to the early 1800s under Dutch influence, the English influence on court procedure in the early 1800s created a legal system which utilizes for the most part an adversarial mode of adjudication.[10] This mode has the inevitable consequence that lawyers play an important role in access to justice, as the South African courts have recognized.[11] Also, South Africa's mixed system of law, together with complex rules of recognition regarding customary law, mean that lawyers are especially important in translating and accessing justice for those who need it.[12]

Lawyers in South Africa have historically comprised a divided profession of advocates and attorneys. Similar to the English barrister and solicitor, advocates practised in the courts but were only allowed to accept briefs through attorneys rather than directly from clients; attorneys primarily advised clients, and while they did appear in court, they did so less frequently and mostly in the lower courts. These professions were governed by different legislation[13] and different regulatory bodies.[14] This long-standing structure of the legal profession has recently changed via the Legal Practice Act.[15] Major changes in this legislation include partial fusion of the profession, centralization of regulatory functions into one statutory body (the Legal Practice Council), and initiatives attempting to provide access to the profession for the most vulnerable persons and persons previously marginalized by the political system. These developments are discussed later in the chapter. The Legal Practice Act provides for a high court to admit all 'legal practitioners' into one of three forms of practice, as an attorney, as an advocate practising on a referral basis only, and as an advocate accepting work directly

8 *The Constitution of the Republic of South Africa, 1996* (as amended 1 February 2013) [*South Africa Constitution*].

9 *South Africa Constitution, supra* note 8, ss 30 and 31.

10 See C. R. Snyman, 'The Accusatorial and Inquisitorial Approaches to Criminal Procedure: Some Points of Comparison between South African and Continental Systems' (1975) 8:1 *Comparative and International Law Journal of South Africa* 100.

11 See for example, *Legal Aid Board* v. *S* [2010] ZASCA 112 (SCA) at [1].

12 See R. S. Suttner, 'African Civil Law – Special Legal Aid Problems' in *Legal Aid in South Africa* (South Africa: University of Natal, 1973) 189 at 191–4.

13 *Attorneys Act 53 of 1979*, South Africa [*Attorneys Act*]; *Admission of Advocates Act 74 of 1964*, South Africa.

14 Attorney membership was required in one of four statutory law societies, but advocates were allowed to choose whether to join the voluntary association of the General Council of the Bar (see General Council of the Bar of South Africa, online: www.gcbsa.co.za/).

15 *Legal Practice Act 28 of 2014*, South Africa [*LPA*]. Transitional provisions came into effect on 1 February 2015 (Proc. R2 / GG 38412 / 20150123). The new regulatory body, the Legal Practice Council, came into effect on 31 October 2018 (see Proc. R31 / GG 42003 / 20181029 and Proc. R31 / GG 42003 / 20181029).

from the public. The last form of practice mentioned is a new type of practice which is meant to cut the costs of an intermediary attorney if the advocate has a trust account.[16]

The structure and type of a legal system obviously impact how justice is accessed, but history must also be considered when interrogating the relationship between the South African legal profession and access to justice. At best this relationship has been an uneasy one, and at its worst it could be described as schizophrenic.[17] The relationship has been the consequence of South Africa's complex political, social, and economic background, as well as its current post-colonial position in a time of economic volatility. South Africa's status as a constitutional democracy is a recent one, established in 1994. Previously, the country was subjected to a system of law, imposed by a minority group on a majority of its people, through oppression, prejudice, and discrimination based primarily on race. This system, which operated informally until the 1940s, was formalized by the government of the day into a system known as 'apartheid', benignly portrayed as a system in which the relationships between the races were treated as 'separate but equal', but which in truth was a system which treated the non-white population as subhuman.

By the 1980s, the political situation in South Africa had become so unstable that it threatened to take the country into civil war. During this time, the vast majority of legal practitioners were white. The country's racial classification system placed obstacles in the way of black people, precluding them from receiving an education that would equip them for the tertiary education necessary to obtain legal qualifications and admission to the profession.[18] In 2000, 85 per cent of the legal profession was white and only 15 per cent was black.[19]

During the apartheid regime, the South African legal profession could be said to have been in both the vanguard and the rear of access to justice. A small but committed group of practitioners forged a human rights culture in a few law firms[20] and litigated against the state, making small inroads against the state's apartheid policy.[21] This work, now commonly referred to in South Africa as public interest litigation, was mostly carried out with international funding, and then with local funding when international funding was banned by the state in the 1960s.[22] This work contributed significantly to two notable outcomes. First, despite gloomy forecasts, the country avoided major bloodshed, although violence did occur. Second, the public interest litigation

[16] *LPA*, *supra* note 15, s 24; see *South African Legal Practice Council* v. *Alves* (1255/2019) [2020] ZASCA 170, at para. 11.

[17] Joel Modiri, 'Transformation, Tension and Transgression: Reflections on the Culture and Ideology of South African Legal Education' (2013) 24 *Stellenbosch Law Review* 455 at 478.

[18] See J. W. Macquarrie, 'The Sociological Background of the African University Student' in J. V. O. Reid and A. J. Wilmot, eds., *Medical Education in South Africa* (South Africa: Natal University Press, 1965) 225 at 227; Izak Smuts, 'Transforming the Transformation Debate' (Address to *Ndifuna Ukwazi* (Dare to Know), an NGO in Cape Town, 10 September 2013), online: www.politicsweb.co.za/news-and-analysis/on-transformation-and-the-legal-profession–izak-s.

[19] David J. McQuoid-Mason, 'The Delivery of Civil Legal Aid Services in South Africa' (2000) 24:6 *Fordham International Law Journal* S111 [*Civil Legal Aid Services*].

[20] Cheadle, Thompson and Haysom Inc.; Lawyers for Human Rights; the Legal Resources Centre, to name a few. See Stephen Golub, 'Battling Apartheid, Building a New South Africa' in Mary McClymont and Stephen Golub, eds., *Many Roads to Justice: The Law Related Work of the Foundation Grantees Around the World* (New York: Ford Foundation, 2000) 19 at 19.

[21] See for example *Komani NO* v. *Bantu Affairs Administration Board, Peninsula Area* (1980) 4 SA 448 (A) (African pass laws) and *Oos-Randse Administrasieraad* v. *Rikhoto* (1983) 3 SA 595 (A) (permanent residency requirements); see also Richard L. Abel, *Politics by Other Means: Law in the Struggle against Apartheid, 1980–1994* (New York: Routledge, 1995).

[22] See South African History Online, 'The International Defence and Aid Fund' (14 February 2013), online: www.sahistory.org.za/article/international-defence-and-aid-fund-idaf.

and its promotion of a human rights culture laid the groundwork for the African National Congress' adoption of a human rights document, titled the Freedom Charter,[23] and contributed to the country's subsequent adoption of one of the world's most progressive constitutions.

Apart from the small pocket of lawyers practising public interest litigation of a mostly political nature, there is a limited history of pro bono, referred to as *pro deo*. *Pro deo* appears to have originated in *in forma pauperis* proceedings, in which litigants were not required to pay court fees, and in 'dock briefs/defences', where a trial judge allowed an accused to brief counsel for a nominal fee in court. Both proceedings were inherited from the English colonizers and imported into South Africa's civil and criminal procedure.[24] Notably, law societies at this stage prohibited attorneys from taking up free work themselves, except in limited circumstances such as a court request in connection with *in forma pauperis* proceedings. This position reflects an anti-competitive, protectionist stance.[25] Anecdotal accounts suggest that these court appointments were relatively rare,[26] and related mostly to advocates rather than attorneys.[27] Nevertheless, there are recorded cases of *pro deo* counsel being appointed by the court in civil matters.[28] In criminal matters, appointment was largely limited to capital cases.[29] At the same time as *pro deo* practices, the terminology *pro amico* was used to refer to the provision of free legal services by counsel, but limited to obligations arising out 'of friendship or familial relationship'.[30]

The first recorded use of terminology '*pro bono publico*' in the context of free legal services for poor or vulnerable persons appears to have been in 1973, when the University of Natal's Faculty of Law[31] held a conference on legal aid in South Africa.[32] A delegate from the US, Professor David S. Nelson, referred to programmes in the US such as the Massachusetts Defenders Committee, and commented that US law firms had displayed a '*pro bono publico* commitment'.[33] He further explained that this commitment prompted US lawyers to volunteer to represent indigent and minority groups.[34] Following this conference, the phrase 'pro bono'

[23] See 'The Freedom Charter', adopted at the Congress of the People at Kliptown, Johannesburg, 25 and 26 June 1955 (*Johannesburg: Historical Papers Research Archive* (2013)), online: www.historicalpapers.wits.ac.za/inventories/inv_pdfo/AD1137/AD1137-Ea6-1-001-jpeg.pdf.

[24] B. R. Bamford, 'Service in the Gown' (1970) 87 *South African Law Journal* 338 [*Service in the Gown*] at 342; E. A. L. Lewis, *Legal Ethics: A Guide to Professional Conduct for South African Attorneys* (Cape Town: Juta and Company, 1982) [*Legal Ethics*] at 27; Lynn Berat, 'Legal Aid and the Indigent Accused in South Africa: A Proposal for Reform' (1988) 18 *Georgia Journal of International and Comparative Law* 239 [*Proposal for Reform*] at 248.

[25] *Rules Regulating the Conduct of the Proceedings of the Supreme Court of Appeal of South Africa*, R. 1523 (1998), r 15; and *Uniform Rules of Court*, South Africa (as amended 26 June 2009) (pertaining to High Courts), r 40; and *Magistrates' Courts Rules of Court*, South Africa, R. 740 (2010), r 53, as collated in Juta's Statutes Editors, *The Supreme Court Act 59 of 1959 and the Magistrates' Courts Act 32 of 1944 and Rules*, 11th edn, revised reprint (Cape Town: Juta and Company, 2013). In the Supreme Court of Appeal and High Courts the programme is called *in forma pauperis*, whereas in the Magistrates' Courts Rule 53 refers to '*pro deo* applicants'. However, the import is the same and the programmes are discussed using the *in forma pauperis* label.

[26] H. R. Hahlo and Ellison Kahn, *The Union of South Africa: The Development of its Laws and Constitution (The British Commonwealth – The Development of its Laws and Constitution)* (Cape Town: Juta and Company, 1960) at 290.

[27] *Legal Ethics*, *supra* note 24, at 206.

[28] *Mtembu* v. *Eagle Star Ins. Co.* 1960 (2) SA 50 (C).

[29] *S* v. *Gibson* (1979) 4 SA 115 (D) 123A–124G; *S* v. *Motsatsi* (1998) 2 SACR 35 (W).

[30] *Legal Ethics*, *supra* note 24, at 28.

[31] Now the University of KwaZulu-Natal.

[32] See *Legal Aid in South Africa: Proceedings of a Conference Held in the Faculty of Law, University of Natal, Durban, from 2nd–6th July, 1973* (South Africa: University of Natal, 1973) [*Legal Aid Conference*].

[33] D. S. Nelson, 'The Lawyer's Role Among Disadvantaged Sections of Community' in *Legal Aid Conference*, *supra* note 32, at 82.

[34] Ibid.

slowly crept into South African legal discourse, and the phrase is evident in increased usage today. It is fair to say that the idea of pro bono was understood and reflected in the related concepts of *pro amico*, *pro deo*, and *in forma pauperis*, but with increased influence of the US, these South African concepts coalesced into and are now packaged as pro bono.

Apart from the express provisions of the *in forma pauperis* rule, some members of the Bar, judges, and local attorney generals during the 1970s recognized that the provision of free legal services was urgently needed.[35] While there was disagreement regarding whether the legal profession had a 'moral duty' or calling to provide free services to the indigent,[36] it appears that with increased need came increased pressure. As reviewed above, the legal profession was persuaded to make some provision for free legal services, and then the legal profession pressured the government to provide state-sponsored legal aid.

Pressure for state-sponsored legal aid was evident as early as 1930, when it was asked why South Africa should not have a law similar to the Poor Prisoners Defence Act 1930, introduced in England and Wales.[37] While legal aid bureaus were set up as early as 1937, and were initially successful in reaching out to the poor, chronic financial shortages and arguments between the government and law societies regarding their independence seriously limited their ability to provide legal aid.[38] By the early 1960s, and with the banning of international funding, the government finally introduced a formal national system known as the Legal Aid Board ('Board'), 'to render or make available legal aid to indigent persons'.[39] The Board was given wide discretion in achieving this goal, and initially it adopted a referral or judicare system which largely outsources matters to private legal practitioners, as opposed to a salaried lawyer approach.[40] By the mid-1980s, it was evident that the Board's methods, together with work by NGOs and rare *pro deo* appearances, still left many people without legal representation.[41] The apartheid state was put under more and more international pressure, internal protests against the state grew, and decisions such as S v. *Khanyile*[42] and S v. *Davids*, S v. *Dladla*[43] illustrated the fact that too many people were imprisoned without the benefit of legal representation.[44] In these cases, a liberal-minded judge attempted to impose a limited duty of legal representation on the state,[45] but the duty was overturned by the Appellate Division, then the highest appellate court.[46] Without clear obligations on either the state or legal professionals, access to justice for the most vulnerable individuals was not an achievable goal. An important turning point, for the country and access to justice, occurred when the apartheid government started negotiating with a variety of

35 *Service in the Gown*, *supra* note 24, at 342–3.

36 G. W. Cook, 'History of Legal Aid in South Africa' in *Legal Aid Conference*, *supra* note 32 [*History of Legal Aid*], at 28; and see M. Zander, 'Legal Aid in a Democratic Society' in *Legal Aid Conference*, *supra* note 32, at 12–13.

37 Note, 'Poor Prisoners Defence Act' (1930) 47 *South African Law Journal* 427.

38 *Proposal for Reform*, *supra* note 24, at 251–7.

39 Preamble, *Legal Aid Act, No. 22 of 1969*, South Africa (as amended 19 April 1996). Prior to the Act, a National Legal Aid Scheme was discussed in 1962 but never came into full operation: see *History of Legal Aid*, *supra* note 36, at 32.

40 *Civil Legal Aid Services*, *supra* note 19, S117.

41 Ibid.

42 (1988) 3 SA 795 (N). For a discussion of this case, see C. J. Ogletree Jr, 'From Mandela to Mthwana: Providing Counsel to the Unrepresented Accused in South Africa' (1995) 75:1 *Boston University Law Review*, 21ff.

43 (1989) 4 SA 172 (N), 173Cff.

44 For a discussion of this issue, see the extracurial comments of a subsequent Chief Justice (2005–9): Pius Langa, 'Pro Bono Work: Making Rights a Reality' (2002) 19:3 *Indicator South Africa* 38 [*Making Rights a Reality*].

45 *Making Rights a Reality*, *supra* note 44, per Didcott J.

46 S v. *Rudman*; S v. *Mthwana* (1992) 1 SA 343 (A) at 371–2.

then-banned political parties to end apartheid.[47] This political development paved the way for the drafting of a Constitution, which in both its interim (1993) and final (1996) versions, embraced and codified the decision in *Khanyile* regarding the right to counsel in criminal cases at state expense if substantial injustice would otherwise result.[48] The Constitution included far-reaching rights of access to justice, explored in the next section.

III. CONSTITUTIONAL GUARANTEES SUPPORTING ACCESS TO JUSTICE IN SOUTH AFRICA

As a result of the legacy of a general lack of access for persons based on socio-economic and racial lines, the South African Constitution adopted in 1996[49] contained explicit access to justice guarantees. In Section 34, a general right of access to the courts was set out.[50] Section 35 established a right of legal representation for those arrested, detained, and accused of crimes,[51] and Section 28 established specific guarantees for minors.[52] Section 35 requires the state to provide legal aid to those facing criminal charges, if substantial injustice would result without it. However, the Constitution does not extend the right to legal aid to civil claims, unless the party is a minor whose failure to have legal aid would similarly result in substantial injustice.[53]

IV. REALIZING CONSTITUTIONAL GUARANTEES: LEGAL AID IN SOUTH AFRICA

Despite the advent of the Constitution, by the mid- to late 1990s there were signs that many persons still remained unrepresented, and that the Board was not meeting demand or had not been adequately restructured to meet the new constitutional guarantees. This failure to provide access is clear from one of the earliest judgments of the Constitutional Court, where the court stated:[54]

> A word or two had better be added … on a subject of public importance which promoted some discussion when the present cases were argued. No counsel on either side could then tell us of any steps taken to establish the financial and administrative structures that were necessary to give effect to the part of Section 25(3)(e) [under the Interim Constitution – now s 35(3)] providing for legal representation at the expense of the State. We gain the impression that nothing of much significance had been done in that direction since the Constitution came into force a year ago. The impression, if true, is most disturbing. We are mindful of the multifarious demands on the

[47] See South African History Online, 'Convention for a Democratic South Africa (CODESA)', online: www.sahistory.org.za/article/convention-democratic-south-africa-codesa.

[48] David J. McQuoid-Mason, 'Legal Representation and the Courts' (1994) 5 *South African Human Rights Yearbook* 162 at 165; John Milton et al., 'Procedural Rights' in D. Van Wyk et al., eds., *Rights and Constitutionalism: The New South African Legal Order* (Oxford: Clarendon Press, 1996) 401 at 414–15.

[49] *South Africa Constitution, supra* note 8.

[50] *South Africa Constitution, supra* note 8, s 34, states that '[e]veryone has the right to have any dispute that can be resolved by the application of law decided in a fair public hearing before a court or, where appropriate, another independent and impartial tribunal or forum'.

[51] *South Africa Constitution, supra* note 8, ss 35(2)(c) and 35(3)(g).

[52] Under the *South Africa Constitution, supra* note 8, s 28(1)(h), every child has the right 'to have a legal practitioner assigned to the child by the state, and at state expense, in civil proceedings affecting the child, if substantial injustice would otherwise result'.

[53] See *Soller NO* v. *G* (2003) 5 SA 430 (W) at [20]–[29].

[54] *S* v. *Vermaas, S* v. *Du Plessis* (1995) 2 SA 292 (CC) at [16].

> public purses and the machinery of government that flow from the urgent need for economic and social reform. But the Constitution does not envisage and surely does not brook an undue delay in the fulfilment of any promise made by it. It is a fundamental right. One can safely assume that, in spite of Section 25(3)(e), the situation still prevails where during every month countless thousands of South Africans are criminally tried without legal representation because they are too poor to pay for it. They are presumably informed at the beginning as the section requires them peremptorily to be, of their right to obtain that free of charge in the circumstances which it defines. Importing such information becomes an empty gesture and makes a mockery of the Constitution, however, if it is not backed by mechanisms that are adequate for the enforcement of that right.

As a result of these realities, the Board moved away from the judicare approach and opted for a legal aid model based largely on salaried lawyers; a limited judicare model was retained for specific instances such as conflicts of interests or a need for particular expertise.[55] By 2008, the Board claimed to have provided criminal legal representation in 45–65% of matters in the District Courts; 50–75% in the Regional Courts; and 80–95% in the High Courts.[56] The model of salaried lawyers is the prevailing model in the offices which administer legal aid (Justice Centres) around South Africa today.[57] In the 2017–18 financial year, 2,627 recruited legal staff including paralegals handled 426,617 new matters.[58] Of these, 371,202 or 87% were criminal matters, and 55,415 or 13% were civil matters.[59]

As noted above, the Constitution requires the state to appoint counsel at its expense only if substantial injustice would otherwise result. The Board, now known as Legal Aid South Africa ('LASA'),[60] must therefore determine when counsel are necessary to avoid substantial injustice. In criminal cases, LASA's decisions are guided by supporting regulations to the Act and the *Legal Aid Manual*, a manual that the enabling statute requires LASA to publish and review every two years.[61]

Currently the regulations set out that LASA may grant legal aid to a sentenced or detained person or an accused person in a criminal trial if it is likely that such person would suffer substantial injustice; it is provided that substantial injustice might occur 'if that person cannot afford legal representation and the possibility that he or she might be imprisoned exists'.[62] The manual,[63] in turn, states that 'substantial injustice' takes place when a person without legal aid would experience significant injustice by being sentenced, or having the possibility of being sentenced, to direct imprisonment of more than three months in a criminal case.[64] Affordability

[55] See David J. McQuoid-Mason, 'The Supply Side: The Role of Lawyers in the Provision of Legal Aid – Some Lessons from South Africa' in *Access to Justice in Africa and Beyond: Making the Rule of Law a Reality* (Illinois: Penal Reform International, 2007) 97 at 102.

[56] Dunstan Mlambo, 'Introduction' in Legal Aid Board South Africa, *Annual Report for 2007/8* (2008) at 3.

[57] In the financial year 2015/16.

[58] Legal Aid South Africa, *Integrated Annual Report 2017–2018* (2018) [*Annual Report 2017–2018*] at 2.

[59] Ibid.

[60] The Legal Aid Board changed its name to Legal Aid South Africa in 2014 via the *Legal Aid South Africa Act 39 of 2014* [*Legal Aid SA Act*].

[61] See *Legal Aid SA Act*, *supra* note 60, s 24. As at the time of writing, the current *Legal Aid Manual* 2020 (version 5) is available online: www.legal-aid.co.za/wp-content/uploads/2020/10/LEGAL-AID-MANUAL-VERSION-5_16-October-2020-gazetted.pdf [*Legal Aid Manual*]. This manual was gazetted in South Africa, *Government Gazette* 43814 of 16 October 2020, Government Notice 572, and the came into effect 60 days after the gazette, 15 December 2020.

[62] Regulation 3(1) published under Government Notice R745 in South Africa, *Government Gazette* 41005 of 26 July 2017, and amended by South Africa, *Government Gazette* 42338, Government Notice 498 of 29 March 2019 [*GN R745 Gov Gaz 41005, as amended*].

[63] See *Legal Aid Manual*, *supra* note 61, at 20.

[64] Ibid.

as per the regulations and the manual is determined primarily by the person's means and the costs of the legal representation. While the reference to costs implies that heightened costs of representation may result in LASA not taking the case, the regulations clarify that no person in a criminal matter facing possible imprisonment should be unrepresented due to unaffordability. The situation is different for civil matters, where the cost of legal representation is important when LASA decides whether to extend representation. This approach is evident from the *Legal Aid Manual*, which includes two factors in a merit report regarding whether to take on a matter: the total expected financial involvement of LASA, and the expected costs of experts and other witnesses in relation to their evidence and testimony.[65] The exception to this approach is where a person applies for legal aid where his or her constitutional or personal rights are affected in a civil matter.[66]

In general the legal aid means test defines indigence as earning under ZAR7,400 (US$438.79)[67] per month, after tax deductions.[68] To put this amount into context, the average teacher, nurse, miner, and police person in South Africa will earn over this amount,[69] while domestic workers generally earn under this amount.[70] In civil matters, the *Legal Aid Manual* states that legal aid will only be granted to a litigant who is indigent *and* the matter has prospects of success on a balance of probabilities. The guide further qualifies civil legal aid as being dependent on the availability of state resources.[71] The regulations of the Legal Aid Act set out the factors to be taken into account when considering granting civil legal aid:[72]

(a) in the opinion of Legal Aid South Africa, the matter has good prospects of success;
(b) in the opinion of Legal Aid South Africa, the matter has good prospects of enforcement of a court order; and
(c) Legal Aid South Africa has the necessary resources available.

The manual doubles down on the costs issue by making it necessary to consider several resource issues, including the availability of evidence and witnesses, the expected costs of their evidence and testimony (where experts are involved), the anticipated duration of the trial, the financial ability of the other side to satisfy the claim and costs if the legal aid applicant is successful, all cost implications of the proceedings to date, and a final all-encompassing issue,

65 *Legal Aid Manual, supra* note 61; see in particular para. 3.8(b)(g) and (h), 'Approving Legal Aid for Merit Report'.

66 The *Legal Aid SA Act* does not define 'indigent person', and LASA establishes a means test: Reg. 27 in *GN R745 Gov Gaz 41005, as amended, supra* note 62.

67 XE Currency Converter, online: www.xe.com/currencyconverter/convert/?Amount=7400&From=ZAR&To=USD. Unless another reference was cited, US$ denominations in the chapter were derived from www.xe.com at the time of publication; they are intended for general reference and may have been rounded up or down for ease of reference.

68 Reg. 27 of *GN R745 Gov Gaz 41005, as amended, supra* note 62.

69 See PayScale, 'Average Department of Education Salary', online: www.payscale.com/research/ZA/Employer=Department_of_Education/Salary; PayScale, 'Average High School Teacher Salary', online: www.payscale.com/research/ZA/Job=High_School_Teacher/Salary; PayScale, 'Average Neonatal Intensive Care Unit (NICU) Registered Nurse Salary', online: www.payscale.com/research/ZA/Job=Neonatal_Intensive_Care_Unit_(NICU)_Registered_Nurse/Salary; PayScale, 'Average Nurse, Intensive Care Unit (ICU) Salary)', online: www.payscale.com/research/ZA/Job=Nurse%2c_Intensive_Care_Unit_(ICU)/Salary; PayScale, 'Average Miner Salary', online: www.payscale.com/research/ZA/Job=Miner/Salary.

70 See Department of Labour, Republic of South Africa, *Basic Conditions of Employment Act No. 75 of 1977: Amendment of Sectoral Determination 7: Domestic Workers Sector, South Africa*, R. 919 (24 November 2014), online: www.gov.za/documents/basic-conditions-employment-act-sectoral-determination-7-domestic-worker-sector-3.

71 *Legal Aid Manual, supra* note 61.

72 *GN R745 Gov Gaz 41005, as amended, supra* note 62, regulation 9(1).

'the total expected financial involvement of [LASA]'.[73] The level of legal aid funding is therefore key in assessing access to civil justice, since LASA simply cannot execute on its mandate where funding is insufficient. This is a challenge, as LASA has itself recognized; in its 2017–18 Annual Report, LASA explicitly identified legislation which mandates legal assistance by the state, but no state funding is given or it is underfunded.[74] Notable areas where no funding is provided despite a legislative mandate include matters relating to labour, land reform, and eviction.[75]

Evaluating the effectiveness of legal aid is always going to be challenging. Budget data are difficult to assess since allocations need to be linked to the actual need for legal services in the indigent population, and considered in light of the government's need to spread its budget across a multiplicity of demands, many related to broader justice issues of access to housing, education, and health care.[76] What is clear is that Legal Aid's financial resources are 'stretched to the limits of their capacity', and even then are insufficient to meet demand.[77] Using a sample comparison to another need, that of basic education, one can compare annual budgets over three financial years. The legal aid budget over the three years constituted 0.007% (0.008% for 2017/18) of the basic education budget.[78] Practically speaking, this means that for approximately every ZAR3,200 (US$227)[79] the state spends on basic education, the state spends ZAR22.40 (US$1.59) on state legal aid.

The budget spent on legal aid appears to be at odds with the strong guarantees in South Africa's Constitution supporting access to justice as well as the country's notorious status as one of the most unequal countries in the world. Presently, the country has a Gini Co-efficient, an international measurement of relative poverty in a country or region, of approximately 0.6. While the ratio of lawyers to the general population, often taken as a rough proxy of access to justice, is 1:1,710,[80] not bad compared to other African countries, the high cost of legal services and the limited budget of state legal aid renders this ratio largely meaningless. The high cost of legal services is exacerbated by the fact that most of the legal practitioners are situated in larger towns and cities, while more than 50 per cent of the population, of whom 81.3 per cent are classed as 'poor', live in rural areas.[81]

73 *Legal Aid Manual*, *supra* note 61, at 35.

74 *Annual Report 2017–2018*, *supra* note 58, at 11.

75 *Labour Relations Act 66 of 1995*, South Africa, s 149; *Restitution of Land Rights Act 22 of 1994*, South Africa, s 22; *Prevention of Illegal Eviction from and Unlawful Occupation of Land Act 19 of 1998*, South Africa, s 4(5); *Land Reform (Labour Tenants) Act 3 of 1996*, South Africa, and *The Extension of Security of Tenure Act 62 of 1997*, South Africa.

76 See for example *Making Rights a Reality*, *supra* note 44, at 38.

77 See *Legal Aid South Africa* v. *Magidiwana* [2015] ZACC 28 at [61], where the Constitutional Court of South Africa accepted this into evidence.

78 The Legal Aid budget for 2014/15 was reported as ZAR1,638,622,972(US$97.17 million) (Legal Aid South Africa, *Annual Report 2014–2015* (2015) at 2), for 2015/16 as ZAR1,751,687,424(US$103.87 million) (Legal Aid South Africa, *Integrated Annual Report 2015–2016* (2016) at 2), and for 2017/18 ZAR1,860,956,466(US$110.35 million) (*Annual Report 2017–2018*, *supra* note 58, at 2); see South African National Treasury, 'National Budget Review 2016', online: www.treasury.gov.za/documents/national%20budget/2016/review/excel.aspx ('All budget review Excel tables').

79 This amount is chosen as the comparison since it was said to represent the average legal aid budget per client, for representation in an entire criminal case, albeit in 2013. See Nathan Geffen, 'The Exorbitant Price of Justice', *The Star* (9 September 2013), online: www.iol.co.za/the-star/the-exorbitant-price-of-justice-1575149. None of LASA's subsequent annual reports set out this amount.

80 2016, provided by the Law Society of South Africa. For comparative purposes, see for example Table 1 in *Access to Legal Aid in Criminal Justice Systems in Africa: Survey Report* (United Nations Office on Drugs and Crime, 2011) at 11, which compares the ratio of lawyers to population in 46 African countries, online: www.unodc.org/pdf/criminal_justice/Survey_Report_on_Access_to_Legal_Aid_in_Africa.pdf.

81 *Poverty Trends in South Africa: An Examination of Absolute Poverty Between 2006 and 2015* (Statistics South Africa, 2015) at 67, online: www.statssa.gov.za/publications/Report-03-10-06/Report-03-10-062015.pdf. See in general Jackie

Addressing the high cost of legal services and its effects, South Africa's Constitutional Court called on the legal profession to carry out a 'duty of diffidence' in relation to fees:[82]

> We feel obliged to express our disquiet at how counsel's fees have burgeoned in recent years. To say that they have skyrocketed is no loose metaphor. No matter the complexity of the issues, we can find no justification, in a country where disparities are gross and poverty is rife, to countenance appellate advocates charging hundreds of thousands of Rands to argue an appeal. No doubt skilled professional work deserves reasonable remuneration, and no doubt many clients are willing to pay market rates to secure the best services. *But in our country the legal profession owes a duty of diffidence in charging fees that go beyond what the market can bear.*

Commenting on the realities of the market, the Deputy Minister of Justice of South Africa noted that:[83]

> A 2016 review . . . into the attorney's profession in South Africa found that 61% of salary partners bill between ZAR1,000 to 3,000 per hour, and that was in 2016. So the amounts, one can assume, have further increased since then. So let us imagine you are a worker earning 7,000 per month after tax. This means that your total monthly wage will give you three billable hours with a salary partner on the bottom end of the scale. This raises many issues, is this fair? Is this what we mean by access to justice?

Given the limits of state legal aid, and South Africa's unequal socio-economic situation, the question that remains is what other measures have been put in place to deal with access to justice, and in particular what is a lawyer's role in this process? First, the public interest organizations and university law clinics, initially set up under apartheid, have continued to operate. They handle matters such as class-action litigation for the enforcement of constitutionally protected socio-economic rights.[84] However, there are reasons related to donor funding, such as donor interests, agenda, and terms of funding, that potentially limit what these organizations can do. Second, court structures such as the small claims court, for certain matters under ZAR20,000 (US$1,419), and the Commission for Conciliation, Mediation and Arbitration ('CCMA') for basic labour matters, provide a form of equality of arms since their procedures are simple and lawyers are not allowed to represent parties in hearings.[85] Third, legal insurance schemes have taken off in South Africa, ostensibly providing access mainly to the middle class.[86] However, the majority of South Africans struggle to access justice, and it is this reality that prompted future Chief Justice of South Africa Langa to write that '[t]he legal community should claim a niche for itself in the construction and development of a South Africa that is as close to our ideals as possible',[87] a niche that includes pro bono legal services.

Dugard, 'Courts and the Poor in South Africa: A Critique of Systemic Judicial Failures to Advance Transformative Justice' (2008) 24:2 *South African Journal on Human Rights* 214 at 216.

[82] *Camps Bay Ratepayers' and Residents' Association* v. *Harrison* [2012] ZACC 17 at [10]–[11] (emphasis supplied); see generally O. Rogers, 'High Fees and Questionable Practices' (2012) 25 *Advocate* 40.

[83] Deputy Minister of Justice and Constitutional Development John Jeffrey, 'Key Note Address' 1 November 2018 at 11–12, online: www.justice.gov.za/salrc/docs/2018-Conf-Costs/20190326-SALRC-AccessToJustice-Conference-Nov2018-Report.pdf [*Key Note Address*].

[84] See Steven Budlender, Gilbert Marcus, and Nick M. Ferreira, *Public Interest Litigation and Social Change in South Africa: Strategies, Tactics and Lessons* (Atlantic Philanthropies, 2014).

[85] See Commission for Conciliation, Mediation and Arbitration, 'Home', online: www.ccma.org.za/.

[86] See David J. McQuoid-Mason, 'Challenges in Increasing Access to Justice in the Next Decade', in Marita Carnelley and Shannon Hoctor, eds., *Law, Order and Liberty: Essays in Honour of Tony Mathews* (South Africa: University of KwaZulu-Natal Press, 2011) 169–205 at 192.

[87] *Making Rights a Reality*, *supra* note 44, at 38.

V. ACCESS TO JUSTICE INITIATIVES BY THE LEGAL PROFESSION

A. *Mandatory Pro Bono Scheme and Future Plans*

Pro bono in the form of *pro deo* and *pro amico* had been part of the South African legal landscape from the time of South Africa's second colonizers in the early 1800s, but while legal professionals undertook these voluntary services, only a few did so and it was not seen as a requirement. No law or policy required practitioners to undertake pro bono work, and the *in forma pauperis* rule was only used intermittently as a basis for appointment of counsel.[88] However, following the imposition of the constitutional guarantees of access to justice, and the initial lead of the Cape Law Society in 2002,[89] all four law societies in the country adopted rules requiring their attorney members to complete a minimum of 24 hours of pro bono work a year. In early 2016, the legal profession introduced new national rules for attorneys via delegated legislation, similar to the provincial rules but in much more detail. These details set out exemptions for the pro bono requirements, the naming of 'recognized structures' through which pro bono could be rendered, and other administrative issues.[90] In the advocate's profession, the General Council of the Bar required local bar associations to set up their own pro bono rules for their jurisdictions. One of the largest associations, the Cape Bar, has since 2004 required its members to complete 20 hours of pro bono service a year.[91]

This attorney rules' scheme operated until 1 November 2018, when the Legal Practice Act came into force (discussed below), but certain aspects of the scheme deserve mentioning.[92] The first, possibly most distinctive, aspect of this mandatory pro bono scheme is that it was only pseudo-mandatory, in that there was no penalty for non-compliance. While law societies were expected to keep a record of pro bono work, no action was taken against a member for failure to do pro bono. The only possible way in which a law society could have taken action against a member was via a complaint by any person that 'a practising member who has still to perform pro bono service hours in any year' refused, without good cause, to deliver pro bono services.[93] It is not clear that a law society could take any punitive measure against a member who had not completed the required number of hours if no one complained about the attorney or his firm. In this sense, the pro bono scheme could be described as encouraged, even institutionalized, but not mandated.

While the failure to enforce mandatory pro bono provisions can be criticized, there is a debate about the consequences, especially for clients, of forced altruism in the representation of the poor and marginalized. Mandatory pro bono has been objected to on the basis that the quality of legal work could be affected by lawyers 'forced' to do it. It has also been argued that making pro bono

[88] The main statute for attorneys, the *Attorneys Act*, *supra* note 13, did not place an obligation on admitted practitioners to perform pro bono work, but it did create non-profit entities such as university law clinics to perform such work.

[89] Willem De Klerk, 'University Law Clinics in South Africa' (2005) 122:4 *South African Law Journal* 929 at 945.

[90] For example, the rules exempt legal practitioners who have practised for more than 40 years and/or who are more than 60 years of age. See *Rules for the Attorney's Profession*, South Africa, 2016, online: www.lssa.org.za/rules-for-the-attorneys-profession/ [*Attorney Profession Rules*], r 25.2.

[91] This is qualified: every member of the Cape Bar of more than three years' standing (including associate members but excluding associate academic members) is required from 1 January 2004 to render a minimum of 20 hours' pro bono service each calendar year. See Cape Bar, 'Pro Bono Rules (2016)', online: capebar.co.za/wp-content/uploads/2015/04/Pro-Bono-rules-after-amendment-in-September-2016.pdf.

[92] The rules came into force on 1 March 2016 and were repealed on 1 November 2018 by the *LPA*, *supra* note 15.

[93] *Attorney Profession Rules*, *supra* note 90, rr 25.15 and 25.16 promulgated in terms of *Attorneys Act*, *supra* note 13, s 74(4).

mandatory undermines the very nature of the concept, being one for the individual conscience. Notwithstanding, and on a far more pragmatic level, it is clear that most law societies in South Africa lacked the capacity to enforce these provisions. While statistics are hard to come by, it is clear that some law societies struggled just to keep up with complaints about the conduct of lawyers.[94] In correspondence with one law society president, he indicated that '[i]t is not possible for us to refer work to all of our 14,600 members [and] ensure their compliance with the 24 hour per annum requirement'.[95] The same law society president, of the biggest law society in South Africa serving the most populated urban area, observed that no member had been disciplined for failing to do pro bono hours.[96] It is more likely that an attorney who accepted a pro bono instruction and then did not attend to it properly would face a charge of failing to give attention to the affairs of the client, rather than for failing to act pro bono.[97]

If the requirement for mandatory pro bono is not enforced, why did the law societies bother with it at all? Those advocating for further and better pro bono by lawyers in South Africa[98] argue that a mandatory rule, even a pseudo-mandatory rule, represents a recognition that lawyers have a responsibility to ensure access to justice. Despite regulatory shortcomings, rules are 'the closest one can come to … a collective statement about [lawyers'] values and ideals',[99] and explicitly mandating pro bono work makes it an increasingly essential feature of a lawyer's daily work. This view is attractive despite the obvious criticism that a mandatory requirement makes lawyers look good from a public relations perspective without much pain to lawyers themselves.[100]

Whether it is due to law firm marketing or the ideals of the profession, larger law firms in South Africa have taken up the cudgels of pro bono. Since the first initiative by the Cape Law Society on mandatory pro bono hours, these firms have set up pro bono policies and departments which are held out as a demonstration that the firm 'is determined to provide its clients and the wider public with the highest level of legal expertise, combined with social sensitivity and responsibility'.[101] However, these initiatives are limited to those in the immediate locale, and often their geographical location is far from the place where the rural poor are based and where these initiatives are also needed.

All in all, by 2014 the legal profession had pulled itself, slowly and unwillingly at times, to the point where, at least formally, it had shown a commitment to addressing unmet legal need

94 See Eberhard Bertelsmann, 'Die rol van en beperkings op die regbank om sociale vrede in Suid-Afrika te bevorder' (2012) 15:2 *Potchefstroom Electronic Law Journal/Potchefstroomse Elektroniese Regsblad* 2 at 15.

95 Letter from Helen Kruuse to President, LSNP (4 May 2017) (copy on file with author).

96 Ibid.

97 Ibid.

98 Jeremy Sarkin, 'Restructuring the Legal Profession and Access to Justice: The Duty of Law Graduates and Lawyers to Provide Legal Services' (1993) 9:2 *South African Journal on Human Rights* 223; Geoff Budlender, 'Access to Courts' (2004) 121:2 *South African Law Journal* 339; Dave Holness, 'The Constitutional Justification for Free Legal Services in Civil Matters in South Africa' (2013) 27:2 *Speculum Juris* 25; Jason Brickhill, 'The Right to a Fair Trial: Duties of Lawyers and Students to Act Pro Bono' (2005) 21 *South African Journal on Human Rights* 293. See also *Making Rights a Reality*, *supra* note 44, at 38.

99 Donald Nicolson and Julian Webb, 'Taking Lawyers' Ethics Seriously' (1999) 6:1 *International Journal of the Legal Profession* 109 at 115.

100 Fiona Mcleay, 'The Legal Profession's Beautiful Myth: Surveying the Justifications for the Lawyer's Obligation to Perform Pro Bono Work' (2008) 15:3 *International Journal of the Legal Profession* 249 at 252.

101 Webber Wentzel's policy statement: see Webber Wentzel, 'Overview', online: www.webberwentzel.com/wwb/content/en/ww-pro-bono-overview.

through pro bono requirements set out by its respective regulatory bodies. While problems with enforcement existed, the law societies accepted that lawyers had a duty in light of, rather than in spite of, the constitutional guarantees set out above. The existence of the state legal aid did not replace their duty, but only supplemented it.[102] However, this situation has changed with the coming into force of the Legal Practice Act.

VI. LEGISLATIVE CHANGES IN ACCESS TO JUSTICE: THE LEGAL PRACTICE ACT

Significant legislative changes via the Legal Practice Act ('LPA') are changing the relationship between the legal profession and access to justice in a profound way in South Africa. These changes include partial fusion of the profession, merging regulatory authorities, and new access to justice mechanisms. A result of consultations commenced in the early 2000s, the LPA has been years in the making. Some of the challenges in bringing the legislation to fruition have been a lack of consensus about the duties of lawyers in providing access to justice. Nevertheless, two important mechanisms will impact on access to justice, and neither uses the language of pro bono.

The most striking change to the legal profession is the introduction of mandatory 'community service'.[103] Section 3(b)(2) states that the purpose of the Act includes broadening access to justice by putting in place 'measures to provide for the rendering of community service by candidate legal practitioners and practising legal practitioners'. Section 29 of the Act requires that candidate attorneys must undertake community service as 'a component of practical vocational training',[104] and that legal practitioners are required to undertake 'a minimum period of recurring community service', upon which their registration as a legal professional is dependent.[105]

The list of what comprises community service indicates that these services should not be categorized as pro bono:[106]

(a) service in the State, approved by the Minister, in consultation with the Council;
(b) service at the South African Human Rights Commission ('SAHRC');
(c) service, without remuneration, as a judicial officer in the case of legal practitioners, including as a commissioner in the small claims courts;
(d) the provision of legal education and training on behalf of the Council, or on behalf of an academic institution or non-governmental organisation ('NGO'); or
(e) any other service which the candidate legal practitioner or the legal practitioner may want to perform, with the approval of the Minister.

The wording in Section 29(2)(c) states that the relevant service, that of a judicial officer, would only constitute community service if it is 'without remuneration'. None of the other services have this restriction. If one applies the *expressio unius est exclusio alterius* rule of interpretation, it appears that the other examples of community service include paid activities. This approach of course conflicts with the idea of pro bono, defined as free or low-cost services for the indigent.

[102] Jones J says as much in *Mackay* v. *Legal Aid Board* (2003) 1 SA 271 (SE) 281G–282B.
[103] See *Transformation of the Legal Profession: Discussion Paper* (General Council of the Bar of South Africa, 1999) [*Transformation of Legal Profession*] at para. 3.4.10, and the current *LPA*, *supra* note 15, s 29.
[104] *LPA*, *supra* note 15, s 29(1)(a).
[105] *LPA*, *supra* note 15, s 29(1)(b).
[106] *LPA*, *supra* note 15, s 29(2)(a)–(e).

A different reading of Section 29 is possible. It could be argued that the legislature saw this section of recurring community service rendered by legal practitioners every year referred to in Section 29(1)(b), as what we know of as pro bono legal service.[107] Thus, the Minister's determination of 'service in the State' could be broadly construed and replicate pro bono in every way. On this latter interpretation, there is still the issue of what is seen as 'community service'. While it is open to the Justice Minister to add other approved services, there is a lack of direct reference to language incorporating access to justice, pro bono, and other duties of the legal profession to provide access to justice to indigent members of society. As a commentator has asked: '[W]ould the LPA not have included a direct and explicit mention to this by stating at s 29(2) that one form of community service could be service for indigent people and the organisations that represent them?'[108]

The activities listed would indirectly support access to justice, but it is perplexing that an express reference to direct legal services for indigent people was not even included as a potential source of community service in this provision. In addition, if the legislature wanted to include pro bono services in the definition of community service, it could have adopted the language recommended in the General Council of the Bar of South Africa's discussion paper on the Act: '[a]ll qualified legal practitioners who have been in practice for more than five years might be required to do 48 certified hours of un-remunerated community service each year'.[109] The natural conclusion here is that Section 29 is not a direct call for lawyers to do pro bono, although it may result in more access to justice generally.

In a final twist, the rush to effect the new legislation (the LPA) produced a rather perverse status quo. With the mandatory pro bono rules repealed due to the legislation coming into effect, and the Minister not having issued regulations on community service, at the time of writing attorneys and advocates had no mandatory obligation to perform pro bono or community service at all. Given that one of the main aims of the Act was to improve access to justice, this situation appears to be a regression from the previous scheme. The Legal Practice Council ('LPC'), the new regulatory body, has all but admitted as much in a communiqué to members, in which the Chair of the LPC encouraged legal practitioners to continue performing pro bono on the basis that it 'reflects the social conscience of the profession'.[110]

The second legislative change related to access to justice addresses the affordability of legal services. Section 35(4) of the LPA mandates that the South African Law Reform Commission ('SALRC') tackle the high cost of legal fees by introducing the possibility of caps. Section 35 of the Act, which came into force on 1 November 2018, gives SALRC two years to investigate and report back to the Minister with recommendations on the following:[111]

(a) the manner in which to address the circumstances giving rise to legal fees that are unattainable for most people;
(b) legislative and other interventions in order to improve access to justice by the members of the public;

[107] Erica Emdon, 'More Clarity on Pro Bono Under Legal Practice Act', *De Rebus* (1 February 2017), online: www.derebus.org.za/clarity-pro-bono-legal-practice-act/.
[108] Ibid.
[109] *Transformation of Legal Profession*, *supra* note 103, at para. 3.4.10.
[110] K. Dlepu (Chair of LPC), 'Legal Practice Council – Pro Bono Services' *Message from the Desk of the Chairperson* (12 March 2019) (copy on file with author).
[111] *LPA*, *supra* note 15, s 35(4).

(c) the desirability of establishing a mechanism which will be responsible for determining fees and tariffs payable to legal practitioners;
(d) the composition of the mechanism contemplated in paragraph (c) and the processes it should follow in determining fees or tariffs;
(e) the desirability of giving users of legal services the option of voluntarily agreeing to pay fees for legal services less or in excess of any amount that may be set by the mechanism contemplated in paragraph (c); and
(f) the obligation by a legal practitioner to conclude a mandatory fee arrangement with a client when that client secures that legal practitioner's services.

In conducting the investigation referred to in subsection (4), the SALRC must take the following into consideration:[112]

(a) best international practices;
(b) the public interest;
(c) the interests of the legal profession; and
(d) the use of contingency fee agreements as provided for in the Contingency Fees Act, 1997 (Act No. 66 of 1997).

There is significant force behind this provision. At the second reading of the Legal Practice Bill in the South African Parliament, a Member of Parliament noted that the Constitutional Court's pronouncements on the exorbitant fees charged by certain members of the profession could not be ignored, and that the organized profession's uniform response to the access to justice challenge, of '[l]egal aid, pro bono; pro bono, legal aid', was simply not enough.[113] In committing to their mandate, the SALRC organized and hosted a conference to stimulate discussion on the issue.[114] While the conference looked at various ways in which access to justice could be achieved, for example, through community-based paralegals, law student representation in court, and increased state-sponsored mediation, the state representatives were clear that they wanted the investigation to focus on making legal services more accessible in what amounts to price control.[115] The provision represents an interesting turn in access to justice in South Africa, and it appears to follow reform trends in some other jurisdictions.[116] The scheme requires more investigation, but the move itself underscores the state's perception that the organized profession has failed to adequately respond to unmet legal need, and that the legal profession will not easily let go of its privileged position. As observed by the Deputy Minister of Justice:[117]

> I would ... caution [the South African Law Reform Commission] that ... in its consultations, [it] does not prioritise the profession over the public because it is almost like asking turkeys to be the authoritative voice on what should be on the table for Christmas dinner, while ignoring the impact of the decision on geese, chickens and pigs.

It appears then that the state's focus is on fee control, and that community service is a secondary concern. This set of priorities is further suggested by the situation set out above regarding pro

[112] *LPA*, *supra* note 15, s 35(5).
[113] South African Law Reform Commission, 'Report on the International Conference on Access to Justice, Legal Costs, and Other Interventions', March 2019, online: www.justice.gov.za/salrc/conf.htm [*Report on International Conference*].
[114] Ibid.
[115] *Key Note Address*, *supra* note 83.
[116] For example, Courts and Tribunals Judiciary, 'Review of Civil Litigation Costs: Supplemental Report – Fixed Recoverable Costs', online: www.judiciary.uk/publications/review-of-civil-litigation-costs-reports/.
[117] *Key Note Address*, *supra* note 83, at 16–17.

bono, as it only needed the Minister to bring community service regulations into force to avoid the regression from mandatory pro bono to 'encouragement', something the Minister has not done to date. While fee control may assist the middle class to a certain extent, bringing into force community service regulations and enforcement mechanisms for pro bono alongside this process is needed for the most vulnerable in the South African community.

VII. CONCLUSION

The South African experience in dealing with access to justice is complex. Access to justice is made difficult to achieve by huge inequalities leading to unmet legal need, which must be viewed in light of South Africa's history of apartheid including summary arrest, detention without trial, and lack of access to material goods.[118] This chapter addresses the role of lawyers in access to justice, and in South Africa, it has been argued that the strongest basis for the responsibility of legal practitioners to provide pro bono is a constitutional obligation, not vague references to tradition or professional duty or 'social conscience'. Considering pro bono in this way provides the regulatory bodies with a basis for introducing more structure and possible coercive measures for those who fail to do pro bono work. But constitutional provisions notwithstanding, state-sponsored legal aid and efforts at pro bono have simply not been able to meet the needs of the majority of South Africans. In this context, the state has taken an alternative view on how to achieve access to justice, first through the introduction of community service for all practitioners, and second through the possibility of capping legal fees. The problem with these legislative changes is the failure to provide content to guarantees and draft regulations for community service provisions in the first instance, and the intractable positions by stakeholders on price control in the second instance.[119] Further, as the community service provisions currently read, they appear to encompass paid work, which immediately raises the question of where remuneration will come from, as LASA already has insufficient funds. In addition, the capping of legal fees raises questions about whether price controls actually work or whether they distort the market, a view held by many in the advocate's profession.[120] On a positive note, proposed caps on fees may be part of a longer game intended to provoke a more enthusiastic response from the legal profession regarding other aspects of access to justice such as pro bono. In its final form, these access to justice reforms should be closely watched by those seeking to provide justice in other countries.

[118] *Public Interest Legal Services in South Africa Project Report: July 2015* (Socio-Economic Rights Institute of South Africa, 2015) at 8–9.

[119] See Melody Emmett, 'How Legal Practice Act Overlooks the Spirit of Pro Bono Work', *Business Day* (2 November 2017), online: www.businesslive.co.za/bd/opinion/2017-11-02-how-legal-practice-act-overlooks-the-spirit-of-pro-bono-work/. See in general, the discussion reported in *Report on International Conference*, *supra* note 113.

[120] For example, see Gerrit Pretorius SC, 'The Legal Practice Bill – Again' (2012) 25:2 *Advocate* 2.

Index

For EU product safety concerns, contact us at Calle de José Abascal, 56–1°,
28003 Madrid, Spain or eugpsr@cambridge.org.

www.ingramcontent.com/pod-product-compliance
Lightning Source LLC
LaVergne TN
LVHW060022210926
848481LV00013B/3766

* 9 7 8 1 0 0 9 0 4 5 4 7 6 *